BEYOND THE
NEW LEFT

Other books by IRVING HOWE

Sherwood Anderson: A CRITICAL BIOGRAPHY
William Faulkner: A CRITICAL STUDY
Politics and the Novel
A World More Attractive
The American Communist Party: A CRITICAL HISTORY
(with Lewis Coser)
Thomas Hardy: A CRITICAL STUDY
Steady Work: ESSAYS IN DEMOCRATIC RADICALISM
The Decline of the New: LITERARY AND CULTURAL ESSAYS

BEYOND THE NEW LEFT

Edited and with an introduction by

Irving Howe

THE McCALL PUBLISHING COMPANY

NEW YORK

CONTENTS

BEYOND THE
NEW LEFT

INTRODUCTION

by Irving Howe

The analysis and critique of the New Left that appears in this book stems, in the main, from the political outlook of democratic socialism. I say in the main, because a few of the authors included here might not care to identify themselves with this or any other political outlook. So it seems best to note that each writer speaks for himself. Here, in this brief introduction, I will avoid repeating what the contributors to this book say, and will confine myself mainly to some historical background.

What *is* the New Left? The phrase has become part of our journalistic currency, but the phenomena to which it points are barely a decade old and remain strikingly diverse in character, scattered in organization, and not always coherent in statement. In any traditional sense, the New Left does not comprise a structured movement. Whenever it has tried to form a national organization, as at the disastrous Conference for a New Politics held in Chicago during the summer of 1967, it has quickly fractured into several hostile groups. As this is being written, Students for a Democratic Society, the major New Left group, is split into three or four embattled factions, with the two main ones using physical violence on one another, as if intent upon reenacting the worst of Stalinism. (Says Mark Rudd, leader of the SDS Weatherman faction, "We sometimes beat them up [the other faction] and they beat us up. What we usually do is beat them up when we find them. . . ." *The New York Times*, 26 September 1969.)

The New Left has become an important force, though only in certain limited segments of American society. It has made no impact on such major institutions as the trade unions or such major social groups as the working class, which is by traditional Marxist expectations the lever of revolution. It has not been able to establish itself as a significant presence in either national or regional politics (e.g., the pitiably small vote received by Eldridge Cleaver and Dick Gregory in the 1968 election, the failure of New Leftists to win even a primary in a stronghold like Berkeley). But the New Left has had a notable effect on campus life; it has exerted an oblique influence on the more extreme black militants; and it has contributed to the growth of a distinctive "youth culture," as well as to the swinging, pop-guerrilla, middle-class culture that has scored commercial successes in our cities.

Some questions about New Left influence are hard to answer. The claim is often made that it has played a major role in mobilizing public sentiment, even if through confrontationist shock tactics, against the Vietnam war. My own judgment is that large sections of both the American population and our political leadership turned to opposing the war mainly out of a realization that it could not be won short of an intolerable escalation. Nevertheless, it seems indisputable that on this score, despite some exaggeration, the New Left deserves credit. It did play a valuable role in stirring dissent against the war, it did serve as a pressure on the conscience of liberals. Yet the paradox that must be noted here is that such credit is of a kind that the New Left can't, in ideological consistency, be very enthusiastic about. For a central New Left dogma has insisted that "the system can't be changed," and that to achieve even limited ends it is necessary to complete a wholesale social transformation, what is loosely called these days "a revolution." (Like many other New Left notions, this one is rarely developed or examined: *Which* limited ends can't be achieved short of revolution? ending the war in Vietnam? the abolition of racial discrimination? reform of the universities?) Insofar as the New Left claims credit for mobilizing popular sentiment in behalf of changing U.S. policy in Vietnam—and I think it has some right to make that claim—it undercuts its "revolutionary" theories and tacitly acknowledges that, despite its intentions and rhetoric, it has played the role of a pressure or reformist group mobilizing sentiment for change within this society. I see nothing dishonorable in playing such a role. I only wish to point to the problems it presents the New Left. And let me also stress that it is not I, or people of my persuasion, who insist that achieving short-range goals within the present society is incompatible with working toward long-range social change.

If, however, we do try to estimate the short-run consequences of New Left activities, we must also look at the other side of the balance. We must ask ourselves, how much sentiment has the New Left helped to mobilize for the far Right? to what extent has it contributed to the victories of Nixon in the country as a whole, Reagan in California, and Stenvig in Minneapolis? Now, there is no completely accurate or "scientific" way of measuring the consequences of any political conduct, not even conduct as abrasive as that of the New Left; but every available source of evidence—from opinion polls to electoral results to the use of common sense—indicates that among large segments of the middle and working classes there has set in a strong, though not yet violent, reaction against New Left methods. My impression is that the more candid New Left spokesmen would not deny this, for believing as they do in "polarization" (that is, in provoking large numbers of people toward the extremes of the political spectrum and thereby dislodging and disabling the liberal center), some of them would actually see the growth of the far Right as a tribute to their own effectiveness. And so it is, though hardly in the way they suppose. For what the New Left, in its feckless hunger for apocalypse, fails to reckon with is the probable lineup of forces in this country if there is to be a "polarization" during the next few years—to say nothing of the probable victor in such a showdown. Soberly estimating the likely consequences of its tactics isn't one of the strong points of the New Left.

Other questions concerning its influence are equally hard to answer. To what extent, for instance, was the recent appearance of that promising political tendency we call the New Politics—the leftist-liberal coalition associated with the campaigns of Senator Eugene McCarthy and the late Senator Robert Kennedy—a consequence of pressures from the New Left? Again, there can't be an assured reply, but I for one would be prepared to say that yes, some credit should go to the New Left. Saying that, however, I would also want to note that most New Left segments, and especially SDS, sneered at and refused to support Senator McCarthy's candidacy when he rallied public sentiment against the war. One New Left spokesman, Tom Hayden, even declared publicly that "a vote for George Wallace would further his objective more than a vote for RFK." (*Village Voice*, 30 May 1968.) Both the morality and the logic of such a view seem too shabby to require an answer.

As writers in Part Two of this book argue, the New Left has made few serious contributions to political thought or cultural experience. Whatever interest the New Left shows in political theory is usually directed toward the work of older writers whose work it appropriates and sometimes twists for its own sake. At the same time the New Left has had a considerable impact on intellectual styles and fashions, reviving radical sentiments in elderly men of letters who found it expedient to restrain themselves during the conservative fifties, providing a rhetoric of excitement for young writers often well-attuned to the demands of the market, and helping to make "radicalism" a hot journalistic property in magazines as various as *Esquire* and *The New York Review of Books*. A series of heroes and gurus from the intellectual world has been raised to fame by the student New Left: Mills, Goodman, Marcuse, and Chomsky at home, and Fanon, Debray, and Guevara abroad. (Goodman, who has a habit of being critical, has recently been dismissed from the role of mentor.) Our intellectual life is especially susceptible to the lures of novelty, and novelty is what some people have supposed the New Left to be providing—especially those whose historical memories extend no further back than a decade or two, or who do not trouble to read books older than themselves.

In its few years of existence, the New Left has already gone through two distinct phases. The first was a phase of populist fraternity, stressing an idealistic desire to make real the egalitarian claims of the American tradition, a non- and even anti-ideological approach to politics, and a strategy of going into local

communities in order to help oppressed minorities. Perhaps the
major stimulant to this early New Left was the upsurge of the
American Negroes in the early 1960s, as they began to struggle
for their dignity as men and for their rights as citizens. And perhaps the most dramatic action of the early New Left was the
journey hundreds of young people took in the summer of 1963 to
live and work in Mississippi, helping Negroes organize themselves for local community and political ends. The main slogan
of that moment—appealing but vague—was "participatory democracy." For those of us committed to democratic socialism,
this first phase of the New Left was, despite occasional tactical
blunders, a profoundly welcome and promising reinvigoration of
American political life. How many of the young people who re-
sponded to the appeal of nonviolence, fraternity, and an undogmatic radicalism would later remain with the New Left we don't
really know. Clearly, many of the founders of the Student Nonviolent Coordinating Committee, black and white youth who
believed in both integration and nonviolence, abandoned that
group once it fell into the hands of people like Stokely Carmichael and Rap Brown.

The second phase of the New Left signifies a sharp turn: away
from fraternal sentiment and back to ill-absorbed dogma, away
from the shapelessness of "participatory democracy" and back to
the rigidity of vanguard elites, away from the loving spirit of
nonviolence and back to a quasi-Leninist fascination with violence. In this second phase the New Left grows in numbers yet
makes certain, through its sterile authoritarianism, that it will not
be more than a blown-up reincarnation of the radical sects of
the past.

What are the causes of this sharp change? The break-up of the
Negro-labor-liberal coalition that had sparked the civil rights
movement and ensured the victory of John F. Kennedy; the despair, most of it warranted and authentic, over U.S. involvement
in Vietnam; the rise of separatist and nationalist sentiment
among black youth; an intense disillusionment not only with liberal politics of the moment but with the whole idea of liberalism; and the growing appeal of the "Third-World Revolution"
conceived (or misperceived) by the New Left as an odd blend
of romantic anarchism and Leninist authoritarianism. In this sec-

ond phase of the New Left, it sometimes seemed as if the SDS were transforming itself into a society for the resurrection of the god that failed. Notions, dogmas, ideologies, and slogans that an earlier generation of radicals had discarded after painful reflection and experience now came back in crude form. The theory of "social fascism," Stalin's contribution to the victory of Hitlerism, was transformed into a theory of "liberal fascism" by SDS leaders. The idea of a self-appointed "vanguard" that will prod the sluggish masses into rebellion—one of the more dubious contributions of Leninist orthodoxy—was uncritically embraced by affluent middle-class students. Confrontationist tactics, often similar to those Lenin had so caustically denounced in *Left-Wing Communism: An Infantile Disorder*, were used by SDS and other New Left groups with no visible concern for how well or poorly they had worked in the past, or what their likely consequences would be in the future. The vulgar-Marxist notion that "bourgeois democracy" is no more than a mask for the domination of capital and therefore not to be valued by radicals, found strong echoes in the sixties. And perhaps most distressing of all, the liberal values of tolerance and respect for the rights of opponents were sneeringly dismissed in accordance with the formulas of Herbert Marcuse. To be sure, not all New Leftists succumbed to this authoritarian debauch; some, like Greg Calvert, former SDS National Secretary, complained sadly about the "Stalinization of the New Left" and looked back wistfully to its earlier years; but, in the main, the drift was toward the sectarian wastelands, marked by the ideologizing of the Maoists and the adventurism of the Guevarists.

(In this book, the two opening essays, by myself and Michael Harrington, respectively, deal primarily with what I've called the first phase of the New Left, though both contain warnings that there is an authoritarian potential in its populist sentiment. These are followed by my critique of the New Left's "confrontation" methods. The next essay, by Richard Lowenthal, is, I think, the most extensive and profound analysis yet to appear of the second phase of the New Left; it offers a fundamental critique such as I cannot pretend to undertake in a brief introduction. And Paul Goodman's essay tries to establish a certain historical distance from contemporary phenomena, so that the New Left is seen not in exclusively political terms at all but rather as a quasi-religious upsurge. The reader will note that these essays, arranged in order of publication, roughly parallel the political development of the New Left.)

It now begins to seem that we are on the verge of still another phase in the development of the New Left. Some elements within it—the Weathermen and the Crazies, for example—seem to be abandoning what they have regarded as orthodox Leninism and to be turning to a mixture of violent adventurism, staged desperation, and even hooliganism, all marked by symptoms of social pathology. Any contrast between the United States today and Russia in the late nineteenth century must of course be made with a maximum of caution, yet it is hard to avoid the impression that the desperado-totalitarian Left, in both the United States and Europe, is a reenactment of the politics of Nechaev, the Russian terrorist of the late nineteenth century. The Weathermen, having given up hope for the proletariat, now see the main revolutionary force in our society as the high school students; their experience may yet lead them to the kindergartens. Nor is it impossible that we may also see in this country the desperate children of the affluent reenacting the terrorism of Russia in the 1880s.

How far some elements—not, it should be said in fairness, the majority—of the New Left have sunk into the pathology of violence can be seen from the following report about a Weatherman gathering, which appeared in the 10 January 1970, issue of *The Guardian*, a New Left weekly. The report summarizes the keynote speech of Bernardine Dohrn, former interorganization secretary of SDS:

> Dohrn characterized violent, militant response in the streets as "armed struggle" against imperialism. . . . "We're about being a fighting force alongside the blacks, but a lot of us are still honkies and we're still scared of fighting. We have to get into armed struggle."
> Part of armed struggle, as Dohrn and others laid it down, is terrorism. Political assassination—openly joked

about by some Weathermen—and literally any kind of violence that is considered anti-social were put forward as legitimate forms of armed struggle. . . .

A 20-foot long poster adorned a wall of the ballroom. It was covered with drawings of bullets, each with a name. Along with the understandable targets like Chicago's Mayor Daley, the Weathermen deemed as legitimate enemies to be offed, among others, *The Guardian* (which has criticized Weatherman) and Sharon Tate, one of several victims in the recent mass murder in California. She was eight months pregnant.

"Honkies are going to be afraid of us," Dohrn insisted. She went on to tell the war council about Charlie Manson, accused leader of the gang which allegedly murdered the movie star and several others on their Beverly Hills estate. Manson has been portrayed in the media as a Satanic, magnetic personality who held near-hypnotic sway over several women whom he lent out to friends as favors and brought along for the murder scene. The press also mentioned Manson's supposed fear of blacks—he reportedly moved into rural California to escape the violence of a race war.

Weatherman, the "Bureau" says, digs Manson . . .

"Dig it, first they killed those pigs, then they ate dinner in the same room with them, then they even shoved a fork into a victim's stomach! Wild!" said Bernardine Dohrn.

It will be said that these sentiments are in no way characteristic for the thousands of young people who have been protesting against the Vietnam war. I entirely agree. It will be said that the Weatherman group isn't representative of the New Left. In one sense, that also is true. No other New Left tendency has abandoned itself so completely to corrupting fantasies of blood. But it needs to be added that Miss Dohrn's ravings have a connection —distorted, extreme yet with the representativeness of caricature—to things one can hear and see these days among portions of the New Left. The cult of violence, the celebration of bombs, the arrogant identification of a tiny group of affluent youth with the "destiny of the revolution," the adulation of charismatic

authoritarian leaders, the crude hatred for liberal values: all
these can be found in most New Left tendencies, even if without
the vivid pathology of the Weathermen.

The most interesting theoretical question concerning the rapid
changes within the New Left has to do with the relation between its earlier and later phases. Those of us who write for
journals like *Dissent*, whatever our many shortcomings, can at
least claim some credit for having foreseen (the evidence appears in these pages) the possibility that a politics of populist
vagueness would lead to a politics of authoritarian rigidity. For
this decline I would suggest two causes:

1. *The crisis and virtual collapse of U.S. liberalism.* During
the 1960s, with the possible exception of John F. Kennedy's brief
tenure as President and Eugene McCarthy's effort to win the
Democratic nomination, American liberalism has been in a bad
way. Without pretending to a full explanation, let me at least indicate a few summary reasons for this decline: the exhaustion of
traditional New Deal politics, alliances, and outlooks; the appearance of moral-political issues which bread-and-butter liberalism was not equipped to deal with; the involvement of certain
liberal leaders (e.g., Humphrey) in a war that large numbers of
young people rightly saw as indefensible.

A rough but useful axiom can be suggested about recent
American politics: The New Left has flourished as a result of, or
in direct proportion to, the failures and failings of liberalism.
When the candidacies of Eugene McCarthy and Robert Kennedy seemed to offer a significant alternative, a way of realizing
the hopes of the idealistic young through electoral politics, then
thousands of young radicals and liberals flocked to their campaigns. Both on and off the campus, the New Left began to
wither into a marginal group, limited for the time to nasty and
impotent sniping. But when there seemed no viable alternative,
and both candidates in the 1968 presidential election spoke as
supporters of the Vietnam war, then moods of despair swept
across the campus, and the New Left could transform these
moods into a disillusionment with liberal politics in particular
and the idea of liberalism in general. The way was then open

for the growth of anarcho-authoritarian sentiment: Castroite, Maoist, Guevarist, and still more exotic varieties.

2. *An internal connection between the thought of the early New Left and the thought of the later New Left.* What both shared was an impatience, sometimes a distrust, and more recently a downright contempt for the methods and norms of democracy—the "cumbersomeness" or "sham" of representative elections, the "irrelevance" of undemonstrative majorities, the "manipulation" of the masses by politicians and the media, the "dullness" of ordinary middle-class people, and so on. Under the guidance of such authoritarian thinkers as Herbert Marcuse, the New Left in both its phases, though more so in the later one, revealed a profoundly elitist bias. It might speak about "the people," and sometimes even "the workers," but it found its base of support mainly among the alienated middle-class young.

When the phrase "participatory democracy" first began to be heard, it gained its impact partly as a response to a genuine problem that had been troubling both socialist and nonsocialist thinkers for some time: What could be done to stop the gradual erosion of democratic institutions, in which the formal appearance of participation by the people continued but the real substance declined?

At first the New Left's emphasis on "participatory democracy" signified mainly a desire to reinvigorate democracy, to give it greater meaning and immediacy—though the New Left rarely had any concrete proposals for achieving this end. Too often "participatory democracy" meant in practice a blithe dismissal of parliamentary rules within the discussions of the New Left groups, a practice that may have encouraged collective expressiveness (and interminable meetings) but also proved to be peculiarly open to manipulation by tight little factions and charismatic figures emphasizing their modesty. At best such procedures helped enliven—were relevant to—the politics of small groups, but they could contribute almost nothing to solving the problem of democratic politics in large societies, where the sheer number of citizens and complexity of competing interests require a system of representative institutions.

The stress on "participatory democracy" proved to be especially damaging in the curious way it prepared the ground for authoritarian politics. There was not too great a distance between the contempt shown for the limitations of representative institutions by the early New Left and the contempt shown for the very idea of representative institutions by the later New Left. To dismiss "formal democracy" in behalf of "participatory democracy" was in effect to jettison the values of both—as if, in reality, democratic rights didn't always require a commitment to "forms," that is, rules both fixed and open to change through agreed-upon procedures. By the late sixties one rarely heard much about "participatory democracy" from the New Left. Now the fashionable phrase was "revolution," unspecified as to social character, political possibility, or ultimate goal and too often reduced to a ritual of expressiveness that required neither thought nor moral justification.

Those of us who want to preserve and extend democracy while simultaneously working toward fundamental social change must acknowledge that the coming decade is likely to be a time of trouble, even peril. There are linked dangers from the irrationalities and violence of both polar extremes, which together could destroy our hopes for an American movement at once democratic, militant, and radical. The New Left plays a double role here. It contributes valuable energy to the needed task of protest and insurgency, but also a political-moral confusion, sometimes verging on nihilism, which threatens liberal values and helps provoke a popular backlash.

Much recent behavior of New Left students goes against the grain. Destroying computers, burning buildings, breaking up meetings, shouting down teachers in classrooms, carrying guns —this has nothing to do with the socialist, or radical, tradition. It is a strange mixture of Guevarist fantasia, residual Stalinism, anarchist braggadocio, and homemade tough-guy methods.

Nor are our objections merely tactical. The kind of "revolution" envisaged by all the SDS factions has nothing to do with the large-scale social transformation this country needs. Who, with a reasonable impulse to self-preservation and democratic survival, would care to test out the dispensation of a Tom Hayden or Mark Rudd? Worthy fellows, perhaps; but better powerless.

The perspective I would advance for the immediate future combines a broad coalition of popular forces to work for immediate social improvements along a liberal course, and a regathering of those people, now a tiny minority in this country, who believe in the values of democratic socialism. This signifies:

> the premise that we are not and will not soon be in a "revolutionary situation";

> the subpremise that if "revolutionary activity" in the next few years comes to more than loud talk, it will have an elitist, desperado, and adventurist character;

> the belief that it is in our interest to preserve and improve the present agencies of democratic politics, marred as they may be, requiring changes as they do, and even liable to sudden collapse as they are;

> the prognosis that the necessary social and economic reforms can be achieved through a reactivated coalition of liberal-left-labor forces, though one that would be different in stress and internal composition from the New Deal–inspired coalition that has slowly been disintegrating these last several years.

I think that the more sensitive and undogmatic elements in and near the New Left will soon have to face the futility of trying to "go it alone." Their movement has grown and it probably will continue to grow; yet, barring some major self-transformation, it will continue to have the character of a sect isolated in fundamental outlook, language, and psychology from the American people. Nevertheless, it contains precious resources of energy and idealism, and this energy and idealism ought to be thrust into the mainstream of American politics.

One can only hope for a slow regathering of forces among the liberal-labor-left in the United States. A movement that fails to understand the needs and aspirations of the American workers and their unions, or which dismisses them contemptuously in the name of some abstract revolutionary purity, is doomed to failure. A movement that fails to understand the urgency of moral protest animating the young, and stays rigidly within the limits of traditional New Deal and post–New Deal liberalism, is also doomed to failure.

Can we then bring together the strategy of coalition with the passions of insurgency? Can we recognize that in the American system wide and loose electoral blocs, inherently unsatisfactory to ideological purists, are essential, while at the same time the idea of stirring the bottom layers of society to speak out for themselves is also urgent? Such a view of things is inherently complex, and this is a moment when many people are seized by a mania for simplicity; but I think it is a political perspective that, no matter how difficult to realize, is required by the present state of things. Oddly enough, if you were to go back to the founding document of SDS, the now-famous Port Huron statement, you would find a view of politics fairly close to what has been said here. One can only hope that many young people will yet return to it.

PART ONE

Analyses and Critiques

NEW STYLES IN "LEFTISM"

by Irving Howe

I propose to describe a political style or outlook before it has become hardened into an ideology or the property of an organization. This outlook is visible along limited portions of the political scene; for the sake of exposition I will make it seem more precise and structured that it really is.

There is a new radical mood in limited sectors of American society: on the campus, in sections of the civil rights movement. The number of people who express this mood is not very large, but that it should appear at all is cause for encouragement and satisfaction. Yet there is a segment or fringe among the newly blossoming young radicals that causes one disturbance—and not simply because they have ideas different from persons like myself, who neither expect nor desire that younger generations of radicals should repeat our thoughts or our words. For this disturbing minority I have no simple name: Sometimes it looks like kamikaze radicalism, sometimes like white Malcolmism, sometimes like black Maoism. But since none of these phrases will quite do, I have had to fall back upon the loose and not very accurate term, "New Leftists." Let me therefore stress as strongly as I can that I am not talking about all or the majority of the American young and not-so-young who have recently come to regard themselves as radicals.

The essay which appears here is a condensed version of a longer study.

The form I have felt obliged to use here—a composite portrait of the sort of New Leftist who seems to me open to criticism—also creates some difficulties. It may seem to lump together problems, ideas, and moods that should be kept distinct. If some young radicals read this text and feel that much of it does not pertain to them, I will be delighted by such a response.

The society we live in fails to elicit the idealism of the more rebellious and generous young. Even among those who play the game and accept the social masks necessary for gaining success, there is a widespread disenchantment. Certainly there is very little of the joy that comes from a conviction that the values of a society are good, and it is therefore good to live by them. The intelligent young know that if they keep out of trouble, accept academic drudgery, and preserve a respectable "image," they can hope for successful careers, even if not personal gratification. But the price they must pay for this choice is a considerable quantity of inner adaptation to the prevalent norms: There is a limit to the social duplicity that anyone can sustain.

The society not only undercuts the possibilities of constructive participation, it also makes very difficult a coherent and thought-out political opposition. The small minority that does rebel tends to adopt a stance that seems to be political, sometimes even ideological, but often turns out to be little more than an effort to assert a personal style.

Personal style: That seems to me a key. Most of whatever rebellion we have had up to—and even into—the civil rights movement takes the form of a decision on how to live individually within this society, rather than how to change it collectively. A recurrent stress among the young has been upon differentiation of speech, dress, and appearance, by means of which a small elite can signify its special status; or the stress has been upon moral self-regeneration, a kind of Emersonianism with shock treatment. All through the fifties and sixties disaffiliation was a central impulse both as a signal of nausea and a tacit recognition of impotence.

Now, to a notable extent, all this has changed since and through the civil rights movement—*but not changed as much as may seem.* Some of the people involved in that movement show an inclination to make of their radicalism not a politics of common action, which would require the inclusion of saints, sinners, and ordinary folk, but rather a gesture of moral rectitude. And the paradox is that they often sincerely regard themselves as committed to politics—but a politics that asserts so unmodulated and total a dismissal of society, while also departing from Marxist expectations of social revolution, that little is left to them but the glory or burden of maintaining a distinct personal style.

By contrast, the radicalism of an earlier generation, despite numerous faults, had at least this advantage: It did not have to start *as if* from scratch, there were available movements, parties, agencies, and patterns of thought through which one could act. The radicals of the thirties certainly had their share of bohemianism, but their politics were not nearly so interwoven with and dependent upon tokens of style as is today's radicalism.

The great value of the present rebelliousness is that it requires a personal decision, not merely as to what one shall do but also as to what one shall be. It requires authenticity, a challenge to the self, or, as some young people like to say, an "existential" decision. And it makes more difficult the moral double-bookkeeping of the thirties, whereby in the name of a sanctified movement or unquestioned ideology, scoundrels and fools could be exalted as "leaders" and detestable conduct exonerated.

This is a real and very impressive strength, but with it there goes a significant weakness: the lack of clear-cut ideas, sometimes even a feeling that it is wrong—or worse, "middle-class"—to think systematically, and as a corollary, the absence of a social channel or agency through which to act. At first it seemed as if the civil rights movement would provide such a channel; and no person of moral awareness can fail to be profoundly moved by the outpouring of idealism and the readiness to face danger which characterizes the vanguard of this movement. Yet at a certain point it turns out that the civil rights movement, through the intensity of its work, seems to dramatize . . . its own insufficiency. Indeed, it acts as a training school for experienced, gifted, courageous people who have learned how to lead, how to sacrifice, how to work, but have no place in which to enlarge upon their gifts.

The more shapeless, the more promiscuously absorptive, the more psychologically and morally slack the society becomes, the more must candidates for rebellion seek extreme postures which will enable them to "act out" their distance from a society that seems intent upon a maliciously benevolent assimilation; extreme postures which will yield security, perhaps a sense of consecration, in loneliness; extreme postures which will safeguard them from the allure of everything they reject. Between the act of rebellion and the society against which it is directed, there remain, however, deeper ties than is commonly recognized. To which we shall return.

These problems are exacerbated by an educational system that often seems inherently schizoid. It appeals to the life of the mind, yet justifies that appeal through crass utilitarianism. It invokes the traditions of freedom, yet processes students to bureaucratic cut. It speaks for the spirit, yet increasingly becomes an appendage of a spirit-squashing system.

New Leftism appears at a moment when the intellectual and academic worlds—and not they alone—are experiencing an intense and largely justifiable revulsion against the immediate American past. Many people are sick unto death of the whole structure of feeling—that mixture of chauvinism, hysteria, and demagogy—which was created during the cold war years. Like children subjected to forced feeding, they regurgitate almost automatically. Their response is an inevitable consequence of over-organizing the propaganda resources of a modern state; the same sort of nausea exists among the young in the Communist world.

Unfortunately, revulsion seldom encourages nuances of thought or precise discriminations of politics. You cannot stand the deceits of official anti-Communism? Then respond with a rejection equally blatant. You have been raised to give credit to every American power move, no matter how reactionary or cynical? Then respond by castigating everything American. You are weary of Sidney Hook's messages in *The New York Times Magazine*? Then respond as if talk about Communist totalitarianism were simply irrelevant or a bogey to frighten infants.

Yet we should be clear in our minds that such a response is not at all the same as a commitment to Communism, even though it may lend itself to obvious exploitation. It is rather a spewing out of distasteful matter—in the course of which other values, such as the possibility of learning from the traumas and tragedies of recent history, may also be spewed out.

Generational clashes are recurrent in our society, perhaps in any society. But the present rupture between the young and their elders seems especially deep. This is a social phenomenon that goes beyond our immediate subject, indeed it cuts through the whole of society; what it signifies is the society's failure to transmit with sufficient force its values to the young, or, perhaps more accurately, that the best of the young take the proclaimed values of their elders with a seriousness which leads them to be appalled by their violation in practice.

In rejecting the older generations, however, the young sometimes betray the conditioning mark of the very American culture they are so quick to denounce. For ours is a culture that celebrates youthfulness as if it were a moral good in its own right. Like the regular Americans they wish so hard not to be, yet, through wishing, so very much are, they believe that the past is mere dust and ashes and that they can start afresh, immaculately.

A generation is missing in the life of American radicalism, the generation that would now be in its late thirties, the generation that did not show up. The result is an inordinate difficulty in communication between the young radicals and those unfortunate enough to have reached—or, God help us, even gone beyond —the age of forty. Here, of course, our failure is very much in evidence too: a failure that should prompt us to speak with modesty, simply as people who have tried, and in their trying perhaps have learned something.

Let me specify a few characteristic attitudes among the New Leftists:

1. *An extreme, sometimes unwarranted, hostility toward liberalism.* They see liberalism only in its current version, institutional, corporate, and debased; but avoiding history, they know very little about the elements of the liberal tradition which should remain valuable for any democratic socialist. And thereby they would cut off the resurgent American radicalism from what

is, or should be, one of its sustaining sources: the tradition that has yielded us a heritage of civil freedoms, disinterested specula- tion, humane tolerance.

2. *An impatience with the problems that concerned an older generation of radicals.* Here the generational conflict breaks out with strong feelings on both sides, the older people feeling threatened in whatever they have been able to salvage from past experiences, the younger people feeling the need to shake off dogma and create their own terms of action.

There are traditional radical topics which no one, except the historically minded, need trouble with. To be unconcerned with the dispute in the late twenties over the Anglo-Russian Trade Union Committee or the differences between Lenin and Luxem- bourg on the "national question"—well and good. These are not quite burning problems of the moment. But *some* of the issues hotly debated in the thirties do remain burning problems: In fact, it should be said for the anti-Stalinist Left of the past several decades that it anticipated, in its own somewhat constricted way, a number of the problems (especially, the nature of Stalin- ism) which have since been widely debated by political scien- tists, sociologists, indeed, by all people concerned with politics. The nature of Stalinism and of post-Stalinist Communism is not an abstract or esoteric matter; the views one holds concerning these questions determine a large part of one's political conduct: and what is still more important, *they reflect one's fundamental moral values.*

No sensible radical over the age of thirty (something of a cut- off point, I'm told) wants young people merely to rehearse his ideas, or mimic his vocabulary, or look back upon his dusty old articles. On the contrary, what we find disturbing in some of the New Leftists is that, while barely knowing it, they tend to repeat somewhat too casually the tags of the very past they believe themselves to be transcending. But we do insist that in regard to a few crucial issues, above all those regarding totalitarian move- ments and societies, there should be no ambiguity, no evasive- ness.

So that if some New Leftists say that all the older radicals are equally acceptable or equally distasteful or equally inconsequen- tial in their eyes; if they see no significant difference between, say, Norman Thomas and Paul Sweezy such as would require them to regard Thomas as a comrade and Sweezy as an opponent—then the sad truth is that they have not at all left behind them the old disputes, but on the contrary, are still completely in their grip, though perhaps without being quite aware of what is happening to them. The issue of totalitarianism is neither academic nor merely historical; no one can seriously engage in politics without clearly and publicly defining his attitude toward it. I deliberately say "attitude" rather than "analysis," for while there can be a great many legitimate differences of analytic stress and nuance in discussing totalitarian society, morally there should be only a candid and sustained opposition to it.

3. *A vicarious indulgence in violence, often merely theoretic and thereby all the more irresponsible.* Not being a pacifist, I believe there may be times when violence is unavoidable; being a man of the twentieth century, I believe that a recognition of its necessity must come only after the most prolonged consideration, as an utterly last resort. To "advise" the Negro movement to adopt a policy encouraging or sanctioning violence, to sneer at Martin Luther King for his principled refusal of violence, is to take upon oneself a heavy responsibility—and if, as usually happens, taken lightly, it becomes sheer irresponsibility.

It is to be insensitive to the fact that the nonviolent strategy has arisen from Negro experience. It is to ignore the notable achievements that strategy has already brought. It is to evade the hard truth expressed by the Reverend Ralph Abernathy: "The whites have the guns." And it is to dismiss the striking moral advantage that nonviolence has yielded the Negro movement, as well as the turmoil, anxiety, and pain—perhaps even fundamental reconsideration—it has caused among whites in the North and the South.

There are situations in which Negroes will choose to defend themselves by arms against terrorist assault, as in the Louisiana towns where they have formed a club of "Elders" which patrols the streets peaceably but with the clear intent of retaliation in case of attack. The Negroes there seem to know what they are doing, and I would not fault them. Yet as a matter of general policy and upon a nationwide level, the Negro movement has chosen nonviolence: rightly, wisely, and heroically.

There are "revolutionaries" who deride this choice. They show a greater interest in ideological preconceptions than in the experience and needs of a living movement; and sometimes they are profoundly irresponsible, in that their true interest is not in helping to reach the goals chosen by the American Negroes, but is rather a social conflagration which would satisfy their apocalyptic yearnings even if meanwhile the Negroes were drowned in blood. The immediate consequence of such talk is a withdrawal from the ongoing struggles.

4. *An unconsidered enmity toward something vaguely called the Establishment.* As the term "Establishment" was first used in England, it had the value of describing—which is to say, delimiting—a precise social group; as it has come to be used in the United States, it tends to be an all-purpose put-down. In England it refers to a caste of intellectuals with an Oxbridge education, closely related in values to the ruling class, and setting the cultural standards which largely dominate both the London literary world and the two leading universities.

Is there an Establishment in this, or any cognate, sense in the United States? Perhaps. There may now be in the process of formation, for the first time, such an intellectual caste; but if so, precise discriminations of analysis and clear boundaries of specification would be required as to what it signifies and how it operates. As the term is currently employed, however, it is difficult to know who, besides those merrily using it as a thunderbolt of opprobrium, is *not* in the Establishment. And a reference that includes almost everyone tells us almost nothing.

5. *An equally unreflective belief in "the decline of the West"* —apparently without the knowledge that, more seriously held, this belief has itself been deeply ingrained in Western thought, frequently in the thought of reactionaries opposed to modern rationality, democracy, and sensibility.

The notion is so loose and baggy, it means little. Can it, however, be broken down? If war is a symptom of this decline, then it holds for the East as well. If totalitarianism is a sign, then it is not confined to the West. If economics is a criterion, then we must acknowledge, Marxist predictions aside, that there has been an astonishing recovery in Western Europe. If we turn to culture, then we must recognize that in the West there has just

come to an end one of the greatest periods in human culture—
that period of "modernism" represented by figures like Joyce,
Stravinsky, Picasso. If improving the life of the workers is to
count, then the West can say something in its own behalf. And if
personal freedom matters, then, for all its grave imperfections,
the West remains virtually alone as a place of hope. There remains, not least of all, the matter of racial prejudice, and here no
judgment of the West can be too harsh—so long as we remember that even this blight is by no means confined to the West,
and that the very judgments we make draw upon values nur-
tured by the West.

But is it not really childish to talk about "the West" as if it
were some indivisible whole we must either accept or reject
without amendment? There are innumerable strands in the Western tradition, and our task is to nourish those which encourage
dignity and freedom. But to envisage some global apocalypse
that will end in the destruction of the West is a sad fantasy, a
token of surrender before the struggles of the moment.

6. *A crude, unqualified anti-Americanism, drawing from every
possible source, even if one contradicts another: the aristocratic
bias of Eliot and Ortega, Communist propaganda, the specula-
tions of Tocqueville, the* ressentiment *of postwar Europe, etc.*

7. *An increasing identification with that sector of the "third
world" in which "radical" nationalism and Communist authoritarianism merge.* Consider this remarkable fact: In the past decade there have occurred major changes in the Communist world,
and many of the intellectuals in Russia and Eastern Europe have
reexamined their assumptions, often coming to the conclusion,
masked only by the need for caution, that democratic values are
primary in any serious effort at socialist reconstruction. Yet at
the very same time most of the New Leftists have identified not
with the "revisionists" in Poland or Djilas in Yugoslavia—or even
Tito. They identify with the harder, more violent, more dictatorial segments of the Communist world. And they carry this au-
toritarian bias into their consideration of the "third world,"
where they praise those rulers who choke off whatever weak im-
pulses there may be toward democratic life.

About the problems of the underdeveloped countries, among
the most thorny of our time, it is impossible even to begin to

speak with any fullness here. Nor do I mean to suggest that an attack upon authoritarianism and a defense of democracy exhaust consideration of those problems; on the contrary, it is the merest beginning. But what matters in this context is not so much the problems themselves as the attitudes, reflecting a deeper political-moral bias, which the New Leftists take toward such countries. A few remarks:

a. Between the suppression of democratic rights and the justification or excuse the New Leftists offer for such suppression there is often a very large distance, sometimes a complete lack of connection. Consider Cuba. It may well be true that United States policy became unjustifiably hostile toward the Castro regime at an early point in its history; but how is this supposed to have occasioned, or how is it supposed to justify, the suppression of democratic rights (including, and especially, those of all other left-wing tendencies) in Cuba? The apologists for Castro have an obligation to show what I think cannot be shown: the alleged close causal relation between United States pressure and the destruction of freedom in Cuba. Frequently, behind such rationales there is a tacit assumption that in times of national stress a people can be rallied more effectively by a dictatorship than by a democratic regime. But this notion—it was used to justify the suppression of political freedoms during the early Bolshevik years—is at the very least called into question by the experience of England and the United States during the Second World War. Furthermore, if Castro does indeed have the degree of mass support that his friends claim, one would think that the preservation of democratic liberties in Cuba would have been an enormously powerful symbol of self-confidence; would have won him greater support at home and certainly in other Latin-American countries; and would have significantly disarmed his opponents in the United States.

b. We are all familiar with the "social context" argument: that for democracy to flourish there has first to be a certain level of economic development, a quantity of infrastructure, and a coherent national culture. As usually put forward in academic and certain authoritarian-left circles, it is a crudely deterministic notion which I do not believe to be valid: for one thing, it fails to show how the suppression of even very limited political-social rights contributes, or is *in fact* caused by a wish, to solve these problems. (Who is prepared to maintain that Sukarno's suppression of the Indonesian Socialists and other dissident parties helped solve that country's economic or growth problems?) But for the sake of argument let us accept a version of this theory: Let us grant what is certainly a bit more plausible, that a full or stable democratic society cannot be established in a country ridden by economic primitivism, illiteracy, disease, cultural disunion, etc. The crucial question then becomes: Can at least some measure of democratic rights be won or granted?—say, the right of workers to form unions or the right of dissidents within a single-party state to form factions and express their views? For if a richer socioeconomic development is a prerequisite of democracy, it must also be remembered that such democratic rights, as they enable the emergence of autonomous social groups, are also needed for socioeconomic development.

c. Let us go even further and grant, again for the sake of argument, that in some underdeveloped countries authoritarian regimes may be necessary for a time. But even if this is true, which I do not believe it is, then it must be acknowledged as an unpleasant necessity, a price we are paying for historical crimes and mistakes of the past. In that case, radicals can hardly find their models in, and should certainly not become an uncritical cheering squad for, authoritarian dictators whose presence is supposed to be unavoidable.

The New Leftists, searching for an ideology by which to rationalize their sentiments, can now find exactly what they need in a remarkable book recently translated from the French, *The Wretched of the Earth*. Its author, Frantz Fanon, is a Negro from Martinique who became active in the Algerian revolution. He articulates with notable power the views of those nationalist-revolutionaries in the underdeveloped countries who are contemptuous of their native bourgeois leadership, who see their revolution being pushed beyond national limits and into their own social structure, who do not wish to merge with or become subservient to the Communists yet have no strong objection in principle to Communist methods and values.

Fanon tries to locate a new source of revolutionary energy: the peasants who, he says, "have nothing to lose and everything to gain." He deprecates the working class: In the Western countries it has been bought off, and in the underdeveloped nations, it constitutes a tiny "aristocracy." What emerges is a curious version of Trotsky's theory of permanent revolution, concerning national revolts in the backward countries which, to fulfill themselves, must become social revolutions. But with one major difference: Fanon assigns to the peasants and the urban declassed poor the vanguard role Trotsky had assigned to the workers.

What, however, has really happened in countries like Algeria? The peasantry contributes men and blood for an anticolonial war. Once the war is won, it tends to disperse, relapsing into local interests and seeking individual small-scale ownership of the land. It is too poor, too weak, too diffuse to remain or become the leading social force in a newly liberated country. The bourgeoisie, what there was of it, having been shattered and the working class pushed aside, what remains? Primarily the party of nationalism, led by men who are dedicated, uprooted, semieducated, and ruthless. The party rules, increasingly an independent force perched upon and above the weakened classes.

But Fanon is not taken in by his own propaganda. He recognizes the dangers of a preening dictator and has harsh things to say against the Nkrumah type. He proposes, instead, that "the party should be the direct expression of the masses," and adds, "Only those underdeveloped countries led by revolutionary elites who have come up from the people can today *allow* the entry of the masses upon the scene of history."(Emphasis added.)

Fanon wants the masses to participate, yet throughout his book the single-party state remains an unquestioned assumption. But what if the masses do not wish to "participate"? And what if they are hostile to "the"—always "the"—party? Participation without choice is a burlesque of democracy: indeed, it is an essential element of a totalitarian or authoritarian society, for it means that the masses of people act out a charade of involvement but are denied the reality of decision.

The authoritarians find political tendencies and representative men with whom to identify in the Communist world; so do we. We identify with the people who have died for freedom, like Imre Nagy, or who suffered in prison, like Djilas. We identify with the "revisionists," those political *marranos* who, forced to employ Communist jargon, yet spoke out for a socialism democratic in character and distinct from both Communism and capitalism. As it happens, our friends in the Communist world are not in power; but since when has that mattered to socialists?

In 1957, at the height of the Polish ferment, the young philosopher Leszek Kolakowski wrote a brief article entitled "What Is Socialism?" It consisted of a series of epigrammatic sentences describing what socialism is not (at the moment perhaps the more immediate concern), but tacitly indicating as well what socialism should be. The article was banned by the Gomulka regime but copies reached Western periodicals. Here are a few sentences.

Socialism is not:

A society in which a person who has committed no crime sits at home waiting for the police.

A society in which one person is unhappy because he says what he thinks, and another happy because he does not say what is in his mind.

A society in which a person lives better because he does not think at all.

A state whose neighbors curse geography.

A state which wants all its citizens to have the same opinions in philosophy, foreign policy, economics, literature, and ethics.

A state whose government defines its citizens' rights, but whose citizens do not define the government's rights.

A state in which there is private ownership of the means of production.

A state which considers itself solidly socialist because it has liquidated private ownership of the means of production.

A state which always knows the will of the people before it asks them.

A state in which the philosophers and writers always say the same as the generals and ministers, but always after them.

A state in which the returns of parliamentary elections are always predictable.

A state which does not like to see its citizens read back numbers of newspapers.

These negatives imply a positive, and that positive is a central lesson of contemporary history: the unity of socialism and democracy. To preserve democracy as a political mode without extending it into every crevice of social and economic life is to allow it to become increasingly sterile, formal, ceremonial. To nationalize an economy without enlarging democratic freedoms is to create a new kind of social exploitation. Radicals and liberals may properly and fraternally disagree about many other things; but upon this single axiom concerning the value of democracy, this conviction wrung from the tragedy of our age, politics must rest.

[1965]

THE MYSTICAL MILITANTS

by Michael Harrington

The young radicals of the early sixties were mystical militants, articulating the authentic miseries of the poor even while maintaining some of the attitudes of the middle class. They were also one of the most significant, hopeful developments in recent American life. I do not emphasize their importance as an uncritical compliment. They have already been subjected to quite enough journalistic flattery, and some of the mass media would probably like to package them as they did the beats. Moreover, I have differences with the young radicals and have on occasion been puzzled, exasperated, and even saddened by them. Yet the happy fact remains that the emergence of a personally committed generation seeking basic social change is momentous. They are a minority of their age group, to be sure, but a creative, activist minority who should place their stamp upon the times. Eventually, and it will probably try the anarchist spirit of some of them, they are going to lead adult movements and change this society. Whatever their shortcomings, the New Leftists hold out the hope for a renewal of American social criticism and action.

When I became a radical in 1948 (the last year of the politics of the thirties), it was taken for granted (on the Left) that the Fourth of July was really a front for the four hundred families. In part, this was a heritage of European socialist theory, in part a legacy of the American experience of a depression which had demystified so many clichés. One did not get angry that the powers-that-be lied and cheated and manipulated. That, after all, was their function in life, just as it was the task of the Left to create a society which would not need to corrupt its avowed values.

The young radicals of today, it seems to me, did not start with this inherited cynicism. They came to teen-age during the American celebration of the Eisenhower years and were, for the most part, not really politically conscious until after both Korea and McCarthyism. They seemed to have believed what they were told about freedom, equality, justice, world peace, and the like. They became activists in order to affirm these traditional values with regard to some ethical cause: defending civil liberties against HUAC, picketing for the life of Caryl Chessman, demanding an end to nuclear testing, fighting for civil rights. The shock generated by the society's duplicity in this or that single issue then opened their eyes to larger, and even more systematic, injustices.

It is, I suspect, this unique fifties-sixties experience which gives the New Left its distinctive flavor: a sense of outrage, of having been betrayed by all the father figures, which derives from an original innocence. And it is also the source of the young radicals' insistence on sincerity and community. They begin, not with an image of the future which was received, in one way or another, from Europe and involves theory and history, but from a sense of the immediate contradiction between democratic posturing and the undemocratic reality. They descend from the abolitionists and Wobblies, not from Marx.

This intense, even painful, consciousness of American hypocrisy has led the young radicals to people who do not, or cannot, play the national rhetorical game: the left-outs, the outcasts. And it has involved them in a clash between mysticism and militancy.

In the iconography of the thirties, the proletarian was a figure of incipient power and a puritan sense of duty. The *lumpen* proletarian was despised because he did not belong to a conscious class, because he floated; and he was feared as a potential shock trooper of fascism. By the fifties, much of the old élan had left the labor movement and, with an overwhelming majority of the people satisfied with Eisenhower, there did not seem to be much of a political perspective for insurgency. At this point a cultural rebellion took place among young people. It was expressed among the beats who contracted out of the system; it informed Norman Mailer's vision of the white man who aspired to the cool and the hip that white society provoked in the Negro.

As disestablishmentarians, the young radicals continue this tradition of the fifties. They identify precisely with the *lumpen,* the powerless, the maimed, the poor, the criminal, the junkie. And there is a mystical element in this commitment which has nothing to do with politics. By going into the slum, they are doing penance for the sins of affluence; by sharing the life of those who are so impoverished that they are uncorrupted, values are affirmed. It is honest and moral and antihypocritical to be on the margin of society *whether the community organization works or not.* Indeed, there is a fear of "success," a suspicion that it would mean the integration of the oppressed into the corruption of the oppressors.

But, on the other hand, the New Leftists are not fifties beats. They are angry militants who see the poor as a new force in America, perhaps even as a substitute for the proletariat that failed. So they insist that the Mississippi and Alabama sharecroppers can choose for themselves. But from this point of view, it does make quite a bit of difference whether the community-organizing campaign works or not.

An analogy from the thirties might illuminate the political hope that is here asserted by the young radicals. In 1932 or 1933, many polite Americans believed that if you gave a worker a bathtub, he would put coal in it. And the skilled AFL members thought it preposterous that mass production machine operators could form *their own* union. On paper, the right to organize was proclaimed by the Wagner Act. In fact, it took at least five tumultuous years of picketing, striking, and sitting-in before the CIO turned the brave words into something of a reality. Similarly in 1964, America declared war on poverty; and most of the well-bred citizenry did not intend by that to have field hands and janitors speaking up for themselves; and the young radicals, who have this knack of taking America's promises seriously, sought a surge from below to give meaning to the phrasemaking on high. But, as I think the New Left realizes, this analogy is faulty in part. The mass production workers were, just as radical theory had said, forced by the conditions of their existence (thousands of men assembled at one miserable place with common problems and interests) into a solidarity which became the basis of union organization. The poor are not grouped into incipient communities. A slum street fragments and atomizes people; the two largest groups of the poor, the young and the old, have little to do with one another; and even if they could get together, the poor are still a minority of the society. Therefore it is going to take even more creativity to help the outcasts into their own than it did to build industrial unionism.

For a number of reasons the New Leftists shied away, until quite recently, from thinking through the problems posed by their own militancy. For one thing, they are indeed "American" in the empirical, activist, antitheoretical sense of the word. For another, they rejected the scholasticism of some of the traditional Left formulae (as well as the genuine profundity of the Left's intellectual heritage) and they were imbued with the spirit of the civil rights movement of the early sixties where the willingness to go to jail was more important than political abstractions. Recently there have been signs that the young radicals are moving into a phase of discussion and debate. And this is necessary if the conflict of mysticism and militancy is to be resolved. For if the poor are seen as Dostoevskian peasants whose beauty is their suffering, then politics and the inevitable alliances with others are a contamination; but if they are to be a social force, then coalition is a necessity.

The New Leftists regard the welfare state, rather than the economic royalists, as the incarnation of the status quo. This is an almost inevitable result of trying to look at America with the eyes of the poor. It is very right—and it is a dangerous half-truth.

The welfare state developed in the thirties was created by, and for, the "middle third" of American society: the liberal middle class and the organized workers. The poor were, and still are, those who were left behind in the depression because of bad geographical, occupational, or political luck: migrants, farm workers, full-time laborers at poverty jobs, racial and ethnic minorities which came into the economic mainstream at the time of the computer rather than of the assembly line. In addition, the poor include all those who have suffered from a *relative deterioration* in various social insurance and income maintenance programs (social security, unemployment compensation, etc.).

The *visible* enemies of the poor are not the captains of industry but the landlords, shopkeepers and, often enough, the agents of the welfare state. For the welfare state is, of course, ill-financed and bureaucratic, and this distorts the good intentions of many of the fine people who work for it and reinforces the vices of the bad. So for the poor the welfare state means a humiliating dependence and fear and requires a constant, cunning battle against authority. The young radicals attempt to articulate these fierce resentments that they discovered in the slums, and the experience does not leave them in a mood for sociological nicety. The welfare state is, they say, a fraud. And the liberals, who actually boast of having created this monster in the name of humane values, are therefore the worst hypocrites.

In formulating this attitude, it is not simply that the New Leftists overlook some history, which youth always does, but that they ignore some *relevant* history. The welfare state did not come out of the thirties as a result of a liberal plot to manipulate the dispossessed. It was created over the violent resistance of most men of property and wealth, and its creation required a major upheaval on the part of the workers, from the bottom up. Business did not begin its conversion to welfare statism until the World War II discovery that a federal agency staffed by corporation executives was not exactly a class enemy of the rich; and its final conversion to "tax cut" Keynesianism waited upon the persuasiveness of Lyndon B. Johnson. There was, and is, a very real element of buying off the restless natives in business acceptance of welfarism.

The relevance of this history is that the current welfare state consensus is not quite so homogeneous as the President and some New Leftists sometimes think. For the apparent agreement conceals the latent conflict between the sophisticated conservatives on the one hand, and the liberal-labor-civil rights forces on the other. One can rightly accuse the liberal welfarists of having been too nostalgically proud of *their* upheaval to understand the terrible urgency of more change now as seen from the bottom of society. But it is something else again to *equate* all present supporters of the welfare state with one another.

And here I think I come to my most serious criticism of the New Left: that they sometimes expect the poor to act out the moral values of the middle-class radical who has come to the slum.

I find, for instance, a genuine poignancy in Tom Hayden's realization that a coalition of the outcasts will not really be able to change the society and that radicalism can only give itself up to, and become part of, "the energy kept restless and active under the clamps of paralyzed imperial society. Radicalism then would go beyond the concepts of optimism and pessimism as guides to work, finding itself working despite odds. Its realism and sanity would be grounded in nothing more than the ability to face whatever comes."

This attitude is a logical deduction from the theory that all the welfare staters, from Henry Ford to Walter Reuther, if you will, are the same kind of manipulative bureaucrats. For if everybody but the poor and outcast are "they," then "we" must inevitably lose, for by definition "we" are not strong enough to transform a fraud and scandal supported by sixty or seventy percent of the society.

The conscious and committed radical can find his solace in such a vision; most of the poor cannot. Indeed, one of the things that has made the poor so inarticulate, so unorganized, so hopeless, is precisely the conviction that they can't win. Are they now to be told stoically to treasure their misery, which, though permanent, is at least not corrupted by the hypocrisy of affluence? That will be cold comfort. And it will not move them to action, but rather reinforce them in their passivity.

The danger is that the poor will thus be assigned roles as abstractions in the morality plays of the disenchanted middle class. To fight this possibility, the New Leftists must come up with a strategy which offers real hope to the other America. And this means making a more sophisticated analysis of the coalition which supports the welfare state.

For the liberal wing of this consensus certainly did not start with the intention to build a manipulative bureaucracy, and it maintains values which *could* provide a basis for transforming the present structure. If the social-change movements of the previous generation must be shaken up by the poor, they must be shaken up in order to be made allies. To do this requires an intensification of the efforts to organize the slums and ghettos and backwoods as an independent political force. But if there is to be honest hope, that organization must be thought of as the catalyst of a new political majority in the United States, and not as a doomed last stand of noble savages.

[1966]

"CONFRONTATION POLITICS" IS A DANGEROUS GAME

by Irving Howe

A new term has entered the American language—"confrontation politics," the equivalent in public life of Russian roulette in private life. Some who play this new political game are authentic desperadoes, mostly young Negro militants; others are white middle-class students acting—or acting out—a fantasy-wish of revolution.

For the black desperadoes, confrontation politics can bring large risks: prison, violence, death. For the white students, the risks until recently were small; but after the ghastliness of Chicago and the growing popular obsession with "law and order," they will surely increase. For the country as a whole, the problem is perplexing. At a time of social disorder, when gross injustices continue to plague us, there arise combative minorities charged with moral idealism and apocalyptic emotion, which have developed tactics of protest going beyond the usual democratic methods yet short of the usual insurrectionary ones.

Like other New Left notions, confrontation politics has not been well articulated as a theory. It is a kind of politics that grows up through improvisation, and it has been improvised as a way of getting around the sense of futility which has usually beset American radicalism. It has been choreographed as an out-of-door explosion, a sort of real-life theater.

The purpose is to prod and incite a dormant, insensitive society into recognizing its moral failures. No longer committed, as were the Marxists, to the idea that the proletariat would be the crucial lever for the transformation of history, the young semi-anarchists who practice confrontation see themselves as a minority probably doomed to remain one for a long time. They have no expectation of creating new electoral majorities and small expectation of persuading large numbers of people; for they see the mass of Americans as brainwashed by "the media" (the very media which give them vast amounts of publicity). Their politics is a politics of desperation, at best moral shock and at worst nihilist irritation. They assign to themselves the task of sacrifice and assault, as a self-chosen vanguard which must destroy the complacence of "corporate liberalism."

What makes this task seem especially urgent is the feeling that in Vietnam the United States is conducting an immoral war which the ordinary democratic process is too slow and cumbersome to cope with.

One source of confrontation politics, seldom acknowledged, is the strategy worked out by the civil rights movement in the South during the fifties. Under strong pacifist guidance at that point, the civil rights movement "confronted" Southern institutions through direct action—that is, through demonstrations, parades, lunch-counter sit-ins. Conceived as a way to force the South into recognizing that Negroes would no longer be dormant, these actions involved a degree of "obstruction" (Jim Crow arrangements in stores were upset) and a kind of "confrontation" (nonviolent minorities exposed themselves to beatings by police and mobs.)

The success of such actions depended on the following conditions:

The demonstrators were demanding rights which had already been recognized, both in law and moral consensus, by the nation as a whole. Despite failures by the federal government to enforce antidiscrimination laws, the demonstrators could count on at least some practical help from the Kennedy and Johnson administrations, as well as large amounts of support from many Northerners. And while the Southern police often remained brutal, it was no longer possible for municipal and state governments in the South to destroy Negro protest through sheer terror.

The demonstrations came at a time when there were growing differences of response among Southern whites. A majority may still have remained convinced that Jim Crow was a practical convenience, but a growing minority seems to have felt it was morally indefensible. Even if that minority did not always act with courage, it did begin to break the monolithic front which the white South had put up for decades. Doubt and guilt pierced the hard shell of white superiority.

The unconditional nonviolence practiced by Dr. King and his friends was a principle that sections of the middle-class South had to respect—indeed, to respect almost as much as white Northerners came to admire. The sight of men willing to turn the other cheek is one that must move, or at least disturb, people who retain even the flimsiest connections with Christianity. Tactically, it bewildered the Southern police, who would have been delighted to trade one hundred blows for one, but didn't know how to cope with men going limp under beatings.

While the Southern demonstrators sometimes broke local ordinances, their actions were justifiable by democratic standards. For they had long been deprived of the right to vote and thereby participate in changing policies through peaceful means —which meant they now had a certain sanction for resorting to partly coercive but completely nonviolent forms of direct action. Furthermore, they were struggling for the enforcement of national laws superseding local ordinances, many of which were deliberately contrived to circumvent federal legislation and were commonly felt to be of dubious constitutionality. Indeed, one reason for breaking local ordinances was to challenge their constitutionality.

The power of Southern protest derived partly from its alliance with major forces in the North: liberals, unionists, churches, and academicians, all pressing for civil rights legislation. One reason the Selma march proved to be so valuable was that it came just at the moment when it could most dramatically induce popular support for the Voting Rights Act. By contrast, demonstrations leading only to other demonstrations, or demonstrations lacking clearly defined goals (e.g., "justice"), or demonstrations with hopelessly unrealizable goals (e.g., a "black republic" in the

South) will result in a dissipation of energies. The civil rights marches during the fifties and early sixties, however, were directed toward concrete local aims and in support of proposed national legislation.

Now, all of these favorable circumstances were special to the South, and it would be naïve to suppose they can now be duplicated on a national scale. When certain kinds of demonstrations are held by anti-Vietnam protestors—especially if they are feckless enough to include Vietcong banners—it can hardly be said that they act in behalf of moral-political opinions shared by a large majority of the people but thwarted by a sectional minority; or that they have been significantly deprived of their right to organize and protest; or that they act out of a principled devotion to nonviolence.

These are not new problems, either in the development of radical movements or the history of democratic states. There are historical precedents, and something can be learned from glancing at them.

Shortly after the Russian Revolution there appeared tendencies within the Communist movement, opposed by Lenin and Trotsky, which led to a strategy of constant assault: endless demonstrations, unremitting "offensives," indeed a precursor of confrontation politics. Some ultraleft German Communists even gave this strategy a name, the "theory of electrification." Through reckless self-sacrifice, the party would "electrify" the masses into revolution. Predictably, this led to disasters in Germany and elsewhere during the early twenties—brave but suicidal coups by Communist combat groups which failed to gain the support of the workers. About the theory of electrification Trotsky remarked with asperity that the probable consequence was that the electrifiers would burn themselves.

In the immediate pre-Hitler period, there was an even more senseless turn toward a kind of confrontation politics. The Communists came up with the insane notion of "social fascism," according to which the Social Democrats, and not the Nazis, were the main danger in Germany. (Today, it is "the liberals" who are the main danger. . . .) The Communists kept staging endless demonstrations which, in Trotsky's phrase, "succeeded only in irritating all classes without winning over any." They antagonized the middle classes; they wore out the patience of the workers; they exhausted their own cadres. They made loud noises about "taking power" but never came within reach of power. Inevitably there appeared a force calling for the restoration of "law and order," behind which a large segment of the population united, actively or passively. It would be an exaggeration to say that the Communist tactics caused the rise of Hitlerism, but no exaggeration at all to say that they helped the Nazis come to power.

Taken simply as a syndrome of going into the streets (what has been called the "Theory of Permanent Demonstrations"), the politics of confrontation would not be a very serious matter. Demonstrations can be useful; demonstrations can be self-defeating. Opposition to the Vietnam war was surely rallied and increased through demonstrations; but some of them, by allowing themselves to be linked with the Vietcong and overtaken by anti-American hatreds not at all essential to the cause of peace, had a counterproductive effect, stiffening the hostility felt by millions of Americans toward dissent. About such matters we can only make estimates based partly on our sense of what this country is like. There is, finally, no science for measuring the consequences of going into the streets.

Far more serious is the political outlook which inspires confrontationist acts. As developed by Herbert Marcuse, the current New Left guru, this political outlook advances the following propositions: We live in an advanced stage of capitalism, a mass society providing bread, circuses, and technology, which has tamed the forces of opposition and thereby undercut hopes for "transcendence." There is no great likelihood, in Marcuse's view, that we will soon witness an end to a social oppression sustained by material plenty but yielding no spiritual gratification. Efforts at reform tend to be superficial, and many of the values of liberalism—tolerance, free speech, electoral activity—are depreciated as devices for adjusting people to the status quo.

Revolution thus being declared all but impossible and reform all but ineffectual, Marcuse's doctrines justify those radicals who turn away from both traditional Leninism and social democracy, in order to launch a series of adventures or "raids," perhaps to usurp, perhaps to unsettle established power, but clearly without much concern for democratic processes. The claim here is that the society can be shaken into change, if shaken at all, only through attacks by marginal groups: the outraged poor, alienated hippies, rebellious students.

Whatever one may think about the analytical portions of Marcuse's thought, his political conclusions offer a simultaneous rationalization for withdrawal and wildness, copping-out and turning-on. Precisely insofar as numbers of students have come under Marcuse's influence, the picture of society he draws seems less and less valid. Men are not slipping into apathy and somnolence, at least not yet; they are disturbed, restless, worried. In the last decade the United States has not become stultified, immobile, and indifferent. The *cul-de-sac* of historical stagnation posited by Marcuse is indeed a nightmare haunting every sensitive man, but one must be able to distinguish between the fears of the dark and the facts of day.

Still, if you hold a version of Marcuse's ideas and believe liberalism is exhausted or corrupt or inseparable from "racist imperialism"; if you further conclude that no major social classes within society can be expected significantly to transform it; you then have no serious alternative to either a Salinger-like withdrawal or the political equivalent of guerrilla raids. By this last phrase I don't mean literally shooting it out—though there are a few free-lance lunatics advocating as much—but rather a series of actions, dramatic, desperate, and provocative, which keep the society in a state of constant turmoil and the university in a state of constant chaos.

This strategy, in my view, can lead only to disaster and a backlash of terrifying proportions. The signs of it are everywhere about us.

A tacit premise behind confrontation politics is that the university largely resembles the surrounding society, or is even identical in nature with it. The result is to damage academic life and distort political action.

Within the university the New Left students engage with more or less liberal faculties, and behind these engagements there is often the assumption that, finally, the university will behave like a middle-class parent. When sometimes it does not, there follow among students considerable shock and rage. At Columbia the students who seized buildings and declared "communes" were engaged in a quasi-revolutionary action—or so some of them said. But when the Columbia administration (quite stupidly, I think) retaliated with the police force which New Left theory says is inevitable but which New Left feelings are often not really prepared for, the students cried foul. They invoked the traditional view of the university as a cloister of intellect from which police should be barred.

At this point they were caught in a dilemma. If they believed it proper to transform the campus into a training ground for revolutionary action, they could hardly complain when the powers-that-be retaliated with force. If they genuinely believed (as I, for one, believe) that the campus should be a center of learning from which the police are barred, then they could hardly treat the university as if it were *no more than* a microcosm of capitalist society. True, they might argue with much cogency that many universities have been contaminated and should be returned to their true purposes of scholarship and teaching; but to say that would be to accept—O dreadful prospect!—a view of the university close to that of liberalism.

The analogy between university and society breaks down in a still more serious way. One reason the tactics of the Students for a Democratic Society have worked on certain campuses is that implicitly they count on that mixture of affection and irritation many faculty people feel toward "the students." In good measure the politics of confrontation as practiced on the campus depends on a benevolent or indecisive response from the liberal professors whom the New Left treats with such contempt. But once such tactics are transferred to the society at large, the result is going to be very different. The professors, who count for a good deal on the campus, count for fairly little in the society; and the society itself is not nearly so pacific or indulgent as are most professors. One needs a talent for self-delusion to say that in the United States liberalism—for all its many faults and failures—represents the main danger to humane aspirations.

No; this society retains large potentials of hatred and violence, its capacities for tolerating what it regards as disruption have a visible limit, and its response to confrontation tactics could well be a crushing display of force which would harm many people who have nothing to do with the New Left. I say none of this by way of approval, only by way of describing hard facts which those of us who believe in radical politics must take into account.

If anything should give the New Left pause, it is the fact that according to the polls, a clear majority of the American people approved of Mayor Daley's treatment of the Chicago demonstrators. I don't mean it should give them pause in their opposition to the Vietnam war, an opposition I share; but it should stir them into rethinking the value of confrontation methods.

Now, when arguments of this kind are put forward in debates with the New Left, one of the usual replies goes like this: "You liberals, you Social Democrats are always trying to hamstring protest by raising the specter of backlash. But where is the backlash? Is it perhaps just a bogey with which you're trying to frighten us? And if we pay attention to it, how can we ever mount an effective protest?"

The backlash is everywhere. Some of us, raised on memories of earlier decades, carry a mental picture of reactionary mobs and American Legionnaires assaulting radicals in the street: That was true in the twenties and thirties; it may yet prove true in the next few years. But just as everything else in modern society becomes bureaucratized, so has backlash. Instead of swarming mobs, there are now trained police. The white workers of Italian or Polish or Slavic origin who have managed to save up enough money to buy themselves little homes in the suburbs aren't likely to organize mobs to invade the black ghettos—at least not yet; but they are inclined, many of them, to vote for George Wallace in the name of law and order. That some twenty per cent of the American electorate could even consider voting for Wallace—surely that's a sufficient sign of backlash.

Is the answer, then, for dissidents to crawl into holes and keep silent? Of course not. But in order to protest the Vietnam war it isn't necessary to rouse all the prejudices millions of Americans hold, and it isn't even necessary to outrage their sincere patriotic sentiments. In order to fight for Negro rights, it isn't necessary to talk blood or to call white men "honkies" and policemen "pigs." That's a way of blowing off steam, and the resulting profit goes to George Wallace.

One aim of confrontation politics is the "polarization" of society. In plain English, this means that by constant assault the activists hope to drive a segment of the liberals into radicalism; thereupon the "mushy middle" of the country will be broken up; and we can then look forward to an apocalypse, with two extremes hardened and ready for a final conflict.

When they invoke this vision the confrontationists are drawing upon political emotions that have been very powerful in the twentieth century—emotions concerning "the seizure of power," a political Second Coming. Having shared these emotions and still being susceptible to them, I can appreciate their force. But I must nevertheless ask: What, in the present circumstances, would be the likely outcome of such a polarization in the United States?

Were anything of the sort to happen, millions of ordinary Americans—for whom student protest-drugs-hippiedom-black rioting forms a stream of detested association—would also be activated. Lower-class white ethnic groups would be stirred up. *Lumpen* elements would be emboldened. Both respectable and marginal classes would turn to demagogues promising order in the streets.

Despite its talk about "the power elite" and the idiotic notion it sometimes proposes that we live under "liberal fascism," the New Left clings to an excessively optimistic view of American society. Its spokesmen have neither memory nor awareness of what fascism—the real thing, *fascist* fascism—would be like. They fail to recognize that there are sleeping dogs it would be just as well to let lie. And they are shockingly indifferent to the likelihood that the first victim of a new reaction in America would be the universities in which they now find shelter.

Only in terms of a theory of polarization can one explain the peculiar intensity with which New Left students kept trying to break up the meetings of Hubert Humphrey, while virtually ignoring those of Richard Nixon. (I am against breaking up anyone's meetings.) They were acting on the premise that liberalism is their main enemy, and some of them have even said that they would find attractive an alliance between far Left and far Right.

Such notions tacitly continue the old Stalinist tradition of "the worse, the better" and *"Nach Hitler, uns."* Yet all of recent history enforces the lesson that misery cannot be the seedbed of progress or chaos of freedom. Polarization helps, not the Left, but the Right; not those with grievances, but those with guns. In any case, is the prospect of polarization an attractive one? How many of us would like to face a choice between an America symbolized by George Wallace and an America symbolized by Tom Hayden? Morally, because he is against racism, Hayden is superior; but politically, neither has much respect for democracy. I for one would fear for my safety almost as much with one as with the other. Wallace might have me pistol-whipped as a Communist, and Hayden have me sent to a labor camp as a Social Democrat. Hayden would be more accurate politically, but what sort of consolation would that be?

For a while confrontation politics seems to work. Caught off-balance, the enemy panics. College administrators aren't sure how to cope with students who seize buildings. But in time, for better or worse, they are going to figure out a way of dealing with this problem.

There is some truth in the claim—it constitutes a damning criticism of our society—that provocative demonstrations spilling over into violence have a way of gaining attention, certainly from TV, which programmatic and disciplined protest does not. But it is a truth easily overstated. The ghetto riots in Detroit and Watts have not brought notable improvements to their communities; they have not led to those increased federal appropriations which are the only serious way of starting to clear the slums. At best they have enabled these communities, at enormous cost to themselves, to gain a slightly larger share of the funds already available. And as the California election of Ronald Reagan showed, the violence helped set off an electoral trend which can only signify a tight-fisted and mean-spirited policy toward the blacks.

Concerning this, let me quote from a discussion between Bayard Rustin, the Negro leader, and myself in the November 1968 *Dissent:*

> *Howe:* I keep encountering the argument in regard to riots: "We know in principle it's not a good thing. But

when you have a society that is not susceptible to pressure or moral appeals, the only way you can get them to pay attention is through raising hell."

Rustin: There are two tragedies here. One is that to some extent they're right. You don't get concessions until there's been trouble. . . . The second tragedy is that although we receive minor concessions from the establishment, once the rioting reaches a certain point there will be repression against the entire Negro community.

Howe: Raising the ante indefinitely isn't going to work. . . .

Rustin: Right. To repress one-tenth of the population will require an assault on the civil liberties of everyone. And in such an atmosphere, no genuine progress in the redistribution of wealth can take place. . . . There's another factor. Sooner or later the unity of the Negroes, small as it is, in making demands on the whole society will be splintered, because the Negro community gets into a debate—are you or are you not for violence?—instead of uniting around a fight for political and economic objectives

The advocates of confrontation seem undisturbed by the fact that they are setting precedents which could lead to a major crisis for democracy. If it is permissible for opponents of the war to burn government records, why may not neo-Fascists do the same thing a few years later? If it is permissible for left-wing students to seize buildings in behalf of virtuous ends, why may not their action become a precedent for doing the same thing in behalf of detestable ends? At the very least, such problems must be discussed.

Some will say that violence and illegality are already rampant in the society, and that they are merely responding to their official use. This has a measure of truth. But I would reply that democratic procedures, incomplete as they may still be, have been established only after decades of struggle, and that it would be feckless to dismiss them as mere sham. Those of us who see the need for radical change have the most interest in preserving democracy.

A few years ago Staughton Lynd wrote about an antiwar demonstration in Washington: "It was unbearably moving to watch the sea of banners move out . . . toward the Capitol. . . . Still more poignant was the perception that as the crowd moved toward the seat of government . . . our forward movement was irresistibly strong . . . nothing could have stopped that crowd from taking possession of its government. Perhaps next time we should keep going, occupying for a time the rooms from which orders issue."

One must ask Staughton Lynd: Under whose mandate were the marchers to occupy the government? And if they did "perhaps next time" arrogate to themselves the privilege of a coup d'etat, even a symbolic one lasting five minutes, how will they keep other crowds, other causes—equally sincere, equally "moving"—from doing the same "perhaps the time after next"?

The politics of confrontation bear an inherent drift toward antidemocratic elitism. Electoral processes are declared irrelevant, majorities mere formalities. Once such notions are indulged, the choice is either to sink back into apathy with pot or to plunge into a desperate elitism which dismisses the people as boobs and assigns the "tasks of history" to a self-appointed vanguard. And in the current atmosphere, it isn't hard to drift from elitism to talk of violence. Mostly, so far, it is talk.

But there are troubling signs. In the summer of 1968 the office of Stanford University's president was set afire, an event that followed in time a season of student sit-ins. I see no reason to connect these two, and would never have dreamed of doing so had I not read the following in a New Left paper, *The Midpeninsula Observer:*

"Most leftists in this area seem to feel that the fire was politically motivated, and a split of opinion has developed with regard to the tactical efficacy of the act. Some believe that the fire was an effective attack on state power and that it was a logical extension of the leftist activity that has been going on at and around Stanford. Others think that the fire itself was a mistake . . . since it is not clearly connected with a political movement and since most of the people who might be educated by such an act are gone for the summer."

Significant here is not the speculation that the fire was politically motivated but the argument offered by those leftists opposed to setting fires. They seem to have a seasonal theory of the revolutionary uses of arson. In the winter, apparently, when more people can be "educated" by such an act, these critics would find arson more acceptable. The whole thing, I must say, reminds one of Dostoevski's *The Possessed*—as also of George Orwell's caustic remark that a certain kind of infantile Leftism is "playing with fire on the part of people who don't even know that fire is hot."

Or here, to cite another instance, is a 25 August 1968 report by Robert Maynard in *The Washington Post* about a feud between SNCC and the Black Panthers. At a meeting between leaders of the two groups, writes Maynard, there was a sharp dispute which "resulted in Panthers drawing guns on James Forman," the SNCC leader. Another SNCC leader, Julius Lester, is quoted by Maynard as having written: "The shoot-out was averted, fortunately, but there was no doubt . . . that whatever merger or alliance may have existed was finished."

As a sign of the fraternal spirit induced by Black Power, this isn't much more convincing than the civil war in Nigeria. No doubt, much of this gun-drawing is a kind of playacting; but playacting can lead to acting.

Nor is the rhetoric of violence likely to diminish soon. The New Left will continue to talk blithely about revolution, but the police will do most of the shooting. Might it not, therefore, be in order to plead with the young confrontationists that if the ethic of democracy seems to them hollow or irrelevant, they at least think in terms of common prudence? And perhaps that they take off an hour to read Lenin's *Left-Wing Communism: An Infantile Disorder* in which the great revolutionist explains why compromise and even retreat are sometimes necessary?

One defense sometimes offered for confrontation politics is that, effective or not, it provides a dramatic way of releasing emotions. Of all the arguments, this seems to me the least tolerable. It means that in behalf of self-indulgence one is ready to bring down on oneself and others the forces of repression, of which the first victims would surely be the Negroes about whom the New Left declares itself so deeply concerned. This is a form of middle-class frivolity; a politics of the kindergarten. About such carryings-on (Yippies' trippies) I would cite a remarkable statement recently made by the English writer, David Caute, himself a New Left sympathizer, after his return from Czechoslovakia:

"These observations reveal to me a certain perversity in my own attitude. Nostalgia for student riots, clashes with the police, and totally exposed thighs suggest a false romanticism, an irritable desire to inflict on an ostensibly sane society a form of chaos which, as a way of life, is superficial and nihilistic. The manner in which the young Czechs are conducting themselves is really a model of civic control and enlightenment, whereas we have become alcoholic on sensation and violence."

Far more serious are those who advance the view that, as a matter of conscience and regardless of consequences, they must break a given law. If a man finds the Vietnam war a moral crime and says he cannot serve in the Army even though the result be his imprisonment, then I think he merits respect and, often, admiration. He is ready to accept punishment for his behavior, ready to pay the price of his convictions. His violation of the law is undertaken in behalf of a higher principle and out of respect for law in general; he hopes to stir the conscience of society or, failing that, to live according to his own. Such a version of civil disobedience, Spiro Agnew notwithstanding, is a legitimate act when seriously undertaken in a democratic society.

What is not legitimate is to use tactics that look like civil disobedience but are meant to further "revolutionary" ends (e.g., blocking draft boards), since these can only lead to displays of impotence and are likely to harm those who genuinely care about civil disobedience. Nor is it legitimate to resort to civil disobedience, or a tactic easily confused with it, every Monday and Thursday morning. Acts of conscience violating the law can be taken seriously only if they are concerned with the most fundamental moral issues. And there is also, I think, an obligation to obey many laws one dislikes, in order to preserve the possibility for peacefully changing them.

This is a bad moment in American politics. The Vietnam war is a scandal and a disaster; social obligations pile up shamefully in the cities; radical measures are called for; the exploited cannot remain silent. Militant protest is therefore needed. Yet we must try to make certain that the methods we use to fight against injustice do not give the opponents of liberty an occasion for destroying both the struggle for justice and the procedures of liberty. That would be to invite disaster through a celebration of mindlessness.

[1968]

UNREASON AND REVOLUTION

by Richard Lowenthal

This is a tentative exploration of what I believe to be a major phenomenon of our time—the rise of a new type of revolutionary movement. Hitherto, we have been familiar with two broad classes of revolutions and revolutionary movements. First, there are the movements which may be understood as resulting when the normal growth, the spontaneous evolution of a society, meets an obstacle in the form of rigid political institutions that are increasingly felt as oppressive. In such cases, sooner or later an acute political crisis occurs in which the obstacle is swept away by revolutionary action. That is, broadly speaking, the formula fitting the great democratic revolutions of modern Western history; it may also be applied to a number of the national movements for independence from colonial rule that have occurred in our time.

In the last fifty years we have learned, to our cost, to distinguish a second type of revolution and revolutionary movements—those which I, for want of a better name, would still describe as "totalitarian revolutions." It seems to be characteristic of them that they do not occur because of the clash between a growing, dynamic society and a static political framework tending to shackle its growth, but because of some elements of stagnation, some major lopsidedness of development *within* the society itself, leading to a deadlock which a dynamic state is then called upon to resolve by the massive use of political force. This appeal from a deadlock in society to the "savior state" has been the background to the rise of German National Socialism as a mass movement and to the long-lasting reign of violence which its victorious regime inflicted on the prostrate body of society. But the overcoming of social stagnation in the midst of change and of lopsided development has also been underlying the rise of Communist regimes in a number of underdeveloped countries—the only ones that have come to power by the victory of indigenous revolutionary movements—and has given them the opportunity for their repeated, forcible transformations of the social structure.

Now it seems to me that in recent years we have begun to be confronted by yet another kind of revolutionary movement. These new movements, both within our Western world and in the so-called underdeveloped countries, use much of the familiar language of Communist ideology, and actually have taken over much of the substance of the Marxist-Leninist critique of Western capitalism and imperialism as well as the Marxist utopia of a society without classes or domination. Nevertheless they are radically different from the Communist movements that had been created in the image of Lenin's Bolshevik party—different in their forms of organization, their strategies of political action, and indeed in the rank order of values that gives operative meaning to their vision of the goal. In fact, one of the preconditions for the rise of these new movements has been the increasingly obvious disintegration of the Marxist-Leninist doctrinal synthesis; they grow out of an ideological soil that has been fertilized by its decomposition. But some of the products of this decay appear to be as virulently destructive as any Leninist movements have been in the past—without, so far, offering any tangible prospect of comparable constructive achievements.

A preliminary survey of these new movements may perhaps best start by marking them off with two negative statements. On one side, they are not the democratic expressions of stable, productive sectors of the societies in which they arise; in other words, they do not originate as class movements, as interest groups, or coalitions of interest groups. On the other hand, they are not disciplined parties of the Communist type, organized from the top downward as instruments of a single will, with a systematic, strategic concept of what they want and how to get there given in advance. On the contrary, it is typical for them that action often precedes thought. Despite the verbal echoes of the Marxist pathos of rationality that may still be heard from the ideological spokesmen of the Western New Left, in practice the urge for violent action increasingly outruns consideration of any precise short-term objectives and of the rational, tactical, and organizational means for achieving them. It is the style of action and the utopian goal that define the movement, while all other ideas and organizational forms remain very much in flux. The goal itself, though it remains a powerful motivating force, never takes the form of a political program with precise institutional content. That, on the contrary, is increasingly rejected: The tendency is to say that the new institutions, if any, will have to emerge from the process of struggle and from the destruction of the old order.

While the New Left in the West thus replaces Communist programs, strategies, and organizational forms by a faith in utopia and a cult of violent action, a number of revolutionary movements in the underdeveloped world show a parallel trend—away from the elaborations of Communist doctrine and the organizational discipline based on ideological authority, and toward the primacy of violent action over social analysis and of military over political and ideological leadership. We may observe this tendency in the practice first of Castro's Cuban revolution and then of the guerrilla actions started in other Latin-American countries under the influence of the Cuban model; and we find its ideological justification sketched out by Che Guevara and elaborated by Régis Debray. A parallel, if delayed, breakthrough of immediate utopianism and immediate violence seems to have occurred in the transformation of Chinese Communism in the course of the last decade, beginning with the Great Leap Foward and the creation of the People's Communes and culminating in the recent Cultural Revolution. Finally, analogous processes seem to be at work in some of those revolutionary nationalist movements which, without ever having become formally Communist, are developing as passionately an anti-Western, antimodernistic, and antirational outlook as the last-named products of the disintegration of world Communism.

This, then, is our theme. Why do those phenomena arise in

various parts of the world at this time? What are the intellectual roots of their beliefs and the social roots of their strength? And what are their significance and possible prospects?

Let us begin with a subject we know fairly well—the role of Marxism and Leninism in the development of revolutionary ideas. If we cast our minds back to the 1840s when Marxism was born, and if we recall Engels' proud phrase about the development of socialism from a utopia into a science, it is evident to us today that the real difference between Marx and many of his socialist precursors was not that Karl Marx was no utopian: His goals were just as utopian, just as rooted in a profound need to discover a road to salvation on earth, as theirs had been. The difference was that Marx turned his back on *romantic* and *immediate* utopianism in favor of a historical and forward-looking version. The birth of utopian socialism in the early nineteenth century had been part of the romantic revolt of the newborn European intelligentsia against the beginning of industrialization and the transformation of human relations by an increasingly specialized division of labor and an increasingly pervasive cash nexus. The new turn which Marx gave to those ideas was that he rejected the romantic element in them, the resistance to modernization based on an idealization of the past, and proclaimed instead that, thanks to the logic of history, utopia would be achieved by ruthlessly carrying through the painful process of industrialization to the end. To quote Raymond Aron, Marx put forward the thesis that the only way to achieve the goals of Rousseau was to follow the precepts of Saint-Simon.

This was a highly original idea at the time, one might even say a rather absurd idea. But it also proved an extremely powerful idea: for it enabled Marx to forge a link between the belief in utopia and the belief in the logic of history. As a result, he was able to inspire a movement that combined the religious fervor of utopianism with a historical and rational element. Utopia, and the violent revolution that was to precede it, were not to be achieved by mere enthusiasm and an act of will. They depended on well-defined economic and social conditions; but the laws of history guaranteed that these conditions would be achieved in the fullness of time. Moreover, one effect of this analysis was to inspire the followers of Marx with a conviction of the vital importance of material progress; for together with the growth of the organization and consciousness of the working class, the rise of productivity was the most important of the conditions that must mature before mankind could enter the realm of freedom. Increasing productivity would eventually lead to abundance, and only abundance would permit the creation of a social order without classes or domination. Thus the utopian goal and the violent overthrow of the old order were not the objectives of immediate action: Their possibility was mediated by the laws of the historical process, by reason as manifested in history—their achievement by a rational strategy based on the insight into that process.

In a sense, the disintegration of this rationalist and historic concept of the road to revolution and utopia may be said to have started with Lenin—as well as with the early "revisionists" at the opposite pole. For while the latter sought to retain the evolutionary optimism of Marx yet to eliminate the revolutionary and utopian perspective, Lenin was the first pupil of Marx deliberately to separate the task of "organizing the revolution" from some of its economic and social preconditions as formulated by the teacher. He argued, under the impact of World War I, that it was the duty of the Socialist party to seize power in backward Russia without waiting for the maturing of the economic conditions for a socialist society. He had even earlier "emancipated" this party from dependence on the actual support of the working class by giving it a highly centralistic, instrumental structure. Implicitly, Lenin had thus attempted to replace the missing "objective" preconditions of socialism by the creation of his new vanguard party as an instrument for the seizure of power and for the subsequent transformation of the immature society, and to that extent had begun to turn Marxism upside down. But even while doing so, Lenin still clung to the Marxist analysis in believing that *some* objective conditions were needed for the victory of the revolution—not indeed the condition of economic abundance, of objective maturity for socialism, but certainly the condition of a profound and acute crisis of capitalist society, and of a mass mood of bitter discontent enabling the revolutionary party to gain a mass following. Only once the crisis had reached that stage, he taught to the end, only once the revolutionary party had won a strategically decisive following among the masses— only then could the violent seizure of power take place. As a result, the role of the party never consisted for Lenin *primarily* in the organization of violence. Violence might play a crucial part in its action at the critical moment, but the primary task of the party was to win over the masses *before* that moment by a policy based on a correct analysis of the crisis of society.

Some of the strategic changes introduced by Mao Tse-tung in transferring revolutionary Marxism to Asian soil and deliberately "adapting" it to Asian conditions may still be interpreted as mere developments along the road shown by Lenin. Striving to conquer power in a country where economic and social conditions were incomparably more backward—and correspondingly more remote from "objective" maturity for socialism in the Marxist sense—than in the Russia of 1917, Mao became the first pupil of Lenin to make use of the structural flexibility of the centralized vanguard party by seeking the necessary mass support among the peasants rather than the urban working class, and that for many years. He thus completed the effective emancipation of a "Marxist" party from working-class support that had been implied as a potentiality in Lenin's separation of the seizure of power from conditions of economic maturity and of the party organization from working-class democracy. Moreover, Mao recognized at an early stage that the role of armed force in the struggle for power was likely to be far more continuous and decisive in China than it had been in Russia—that here, power would "grow out of the barrel of a gun." But this greatly expanded role of violence in Mao's revolutionary strategy was still tied to objective political and social conditions in two important ways.

In the first place, it was in Mao's own view only made possible by the special conditions of a semicolonial country, in which neither a single native government nor a single colonial power enjoyed an effective monopoly of armed force. That, at least, was Mao's view at the time of his own struggle for power, though after his victory he came to persuade himself that similar "protracted war" strategies would prove appropriate for *all* the colonial and underdeveloped coutries of the world.[1]

In the second place, Mao never ceased to insist that the success of the strategy of armed struggle depended not only on developing the correct military tactics for guerrilla warfare, but on winning and retaining the support of the peasant population in the regions concerned, by correct policies and effective forms of political and economic organization. Only a policy based on a realistic analysis of the conditions and needs of the people in the area, and a type of organization that maintained communication with them, could enable the guerrillas "to live among the population like a fish in water," preventing their isolation by the militarily superior enemy and assuring them of intelligence, of supplies, and of a reservoir for new recruitment. This insistence on maintaining mass support by policies based on a study of the concrete social situation constitutes the indispensable corollary to the Maoist emphasis on armed struggle and its link with the Marxist-Leninist tradition: It is the foundation for Mao's dictum that while power grows out of the barrel of a gun, the party must command the gun. For, though the party no longer represents (as with Marx) the actual evolving consciousness of a working class increasingly aware of its true historical interests, it still represents (as with Lenin) the leaders' "scientific," analytical consciousness of the total social situation, its contradictions and tendencies, and hence of the objective possibilities for action which any successful political strategy must take into account. To that extent, Mao's concept of the leading role of the party preserves, like Lenin's concept, the Marxian idea of a rational strategy based on perception of the rational laws of history.

Yet there is in Mao's emphasis on the decisive role of armed struggle also the germ of a different, more basically "voluntaristic" approach to social reality. This is to be found in his view that the use of violent action by itself may be one of the most effective means for changing the relation of forces between revo-

---

[1] Mao's original view of the special conditions permitting protracted guerrilla warfare in China is contained in his 1928 resolution "Why Can China's Red Political Power Exist," printed in *Selected Works*, vol. 1 (London, 1954); see particularly p. 65. The later view generalizing this method is expressed in the editorial note 7 to this document, p. 304.

lution and reaction, because the right technique of armed struggle may enable an initially much inferior, revolutionary force to whittle down step by step the initial superiority of its enemy—to tire him out by exhaustion, cause splits in his ranks, and finally wear down his will to fight. In a sense, the art of ensuring the survival and regeneration of inferior forces resisting a stronger and better-armed enemy is, of course, the essence of *all* guerrilla tactics, and the hope that this will enable the guerrillas to outlast the enemy's determination has always been their rationale. But the fulfillment of that hope depends clearly not on the dedication and skill of the guerrillas alone, but on a number of independent factors—such as the enemy's fighting commitments outside the theater of guerrilla warfare, the importance of that theater in relation to his general policy objectives, and the cohesion of his political system as reflected in the support for the antiguerrilla campaign and the loyalty of his troops.

In the Chinese case, the evidence does not show that the Communists were effectively wearing down the Kuomintang regime (or even substantially increasing its divisions) before the attack of Japan, nor that they had any chance to defeat the Japanese occupants (who regarded control of China as vital to their purposes), until their will to fight was broken by defeat on other fronts. Similarly, nobody has ever suggested that the Yugoslav Communists could have evicted the armies of Hitler Germany independent of the outcome of World War II. Conversely, guerrilla "wars of liberation" in Vietnam and Algeria could achieve political victory by military means because neither area was truly vital for the French republic; and Mao's own final civil war defeated a nationalist regime whose political and moral cohesion had been gravely undermined by the disastrous effects of the long-lasting Japanese invasion.

Mao's original doctrine of protracted warfare, so far from neglecting the crucial importance of these "objective conditions," took them into account by laying down what conditions must be fulfilled for passing from guerrilla tactics proper to the stage of decisive battles, and thus implying that these conditions cannot be created at will but must be patiently waited for. (There have been echoes of that realistic approach even in fairly recent Chinese advice to the Vietnamese Communists.) Yet, on the other hand, the attempts of the victorious Chinese Communists to recommend the Maoist strategy of armed struggle as a model for colonial revolutions in general (which became prevalent since about 1959, in the context of their ideological rivalry with the Soviet Communists) have increasingly treated the revolutionary faith and tactical military skill of the guerrillas as universal and sufficient prescriptions for victory in "wars of liberation" that would achieve their magic effects *independent* of the objective conditions in any particular case.

This growing tendency to separate the use of armed revolutionary force from any analysis of political and social conditions, implicit in the transformation of Maoist doctrine under the impact of the ideological rivalry with Russia for leadership of the revolutionary movements of the underdeveloped world, has become quite explicit with the leaders of the Cuban revolution and its would-be imitators in Latin America—with Fidel Castro, Che Guevara, and Régis Debray.

Long before Fidel Castro ever dreamed of calling himself a Marxist-Leninist, and presumably before he read any serious Marxist literature, he acted on the assumption that armed minority action would by itself be sufficient to *create* a revolutionary situation. After this prescription had proved successful in Cuba, Guevara spelled out this new doctrine in so many words as early as 1960. Guevara, of course, did have a background of Marxist knowledge, and in 1960 he still made the validity of the new strategy dependent on one objective condition: the existence of a —presumably unpopular—dictatorial regime. Armed minority uprisings, he then suggested, would not be effective against a government which enjoyed some degree of democratic legitimacy. However, this qualification was dropped by the *Fidelistas* a few years later, when the democratic government of Venezuela became the main target of their effort to export the strategy— and to some extent the leading personnel—of guerrilla insurrection.[2] Since then it has become an official dogma of

---

[2] In 1960, Guevara wrote: "Where a government has come to power by popular vote, of whatever kind, whether falsified or not, and preserves at

"Castroism" that a small but determined and well-led *foco* of professional guerrillas is in principle sufficient to shake the stability of *any* political system in Latin America, and thus to create eventually, by its own action alone, the conditions for the seizure of power.

The consequences of this separation of armed violence from any analysis of social and political preconditions, and hence from any rational political strategy, have been most fully developed in Régis Debray's book *Revolution in the Revolution*. The political significance of this statement of the new doctrine lies in the fact that it represents more than its author's individual opinion. It was written on the basis of long conversations with Castro and other Cuban leaders, who had made the diaries and other documents of their struggle for power accessible to the author, and it was published for mass circulation and used as training material by the ruling party in Cuba.[3] Hence it must be regarded as an authorized summary of Castro's and Guevara's own views of the "Cuban model" for the conquest of power. Now Debray has become the first to state plainly that it is positively harmful for the chances of armed struggle if it arises from the defense of the interests of a particular productive group; for such a struggle by people who are tied to their place of production— like the miners in Bolivia or the peasants of the most impoverished region of Colombia—tends to take the form of "armed self-defense" also in military tactics. People who lead normal working lives, however poor and oppressed, have something

---

least the appearance of constitutional legality, guerrilla warfare cannot be started because the possibilities of peaceful struggle have not yet been exhausted." *La guerra de guerrillas* (Havana, 1960), p. 13. But in September 1963 he wrote that *all* Latin-American regimes were oligarchic dictatorships, and that the struggle could be successfully intensified by forcing them to drop their legalistic mask. "Guerra de guerrillas: un método," in *Cuba socialista*, no. 25 (1963).

[3] For Debray's privileged sources, see the preface to the Cuban edition by its publisher, Roberto Fernandez Retamar, *Revolución en la revolución*, p. 5. For its use as official training material, see Raoul Castro's attack on the pro-Soviet "microfaction" (which had complained about it) in *Granma*, 30 January 1968. I am indebted to Dr. Wolfgang Berner's study: *Der Evangelist des Castroismus-Guevarismus: Régis Debray und seine Guerilla-Doktrin* (1969).

to lose—their working place, their houses with their families—
which they want to defend; hence they are militarily too
vulnerable and are bound to be defeated in the end by the government's regular forces. In order to have a chance of success, the
revolutionary struggle must be conducted by perfectly rootless,
and therefore perfectly mobile, professional guerrillas alone!

In the context of this complete dissociation of the "revolution"
from any concrete social basis, it is only logical that Debray goes
so far as to give his own, arbitrary new meaning to the familiar
Marxist terms of "bourgeois" and "proletarian." According to
him, only the uprooted guerrilla is the true "proletarian," because he has chosen a life of extreme deprivation and constant
danger; he has nothing more to lose but his life, and is willing to
sacrifice that. Conversely, the industrial worker in the towns of
Latin America is in the eyes of Debray a "bourgeois," simply because he has a regular job and values it. Now any writer is, of
course, free to choose and define his own terminology. But an ide-
ologist who uses the terms of "bourgeois" and "proletarian" in
this purely moralistic and emotional way, and defines his "proletarian" as a figure wholly divorced from the productive process,
has evidently completely abandoned the method of social analysis which Karl Marx inaugurated by *his* use of those terms in the
Communist Manifesto.

Finally, the cutting of all ties between the revolutionary movement and any defined social basis leads Debray with equal logic
to a reversal of the relation between military and political leadership and to a new view of the role and formation of the revolutionary party. He argues that it is futile to concentrate first on
creating a Marxist-Leninist party which would then organize a
guerrilla movement in due course, because the party could only
develop in the towns and its leaders might then be afraid to
leave the towns. Instead, the only promising way in Latin America will be to begin by recruiting a band of armed volunteers
who will form a guerrilla focus. The volunteers may have little
or no previous political experience; they should be attracted on
no narrower basis than their willingness to risk their lives in
fighting Yankee imperialism and its ruling native stooges. As their
ideas become more clearly defined due to the experience of the
common struggle, a party will eventually arise—usually only

after victory—with the proven guerrilla leaders at its head. Thus military leadership precedes political leadership both in time and as a source of authority.

It is no longer the party that commands the gun—it is the gun that creates the party.

So far I have discussed the progressive dissociation of the revolutionary struggle *for* power from "objective conditions"—first from the maturity of the productive forces and of the consciousness of a large, organized working class for a socialist society, then from any objectively given crisis of society and any defined social basis—along the road leading from Marx via Lenin and Mao to Castro.

If we now turn to the problems of a Communist regime *in* power, we notice in some countries a progressive dissociation of the effort to achieve the utopian goal from the objective conditions of economic development. This is a fairly recent phenomenon. For while Lenin was the first to sanction the seizure of power independent of the conditions of economic maturity, it would never have occurred to Lenin (or, for that matter, to Stalin or any other Russian party leader) to suggest that the criteria of the higher stage of the classless society—work according to ability and distribution according to needs—could become reality before a state of economic abundance had been reached. Stalin was emphatic that the basic task in "building socialism" was to create, at high pressure, those economic preconditions which had been lacking at the moment of political victory. Pending the achievement of economic abundance, the link between individual contribution and individual reward—distribution of scarce goods not according to needs but according to performance— was an indispensable incentive to rapid economic progress. Yet in recent years, conscious attempts to cut this link and to introduce the distributive principles of the "higher stage" of Communism in conditions of poverty and want have been made both in China and in Cuba.

In China, this occurred first at the time of the Great Leap Forward in 1958, when the creation of the People's Communes was accompanied by a major effort to introduce specifically "Communist" relationships, with distribution approaching complete equality, as the share of equal "free supplies" in kind in the members' income rose quickly at the expense of the still unequal cash wages. Thus, the peasants were expected to work less and less for material incentives and more and more from enthusiasm for the common good. In fact, this armylike system of equal supplies in kind was for a time described as "distribution according to needs," even though on the basis of the existing poverty the "needs" were assessed by the authorities, and not by the individuals themselves as Marx had envisaged on a basis of abundance. This attempt was severely criticized by the Soviets at the time, and the Chinese themselves soon backtracked under the impact of its disastrous economic consequences. Yet in the course of the Cultural Revolution, they have largely returned to the same basic view that the use of material incentives and income differentiation, which Lenin and Stalin had regarded as necessary tools of economic development, was really a "revisionist" concession to the capitalist spirit. Mao's decisive argument seems to be that, in the light of Russian experience, a desperate effort must be made to educate the new Communist man here and now, without waiting for the achievement of economic abundance, because otherwise he may never be created at all. The remolding of the people to create the new, collectively motivated man should be given priority over the immediate need for increasing productivity by material incentives, because the latter tend to create not the "new socialist man," but the familiar type of economic man—which to Mao means "capitalist man." [4]

To an increasing extent, the same principles have lately come to be applied in Cuba as well. The use of youthful "volunteer" labor to work under discipline in the rural *campamento* recalls both the earlier Chinese communes and the more recent mass transfer of Chinese students to work in the countryside. It has lately been supplemented by a general ban on overtime payments, based on the same principle that, in the interest of socialist education, the needed increases in output must be achieved by appealing only to collective solidarity and enthusiasm, not to ambition and avarice. In other words, here, too, the connection

---

[4] See my discussion of "Mao's Revolution" in *Encounter,* April 1967.

between the achievement of utopia and the stage of economic development is being denied in action: The goal is dissociated from the objective conditions stipulated by Marx.

Finally, just as the dissociation of the revolutionary struggle for power from an analysis of objective social conditions leads ultimately to the replacement of the primacy of the party and the political leadership by the primacy of the guerrilla *foco* and the military leadership, so the dissociation of the attempt to build a Communist utopia from the effort to achieve its economic preconditions leads to a change in the basic legitimation for ruling a country engaged in that attempt. It issues in a transfer of the claim to legitimate leadership from the exponents of the "scientific" road to socialism and Communism to the exponents of heroic determination, from the technicians skilled in adopting the ideology to economic needs by interpretation to the technicians skilled in enforcing ideological conformity by violence. This is a development that has not, so far, been fully consummated, but is recognizable as an increasingly powerful tendency in both China and Cuba.

In Cuba, the old Communist party had a much clearer economic program as well as a much more effective centralistic discipline than the ideologically heterogeneous crowd of Castro's original followers, and up to a point Castro was eager to learn from them as well as to use their disciplined apparatus. But ultimately it was the charismatic prestige of the successful insurrection rather than the bureaucratic merits of long-term party-building, the military prowess of Castro and a few men around him rather than the ideological certainty of the old Communists that legitimated the new leadership. The resulting regime is probably as much a pseudomorphosis—a similar shape without similar substance—of a Communist party dictatorship as many Latin-American "democracies" have been of true parliamentary or presidential democracies. The Marxist-Leninist party is supposed to rule and its offices are everywhere, but its central organs hardly ever meet. Actual power is exercised by the revolutionary *caudillo,* using his personal impact on television on one side and the armed force of the militia on the other.

In China, the virtual destruction of the Communist party ma-

chine as well as of much of the state administration in the course
of the Cultural Revolution seems to have started a similar shift
of the basis of legitimacy. For Mao turned on the bureaucracy of
party and government with its growing preference for routine
and economic rationality in the name of the heroic traditions of
the Long March and in an effort to train the young generation in
the spirit of its veterans. He found it much easier to revive the
utopian spirit of the heroic period in the army than in the party
or in economic life, and since 1964 increasingly called on all
other organizations to "learn from the army." Having undermined the discipline of all other organizations by proclaiming
the "right to rebel" in the Cultural Revolution, while leaving only
army discipline intact, he has now proceeded to reorganize the
shattered party from the top with an unprecedentedly high share
of military men in the leadership, on the principle of sworn personal loyalty to him and to the head of the Military Council
which is his designated successor.

There seems to be a significant parallel here with developments in some of those revolutionary nationalist single-party regimes, particularly in the Arab world, in which the official
ideological doctrine was poorly developed from the beginning,
and in which military prestige has therefore sooner or later
proved superior to party legitimacy. The case of Nasser's Egypt
may be regarded as too obvious to be really significant in our
context, because there the military *junta* was first, and the suc-
cessive attempts to create a state party have only confirmed its
character as at best an auxiliary to charismatic rule by a military
leader. But it seems symptomatic that the Algerian *FLN*,
which originated as a fighting guerrilla organization under
political nationalist leadership, proved unable to provide stable
one-party rule until a full-time military commander took political
control by force barely bothering to have himself confirmed by
the legitimate party organs afterwards. The transformation of
the *Ba'ath* party, which started with a more elaborate nationalist-
socialist ideology than either the Algerians or the Nasserites, yet
has degenerated into little more than a congeries of rival officers'
clans in both Syria and Iraq, the two countries in which it officially governs, seems even more eloquent testimony to the

strength of a general tendency. It may be at least worth inquiring whether this parallel tendency to a decline in the role of political leadership and ideological guidance, and to a reversion of legitimacy to the military hero (or would-be hero), to the charismatic specialist in the techniques of violence, in a number of underdeveloped countries under both Communist and national-revolutionary regimes is not due to the impact of similar causes.

The dissociation of revolutionary passion and action from the Marxist belief in the rationality of history is not confined to the particular examples I have analyzed. On the contrary, it appears to be a universal process, in which movements and regimes that remain strongly influenced by a Marxist outlook are ceasing to be revolutionary, while those that remain revolutionary renounce essential parts of the Marxist analysis.

Thus we observe that the Communist party regime in the Soviet Union—as it comes increasingly to regard the development of its productive capacity as the only decisive factor for its advance towards the "higher stage" of Communism and as its principal contribution to the victory of its cause on a world scale—is becoming less concerned with either forcibly imposing "revolutions from above" on its own people or actively fostering revolutionary movements elsewhere.[5] It has retained the belief that the final, world-wide achievement of Communism is guaranteed by the laws of history—but it interprets those laws in an increasingly revisionist spirit as working mainly through the logic of economic development, so that the eventual attainment of utopia will not require further revolutionary action on its part. Even more explicitly, Communist parties in some advanced Western countries, particularly those with a strong following in a modern, industrial working class, are proposing revisionist strategies for the socialist transformation of their countries by peaceful, democratic methods, based on the expectation that the inherent trends of modern industrial societies will enable them to join the gov-

---

[5] For a fuller analysis of this development, see my "Has the Revolution a Future?" *Encounter,* January–February 1965.

ernments and carry out their program with majority support, and preferably without violence.

Conversely, those New Left movements in the same countries, recruited chiefly from students and other adolescents divorced from production, that are preoccupied with the need for violent action and the revolutionary overthrow of the social order, have come increasingly to reject the Marxist belief in the rationality of history and the link between the progress of industrialization, the growth of the working class, and the utopian goal. Instead, they are looking for support to the peoples of the underdeveloped "countryside of the world" whose revolutionary ardor has not yet been dampened by material comfort, and for guidance to Mao and Castro who promise to solve the economic problems of their poor countries through an upsurge of collective effort called forth by an appeal to solidarity rather than to egoistic self-interest. Nor is their choice difficult to understand in view of the fact that the working class in the industrially advanced countries has become less and less revolutionary, and that the successful industrialization of Russia has evidently not created a society without classes and domination, but a bureaucratic class society still ruled by a harsh party dictatorship after fifty years.

To return to the remark of Raymond Aron's that I quoted earlier, it has become obvious that the world has not come the least bit closer to the goals of Rousseau after following the precepts of Saint-Simon for more than a century. Hence those who will not abandon utopianism have at long last decided to try and approach those goals directly. The intellectual importance of Herbert Marcuse for the development of the Western New Left is that he has classically formulated this disappointment of the Marxist utopian who feels betrayed by the logic of history. The author of *Reason and Revolution* still puts his trust in that Goddess; to the author of *One-Dimensional Man,* the Devil is the Prince of the Modern World. But once the assurance is gone that justice will triumph when the millennium comes in the fullness of time, the only alternative left to the believer is to try and bring it about by storming the heavens here and now. We are faced with a regression to a more primitive kind of secular religion—as different from that of Marx as was the faith of the Bohemian

Taborites and the Muenster Anabaptists from the mainstream of Western Christianity.

As the term "regression" implies, the breakdown of the rationalist and historical constructs by which Marx had "mediated" the revolutionary struggle for utopia, and the consequent return to immediate utopianism and immediate violence links the contemporary New Left to an earlier type of revolutionary tradition. It is a tradition which, in contrast to Marx, directly expressed the romantic resistance to the growth of mechanized industry and to the destruction of "natural" communities by the process of modernization, and exalted the values of "life," community feeling, and spontaneous, violent action in opposition to "calculating" reason. There are, in fact, two distinct but frequently entangled strands of this romantic-revolutionary tradition, which we may provisionally designate by the names of two friends who were together involved in the Dresden insurrection of 1849: Mikhail Bakunin and Richard Wagner.

It is hardly accidental that Bakunin has lately been rediscovered by sections of the New Left in a number of countries. What seems to attract them is not just his anarchist vision, the goal of a stateless society of free associations of producers (which others have developed more fully both before and after him), but his passionate opposition to the bureaucratic rationality of the rising industrial age; his readiness to assign priority to the "creative passion for destruction" over any program for what was to come afterward; his hatred and contempt for liberalism, reform, and all representative institutions, not only in Russia but everywhere; his belief that a cumulation of uncoordinated, spontaneous acts of local violence could bring down both the Czarist regime and the ruling economic and social system (alternating with fantasies of a supercentralistic, conspirative organization which were never put into practice), and his tendency to rely on the uprooted peasant (the "bandit") as the true revolutionary, and on the backward regions on the eastern and southern periphery of Europe—on Russia, Spain, southern Italy—for the ultimate revolutionary assault on the modern core that was already corrupted by capitalism and bureaucracy. Yet Bakunin's Pan-

Slavism, his hatred of Germans and Jews, and his abiding hostility to liberalism (which he did not disdain to use as arguments in the *"Confession"* he sent to the Czar from prison in the hope of being reprieved) constitute a bond with other ideologies of antimodern violence directed not to the goal of egalitarian anarchy, but to that of the dictatorship of an elite in the name of nationalism. Richard Wagner, who was to become one of the intellectual ancestors of Nazism, already dreamed—and spoke and wrote—of the destruction of the bankers' rule by a popular emperor and of the replacement of Westernized, liberal pseudoculture by a truly national German folk culture at the time of his youthful friendship with Bakunin.[6] The kinship between the more violent and irrational forms of anarchism and fascist tendencies has since been repeatedly demonstrated in other countries and later generations.

Thus Georges Sorel, whose special contribution to the syndicalist movement has been to give it an irrationalist turn and to exalt the role of violence as the test of social vitality, came for a time to support the extreme right-wing *Action Française* and influenced the elitism of Pareto and Mussolini. Again, if one asks to what historical model Fidel Castro's early intellectual background, his style of governing Cuba by harangues, and his reliance on a mixture of nationalist and socialist appeals bear the most striking resemblance, the picture that comes to mind is not that of any victorious Communist leader, but of Gabriele D'Annunzio, his "Republic of Fiume," and his highly original witches' brew of nationalist passion, anarchist ideals, and plebiscitary techniques of government (though Castro, no doubt, has shown less poetical and more political ability than his illustrious predecessor). And D'Annunzio's movement, by its ideological prestige and its practical failure, helped to recruit many of the cadres for Italian Fascism.

Finally, the semianarchist violence of Benito Mussolini's antimilitarist agitation during the Libyan war of 1911, when he was at the height of his New Left period as editor of the Social-

---

[6] For Wagner's views at the time, see the chapter on Wagner in Hans Kohn, *The Mind of Germany* (1960), particularly pp. 196–197. For the Dresden episode in Bakunin's life, see E. H. Carr, *Michael Bakunin* (1937), pp. 186–194.

ist party daily, fed on the same emotional and partly on the same ideological sources which enabled him in 1914–15 to break with the Socialist workers' movement as a violent advocate of a "revolutionary" war for nationalist objectives on the side of the Entente, and later to become the founder of Fascism and lead it to victory through terror. I might also mention as belonging to the same spiritual family those German ideologues of the 1920s —the period preceding the victory of National Socialism—who were then known as "National Bolsheviks" or "*Linke Leute von Rechts.*" They sought to combine an anticapitalist social radicalism (which in their case was much more genuine than with the Nazi party) with an anti-Western but often explicitly pro-Russian nationalism and with a cult of heroic violence based on the memory of the "frontline experience"—of the true community of those who had been ready to die (and to kill) for the fatherland.

In short, those ardent believers in salvation on earth by political revolution who rejected the historical and rationalist "mediation" of their goal in favor of irrational passion and immediate violence have always tended to rely on romantic ideologies using varying mixtures of arguments of the Bakunist and the nationalist-fascist type. It is typical that in the later writings of Marcuse, his earlier Hegelian-Marxist rationalism is getting increasingly overlaid by the elitist anti-Western cultural pessimism of Martin Heidegger—his first teacher.

The revival of both strands of the romantic ideological tradition in the irrational revolt of the Western New Left indicates a revival of the basic emotional attitude underlying them both. The rebels reject the modern industrial world in both its Western-capitalist and Soviet-Communist forms—the crude materialism of its values, the pervasive bureaucratism of its organization, the purely instrumental character of its rationality. Indeed, their despair is a reaction to the discovery that the process of "rationalization" in the instrumental sense, which Max Weber recognized as a universal law of the modern world, does not assure the triumph of "Reason" in the sense of the achievement of utopia. It is the same rejection of the industrial order that also constitutes the fundamental link between the Western New Left and some of the revolutionary movements of the poor nations. To the new romantics, Mao Tse-tung and Castro embody the promise of a spontaneous community without conflict, hence without need for rational rules and institutions—just as to Frantz Fanon, Sorel has revealed the liberating dignity of irrational violence.

But this means that in some of the revolutionary movements of the excolonial and semicolonial peoples, we are now facing a "revolt against the West" in a new and different sense. The classical nationalist movements for colonial liberation and for the independent development of the underdeveloped countries have always been, and many of them still are, characterized by ambivalence toward the West. They have been fighting for political independence from the Western powers, for economic independence from Western capital, to some extent also for the chance to preserve their cultural identity, to keep their own soul. But they have also wished to learn from the West in order to imitate it successfully in the techniques of production and power, to catch up with it in science and material development. For the classical movements of national liberation from colonialism or semicolonialism, one essential goal has been to make their country as rich and powerful as its former Western masters, though this goal could only be achieved by a struggle for independence which often required prolonged conflicts with the Western powers. This was an ambivalent attitude in that it was *not* inspired by a total rejection of Western models and values, but in part by a desire to emulate Western achievements—even though the road there led through a struggle against Western domination.

The new attitude which we encounter in Mao's cultural revolution, in Castro's Cuba, and potentially in other movements influenced by them (whether formally Communist or not) *is* a total rejection of some Western values. It is a determination to stay poor-but-honest rather than imitate the West in promoting the development of economic man (as the Soviets have done), to accept some of the consequences of nondevelopment (though not all) rather than assimilate to Western civilization. Indeed, we observe for the first time since the decline of the early nativistic movements in those countries, for the first time in movements that claim to be not traditionalist but modern, nationalist, and revolutionary, a fundamental resistance not just to Western power and Western capital, but to the pull of Western civilization that had hitherto been inseparable from any effort at the modernization of non-Western countries.

This in turn throws further light also on the revolt of part of the young generation in the West; for that revolt, too, is directed against important aspects of Western civilization.

This is often denied by well-meaning liberals who, in trying to understand the young rebels, argue that the latter "really" share our liberal values—that they merely take them more seriously than their hypocritical elders and want to *act* on principles which the establishment merely *talks* about. If that were all, we should be faced with a political and social movement of a familiar type, for that is indeed the classical role of revolutionary (and also of reformist) movements within a growing civilization —to regenerate the traditional values of that civilization by giving them a new institutional content corresponding to changed social conditions. Thus the basic Western idea of the rights of the human person has been reinterpreted in course of time from referring to "the rights of each according to his station" to meaning "equal political rights for all," and more recently to imply the rights of each to equal opportunity and social security. But this, it seems to me, no longer applies to many of either the politically active or the passive and nonpolitical young rebels of our time.

For while it is true that they generally accept the familiar values of love and individual freedom, of truth and social justice, merely seeking to turn these values into an indictment of the older generation, it is also true that they have increasingly come to reject the values of material and in part even of intellectual achievement and of the effort and discipline needed to accomplish it, including the discipline of reason—values which are equally essential parts of the cultural heritage of the West. The same is apparent in their rejection of any time perspective in the name of a cult of immediacy; for the sense of measured time and the gearing of action to foresight have been basic for all Western civilization from the age when Western church towers were first endowed with clocks to the latest achievements of science and industry. In other words, we are witnessing a major failure to transmit an important part of our basic values to a significant part of the young generation.

Indeed it seems to me that the rebellion of the young which is taking place in all advanced Western countries, and which is assuming both politically revolutionary forms and the form of a passive nonpolitical refusal to grow into roles within the industrial society and submit to its pressures, is not primarily a political phenomenon. It is, above all, a sign of a crisis in our civilization.

For there are, I believe, two basic tests for the vitality of a civilization. One is the ability to transmit to the young generation its essential values even while adapting their concrete, practical meaning to changing conditions. The other is its capacity to attract and assimilate outsiders, "barbarians," who come within range of its material influence—and not only subject them and disrupt their traditional forms of life.

As recently as the last generation, this vitality of Western civilization was subjected to extremely serious strain, for the destructive outbreak of Nazism constituted a radical, nihilistic revolt against that civilization from within. Yet following its military defeat, the reassimilation of Germany by the West has been extremely successful, and even the Soviet Union, for all the rigidity of its political structure and all the seriousness of its continuing conflicts with the Western powers, shows unmistakable signs of a progressive *cultural* "convergence" with the West. Now for the first time, the West is faced simultaneously with growing evidence of a crisis both in its capacity to assimilate its "external proletariat" (in the sense given to this term in Toynbee's *Study of History*), the poor, underdeveloped, non-Western peoples, and in its ability to transmit its heritage to its own youth.

This diagnosis is confirmed by the fact that the quasi-religious character of some of the new movements is manifested not only in their commitment to chiliastic goals, but in their cult of savior-leaders and in their search for a new code of conduct. Thus the asceticism and heroic self-sacrifice of Che Guevara have permitted the growth of a legend around him that combines Christ-like features with those of a militant secular leader. The official cult of Mao Tse-tung no longer describes him as a mere creative continuator of the Marxist-Leninist revolutionary tradition, not even merely as the unique architect of the political rebirth of the Chinese nation and state: He is presented as the author of a totally new system of thought and action—a system that will enable all those to work miracles who believe in Mao and live by his new rules. Many of the "Quotations from Chairman Mao" in the little *Red Book,* from which hundreds of millions of Chinese are taught to recite several times a day, stand in competition not with any Western or Soviet political document, but with the *Analects* of Confucius and the Bible.

Yet while the new movements are largely united in their rejection of the Western way of life (or, at any rate, of major aspects of it), they diverge widely in seeking to define their alternatives. Castro and Mao reject Western materialism, and, at least Mao, also Western individualism. But both believe in the need for collective effort and discipline which are rejected by large parts of the Western New Left as well as by the nonpolitical Western hippies, dropouts, and drug-takers. Conversely, many of the would-be revolutionaries of the New Left retain an anarchist type of individualism; but "petty bourgeois anarchism" remains a term of abuse in Cuba and China as much as in Russia, while the prophets of a nonpolitical drug culture clearly believe that community can only be established by escaping from individuality.

There is thus no unity of values among the new movements except in their common target of attack—their negation of the modern industrial society. Beyond that the New Left's admiration for Castro and Mao is based on a romantic misunderstanding that sees those hard-striving, hard-driving taskmasters of their peoples as the Noble Savages of our time.

This, then, is the tentative conclusion at which we have arrived. The new type of revolutionary movements, both on the outer fringes of our Western-centered world and in the advanced Western countries, as well as some phenomena within the latter that are not "revolutionary" in the conventional, political sense of the term, can best be understood as symptoms of a crisis of Western civilization. It is this which explains their increasing turning away from the Marxist type of analysis and strategy: for Marxism, in its origin, its values, and its commitment to rationality, is indissolubly linked to its Western heritage.

I am conscious that while that conclusion may help us to grasp the historical significance, intellectual background, and spiritual character of the new movements, it does not answer the further questions about their concrete social roots, the reasons for their appearance at this time, and their prospects of political success. Nor can I even attempt to deal seriously with those questions in the framework of the present essay. All that is possible here is to sketch out some of the directions in which the answers may be looked for.

The main point I should like to make here is that the crisis in our civilization has followed an unprecedented acceleration both of the external expansion of its influence and of the pace of its internal change.

Externally, Western expansion over the last two centuries has effectively disrupted the traditional societies created by other civilizations all over the globe. The political reflux of that expansion, the extrusion of Western dominance from the former colonial areas in the last few decades, has not reversed its disruptive effects and has left the new nations with problems of "modernization" which in most cases are proving far more difficult than anticipated.

As I have already suggested, the goal of modernization was at first generally conceived as implying at least a partial imitation of the West, even if often by different institutional means—for instance, industrialization not by free enterprise but by state planning, or political mobilization by single-party rule rather than by multi-party competition. But it now looks as if in countries where "development" in this sense proves particuarly difficult—owing to the pressure of population, or to the extreme shortage of cadres with modern training, or simply to the strength of traditionalist cultural resistance, or to any combination of those factors—important aspects of the goal itself are coming to be doubted. Total rejection of the Western model is proclaimed in the accents of revolt in order to avoid the confession of failure and the disappointment of the expectations aroused. As the West can always be blamed for having started the whole agonizing process by its intrusion, and for either having refused to help the development of the latecomers or at any rate having failed to give enough aid to be effective, the rejection of the unattainable model is accompanied by a deepening of resentment against its possessors.

Internally, the acceleration of change in technology, and with it, in social structures and habits of living, has in the last few decades created intense moral uncertainty in many Western countries. That moral uncertainty of a generation of parents who on many issues are no longer sure what is right or wrong is probably at the root of their failure to transmit their values effectively, and of the consequent revolt among the young. What appears today as a widespread rebellion of youth against authority is, I suspect, largely born of frustration caused by the absence of authority—in the sense of a lack not of severity, but of convinced and therefore convincing models of conduct. For a growing civilization to survive in a climate of unending social change, as is the fate of ours, the central problem is to combine a belief in the absolute validity of its fundamental values with flexibility in the practical rules derived from them. As the pace of change accelerates, the difficulty of solving this problem increases, and the tendency towards a polarization of attitudes between a combination of firm belief with impractical rigidity on one side and of pragmatic flexibility with fundamental relativism on the other becomes stronger.

In the Western industrial societies of today, this basic problem of preserving a continuity of values in the flux of changing conditions and rules appears in a variety of concrete shapes. Probably the most important of those is the loss of a sense of common purpose in the midst of enormous, accelerating material progress. While that progress has not abolished scarcity and made effort and discipline superfluous (as the new utopians believe), it has indeed created an unprecedented degree of relative affluence, solved the crucial problem of steadiness of employment, and permitted improvements in the standards of living, leisure, and social security on so broad a front as to deprive traditional class conflicts of their revolutionary potential.

Yet this tremendous progress has been achieved at the price of a concentration on individual material advantage and been accompanied by the loss of a sense of common purpose, as first the traditional certainties of religious faith and then the substitutes offered by national loyalties were undermined. The moral sensitivity of the young is shocked by the contrast between the intense effort devoted by their elders to the pursuit of minor individual advantages or to expenditure for national military power on one side, and their lack of concern for the suffering of the marginal poor inside and the undernourished majority of mankind outside the industrial world on the other. The young are all the more assured of the righteousness of their criticism because they have experienced the moral uncertainty of their elders from an early age. As a result, many of them perceive an acute moral conflict between the ideals they have been taught and the competitive conformism into which they are expected to grow—a conflict all the more insoluble because the society which they reject as "empty" is technically well-functioning and is apparently accepted without question by the large majority of adults. Now where intolerable moral conflict is not confined to individuals but expresses a crisis of civilization, the response has always been an upsurge of utopian beliefs—a collective escape into the dream of a perfect society where every conflict would be solved in advance. The difference this time is that we are dealing with a utopianism inspired not by hope, but by despair. That is the ultimate reason for its lack of a time perspective, its irrationality, and its violence.

As for the social locus of the revolt, just as a turn toward total rejection of the Western model is most likely to occur among those non-Western nations which experience the most discouraging difficulties in their effort at modernization, so a radical denial of the need for material effort and discipline appears to prove most attractive to those strata of Western youth that have remained longest and furthest removed from the productive process—be it as students from upper- and middle-class families or as undereducated members of minority groups who find themselves virtually unemployable through no fault of their own.

Indulgence in pipe dreams about the effortless abundance possible in the "postindustrial society" is most natural for those who have either been preserved from any contact with the productive sources of our relative affluence by the economic security of their parents, or have been barred from both those sources and their benefits by the underprivileged position of theirs. Karl Marx once pointed out that while the (nonproductive) proletariat of ancient Rome lived on society, modern capitalist society lived on its (industrial) proletariat. But the "internal proletariat" that is coming to be as disaffected from Western civilization as some parts of its "external proletariat" does not consist of the industrial workers for whom Marx reserved the term. It is a "proletariat" in the ancient Roman sense, divorced from production but convinced that society owes it a living, and willing only to supplement the publicly supplied bread by providing its own circuses. For today as in Rome, the only forms of separate collective action open to a group that cannot withdraw its productive contribution, because it makes none, are highly emotional and violent. The neo-Bakuninism of the New Left appears to be the ideological expression of this transfer of the revolutionary mission from the industrial working class to the neo-Roman proletariat of our time. As its purely destructive forms of action repel all productive sectors of society but attract its marginal and semicriminal elements, the danger of its degeneration into a movement of the *Lumpenproletariat* becomes manifest.

There remains the question of the political prospects of these new movements. In terms of "power politics," I do not rate their chances of success very high; that is indeed implied in what I have described as their lack of rationality. Because of Maoist irrationality, China seems to have made very little progress in the last decade, except on the narrowest sector of nuclear weapons; and it will not become an effective model of development so long as it remains Maoist in this sense. Nor has the model of Castroism, and the strategy of small guerrilla bands starting operations regardless of social and political conditions, gained much influence in Latin America or shown much promise of doing so in the foreseeable future—unless widespread failures of development give them a chance. Finally, today's campus rebels are not, like the student movements of Czarist Russia or Weimar Germany or British India, the forerunners of a political revolution. They do not operate in stagnant or politically oppressed societies and are not the articulate expression of the inarticulate mood of large masses of people. Moreover, for all the traits of kinship we have mentioned, the New Left students are not fascist—and Bakuninists have never and nowhere taken power: Indeed, they would not know what to do with it.

Nevertheless, the danger to Western society from these new movements is serious. It is not the danger of a "Third World bloc" abroad or "revolution" at home; it is the prospect of destruction, decay, and barbarization. The real threat is not that Mao will be able to overrun Asia or that Castro will revolutionize Latin America. It is that overpopulation and hunger, indigenous governmental incompetence, and Western self-satisfied indifference will cause the festering sores of despair, political instability, and violence to spread. Again, the real menace within the West is not that young extremists will "take over"; they cannot even take over the universities. But they can paralyze and, in some cases, destroy them by first destroying the climate of tolerance and rational discourse which is the breath of academic life. They can deprive our societies of an important part of the well-trained and loyal elites needed for the steady renewal of administration and economic management, of research and education. And they can create a backlash of police brutality and right-wing extremism which will in effect help them to obstruct the working of democracy and the constructive solution of urgent problems.

I do not, of course, know any simple answer to these problems, any magic prescription for coping with them. All I should like to state in conclusion is that, in dealing with the danger constituted by the new type of revolutionary movements, it is wrong —even more wrong than it was with the old type of Communist movements—to be obsessed with "the enemy" as if he were a devil suddenly appearing out of nowhere, a *diabolus ex machina*. The forces of destruction have, of course, to be resisted; civilization cannot be defended by surrendering to violence. But this is only the minor part of the task. Above all, civilization must be defended by upholding and renewing its standards in action, by combining a faith in its values with the determination to apply them constructively in a changing world—and therefore to make sacrifices for them—inside and outside the West. Only if we can restore hope by doing that will the West survive. Otherwise it will succumb to barbarization—and that means (as the whole of history is there to teach us) succumbing not to some particular barbarian ideology, movement, or tribe, but to its own failure.

[1969]

THE NEW REFORMATION

by Paul Goodman

For a long time modern societies have been operating as if religion were a minor and moribund part of the scheme of things. But this is unlikely. Men do not do without a system of "meanings" that everybody believes and puts his hope in even if, or especially if, he doesn't know anything about it; what Freud called a "shared psychosis," meaningful because shared, and with the power that resides in deep fantasy and longing. In advanced countries, indeed, it is science and technology themselves that have gradually, and finally triumphantly, become the system of mass faith, not disputed by various political ideologies and nationalisms that have also had religious uses.

Now this basic faith is threatened. Dissident young people are saying that science is antilife, it is a Calvinist obsession, it has been a weapon of white Europe to subjugate colored races, and scientific technology has manifestly become diabolical. Along with science, the young discredit the professions in general, and the whole notion of "disciplines" and academic learning. If these views take hold, it adds up to a crisis of belief, and the effects are incalculable. Every status and institution would be affected. Present political troubles could become endless religious wars. Here again, as in politics and morals, the worldwide youth disturbance may indicate a turning point in history, and we must listen to it carefully.

In 1967 I gave a course on "Professionalism" at the New

School for Social Research in New York, attended by about twenty-five graduate students from all departments. My bias was the traditional one: Professionals are autonomous individuals beholden to the nature of things and the judgment of their peers, and bound by an explicit or implicit oath to benefit their clients and the community. To teach this, I invited seasoned professionals whom I esteemed—a physician, engineer, journalist, architect, etc. These explained to the students the obstacles that increasingly stood in the way of honest practice, and their own life experience in circumventing them.

To my surprise, the class unanimously rejected them. Heatedly and rudely they called my guests liars, finks, mystifiers, or deluded. They showed that every professional was co-opted and corrupted by the System, all decisions were made top-down by the power structure and bureaucracy, professional peer-groups were conspiracies to make more money. All this was importantly true and had, of course, been said by the visitors. Why had the students not heard? As we explored further, we came to the deeper truth, that they did not believe in the existence of real professions at all; professions were concepts of repressive society and "linear thinking." I asked them to envisage any social order they pleased—Mao's, Castro's, some anarchist utopia—and wouldn't there be engineers who knew about materials and stresses and strains? Wouldn't people get sick and need to be treated? Wouldn't there be problems of communication? No, they insisted; it was important only to be human, and all else would follow.

Suddenly I realized that they did not really believe that there was a nature of things. Somehow all functions could be reduced to interpersonal relations and power. There was no knowledge, but only the sociology of knowledge. They had so well learned that physical and sociological research is subsidized and conducted for the benefit of the ruling class that they did not believe there was such a thing as simple truth. To be required to learn something was a trap by which the young were put down and co-opted. Then I knew that I could not get through to them. I had imagined that the worldwide student protest had to do with changing political and moral institutions, to which I was sympathetic, but I now saw that we had to do with a religious crisis of the magnitude of the Reformation in the fifteen-hundreds, when not only all institutions but all learning had been corrupted by the Whore of Babylon.

The irony was that I myself had said ten years ago, in *Growing Up Absurd*, that these young were growing up without a world for them, and therefore they were "alienated," estranged from nature and other people. But I had then been thinking of juvenile delinquents and a few beats; and a few years later I had been heartened by the Movement in Mississippi, the Free Speech protest in Berkeley, the Port Huron statement of SDS, the resistance to the Vietnam war, all of which made human sense and were not absurd at all. But the alienating circumstances had proved too strong after all; here were absurd graduate students, most of them political "activists."

Alienation is a Lutheran concept: "God has turned His face away, things have no meaning, I am estranged in the world." By the time of Hegel the term was applied to the general condition of rational man, with his "objective" sciences and institutions divorced from his "subjectivity," which was therefore irrational and impulsive. In his revision of Hegel, Marx explained this as the effect of man's losing his essential nature as a cooperative producer, because centuries of exploitation, culminating in capitalism, had fragmented the community and robbed the workman of the means of production. Comte and Durkheim pointed to the weakening of social solidarity and the contradiction between law and morality, so that people lost their bearings—this was anomie, an acute form of alienation that could lead to suicide or aimless riot. By the end of the nineteenth century, alienation came to be used as the term for insanity, derangement of perceived reality, and psychiatrists were called alienists.

Contemporary conditions of life have certainly deprived people, and especially young people, of a meaningful world in which they can act and find themselves. Many writers and the dissenting students themselves have spelled it out. For instance, in both schools and corporations, people cannot pursue their own interests or exercise initiative. Administrators are hypocrites who sell people out for the smooth operation of the system. The budget for war has grotesquely distorted reasonable social priorities. Worst of all, the authorities who make the decisions are incompetent to cope with modern times: We are in danger of extinction, the biosphere is being destroyed, two-thirds of mankind are starving. Let me here go on to some other factors that demand a religious response.

There is a lapse of faith in science. Science has not produced the general happiness that people expected, and now it has fallen under the sway of greed and power; whatever its beneficent past, people fear that its further progress will do more harm than good. And rationality itself is discredited. Probably it is more significant than we like to think that intelligent young people dabble in astrology, witchcraft, psychedelic dreams, and whatever else is despised by science; in some sense they are not kidding. They need to control their fate, but they hate scientific explanations.

Every one of these young grew up since Hiroshima. They do not talk about atom bombs—not nearly so much as we who campaigned against the shelters and fall-out—but the bombs explode in their dreams, as Otto Butz found in his study of collegians at San Francisco State, and now George Dennison, in *The Lives of Children,* shows that it was the same with small slum children whom he taught at the First Street School in New York. Again and again students have told me that they take it for granted they will not survive the next ten years. This is not an attitude with which to prepare for a career or to bring up a family.

Whether or not the bombs go off, human beings are becoming useless. Old people are shunted out of sight at an increasingly earlier age, young people are kept on ice till an increasingly later age. Small farmers and other technologically unemployed are dispossessed or left to rot. Large numbers are put away as incompetent or deviant. Racial minorities that cannot shape up are treated as a nuisance. Together, these groups are a large majority of the population. Since labor will not be needed much longer, there is vague talk of a future society of "leisure," but there is no thought of a kind of community in which all human beings would be necessary and valued.

The institutions, technology, and communications have infected even the "biological core," so that people's sexual desires are no longer genuine. This was powerfully argued by Wilhelm Reich a generation ago and it is now repeated by Herbert Marcuse. When I spoke for it in the nineteen-forties, I was condemned by the radicals, for example, C. Wright Mills, as a "bedroom revisionist."

A special aspect of biological corruption is the spreading ugliness, filth, and tension of the environment in which the young grow up. If Wordsworth was right—I think he was—that children must grow up in an environment of beauty and simple affections in order to become trusting, open, and magnanimous citizens, then the offspring of our ghettos, suburbs, and complicated homes have been disadvantaged, no matter how much money there is. This lack cannot be remedied by art in the curriculum, nor by vest-pocket playgrounds, nor by banning billboards from bigger highways. Cleaning the river might help, but that will be the day.

If we start from the premise that the young are in a religious crisis, that they doubt there is really a nature of things, and they are sure there is not a world for themselves, many details of their present behavior become clearer. Alienation is a powerful motivation, of unrest, fantasy, and reckless action. It leads, as we shall see, to religious innovation, new sacraments to give life meaning. But it is a poor basis for politics, including revolutionary politics.

It is said that the young dissidents never offer a constructive program. And apart from the special cases of Czechoslovakia and Poland, where they confront an unusually outdated system, this is largely true. In France, China, Germany, Egypt, England, the United States, and so on, most of the issues of protest have been immediate gut issues, and the tactics have been mainly disruptive, without coherent proposals for a better society. But this makes for bad politics. Unless one has a program, there is no way to persuade the other citizens, who do not have one's gut complaints, to come along. Instead one confronts them hostilely and they are turned off, even when they might be sympathetic. But the confrontation is inept too, for the alienated young cannot take other people seriously as having needs of their own; a spectacular instance was the inability of the French youth to communicate with the French working class, in May 1968. In Gandhian theory, the confronter aims at future community with the confronted; he will not let him continue a course that is bad for *him,* and so he appeals to his deeper reason. But instead of this *Satyagraha,* soul force, we have seen plenty of hate. The confronted are *not* taken as human beings, but as pigs, etc. But how can the young people think of a future community when they themselves have no present world, no profession or other job in it, and no trust in other human beings? Instead, some young radicals seem to entertain the disastrous illusion that other people can be compelled by fear. This can lead only to crushing reaction.

All the "political" activity makes sense, however, if it is understood that it is not aimed at social reconstruction at all, but is a way of desperately affirming that they are alive and want a place in the sun. "I am a revolutionary," said Cohn-Bendit, leader of the French students in 1968, "because it is the best way of living." And young Americans pathetically and truly say that there is no other way to be taken seriously. Then it is not necessary to have a program; the right method is to act, against any vulnerable point and wherever one can rally support. The purpose is not politics, but to have a movement and form a community. This is exactly what Saul Alinsky prescribed to rally outcast blacks.

And such conflictful action has indeed caused social changes. In France it was conceded by the Gaullists that "nothing would ever be the same." In the United States, the changes in social attitude during the last ten years are unthinkable without the youth action, with regard to war, the military-industrial, corporate organization and administration, the police, the blacks. When the actors have been in touch with the underlying causes of things, issues have deepened and the Movement has grown. But for the alienated, again, action easily slips into activism, and conflict is often spite and stubbornness. There is excitement and notoriety, much human suffering, and the world no better off. (*New Left Notes* runs a column wryly called, "We Made the News Today, Oh Boy!") Instead of deepening awareness and a sharpening political conflict, there occurs the polarization of mere exasperation. It often seems that the aim is just to have a shambles. Impatiently the ante of tactics is raised beyond what the "issue" warrants, and support melts away. Out on a limb, the leaders become desperate and fanatical, intolerant of criticism, dictatorial. The Movement falls to pieces.

Yet it is noteworthy that when older people like myself are critical of the wrongheaded activism, we nevertheless almost invariably concede that the young are *morally* justified. For what is the use of patience and reason when meantime millions are being killed and starved, and when bombs and nerve gas are being stockpiled? Against the entrenched power responsible for these things, it might be better to do something idiotic now than something perhaps more practical in the long run. I don't know which is less demoralizing.

Maybe the truth is revealed in the following conversation I had with a young hippie at a college in Massachusetts. He was dressed like an (American) Indian—buckskin fringes and a headband, red paint on his face. All his life, he said, he had tried to escape the encompassing evil of our society that was trying to destroy his soul. "But if you're always escaping," I said, "and never attentively study it, how can you make a wise judgment about society or act effectively to change it?" "You see, you don't dig!" he cried. "It's just ideas like 'wise' and 'acting effectively' that we can't stand." He was right. He was in the religious dilemma of Faith vs. Works. Where I sat, Works had some reality; but in the reign of the Devil, as he felt it, all Works are corrupted, they are part of the System; only Faith can avail. But he didn't have Faith either.

Inevitably, the alienated seem to be inconsistent in how they take the present world. Hippies attack technology and are scornful of rationality, but they buy up electronic equipment and motorcycles, and with them the whole infrastructure. Activists say that civil liberties are bourgeois and they shout down their opponents; but they clamor in court for their civil liberties. Those who say that the university is an agent of the powers that be, do not mean thereby to reassert the ideal role of the university, but to use the university for their own propaganda. Yet if I point out these apparent inconsistencies, it does not arouse shame or guilt. How is this? It is simply that they do not really understand that technology, civil law, and the university are *human* institutions, for which they too are responsible; they take them as brute-given, just what's there, to be manipulated as convenient. But convenient for whom? The trouble with this attitude is that these institutions, works of spirit in history, are how Man has made himself and is. If they treat them as mere things, rather than being vigilant for them, they themselves become nothing. And nothing comes from nothing.

In general, their lack of a sense of history is bewildering. It is impossible to convey to them that the deeds were done by human beings, that John Hampden confronted the king and wouldn't pay the war tax just like us, or that Beethoven too, just like a rock 'n' roll band, made up his music as he went along, from odds and ends, with energy, spontaneity, and passion—how else do they think he made music? And they no longer remember their own history. A few years ago there was a commonly accepted story of mankind, beginning with the beats, going on to the Chessman case, the HUAC bust, the Freedom Rides, and climaxing in the Berkeley Victory—"The first human event in forty thousand years," Mike Rossman, one of the innumerable spokesmen, told me. But this year I find that nothing antedates Chicago '68. Elder statesmen, like Sidney Lens and especially Staughton Lynd, have been trying with heroic effort to recall the American antecedents of present radical and libertarian slogans and tactics, but it doesn't rub off. I am often hectored to my face with formulations that I myself put in their mouths, that have become part of the oral tradition, two years old, author prehistoric. Most significant of all, it has been whispered to me—but I can't check up, because I don't speak the language—that among the junior-high-school students, aged twelve and thirteen, that's really where it's at! Quite different from what goes on in the colleges that I visit.

What I do notice, however, is that dozens of Underground newspapers have a noisy style. Though each one is doing his thing, there is not much idiosyncrasy in the spontaneous variety. The political radicals are, as if mesmerized, repeating the power plays, factionalism, random abuse, and tactical lies that aborted the Movement in the thirties. And I have learned, to my disgust, that a major reason why the young don't trust people over thirty is that they don't understand them and are too conceited to try.

Having grown up in a world too meaningless to learn anything, they know very little and are quick to resent it.

This is an unpleasant picture. Even so, the alienated young have no vital alternative except to confront the Evil, and to try to make a new way of life out of their own innards and suffering. As they are doing. It is irrelevant to point out that the System is not the monolith that they think and that the majority of people are not corrupt, just browbeaten and confused. What is relevant is that they cannot see this, because they do not have an operable world for themselves. In such a case, the only advice I would dare to give them is that which Krishna gave Arjuna: to confront with nonattachment, to be brave and firm without hatred. (I don't here want to discuss the question of "violence"; the hatred and disdain are far more important.) Also, when they are seeking a new way of life, for example when they are making a "journey inward," as Ronald Laing calls it, I find that I urge them occasionally to write a letter home.

As a citizen and father I have a right to try to prevent a shambles and to diminish the number of wrecked lives. But it is improper for us elders to keep saying, as we do, that their activity is "counterproductive." It's our business to do something more productive.

Religiously, the young have been inventive, much more than the God-is-dead theologians. They have hit on new sacraments, physical actions to get them out of their estrangement and (momentarily) break through into meaning. The terribly loud music is used sacramentally. The claim for the hallucinogenic drugs is almost never the paradisal pleasure of opium culture nor the escape from distress of heroin, but tuning in to the cosmos and communing with one another. They seem to have had flashes of success in bringing ritual participation back into theater, which for a hundred years playwrights and directors have tried to do in vain. And whatever the political purposes and results of activism, there is no doubt that shared danger for the sake of righteousness is used sacramentally as baptism of fire. Fearful moments of provocation and the poignant release of the bust bring unconscious contents to the surface, create a bond of solidarity, are "commitment."

But the most powerful magic, working in all these sacraments, is the close presence of other human beings, without competition or one-upping. The original sin is to be on an ego trip that isolates; and angry political factionalism has now also become a bad thing. What a drastic comment on the dehumanization and fragmentation of modern times that salvation can be attained simply by the "warmth of assembled animal bodies," as Kafka called it, describing his mice. At the 1967 Easter Be-In in New York's Central Park, when about ten thousand were crowded on the Sheep Meadow, a young man with a quite radiant face said to me, "Gee, human beings are legal!"—it was sufficient, to be safe, to be exempted from continual harassment by officious rules and Law and Order.

The extraordinary rock festivals at Bethel and on the Isle of Wight are evidently pilgrimages. Joan Baez, one of the hierophants, ecstatically described Bethel to me, and the gist of it was that people were nice to one another. A small group passing a joint of marijuana often behaves like a Quaker meeting waiting for the spirit, and the cigarette may be a placebo. Group therapy and sensitivity training, with Mecca at Esalen, have the same purpose. And I think this is the sense of the sexuality, which is certainly not hedonistic, nor mystical in the genre of D. H. Lawrence; nor does it have much to do with personal love—that is too threatening for these anxious youths. But it is human touch, without conquest or domination, and it obviates self-consciousness and embarrassed speech.

Around the rather pure faith there has inevitably collected a mess of eclectic liturgy and paraphernalia. Mandalas, beggars in saffron, (American) Indian beads, lectures in Zen. Obviously the exotic is desirable because it is not what they have grown up with. And it is true that fundamental facts of life are more acceptable if they come in fancy dress, e.g., it is good to breathe from the diaphragm and one can learn this by humming "OM," as Allen Ginsberg did for seven hours at Grant Park in Chicago. But college chaplains are also pretty busy, and they are now more likely to see the adventurous and off-beat than, as used to be the case, the staid and square. Flowers and strobe lights are indigenous talismans.

It is hard to describe this (or any) religiosity without lapsing into condescending humor. Yet it is genuine and it will, I am convinced, survive and develop—I don't know into what. In the end it is religion that constitutes the strength of this generation, and not, as I used to think, their morality, political will, and common sense. Except for a few, like the young people of the Resistance, I am not impressed by their moral courage or even honesty. For all their eccentricity they are singularly lacking in personality. They do not have enough world to have much character. And they are not especially attractive as animals. But they keep pouring out a kind of metaphysical vitality.

Let me try to account for it. On the one hand, these young have an unusual amount of available psychic energy. They were brought up on antibiotics that minimized depressing chronic childhood diseases, and with post-Freudian freedom to act out early drives. Up to age six or seven, television nourished them with masses of strange images and sometimes true information —McLuhan makes a lot of sense for the kindergarten years. Long schooling would tend to make them stupid, but it has been compensated by providing the vast isolated cities of youth that the high schools and colleges essentially are, where they can incubate their own thoughts. They are sexually precocious and not inhibited by taboos. They are superficially knowledgeable. On the other hand, all this psychic energy has had little practical use. The social environment is dehumanized. It discourages romantic love and lasting friendship. They are desperately bored because the world does not promise any fulfillment. Their knowledge gives no intellectual or poetic satisfaction. In this impasse, we can expect a ferment of new religion. As in Greek plays, impasse produces gods from the machine. For a long time we did not hear of the symptoms of adolescent religious conversion, once as common in the United States as in all other places and ages. Now it seems to be recurring as a mass phenomenon.

Without doubt the religious young are in touch with something historical, but I don't think they understand what it is. Let me quote from an editorial in *New Seminary News,* the newsletter of dissident seminarians of the Pacific School of Religion in Berkeley; "What we confront (willingly or not we are thrust into it) is a time of disintegration of a dying civilization and the emergence of a new one." This seems to envisage something like the instant decline of the Roman Empire and they, presumably, are like the Christians about to build, rapidly, another era. But there are no signs that this is the actual situation. It would mean, for instance, that our scientific technology, civil law, professions, universities, and so forth, are about to vanish from the earth and be replaced by something entirely different. This is a fantasy of alienated minds. Nobody behaves as if civilization would vanish, and nobody acts as if there were a new dispensation. Nobody is waiting patiently in the catacombs, and the faithful have not withdrawn into the desert. Neither the yippies nor the New Seminarians nor any other exalted group have produced anything that is the least bit miraculous. Our civilization may well destroy itself with its atom bombs or something else, but then we do not care what will emerge, if anything.

But the actual situation *is* very like 1510, when Luther went to Rome, the eve of the Reformation. There is everywhere protest, revaluation, attack on the Establishment. The protest is international. There is a generation gap. (Luther himself was all of 34 when he posted his 95 theses in 1517, but Melanchthon was 20, Bucer 26, Münzer 28, Jonas 24; the Movement consisted of undergraduates and junior faculty.) And the thrust of protest is not to give up science, technology, and civil institutions, but to purge them, humanize them, decentralize them, change the priorities, and stop the drain of wealth.

These were, of course, exactly the demands of the 4 March 1969 nationwide teach-in on science, initiated by the dissenting professors of the Massachusetts Institute of Technology. This and the waves of other teach-ins, ads and demonstrations have been the voices not of the alienated, of people who have no world, but of protestants, people deep in the world who will soon refuse to continue under the present auspices because they are not viable. It is populism permeated by moral and professional unease. What the young have done is to make it finally religious, to force the grown-ups to recognize that they too are threatened with meaninglessness.

The analogy to the Reformation is even closer if we notice that the bloated universities, and the expanded school systems under them, constitute the biggest collection of monks since the time of Henry VIII. And most of this mandarinism is hocus-po-

cus, a mass superstition. In my opinion, much of the student dissent in the colleges and especially the high schools has little to
do with the excellent political and social demands that are made,
but is boredom and resentment because of the phoniness of the
whole academic enterprise.

Viewed as incidents of a Reformation, as attempts to purge
themselves and recover a lost integrity, the various movements of
the alienated young are easily recognizable as characteristic
Protestant sects, intensely self-conscious. The dissenting seminarians of the Pacific School of Religion do not intend to go off to
primitive love feasts in a new heaven and new earth, but to form
their own Free University; that is, they are Congregationalists.
The shaggy hippies are not nature children as they claim, but
self-conscious Adamites trying to naturalize Sausalito and the
East Village. Heads are Pentecostals or Children of Light. Those
who spindle IBM cards and throw the dean down the stairs are
Iconoclasts. Those who want Student Power, a say in the rules
and curriculum, mean to deny infant baptism; they want to
make up their own minds, like Henry Dunster, the first president
of Harvard. Radicals who live among the poor and try to organize them are certainly intent on social change, but they are also
trying to find themselves again. The support of the black revolt
by white middle-class students is desperately like Anabaptism,
but God grant that we can do better than the Peasants' War.
These analogies are not fanciful; when authority is discredited,
there is a pattern in the return of the repressed. A better scholar
could make a longer list; but the reason I here spell it out is that,
perhaps, some young person will suddenly remember that history was about something.

Naturally, traditional churches are themselves in transition. On
college campuses and in bohemian neighborhoods, existentialist
Protestants and Jews and updating Catholics have gone along
with the political and social activism and, what is probably more
important, they have changed their own moral, esthetic, and personal tone. On many campuses, the chaplains provide the only
official forum for discussions of sex, drugs, and burning draft
cards. Yet it seems to me that, in their zeal for relevance, they
are badly failing in their chief duty to the religious young: to be
professors of theology. They cannot really perform pastoral serv-

ices, like giving consolation or advice, since the young believe they have the sacraments to do this for themselves. Chaplains say that the young are uninterested in dogma and untractable on this level, but I think this is simply a projection of their own distaste for the conventional theology that has gone dead for them. The young are hotly metaphysical—but, alas, boringly so, because they don't know much, have no language to express their intuitions, and repeat every old fallacy. If the chaplains would stop looking in the conventional places where God is dead, and would explore the actualities where perhaps He is alive, they might learn something and have something to teach.

[1969]

PART TWO

Figures and Themes

INTRODUCTION

Having offered a series of general analyses of the New Left, we now turn to some of the topics that have figured most prominently in its responses to contemporary politics. The opening essay, by David Spitz, is a detailed examination of a notion that has achieved a disturbing popularity on the American campus, mostly through the writings of Herbert Marcuse: The notion that the liberal virtue of tolerance has become, in present-day society, a form of repression and a device for avoiding basic social change. Marcuse's thought, perhaps the most influential in the New Left, is subjected to a wide-ranging critique by Allen Graubard, both on philosophical and political grounds.

The remaining essays touch upon, and criticize, key elements in New Left thought and feeling. Two of its international heroes, Frantz Fanon and Régis Debray, are sharply examined by Lewis Coser, who notes in them a characteristic blend of utopian sentiment and authoritarian method. In a lengthy study Henry Pachter turns to another subject that has occupied much attention on the New Left: The effort of "revisionist" historians to provide a new picture of the conflict between East and West during the cold-war years.

Other essays in this part of the book deal with a wide range of topics—from problems of university life (Robert Brustein) to the politics of the Black Panthers (Theodore Draper), from the snobbism sometimes displayed toward workers by the New Left (Brendan Sexton) to the cultural styles of New Left youth (Erazim V. Kohák). Certain topics that ideally should appear in the following pages, do not: a discussion of imperialism, a political critique of Che Guevara. There will, we hope, be other occasions. Meanwhile, here is abundant material for a democratic Left critique of the New Left.

PURE TOLERANCE:

A Critique of Criticisms

by David Spitz

Ever since men climbed down from the trees and found it necessary to establish ground rules, they have fought over what those rules shall be. They have fought longest, and perhaps most bitterly, over the most fundamental rule of all—the rule by which the ground rules themselves shall be determined. For he who controls the ground rules is in a position to control the game.

That the rule of tolerance is this fundamental rule is revealed by the fact that dictatorships exclude it and democratic states make it central to their enterprise. Only in democratic states are governments established and changed in response to the free play of conflicting opinions.

This—the securing of responsible government—is not, of course, the only reason for supporting tolerance. Those who defend it also contend that tolerance makes for diversity, which is essential to progress and the development of individuality, and thus to the common good. They also believe that tolerance, at least in a pluralist society, is the only principle under which diverse groups can live together without resorting either to mutual slaughter or to an authoritarian regime that will impose one group's creed on others.

The argument for intolerance, in contrast, is generally put forward by men who mean to have their way but fear that free discussion will "mislead" other men—either because those others are less wise or virtuous than they or because conditions are such as to favor the false doctrine.

Now, the classic case for tolerance has been set forth in John Stuart Mill's celebrated essay *On Liberty*. Ever since Mill published that essay in 1859, the critics of tolerance have been diligently at work refuting him. It needs to be said, if unkindly, that one obvious reason for this is that later critics have recognized the difficulties that earlier critics have had with him. It is a mark of no mean significance that this process still continues; indeed, it has become the foundation of a flourishing industry.

As a part-time member of this guild (though one essentially in sympathy with Mill), I can do no other than commend it to the newcomers. I ask only that they first familiarize themselves with already existing products. Then they might spare their readers, if not themselves, the labor of reencountering ancient formulations under the guise of a new suit of phrases; and in doing so they might also learn to distinguish reputable from shoddy merchandise. For it needs also to be said that much of what is produced by this industry today is neither novel nor imaginative nor important. That is the judgment I propose in regard to *A Critique of Pure Tolerance*, co-authored by Herbert Marcuse, Barrington Moore, Jr., and Robert Paul Wolff (Boston: Beacon Press, 1965).

What distinguishes the three essays that constitute this book is *not* an awareness, and hence transcendence, of these elementary considerations. It is rather the marshaling and ocasionally the revision of old arguments to attack Mill from what might (for the moment) be called radical perspectives. Traditionally, Mill has been identified with the Left and his critics with the Right. This ideological cleavage by no means accounts for all of Mill's critics; some of them—Dorothy Fosdick, J. C. Rees, and Isaiah Berlin, for example—have dealt with Mill and his arguments in terms divorced from such partisanship. But it accounts for a good many of them, including, I venture to think, the three critics who here attack Mill's plea for complete freedom of thought and expression on the ground, so they say, that it prevents, or at the very least militates against, the supremacy of "correct" ideas, that is, "their" ideas. And because they profess to be of the radical Left, Mill stands condemned (in their eyes) as a protagonist of the "wrong" ideas, as a purveyor of a political philosophy that safeguards the *status quo*.

The keynote of their argument—on which, despite other differences, they are agreed—is contained in this introductory sentence: "For each of us the prevailing theory and practice of tolerance turned out on examination to be in varying degrees hypocritical masks to cover appalling political realities." And here I must begin with a confession of inadequacy: I have tried, but I am unable to make sense of this statement. What, apart from its strident terminology, does it mean? Is the theory referred to one that accounts for the practice or one that articulates an ideal to which that practice should conform? If it accounts for the practice, then the theory is not a mask but a revelation of the realities. If it articulates an ideal, then the theory stands not as a description of what is but as a prescriptive norm, and hence as a criterion of judgment by which those realities are to be judged. If it is replied that theory here means what people say, then we are simply confronted by the usual dichotomy between rhetoric and performance, between espoused or intended conduct and actual behavior. But a theory is never this; it is always an attempt to describe the true reality—our function, Klee somewhere said, is "not to reveal the visible but to make visible the real"—or to prescribe the proper conduct. Then, if we omit the word "theory" and look only at the word "practice," all that the statement seems to mean is that people do not behave very nicely, which is hardly a piercing insight.

In what sense, then, can the theory or practice of tolerance be termed hypocritical? Presumably in the sense that the theory is at odds with, and a rationalization of, the practice. But this means only that the theory (as explanation rather than as prescription) is deficient, that in fact it is not a theory at all but an ideology.

What, finally, is meant by the phrase "prevailing theory"? Is it Mill's theory of liberty, or what the writers call the doctrine of "pure tolerance"? If so, there is obviously a considerable gap not only between Mill's teaching and current (e.g., American) practice, but also, I think, between that teaching and whatever may be said to be the dominant legal and political view (or views) of liberty. Is it some other theory, a doctrine more in keeping with what our three writers are pleased to call the realities of an industrial democracy? If so, this is not identified. What they attack, then, is not *the* prevailing doctrine of liberty, and not always, as will become clear, Mill's doctrine, but doctrines and conditions imputed to Mill and which, in their view, constitute the hallmark of a sorry liberalism.

Let us consider the contentions of our three critics.

Take, first, the argument of Robert Paul Wolff. I am not altogether sure whether he misunderstands Mill or intends his readers to misunderstand Mill, but to the extent that I may read him correctly he depicts Mill at one point as an exponent of psychological egoism and at another as an advocate of individual liberty free of all social restraints. Neither of these characterizations accurately describes Mill. He also asserts that Mill defended the freedoms of thought and of action so long as these did not harm others. But Mill clearly and explicitly distinguished his defense of freedom of thought, which he made an absolute, from freedom of action, which was conditioned by its consequences. Wolff makes the important point that tolerance should not be confused with neutrality or condescension but should be recognized as a positive good; however, though Wolff does not mention it, this is also central to Mill's thought.

What is of interest, then, is not Wolff's critique of Mill—which is, strictly speaking, essentially irrelevant—but the fact that his essay, though it is entitled "Beyond Tolerance," deals less with tolerance than with the conditions that make it ineffective. Wolff believes that tolerance is a doctrine that has emerged from and is only appropriate to a particular stage of historical development, namely, the stage of democratic pluralism. But—and this is what he is most concerned to show—democratic pluralism is no longer adequate to the so-called stage of modernity in which we now find ourselves, and for two reasons primarily: It discriminates against certain disadvantaged social groups or interests—those that are outside the Establishment, that lack "legitimate representation," and that are not consequently given a place or a

voice in society—and it discriminates against certain social policies, most directly those that look to the promotion of the common good rather than to the satisfaction of diverse particular interests or claims. As a result, democratic pluralism in its concrete
application—though not, Wolff adds, in its theory—supports
inequality, maintains the *status quo*, blocks social change. What
is required, Wolff concludes, is a new philosophy of community,
of the common good, one that goes "beyond pluralism and beyond tolerance."

Now it is curious that one who, like Wolff, relates ideas in
near-deterministic fashion to particular stages of historical development—and I must bypass here the familiar and age-old controversy over this asserted but still unproved thesis—should ignore the fact that earlier theories of tolerance, those of Locke
and Milton, for example, and perhaps even of Socrates in the
Apology before them, were not merely arguments for a *qualified*
tolerance, but were in a very real sense also arguments consistent
with a kind of homogeneous, or largely homogeneous, society.
To go beyond pluralism is presumably to plead for a new type of
homogeneity, and hence for a new kind of orthodoxy; for from
what individuals or groups, and for what purpose, will new and
diverse ideas then emerge?

What makes Mill distinctive, and vitally important, is that
while he recognized and even pleaded for a sense of national
cohesion and for the pursuit of the public interest, he insisted
along with this that it was necessary to respect and to build
upon a certain heterogeneity, that progress required *both* the
promotion of the common good and furtherance of individual
and group differences. Consequently, in line with his utilitarian
philosophy, he argued for the absolute toleration of ideas and for
the maximum toleration of variety in practices. He sought a
unity that would contain rather than eliminate diversity. In these
terms, to argue against pluralism and for the idea of a common
good, as if these were opposing and mutually exclusive principles, is to argue for a self-defeating proposition; for it may well
be—and I am convinced it is—that democratic pluralism, properly understood and properly institutionalized, is precisely what
defines or constitutes the core of the common good.

It is noteworthy that Wolff nowhere defines or articulates the nature of his common good; nor does he set out a program for its realization. Were he to attempt to do so, he might find, as many another writer has found, that in a multigroup society the common good requires not the rejection of pluralism but the determination of the appropriate kinds and degrees of pluralism compatible with a political goal. Otherwise there can emerge only a deadening, even if new, conformity. However this may be, if it is true, as Wolff admits, that the fault is not in the theory of pluralism, or of tolerance, but in the shortcomings of its practice, why does he attack the theory of pure tolerance? Why does he not focus instead on the conditions—whether of structure, institutions, attitudes, or all of these combined—that hinder its attainment and impair or delimit its free exercise, and on measures calculated to redress those deficiencies? For it is not Mill and his theory of liberty but the arrangements and practices of modern industrial society that are clearly the issues at stake.

Barrington Moore's essay, "Tolerance and the Scientific Outlook," is a more sophisticated and relevant effort. In part, this is because Moore is aware of many of the foregoing considerations and avoids certain elementary confusions. In part, it is because Moore restates and builds upon a number of Mill's arguments—though he does not, curiously, acknowledge this indebtedness. In part, finally, it is because Moore advances an interesting argument of his own.

With respect to Mill, the most important of Moore's restatements is the proposition that the intellectual's task is not to agitate or fight for a particular doctrine or ideal "but to find and speak the truth, whatever the political consequences may be." The latter part of this proposition is, of course, standard Millian doctrine, as may be evidenced by Mill's familiar plea (in his essay "On Civilization"), that the very cornerstone and object of education "is to call forth the greatest possible quantity of intellectual *power,* and to inspire the intense *love of truth;* and this without a particle of regard to the results to which the exercise of that power may lead. . . ." But the first part of Moore's statement does not, alas, confront the obvious question: What if one's discovery of the truth is at the same time the discovery of a correct doctrine or ideal? Does one's commitment to the truth not require one then to advocate, even agitate for, that doctrine? Does the intellectual not then become a partisan *malgré lui?* If I am to infer Moore's answer from the content of this essay, it is clearly positive. But Moore does not explicitly say so; nor does he pursue the implications of that conclusion. Mill, of course, essayed both roles, precisely because he saw no necessary incompatibility between them.

Moore properly maintains that historical disputes can often be settled by an appeal to the evidence. But does it follow that "tolerance for different 'interpretations' based on different *Weltanschauungen* merely befuddles the issue"? Or that "a scientific attitude toward human society [does not] necessarily induce a conservative tolerance of the existing order"? Clearly, what constitutes relevant evidence is itself a matter of interpretation; and the issue is not whether tolerance or a scientific attitude implies acceptance (or, for that matter, rejection) of a particular interpretation or social order—it does not—but whether it implies acceptance of one's right to entertain and advance *ideas* that defend (or reject) a particular interpretation or social order. When Moore says, as he does, that tolerance of conflicting interpretations befuddles the issue, does he mean to suggest that the natural consequences of a serious examination of alternative doctrines will always, or mostly, lead to the adoption of the wrong doctrine? This, I think, can only be affirmed by repudiating the value of reason itself, which Moore does not and of course will not do. But if reason itself is not at fault, the rational examination of alternatives cannot lead to befuddlement. What makes for confusion, instead, is the intrusion of unreason, of prejudices or interests or the operation of weighted conditions that militate against the free play of intellect. But then Moore's indictment should turn not on the principle of tolerance but (as with Wolff) on the social conditions in which tolerance is practiced —conditions that deny reason its day in court or that perpetuate the deficiencies of reasoners. All of which would seem to be confirmed by Moore himself when he says that "every idea, including the most dangerous and apparently absurd ones, deserves to have its credentials examined."

This, however, is not the message that Moore is most anxious to communicate. He is concerned rather to argue three things: (a) that the secular and rational (i.e., scientific) outlook, by which he means neither "technicist science" nor "academic humanism" but a conception of science that embraces "whatever is established by sound reasoning and evidence," is adequate both for understanding and evaluating human affairs; (b) that this outlook is able, in principle, to yield clear-cut answers to important questions, including the question of "when to be tolerant and when tolerance becomes intellectual cowardice and evasion"; and (c) finally, and most importantly, that in the present historical moment it may well behoove us to abandon the "nauseating hypocrisy" of "liberal rhetoric," to refuse to work under the prevailing system, and to consider "the conditions under which the resort to violence is justified in the name of freedom."

This is a hard teaching, but not for that reason to be avoided. We must first ask, however, whether it is also true. And here, it seems to me, the answer is by no means as simple as Moore takes it to be.

Consider Moore's claim—(a) and (b)—that objective knowledge and objective evaluation of human institutions are possible, thereby yielding correct and unambiguous answers, independent of individual whims and preferences. If Moore really admires Morris R. Cohen, whom he cites approvingly, he should have borne in mind Cohen's important distinction between the meaning of what is asserted in verified scientific theory and the degree of certainty of its verification. This certainty is always a matter of degree; it is never absolute; for what is verified is the theorems, not the postulates, of the theory. This is why Cohen, like Mill, believed that scientific *method* encourages toleration even as it enables us to differentiate beliefs and opinions that have been confirmed from those which have not.

Now Moore avows his commitment to scientific method. He recognizes that as a method it is a procedure for the testing of ideas, from which it follows that no conclusion, including the contents and very conception of science itself, is permanently above and beyond criticism and, possibly, fundamental change. How, then, can he confuse the principle of tolerance, which at one point he explicitly equates with this scientific procedure, with the acceptance of a particular doctrine or system of order, or assert the possibility not merely of objective knowledge but of objective evaluation, of correct answers to human problems? This is not to deny the relevance and utility of scientific method in the evaluation and solution of such problems; it is only to suggest that the most scientific evaluation, along with its alleged clear-cut answers, is still but tentative rather than absolute, relative to our assumptions and values, and always subject to revision.

Moore, however, confident of his "truths," seems prepared to reject the prevailing system and to adopt a revolutionary attitude. So long as three conditions are met—that the prevailing regime is unnecessarily repressive, that a revolutionary situation is in fact ripening, and that through a rough calculus of revolutionary violence one can reasonably believe that the costs in human suffering inherent in the continuation of the *status quo* outweigh those to be incurred in the revolution and its aftermath—the resort to violence, Moore holds, is justified in the name of freedom.

It is not easy for one who views the prevailing regime (or regimes) with considerable unhappiness, and who would consequently welcome certain fundamental changes in the social order, to cavil at Moore's revolutionary posture. Clearly, unless one is prepared to say that under no circumstances may men rebel, that men must remain always at the base of even the most burdensome pyramids of unjust power, there are moments in history when the resort to violence is fully warranted. That many contemporary nations, including the United States, celebrate their own past revolutions is only the more obvious of many instances in point. Thus, as an abstract statement of conditions that require and justify violence to overturn an indecent social order, Moore's argument merits respect. (Though it should not go unnoted that he here goes counter to his own earlier contention that the intellectual is not to be a partisan in the cause of this, or any other, ideal.)

Nevertheless, if we apply his (very far from precise) conditions to the modern industrial societies of the Western world, his argument becomes less than conclusive. For one thing, it is not at all clear that Western industrial societies are so oppressive that violent overthrow of the entire system is justified. For another, it is questionable that the cultural and human drabness to which Moore presumably objects is, in fact, amenable to correction through political action. For still another, the applicability of his second and third conditions is more than problematical. Nor do his conditions take into account certain useful and perhaps necessary distinctions: those, for example, between a class and a national revolution, or between a revolution initiated to seize power and a revolution, like the National Socialist Revolution, imposed after power has been effectively seized. Finally, his argument either neglects or gives insufficient weight to certain risks attendant upon all revolutionary efforts. Of these inconvenient but ever-present risks, I have space here to note only two.

One is the corrupting effect of the revolution itself, which often degrades and alters the characters and principles of the revolutionaries themselves, so that men who emerge at the top after a successful revolution are rarely the same men (even if they retain the same names and carry the same bodies) as those who made the revolution, with all that this implies in the way of altered ends, new hatreds and antagonisms, and new repressions. To be sure, some consequences of a successful revolution may be praiseworthy, e.g., the institution of certain reforms designed to eliminate or abate injustices and discontents. But other consequences are more than likely to be catastrophic. Of these the most immediately probable is the suppression of freedom of speech and political opposition. For it is not uncommon that governments which have survived revolutionary attempts, or which have come to power through revolution, seek with grim determination to eliminate the possibility of further revolutionary efforts. This, certainly, would seem to be one of the more evident lessons of revolutionary movements that have come to power since, say, the Second World War. Thus the appeal to revolution often invites the destruction of the very principle that makes the revolution possible—the principle of tolerance.

The second dangerous risk is the high improbability of success. Paul Kecskemeti has called attention to the striking fact that, despite all the revolutionary talk of the past century, if we except the Iberian peninsula, there have been no serious attempts at internal revolution in peacetime Europe since 1848–49; and if we consider the abortive Hungarian Revolution of 1956 (which took place after Kecskemeti wrote), the point is underscored that in the modern industrial state, with its specialized technology and advanced systems of weaponry, and with the support of powerful external armies and governments, civil revolt is in the ordinary course of events most unlikely to succeed. In fact, the normal complement of apathy, contentment, and especially fear—not of sporadic outbreaks but of wholesale violence and disorder—makes it more than unlikely that the masses will venture to disrupt the prevailing system of order by revolutionary means. It is, then, one thing to call for a revolutionary attitude, quite another to call for and expect revolutionary action. (I speak, let it be emphasized again, not of primitive or developing societies, but only of modern industrial societies; for it is only to such states that our authors apply their arguments.)

Once again, therefore, we are back to the central confusion inherent in this criticism: that which equates the principle of tolerance with the restrictive practices of states avowedly committed to that principle. The criticism actually testifies only to the limitations of those practices, and thus leaves untouched—at least at this level of argument—Mill's plea for freedom of thought and expression.

We come now to the most extreme and convoluted, yet in some ways the most intriguing, of our three indictments of pure tolerance: Herbert Marcuse's essay "Repressive Tolerance." It may seem outrageous to suggest that this very title is a contradiction in terms, as are also other phrases employed by Marcuse, for example "totalitarian democracy" and "the democratic educational dictatorship of free men"; but I shall make this suggestion nonetheless. I am aware that Marcuse, as a neo-Hegelian (also a neo-Marxist and neo-Freudian), prides himself on his dialectical thinking. But the dialectic—or, as Marcuse likes to say, the negation of the negation—aims to produce not a conjunction of two opposites but a synthesis which is different from either of them. And expressions like "repressive tolerance," "totalitarian democracy," and "democratic dictatorship," because they mismate rather than synthesize opposites, are self-contradictory and therefore meaningless. They should be banished from the literature. It is necessary to say this at the outset because Marcuse has

dwelt harshly and at length on the inadequacies, even the Or-
wellian evils, of ordinary language, yet has also condemned philosophers who employ linguistic analysis in an effort to avoid the
pitfalls of meaninglessness. Why, then, does he himself foster
rather than transcend obscurity?

I will have occasion to return to this problem. Let me first,
however, try to state the essentials of Marcuse's argument.
Briefly, for it is a reiteration and extension of his argument in
One-Dimensional Man, it comes to this: We—and by "we" Marcuse means the peoples of *all* modern industrial societies,
whether "democratic" or otherwise—live today in a totalitarian
system. It is totalitarian because, with the concentration of economic and political power and the use of technology as an instrument of domination, and under the rule of monopolistic
media, "a mentality is created for which right and wrong, true
and false are predefined wherever they affect the vital interests
of the society." Rational persuasion is thus all but precluded. In
such a situation tolerance "is administered to manipulated and
indoctrinated individuals who parrot, as their own, the opinion
of their masters." It is a tolerance abstractly "pure" but concretely "partisan," for "it actually protects the already established machinery of discrimination." It is thus repressive rather
than true tolerance. For tolerance to be real, it must discriminate
instead against falsehood and evil; it must cancel the liberal
creed of free and equal discussion; it must preclude harmful
ideas and harmful behavior. It must in fact encourage subversion
of the existing order, even if this requires "apparently undemocratic means."

Marcuse articulates these "apparently undemocratic means" as
follows:

> They would include the withdrawal of toleration of
> speech and assembly from groups and movements which
> promote aggressive policies, armament, chauvinism, dis-
> crimination on the grounds of race and religion, or which
> oppose the extension of public services, social security,
> medical care, etc. Moreover, the restoration of freedom of
> thought may necessitate new and rigid restrictions on
> teachings and practices in the educational institutions

which, by their very methods and concepts, serve to en-
close the mind within the established universe of discourse and behavior—thereby precluding a priori a rational evaluation of the alternatives.

All this, Marcuse admits, is censorship, "even precensorship,"
but warranted because the distinction between liberating and
repressive teachings and practices "is not a matter of value-
preference but of rational criteria"; and these, Marcuse insists,
are empirical in nature, turning on the real possibilities of
attaining human freedom in a particular stage of civilization. To
the question: Who is to draw these distinctions and make these
decisions?—the answer (and here Marcuse mistakenly believes
he is following Mill) is: Everyone in the maturity of his faculties
as a human being, that is, "everyone who has learned to think
rationally and autonomously." To be sure, such men will constitute a minority, but since all systems—even "democratic democracies"—are in fact controlled by a few, the only questions
are whether they are the correct few and whether they act in the
interests of the many, in short, whether they are qualified to
exercise Marcuse's "democratic educational dictatorship of free
men." Such free men are not to be identified with any social class;
they are rather "fighting minorities and isolated groups . . .
hopelessly dispersed throughout the society." To liberate these
few, and through them the society as a whole, it is necessary
"officially" to practice intolerance—both in speech and in action
—against movements from the Right and to be tolerant only of
movements from the Left. Through such "repressive tolerance"
alone, Marcuse concludes, we can hope to realize the objective
of "true tolerance."

Of the many things that might be said by way of analysis of
or in reply to this argument, I shall limit myself here to three
points: (1) Marcuse confuses the meaning of freedom with its
conditions and consequences and hence misunderstands tolerance. (2) Marcuse's argument is essentially, though in reverse,
the argument of Dostoevski's Grand Inquisitor, of the Right. (3)
Marcuse's solution is contradicted and rendered impossible of attainment by his own analysis.

(1) Freedom is not, as Marcuse variously affirms it to be,

"self-determination, autonomy" or "a specific historical process." It is rather, as Hobbes properly said, the absence of chains. Since in the real world men who are unrestrained come into collision with one another, societies have always and everywhere confronted—and each in its own way resolved—the problem of determining which liberties are worth protecting, for whom, under what conditions, and to what degree, and, as a necessary consequence, which restraints must be imposed. Freedom then becomes an ordered system of liberties and restraints. Men may differ as to the right order of priorities with respect to such liberties, but some order of priorities there must be. Thus, in democratic states a high value is given to freedom of political opposition; in dictatorships it is not. But to assure and protect this freedom, restraints must be imposed on those men (and practices) who would interfere with it. This is one, though not the only, function of law; but it is not, of course, merely a matter of law, for it involves a complex set of attitudes and appropriate behavior in other realms of social life as well.

Now Marcuse may deplore the particular freedoms granted in a specific society. He may properly object that a formal or legal freedom is in fact negated by informal or social pressures. But freedom as a principle is always a matter of specific liberties and concomitant restraints. It is not self-determination, though a measure of self-determination may be achieved through a particular combination of liberties and restraints. Nor is it a specific historical process, though the specific combination of liberties and restraints may be conditioned by and reflect the values of a particular historical period. Nor, again, is freedom limited to rational and autonomous men. While Mill clearly preferred a society made up of such men, he was realistic enough to recognize that this could not be a necessary condition of freedom. Thus, while he would not apply his principle of liberty to children and immature peoples, i.e., those not capable of improvement by free and equal discussion, he would and did apply it to all mature (not necessarily "autonomous") men, and not simply to Marcuse's elites. Nor, finally, is freedom vindicated only by "good" results, or rightfully "confined by truth." Freedom is in part a value in itself, in part an instrument of individual development, in part a necessary means of social change. That men and societies might make the "wrong" or "false" choices is clearly possible, but this too is an essential aspect of freedom. Otherwise a select group of allegedly wise men will make these choices for them, and this, by whatever name it may be called, is not freedom.

From all of which it follows that tolerance is not the freedom to express only the right ideas, but the freedom to express even stupid or loathsome ideas. The results may improve or depress the lot of men or societies, but the results are distinct from the principle of tolerance itself. And those who argue for tolerance, even absolute tolerance of ideas, do so because they believe that reason and experience are not calculated to lead men to the wrong decisions. Marcuse's rejection of pure tolerance is in these terms either a distrust of reason itself or a belief that the conditions under which reason operates today are such as to vitiate the process of reason, and probably both. But to the extent that it is the second, his attack is properly directed to those conditions and not to the principle of tolerance. Clearly, the "tolerance" he espouses is intolerance, and so it should be called, lest we abandon all semblance of meaning in our ordinary use of terms.

(2) Those who believe not merely that there is an objective truth but that, by some mystery of incarnation, it has been given to them to know it, have rarely been willing to respect the claim to such knowledge by others. For such True Believers, allowing others to disseminate what is believed to be true, but what in fact is false, is to make possible the adoption of error. For error, seductively presented, may prevail over truth even in free and equal discussion. How much more likely is it to prevail when the conditions are not free and equal, when those who propound the error (because it gratifies their passions or promotes their conceived interests) also control the sources of information and media of communication, and where the objects of the debate are neither rational nor autonomous but "conditioned" men! In such circumstances to trust to an abstract but spurious toleration is to yield the cause. For truth to prevail, the "right" men must impose it—either by altering the conditions or by directing otherwise irrational men, and generally both. In this way men will be governed by truth, and thus, even though forced, they will also be free.

This, it is clear, is the argument of Socrates in the *Republic*. It is the argument of Rousseau in the *Social Contract*. It is the argument of the Grand Inquisitor, both of the Roman Catholic Church and of Stalin's Russia. It is the traditional argument of the Right, of all who would usurp the gates of heaven and in the name of a higher morality insist as with Gerhart Niemeyer, upon "a firm official stand for what is known as right, true, and good." And it is, in all essentials, the argument of Marcuse. But it is not the argument of John Stuart Mill.

For Mill, as for all democrats committed to the liberal idea of freedom, to believe in Man is not to dispel one's doubts about men. Men are fallible and cannot presume to know the whole truth. Room must therefore be left for the rectification of error and the discovery of additional knowledge. This requires tolerance, the free exploration and articulation of ideas. It may well be that there are deficiencies in the intellectual marketplace, but the remedy is not to mistake Marcuse's authority for truth; it is rather to correct those deficiencies. To substitute one allegedly right authority for another, to compel or manipulate men to do what Marcuse (or anyone else) is convinced it is proper for them to do, is not to force them to be free. It is simply to subject them to Marcuse's (or another's) will. This, by any name, is coercion. It ill accords with the purposes of one who professes to respect humanity.

(3) Finally, and briefly, Marcuse's argument collapses because the reality he portrays renders unattainable, and is in turn contradicted by, the proposals he recommends. If it is true that we live "in a democracy with totalitarian organization" and that this "coordinated society" rests on "firm foundations," how is it humanly possible to change it? Surely not by election, for the "conditioned" masses will simply acquiesce in the opinions of their masters. Surely not by education, for the rulers control both the educators and their media of communication. Surely not by revolution, for who will revolt but "hopelessly dispersed" minorities? It may well be, as Marcuse thinks, that in such a situation the alienated man is the "essential" rather than the sick man, and that rebellious men merit applause rather than condemnation. But such men, however viewed, cannot overturn a firmly established order. Then to whom, and for what purpose, does

Marcuse speak? Is his message really more than a tocsin of futility, a summons to surrender?

If on the other hand, we are to take seriously his plea for fundamental social and political change, for the establishment of "real" tolerance (or, as he says, "official" intolerance), it can only mean that the society is less than totalitarian, that its foundations are not altogether firm, that there are chinks in the monopolistic concentration of power.

Marcuse cannot have it both ways: Either his analysis is correct and his recommendations are unrealizable, or his recommendations are meaningful and appropriate, in which case his analysis cannot stand.

It would be less than just to conclude these remarks without noting the deep anguish and high moral commitment that animate all three of our critics. They are disturbed, and properly so, by the injustices that disfigure modern societies. They are distressed by the realization that these injustices are maintained by an indifferent, because unseeing, or acquiescent public opinion. Consequently they probe to the roots in an effort to uncover the sources and the interests that mold that opinion. And they have found, as every sensitive observer of human societies has always found, that within our cities there are still two cities—the city of the rich and the city of the poor, with all that this implies in inequalities of power, of access to privileges, and of opportunities. One need not accept everything that A. J. Liebling has written in *The Press*, or that C. Wright Mills has written in *The Power Elite*, to recognize that freedom of speech, for example, has a different meaning for those wealthy enough to buy a newspaper company or to purchase time on radio or television, than it has for the masses of individuals who may wish to express their thoughts but have no effective access to the various media of communication. Nor does it require undue imagination to note that men cannot choose what they do not know exists, or will not choose what they have been taught to believe is evil. For these and other reasons, it is less than convincing to argue that the principle of equality accurately characterizes the world of public opinion, or that the free play of ideas does in fact afford people a full range of alternatives.

In underscoring these objectionable features of contemporary life and in urging their correction, our three critics manifest a concern for Man rather than for rich or powerful or prestigious men. Further, in their readiness to foster even revolutionary social and political change in an effort to elevate Man from what he presently is to what he ought to be, to what he *can* be, they identify themselves with an abiding radical tradition. They are legitimately of the Left.

But a wise radicalism seeks to overturn not all things, only unjust and harmful things; and not everything that men have thought and done in the course of human history demands repudiation. There have been achievements, too, and of these not the least noble has been the slow and painful liberation of the human mind. Whatever the merits or demerits of liberalism as a political and economic doctrine, in the realm of the intellect it should command our supreme allegiance: for it has freed reason from the chains of dogma and superstition; it has broken the back of orthodoxy; it has given us a method by which we may continue to correct our errors and improve our understanding. And whatever the merits or demerits of a particular social system in observing, or failing to observe, the principle of liberalism in the intellectual sphere, it is necessary—and I believe that even under circumstances that most humanly approximate the ideal, it will remain necessary—always to distinguish the fact of public opinion, what may be called the will of the people, from the motives and influences that elicit it. Democracies rest on the volume, not on the quality, of that will; and though no one would contend that it is better to have a stupid or misguided will, what distinguishes democratic from nondemocratic governments is that the former rest upon that will even though oligarchic or plutocratic influences may have been powerful in creating it, while the latter reject that will, or at most seek to mold it in support of their policies; it is not, as in democratic states, an initiating and controlling will. To render that will a purer or wiser will is surely a proper concern of democratic (whether liberal or radical) theorists, but this means that they must look not to the removal of that will, or of the process that alone gives it the opportunity to be formed after a consideration of alternatives, but to the correction of those conditions that limit or block the introduction of new and conflicting ideas. In any case, the fact of will and not its purity or disinterestedness remains the foundation of the democratic state.

Those who, therefore, in the name of a social revolution, would destroy not merely the conditions that still constrain reason but the principle of tolerance that alone gives reason its chance to prevail, defy the grim lessons of history. What, then, can one say of those who, like Marcuse, seek to reverse history by substituting for even the imperfect democracies of our day an intellectual and political authoritarianism that would allegedly act *for* the people, on the ground that a government that really acts in the interests of the people is better (and more democratic) than a goverment *by* the people that may, through ignorance or irrationality, act contrary to those best interests? Such men are neither radical nor liberal but, let us use the cruel word, reactionary. This is why, despite all the legitimate criticisms that might be (and in the course of the past century have been) made of Mill's philosophy, or of his political and economic teachings, or even of the subsidiary doctrines and incidental observations in his essay *On Liberty*, the central argument of that essay remains fundamentally unimpaired.

Not Mill's theory of pure tolerance but the repressive intolerance of our critics is, then, to be condemned.

[1966]

FANON AND DEBRAY:

Theorists of the Third World

by Lewis Coser

Three figures associated with the Third World—Che Guevara, Frantz Fanon, and Régis Debray—have become intellectual heroes of the New Left. Guevara has left no significant literary remains, since he taught by example mainly; the other two have produced writings worthy of attention.

1. THE MYTH OF PEASANT REVOLT

Only rarely does a book immediately convey a sense that it will rank among the influential works of the time. Frantz Fanon's *The Wretched of the Earth* is just such a book. It is badly written, badly organized, and chaotic. The author's reasoning is often shoddy and obviously defective. But all this is finally unimportant. This is not a work of analysis. Its incantatory prose appeals not to the intellect but to the passions. Its author wished to create a modern myth, and he must be ranked among the very few great mythopoeists of our age even by those who, like myself, think he has created an evil myth.

"Myths," wrote Georges Sorel, "are not descriptions of things, but expressions of a determination to act. . . . A myth cannot be refuted, since it is, at bottom, identical with the conviction of a group, being the expression of these convictions in the language of movement." "One must not try to analyze such complexes of pictures," he added, "as one would break down a thing into its elements; one must take them as a whole, as historical forces, and . . . must above all refrain from comparing actual accomplishments with the images of them that had been generally accepted before the action." It is such a myth that Frantz Fanon has created and I venture to think that it will have an enduring influence in the world of politics and ideas, perhaps more so than Sorel's own myth of the General Strike.

Frantz Fanon was born in 1925, on the island of Martinique in the French West Indies. He studied medicine in France and specialized in psychiatry. During the Algerian revolt against French domination, Fanon was assigned to an Algerian hospital and soon threw in his lot with the revolutionists to become one of their major ideological spokesmen. Out of this experience came two books, *The Year V of the Algerian Revolution* and the present volume, first published in France in 1961. Fanon died of cancer, at the age of thirty-six, soon after the book appeared.

The Wretched of the Earth could be read as yet another indictment of the evils of colonialism, but so to understand it would bypass its real importance. Fanon wishes to do a great deal more. He wishes to show how the native, degraded by his conquerors, can reconquer himself. The book is, above all, an apologia for violence. The violence of the conquest, he argues, has dehumanized the native and only counterviolence can make him whole again. ". . . Violence is a cleansing force. It frees the native from his inferiority complex and from his despair and inaction; it makes him fearless and restores his self-respect. . . . For the native, life can spring up again out of the rotting corpse of the settler." Violence is the only effective individual and social therapy; it helps overcome a schism of the soul which has been caused by colonialist contempt, and it wields together a body social which had been rent by the colonial system. "Violence unifies the people."

In Sorel's hands the myth of violence had a somewhat bloodless character. Sorel was, to be sure, a man given to apocalyptic visions, yet upon inspection his heroic violence turns out to be more literary than real, more a figure of speech than a concretely envisioned event. This safely settled petty-bourgeois moralist dreamed of heroic virtues, but fantasies of a real bloodbath seem

to have been utterly alien to him. Matters stand very differently
with Fanon. He was a marginal man, torn from his moorings,
most of his adult life working in the world of French medical
professionals without being of that world. Scarred and humili-
ated, stripped of his previous identity, he searched for redeeming
wholeness through a cataclysmic destruction. To him, the call to
violence, the belief in its redeeming quality, is no rhetorical device; he means it. He believed in the cleansing quality of the
knife, the gun, the bomb. Only these, he thought, can make colonial man whole again. During the Mau-Mau revolt, it was required, he writes, "that each member of the group should strike
a blow at the victim. Each one was thus personally responsible
for the death of that victim. To work means to work for the
death of the settler. This assumed responsibility for violence
allows both strayed and outlawed members of the group to come
back again and to find their place once more, to become integrated. Violence is thus seen as comparable to a royal pardon.
The colonized man finds his freedom in and through violence.
This rule of conduct enlightens the agent because it indicates to
him the means and the end."

Anticolonial violence is to Fanon the only way to bring about
a total transformation in the former colonies. It leads to a com-
prehensive transvaluation of values. "Without any period of transition, there is a total, complete, and absolute substitution." All
decolonization creates a *tabula rasa* at the outset, and this is the
precondition for all further advances. Decolonization does not
mean the substitution of one kind of regime for another; it
signifies total rebirth and it can only be the work of new
men, men reborn through acts of violence.

Fanon is at his most original when he attempts to locate potential revolutionary actors within the structure of colonial societies. Here he departs most markedly from classical Marxist
theory. Very little, he argues, can be expected of the embryonic
working class. The workers enjoy a comparatively privileged position. They may be the most faithful followers of the nationalist
parties, but when the chips are down, they realize that they have
much to lose when the colonial regime is overthrown. By virtue
of the privileged position they hold in the colonial system, they
constitute a "bourgeois" faction of the colonized people. Pam-

pered, and sheltered from the worst slights and the worst misery, they can easily be bought off. So much for the traditional proletarian vanguard of the Marxist textbooks.

Nor is there reason to believe that the national bourgeoisie can play a role. It has none of the characteristics of its Western counterpart. "It is not engaged in production, nor in invention, nor building, nor labor; it is completely canalized into activities of the intermediary type. Its innermost vocation seems to be to keep in the running and to be part of the racket." Fanon treats this national bourgeoisie with a withering contempt that is only matched by his contempt for the assimilationist and partly Westernized intelligentsia. If the working class can be bought off and the national bourgeoisie is "good for nothing," where, then, can the true agents of total transformation be found? Here Fanon, true to an age-old millenarian tradition which, by the way, strongly informed the thought of the young Marx, answers: Only those who are totally disinherited, those who have nothing to lose in the old system can be the architects of the new. The biblical "the last shall be first and the first last" runs like a refrain through the book.

The last in colonial society are the peasants and they are hence the true agents of the revolution. ". . . The peasants alone are revolutionary, for they have nothing to lose and everything to gain. The starving peasant, outside the class system, is the first among the exploited to discover that only violence pays. For him there is no compromise, no possible coming to terms." The anti-colonial revolution must hence be a peasant revolution. Yet this revolution, in order to succeed, must of necessity spread from the countryside into the towns. A peasant *maquis* can hardly be expected to take the cities. Here the mass of ex-peasants, settled in the huts and shantytowns around the fringe of the city, assumes a major strategic role. The city *Lumpenproletariat* is the predestined ally of the rural masses. "The *Lumpenproletariat,* that horde of starving men, uprooted from their tribe and from their clan, constitutes one of the most spontaneous and the most radically revolutionary forces of colonized people." They have not yet found "a bone to gnaw in the colonial system." They are physically near the city but spiritually very far from it. Their very presence is "the sign of the irrevocable decay, the gangrene ever present at the heart of colonial domination. So the pimps, the hooligans, the unemployed, and the petty criminals, urged on from behind, throw themselves into the struggle for liberation like stout working men. These classless idlers will by militant and decisive action discover the path that leads to nationhood." Truly, the last will be the first.

Fanon plays many variations upon the theme of the revolt of the wretched, the eruption of colonial society, bringing to the fore the new heroic man created in and through revolutionary violence. But what after the morrow of victory? Will the heroic days of struggle not be followed by the dullness of quotidian routine? This is a persistent danger of which Fanon is acutely aware. "During the struggle for liberation the leader awakened the people and promised them a forward march, heroic and unmitigated. Today, he uses every means to put them to sleep, and three or four times a year asks them to remember the colonial period and to look back on the long way they have come since then. . . . After independence, the party sinks into an extraordinary lethargy . . . the local party leaders are given administrative posts, and the party becomes an administration, and the militants disappear in the crowd and take the empty title of citizen. . . ." When the revolution grows cold, its leaders tend to develop into cold and calculating monsters. Once it freezes into bureaucratic mold, it becomes but a means for the advancement of its functionaries, and the pursuit of their private pleasures replaces the heroic dedication to public revolt. But all of this, thinks Fanon, while an ever-present danger, is not a necessary outcome.

The revolution can be saved provided it is not halted prematurely, and provided it remains permanent. The soft life of the city must not be allowed to corrupt the new governing elites. The city, to Fanon, is always corruption. He hates it with the traditional hatred of the peasant; it is to him the true whore of Babylon. The city represents softness and relaxation in contrast to the lean and hard energy and dedication of the countryside. Hence only geographic decentralization of power can save the revolution. Revolutionary virtue can be maintained in the village square; it will inevitably succumb to the vices of the city if power comes to be centered in the capital.

The anticolonial revolution is primarily a revolution of the peasant people, and it can maintain itself only as long as it remains rooted in that people. The party, the leaders, once arrived in power will attempt to exclude the people from participation. They will say that the people are too ignorant, that they do not understand the intricacies of political decision-making. These are self-serving lies. "Everything can be explained to the people, on the single condition that you really want them to understand . . . when the people are invited to partake in the management of the country, they do not slow the movement down but on the contrary speed it up." Hence the birth of a national bourgeoisie or of a privileged caste of bureaucrats must be vigorously opposed. The masses must be educated so that they can form the politically decisive arms of the revolution. If this is done, the nation will become a living reality to each of its citizens.

The book closes with a violent diatribe against European civilization. "Europe undertook the leadership of the world with ardor, cynicism, and violence. . . . Europe has declined all humility and all modesty; but she has also set her face against all solicitude and all tenderness . . . she has only shown herself parsimonious and niggardly where men are concerned; it is only men that she has killed and devoured . . . today we know with what sufferings humanity has paid for every one of their [the Europeans'] triumphs of the mind." European civilization, Fanon argues, by its very success in taming the forces of nature, has only succeeded in dehumanizing man—colonial man in the first place, but ultimately, European man also. Hence Fanon's message, and this distinguishes him from almost all previous colonial rebels, rejects the whole heritage of Europe. He declines to accept guidance even from the West's revolutionaries. Corrupted to the core, the West can teach nothing but death of the soul. "So, comrades," says Fanon on his last page, "let us not pay tribute to Europe by creating states, institutions, and societies which draw their inspiration from her." Most previous colonial revolutionaries paid tribute to the West in the very act of revolting against it. Fanon's myth involves a much more profound rejection than do the ideologies of a Gandhi or of a Nehru, a Lenin, or a Stalin. He warns the nations of the Third World that they should not create a Third or Fourth Rome, a pale imitation of a civilization decaying at its very roots.

Spengler coined the term "historical pseudomorphosis" to "designate those cases in which an older alien culture lies so massively over the land that a young culture, born in this land, cannot get its breath and fails not only to achieve pure and specific expression-forms, but even to develop fully its own self-consciousness. All that wells up from the depth of the young soul is cast in the old molds, young feelings stiffen in senile works, and instead of rearing itself up in its own creative power, it can only hate the distant power with a hate that grows to be monstrous." It is to prevent such a state of affairs that Fanon has fashioned his myth.

If, contrary to Sorel's prescription, one compares actual accomplishments with the mythical images that Fanon set forth only a few years ago, one is brought up against the fact that the book is already dated. The Algeria of Boumédienne bears but little resemblance to the peasant democracy of which Fanon dreamed. The tough military men who now run independent Algeria presumably look at men like Fanon as ideologists whose usefulness to the regime has long been exhausted. African rulers have grown fat on resources pumped out of the countryside, and they have flocked to the central cities where they build skyscrapers and airports, slavishly imitating Western models. The peasants have fallen back into the immemorial routines of traditional lifestyles; sometimes they are prodded into the world of modernity by tax collectors, recruiting sergeants, or party organizers. The peasants' lot differs in the various new nations, to be sure, but in none of them have they become history-making subjects, as Fanon expected and hoped. Everywhere they are the subjects of historical processes over which they have, at best, only minimal control. The specific weight of the peasantry in the political life of the underdeveloped nations is low indeed, and the tutelary power of the new states comes to lie as heavily on today's peasantry as it rested upon them in the colonial past.

Fanon's picture hardly fits the contemporary reality. Yet it would be foolish to dismiss his work as a mere regressive fantasy —though it may be that, too. The myth that he has helped to create will stay alive, I believe, precisely because the reality of the new nations departs so very crucially from the image he has drawn. The peasantry does make up the great majority in these nations and will remain so for a very long time to come. Peasant discontent will persist as a consequence of the dislocation of traditional styles of life which the modernizing regimes attempt to institute. Fanon was quite right, of course, when he noted that the young working class and the bulk of the Westernized intelligentsia would not, as a whole, play a revolutionary role in the history of the new nations. They have tasted power or gained at least a modicum of higher standards of living, and they are most probably not willing to risk these. But it is conceivable that dissatisfied peasants may come to learn of this book in due course and make it a kind of breviary for their aspirations. Yet while the future, contrary to what Fanon believed, belongs to the city and not the countryside, the death throes of traditional peasant society will last for a very long time and may well be punctured by uprisings and revolts, a variey of peasant *Jacqueries*. And even though I believe these peasant revolts ultimately doomed to failure, they may for a time, perhaps in alliance with disaffected city intellectuals, create large revolutionary movements. Africa may see a repeat performance of Europe's peasant revolts before it enters the new world of modernity. For quite some time to come, the new rulers of the African nations will be faced by the specter of peasant uprisings and disaffection—and Fanon's myth will haunt them, much as the *Communist Manifesto* and its myth haunted the millowners of Victorian Europe.

In the West this book will be read for a long time and will become a bible for romantic rebels and sophisticated university students in quest of primeval revolutionary innocence. Jean-Paul Sartre's incredibly naive introduction gives a foretaste of what may be in store. A man who can speak in earnest about North African Arabs, of all people, "recovering their lost innocence" can believe anything—anything, that is, which feeds his anti-Western masochism.

It seems hardly necessary to say here that I consider Fanon's myth an evil and destructive vision. I find his view of violence as a healer profoundly mistaken. Violence may sometimes be necessary, but those who wield it systematically cannot help becoming brutalized by it. And this holds true for colonizer and native alike. Similarly, I think that the course Fanon charts for the new nations is not only morally dubious but politically inept and self-defeating. What I have tried here is to convey Fanon's symptomatic importance rather than engage in refutations of his views.

One must never forget while reading Fanon's book that it was written in anguish and heartbreak, even though one might recognize in it elements of a "paranoid style" with which we have become familiar in many a sinister context. The vision which informs the book may be profoundly repellent, but we must not forget that the violence and hatred it breathes on every page is a reactive violence, a testimony to the havoc the white man has loosed upon Africa. Finally, one might hope that the myth Fanon has wrought may move some Western men to that compassion and sense of fraternity with the downtrodden of Africa which Fanon—who expected only white hatred and, at best, condescension—plainly believed impossible.

2. NECHAEV IN THE ANDES

"The emancipation of the working class is the work of the working class itself," wrote Marx and Engels in the *Communist Manifesto*.

One of the tragic paradoxes of the Marxist movement has been that impatient revolutionaries—appalled by the sluggishness of history and the apparent unwillingness of the working class to be interested in its alleged interest—have ever since been in search of substitute agents of historical transformation.

Lenin, convinced that unaided working-class spontaneity could create trade-union but not political consciousness, bent all his energies to organizing a devoted sect of professionals who would become the real agents of the revolutionary transformation, even though initially they might be mainly intellectuals of middle-class origin. The emancipation of the working class, Lenin believed, could never be accomplished except through the Bolshevik party. And in due course, the party substituted itself for the working class.

In Lenin's day the Russian working class was numerically small, almost drowned in a sea of peasants. But it carried considerable specific weight due to its high degree of social concentration. In China, by contrast, when the Chinese Communist party was created, there was hardly an industrial working class at all. In consequence, after the bloody repression of revolutionary attempts in a few port cities, Mao Tse-tung turned to the peasantry, which was led by cadres of *déclassé* intellectuals, as the major revolutionary force. That very peasantry toward which Marx had expressed his withering contempt, and that he had judged to be incapable of concerted action due to its isolation from the major centers of political and economic power, became the basis for the second major revolution to call itself—such are the ironies of history—"Marxist."

In our day a significant theorist of revolution in the underdeveloped countries, Frantz Fanon, created a powerful myth according to which, the proletariat having been corrupted and softened by the exploiting colonialists, only a pure and uncontaminated peasantry allied to the *Lumpenproletariat* of the city—that *Lumpenproletariat* Marx had thought incapable of any constructive political initiative—would constitute the motor force of revolutionary transformation.

But the end is not yet. *The Monthly Review,* the organ of Paul Sweezy, a man who thinks of himself as the upholder of Marxist orthodoxy in the United States, published a special issue (July–August 1967) presenting a full translation of Régis Debray's book *Revolution in the Revolution,* in which it is argued that neither the working class nor the peasantry, neither professional political revolutionaries nor city *Lumpen,* but armed guerrillas made up of students and revolutionary intellectuals will "initiate the highest forms of class struggle." Debray and Sweezy thus have come full circle in their distorted form of "Marxism"; the emancipation of the working class is now to be the work of *déclassé* intellectuals.

Yet Debray's work is by no means without historical precedent. He is a lineal descendant of that long line of Russian revolutionary terrorists and *enragés* from Nechaev to Tkachev, who, appalled by the weakness of the liberal bourgeoisie, the subservience of the enlightened nobility, and the primordial passivity of the peasantry, concluded that only the heroic deeds of small elites of dedicated revolutionaries could propel Russian society into freedom. Despairing of the slow course of history, despairing also of all existent social forces, they concluded that only terroristic acts of a self-chosen few would be able to mold the resistant paste of social reality.

Since history was unwilling to go in the direction of their desires, they would have to rape it. They would take it upon themselves to break the thick cake of customary resistance, they would pit their naked will against the inert force of history. And they would prevail.

> Neither in the present nor in the future [wrote Tkachev], can the people, left to their own resources, bring into existence the social revolution. Only we revolutionists can accomplish this. . . . Social ideals are alien to the people; they belong to the social philosophy of the revolutionary minority.

Debray is a follower of these Russian revolutionaries, though he seems to suffer under the strange illusion that he is a Marxist. A young French philosopher of impeccable upper-class origin, he has turned his intellectual gifts to developing the theoretical underpinnings for Castro's political adventurism in Latin America.

His book is not without its pathos. One sometimes feels sympathy for this young revolutionary who is engaged in what he himself surely considers a promethean effort at liberation in the face of hard and seemingly untractable realities. Nevertheless, what strikes one most forcefully in the book is his deep and abiding contempt for the common run of humanity.

All previous Marxist theory took as its point of departure an assessment of the preparedness, or readiness for basic change, of the class or classes which were to be the targets of revolutionary agitation and propaganda. Though they may have differed as to the extent to which voluntaristic action by the vanguard elite could hasten the process of radicalization in the population, no Marxist theorist ever considered it possible or desirable to engage in revolutionary activity without the assurance of large-scale disaffection and at least an inchoate desire for fundamental change among oppressed classes.

Debray breaks with that tradition. He is basically unconcerned with the wishes and desires of the people. His revolutionary guerrilla units are to be "organizationally separate from the civilian population." They will function in its midst, but they will "not assume the direct defense of the peasant population." In other words, they will not feel responsible if this population is subject to reprisal by virtue of nearby guerrilla actions. Debray, in fact, is at pains to point out that the revolutionary warfare he advocates has nothing to do with the age-old tradition of peasant self-defense. "Self-defense," he argues, "is partial; revolutionary guerrilla warfare aims at total war by combining under its hegemony all forms of struggle at all points within its territory."

The guerrillas are not responsible to the peasants among whom they fight; nor are they responsible to urban-based political party leaders. Debray, like Fanon, distrusts the city; it softens and corrupts. "These lukewarm incubators [of the cities] make one infantile and bourgeois." Or: "When a guerrilla group communicates with city leadership or its representatives abroad, it is dealing with 'its' bourgeoisie." The city, that whore of Babylon, is lost; parties, being city-based organisms, are inherently suspect.

Not only can the armed units of youthful adventurers operating in the remoteness of the hinterland not trust the city; they cannot even trust older men, no matter what their politics or previous experience. "There is a close tie between biology and ideology. . . . That an elderly man should be proven militant—and possess revolutionary training—is not, alas, sufficient for coping with guerrilla existence, especially in the early stages. Physical aptitude is the prerequisite for all other aptitudes."

In Debray's picture, the guerrilla fighter who presumes to unleash the forces of revolution looks a bit like a caricature of a Nietzschean superman. He needs to be young lest he suffer from "the vices of excessive deliberation," and "a perfect Marxist education is not at the outset an imperative condition." If he can shoot straight, he need not be burdened with theoretical baggage. Too much ratiocination may only cramp his style.

"The guerrilla army assumes the prerogatives of political leadership" even though it is, at least in the initial stages of insurrection, cut off from all strata of the underlying population. The guerrillas "are the foreigners, lacking status, who at the begin-

ning can offer the populace nothing but bloodshed and pain."
They must live like perpetual nomads moving from camp to
camp. Mao taught that the guerrillas should remain unnoticed,
living in the midst of peasant sympathizers "like fish in water,"
but Debray thinks this impossible under Latin-American conditions. The guerrillas must cut themselves loose from all sectors of
the population, all of which are either hostile or lukewarm. The
world is corrupt, and only a tiny revolutionary elite can be
trusted. But why can they be trusted, why should they be
trusted? Because they act, because they wield guns. It is perhaps
harsh to say so, yet I cannot help but feel that Debray's view of
the matter has more affinity with the rhetoric of fascism than with
that of classical Marxism.

Nowhere is Debray's distrust of reason and his elitist anti-intellectualism more apparent than in his discussion of the relationships between the guerrilla units and the revolutionary party.
Here again he seems nearer to fascist than to Marxist thought.
For all Marxists the forging of a revolutionary party was
always a *sine qua non,* because the party and its program
embodied the theoretical and ideological thrust of the movement. Its program was the intellectual distillation of the movement's philosophy and ideology. But to Debray the party counts
for very little, because ideas and ideologies count for very little.
What Karl Mannheim once said of fascism seems eminently ap-
plicable to Debray's vision:

> At the very heart of its theory and its practice lies the
> apotheosis of direct action, the belief in the decisive *deed,*
> and in the significance attributed to the initiative of a
> leading elite. The essence of politics is to recognize and to
> grapple with the demands of the hour. . . . History is
> made neither by the masses, nor by ideas . . . but by the
> elites who from time to time assert themselves. . . . This
> idea of history as an intelligible scheme disappears in the
> face of the irrationality of the fascist apotheosis of the
> deed.

Someone once said that everywhere else armies were the instruments of states, but in Prussia the state was an instrument of

the army. Debray has a "Prussian" view of the relations between the party and the army: "The people's army will be the nucleus of the party, not vice versa." "Eventually, the future People's Army will beget the party of which it is to be, theoretically, the instrument: Essentially the party is the army." Ideology and organization, it would appear, all grow out of the barrel of a gun.

Personally, Debray may be a man of heroic cast and admirable virtues, but what he stands for is an evil and mischievous doctrine. His is a politics of despair, a politics that has lost all belief in the political capacities of ordinary human beings. His violent and apocalyptic fantasies are rooted in his distrust of men. He would force them to be free at the point of a gun. Debray thinks of the guerrillas as promethean rebels, but had they any power, they would more likely become the terroristic scourges of the people of Latin America.

Defenders of Debray's doctrine might contend that he proposes guerrilla activity in Latin America not because he is drawn to such solutions in principle but only because, given the reality of Latin-American dictatorships, other methods are not available. How can you consult the masses, they might argue, if they are gagged by a military regime? Debray's defenders may so argue, but it is important to note that he himself does not employ this rationale. He makes no distinction whatever between political activities in relatively democratic countries, such as Venezuela and Chile, and in military dictatorships, such as Bolivia. He offers the same terroristic solution for all of them—and hence shows quite clearly that he has only contempt for democratic methods and alternatives.

There is no doubt in my mind that the liberation of Latin America from internal and external oppression will be a prolonged ordeal. It would be foolish to expect that this will not be accompanied in many situations by violence and bloodshed. Guns will probably have to be used. But recourse to guns always corrupts, absolute reliance on guns corrupts absolutely, and those who make a mystique out of guns are already corrupted in advance.

Ché Guevara was killed after his guerrilla band was discovered by the Bolivian military. And Régis Debray faced a military court in Bolivia, which accused him of having been a participant in guerrilla activities and sentenced him to thirty years' imprisonment—the maximum penalty according to Bolivian law. What has been reported about the proceedings of the court does not give one the impression that it acted with anything resembling judicial impartiality. International pressures should be brought upon the Bolivian junta to induce it to expel Debray from the country rather than impose so severe and vindictive a sentence.

In the meantime it ought to be said without equivocation: Those of us who sympathize with the Latin-American masses, and are moved by the misery and oppression in which they now live, must hope that they will not fall prey to the sick adventurist fantasies of Debray and his ilk. Whatever the Andes need, it is not Nechaevs from Paris.

[1968]

A DAY IN THE LIFE OF A
SOCIALIST CITIZEN

by Michael Walzer

Imagine a day in the life of a socialist citizen. He hunts in the morning, fishes in the afternoon, rears cattle in the evening, and plays the critic after dinner. Yet he is neither hunter, fisherman, herdsman nor critic; tomorrow he may select another set of activities just as he pleases. This is the delightful portrait that Marx sketches in *The German Ideology* as part of a polemic against the division of labor. Socialists since have worried that it is not economically feasible; perhaps it isn't. But there is another difficulty that I want to consider: that is, the curiously apolitical character of the citizen Marx describes. Certain crucial features of socialist life have been omitted altogether.

In light of the recent discussions about participatory democracy, Marx's sketch needs to be elaborated. Before hunting in the morning, this unalienated man of the future is likely to attend a meeting of the Council on Animal Life, where he will be required to vote on important matters relating to the stocking of the forests. The meeting will probably not end much before noon, for among the many-sided citizens there will always be a lively interest even in highly technical problems. Immediately after lunch, a special session of the Fishermen's Council will be called to protest the maximum catch recently voted by the Regional Planning Commission. And the Marxist man will participate eagerly in these debates, even postponing a scheduled discussion of some contradictory theses on cattle-rearing. Indeed, he will probably love argument far better than hunting, fishing, *or* rearing cattle. The debates will go on so long that the citizens will have to rush through dinner in order to assume their roles as critics. Then off they will go to meetings of study groups, clubs, editorial boards, and political parties where criticism will be carried on long into the night.

Socialism, Oscar Wilde once wrote, would take too many evenings. This is, it seems to me, one of the most significant criticisms of socialist theory that has ever been made. The fanciful sketch above is only intended to suggest its possible truth. Socialism's great appeal is the prospect it holds out for the development of human capacities. An enormous growth of creative talent, a new and unprecedented variety of expression, a wild proliferation of sects, associations, schools, parties: This will be the flowering of the future society. But underlying this new individualism and exciting group life must be a broad, self-governing community of equal men. A powerful figure looms behind Marx's hunter, fisherman, herdsman, and critic: the busy citizen attending his endless meetings. "Society regulates the general production," Marx writes, "and thus makes it possible for me to do one thing today and another tomorrow. . . ." If society is not to become an alien and dangerous force, however, the citizens cannot accept its regulation and gratefully do what they please. They must participate in social regulation; they must be social men, organizing and planning their own fulfillment in spontaneous activity. The purpose of Wilde's objection is to suggest that just this self-regulation is incompatible with spontaneity, that the requirements of citizenship are incompatible with the freedom of hunter, fisherman, and so on.

Politics itself, of course, can be a spontaneous activity, freely chosen by those men and women who enjoy it and to whose talents a meeting is so much exercise. But this is very unlikely to be true of all men and women all the time—even if one were to admit what seems plausible enough: that political life is more intrinsic to human nature than is hunting and cattle-rearing or even (to drop Marx's rural imagery) art or music. "Too many evenings" is a shorthand phrase that describes something more

than the sometimes tedious, sometimes exciting business of reso-
lutions and debates. It suggests also that socialism and participatory democracy will depend upon, and hence require, an extraordinary willingness to attend meetings, and a public spirit and
sense of responsibility that will make attendance dependable
and activity consistent and sustained. None of this can rest for
any long period of time or among any substantial group of men
upon spontaneous interest. Nor does it seem possible that spontaneity will flourish above and beyond the routines of social regulation.

Self-government is a very demanding and time-consuming
business, and when it is extended from political to economic and
cultural life, and when the organs of government are decentralized so as to maximize participation, it will inevitably become
more demanding still. Ultimately, it may well require almost
continuous activity, and life will become a succession of meetings. When will there be time for the cultivation of personal
creativity or the free association of like-minded friends? In the
world of the meeting, when will there be time for the tête-à-
tête.

I suppose there will always be time for the tête-à-tête. Men
and women will secretly plan love affairs even while public business is being transacted. But Wilde's objection isn't silly. The
idea of citizenship on the Left has always been overwhelming,
suggesting a positive frenzy of activity, and often involving the
repression of all feelings except political ones. Its character can
best be examined in the work of Jean Jacques Rousseau, from
whom socialists and, more recently, New Leftists directly or indi-
rectly inherited it. In order to guarantee public-spiritedness and
political participation, and as a part of his critique of bourgeois
egotism, Rousseau systematically denigrated the value of private
life:

> The better the constitution of a state is, the more do pub-
> lic affairs encroach on private in the minds of the citizens.
> Private affairs are even of much less importance, because
> the aggregate of the common happiness furnishes a
> greater proportion of that of each individual, so that there
> is less for him to seek in particular cares.

Rousseau might well have written these lines out of a deep awareness that private life will not, in fact, bear the great weight that bourgeois society places upon it. We need, beyond our families and jobs, a public world where purposes are shared and cooperative activity is possible. More likely, however, he wrote them because he believed that cooperative activity could not be sustained unless private life were radically repressed, if not altogether eradicated. His citizen does not participate in social regulation as one part of a round of activities. Social regulation is his entire life. Rousseau develops his own critique of the division of labor by absorbing all human activities into the idea of citizenship: "Citizens," he wrote, "are neither lawyers, nor soldiers, nor priests by profession; they perform all these functions as a matter of duty." *As a matter of duty:* Here is the key to the character of that patriotic, responsible, energetic man who has figured also in socialist thought, but always in the guise of a new man, freely exercising his human powers.

It is probably more realistic to see the citizen as the product of collective repression and self-discipline. He is, above all, *dutiful,* and this is only possible if he has triumphed over egotism and impulse in his own personality. He embodies what political theorists have called "republican virtue"—that means, he puts the common good, the success of the movement, the safety of the community, above his own delight or well-being, *always.* To symbolize his virtue, perhaps, he adopts an ascetic style and gives up every sort of self-decoration: He adopts a sansculotte style or wears unpressed khakis. More important, he foregoes a conventional career for the profession of politics; he commits himself entirely. It is an act of the most extreme devotion. Now, how is such a man produced? What kind of conversion is necessary? Or what kind of rigorous training?

Rousseau set out to create virtuous citizens, and the means he chose are very old in the history of republicanism: an authoritarian family, a rigid sexual code, censorship of the arts, sumptuary laws, mutual surveillance, the systematic indoctrination of children. All these have been associated historically (at least until recent times) not with tyrannical but with republican regimes: Greece and Rome, the Swiss Protestant city-states, the first

French republic. Tyrannies and oligarchies, Rousseau argued, might tolerate or even encourage license, for the effect of sexual indulgence, artistic freedom, extravagant self-decoration, and privacy itself was to corrupt men and turn them away from public life, leaving government to the few. Self-government requires self-control: It is one of the oldest arguments in the history of political thought.

But if that argument is true, it may mean that self-government also leaves government to the few. For, if we reject the discipline of Rousseau's republicanism (as we have, and for good reasons), then only those men and women will be activists who volunteer for action. How many will that be? How many of the people you and I know? How many ought they to be? Certainly no radical movement or socialist society is possible without those ever-ready participants, who "fly," as Rousseau said, "to the public assemblies."

Radicalism and socialism make political activity for the first time an option for all those who relish it and a duty—sometimes —even for those who don't. But what a suffocating sense of responsibility, what a plethora of virtue would be necessary to sustain the participation of everybody all the time! How exhausting it would be! Surely there is something to be said for the irresponsible nonparticipant and something also for the part-time activist, the half-virtuous man (and the most scorned among the militants), who appears and disappears, thinking of Marx and then of his dinner? The very least that can be said is that these people, unlike the poor, will always be with us.

We can assume that a great many citizens, in the best of societies, will do all they can to avoid what Mel Tumin has nicely called "the merciless masochism of community-minded and self-regulating men and women." While the necessary meetings go on and on, they will take long walks, play with their children, paint pictures, make love, and watch television. They will attend sometimes, when their interests are directly at stake or when they feel like it. But they won't make the full-scale commitment necessary for socialism or participatory democracy. How are these people to be represented at the meetings? What are their rights? These are not only problems of the future, when popular participation has finally been established as the core of political and economic life. They come up in every radical movement; they are the stuff of contemporary controversy.

Many people feel that they ought to join this or that political movement; they do join; they contribute time and energy—but unequally. Some make a full-time commitment; they work every minute; the movement becomes their whole life and they often come to disbelieve in the moral validity of life outside. Others are established outside, solidly or precariously; they snatch hours and sometimes days; they harry their families and skimp on their jobs, but yet cannot make it to every meeting. Still others attend no meetings at all; they work hard but occasionally; they show up, perhaps, at critical moments, then they are gone. These last two groups make up the majority of the people available to the movement (any movement), just as they will make up the majority of the citizens of any socialist society. Radical politics radically increases the amount and intensity of political participation, but it doesn't (and probably oughtn't to) break through the limits imposed on republican virtue by the inevitable pluralism of commitments, the terrible shortage of time, and the day-to-day hedonism of ordinary men and women.

Under these circumstances, words like citizenship and participation actually describe the enfranchisement of only a part, and not necessarily a large part, of the movement or the community. Participatory democracy means the sharing of power among the activists. Socialism means the rule of the men with the most evenings to spare. Both imply also an injunction to the others: Join us, come to the meetings, participate!

Sometimes young radicals sound very much like old Christians, demanding the severance of every tie for the sake of politics. "How many Christian women are there," John Calvin once wrote, "who are held captive by their children!" How many "community people" miss meetings because of their families! But there is nothing to be done. Ardent democrats have sometimes urged that citizens be legally required to vote: That is possible, though the device is not attractive. Requiring people to attend meetings, to join in discussions, to govern themselves: That is not possible, at least not in a free society. And if they do not govern themselves, they will, willy-nilly, be governed by their activist fellows. The apathetic, the occasional enthusiasts, the part-time workers: All of them will be ruled by full-timers, militants, and professionals.

But if only some citizens participate in political life, it is essential that they always remember and be regularly reminded that they are . . . only some. This isn't easy to arrange. The militant in the movement, for example, doesn't represent anybody; it is his great virtue that he is self-chosen, a volunteer. But since he sacrifices so much for his fellowmen, he readily persuades himself that he is acting in their name. He takes their failure to put in an appearance only as a token of their oppression. He is certain he is their agent, or rather, the agent of their liberation.

He isn't in any simple sense wrong. The small numbers of participating citizens in the United States today, the widespread fearfulness, the sense of impotence and irrelevance: All these are signs of social sickness. Self-government is an important human function, an exercise of significant talents and energies, and the sense of power and responsibility it brings is enormously healthy. A certain amount of commitment and discipline, of not-quite-merciless masochism, is socially desirable, and efforts to evoke it are socially justifiable.

But many of the people who stay away from meetings do so for reasons that the militants don't understand or won't acknowledge. They stay away not because they are beaten, afraid, uneducated, lacking confidence and skills (though these are often important reasons), but because they have made other commitments; they have found ways to cope short of politics; they have created viable subcultures even in an oppressive world. They may lend passive support to the movement and help out occasionally, but they won't work, nor are their needs and aspirations in any sense embodied by the militants who will.

The militants represent themselves. If the movement is to be democratic, the others must *be represented*. The same thing will be true in any future socialist society: Participatory democracy has to be paralleled by representative democracy. I'm not sure precisely how to adjust the two; I am sure that they have to be adjusted. Somehow power must be distributed, as it isn't today, to small groups of active and interested citizens, but these citizens must themselves be made responsible to a larger electorate.

Nothing is more important than that responsibility; without it we will only get one or another sort of activist or *apparatchik* tyranny. And that we have already.

Nonparticipants have rights; it is one of the dangers of participatory democracy that it would fail to provide any effective protection for these rights. But nonparticipants also have functions; it is another danger that these would not be sufficiently valued. For many people in America today, politics is something to watch, an exciting spectacle, and there exists between the activists and the others something of the relation of actor and audience. Now for any democrat this is an unsatisfactory relation. We rightly resent the way actors play upon and manipulate the feelings of their audiences. We dislike the aura of magic and mystification contrived at on stage. We would prefer politics to be like the new drama with its alienation effects and audience participation. Fair enough.

But even the new drama requires its audience, and we ought not to forget that audiences can be critical as well as admiring, enlightened as well as mystified. More important, political actors, like actors in the theater, need the control and tension imposed by audiences, the knowledge that tomorrow the reviews will appear, tomorrow people will come or not come to watch their performance. Too often, of course, the reviews are favorable and the audiences come. That is because of the various sorts of collusion which presently develop between small and co-opted cliques of actors and critics. But in an entirely free society, there would be many more political actors and critics than ever before, and they would, presumably, be self-chosen. Not only the participants, but also the nonparticipants would come into their own. Alongside the democratic politics of shared work and perpetual activism, there would arise the open and leisurely culture of criticism, second-guessing, and burlesque.

It would be a mistake to underestimate the importance of all these, even if they aren't marked, as they generally won't be, by responsibility and virtue. They are far more important in the political arena than in the theater. For activists and professionals in the movement or the polity don't simply contrive effects; their work has more palpable results. Their policies touch us all in material ways, whether we go or don't go to the meetings. And those who don't go may well turn out to be more effective critics than those who do: No one who was one of its first guessers can usefully second-guess a decision. That is why the best critics in a liberal society are men-out-of-office. In a radically democratic society they would be men who stay away from meetings, perhaps for months at a time, and only then discover that something outrageous has been perpetrated that must be mocked or protested. The proper response to such protests is not to tell the laggard citizens that they should have been active these past many months, not to nag them to do work that they don't enjoy and in any case won't do well, but to listen to what they have to say. After all, what would democratic politics be like without its kibbitzers?

[1968]

ONE-DIMENSIONAL PESSIMISM:

A Critique of Herbert Marcuse's Theories

by Allen Graubard

Herbert Marcuse's *One-Dimensional Man* appeared four years ago. Since then it has been widely and, on the whole, favorably reviewed, read, and discussed. Accepted by many as the long-awaited work that "tells it like it is," Marcuse's essay has assumed near-canonical status among some of the most serious and thoughtful of the New Left. An incisive and original discussion of community organizing in *Studies on the Left* led off by announcing that *One-Dimensional Man* was to be assumed as the theoretical underpinning for the detailed and specific analysis that followed—though the philosopher's theory could be taken to be sometimes downright incompatible with the authors' practice. In *New Left Notes*, the SDS internal journal, Marcuse's special philosophical vocabulary appears as unproblematically as if it were part of ordinary language. Marcuse's reputation in Europe is tremendous, as attested by a news item in *The New York Times* in the summer of 1967 described the tumultuous reception he received from crowds of Berlin students. A weighty *Festschrift* for Marcuse has also appeared, and a front-page review in the Sunday *New York Times Book Review* section proclaimed him as "the foremost philosopher of the New Left." Even in the "bourgeois" press, Marcuse has made it.

Clearly the work has wide appeal. But in my view it is a great disappointment. Given the real and pressing needs of theory-hungry American radicalism and the danger of overvaluing any attempt, especially one which seems to be deeply rooted in profound if obscure philosophical traditions, it is worthwhile even at this time to try to account for both the appeal and the disappointment. *One-Dimensional Man* is an attempt to give a "total" analysis of our society, encompassing all major aspects of thought and action. It claims to unmask hopes for any significant possibilities of change from within the system. The note of pessimism struck is so profound that to be critical is to appear superficial, unaware of the despair which must accompany true insight. An example can serve to show how the tone of the book can evoke such feelings. At one point, Marcuse inserts a quote from Ionesco, without comment, though clearly with approval.

> The world of the concentration camps . . . was not an exceptionally monstrous society. What we saw there was the image, and in a sense the quintessence, of the infernal society into which we are plunged every day.

The quote is not explicitly related to the discussion of technological rationality in the midst of which it appears. What should one say? My feeling is *no,* but I feel hesitant and defensive about it. I do think the camps were exceptionally monstrous, and I don't think they are, even "in a sense," the "quintessence" of the society I am plunged into daily (or Professor Marcuse either). Which isn't to defend the goodness of this society unless one's position is so "profound" that "not as bad as Auschwitz" is considered a positive defense.

The kind of position here taken by Marcuse makes profundity a little too easy and smothers analysis. From such a stance all qualifications can seem unessential, petty, and superficial. The total statement is tougher, more absolute, more powerful, and more satisfying; but finally, if offered as description and explanation, it fails. For precisely the differences and qualifications it overlooks are essential for understanding our situation, especially if understanding is related to decision and action. The vision of pessimism may express part of our mood, as in the Beckett novels which Marcuse commends, but offered as multidimensional analysis it can be numbing. It can lead to a sense that no action is really relevant or significant in a situation so totally awful and devoid of possibilities.

The book is an essay in philosophical sociology, an attempt to grasp the essential defining characteristics of a form of society by means of an analysis of its ideology. Marcuse's mode is to specify *the* ideology of the society as a whole in terms of particular realizations of general categories. We are given descriptions of particular uses of propaganda as exemplifications of the general category of "*the* language of the society," a particular view of modern atomic physics as *the* philosophy of science, a particular style of philosophy now dominant in England and important in America as *the* philosophy of "advanced industrial society," a particular approach to method in social science ("functionalism" and "behaviorism") as *the* social science of the society, and so on.

This style is carried through even in the more rhetorical passages, as in Marcuse's statement that *the* face of our time is seen in the novels of Samuel Beckett. The unqualified nature of this style incorporates fundamental ambiguities, empirical and methodological. First, a characterization of the general category—Art, Philosophy, Science, Language—is stated. As usual, such general descriptions of what Art or Philosophy has always been are at best dubious. Then the realization of the general category for advanced industrial society is described in terms of the root metaphor of "one-dimensionality." *The* art, *the* politics, *the* language, *the* social science, *the* philosophy are one-dimensional; they lack the possibility of transcendence or negation, possibilities always present in previous societies. These realizations are expounded in terms of particular examples, often extreme examples, the worst aspects of whatever activity or category is being considered. The argument is not an inductive empirical one, though empirical pronouncements are often made in the course of the argument. (We are told what *the* people think, how *Time* magazine affects *the* leader. No empirical basis for such claims is given, no qualifications are offered; exceptions are not analyzed.)

The effect of the empirical claim is really dependent upon the conceptual claim that the "totalizing" syntax is justified; that the examples or particular realizations of the general category are the defining, essential ones. No real argument justifying the "essential" constructions is, in fact, given (just as there is no argument to support the claim that the Nazi death camps are the quintessential image of the society we live in). What drives the discussion along is the repetition of the root image, the emotional appeal of extreme and powerful examples, and crucial confusions between empirical and conceptual questions involved in notions like "prevailing universe of discourse and action," and "possibility of transcendence."

However difficult the language often is to those who are not at ease in Marcuse's Hegelian idiom, the general thesis and overall structure of the argument are quite clear. The thesis is as follows:

The avance of modern post-Galilean science and the technology based upon this science have made possible an industrial society that is able to achieve a tremendous and constantly increasing productivity. Politically, the effect of this development has been to destroy the basis of revolutionary protest, to damp down social conflict to the point where historical agencies of social change disappear. In Marcuse's words:

> Contemporary society seems to be capable of containing social change—qualitative change which would establish essentially different institutions, a new direction of the productive process, new modes of human existence.
>
> . . . the capitalist development has altered the structure and function of these two classes [bourgeoisie and proletariat] in such a way that they no longer appear to be agents of historical transformation. An overriding interest in the preservation of the institutional status quo unites the former antagonists in the most advanced areas of contemporary society.

What follows is the disappearance of meaningful protest as a society develops which instills the false needs it then satisfies. Society conditions a population to support its own irrational domination while thinking itself to be free and rational.

> . . . the technological controls appear to be the very embodiment of Reason for the benefit of all social groups

and interests—to such an extent that all contradiction seems irrational and *all* counteraction impossible. . . .

The intellectual and emotional refusal "to go along" appears neurotic and impotent. This is the socio-psychological aspect of the political event that marks the contemporary period: the passing of the historical forces which, at the preceding stage of industrial society, seemed to represent the possibility of new forms of existence.

(Italics added.)

The result is a false consciousness, a deceptive "Happy Consciousness," a "preconditioning," an indoctrination which securely integrates the society around its productive apparatus and makes impotent or meaningless any protest.

Thus emerges a pattern of *one-dimensional thought and behavior* in which ideas, aspirations, and objectives that by their content transcend the established universe of discourse and action are either repelled or reduced to terms of this universe. They are redefined by the rationality of the given system and its quantitative extension.

At the conclusion of the book, Marcuse writes:

The enchained possibilities of advanced industrial society are: development of the productive forces on an enlarged scale, extension of the conquest of nature, growing satisfaction of needs and faculties. But these possibilities are gradually being realized through means and institutions which cancel their liberating potential, and this process affects not only the means but also the ends. The instruments of productivity and progress, organized into a totalitarian system, determine not only the actual but also the possible utilizations.

Marcuse's discussions of particular topics are designed to illustrate and substantiate this general theme. The metaphor of "one-dimensionality" expresses the disappearance of fundamental oppositions in our society, those oppositions which can be indicated by such traditional pairs as "fact-value," "is-ought," "reality-appearance," "potential-actual." The dimension which is dissolving is that of man's perception of the injustice, irrationality, and oppression which characterize the actual existence of all historical societies. This perception was always accompanied by a vision of a better, truer, freer existence, as has been conceived in art, philosophy, and religion; though such vision was presented necessarily in a disguised and sublimated form.

This metaphor expresses Marcuse's sense of the frightening uniqueness of advanced industrial society. The very society which has, in Marxian terminology, produced the material means for the leap from the realm of necessity into the realm of freedom, has accomplished this in such a manner as to perpetuate "domination." Even more important, this domination, characteristic of "technological rationality," destroys the possibility of transcending the domination. This unique closing-off of possibility, this destruction of an entire dimension of human existence cannot but be the most frightening and depressing development in man's history. In an obvious sense—implies Marcuse—this is the best and the worst of times, but the "bestness" is superficial and the "worstness" profound.

The first "study" in the book is of "one-dimensional society." The thesis is that technological society has made it possible to incorporate the proletariat into the system, in fact as well as in consciousness, by means of the welfare state. Using as background this conception of the welfare state as a stable form of oppression, Marcuse describes the concomitant cultural integration under the heading "The Conquest of the Unhappy Consciousness: Repressive Desublimation." The claim here is that "high culture," by being absorbed by the system which uses it as a commodity, loses its essential function of being sublimated protest. The alienation, the embodying of the tension between the actual and the possible, beauty as the *promesse de bonheur*— these essential characteristics of all art are disappearing. The massification of culture as a by-product of democratization and technological advance has undermined the very substance of art, its critical potential, and its alienated truth.

In the sphere of sexuality also, apparent progress is seen as really a worsening of the situation. Admittedly, erotic energy is

freed in contemporary society. But Marcuse conceives of the
"sexual revolution," the "desublimation," as worse than the
former repression since

> the greater liberty involves a contradiction rather than ex-
> tension and development of instinctual needs . . . it works
> *for* rather than *against* the status quo of general repres-
> sion—one might speak of "institutionalized desublima-
> tion."

Pleasure is allowed, but only in acceptable forms which dissolve
those claims that are unreconcilable with the established society.
In this manner, further submission is generated. The result is
"The Happy Consciousness," "the belief that the real is rational
and that the system delivers the goods."

Marcuse extends this cultural analysis to the "closing of the
universe of discourse." He wishes to show how "behaviorism"
and "functionalism" characterize the language and thought of
our society and destroy the capacity for critical two-dimensional
language and thought.

> Discourse is deprived of the mediations which are the
> stages of the process of cognition and cognitive evalua-
> tion. The concepts which comprehend the facts are losing
> their authentic linguistic representation. Without these
> mediations language tends to express and promote the im-
> mediate identification of reason and fact, truth and estab-
> lished truth, essence and existence, the thing and its func-
> tion.

Marcuse uses the term "operationalism," as expounded by the
physicist P. W. Bridgman, to characterize the identification of a
concept with a set of operations. This "total empiricism" restricts
the meaning of concepts to the representation of particular operations and behavior. Marcuse considers this type of "operationalism" and its counterpart "behaviorism" to be the "predominant
trend in philosophy, sociology, and other fields."

This is a very substantial claim, but Marcuse does little to
substantiate it. Bridgman's views, along with the logical positiv-

ist position of which they were the most extreme expression, have been subjected to quite devastating critiques, both from within and without the "neo-positivist" tradition. Similarly, such methodologies in social science continue to receive effective criticism; and for many scientists and philosophers, such extreme behaviorism as Marcuse constructs is a thoroughly refuted position. (See, for example, Noam Chomsky's brilliant and scathing review of Skinner's *Verbal Behavior,* and Charles Taylor's *The Explanation of Behavior,* a subtle attack on behaviorism in psychology written by an analytical philosopher who was a leading figure in the English New Left of the late 1950s.) The same dialectical situation of accepted position and critique applies to anthropology, sociology, and political science as well.

In a broader and vaguer sense of "behaviorism" and "positivism" than Marcuse's, there is such a predominance in American social science. The kind of "scientism" with its proclaimed "value neutrality," which characterizes much work in social science, often cloaks ideological support for the system in the guise of "scientific objectivity," as Marcuse shows in unmasking some examples of such work. But this sort of predominance is not startling to a radical, especially one who is conscious of Marx's contributions to the theory of ideology. This society is not exceptional in having key institutions like universities dominated by trends and approaches that are ideologically tied to and supportive of the status quo. What would be exceptional and uniquely "one-dimensional" is the disappearance of an opposition. But Marcuse does not demonstrate this, and the book misses what would be helpful and revealing in this context, namely a sense of the dialectic of the disputes and radical critiques being made within the disciplines.

Marcuse's view would clearly be that my comments are totally superficial; that these positions are not merely dominant but actually definitive of the activity for *this* society because they are truly the expression of the form of Reason which is embodied in advanced industrial society. The opposition is ignored and implicitly ruled out of being part of *the* society, and the ideological and institutional dominance is transformed into a monolithic conceptual bind. This form of argument comes out quite clearly in the use of examples. The author explicitly puts forward his ex-

amples as illuminatingly representative, although little argument
is offered other than the feel of how, being extreme examples,
they appeal to and reflect our fears. What results is a kind of
armchair sociology of knowledge, a truncation of reality, and a curious ambiguity in the extension of crucial terms.

For example, in the discussion of "functional," "operational,"
and "behavioral" language referred to, Marcuse wants to characterize the "prevailing modes of speech" as making the expression
of opposition impossible. The explication of concepts in terms of
functions is said to result in a one-dimensional language of
"magic-ritual formulas."

Marcuse attempts to illustrate the thought-impeding style of
this language in terms of advertisements for luxury fallout shelters, RAND Corporation "war game" instructions, specimens of
political huckstering, news-column heads, and a passage from
Time. The claim is that "clean bomb" and "harmless fallout" are
"only extreme creations of a normal style." The passage from
Time, also noted as an "extreme example," is analyzed in this
manner:

> A hyphenated attributive construction creates a fixed syn-
> drome: "Georgia's high-handed low-browed governor . . .
> had the stage all set for one of his wild political rallies
> last week." . . . The governor, his function, his physical
> features, and his political practices are fused together into
> one *indivisible* and *immutable* stucture which, in its natu-
> ral innocence and immediacy, overwhelms *the reader's*
> mind. . . . Terms designating quite different spheres or
> qualities are forced together into a solid, *overpowering*
> whole. . . . The effect is again a *magical* and *hypnotic*
> one.

The kind of "good" language characterizing the possibilities of
previous societies is exemplified for Marcuse by *The Communist
Manifesto*. (I think this might be called "loading the comparison.") Are we to take it that *the* language of nineteenth-century
bourgeois-feudal Germany, the "prevailing universe of discourse," is best represented by the writings of Karl Marx and
Friedrich Engels? If not, why this particular sort of comparison?

A critical aspect of this *a priori* sociology can be brought out by noting an ambiguity in the reference of crucial terms, a tacit amendment to the "total" claims of Marcuse's syntax. Take the analysis of *Time* language: *The* reader's mind is "overwhelmed," the structure is "indivisible and immutable," the whole is "solid and overpowering," the effect is "magical and hypnotic." At another point, Marcuse says: "The people recognize themselves in their commodities; they find their soul in their automobile, hi-fi set, split-level home, kitchen equipment." The tacit amendment to such characterizations is that neither the author nor the radical reader is included in "the reader" or "the people" (even if one sometimes looks, with anger and disgust, at an issue of *Time,* or if one owns a car and a stereo). My question is—how does Marcuse know so much and so exactly about *the* reader's responses? From a brief analysis of *Time*-ese, from the evidence of syntax? The sociological questions—who reads *Time,* what variety of responses are there, is there skepticism, do the same "language" and response characterize, say, *The New Yorker, Scientific American, Partisan Review, Fortune,* and *Ramparts*—are immediately raised in my mind. The author, however, does not seem to feel that there is anything more to be learned or that what might be discovered could make a difference in one's understanding.

But Marcuse also says: "The new touch of the magic-ritual language rather is that people don't believe it, or don't care, and yet act accordingly." Is it really all so clear? Is there any range between being hypnotized and "not believing"? No complexity or shading of response? Isn't there anything to be discovered about the nature of compliance and support, the apathy, the areas of dissent? What is the implication of the fact that *we* are not included—we have seen through it, we fight against it, write critical books, publish magazines, organize "free universities"? Why is it that the others don't (can't, won't)? Marcuse's "totalizing" analysis of extreme examples is not a sufficient answer.

The most detailed critique of the possibilities of the "language" of the society is presented in the central section of the essay, the discussion of "one-dimensional thought." This is the most "ideological" of the analyses, for Marcuse assumes that "it is the sphere farthest removed from the concreteness of society which may show most clearly the extent of the conquest of thought by society."

Unfortunately, this section is the weakest part of the book. The subjects are no less than science and philosophy in general and specifically in our society. The discussion of the essential nature of philosophy and its origins among the Greeks is extremely compressed, and, for me, almost impossible to follow with any confidence. The intent is to characterize good philosophy as "two-dimensional," dialectical, contradictory, able to come "to grips with reality," in Marcuse's phrase. Only "dialectical thought," he seems to be saying, retains the tension between "is" and "ought" (and of the other oppositions mentioned at the beginning of this article). This kind of thought emphasizes the necessity of changing the apparent reality in order to bring into being a truer, more rational, and hence more real reality. (In Marcuse's words, "Dialectical thought understands the critical tension between 'is' and 'ought' first as an ontological condition, pertaining to the structure of Being itself.") This "two-dimensionality" involves the notion of "another logic," "another universe of discourse."

There is good rhetoric here, but not much more. At no point does Marcuse clarify the notion of a "logic" or of "laws of thought." This would be necessary if one wanted to show how "formal logic" is a narrow and essentially conservative mode of thinking, a "logic of domination," "nontranscendent in its very structure."

The discussion depends upon unexamined ambiguities in the use of "logic," "contradiction," "real," and other related terms. Although we are supposedly given a contrast between "good" logic and "bad" logic, at no point is the formal study of "logic," as in Aristotle or Frege, distinguished from the idea of "logic" as referring to coherence and consistency of thought and communication. "Logic," in this general sense of deductive logic or rules of inference, seems to exist in all languages and in all societies. In this sense, "logic" is a "linguistic universal." The "dialectic" as a style, a recommendation to conceive the world in terms of conflicting forces, within a context which should always be seen as characterized by possibilities for transformation, is not, therefore, a question of "logic," properly conceived. It is one of intelligence and insight. A logical contradiction will be invalid even in a good society, when all social "contradictions" will have been dissolved.

The discussion of "good" thought is the context for an analysis of the nature of science and its philosophy. The line taken is the familiar one that science took man out of nature, separated value and fact, destroyed a nature conceivable in terms of "final causes," dissolved matter into abstract equations.

Marcuse's analysis of mathematical physics and the philosophy associated with it is singularly unenlightening. It is dogmatically stated, based on a pastiche of quotes from various philosophers and philosophically minded scientists. We get little sense of the kind of discussions these quotes may be part of; or why a certain philosopher's statement, say W. V. Quine's personal and controversial formulation that "objects continue to persist only as 'convenient intermediaries,' as 'obsolescent cultural posits,'" is to be taken as properly and essentially characterizing the general terms "physics" and "modern philosophy of science." ("Obsolescent" is Marcuse's own misinterpretive interpolation.) Without a proper "dialectical" sense of the debates, such use of quotes gives only an arbitrary picture of Marcuse's own construction, especially misleading if it can be assumed that most readers don't know much about quantum mechanics or special relativity theory.[1]

The key claim is that science "develops under the *technological a priori* which projects nature as potential instrumentality, stuff of control and organization." For Marcuse this means that

---

[1] It is interesting to note that this approach to science and its philosophy is almost identical with that given by Hannah Arendt in *The Human Condition*, a book which in many ways resembles *One-Dimensional Man*. (Neither writer will thank me for this comparison.) The same essays by Heisenberg, giving philosophical interpretations that are highly controversial and are in any case obscurely and inadequately argued, are accepted without question as definitive of modern science and its philosophy. There are also striking similarities in the respective analyses of "functionalism" and "behaviorism" and the dreaded but expected "brave new world"-style behavioristic future for postindustrial mass society. But ironically, Miss Arendt writes from a profoundly conservative antirevolutionary perspective while Marcuse is revolutionary and utopian.

scientific rationality determines a society of technological domination in which everything, including man, is treated "functionally" and "instrumentally." He wants

> to demonstrate the *internal* instrumentalist character of this scientific rationality by virtue of which it is *a priori* technology, and the *a priori* of a *specific* technology — namely, technology as a form of social control and domination. . . . Science, *by virtue of its own method* and concepts, has projected and promoted a universe in which the domination of nature has remained linked to the domination of man.

Since Marcuse's discussion of science and its philosophy is so inadequate and mistaken, the claimed connection between science in general and domination is left completely undemonstrated.

But isn't the question itself wrongly posed? Science has not *led* to domination, even to a particular form of domination. It has been a crucial factor, of course, in the material and ideological transformation of the West, and now, increasingly, of the entire world. But the activity of science arose in a society which was characterized by all sorts of tyrannies and domination, and many of the liberating forces of our age are essentially related to ideas of science and the various ways in which these have been interpreted. These include the development of socialism, Marxism, psychoanalytic theory. I don't mean to say hurrah for science; like logic, it is part of the general framework in which we think and act. The question should not be how science has maintained domination, which would have been better maintained by "non-science," but why didn't the development of scientific thought, by and of itself, lead to the free society? To ask the question this way is to see immediately that blaming or exonerating science is unhelpful at best. Why should science have accomplished this? What about everything else—the social institutions, character structures, beliefs, vested interests—which characterized the society within which science developed? What we need and Marcuse doesn't supply is a sense of the interplay between scientific ideas, technological developments, and the beliefs and values of man, as this interplay works itself out in history.

For Marcuse, the "one-dimensional thought" toward which science has led is seen most clearly in the "positive thinking" of "one-dimensional philosophy." This philosophical ideology, the "school" of linguistic analysis, is claimed to be a travesty, a pseudophilosophy, at best inconsequential, at worst tragically dangerous.

Marcuse's discussion of linguistic philosophy raises the general question of ideological analysis, as much by what it doesn't say as by what it does. If we take examples of ideological analysis like Mannheim's study "Conservative Thought" or Sutton's *The American Business Creed*, we find an analysis of "ideological productions" related to the individuals who produced them or adhere to them. These individuals are described as members of particular groups, characterized in terms of roles, institutions, and social structure. Thought and social structure are mediated by a theory of some sort—crude self-interest theories, Marxist theories of class interest, "strain" theories of the sort prominent in American social science.

Marcuse's critique of linguistic analysis completely ignores the questions raised by this schema of ideological analysis. Social and institutional questions are not raised. Nor are the political positions of the people involved. The national traditions of English philosophy and its relation to linguistic analysis are not discussed. The claim is that, in crucial ways, this philosophy represents a radical break with all previous philosophy, even with the "two-dimensional" empiricism it evolves from.

What Marcuse hopes to show is that this philosophy reflects the positive thinking of advanced industrial society. This project would seem to entail a subtle and accurate description and analysis of linguistic philosophy. What we find instead is another instance of the fallacious kind of argument used throughout the book.

Marcuse takes as given that linguistic philosophy is a philosophy with clear and definite doctrines. "It identifies as its chief concern the debunking of transcendent concepts; it proclaims as its frame of reference the common usage of words, the variety of prevailing behavior." According to Marcuse, such philosophy permits no negativity toward the existing practices of society.

> The self-imposed restriction to the prevalent behavioral universe makes for an intrinsically positive attitude . . .

the prebound analysis succumbs to the power of positive thinking.

How these doctrines were proclaimed we are not told. Would the God believed in by religious linguistic philosophers count as a "transcendent concept"? What exactly is meant by "debunking"? Does Marcuse mean that any attempt to criticize society is considered meaningless by the linguistic philosophers? What is meant by "the variety of prevailing behavior"? And what is his evidence for characterizing linguistic analysis as adhering to "philosophical behaviorism"? (This subject of "action" and "behavior" is one of the most important areas of dispute *within* the "style," though if Marcuse's analysis were a reader's only acquaintance with this philosophy, he would not have the slightest idea of the existence or nature of such disputes.) As usual, we find the monolithic tone—Linguistic Analysis believes this and Linguistic Analysis makes it impossible to do that.

The examples Marcuse cites to illustrate his claims are from Wittgenstein and Austin, the two major figures of postwar British philosophy. Marcuse tells us that "silly scraps of language that sound like baby talk" guide the analysis of such philosophers. For example, he says: "Wittgenstein devotes much acumen and space to the analysis of 'My broom is in the corner.'" A lengthy quote from Austin's essay "Other Minds" is added. These examples are supposed to support Marcuse's claim that this style of philosophy is destructive of philosophic thought, "and of critical thought as such."

This is a rather damning indictment, and one would have expected some sense of context, *at least* to be told what the analyses mentioned were used for. As it is, Marcuse does not give the slightest hint of the purpose of Wittgenstein's analysis of "silly scraps of language."

However, Marcuse does assure us that if such scraps appeared in Hegel, "they would be revealed as inappropriate or even false examples." But inappropriate or false examples of what? Does the sentence "My broom is in the corner" carry written on it that it will always and in all circumstances be an inappropriate or a false example? Since we are never told what Wittgenstein uses it as an example of, how are we to know even that he takes it to be a true example, in the sense that a truly profound philosopher would show it to be false? Similarly for the quote from Austin, on the basis of which a reader might think that Austin had written an essay on ways of being hesitant or on the taste of pineapples. But in fact the essay quoted deals with basic problems of epistemology. Professor Stanley Cavell, one of the most provocative interpreters of both Austin and Wittgenstein, characterizes Austin's methods and their effects in the following manner:

> He asks for the difference between being sure and being certain, but what is uncovered is an initial survey of the complex and mutual alignments between mind and world that are necessary to successful knowledge. He asks for the difference between expressing belief and expressing knowledge (or between saying "I believe" and saying "I know") and what comes up is a new sense and assessment of the human limitations, or human responsibilities, of human knowledge, and so on. (S. Cavell, "Austin at Criticism," *Philosophical Review,* April 1965.)

Of course there is disagreement even among those who are vaguely called "analytical philosophers" on the worth and implication of the work of Wittgenstein or Austin. But Marcuse is clearly not interested in this nor in recognizing how such stuff could have ever been considered as possibly fruitful philosophical activity. I think that there is a difficult and important task to be done in the analysis of thought-styles and emphases and their relation to more general social circumstances (and analytical philosophy is a good case to work on). But this implies that the works themselves must be treated with appropriate subtlety and even sympathy. To put Wittgenstein down by mentioning a sentence he uses as an example really smacks of philistinism and is unworthy of Marcuse. One could apply this sort of critique to Kant or Descartes with the same result. Making the relevant substitutions in the Marcusean argument, we come up with: "Kant devotes much acumen and space to the analysis of '$5 + 7 = 12$'" (a piece of second-grade arithmetic); "Descartes devotes much acumen and space to describing the melting of a piece of wax." The last step in the argument is to leave the reader to try to discover what on earth could have been in the minds of these so-called philosophers.

The crucial point in Marcuse's attack is the repeated insistence that linguistic analysis makes "negative thinking" impossible; that it surrenders to "ordinary language"; that it doesn't subvert the given facts, as true philosophy should; that it leaves language in "the repressive context of the established universe of discourse"; that it gives a "behavioral explication of meaning." The contention is that this philosophy makes it impossible to think critically about our society because of its unquestioning acceptance of "the established universe of discourse and action."

This last phrase is basic to Marcuse's critique and appears frequently throughout the book. It is based upon a fundamental ambiguity of Marcuse's analysis which emerges most clearly in his polemic against analytical philosophy. In philosophy of this sort, questions of language are in general questions of meaning, and, as Cavell emphasizes, are simultaneously questions about the "world." One concern, among others, is getting clear on how we use words and thus on the conditions and problems of meaning and understanding. This is *not* equivalent to accepting the limiting of "meaningful" to "what most people say" or what is politically or socially acceptable to the majority or to the ruling elites. What is at stake is what *we* ourselves say and mean, when we talk about pain or love or fear or truth or freedom. And it is simply not the case, as Marcuse dogmatically states, that "to begin with, an irreducible difference exists between the universe of everyday thinking and language on one side, and that of philosophic thinking and language on the other." It is not the case because I grew up and live in a "universe of everyday thinking and language," and it is by means of this language, used subtly, intelligently, and critically, that I learn valuable new concepts and new possibilities of meaning, including "philosophic" meaning.

If the difference were truly "irreducible," it would be impossible to explain the meaning of new terms, say "dialectic" or "transcendent." "The established universe of discourse and action" should be taken to mean "what can be meaningfully said and done." (This universe includes radical ideas and radical actions, as well as conforming behavior and television commercials.) The sliding between the statistical and conceptual connotations of this key phrase has been noted several times before. In the derogatory sense of "established universe," to be within it or to accept it uncritically is to lose the possibility of being negative, radical, critical, original, and so is to be "one-dimensional." But in the other sense, and it is this sense I associate with the best possibilities of analytical philosophy, there is no limit except meaningfulness (and establishing this is a problem, not an assumption to begin with).

What can be said in "ordinary language" is that this society is lousy in many ways; that it is immoral to waste vast resources in maintaining irrational and oppressive institutions while most of the world starves; that the lives of many people, both in the United States and in the countries with which it is involved, are twisted and their potentialities distorted by the prevailing values and practices of this affluent society; that there could and should be more beauty and truth and justice in the world. The refusal to accept the propaganda of the Establishment, the decision to protest and to live in socially and politically disapproved ways are as much a part of the universe of meanings as are the most conformist actions. That the number of such radicals may be small does not settle the question of what can be *meant*. It implies that, as always, those who are willing to go beyond generally accepted arrangements and values will be in a minority and can have no guarantee that their vision will win out.

This core ambiguity causes much of Marcuse's critique to miss the mark. That philosophers discuss academic topics at all instead of attacking current political and social arrangements might seem to present a problem, given Marcuse's conception of philosophy. But then every other life activity except direct political action or critique would fall under a similar criticism. Why discuss problems of causality in physics when this is the world of Hiroshima and Auschwitz; why take time listening to music and going to see movies when every minute our government is committing murderous atrocities; why produce Molière comedies or paint abstract canvases when people are starving? I don't find these questions silly, but each of us has to find and live out his own answers.

Why then does Marcuse pour so much scorn and ridicule on

this little-known part of the academy, so out of proportion as a target, given the subjects of the other parts of the book? My feeling is that Marcuse is expressing his anger and frustration at the apparent impotence of thought to break through, to bring about the necessary radical changes in consciousness he sketches in the concluding section on "The Chance for Alternatives."

This whole section should be read against the background of Marcuse's *Eros and Civilization,* an essay that developed at greater length the utopian concepts which constitute Marcuse's vision of a "good" future. In *One-Dimensional Man,* the key concepts are "pacification of existence," "freedom," "liberation." The vision is that the "project" of scientific rationality would surpass its present structure and direction, and would become "metaphysical" again; industrialization would take new forms. Values would be translated into needs that would develop on the basis of "nonrepressive sublimation." The vision must necessarily be sketched programmatically ("liberation of the imagination," "redefinition of needs"), for there is a real limitation of the established universe of discourse.

The ambiguity between the conceptual and the empirical accounts both for the power of Marcuse's vision to express despair and for the confusions of his analysis. It reappears strikingly in his somber conclusion. He reaffirms his faith in "critical reason" but finds its powerlessness a source of despair. The quality of the despair can be related to Marcuse's Marxian framework. One-dimensional society, however wasteful, ugly, oppressive, and crippling for man, seems increasingly capable, by its irrational rationality, of containing social change, and containing it by consent, as it were. This implies the disappearance of real forces, of definite social groups whose existence would compel them toward the abolition of oppression. Without these social groups, determined in their very existence by the nature of the society which brought them into being, can any change come? Can theory, however critical, become practice in some other way; by changing consciousness within the affluent society, for example?

For Marcuse it seems that the answer must be no. This is the way history *must* work. His despair and anger translate themselves into the depressing sense that thought itself is becoming impossible. Even those seemingly favorable signs, like the civil-

rights movement, must be seen as part of "the catastrophe of liberation," as signs of how totalitarian the society is becoming. For
now even the most materially oppressed groups will be brought
into the system; and whereas a blatantly oppressed and despised
Negro population was by its very existence, if not in its consciousness, a threat to the system, a Negro population with apparent political power and opportunities for seeking significant
economic advance will lose this existential aspect of "negativity."
It would seem to follow that peace movements, SDS, left-wing
magazines and books can be taken most significantly as signs of
the increasing power of the system, ways of letting off steam,
part of the society's fooling itself into thinking it is free and open
whereas the true reality is otherwise. Better, it would appear, the
old McCarthyite terror or worse, outlawing of student protests,
police censorship of political publications; at least this would
force some people to face the underlying truth.

This contemporary version of "the worse, the better" could
hardly be more despairing and pessimistic. That hardly anyone
in his most thoughtful moods could desire such a situation seems
obvious. We want our freedoms and rights, and we think it is
worthwhile to work for simple material gains, however small, for
people whose lives are ground down by poverty. But, given the
frustrations of a commitment to a vision of radical social change,
the frequent failure to accomplish small goals—let alone the
great transformations which are the ultimate motivations of
hopefully "radical" projects like organizing a community union
project in the Newark ghetto, being a SNCC worker in Mississippi, or forming a draft resistance movement—how can one
avoid moods of deep pessimism? Such moods are not, finally, an
accurate indication of our complex sense of where we are and
what we can do. But my feeling is that much of the appeal of
the book stems from Marcuse's evocation of this mood of blan-
keting and apparently omniscient pessimism, his rooting the frustrations of failure in an impressive if obscure philosophical frame
which projects a society that makes "transcendence" in any area
impossible.

To a great extent this Marcusean pessimism is related to a romantic involvement with the image and rhetoric of the great revolutionary moment, the kind of apocalyptic transformation

where one can see with satisfying certainty the success of one's efforts in reaching the deepest goals of the radical vision. For Marcuse, the disappearance of the possibility of realizing this vision (for all the reasons that the book notes) provides a simplifying if despairing canon of historical interpretation. If rising standards of living, the elimination of sheer material oppression, the development of a semi–welfare state, the liberation of sexuality, etc., are factors in the conditions making the vision of revolutionary transformation completely illusory, then they are finally bad. What is ignored is the actual meaning of these changes to the people who experience them as real improvements, however meager they seem in the light of the utopian vision of the end of all psychic repression and the transformation of man's instinctual structures.

The analyses in the book are attempts to justify this simplifying pessimism. But as I have tried to demonstrate, Marcuse's argument fails to support his thesis which, itself, is not interestingly new. In various forms it is the recurrent nightmare of an automated, sterile, passive "brave new world." Finally, the argument misleads by not matching our sense of the ambiguity of our situation, its confusing "two-dimensionality": as regards our political possibilities, the art we respond to, the dynamic of science, the meaning of sexuality. By denying this felt ambiguity within our own lived experience and by assuming an almost *a priori* pessimistic knowledge of the state of "the people," the meaning of increasing prosperity and welfare, the possibilities of art and sexuality, Marcuse has translated a justified sense of staggering and sometimes unique difficulties of successful "transcendence" and opposition into an unjustified vision of an almost complete conceptual impossibility. In this way, Marcuse has been able to construct a frightening metaphor of bleak pessimism.

But the real help we need is not in giving nightmares an intellectual structure. It is in beginning to answer questions about the politics of the "totalizing" and "post-totalized" society. The old agents of history may disappear or be absorbed, but what will the new social and psychic strains and discontents be like in the prosperous, postindustrial society, and how will the discontent, dissatisfiaction, and alienation be made politically relevant, at least potentially? Should the movement be one of resolute opposition, gathering in and giving activity and space to those who become conscious of their alienation, thus hopefully building an area of "negativity" in American society which could become relevant in future situations the nature of which we can't yet clearly conceive? Or should attempts be made to work at least partly within the established institutions of the society, to attempt to affect, even if only marginally, the actual and potential destructiveness of American power, and to help in the totalizing process which is going on and will provide the context for a possible new politics? These questions are hard to formulate in a clear way appropriate to the ambiguity of our situation, just as it is hard to explain the meaning of the unexpected phenomenon of the transformation not of "high culture" which Marcuse fastens on, but of mass culture in the form of, say, the Beatles or Bob Dylan or the movies.

A discouraging projection of despair built up by bad argument doesn't touch these questions; and despite the appeal of the tone to many young radicals, the analysis is indifferent between radical perspectives of community organizing and uncompromising opposition and, so to speak, "moderate" perspectives of coalition politics and working within the system. The whole spectrum of possibilities is swallowed up in the "catastrophe of liberation." We may not reach the understanding we need, but if we do, it will be with a little help from our friends; and that Marcuse, for all his intelligence, passion, and commitment, does not help, is the measure of the book's failure and my disappointment.

[1968]

REVISIONIST HISTORIANS AND THE COLD WAR

by Henry Pachter

Not only the East has its revisionists. In this country, too, and even more insistently in Western Europe, honest research has led to a thorough and often painful reappraisal of recent history. The conventional view of the so-called cold war, as it still appears in such widely used textbooks as Spanier and Lukacz,[1] is under attack. This view may be crudely presented in three propositions:

> *After World War II the Soviet Union tried to expand its power through military conquest and Communist uprisings in as many countries as possible.*

> *But it was restrained by vigorous counteraction of the Western powers, which "contained" the Soviet advance by measures of mutual assistance short of war.*

> *Fortunately, United States opinion had abandoned isolationism and America now was ready to assume its responsibilities as a great world power dedicated to the principle of collective security.*

---

[1] John Lukacz, *A History of the Cold War* (Garden City: Doubleday, 1961; rev. ed., *A New History of the Cold War*, 1966); rev. ed. somewhat more critical. John Spanier, *American Foreign Policy Since World War II* (New York: Praeger, 1967).

In this view we appear virtuous, restrained, and almost passive; our policy was largely defensive, and if we sent soldiers abroad, it was only to help the oppressed or to ward off aggression. Moreover, such moves were clearly meant as "deterrence." Only twice were we unfortunate enough to be drawn into military actions—in Korea and in Vietnam, both places where we had to fight under conditions not of our own choosing—and on two occasions we barely avoided military conflict: in Berlin and in Cuba. But on the whole we managed to keep the war "cool" in spite of tempting provocation, as in Hungary, Czechoslovakia, Sinai.

The professional historian will instinctively distrust such a pat presentation. He can hardly remember a twenty-year period in history where right has been consistently on one side and wrong with equal regularity on the other. He is used to the play of force and counterforce with little reference to good and evil, and he expects to see every hero debunked in due time, every patriotic myth destroyed in the light of newly found documents, and every decision that had been deemed "inevitable" or "forced upon us" after diligent research proven avoidable. Therefore, he is not surprised to read, in Mr. Louis Halle's magisterial study of *The Cold War as History* that diametric labels such as "wicked" and "virtuous," or "aggressor" and "peace-loving nation" have little meaning in a conflict that on both sides was experienced as an irreducible dilemma.[2]

Taking a cool view of the East-West conflict, Mr. Halle pleads for an understanding of the Kremlin's motives and concludes that Stalin was as much afraid of us as we were afraid of him. He does not claim that newly unearthed evidence changed his mind. Rather, his dispassionate view of both sides is a matter of interpretation, and whatever new insight is gained by his method is due to his attitude: Having participated in many cold-war decisions as a member of the State Department's Policy Planning staff, he now sits back and reflects on the impact these decisions may have had on the other side, and he comes rather close to the admission that some of the early critics of the con-

---

[2] Louis Halle, *The Cold War as History* (New York: Harper & Row, 1967). A superb work, both personal and scholarly.

tainment policy, like Henry Wallace, Water Lippmann, and P. M. S. Blackett,[3] may have had a point: The Russians refused to play the game according to our rules, and instead of being contained they strained every effort to break out of the "iron curtain" which from their side looked like "capitalist encirclement."

The view that Mr. Halle presents would contrast with the three propositions of the conventional view in the following way:

> *After the defeat of Hitler, the balance of power was not restored in Europe, and from both sides of its outer fringe, therefore, attempts were made to establish a new equilibrium.*

> *The cold war, though widened to encompass worldwide conflicts, is essentially the continuation of the international power contest which has raged from the time of the Seven Years' War through the Napoleonic wars and the two world wars of this century to the present day.*

> *The United States was drawn into this conflict because it is basically a European-Atlantic nation, and this entanglement seems to have been fatefully inevitable; but accidental outbreaks of military hostilities in Asia created a climate of "crusading" which needlessly embroiled the United States in areas where it had little interest, less power, and no traditional ties.*

Even before Mr. Halle, similar views had been expressed by conservative critics like George Kennan and Hans Morgenthau who warned that the cold war must not be escalated into a military confrontation, must not be extended to areas outside Eu-

---

[3] Walter Lippmann, *The Cold War* (New York: Harper, 1948). Consists of 12 articles originally printed in the *New York Herald Tribune* in reply to George F. Kennan's "Mr. X" article. P. M. S. Blackett, *Fear, War and the Bomb: Military and Political Consequences of Atomic Energy* (London, 1948; New York: McGraw-Hill, 1949). The famous British weapons expert was the first to criticize the concepts of nuclear deterrence. Henry Wallace, former Vice President, left the Truman Administration and campaigned in 1948 on a "Peace" platform.

rope, and must not be conducted in the name of one ideology against the other.

Mr. André Fontaine, foreign editor of the Paris *Le Monde*, also abandons the black-and-white view of history in his two-volume *History of the Cold War*.[4] Each side, he laments, sees the enemy as an outlaw against whom no holds are barred, and each feels righteous about its cause. Viewing a confrontation of two *righteous* causes makes tragedy and history close neighbors. But is the cold war so much past history that we can look at it in this way? We shall see that, on the contrary, the revision of our views on the cold war is no academic exercise—like admitting that George III was a fool rather than a tyrant—but a passionate matter of partisanship. Even the contention that the cold war is over is a partisan slogan.

Nevertheless, the new view is associated with deep-seated attitudes of the academic mind. The statesman must act from a conviction of righteousness. But a dispassionate view of our own and a compassionate view of the other side naturally appeals to intellectuals, who not only are more immune to propaganda but also disgusted by its methods and distrustful of its aims. From their vantage point, the cold war appeared as a contest between two brainwashing crews, and perhaps even as the outgrowth of hate ideologies.

However, one can go too far in trying to be fair and even-handed.

Professor Walter La Feber has rendered a valuable service in tracing the relationship between the domestic and the international phases of the cold war and in describing the struggle between the cold-war ideology and the critical forces in this country.[5] He shows how much of the cold-war anxieties and of

---

[4] André Fontaine, *History of the Cold War* (New York: Pantheon, 1968 and 1969). The scope and point of view of this brave attempt is indicated by its starting date—the October Revolution. Writing from the vantage point of French politics, M. Fontaine usefully reminds us that in 1944 Ho Chi Minh liberated part of Vietnam with the help of the CIA (or its predecessor) and that Maurice Thorez, then the French Communist leader, told the Vietnamese that he "would not like to be considered the liquidator of French positions in Indochina."

[5] Walter La Feber, *America, Russia and the Cold War 1945–1966* (New York: Wiley, 1967). Probably the best of the historical narratives.

our responses was due not to enemy action but to our interpretation of it. Regrettably, language difficulties and lack of access to
Russian documents bar him from attempting a similar study of
the cold-war climate in the Kremlin. But like other revisionists,
he tends generally to attribute too much of what happened in
the last eighty years to American initiatives. *We* did this, *we* did
that—as though diplomacy were not an interaction of many
powers. Revisionists have justly criticized the self-centered, arrogant view that this country is called to maintain the world order
single-handedly. They are no less provincial in assuming that different attitudes in this country alone could at will have changed
a course of events that was largely determined by others and by
its starting point. Mr. La Feber neither quotes the European pro-
moters and critics of the cold-war policies nor does he analyze
the *European* interests and forces that drew or pushed the
United States into the cold war. Revisionists fail to combat but
rather tend to amplify the legend that Europe was a mere object
of American policies. This is not true. Reading La Feber or any
other revisionist book, no one would guess that British Foreign
Minister Ernest Bevin did more than anybody else to muddle a
postwar settlement in Europe, or that Berlin's Mayor Ernst Reu-
ter single-handedly forced us to fight for the freedom of his city.
In 1968 our European allies asked us to punish Moscow for the
invasion of Czechoslovakia.

Nor does Mr. La Feber disclose the full measure of Stalin's
contribution to the cold war. This book begins with the statement
that in October 1945 the magazine *Bolshevik* and President Truman more or less simultaneously ("meanwhile") sounded warlike trumpets. Only in the footnote does he acknowledge that
when Truman spoke, *Bolshevik* was already three months old,
i.e., it had appeared *before* the end of World War II. Even earlier, at the time of Roosevelt's death, two public statements announced a reversal in Kremlin policies: One was Jacques Du-
clos's "Open Letter" in *Cahiers du Communisme* for April 1945;
the letter has been quoted frequently because it denounced the
wartime truce between the Allies, deposed Earl Browder as
leader of the Communist Party in the United States, and rein-
stated the slogan of fighting capitalism in all its forms. Mr.

Christopher Lasch, another revisionist, writing in the *New York Times Magazine*,[6] brushes this letter off as just a quibble about electoral tactics and takes Arthur Schlesinger, Jr., to task for considering it a key document. Mr. Lasch displays ignorance of Communist affairs; an open letter was about the most solemn announcement, next to a speech by Stalin himself, of a shift of policy in Comintern usage. Messrs. Lasch and La Feber also omit the real opening shot of the cold war—Soviet Foreign Minister Molotov's speech at the opening session of the United Nations, 26 April 1945, where he accused the Western powers of complicity with Hitler.

Leaning over backward is a laudable attitude, but this is going rather far. American intellectuals have been angered by cold-war lies; but instead of concluding, like Mr. Halle, that both sides lie, many seem to feel that if we lie, the other side must be telling the truth. Mr. Halle carefully says that in such a great conflict where two historic forces meet, it really does not matter "who started it." In fact, every experienced historian will agree that this is a question for nursery-school teachers. To the younger (and some not so young but equally naïve) revisionists, however, this question seems to matter: In order to prove the U.S. government wrong they must prove Stalin right. This calls for three kinds of operations:

> *Finding a suitable date for the beginning of the cold war;*
> *finding documents which disprove Western propaganda claims and prove the claims of Soviet peacefulness;*
> *reinterpreting or ignoring documents which up to now have formed our view of the cold war.*

This endeavor goes beyond the intentions of moderate critics like Halle and La Feber. They assume that any errors of judgment or mistakes of policy were made in good faith, perhaps under the pressure of circumstances or as the consequence of honest miscalculation, misinformation, and misunderstanding;

---

[6] *New York Times Magazine*, 14 January 1968.

that even in ideological warfare the participants believed in what they were saying and that indeed the conflict came about rather like a Greek tragedy—through a confusion of the minds wrought by jealous gods. We shall hear about those gods later on; first we must speak of the new revisionists who charge that vicious men with malicious purposes started the cold war.[7] For obvious reasons we shall give them the name they prefer, radicals.

The liberal critic of the cold war laments the alleged fumbling of our policies and deplores the fateful but involuntary military and ideological escalation; establishment historians impute all criminal initiative to Stalin—the radical says it just was not so. Nor is he content with giving merely his own interpretation to known facts. He cites a different set of facts and he sets out to prove with documents that the real course of events was quite different from what people believe. The most impressive and best documented work of this sort has been presented by Gar Alperovitz in his analysis of the Potsdam Conference of July–August 1945.[8] It will be remembered that President Truman was on his way to Potsdam when he received the "good news" from Alamogordo, that the first atomic bomb had been successfully tested. He relayed this top secret to Stalin in such a way as to minimize its importance, and he chuckled when he told Churchill that the Russian apparently had not grasped the significance

---

[7] Some have suggested that Truman could have avoided the cold war if he had not abruptly stopped Lend-Lease operations after V-E Day, or if he had granted Stalin a loan. Lend-Lease was stopped not only to Russia but to England as well since the program's authorization automatically ended when it had fulfilled its purpose—victory in Europe. As to the loan, the Kremlin could have used drawing rights in the amount of $1.5 billion had it ratified the Bretton Woods agreements. Later, Molotov appeared with a large staff of experts to participate in setting up the Marshall Plan machinery; but he was called out of the meeting by a telegram from Moscow and never returned. I cannot understand why most Americans think that peace could be bought with money.

[8] Gar Alperovitz, *Atomic Diplomacy: Hiroshima and Potsdam* (New York: Simon & Schuster, 1965). Mr. Alperovitz impresses his point of view on the reader by an excessive display of irrelevant scholarship. I have no quarrel with a careful study of the documents. But the results have been meager: The documents show only that the relations between the allies were distrustful throughout the war. This could surprise the naïve.

of the information. In fact he still chuckles when he remembers the incident in his Memoirs.[9] Mindful of the coming election year, eager to "bring the boys home" and also aware that an early victory over Japan would give "Uncle Joe" no chance to claim his part of the spoils, Truman made the fateful decision to use the bomb at once. The world has since questioned the wisdom of this decision but not the alleged reasons. These seem to me quite sufficient to explain Truman's action, given his background and position.

Alperovitz, however, amasses documents to show that the real reason for an early use of the bomb was not victory in Asia over the Japanese, but intimidation of the Russians in Europe. At Potsdam, indeed, where the powers implemented the Yalta arrangements for the future of Europe—we must now say for the partition of Europe—the Western statesmen tried to secure some measure of freedom for their friends in the Eastern countries which they had abandoned to Russian hegemony. Mr. Alperovitz shows how possession of the bomb made the Anglo-Saxons feel much more "confident" that they might be able to negotiate from strength. Lasch flatly maintains that they "asked Stalin to accept hostile governments" or even "tried to force the Soviet Union out of Europe." [10] Alperovitz tells us how: Truman wished to show Stalin his real strength; for that purpose he needed a demonstration of the awesome power of the atom. Therefore he ordered the bombing of Hiroshima—in order to gain room for maneuver in Eastern Europe!

To the odious crime of releasing the jinn that since has hovered over the future of mankind, Alperovitz adds the indictment that this was done wantonly, for an unrelated purpose, in an action that was not even directed against the enemy but against an ally. Since we agree that the use of the bomb was heinous, we are tempted to grant Mr. Alperovitz that the reason for this crime must have been at once sinister and ludicrous. Since Mr. Alperovitz names such a sinister and ludicrous reason, we are further tempted to agree that he must be right, and from there it

---

[9] Harry S. Truman, *Memoirs,* Vol. 1 (Garden City: Doubleday, 1955), p. 419.
[10] *New York Times,* 14 January 1968.

is only one step to the conclusion that, since all this is so shameful, Truman's hope to save a little democracy in Eastern Europe must also be condemned. On such notions radical revisionism builds its case against the U.S. government's actions in the early months of the cold war.

But the entire deduction is fantastic. If Truman wished to frighten Stalin, why did he chuckle instead of plopping the bomb with all its awful statistics on the conference table? Why could he not have ordered a public demonstration of its power? Why does Mr. Alperovitz fail to mention the Oppenheimer-Compton report which recommended the military use of the bomb without making reference to Europe? Why did Secretary of State Byrnes publicly concede that the "Soviet Union has a right to friendly governments along its borders" and Under-Secretary, later Secretary, Acheson even speak of "a Monroe Doctrine for Eastern Europe"? [11] Why, in fact, did they all look on meekly while brutal ultimatums expelled their friends from the governments of Bulgaria, Rumania, Poland, Hungary, and later of Czechoslovakia? All this happened while the United States still enjoyed its atomic monopoly, and Mr. Halle usefully reminds us that the United States demobilized its armies, did not prevent the development of atomic energy elsewhere, and did not try—as I think it should have—to barter its monopoly against the withdrawal of Soviet troops from Eastern Europe. In all the quotations with which Mr. Alperovitz smothers the reader, we do not find a shred of evidence for his contention that Truman tried to force Stalin's retreat from Europe, which is based on pure conjecture. Immersed in documents, he fails to look at the acts of the governments and to reconstruct the climate of the year 1945. So obsessed is he indeed with the search for secret evidence of evil that he never notices the evil which was being done in plain daylight.

Radical revisionism, we see, is not content with suggesting that wrong may be evenly distributed over both sides; it reverses the roles of hero and villain completely. Where we had pointed

---

11 *New York Times,* 1 and 15 November 1945. Mr. Alperovitz indeed has an answer: Byrnes was trying to lull Stalin into complacency. That kind of logic can prove anything.

an accusing finger at Stalin, charging him with bland disregard of the Yalta agreements, we now find ourselves in the defendant's dock, indicted not with an isolated misdeed but with the consistent, systematic, and—one is tempted to say—congenital pursuit of Empire. Mr. Ronald Steel gives his book the angry title *"Pax Americana—The Cold War Empire,"* [12] and begins by quoting de Gaulle to the effect that the United States "feeling that she no longer had within herself sufficient scope for her energies . . . yielded in her turn to that taste for intervention in which the instinct for domination cloaked itself." The general merely was repeating the anguished outcry of his compatriot, Alexis de Tocqueville, 130 years earlier, that "there are today two great peoples which, starting out from different points of departure, advance towards the same goal—the Americans and the Russians. . . . Each of them will one day hold in its hands the destinies of half of mankind." [13]

Tempting as it may be to trace the European roots of revisionism, we must now inquire what is the nature of this American imperialism which has motivated American initiatives in the cold war. There are three main lines of thought indicating long-term American commitments:

To the first proposition of the conventional view, Professor Denna F. Fleming answers that the world need not be concerned with Soviet expansionism—but with the systematic and consistent encirclement policies of the West, beginning with the interventions of 1917–20, and later methodically enlarged to form coalitions threatening the Soviet Union with atomic destruction and organizing the cold war as a holy crusade. [14] No Soviet actions but the mere existence of the Soviet Union called up Western ire.

To the second proposition Professor William Appleman Williams replies that American interventionism abroad needed no provocation by the Soviets. [15] He maintains that it dates back to

---

[12] Ronald Steel, *Pax Americana* (New York: Viking, 1967).
[13] See concluding page of Vol. 1 of *Democracy in America*.
[14] Denna F. Fleming, *The Cold War and Its Origins 1917–1960*, 2 Vols. (Garden City: Doubleday, 1961).
[15] William Appleman Williams, *The Tragedy of American Diplomacy* (Cleveland: World, 1959).

well before the October Revolution, to be precise to the open-door policy of the nineties of the last century, a policy designed to "keep China sovereign for purposes of exploitation by the burgeoning U.S. industrial complex while the Russians who could not compete, tried to assure themselves political leverage by creating spheres of influence." [16]

To the third proposition David Horowitz replies that not idealism led the United States into an internationalist policy but the defense of narrow economic interests,[17] to wit those of the rich. He concludes by quoting Arnold Toynbee, that America is today "the leader of a worldwide antirevolutionary movement in defense of vested interests." [18]

In all the last-named books the scholarship is unbelievably poor. Professor Fleming's work reads in places like a scrap book of newspaper clippings; he never distinguishes between opinion and document, as he will triumphantly exhibit a silly Letter to the Editor of the *Ashville Courier* as though its author were speaking for the U.S. government, while glossing over the most important statements by Lenin, Stalin, and their successors. Mr. Horowitz requotes Fleming's quotes with admiration and adds nothing but vulgar Marxist explanations or plain misinformation. For instance, he wishes to show that Stalin did not plan to hold on to the imposed Communist regime in East Germany; for that purpose he quotes Molotov's unification plan of 10 March 1952. But he fails to mention that Molotov refused to allow free elections under U.N. supervision. Moreover, he fails to mention that the entire "peace plan" was nothing but a desperate, last-minute bait to prevent West Germany from joining NATO. I happen to think that the Western powers should have taken Molotov's

---

[16] La Feber, op. cit; see also the contributions by Lloyd Gardner and Robert Freeman Smith to the New Left anthology *Towards a New Past,* Barton J. Bernstein, ed. (New York: Pantheon, 1968). All three authors acknowledge W. A. Williams as their master. With the exception of Professor Genovese's contribution, the scholarship in Mr. Bernstein's volume leaves much to be desired.

[17] David Horowitz, *The Free World Colossus* (New York: Hill & Wang, 1965).

[18] Arnold Toynbee, *America and the World Revolution* (New York: Oxford University Press, 1961).

offer and trusted the dynamics of further development—the German uprising a year later then might have been a different affair! Had Horowitz analyzed the episode instead of quoting propaganda notes, he would have seen that it provides an argument for, not against cold-war tactics: Molotov had never made even as limited an offer as his 10 March plan until the Germans actually threatened to join NATO! If Acheson needed proof for his theory of "positions of strength," it is here; but though German revisionists have asked why Molotov failed to follow suit, American revisionists remain silent—for good reason; they try to avoid the issue of power.

Mr. Horowitz's treatment of the episode is a rather typical example of the half-truths on which much revisionist writing is based. As for his teacher Fleming, his file of episodes, which throws a bad light on Western governments, may be a good thing to have handy when a government apologist offers nothing but a similar file indicting the Soviet government. But as a serious historical work the Fleming book is beneath discussion. A series of episodes does not show consistency of a policy; by merely suppressing the long periods of coexistence, by ignoring the differences between the attitudes of various Western governments in their relations with the Soviet Union, and by taking the Soviet-Western relationships out of the context of the constantly shifting play of coalitions and constellations, Mr. Fleming misses every point.

Moreover, if Fleming is right, William Appleman Williams must be wrong: If the United States interventions antedate the October Revolution, as Mr. Williams maintains, they cannot have been provoked by it, as Fleming will have it. As George Kennan has shown,[19] Wilson's decision to intervene had no cold-war motivation.

Professor Williams, the most influential writer in this field, ostensibly follows the classical lead of Scott Nearing,[20] in his attempt to reduce U.S. foreign policy to economic causes. He is no

[19] George F. Kennan, *The Decision to Intervene* (Princeton: Princeton University Press, 1958; paper, New York: Atheneum, 1967).
[20] Scott Nearing and Joseph Freeman, *Dollar Diplomacy: A Study in American Imperialism* (New York: Viking, 1925).

Marxist however, but a Christian populist who became a convert
to mercantilism. He is fanatically devoted to the idea that closed
economic areas are healthy for development and for peace.
Whatever disturbs this imaginary idyll is bad, above all the
American efforts to prevent any pieces of geography from being
fenced off as empire. He calls the open-door policy "anticoloni-
alist imperialism" and condemns the Marshall Plan as another attempt to force a door open—an attempt which apparently left
Stalin no choice but to save Europe from U.S. control.

As to the economic motive, the trouble is that our China trade
never lived up to the expectations of the "hundred million
lamps," [21] but remained 1–2 percent of our total imports and ex-
ports. Nor were American capitalists eager to invest in China as
the modern theory of the "surplus" would require. At the beginning of the century the State Department vainly tried to encourage American bankers and railway magnates to help in offsetting
the Japanese and European influence; but to no avail. Far from
practicing "dollar imperialism" the United States was not even
capable of practicing dollar diplomacy—the use of dollars for
political ends. The indifference of U.S. capital made it necessary
for Dr. Sun Yat-sen to turn to Lenin for help.

Nor has Professor Williams been very fortunate in the quality
of his followers. Robert F. Smith descends to the following
trick [22]: To show that U.S. policy was antisocialist even when it

---

[21] Title of a prewar book exhorting America to deny the great Chinese market to the Japanese. Critics of U.S. Asian policies have always argued that
we have no substantial "interests" there. If this is true, Professor Williams
would have to postulate that potential development of hypothetical interests
has the same effect on policy-making decisions as actual interests. I am
not contending, of course, that the "open-door" policy was disinterested or
that it was morally superior: In fact, the United States demanded no real
open door but only equal rights with the Japanese and other colonialists.
However, it so happened that U.S. interests coincided with Chinese interests.
Many critics of U.S. policies think their job has been done when they can
prove an "interest." They forget that all business relations between people,
institutions, and states are based on "interest," which may be beneficial
either to both or to only one side. Opprobrium should properly be cast not
on interests as such but on exploitative interests that subordinate other
interests.

[22] Bernstein, op. cit., p. 247.

seemed to be antifascist, he quotes *Foreign Affairs* for July 1937 to the effect that "capitalism is lost where it is not built on liberalism." On closer inspection, the quoted passage turns out to be by a German exile, editor of a respected business magazine, trying to warn American business to beware of Hitler. In the cold war, too, the economic tools of propaganda and of diplomacy are often mistaken for ends or motivations. Thus Professor La Feber quotes A. A. Berle testifying in 1947 that "within four years the world will be faced with surplus production." He then proceeds to interpret this threat as "one paramount motivation" for the Truman Doctrine and the Marshall Plan.[23] It is, of course, much more correct to say that the Marshall Plan was the economic arm of the Truman Doctrine. Berle then was Under-Secretary for Economic Affairs, and he was particularly concerned with promoting the "Point Four" program which was designed to win the friendship of underdeveloped countries in the world struggle between the United States and the USSR for supremacy. The aim of this policy, including its economic measures, was not economic penetration but the preservation of independent states in all areas of the world. So much for "the economic motive," the search for which only shows that American liberals rarely understand power as a motive. Now let us see how power has been understood by U.S. policy-makers.

As originally conceived, the policy of containment meant the creation of strong, self-reliant states along the periphery of the Soviet empire, but especially in Europe. It meant measures short of war, and there was then no premonition of NATO or other military confrontations. Therefore, Bernard Baruch quipped that we were engaged in a "cold war"; he was varying the coinage "dry war," which had been used before World War I.

This policy was consistent with Wilson's policy of creating independent national states in place of the old empires, and with FDR's anticolonial thrust during and after World War II. Long before he had ever heard of Bolshevism, Colonel House warned Woodrow Wilson that "an Entente victory would mean domina-

---

[23] La Feber, op. cit., p. 43.

tion of Russia on the Continent," [24] and thirty years later George Kennan expressed the same fear in the now-famous "long telegram." As a remedy he recommended the "containment" policy spelled out in the controversial "Mr. X" article.[25]

This indeed has been the red-white-and-blue thread that runs throughout American foreign policy. Shorn of the anti-Communist rhetoric to which Kennan objected, this was the message of the Truman Doctrine of which Kennan approved. It said "hands off" to Stalin, and so did Eisenhower in his first inaugural, as had FDR's "Quarantine Speech": Irrespective of the expansionist's philosophy, the United States has been opposed to closed doors indeed, everywhere and at all times. There is something incomprehensibly sectarian in the revisionist charge that all American and indeed all Western policies have always been directed against Russia. The open-door policy clearly was directed first of all against Japan, second against Western colonialists, and only third against Russia, imperial as well as Soviet. For we are dealing here with the kind of tension between powers that is the usual stuff of history. Its permanence is reflected, for instance, in A. J. P. Taylor's title *The Struggle for Mastery in Europe 1848–1918.* Ideology has done very little to embitter or alleviate these conflicts. World War I started between nations of like ideology, and World War II saw nations with opposing ideologies allied nevertheless. The United States conducted the cold war by helping Tito, a Communist—but Mr. La Feber can quote senatorial diaries endlessly to the effect that Acheson was staunchly anti-Communist, yet forget to mention that he supported Tito's Communist economy. (Since this was written, Acheson's memoirs have appeared, reminding us that at the time the Right attacked Acheson as "fool of Communism.")

In a strange way, revisionists reflect the mirror image of their opponents: Both think that "ideology" was the cause of the cold war or that some conspirational power was hiding behind the ideology—be that power the Communist world leadership, or

---

[24] Quoted by La Feber, from A. S. Link, *Wilson: The Struggle for Neutrality* (Princeton: Princeton University Press, 1960), p. 48.
[25] *Foreign Affairs,* July 1947. Both documents are now contained in his *Memoirs* (Boston: Little, Brown, 1967).

America's military-industrial complex. They find it difficult to admit that conflicts arise out of the fact that "we live in a system of states" (Lenin), and that in such a system of conflicting and converging interests all combinations are possible.

The cold war is such a conflict for the "mastery of Europe" in which political, diplomatic, psychological, and economic pressures are the principal weapons but military deployment is used in a symbolic and logistic fashion short of warlike action. It makes no sense to apply the term "cold" war to the hot wars in Korea and Indochina or to areas where no such conflict rages. The Asian and African wars must be explained in terms of their specific origins; they were fought in a different area, with different means, and against a different enemy. But there is not the slightest connection between "Communism" or "anti-Communism," and the quarreling factions in, say, the Congo or Nigeria.

Cold-war ideologists, of course, like to subsume all the post-1945 wars under the heading of anti-Communism or of the "Sino-Soviet bloc." These efforts must be strongly resisted—if only for the practical reason that one may disagree with U.S. conduct in Asia while agreeing with it in Europe, or agree in 1950 but not today. It is regrettable that the revisionists here do not go far enough. Instead of accepting Mr. Rusk's cold-war generalizations—which they denounce in another context—they should analyze each of these wars in terms of its particular condition, its weapons and conduct, its particular ideology, and, above all—its particular enemy. It will then be found that the cold war proper, as we knew it in the forties and fifties, may soon be over. Like many great wars, it was not settled, had no victors or vanquished, but is simmering down. Both sides in that war recognized rather early in the game that its solution could only be a confirmation of the status quo: For all his propaganda antics about the "liberation" of "captive nations" and the "rollback" of the Iron Curtain, the late John F. Dulles did the most to "freeze" the cold war where it stood. In Asia, on the contrary, even the most ardent Kremlin partisan of coexistence never wavered in his support of "wars of liberation."

Back to the cold war. This conflict arose out of the postwar situation: Russia had just emerged from her most excruciating trial. Even without resorting to Stalin's paranoia one must understand his desire for a protective glacis. The United States, on the other hand, could not allow any power to combine the potential of a reconstructed Europe with the resources of Asia. She is always opposed to the building of empires, as we saw.

But it was not just the actual fear and the recent experience which determined Stalin's expansionism. Rather, Mr. Halle impresses on our sympathetic heart, the Russians are suffering from a deep-seated, historical encirclement complex, an anxiety which the Western powers have clumsily fostered instead of allaying. The Cold War, Mr. Halle gravely informs us, cannot be understood unless we go back into history—not to Churchill's Fulton speech that some use as the date of its beginning, nor to Yalta that to me seems the most reasonable date, not even to 7 November 1917, as Messrs. Fontaine and Fleming suggest, and not to the Pan-Slav agitation that led to World War I. No, we must go back to the Day of Creation when Nature failed to endow Russia with frontiers that can easily be defended. The rulers of her wide-open plains, we learn, could protect themselves only by seizing adjacent territory, a strategy called "defensive expansionism." What with the understandable reaction of her neighbors Russia unhappily acquired, over the centuries, that feeling of insecurity and the resulting ferocity which can be appeased only by giving her mastery over other nations. (Never mind how *their* anxiety is to be soothed.) The pattern which the Czars established reproduced itself in the relations of the Bolsheviks with their neighbors and even (this was written at the peak of the Czechoslovak crisis) with other "socialist" countries. Long before the end of World War II, it was therefore clear to Professor Halle, who then was in the State Department, that ultimately a confrontation between the victors could not be avoided: "The dynamics of the postwar situation produced an expansion of Moscow's tyranny that was not altogether voluntary but provoked a reaction in the West that in turn awoke Moscow's persecution mania. Had it not been for this persecution mania, the Western reaction might have provided the basis for a settlement." The finger of God driving men into mad confusion and conflagration!

With all due respect to Professor Halle's eminence and scholarship, this is history stood on its head. Russia's open plains indeed were invasion roads for Napoleon and Hitler. But the Tatars had come through the inhospitable Urals; the Varangians and the Swedes had come across the sea, and so did the allies in the Crimean War. On the other hand, Russia's open frontiers permitted the Cossacks to invade Poland-Lithuania and to conquer Asia. It was Russia's neighbors who had reason to complain about Nature's disfavor, and Russia's belligerency was a product of her military, absolutist state rather than of her geography. Neither Lenin nor—emphatically—Trotsky needed any "persecution mania" to conceive of the Soviet state as a revolutionary bastion in a worldwide uprising of the underprivileged proletarians and colonial peoples. Zhdanov revived these conceptions when the power vacuum in postwar Europe opened an opportunity, and Stalin felt "secure" only with Communist governments installed in each European capital. Khrushchev felt encircled by the free city of West Berlin, and today Brezhnev does not feel secure behind the Carpathian mountains. "In a conquered country," Stalin varied Machiavelli, "each of the hegemonic powers must install its system." As Engels said, no border is ever strategically safe.

An important function of the cold war was to keep the bloc allies in line. This aspect has been very little commented upon by the revisionists although it is the one which is least likely to disappear so soon, and it is also the one that keeps the cold-war ideology alive. I do not think the Russians had to march into Czechoslovakia because they were afraid of internal reform—after all, the Czech economy is still one hundred percent socialist and Czech agriculture is the most collectivized of all the satellites. What the Russians were unable to tolerate was the softening of Czech relations with West Germany, and for that reason they had to insist on ideological conformity throughout the satellite empire, too.

The revisionists' ability to empathize with Stalin's tender nerves is at times limitless. Christopher Lasch laments that it was inconsiderate of Mikolajczyk to inquire how four thousand Polish officers came to be buried in a mass grave in Katyn. Could Stalin really be expected to tolerate such a man in a Polish cabinet, even a cabinet totally dominated by Communists? Small nations, on the other hand, have no right to tender nerves. Exalting Stalin's magnanimity, Mr. Brian Thomas reminds us that Groza was not even a Communist.[26] Correct! Nor was Laval a Nazi. Groza was only the man on top of the list of the ministers which Vishinsky handed the king of Romania with an ultimatum to appoint them within two hours.

The examples of revisionist writers exculpating Soviet policies by psychosociological explanations, or even by doing a touch-up job on the events, are as numerous as the apologetic somersaults of our Establishment champions. After all, reasoning from insecurity is available to all parties and every nation may need "defensive expansion."

This is the domino theory in reverse, and we must ask ourselves how far it may lead. Would it not justify a Hitler, too? Strangely enough, some revisionist writers have drawn this uncouth consequence. It is not Dean Rusk who proposes the false analogy between Hitler and Stalin or Ho Chi Minh; it is Mr. Robert Freeman Smith, writing in a New Left collection, who suggests that the conformist interpretation of World War II supports the cold-war arguments.[27] Mr. Smith is amused by "simplistic" people who still believe in "the Adolf Hitler syndrome"; he cannot conceive that Hitler and Hirohito had any design to rule the world, and Pearl Harbor to him "revealed the full implication of [Brooks Adams's] imperial logic," which also made the cold war inevitable. For it was not Japan but the United States which "in 1941 rigidly asserted that any order in Asia would have to be in terms of its objectives." Again, history stood on its head.

Professor A. J. P. Taylor, in his turn, author of a book which absolved Hitler of all guilt in unleashing World War II,[28] writes in—of all places!—the *New York Review of Books:*

"Germans were no more wicked in aspiring to dominate Europe . . . than others were in resolving to stop them. They were in a sense less wicked. For their domination was achieved with little physical destruction and comparatively few casualties, whereas the effort to resist them produced general devastation."

[26] Brian Thomas, in the *Journal of Contemporary History* (London), January 1968.
[27] Bernstein, op. cit., p. 237.
[28] A. J. P. Taylor, *The Origins of the Second World War* (New York: Atheneum, 1962).

The wanton destruction of Guernica in the Spanish Civil War, of Lidice, of Coventry, of Amsterdam, and Kharkov—all brought about by the wicked resistance of the victims. The six million Jews were so wicked as not to see that Hitler was merely trying to do them a favor. Not the murderer but the victim is guilty! This atrocious statement is followed by more sick jokes and by an interesting aside which reveals the purpose of Taylor's revisionist effort. Citing Poland's quixotic refusal to become either Hitler's or Stalin's satellite, he says: "Western historians exaggerate Soviet faults as much as they condone Polish ones. This is only to be expected in the era of the cold war, which historians are still loyally fighting when most sensible people have forgotten about it." [29]

Professor Taylor meant to buy peace for England by encouraging Hitler to acquire an Eastern empire. He still thinks that in September 1939 the peace might have been preserved if Poland had yielded some territory and in exchange had been compensated, perhaps, with a piece of the Ukraine. The English have always been very generous with land that did not belong to them —but why does the *New York Review* lend its columns to this kind of eighteenth-century statecraft? Do the revisionists of World War I, World War II, and of the cold war have more in common than the name?

It may be possible to point to an aversion which they share— the fear of ideologies and in particular of the idea of collective security. The Astor set had to resist the pressures which came from the Popular Front in the name of both antifascism and collective security. These two themes were intimately linked with each other since the fascist governments were by nature and ideology aggressors, and to resist them was tantamount to the creation of international police forces against the disturbers of the peace.

One needs no imagination to see the trap here: The cold war,

[29] *New York Review of Books,* 6 June 1968. Taylor claims that he was no member of the famous Astor clique but "denounced it often." I cannot find any evidence of this, the last occasion to denounce Chamberlain was his *English History 1914–1945* (London: Oxford University Press, 1965). There he defends Chamberlain's policy of appeasement and specifically denies (p. 436) that Hitler's policy was aggressive.

too, has been fought on this side under the ideology of collective security against a power that had openly proclaimed itself as the challenger of the status quo. The New Left, which accepts the arguments of radical revisionism, sees the similarities between the cold-war ideology and the ideologies which were used to bring America into both world wars:

In all three cases the United States was defending the status quo against challengers who attacked the traditional power of the Western, colonialist states.

In each case ideology was used more or less deliberately to proclaim a "crusade" against a militant force of change.

In each case the notion of collective security was propagated to justify American involvement in alliances which allegedly were contrary to its interests and which perhaps overtaxed its power.

We can now understand the importance of this ideological identification. To the liberal it matters whether Ho Chi Minh can be compared to Stalin or maybe even to Hitler; to the radical it does not matter at all. He may even find it easier to proclaim his solidarity with a frankly revolutionary Ho Chi Minh than with a pacific one. What matters to him is not whether this country has obligations to come to the aid of others, but that it returns to the isolationist stance which was imparted to it in George Washington's Farewell Address.

Liberals usually know that this is not possible. Conservatives and radicals cherish the pious legend that once this country lived in a state of innocence but at some point evil spirits—power-hungry politicians and greedy capitalists—contrived to entangle it in foreign alliances and wars. Though a superficial glance at nineteenth-century history should dispel such fantasies, most criticism of U.S. policies is based on some version of a Fall. A particularly flattering version of the legend is the Woodrow Wilson myth: that a misguided "idealism," an arrogant, puritanical sense of mission drove this country to assume the mantle of world policeman, which sat awkwardly on its shoulders; it had not been created to "take up the white man's burden" and was not fit for empire. The country was able, therefore, to play a role in world politics only if armed with a righteous ideology. The late John Foster Dulles, with his solemn countenance, was ideally suited to make this image plausible. But let us note that for all his talk about brinkmanship Dulles failed to come to the aid of East Berlin in 1953, or Hungary in 1956; he kept Chiang Kai-shek on the leash and made no move to get the Russian armies out of Europe. He concluded armistices in Korea and Vietnam and seemed reasonably happy with a world divided between "theirs" and "ours": His rhetoric was no guide to his politics, which were defensive and unimaginative. While he sought to contain the Communists, he also recognized that they were containing us.

Moreover, this policy was bipartisan. Rusk took it over from his predecessor, and Stevenson endorsed it shortly before his death (in a letter to Paul Goodman).

Dean Acheson makes it clear in his memoirs that to him and Marshall, the essence of this policy was not ideology or anti-ideology, but collective security (even the Communist scare was mobilized only to make containment acceptable to a reluctant Congress and a war-weary public). As formulated by Niebuhr: *For peace we must risk war.* In the less poetic language of the Secretary of State Rusk: "Let no would-be aggressor suppose that the absence of a formal defense treaty . . . grants immunity to aggression." [30]

The "cool," sophisticated postwar generation feels superior to the generation of its parents which stumbled into two or three wars because they either believed in ideas or placed their faith in collective security. The New Left rejects these illusions: Containment policy, the Truman Doctrine, the Marshall Plan, and NATO have led to other alliances and to wars in Asia; they have dispelled the world political dream of the liberals that peace can be won by power. Conservative and radical critics of the cold war may differ on the precise phase of it which they began to reject: Some started the day Henry Wallace was fired, others after the proclamation of the Truman Doctrine, the more moderate would still go along with the European confrontation until after the death of Stalin, [31] or even side with the U.S. government in

---

[30] Senate Preparedness Committee, quoted in *The Washington Post,* 26 August 1966.
[31] Ronald Steel, op. cit.

the first phase of the Korean War [32]—but all share an almost pathological contempt for "idealism":

> He [Rusk] is a meliorist, a liberalist and moralist . . . the heir to the Wilsonian tradition. . . . Ultimately it was Wilson's effect to convert the First World War, initially a European [!] dynastic and commercial carnage, into a war for the unattainable goal of universal peace and justice. . . . It has escaped notice that the "war to end all wars," that black joke of the Wilson era, has emerged once more in our day as the war to end all insurgency.[33]

It may not be easy to recognize in this caricature the person of the unflamboyant Dean Rusk but it is not difficult to recognize the bastard that conservative *realpolitik* has begotten on Populist pacifism. The noblest principle of American foreign policy, or perhaps the noblest principle in the foreign policy of all ages, has been ridiculed in order to disparage the policies of a particular Secretary of State. Instead of attacking him for misapplying the principle, the principle itself is attacked; instead of denouncing the use of great ideas for petty ends, ideas as such are held up to ridicule.

The revisionists are poor historians if they don't understand the importance of principles and ideas, either in guiding or in moving the men who act.[34] No part of history, not even foreign

---

[32] Edmund Stillman and William Pfaff, *The New Politics* (New York: Harper, 1961), and *The Politics of Hysteria* (New York: Harper, 1964).

[33] Edmund Stillman, "Dean Rusk: In the American Grain," *Commentary*, May 1968, p. 36.

[34] Revisionists of the conservative school reject "ideologies" but at least are aware that "principles" or political concepts are necessary to understand and to shape foreign policy. Such a principle is the old-fashioned "balance of powers." A more modern one would be "collective security"; very ancient ones are "empire" and "hegemony." The New Left, in its general waste land of theory, does not understand the difference between ideologies, which supply rationalizations or justifications for action, and theories or concepts and principles, which are tools. A genuine difficulty is that some principles may be used as ideologies. A perfectly good tool of foreign policy, such as "arbitration," may be used as an excuse for having no policy. But even such debased principles are easy to distinguish from ideologies, such as Com-

policy, is a game on a checkerboard where every move can be figured out coldly with all its consequences. The responsible statesman is distinguished from the chess player in that he does not
see all his enemy's forces on the board and has no way of knowing his true intentions. The revisionist, who can study the ar-
chives at his leisure, has the advantage over the statesman who
was in the middle of the rumble. He knows what each of the acting governments should have done, and he can read all the perti-
nent documents but can ignore the pressures of time, opinion,
and other business that act on the statesman. Nor do his documents reveal the anxieties of contemporaries.[35]

Professor Taylor can calmly assure us that we only needed to
give Hitler one more country to have eternal peace—he does not
choose to remember the anxious moments when Hitler's, Mussolini's, and Hirohito's ultimatums followed each other with the
inexorable regularity of a military march. Mr. La Feber may
blame Acheson for throwing the Communist scare into the Congress debate when obdurate isolationists like Taft would not
grant Greece the aid she needed; fortunately Mr. Halle, writing
from personal memories, conveys the sense of urgency that set
the pace for those who had to respond to a sudden change of the
situation. He also makes it clear that the somewhat confused
message which soon was to be called "the Truman Doctrine"
was hardly conceived as the blistering *pronunciamento* which it
seems in retrospect.

To the orderly mind of the political scientist, historical events
always seem to be planned, or at least conceived, to suit some
idea or conception. In real history nothing ever happens that
way. No one had conceived of the "cold war"; the statesmen re-
acted to situations into which they tumbled. No one seemed to

---

munism and anti-Communism, which cannot serve as guides for a policy and
never have served so, but merely described an imputed motivation.

[35] There is no more dangerous trap for the inexperienced historian, nor any
more dangerous weapon in the hands of the experienced propagandist, than
the pseudo-fact: a well-documented record of irrelevant events. Fortunately,
Professor H. Stuart Hughes has undertaken the necessary and ungrateful task
of setting the record straight in the August 1969 issue of *Commentary*
magazine. He re-creates the atmosphere in which the decisions of 1946–48
were taken.

have planned a crusade, many wondered later on how they came
to be in one. We have to accept as the lesson of history that
forces that were more or less blind and guided by their own dy-
namism clashed in conflict and therefore had to hate each other.
It was the diplomats' business to keep this conflict under control,
not to fan it. We must judge them by their success in disen-
tangling the entanglement, because they could not avoid it in the
first place.

This does not mean, of course, that we must absolve the governments of the charge that they blundered, or that at least some
of the blunders were avoidable. But the revisionists have failed to
prove that the postwar coexistence could be anything but antag-
onistic; it might even be possible to argue that the cold confrontation was among the milder forms which that antagonism was
capable of taking. In certain respects it might even be said that
the phrase "cold war" exaggerates the gravity of the situation.
There was no war plan and no concerted effort to achieve well-
defined aims; no proof has been given that either Stalin or Truman was having designs for the destruction of the other's power.
What we see, rather, is a series of disconnected actions which
happened at opportune moments, of opportunities seized and of
weaknesses exploited. We also see a certain awareness on both
sides to spare the other's susceptibilities and to carry provoca-
tions just to the threshold but not beyond. This must be said
even of Dulles, whose often misquoted simile emphasized the
need to step to the brink *and back.*

Speaking of Dulles, finally, one remembers the worst feature
of the cold war, its ideological aggressiveness, its crusading
spirit, its grandiloquent militancy. Well, Homer's heroes are hol-
lering at each other when they are not giving battle, and ideology
in the cold war served the most degrading purpose to which an
ideology can finally be put—as a cover for inaction. We won all
the battles of righteousness but, thank God, the cold war did not
really break out into a hot war. Most of it was shouting.[36]

---

[36] U.N. debates provide good examples of "cold war" language signifying
nothing. After the invasion of Czechoslovakia by the armies of five Warsaw
Pact powers, Mr. George Ball, our delegate in the Security Council, de-
plored, berated, and condemned the Soviet Union, but carefully avoided
key words such as "aggression" which might have obligated the United

Ideologies rarely are the cause of action; they provide rationalizations for actions, they justify the division into parties. Once created, however, ideas may transcend the immediate propaganda purpose and become myths or rigid doctrines which tend to alienate the faithful from reality, freeze hostilities whose real causes have long been forgotten, and prolong loyalties that no longer make sense. By searching for the sources of the cold war, revisionists might contribute to the thawing-out process, to loosening up the ideological rigidities, and on the whole to deideologizing the antagonisms.

Unfortunately, most revisionists are doing the exact opposite: Instead of understanding how the ideologies were first manipulated and then began in turn to manipulate the manipulators, the revisionists have become victims of the ideological impact. Instead of separating the cold-war ideologies from the power conflict, they have carried them into more areas of conflict, such as the wars in Africa and in the Middle East. They have fallen down on their self-assigned task; instead of questioning the ideological foundations of the crusade, they have simply changed the labels of villain and victim.

[1968]

States to take or support countermeasures. The invasion of Hungary in 1956 was subjected to the same "cold war" treatment. Yet, some political scientists still seize upon such rhetoric to prove that there is a "cold war." One may criticize this rhetoric on many grounds, except on the assumption that the Russians take it seriously. This they leave to our simpletons on the Right and Left.

"MIDDLE-CLASS" WORKERS AND THE NEW POLITICS

by Brendan Sexton

Much of my life has been split between two worlds: blue-collar unions and the intellectual-academic arena—a sort of long-haired working stiff, or at least an uncommon marginal man.

Born in a tough Irish working-class neighborhood and reared on Catholicism, Irish rebellion, and later socialism, I fell into the life of an organizer during the great depression and the early days of the CIO. As a reader of everything in reach, I have followed with great regret the growing schism between organized labor and middle-class liberals during the past decade. Like others, I was stunned to see the old liberal coalition finally fragment during the presidential election under the separate discontents of workers (out of sight and mind to most observers, but not, alas, to George Wallace) and the middle-class liberal antagonists of LBJ. What the consequences of the fragmentation will be only Nixon and Agnew may know.

Yet I continue to believe, in my old-fashioned, radical-populist way, that a broad alliance between these two groups at their center remains the best hope for reconstructing our society along democratic-humanist lines.

Many issues need clarifying if we are to halt a national move to the Right. I wish to explore only one here: the assumption that blue-collar workers are "middle-class" and sitting pretty. I'd also like to suggest some of the political consequences of both the assumption and the reality of workers' lives.

In December of 1967 the "average production worker" with three dependents took home $90.89 for a full week's work. Measured against the previous year, his dollar income rose about $2.34 a week. In fact, however, his actual purchasing power *declined by about six cents per week.* He was worse off in 1967 than in 1966, and probably even more so in 1968.

Now $90.89 take-home is not "middle-class," especially if you are an "average" family head with three dependents. If such a man puts aside $25 a week for house or rent payments (a modest enough sum), he's left with a little less than $66 a week to pay for food, clothing, medicines, school supplies, etc., for two adults and two children. That comes to roughly $2.37 per day, per person, for a family of four—about the amount a big-city newspaper reporter (or any of us in the real middle class) is likely to spend for lunch.

These figures are distorted a bit by the inclusion of Southern, and largely unorganized, workers. But in 1967, *manufacturing* workers (most of whom are organized) with three dependents averaged only $101.26 in take-home pay. As against the previous year, they also experienced a slight dip in real income and purchasing power.

In New York, the locale of many observers who write so expertly about "middle-class" workers, manufacturing workers averaged a gross income of $114.44. Only in Michigan, among all continental states, where the weekly gross was $145.78, could an average manufacturing worker come close to the national family median (about $8,000) with a full year of work.

At the other end of the scale, retail workers averaged just slightly less that $7 per week during 1967. The retail worker, if he worked a full year, earned a gross income high enough to lift him barely above the "poverty line" of $3,000, but low enough to leave him with less than half the national family median income. This is the extreme example. Still, there are more than eight million workers in retail trade. Even when they wear white collars, they can't, at this rate, be factored into the middle class.

Skilled workers are the aristocrats of labor, yet the median earnings of male craftsmen who were employed full-time in 1966 were only $6,981.[1] Of course, a good many of the elite and highly organized urban craftsmen—electricians, typographers, lithographers, etc.—rise to and above $10,000 a year. For a blue-collar worker, this is really "making it." For the new college professor, fresh out of graduate school, it's just so-so.

Where affluence begins and ends no one knows, but it must be above the levels cited. In late 1966, the U.S. Department of Labor said that an income of $9,191 would enable a city family of four to maintain "a moderate standard of living." Only about one-third of *all* American families reach that now-dated standard. Certainly, the typical production worker is much better off than a Mississippi farm tractor driver or a city mother living on welfare, but he hardly lives opulently. He treads water, financially and psychically.

The myth of the "middle-class" worker is kin to the Negro of folklore who "lives in the slums but drives a big new Cadillac." He's there, all right, but his numbers are grossly exaggerated.

Workers with small families and two or more paychecks coming in each week may be able to make it. Among all American families with incomes of $10,000, the multi-incomes are twice as numerous as the single income. Still, millions of families combine two or even three paychecks and yet earn less than $5,000 a year.

The young worker is hardest hit and hence most discontented. He often holds down the lower-paid and more onerous jobs. He is somewhat less likely to work overtime at premium rates and more likely to be caught in temporary layoffs, though in some union contracts he is now protected against loss from the latter.

No less than others of his generation, the young worker expects more. Why not? He belongs to a generation with rapidy rising expectations. As long as he's single, his first paychecks may give him more money than he's ever seen before. He dresses well, owns a new car, and generally lives it up.

But once married, his problems multiply. He furnishes a home, perhaps buys it. He does it "on time." He pays more for furniture and appliances than anyone ever did before. The house that cost his father $12,000, with a mortgage at five percent, now may sell

---

[1] Gaps of a year or more sometimes occur in government statistics. In all cases, I have used the most recent annual reports available.

for twice that and be financed at seven percent. The young married worker age twenty-five or thirty will probably carry twice the burden of debt as the worker age forty or forty-five. When children come, the wife of the young worker will probably drop out of the labor market, leaving him as sole support for perhaps fifteen or twenty years. In these years, his financial needs increase with the size of his family, but his paycheck does not respond to need.

These economic realities confront workers with a long list of harrowing problems. How, for example, do they provide equal opportunity for their children? How do they shelter them against the draft for four years when the cost of sending a son to the state university now averages nearly $2,000 a year? *Perhaps less than a quarter of all high school graduates who are children of factory workers enter college.* (The myth that something like half of all young Americans go to college is very nearly unshatterable. Actually, 46.3 percent of the 18- and 19-year-olds, but only 19 percent in the age group of 20–24 are "in school." U.S. Office of Education reports are so unclear here that I suspect the agency of misleading us regarding the accessibility of college opportunities.)

Children of workers are overrepresented in the mass of those excluded from college. Working-class kids make their trips abroad as members of the armed forces, while some middle-class youths, student deferments in hand, spend a junior year at European universities. While the college boy steps on an escalator that moves rapidly upward, the worker's son may step on his father's assembly line and into a job without much promise.

Relatively few colleges, social agencies, schools, or other public institutions mount programs to meet special needs of workers. In many places, even the services provided by "Red Feather" agencies seem more closely geared to middle- than working-class needs.

Inevitably, many workers come to feel they are being dunned and taxed for the benefit of others. Considering the notorious imbalance of our tax structure, they have a point. *In general, the rate of taxation declines as income rises.* This is most obviously true of the state sales taxes. It is almost as true of the federal income tax, under which, in the most extreme cases, some individuals and corporations pay little or no tax at all, though their incomes may exceed $5 million annually. Estimates of total tax loads indicate that thirty-three percent of the income of those earning $3,000 to $5,000 goes to taxes, and only twenty-eight percent of those earning $15,000 or more.

So we have the case of the "invisible" and aggrieved worker. Many of his breed are even found among Mike Harrington's invisible poor. In fact, about one-third of all heads of impoverished families hold down full-time jobs. They are generally not organized, but they are workers. While millions of workers live in poverty, millions more barely escape it. Most are in income brackets between $3,000 and $10,000 (which include some fifty-six percent of all American families), with probably more workers near the bottom than the top.

Reporters often talk about the sweeper who "makes more than a teacher." True, a sweeper in an auto plant in Michigan or New Jersey probably earns more than a teacher in a backwoods school in Mississippi, but his pay is hardly a pot of gold. The sweeper seems to fit a set of hidden assumptions according to which the society is divided, at a magical line, between rich and poor. The premise of this stereotype is that our class structure is a dualism—rich and poor. In this simplified pseudo-Marxian schema, organized workers are seen as part of the richer half, along with bankers, businessmen, professionals. They are, it is assumed, well fed, well cared for, up to their hip in "things," and all-around partners in an open and affluent society.

According to this hidden assumption, all or nearly all the poor are black. They are mostly mothers of large families living on welfare in big city ghettos. The rest (except for a few Appalachian whites) are young blacks who can't find jobs because they are school dropouts or because they are excluded from unions by corpulent and corrupt union bosses. So goes this version of things, especially popular in some college circles. But in fact about eighty percent of the poor are white, and a startling proportion of them work full-time.

In real life the typical worker has lived on a treadmill, except where union contracts have protected him from rises in the cost of living. Everyone else—including the poor and the militant blacks (at least as their image was cast by the media)—*seemed* to be moving forward, while only *they* stood still, waiting in a twilight zone somewhere between hunger and plenty. Some comforts came to them through expanded consumer credit, but the credit exacted high costs in tension, insecurity, and interest rates. They gave increasing taxes to the government, their sons to the army. They seemed to get little in return: only conflict, and sometimes mortal combat with the emerging black poor over jobs, neighborhoods, and schools.

Here is fertile soil for the growth of resentment. For a time, it grew like a weed under the cultivation of George Wallace. A turning point in the presidential campaign may have come when Hubert Humphrey began to see something Wallace always understood: that while many "experts" said the "old issues" were dead, millions of American workers angrily disagreed and wanted a better life. Many workers were ready, in short, for a campaign resembling Harry Truman's historical effort of 1948, a hell-raising campaign about the "old" economic issues (social justice, more and better jobs, more opportunity, good schools, health care, and so forth).

The trap almost sprung by Wallace was set by those "opinion-makers" who dismissed all Wallace supporters as red-necked bigots and opponents of Negro aspirations. Fortunately, they were mistaken. While many workers have no doubt been shook up quite a bit by the black revolt, they have been even more shaken by their own failure to get on in life. Being far wiser than we think, they knew this was not the fault of blacks.

Sadly, some of the Wallaceite resentment was, of course, turned against the poor and the black. Yet it is possible that Wallace's exposed bigotry finally did him in among Northern workers. Industrial workers generally have closer relations with Negroes than any other class, and the big factories in steel, auto, rubber, glass, etc., are probably the most integrated workplaces in the society. Most workers who were drawn to Wallace because he spoke their economic language must have had problems of conscience about blacks with whom they worked and had friendly relations. As Wallace's campaign became more violent in tone, many of them probably grew uneasy and fell away from his camp.

When "opinion-makers" bothered to talk with workers, they

found to their surprise that not all were racists. After talking with Wallace supporters in Flint, Michigan (said to be a hotbed of Wallace sentiment), Mike Hubbard, a student editor of the University of Michigan *Daily*, wrote:

> Certainly these Americans do not identify with red-necked racism. . . . No one ever taught them Negro History, but they grew up with blacks. . . . They don't dislike blacks, they just feel black men shouldn't be given a bigger break than anyone else. The white UAW members as a whole do not believe Wallace is a racist. All they know is what he told them, and he never said he hated blacks. Even the most militant Negro workers I talked to didn't feel there was large-scale prejudice in the Union. They dislike Wallace, but not the men who are voting for him.

Others found many Wallace supporters who would have preferred Robert Kennedy, and some even Eugene McCarthy. *Time* found many such in its 150 interviews across the country, and Haynes Johnson of *The Washington Star* reported this comment from a leader of the Wallace movement in Duluth, Minnesota: "The reason I got into this actually was when Robert Kennedy was shot. . . . That assassination—plus that of Martin Luther King—pointed up for me just how sick it was in this country, and I decided to do something for my country."

The "new issues"—the war on poverty and bureaucracy, the struggles for racial justice and world peace—can be lost unless they are paralleled by campaigns on issues that are important to those millions who are often ignored except by demagogues.

The mythology that obscures the realities of working-class life derives in large part from the success story of unions and what various observers have made of that story. Unions have made great gains in wages, working conditions, fringe benefits, politics; but they started from very far back, and they are still very far from the millennium. Since our society has been late and miserly in providing social insurance, unions have had to push hard in collective bargaining for benefits that don't show up in paychecks. Their focus on such goals has had some negative side effects. Fringe benefits mean more to older than to younger workers—and it is the young who are drawn to men like George Wallace.

Unless unions were to act irresponsibly toward the aging (one of the most impoverished and helpless groups among us), pensions had to be won. Pensions cost money, and that money was subtracted from the wage package won at the bargaining table. Also, older workers need and make more use of hospitalization, medical, and sickness insurance. These too came out of the total package, leaving less for wages. It was humane to help the older worker, and it helped him retire and make way for younger workers. But it was costly. *In the UAW alone, more than 200,000 members have retired and received pension benefits of over $1.5 billion.* Unions sometimes may have overresponded to the older workers, as in seniority and vacation benefits, but one can hardly look at the life of the aging worker and say he has too much.

Unions need to make a new beginning, paying more attention to the needs of the young. An aging and sometimes feeble union leadership needs to refresh itself with activists and new leadership recruited among younger generations. Unless the young become partners in the union movement, they may end up wrecking it. The dramatic rise in the rate of rank-and-file rejection of union contract settlements is a clear signal of distress among workers. Usually, veteran unionists report, the increased rejections result from organized opposition among young workers.

Unions need to do a lot of things, far more than I can mention in this piece. I come from a union that has split from the AFL over some of these issues, including foreign policy, interest in the poor and minorities, and general militancy. I have opposed the Vietnam war, and I think labor should have. I have been involved in the war on poverty, along with many other unionists—though it is remote from many others. Still, one observer says, "If the labor movement in this country moves to the Right, it's not least the fault of those, like Sexton, who will not say a word of criticism of its policies." I leave nothing to the imagination of readers, for we are all deeply aware of the shortcomings of unions. I do not dwell on these flaws for another reason: Whatever their blemishes, unions have given workers the only support and attention they have had—and they needed a lot.

Unions are, however, limited in what they can do for members. They are limited by their own willingness and that of their members to go into battle, to strike. They are limited by the public's willingness to accept strikes. The middle-class liberal himself is often offended, sometimes outraged, by strikers. He may say, "They're selfish and out for themselves." When the desperately poor hospital worker strikes, the liberal will see only the patient as victim; but he will offer no clues as to how else the hospital worker can win a measure of justice. When subway and sanitation workers in New York strike for a modest $3.50 or so an hour (to perform some of the most disagreeable jobs known to man), many middle-class liberals complain bitterly, without also noting that New York's affluent can afford to pay men decent wages to do hard, often dangerous, always unpleasant work.

Many liberals dismiss as unimportant, if not irrelevant, every claim workers make for their attention and support. In few cases do they distinguish workers from union leaders, for some of whom their contempt may be warranted. It is not surprising, considering their mentors, that so much of the young New Left seems to despise the working class.

Not since the early and dramatic days of the CIO have liberals and intellectuals (with some honorable exceptions) shown much sympathetic interest in workers or unions. Now workers come sharply to their view only when they threaten to make life inconvenient or dangerous. A subway strike, shutdown at *The New York Times,* a large vote for Wallace may do the trick—momentarily.

I believe that liberals and moderate leftists—in whose circle opinion-makers are heavily represented—are out of touch with the reality of American working-class life. Many of them live at rarified levels where almost everyone's income is at least $15,000 a year. *Less than ten percent of the nation's families earn that much;* still, they form a mass of between 18 and 20 million people. Those who live within it can easily come to think that all

Americans, except the poor, are living just about as they and
their colleagues and neighbors do. Having little contact outside
their own circles, and having heard so much about the great
gains of unions, they may naturally assume that workers have
made it too.

Many of these opinion-makers are men of my generation or
near it. Forgetting the ravages of inflation, they may think of
$6,000 a year as a fairly substantial income. They may remember
maintaining a modest existence on even less. I recall that I was
thirty-five years old when I first earned $5,000 a year as presi-
dent of the nation's second largest local union. Now when I hear
that auto workers gross more than $8,000, I too sometimes forget
the dollar's decline and assume they've got it made. Relative to
most other workers, they have; but they are still far from well-
off. These opinion-makers greatly influence what appears in periodicals and dailies, and what is said on TV and radio. They
often draft political platforms and write candidates' speeches.
When they don't, their readers do. They think of themselves as
open-minded and sensitive, and sometimes they are. But too
often their politics are introspective—concentrated only on issues
that touch them, plus a now-fashionable interest in the
poor. . . .

Young workers outnumber all college students, and there are
perhaps fifteen or twenty of them for every one disaffected youth
upon whom various advocates of a New Politics are counting.
The big three in auto alone employ about 250,000 workers who
are thirty or under. Total UAW membership of that age group
may reach 600,000, with perhaps half of these under twenty-five.
Among organized workers, possibly five million are young people
under thirty.

Young workers seem to be tougher and to have more staying
power than students. Their stake in social change may turn out
to be greater and more compelling. Most will never experience
the softening effects of well-paid, high-status jobs in the professional, academic, artistic, or business worlds—jobs to which most
student rebels are on their way. Knowing they're unlikely to escape individually, workers can grow desperate when denied political hope.

One pollster puts many workers in the "no change" coalition. He misunderstands. Workers simply oppose changes that benefit or seem to benefit others while increasing their own burdens.

The auto industry average wage of $3.80 per hour, though the highest in manufacturing, still does not mean affluence, The UAW (like many other unions) has won comprehensive medical protection, including coverage for psychiatric care of a million members. Its contracts now provide tuition remission plans for members who wish to take classes that may help them escape from dead-end factory jobs. In December of 1968, the hourly wage system came close to ending for perhaps a million UAW members; thus, in one industry, workers have almost scaled an important barrier between them and the middle class; they will be salaried rather than hourly workers. UAW contracts have moved toward the guaranteed annual income and retirement with decent security. Gains have been made, yes; but even auto workers still have far to go.

One friend tells me, "intellectuals still cling to a hopeful and perhaps incorrect view, idealizing the union members as an instrument of class struggle." What members and their unions try to do, at best, is not class struggle in any classic sense. Their conscious antagonists are the employer and the conservative legislator, not the "capitalist system." Yet their efforts have profoundly influenced American life. And unionists have tasted enough of victory so that they generally do not believe in the "final conflict" for which the "prisoners of starvation" must arise.

Those publicists who seek such an apocalypse will not find unionists mounting the barricades with the swiftness and pleasure of student rebels or black militants. Unionists have learned a hard lesson after almost a century of fierce bloodletting on the picket line: *That combat is the last, not the first, resort.* Unionists have possibly been too moderate in this respect, for open conflict sometimes is the only way to rally people and get what you want. But they have learned many other good ways to get on with it. They will not be found burning down their own neighborhoods to prove a point, or otherwise sacrificing their own ranks in unproductive, self-destructive conflict. In this respect, interestingly, some black militants seem to be taking a rather active interest in labor studies. Most militants, coming from poor families, are interested in the "old issues" (opportunity, jobs, etc.) and in ways of organizing people for effective action. A similar interest in unions has not come to the campus, thanks to the myth of the middle-class worker and other academic folklore.

Workers and their unions have many problems and they need lots of help. On the other side, the middle-class Left may find itself isolated if it accepts the standard mythology about workers. If they are to create a New Society, liberals and radicals need to become aware of socially excluded workers and find avenues of communication with them, as well as with Negroes, Latin Americans, and the oppressed poor generally.

[1969]

BLACK STUDIES:

Trouble Ahead

by Eugene D. Genovese

No problem so agitates the campuses today as that posed by the growing pressure for black studies programs and departments. The agitation presents special dangers since it can be, and sometimes is, opportunistically manipulated by the nihilist factions of the radical white student movement. For the most part, black students have shown considerable restraint in dealing with dubious white allies and have given strong indication of being much more interested in reforming the universities than in burning them down. The black student movement, like some parts of the white radical student movement and very much unlike others, represents an authentic effort by young people to take a leading role in the liberation of an oppressed people and, as such, exhibits impressive seriousness and developing sophistication. The political forms that the agitation takes and the deep frustrations from which it stems nonetheless open the way to reckless elements among black, as well as white, student militants.

The universities must now choose between three courses: a principled but flexible response to legitimate black demands; a dogmatic, repressive adherence to traditional, liberal, and essentially racist policies; and a cowardly surrender to all black demands, no matter how destructive to the university as an institution of higher learning or to American and Afro-American society in general. This last option, which has been taken in a notable number of places, ironically reflects as much racism in its assumptions and implications as the second, and it takes little skill in prophecy to realize that its conclusion will be a bloodbath in which blacks are once again the chief victims. Yet the debate over black studies proceeds without attention to the major features of the alternatives; it proceeds, in fact, in a manner that suggests the very paternalistic white racism against which so many blacks are today protesting.

The demand for black studies and for special black studies departments needs no elaborate explanation or defense. It rests on an awareness of the unique and dual nature of the black experience in the United States. Unlike European immigrants, blacks came here involuntarily, were enslaved and excluded from access to the mainstream of American life, and as a result have had a special history with a profoundly national-cultural dimension. Unlike, say, Italo-Americans, Afro-Americans have within their history the elements of a distinct nationality at the same time that they have participated in and contributed immensely to a common American nationality. Despite the efforts of many black and some white scholars, this paradoxical experience has yet to be explored with the respect and intellectual rigor it deserves.

This essential justification for black studies, incidentally, raises serious questions about the demands by white radicals for "ethnic studies" and for special attention to people from the "third world," especially since the term "third world" is, from a Marxist and revolutionary point of view, a reactionary swindle. These demands, when sincere, have their origin in a proper concern for the fate of Mexican-Americans, Puerto Ricans, Asians, and other ethnic groups in a white-racist culture, but the study of the attendant problems does not, at least on the face of it, require anything like an approach similar to that of black studies. For the most part, the discrimination against these groups is largely a class question, requiring sober analysis of class structure in America; for the rest, much of the racism directed against these minorities can be traced directly to the by-products of the enslavement of blacks by whites and the ideology derived therefrom. In any case, the issues are clearly different, for the black question is simultaneously one of class and nationality (not merely minority ethnic status), and it is therefore a disservice to the cause of black liberation to construct a politically opportunist equation that can only blur the unique and central quality of the black experience in the United States.

The duality of the black experience haunts the present debate and leads us immediately into a consideration of the ideological and political features of the black studies programs. It is, at best, irrelevant to argue, as DeVere E. Pentony does in the April 1969 issue of the *Atlantic,* that all professors of history and social science bring a particular ideology and politics to their classroom and that a black ideological bias is no worse than any other. There is no such thing as a black ideology or a black point of view. Rather there are various black-nationalist biases, from left-wing versions such as that of the Panthers to right-wing versions such as that of Ron Karenga and other "cultural nationalists." There are also authentic sections of the black community that retain conservative, liberal, or radical integrationist and antinationalist positions. Both integrationist and separatist tendencies can be militant or moderate, radical or conservative (in the sense generally applied to white politics in relation to social questions). The separatists are riding high today, and the integrationists are beating a retreat; but this has happened before and may be reversed tomorrow. All these elements have a right to participate in the exploration of black historical and cultural themes. In one sense, the whole point of black studies programs in a liberal arts college or university ought to be to provide for the widest and most vigorous exchange among all these groups in an atmosphere of free discussion and mutual toleration. The demand for an exclusively black faculty and especially the reactionary demand for student control of autonomous departments must be understood as demands for the introduction of specific ideological and political criteria into the selection of faculty and the composition of programs. Far from being proposals to relate these programs to the black community, they are in fact factionally based proposals to relate them to one or another political tendency within the black community and to exclude others. The bloody, but by no means isolated, feud between black student factions on the UCLA campus ought to make that clear.

One of the new hallmarks of white racism is the notion of one black voice, one black experience, one black political community, one black ideology—of a black community without an authentic inner political life, wracked by dissension and ideological struggle. In plain truth, what appears on the campuses as "what the blacks want" is almost invariably what the dominant faction in a particular black caucus wants. Like all people who fight for liberation, blacks are learning the value of organizational discipline and subordination to a firm and united line of action. Sometimes, the formulation of particular demands and actions has much less to do with their intrinsic merits or with the institution under fire than with the momentary balance in the struggle for power within the caucus itself. This discipline presents nothing unprincipled or sinister, but it does present difficult and painful problems, which must be evaluated independently by those charged with institutional and political responsibility in the white community.

The pseudo-revolutionary middle-class totalitarians who constitute one temporarily powerful wing of the left-wing student movement understand this dimension, even if few others seem to. Accordingly, they support demands for student control as an entering wedge for a general political purge of faculties, a purge they naïvely hope to dominate. These suburban putschists are most unlikely to succeed in their stated objectives of purging "reactionaries," for they are isolated, incoherent, and without adequate power. But they may very well help to reestablish the principle of the campus purge and thereby provide a moral and legal basis for a new wave of McCarthyism. The disgraceful treatment of Professors Staughton Lynd and Jesse Lemisch, among many who have been recently purged from universities by both liberal and right-wing pressure, has already set a tone of renewed repression, which some fanatical and unreasoning left-wing militants are unwittingly reinforcing. If black studies departments are permitted to become political bases and cadre-training schools for one or another political movement, the door will be open for the conversion of other departments to similar roles; that door is already being forced in some places.

Those blacks who speak in harsh nationalist accents in favor of all-black faculties, departmental autonomy, and student power open themselves to grave suspicions of bad faith. The most obvious objection, raised sharply by several outstanding black educators in the South, concerns the systematic raiding of black colleges by financially stronger white ones. The shortage of competent black specialists in black history, social science, and black culture is a matter of general knowledge and concern. Hence, the successful application of the all-black principle in most universities would spell the end of hopes to build one or more distinguished black universities to serve as a center for the training of a national Afro-American intelligentsia. One need not be partial to black nationalism in any of its varieties to respect the right of black people to self-determination, for this right flows directly from the duality of their unique experience in the United States. Even those who dislike or distrust black nationalism as such should be able to view the development of such centers of higher education as positive and healthy. If there is no place in the general American university for ideological homogeneity and conformity, there is a place in American society for universities based on adherence to a specific ideology, as the Catholic universities, for example, have demonstrated.

Responsible black scholars have been working hard for an end to raiding and to the scattering of the small number of black professors across the country. Among other obstacles, they face the effort of ostensibly nationalist black students who seek to justify their decision to attend predominantly white institutions, often of high prestige, by fighting for a larger black teaching staff. The outcome of these demands is the obscurantist nonsense that black studies can and should be taught by people without intellectual credentials since these credentials are "white" anyway. It is true that many black men are capable of teaching important college-level courses even though they do not have formal credentials. For example, the Afro-American tradition in music, embracing slave songs, spirituals, blues, jazz, and other forms, could probably be taught best by a considerable number of articulate and cultured, if sometimes self-taught, black musicians and freelance critics who are largely unknown to the white community. But few good universities have ever refused to waive formalities in any field when genuine intellectual credentials of a non-academic order could be provided. What has to be resisted firmly is the insanity that claims, as in one recent instance, that experience as a SNCC field organizer should be considered more important than a Ph.D. in the hiring of a professor of Afro-American history. This assertion represents a general contempt for all learning and a particular contempt for black studies as a field of study requiring disciplined, serious intellectual effort—an attitude that reflects the influence of white racism, even when brought forth by a black man.

The demand for all-black faculties rests on the insistence that only blacks can understand the black experience. This cant is nothing new: It forms the latest version of the battle cry of every reactionary nationalism and has clear antecedents, for example, in the nineteenth-century German Romantic movement. To be perfectly blunt, it now constitutes an ideologically fascist position and must be understood as such. The general reply to it —if one is necessary—is simply that the history of every people can only be written from within and without. But there is a specific reply too. However much the black presence has produced a unique and distinctly national Afro-American experience, it has also formed part of a broader, integrated national culture. It would be absurd to try to understand the history of, say, the South without carefully studying black history. Any Southern historian worth his salt must also be a historian of black America —and vice versa—and if so, it would be criminal to deny him an opportunity to teach his proper subject. Certainly, these remarks do not add up to an objection to a preference for black departmental directors and a numerical predominance of blacks on the faculty, if possible, for every people must write its own history and play the main role in the formation of its own intelligentsia and national culture. These measures would be justified simply on grounds of the need to establish relations of confidence with black students, for they involve no sacrifice of principle and do not compromise the integrity of the university. But preference and emphasis are one thing; monopoly and ideological exclusion are quite another.

We might mention here the problem of the alleged "psychological need" of black people to do this or that or to be this or that in order to reclaim their manhood, reestablish their ostensibly lost dignity, and God knows what else. There is a place for these questions and in certain kinds of intellectual discussions and in certain political forums, but there is no place for these questions in the formation of university policy. In such a context they represent a benevolent paternalism that is neither more nor less than racist. Whites in general and university professors and administrators in particular are not required to show "sympathy," "compassion," "understanding," and other manifestations of liberal guilt feelings; they are required to take black demands seriously—to take them straight, on their merits. That is, they are required to treat political demands politically and to meet their responsibility to fight white racism while also meeting their responsibility to defend the integrity and dignity of the university community as a whole.

Only if the universities have a clear attitude toward themselves will they be able to fulfill their duty to the black community. Our universities, if they are to survive—and their survival is problematical—must redefine themselves as institutions of higher learning and firmly reject the role of cadre-training schools for government, business, or community organizations of any kind. Blame for the present crisis ought to be placed on those who, especially after World War II, opened the universities to the military, to big-business recruitment, to the "fight against Communism," to the CIA, and to numerous other rightist pressures. If Dow Chemical or ROTC belongs on a college campus, so does the Communist Party, the Black Panthers, the John Birch Society, the Campfire Girls, or the Mafia for that matter. Students have a clear political right to organize on campuses as Democrats, Republicans, Communists, Panthers, or whatever, provided their activities are appropriate to campus life, but the universities have no business making special institutional arrangements with this or that faction off campus and then putting down other factions as illicit. And government and business represent political intrusions quite as much as do political parties. The same is true for the anachronistic and absurd practice of having American universities controlled by boards of trustees instead of by their faculties in consultation with the students. In short, the black studies question, like the black revolt as a whole, has raised all the fundamental problems of class power in American life, and the solutions will have to run deep into the structure of the institutions themselves.

What the universities owe to black America is what they owe to white America: an atmosphere of freedom and dissent for the pursuit of higher learning. Black people have largely been excluded in the past, for the atmosphere has been racist, the history and culture of black people have been ignored or caricatured, and access to the universities themselves has been severely circumscribed. Black studies programs, shaped in a manner consistent with such traditional university values as ideological freedom and diversity, can help to correct this injustice. So can scholarships and financial assistance to black students and special facilities for those blacks who wish to live and work with some degree of ethnic homogeneity. But no university is required to surrender its basic standards of competence in the selection of faculty or the admission of students. If not enough black students are equipped to enter college today, it is because of atrocious conditions in lower education. The universities can take a few steps to correct this injustice, but the real fight must take place elsewhere in society and must be aimed at providing black communities with the financial resources, independence, and autonomy necessary to educate their people properly from the earliest appropriate ages. There are limits to what a particular institution like a university can do, and it dare not try to solve problems that can be solved only by the political institutions of society as a whole. And above all, no university need surrender its historical role and essential content in order to right the wrongs of the whole political and social system; it need only reform itself to contribute to a solution of the broader problems in a manner consistent with its character as a place of higher learning with limited functions, possibilities, and responsibilities.

Black studies programs have two legitimate tasks. First, they can, by their very nature, provide a setting within which black people can forge an intelligentsia equipped to provide leadership on various levels of political and cultural action. Black studies programs themselves can do only part of this job. For that reason many able and sophisticated sections of the Black Student Alliance organizations wisely call on their brothers and sisters to participate in these programs, but also to specialize in medicine, engineering, sociology, economic analysis, or in fact any scientific or humanistic field. They know that only the emergence of a fully developed intelligentsia, with training in every field of knowledge, can ultimately meet the deepest needs of the black community. In this respect, notwithstanding strong elements of nihilism in their own organizations, their seriousness, maturity, discipline, and realism stand in striking contrast to the childish anti-intellectualism of those bourgeois whites who currently claim to speak for the radical student movement and who impose upon it their own version of generational revolt.

Second, black studies can help immeasurably to combat the racism of white students. The exclusion of whites from the faculty and student body of the black studies programs would therefore defeat half the purpose of the programs themselves. Undoubtedly, there are problems. To the extent that black students view these courses as places of refuge where they can rap with their brothers, they are certain to resent the white presence, not to mention a possible white numerical predominance among the student body. Black students who want an exclusively black setting are entitled to it—in a black university. They are not entitled to tear any institution apart to suit their present mood. The universities owe black people a chance to get a liberal or technical education, but that debt can only be paid in a way consistent with the proper role of the university in society. Beyond that, no university may safely go. If it tries, the result can only be the end of any worthwhile higher education. The inability of so many radical whites to grasp this obvious point is especially galling. It ought to be obvious that the elite schools will protect themselves from this kind of degradation, even if they continue to accept the degradation that accompanies complicity with the war machine and with big business. It is the others—the ones serving the working-class and lower-middle-class youth—that will perish or be transformed into extensions of low-grade high schools. Universities must resist the onslaught now being made against them by superficially radical bourgeois students who have exploited the struggles over black studies programs to advance their own tactical objectives. Fortunately, these elements do not speak for the radical student movement as a whole but represent only a tendency within it; the internal diversity of organizations like SDS, for example, far exceeds the level revealed in the press.

No matter how painful some of the battles are or will become, the advent of black studies programs represents a momentous step toward the establishment of relations of equality between white and black intellectuals. But if these programs are to realize their potential in support of black liberation and in the fostering of genuinely free and critical scholarship, our universities must resolve honestly the questions of limits and legitimacy. Those who blindly ignore or cynically manipulate these questions, and the reforms they imply, corrupt the meaning of black studies and risk the destruction of institutions necessary to the preservation of freedom in American life.

[1969]

THE CASE FOR PROFESSIONALISM

by Robert Brustein

---

*In such a state of society [a state of democratic anarchy],
the master fears and flatters his scholars, and the scholars
despise their masters and tutors; young and old are alike;
and the young man is on a level with the old, and is ready
to compete with him in word and deed; and old men
condescend to the young and are full of pleasantry
and gaiety; they are loth to be thought morose and authoritative, and therefore they adopt the manners of
the young. . . .*

PLATO, *The Republic,* BOOK VIII

Among the many valuable things on the verge of disintegration
in contemporary America is the concept of professionalism—by
which I mean to suggest a condition determined by training, experience, skill, and achievement (by remuneration, too, but this
is secondary). In our intensely Romantic age, where so many activities are being politicalized and objective judgments are con-
tinually colliding with subjective demands, the amateur is exalted as a kind of democratic culture hero, subject to no
standards or restrictions. This development has been of concern
to me because of its impact upon my immediate areas of interest
—the theater and theater training—but its consequences can be
seen everywhere, most conspicuously in the field of liberal education. If the amateur is coequal—and some would say, superior

—to the professional, then the student is coequal or superior to the professor, and "the young man," as Plato puts it in his discourse on the conditions that lead to tyranny, "is on a level with the old, and is ready to compete with him in word and deed."

As recently as five years ago, this proposition would have seemed remote; today, it has virtually become established dogma, and its implementation is absorbing much of the energy of the young. Although student unrest was originally stimulated, and rightly so, by such external issues as the war in Vietnam and the social grievances of the blacks and the poor, it is now more often aroused over internal issues of power and influence in the university itself. Making an analogy between democratic political systems and the university structure, students begin by demanding a representative voice in the "decisions that affect our lives," including questions of faculty tenure, curriculum changes, grading, and academic discipline. As universities begin to grant some of these demands, thus tacitly accepting the analogy, the demands escalate to the point where students are now insisting on a voice in electing the university president, a role in choosing the faculty, and even a place on the board of trustees.

I do not wish to comment here on the validity of individual student demands—certainly, a student role in university affairs is both practical and desirable, as long as that role remains advisory. Nor will I take the time to repeat the familiar litany of admiration for the current student generation—it has, to my mind, already been sufficiently praised, even overpraised, since for all its intrinsic passion, intelligence, and commitment, the proportion of serious, gifted, hardworking students remains about what it always was (if not actually dwindling, for reasons I hope soon to develop). I do want, however, to examine the analogy, which is now helping to politicize the university, and scholarship itself, because it seems to me full of falsehood.

Clearly, it is absurd to identify electoral with educational institutions. To compare the state with the academy is to assume that the primary function of the university is to govern and to rule. While the relationship between the administration and the faculty does have certain political overtones, the faculty and administration can no more be considered the elected representatives of the student body than the students—who were admitted after voluntary application on a selective and competitive basis—can be considered freeborn citizens of a democratic state: The relationship between teacher and student is strictly tutorial. Thus, the faculty member functions not to represent the student's interests in relation to the administration, but rather to communicate knowledge from one who knows to one who doesn't. That the reasoning behind this analogy has not been more frequently questioned indicates the extent to which some teachers are refusing to exercise their roles as professionals. During a time when all authority is being radically questioned, faculty members are becoming more reluctant to accept the responsibility of their wisdom and experience and are, therefore, often willing to abandon their authoritative position in order to placate the young.

The issue of authority is a crucial one here, and once again we can see how the concept of professionalism is being vitiated by false analogies. Because *some* authority is cruel, callow, or indifferent (notably the government in its treatment of certain urgent issues of the day), the Platonic *idea* of authority comes under attack. Because some faculty members are remote and pedantic, the credentials of distinguished scholars, artists, and intellectuals are ignored or rejected, and anyone taking charge of a classroom or a seminar is open to charges of "authoritarianism." This explains the hostility of many students toward the lecture course—where an "authority" communicates the fruits of his research, elaborating on unclear points when prodded by student questioning (still a valuable pedagogical technique, especially for beginning students, along with seminars and tutorials). Preferred to this, and therefore replacing it in some departments, is the discussion group or "bull session," where the student's opinion about the material receives more attention than the material itself, if indeed the material is still being treated. The idea—so central to scholarship—that there is an inherited body of knowledge to be transmitted from one generation to another loses favor because it puts the student in an unacceptably subordinate position, with the result that the learning process gives way to a general free-for-all in which one man's opinion is as good as another's.

The problem is exacerbated in the humanities and social sciences with their more subjective criteria of judgment; one hardly senses the same difficulties in the clinical sciences. It is unlikely (though anything is possible these days) that medical students will insist on making a diagnosis through majority vote, or that students entering surgery will refuse anesthesia because they want to participate in decisions that affect their lives and, therefore, demand to choose the surgeon's instruments or tell him where to cut. Obviously, some forms of authority are still respected, and some professionals remain untouched by the incursions of the amateur. In liberal education, however, where the development of the individual assumes such weight and importance, the subordination of mind to material is often looked on as some kind of repression. One begins to understand the current loss of interest in the past, which offers a literature and history verified to some extent by time, and the passionate concern with the immediate present, whose works still remain to be objectively evaluated. When one's educational concerns are contemporary, the material can be subordinated to one's own interests, whether political or aesthetic, as the contemporary literary journalist is often more occupied with his own ideas than with the book he reviews.

Allied to this problem, and compounding it, is the problem of the black students, who are sometimes inclined to reject the customary university curriculum as "irrelevant" to their interests, largely because of its orientation toward "white" culture and history. In its place, they demand courses dealing with the history and achievements of the black man, both in Africa and America. Wherever history or anthropology departments have failed to provide appropriate courses, this is a serious omission and should be rectified: Such an omission is an insult not only to black culture but to scholarship itself. But when black students begin clamoring for courses in black law, black business, black medicine, or black theater, then the university is in danger of becoming the instrument of community hopes and aspirations rather than the repository of an already achieved culture. It is only one more step before the university is asked to serve propaganda purposes, usually of an activist nature: A recent course, demanded by black law students at Yale, was to be called something like "white capitalist exploitation of the black ghetto poor."

On the one hand, the demand for "relevance" is an effort to make the university undertake the reparations that society should be paying. On the other, it is a form of solipsism, among both black students and white. And such solipsism is a serious threat to that "disinterestedness" that Matthew Arnold claimed to be the legitimate function of the scholar and the critic. The proper study of mankind becomes contemporary for future man; and the student focuses not on the outside world, past or present, so much as on a parochial corner of his own immediate needs. But this is childish, in addition to being Romantic, reflecting as it does the student's unwillingness to examine or conceive a world beyond the self. And here, the university seems to be paying a debt not of its own making—a debt incurred in the permissive home and the progressive school, where knowledge was usually of considerably less importance than self-expression.

In the schools, particularly, techniques of education always seemed to take precedence over the material to be communicated; lessons in democracy were frequently substituted for training in subjects; and everyone learned to be concerned citizens, often at the sacrifice of a solid education. I remember applying for a position many years ago in such a school. I was prepared to teach English literature, but was told no such subject was being offered. Instead, the students had a course called *Core,* which was meant to provide the essence of literature, history, civics, and the like. The students sat together at a round table to dramatize their essential equality with their instructor; the instructor—or rather, the coordinator, as he was called—remained completely unobtrusive; and instead of determining answers by investigation or the teacher's authority, they were decided upon by majority vote. I took my leave in haste, convinced that I was witnessing democracy totally misunderstood. That misunderstanding has invaded our institutions of higher learning.

For the scholastic habits of childhood and adolescence are now being extended into adulthood. The graduates of the *Core* course, and courses like it, are concentrating on the development of their "life styles," chafing against restrictions of all kinds (words like "coercion" and "co-option" are the current jargon), and demanding that all courses be geared to their personal requirements and individual interests. But this is not at all the function of the university. As Paul Goodman has observed, in *The Community of Scholars,* when you teach the child, you teach the person; when you teach the adolescent, you teach the subject through the person; *but when you teach the adult, you teach the subject.* Behind Goodman's observation lies the assumption that the university student is, or should already be, a developed personality, that he comes to the academy not to investigate his "life style" but to absorb what knowledge he can, and that he is, therefore, preparing himself, through study, research, and contemplation, to enter the community of professional scholars. In resisting this notion, some students reveal their desire to maintain the conditions of childhood, to preserve the liberty they enjoyed in their homes and secondary schools, to extend the privileges of a child- and youth-oriented culture into their mature years. They wish to remain amateurs.

One can see why Goodman has concluded that many of the university young do not deserve the name of students: They are creating conditions in which it is becoming virtually impossible to do intellectual work. In turning their political wrath from the social world, which is in serious need of reform (partly because of a breakdown in professionalism), to the academic world, which still has considerable value as a learning institution, they have determined, on the one hand, that society will remain as venal, as corrupt, as retrogressive as ever, and, on the other hand, that the university will no longer be able to proceed with the work of free inquiry for which it was founded. As an added irony, students, despite their professed distaste for the bureaucratic administration of the university, are now helping to construct—through the insane proliferation of student-faculty committees—a far vaster network of bureaucracy than ever before existed. This, added to their continual meetings, confrontations, and demonstrations—not to mention occupations and sit-ins—is leaving precious little time or energy either for their intellectual development, or for that of the faculty. As a result, attendance at classes has dropped drastically; exams are frequently skipped; and papers and reports are either late, underreserached, or permanently postponed. That the university needs improvement goes without saying. And students have been very helpful in breaking down its excesses of impersonality and attempting to sever its ties with the military-industrial complex. But students need improvement too, which they are hardly receiving through all this self-righteous bustle over power. That students should pay so much attention to this activity creates an even more serious problem: The specter of an ignorant, uninformed group of graduates or dropouts who (when they finally leave the academic sanctuary) are incompetent to deal with society's real evils or to function properly in professions they have chosen to enter.

It is often observed that the word *amateur* comes from the Latin verb "to love"—presumably because the amateur is motivated by passion rather than money. Today's amateur, however, seems to love not his subject but himself. And his assault on authority—on the application of professional standards in judgment of his intellectual development—is a strategy to keep this self-love unalloyed. The permanent dream of this nation, a dream still to be realized, has been a dream of equal opportunity —the right of each man to discover wherein he might excel. But this is quite different from that sentimental egalitarianism which assumes that each man excels in everything. There is no blinking the fact that some people are brighter than others, some more beautiful, some more gifted. Any other conclusion is a degradation of the democratic dogma and promises a bleak future if universally insisted on—a future of monochromatic amateurism in which everybody has opinions, few have facts, nobody has an idea.

[1969]

THE BLACK PANTHERS

by Theodore Draper

The Black Panther Party was formed in Oakland, California, in October 1966 by two young black nationalists, Huey P. Newton, then twenty-five, and Bobby Seale, five years older. The guiding spirit and dominant personality was—and is—Newton. His family, which he once described as "lower class, working class," moved from Louisiana, where he was born, the youngest of seven children, to California. He graduated from two-year Merritt College, in Oakland, where he met Seale. At the school they took their first step toward nationalist political activity by joining a local Afro-American Association, which soon proved insufficiently militant for them. Newton wanted to become a lawyer, Seale an actor. About a year at San Francisco Law School convinced Newton that he was not cut out to be a lawyer. Seale spent almost four years in the army, the last six months in the stockade because, he later claimed, "I opposed racism in the top brass, [in] a lieutenant colonel," and he was given a "bad conduct discharge" one month before the end of his four-year term. He then drifted from odd job to odd job without getting very far in his chosen career. One evening, during an argument at a party, Newton slashed a black auto worker with a steak knife, and spent eight months in jail for the assault. After his release, he and Seale got together again, and according to one version, Seale stimulated his renewed political activity by giving him *The*

Wretched of the Earth by Frantz Fanon to read.[1] When some of
their younger friends at Merritt formed a Soul Students Advisory
Council to demand a "black curriculum," they took an interest in
it. An incident in Berkeley apparently led them to go much further. It seems that a white policeman tried to arrest Seale for re-
citing poems from a chair at an outdoor café and thereby blocking the sidewalk. A fight ensued; no one was arrested. But
Newton and Seale thereupon decided to give up the Soul Students Advisory Council and to form a broader organization
called the Black Panther Party for Self-Defense. The panther
reference came from the symbol of the Lowndes County Freedom Organization which had been launched in Alabama six
months earlier. The name was later shortened to Black Panther
Party to emphasize a larger goal than "self-defense." While working in the Poverty Office in Oakland in October 1966, they wrote
a 10-point Platform and Program for the new party.

The Panthers seemed at first little more than another self-appointed local band of black nationalists in an urban ghetto
Their chief claims to publicity were their armed patrols which
drove through the streets of Oakland and their mannerism of
saying "right on" as often as possible.[2] Their first important con-

---

[1] Fanon is another author who might be read more carefully by some black
nationalists in America. Of the first congress of the African Cultural Society held in Paris in 1956, he wrote: "But little by little the American
Negroes realized that the essential problems confronting them were not the
same as those that confronted the African Negroes. The Negroes of Chicago
only resemble the Nigerians or the Tanganyikans in so far as they were
all defined in relation to the whites. But once the first comparisons had
been made and subjective feelings were assuaged, the American Negroes
realized that the objective problems were fundamentally heterogeneous. . . .
Negritude therefore finds its first limitation in the phenomena which take
account of the formation of the historical character of men. Negro and
African-Negro culture broke up into different entities because the men who
wished to incarnate these cultures realized that every culture is first and
foremost national, and that the problems which kept Richard Wright or
Langston Hughes on the alert were fundamentally different from those
which might confront Leopold Senghor or Jomo Kenyatta." *The Wretched
of the Earth* (New York: Grove Press, 1964), p. 216.

[2] "Well, its time for us right now to decide what we're gonna do, where
we gone do it, how we gone do it, and when we gone do it. If you ain't
decided whether if you gone do it, then go on home, right on. Because when

vert early in 1967 was Eldridge Cleaver, author of *Soul on Ice*, who, like Malcolm X, had been converted to Elijah Muhammad's Black Muslims in prison and had sided with Malcolm X after the latter's break with them. Newton impressed Cleaver, who was then working for *Ramparts*, by leading a group of armed Panthers into the office of the magazine and daring a policeman to shoot him. The police flinched that time, but in a shoot-out in Oakland in October 1967, Newton was wounded, one policeman was killed, another was wounded, and Newton was given a two-to-fifteen year sentence for manslaughter.

From this unlikely beginning, the Black Panthers have become a formidable national movement. In three years, they claimed to have set up about thirty chapters, the largest in the Oakland-San Francisco area and Chicago, which may have had a membership of about five thousand at its peak, but this was probably cut to about half or less by the end of 1969 as a result of police persecution. Besides Cleaver, the movement was able to win over, though only for a time, such well-known figures as H. Rap Brown and Stokely Carmichael of SNCC. It entered into a coalition with the white-based Peace and Freedom Party, which ran Cleaver for President in the 1968 election. Its program of black nationalism was endorsed by the Students for a Democratic Society in March 1969, and it precipitated the SDS split in June that same year. It is allied with a new League of Revolutionary Black Workers, which has sprung up in the automobile industry and particularly threatens the United Auto Workers' Union. It has provided much of the inspiration, leadership, and program of the black student unions in universities, colleges, and high schools.

The Black Panther ideology, which is all that concerns us here, is only partially revealed by the official platform and rules. Point 1 of the 10-point Platform and Program adopted in October 1966 reads: "We want freedom. We want power to determine the destiny of our Black Community." Other points call for full employ-

---

we say free Huey, that's only the first step to freeing all people. . . . Huey's gonna be set free or nobody gone be free, right. Right on. If Huey can't be free what goddamn bit of difference does it make if you're free, right on. FREE HUEY NOW." (Kathleen Cleaver at the May Day 1969 rally in San Francisco, *The Black Panther,* 11 May 1969, p. 11.)

ment, decent housing, education, and the liberation of all black
prisoners from all prisons and jails. Point 10, the most nationalis-
tic, states: "We want land, bread, housing, education, clothing,
justice, and peace. And as our major political objective, a United
Nations-supervised plebiscite to be held throughout the black
colony in which only black colonial subjects will be allowed to
participate, for the purpose of determining the will of the black
people as to their national destiny." The rest of the document
hints at the meaning of this demand by quoting the justification
for secession in the Declaration of Independence of 1776. But
this was hardly a fully thought out program of black nationhood.
It left the decision to a vaguely formulated plebiscite, and even
if the "black colony" decided to "dissolve the political bands"
connecting it to the existing United States, it did not make any
effort to suggest what the next step might be.

The full Black Panther ideology emerges only in the pages of
its official organ, *The Black Panther,* published weekly in Berkeley, California, and especially in the articles, speeches, and interviews of its main leaders. Some early columns by Newton in
The Black Panther in 1967, before he was imprisoned, have been
collected in a little pamphlet. These essays show that Newton's
basic ideas were formed before his shoot-out with the Oakland
police and derived mainly from Fanon, Malcolm X, Mao Tse-
tung, and Fidel Castro.

For Newton, the "Black colony of Afro-America" has a unique
and universal mission. "The Black people in America are the
only people who can free the world, loosen the yoke of colonialism, and destroy the war machine." No other country can defeat
this "monster" as long as it continues to function. "But Black
people can make a malfunction of this machine from within." In
order to do so, however, "they must have the basic tool of liberation: the gun"—a lesson attributed to Mao Tse-tung and Malcolm X. Guerrilla warfare is the tactical method that goes with
the basic tool. As a self-styled "Vanguard Party," the Black
Panthers do not think they have to do the whole job by themselves. They need only set an example and the masses will fol-
low. Newton's own example leaves little to the imagination:
"When the masses hear that a gestapo policeman has been exe-
cuted while sipping coffee at a counter, and the revolutionary ex-

ecutioners fled without being traced, the masses will see the validity of this type of approach to resistance." The pamphlet, however, tells little about the ultimate objective beyond proposing that "Black people must now move, from the grassroots up through the perfumed circles of the Black bourgeoisie, to seize by any means necessary a proportionate share of the power vested and collected in the structure of America."

Since 1967, Black Panther ideology has become a more fully developed, if not essentially different, system. In essence, it is a hybrid made up of revolutionary black nationalism and what is by now an old friend, "Marxism-Leninism." As a result, it is not quite like any other black nationalism or any other Marxism-Leninism. For example, no other "Marxist-Leninists" have ever identified themselves with the *Lumpenproletariat,* the most rootless and degraded elements in capitalist society, whom Marx and Engels regarded as a "dangerous class" whose conditions of life destined it to play a reactionary role.[3] The peculiar "amalgam," as Trotsky would have called it, of bits and pieces from Frantz Fanon, Malcolm X, Mao Tse-tung, Ernesto Che Guevara, Régis Debray, and others, is typical of the kind of do-it-yourself Marxism-Leninism that has come into vogue.[4] It is especially charac-

---

[3] A statement by Chief of Staff David Hilliard was headed "Lumpen-Proletarian Discipline Versus Bourgeois Reactionism," the former representing the Panther ideal. (*The Black Panther,* 9 August 1969, p. 11.) Later, Hilliard wrote of "our duty as revolutionaries, as members of the lumpen proletariat (field niggers)." (Ibid., 6 September 1969, p. 2.) According to Gene Marine, Huey Newton's brother Melvin recalled that Huey from the outset "saw the Panthers even then as a potential mass movement, something that the *Lumpenproletariat* could relate to. Huey had a lot of confidence in the *Lumpenproletariat;* he believed it could be rallied to its own cause." (Gene Marine, *The Black Panthers,* New York: New American Library, 1969, p. 37.) In *The Communist Manifesto* of 1848, Marx and Engels referred to the *Lumpenproletariat* as follows: "The 'dangerous class,' the social scum, that passively rotting mass thrown off by the lowest layers of old society, may, here and there, be swept into the movement by a proletarian revolution; its conditions of life, however, prepare it far more for the part of a bribed tool of reactionary intrigue." (Section 1: "Bourgeois and Proletarians.") I know of no other self-styled Marxist or Marxist-Leninist group which has ever before tried to glorify the *Lumpenproletariat.*

[4] The Panthers are nothing if not catholic in their revolutionary taste. To the list above should be added Lumumba, Garvey, Ho Chi Minh, as well as

teristic of movements that have invited themselves into the
Marxist-Leninist tradition from the outside, bringing with them
their own national or particularist folkways and shopping among
all the current versions of the doctrine for those features or formulas which happen to suit or please them the most. In this respect Black Pantherism resembles Castroism but has gone much
farther in asserting its individuality.

Organizationally, the party also shows its hybrid makeup. It is
headed by a Central Committee, a term traditionally used in the
Communist movement. But unlike such parties, which are
headed by Secretaries or General Secretaries, the Panthers' No. 1
leader is the Minister of Defense—Huey P. Newton. The idea
that the top leadership should reside in the military commander,
who simultaneously fulfills the chief political role, derives di-

---

Marx, Lenin, Stalin, and Trotsky, judging from the following testimonials:

George Murray: "Our thinking is inspired by Che Guevara, Malcolm X,
Lumumba, Ho Chi Minh and Mao Tse-tung." (*The Black Panther*, 12 Octo-
ber 1968, p. 14.) Huey P. Newton: "Brother Mao put that quite well, and
we will follow the thoughts of Chairman Mao." (Ibid., 3 March 1969, p. 2.)
Field Marshal D. C. [Don Cox]: "And we dig on all the people that held up
the light before: Marx, Lenin, Stalin, Mao, Fidel, Che, Lumumba and
Malcolm. And we dig on all the people who are holding up the light now,
Ho Chi Minh, those brothers and sisters in Al Fatah, those bad Palestinian
Guerrillas, those comrades in arms in Asia and Latin America. . . ." (Ibid.,
20 April 1969, p. 16.) Bobby Seale: "You got your Red Books, hold your
Red Books up and tell the brothers where we getting some new ideology
from. We're saying like Huey P. Newton said, 'that we're going to follow
the thoughts of Chairman Mao.'" (Ibid., 11 May 1969, p. 11.) Ray "Masai"
Hewitt: "We dig Chairman Mao, Ho Chi Minh, we have a profound love
for Fidel Castro." (Ibid., 31 May 1969, p. 16.) For Trotsky, see footnote 9.

Toward the end of 1969, *The Black Panther*'s favorite foreign Communist seemed to be Kim Il Sung, President of North Korea, judging from
the space alloted to his statements and speeches.

As for supporting Al Fatah, the Panthers are so anti-Israel that their
organ attempted to justify the assassination of Senator Robert Kennedy
instead of President Richard Nixon or California's Governor Ronald Reagan
on the ground that "Kennedy was a fence-sitter on the Middle East situation," whereas "the Nixons and Reagans are consistent, open fascists." *The
Black Panther* explained: "But when a liberal asks for respect from third-
world people by 'helping' and then deceived them by representing enemy
interests, the liberal can expect retaliation." ("Sirhan—A Revolutionary,"
ibid., 23 March 1969, p. 14.)

rectly from Régis Debray. After Newton comes Bobby Seale, the Chairman, reminiscent of Mao Tse-tung's favorite title. The next in line is the Minister of Information, Eldridge Cleaver (in absentia). No. 4 is the Chief of Staff, David Hilliard, an ex-longshoreman. The Central Committee also contains Field Marshals (Underground); Minister of Education, Ray "Masai" Hewitt; Minister of Foreign Affairs (unnamed); Minister of Justice (unnamed); Prime Minister (unnamed); Communications Secretary, Kathleen Cleaver, wife of Eldridge Cleaver; and Minister of Culture, Emory Douglas, who is also the party's Revolutionary Artist.[5] With Newton in prison and Cleaver in exile, the two main leaders have been Seale and Hilliard. Local Panther groups duplicate the national setup with a Deputy Chief of Staff and Deputy Ministers.

What is most individual about the Black Panthers is, of course, what concerns them most—the "national liberation" of the "black colony" in the "white mother country."

The last term was apparently originated by Eldridge Cleaver —probably out of Frantz Fanon, who also used the term "mother country" for the French colonial regime. It indicates the difference between the Panthers and the Back-to-Africa nationalists. The mother country of the Panthers' black colony is white America, not Africa. Since the mother country is not Africa, there is no reason to go back to it. Without denying the existence of vestigial ties with Africa, the Panthers strongly reject and oppose the Back-to-Africa line, even in an attenuated form which they contemptuously call "cultural nationalism."

Newton has sternly disapproved of the return to African culture.

---

[5] On 11 February 1968 Eldridge Cleaver announced publicly that the Black Panthers and SNCC had "worked out a merger." SNCC sources claimed that he had gone too far and that the two groups had merely formed an "alliance." In any case, three SNCC leaders were appointed to leading posts in the Panthers' Central Committee—Stokely Carmichael as Prime Minister, H. Rap Brown as Minister of Justice, and James Forman as Minister of Foreign Affairs. Brown and Forman resigned from their posts in August 1968, Carmichael in July 1969. For a version of the Panthers-SNCC tie-up and possible misunderstanding, see Julius Lester, *Revolutionary Notes* (New York: Richard W. Baron, 1969, pp. 144–49).

Cultural nationalism deals with a return to the old culture of Africa and that we are somehow freed by identifying and returning to this culture, to the African cultural stage of the 1100s or before then. . . . Somehow they [cultural nationalists] believe that they will be free through identifying in this manner. As far as we are concerned, we believe that it's important for us to recognize our origins and to identify with the revolutionary Black people of Africa and people of color throughout the world. But as far as returning per se to the ancient customs, we don't see any necessity in this.

Other Panther leaders have been less polite. Former Minister of Education George Mason Murray has called this kind of pro-African cultural nationalism "a fixation in a people's development like a half-formed baby," "reactionary and insane and counterrevolutionary," "a bourgeois-capitalist scheme, to confuse the masses of people, so that they will not assault the city halls, the bank tellers, and managers, or seize control of community schools." A programmatic article in *The Black Panther* ridiculed the "fools running around who declare that they are 'just trying to be black' by wearing dashikis and bubas and who tell black people that they should relate to African customs and African heritage that we left 300 years ago, that this will make them free, that reading black history will make them better."

Ironically, therefore, the Panthers have decided that the emphasis on Black Studies programs has gone too far. In May 1969 the present Minister of Education, Ray "Masai" Hewitt, denounced Black Studies as a "new trick bag." He told of having talked with "many brothers from Africa" who "are not hung up on Swahili or Arabic." Of the new vogue for the "natural head," he reported: "Very few of the African brothers that we met had what could be called a 'Natural head.' They just had hair. You couldn't call it one of those custom-tailored natural heads. They never spoke Swahili and every time we told them that there were brothers here studying Swahili for the revolution, they burst out laughing." He added: "The movement toward Black Studies in colleges and other Black cultural programs have become a fixation. At one point in the revolutionary development of our people it was a revolutionary step. Instead of taking it as a beginning step many cultural nationalist opportunist boot-licking cowards and freaks have latched onto it."

The nationalist side of the Panthers' ideology makes them emphasize black unity; the "Marxist-Leninist" side makes them emphasize a social revolution by both blacks and whites. Unlike other nationalist groups, the Panthers do not believe that the "black colony" can liberate itself alone. "We have two evils to fight, capitalism and racism," Newton says. "We must destroy both racism and capitalism." The Panthers realize that they cannot destroy capitalism and install socialism in the black community without destroying capitalism and installing socialism in the white community. As a programmatic statement put it: "There must be a revolution in the white mother country, led by white radicals and poor whites, and national liberation in the black and third-world colony here in America. We can't triumph in the colony alone because that is just like cutting one finger off a hand. It still functions, you dig it. No, when we deal with this monster we must deal with it totally."

This suggests that the Panthers expect the black nationalist revolution to be part of, or accompanied by, a larger white social revolution. In this respect, therefore, they do not belong in the line of pure black nationalist movements, such as Garvey's. In fact, by the summer of 1969, Newton seemed to be appealing to all "people," not merely to black people. In a significant restatement of his party's position in a Negro magazine of mass circulation, he immediately struck a populist, rather than a nationalist, note: "The Black Panther Party is the people's party. We are fundamentally interested in one thing, that is, freeing all people from all forms of slavery in order that every man will be his own master." He blamed capitalism for all that was wrong, and made socialism the precondition for freedom of any kind, including self-determination. "All members of the working class must seize the means of production," he wrote. "This, naturally, includes black people." He might have added that this, naturally, includes even more white people. Though the Black Panthers remained a purely black organization, its leaders found a way around that restriction, too. In July 1969, they sponsored a National Conference for a United Front Against Fascism in Oakland, California, out of which came local National Committees to Combat Fascism. One black-nationalist organ noted caustically that over ninety percent of those attending the Oakland conference were white. These National Committees were designed to take in whites, especially those who, as Chairman Seale put it, had been asking why they could not join the Panther Party. "We see the National Committees as the political organizing bureaus of the Black Panther Party," Seale declared. In another period, these committees might have been called front organizations, but something was different—this was a black movement with a white front instead of a white movement with a black front. At the conference itself, Seale also disclosed that the Panthers favored creating a "new party, the new workers' party, or what have you," on the model of the "liberation fronts" in Africa and Latin America, "an American Liberation Front composed of all the people of this nation." The National Committees were presumably conceived as "organizing bureaus" of the new party as well as of the Black Panther Party.

Thus the Panthers had changed in three short years from a largely black nationalist organization to a black revolutionary organization, and the latter in turn had led it to become a black organization with white appendages. Nevertheless, at the Oakland conference and elsewhere, Panther leaders have always made clear that they consider themselves to be the vanguard of the social as well as of the nationalist revolution. Those white organizations which recognize their leadership must expect the treatment meted out to the Students for a Democratic Society at the Oakland conference. When the SDS delegates objected to the Panther proposal for "community control of the police," they were given a dose of the special brand of Pantherite polemics. Seale soon called them "those little bourgeois, snooty nose motherfucking S.D.S's." [6] Only that faction in the SDS which was willing to accept this type of "criticism" and come back for more

---

[6] Panther political style is *sui generis*. In his rebuke of the SDS, Seale continued: ". . . And that we're gonna kick their motherfucking ass, if they don't freeze on their shit, and we want to make that clear to them. . . . And we'll beat those little sissies, those little school boy's ass if they don't try to straighten up their politics. So we want to make that known to S.D.S. and the first motherfucker that gets out of order had better stand in line for some kind of disciplinary actions from the Black Panther Party." (*The Black Panther*, 9 August 1969, p. 12.) Another Panther leader once defined the revolution as follows: "The only way we can do this is to pick up the

was permitted to remain in the Panthers' good graces. The Panthers' relations with various white organizations and groups have varied from time to time. At the Oakland conference, the Panthers found the official American Communist Party most useful, and a well-known party intellectual, Dr. Herbert Aptheker, who has specialized in American Negro history, was permitted to make an interminable theoretical address to the meeting. Seale later explained that the American Communists had taken the Panther's criticism to heart and had done more work for the conference than any other white organization.[7]

Despite these good marks for the American Communists, the Panthers' favorite white revolutionary group continued to be the Young Patriots, a band of transplanted young Southerners located in Chicago. Another Chicago-based group, the Young Lords Organization, originally a street gang in a Puerto Rican community, has also been recognized by the Panthers as authentically revolutionary. A Chinese-American "Red Guard" in San Francisco has copied the Panthers' style and program, and there is an American Indian satellite group known as NARP.

This Pantherite shift in line—or, at least, in emphasis—was primarily behind the resignation of Stokely Carmichael. In June 1967, Carmichael had been the beneficiary of Executive Mandate

---

gun. We are gonna walk all across this motherfucking government and say Stick 'em up, motherfuckers—this is a hold up: we come to get everything that belongs to us." (Virgil Morrell, Ibid., 12 October 1968, p. 5.) And in an order purging nineteen members from the Jersey City branch: "The Party will no longer tolerate these counterrevolutionary m——f——s, who by their deeds are harming the interest of the Party and the People. These degenerates have aroused the anger of the people, the people will kill them, and we gonna kill every m——f—— who went along with their s——t." (Ibid., 4 May 1969, p. 7.) The language of "Marxism-Leninism" was never like this.

[7] Seale's exact words were: "And that's just a fascist pig tactic to try to say that the Black Panther Party is led by the Communist Party, and we're not against Communism—we dig Communism. And we have criticisms of the American Communist Party, and lately they're relating to the criticism because we told them they had to put more things into practice, and it seems that they did better than some of the other organizations, because they actually came out and did some degree of work to put the conference over, when we sat down and talked to them." (*The Black Panther,* 9 August 1969, p. 13.)

(as Minister of Defense Newton's early *pronunciamentos* were called) No. 2. In recognition of his distinguished services "in the struggle for the total liberation of Black people from oppression in racist white America," it had invested him with the rank of Field Marshal. In February 1968, Carmichael was elevated to the largely ornamental post of Prime Minister. But Carmichael had come into the Panthers from SNCC, which he had purged of all whites during his chairmanship. He never seems to have been reconciled to the Panthers' idea of coalition with white organizations, let alone a black-white social revolution, and the break on this issue came in July 1969. From his self-imposed "exile" in Guinea, Carmichael charged that the Panthers were "dogmatic, dishonest, vicious and in collusion with whites"—of which derelictions the last was probably the least forgivable. Carmichael charged: "The alliances formed by the party are alliances which I cannot politically agree with, because the history of Africans living in the U.S. has shown that any premature alliance with white radicals has led to complete subversion of blacks by the whites through their direct or indirect control of the black organizations." Cleaver answered for the Panthers that "you cats in SNCC" suffered from a "paranoid fear" of whites because they had had to wrest control of their organization from whites, unlike the Panthers, who had never been in that situation. In fact, the difference between them was not so much that of white control of black organizations as of a black-against-white nationalist revolution versus a black-and-white social-plus-nationalist revolution. The Panthers' "coalitions" with whites have thus far been arranged on the Panthers' terms, though Carmichael obviously doubted that they could continue to have their way in a white-black mass movement "of all the people of this nation." Once Carmichael broke away from the Panthers, he was denounced as nothing more than "a running dog and a lackey."

The loss of Carmichael to the Panthers was less important for the man than for the policy which he represented. The Carmichael-Cleaver dispute reminded one black nationalist editor of the Garvey-Du Bois feud almost fifty years earlier. In both cases, pure-and-simple black nationalism that totally rejected whites was opposed by a more complex and social-minded black nationalism which linked the fates of black and white. In this sense, a historic rift in black nationalism was taking a new but no less irreconcilable form.

Nevertheless, the membership of the Panthers is wholly black, and for that reason they may stand or fall on the persuasiveness of their black nationalist program. Yet it is precisely in this area that they are ideologically most vague and uncertain.

The original proposal in the Platform and Program of October 1966—to hold a United Nations-supervised plebiscite—was clearly an evasion of the issue. It is, of course, highly improbable that the U.N. would or could hold such a plebiscite; at best the proposal passed the problem on to the black voters; and it did not tell them how the Panthers wanted them to vote. There is reason to believe that this evasiveness was deliberate and that the Panther strategists considered any more concrete position premature. At a Peace and Freedom Party forum on 11 February 1968, Cleaver remarked: "It's very important to realize that in moving to gain power, you do not conceal or repudiate the land question, you hold it in abeyance. What you're saying is that we must first get ourselves organized, and then we can get some of this land." Since then, the Panther leaders seem to have had a hard time making up their minds. In an early phase, Newton would go no farther than: "Our problem is unity at this point. We have to unify ourselves. We can handle the colony better than anyone else. We are a colonized people. Many Black communities are like decentralized colonies throughout this country." But what this implied for black American nationhood, he did not say.

A later effort by Chairman Seale at the Anti-Fascist Conference in Oakland in July 1969 was also somewhat tantalizing, if seemingly more definite:

> We are not saying that self-determination of the black people in the black communities is not correct. It is necessary. But we are not saying that black people are a nation just because they are black. We are saying that black people are a nation because they have the same economic oppression that they are subjected to; because they have, number two, a basic psychological makeup in how they react to that environment they exist in; third, because

they describe what's happening; because black people in the black community, understanding genocide (with number 4 coming up) that the language, psychological makeup, economic conditions and the (4) geographical location that black people exist in, generally defined as ghettos. The geographical location defines, with all four of those points, black people as a nation, defines Mexican American people as a nation where they are. Whether they're split or divided because we are colonialized, because the Third World people are colonialized. That's what defines a nation. We are not basing it on racism. We understand nationalism in terms of what a nation is, and we understand internationalism.[8]

Whatever may be thought of Seale's reasons, this statement seemed to commit him to the proposition that there was a black nation in the United States, as well as a Mexican-American nation, even if they were made up of congeries of far-flung ghettos.[8] Soon afterward, Chief-of-Staff Hilliard added a new note for which he may go down in history as the originator of a genuinely novel concept in the annals of international socialism. He was talking about the SDS opposition to the Pantherite demand for community control or decentralization of the police, when it occurred to him to say:

To decentralize the community imperialists, and implement probably on just the community level—Socialism. And that's probably too Marxist-Leninist for those motherfuckers to understand, but we think that Stalin was very clear in this concept—that socialism could be implemented in one country, we say it can be implemented in one community.

And so, if Stalin could have "socialism in one country," the Panthers, if their Chief of Staff can be trusted, see no reason why they cannot have "socialism in one community."[9]

[8] I have thought it best to give Seale's statement in his own words. *The Black Panther*'s practice of publishing verbatim texts of verbal statements makes for colorful if sometimes confusing reading.

[9] This is not the first time that Hilliard invoked the name of Stalin. He had previously "discovered" Stalin, Lenin, and Trotsky in the following way:

After all this, however, the Panthers' maximum leader, Huey P. Newton, published an article in August 1969 in which he explicitly referred to the blacks in America as a "national minority" and, inferentially, as an "ethnic minority," not a nation. He demanded the freedom "to structure our own communities so that we can determine the institutions of the community that will perpetuate our culture." But it would clearly make a difference to that structure if it were based on the concept of a nation or merely of a national minority.

In September 1969, Newton also decided to change his mind —or at least his "rhetoric"—on what being "colonized" meant. "At one time I thought that only Blacks were colonized," he announced. "But I think we have to change our rhetoric to an extent because the whole American people have been colonized, if you view exploitation as a colonized effect, now they're exploited." In effect, Newton had decided to equate "colonization" with "exploitation." Inasmuch as the whole American people were to his mind "exploited," they were at the same time "colonized." In effect, the change in "rhetoric" enlarged the formerly "black colony" to take in the whole American people, black and white. By enlarging it to take in everyone, Newton effectively emptied the concept of an internal American "colony" of all specific content. If "colonization" means nothing more than "exploitation," there is really no need of the former. Far from making the concept of "colony" more inclusive, the concept of "exploitation" does away with it altogether.

At about the same time, Newton argued that even a separate black America of five or six states could not survive if the rest of the United States remained capitalistic. "We also take into consideration the fact that if Blacks at this very minute were able to secede the union, and say have five states, or six states [sic]. It would be impossible to function in freedom side by side with

---

". . . Our whole thing about discovering the triumvirate of Lenin, Trotsky, and Stalin. It is just a matter of trying to give a very complete picture of history. . . . The reason that they fear Joseph Stalin is because of the distorted facts that they have gained through the Western press. The one thing that we respect about Stalin, is that Stalin was able to capture the will of the people." (*The Black Panther,* 20 April 1969, p. 18.) One wonders whether Stalin or Trotsky would be more displeased by the company he was made to keep.

a capitalistic imperialistic country." He implied that enclaves and ghettos made for good "strategy" but might not make for good nationhood:

> In other words we're not really handling this question at this time because we feel that for us that it is somewhat premature, that I realize the physiological value of fighting for a territory. But at this time the Black Panther Party feels that we don't want to be in an enclave type situation where we would be more isolated than we already are now. We're isolated in the ghetto areas, and we think this is a very good location as far as strategy is concerned, as far as waging a strong battle against the established order.

The Panther ideologists, if they can be called that, have thus struggled not too successfully with the "nation" that is presumably inherent in their "nationalism." The only one who has tackled the hardest question—the problem of the land—has been Eldridge Cleaver. He once tried to deal directly with "The Land Question and Black Liberation." At one point he came close to what the trouble has been: "Thus, it is not surprising that the average black man in America is schizoid on the question of his relationship to the nation as a whole, and there is a side of him that feels only the vaguest, most halting, tentative and even fleeting kinship with America. The feeling of alienation and dissociation is real and black people long ago would have readily identified themselves with another sovereignty had a viable one existed." Cleaver then went on to argue that no viable alternative sovereignty had ever existed. He had high praise for Marcus Garvey, but it turned out that Garvey "did not solve the specific question of Afro-America and its immediate relationship to the land beneath her feet. The practical prospect of Garvey's actually transporting blacks back to Africa turned most black people off because of a world situation and balance of power that made such a situation impossible." He gave Elijah Muhammad credit for knowing "that he had to deal with Afro-America's land hunger." But Cleaver considered Muhammad tactically wise enough to be "very careful never to identify any specific geographical location when he issued his call for land for Afro-

America." Stokely Carmichael's thesis of Black Power, Cleaver said, "does not attempt to answer the land question. It does not deny the existence of that question, but rather frankly states that at the present moment the land question cannot be dealt with, that black people must put first things first, that there are a few things that must be done before we can deal with the land question."

Yet Cleaver went on to insist: "The necessity upon Afro-America is to move, now, to begin functioning as a nation, to assume its sovereignty, to demand that that sovereignty be recognized by other nations of the world." But where? The closest Cleaver came to meeting the issue was: "Black Power must be viewed as a projection of sovereignty, an embryonic sovereignty that black people can focus on and through which they can make distinctions between themselves and others, between themselves and their enemies—in short, between the white mother country of America and the black colony dispersed throughout the continent on absentee-owned land, making Afro-America a decentralized colony. Black Power says to black people that it is possible for them to build a national organization on somebody else's land."

What is "sovereignty" without land to be sovereign of? How project "sovereignty" on "somebody else's land"? What is a "decentralized colony"? Is it made up of black ghettos in New York, Chicago, Oakland, and elsewhere, separated from each other by hundreds of miles? Is ghetto "sovereignty" a truly embryonic form of national sovereignty? It may be possible to build a national organization on somebody else's land, but how build a nation on that land?

Cleaver did not raise these questions, but he was not unaware that his notion of "embryonic sovereignty" might need some clarification. He therefore seized on what he considered to be the "parallel" between early Zionism and present-day black nationalism. The Jews, he pointed out, had also been cooped up in Eastern European ghettos. Argentina and Uganda were considered as possible sites for a Jewish homeland before the decision was finally made in favor of Palestine. The Zionists founded a virtual government in exile for a people in exile. Cleaver concluded: "They would build their organization, their government, and then later on they would get some land and set the government and the people down on the land, like placing one's hat on top of one's head. The Jews did it. It worked. So now Afro-Americans must do the same thing."

Cleaver could hardly have chosen a more unfortunate "parallel" for his cause. It is entirely based on the circumstance that the Jewish Zionists in the beginning did not have a national territorial base and were not even sure where it might be. But of one thing the Jewish Zionists were always sure—that they could not set up a national homeland in their East European ghettos. If black nationalism in the United States were prepared to get out of the American ghettos and set up a nation in Africa or elsewhere, the Zionist "parallel" might be helpful, though here again historical differences might dictate against pushing it too far. Black nationalist "Zionism" inevitably heads toward a Back-to-Africa conclusion, which Cleaver and the Black Panthers reject. The "parallel" begins promisingly but ends disastrously for American black nationalism.

In an interview with *Playboy* (October 1968) Cleaver was questioned about the plan adopted by a National Black Government Conference, which met in Detroit in April 1968 for a "Republic of New Africa" to be made up of five Southern states. "Do you think that's a viable plan?" Cleaver was asked. "I don't have any sympathy with that approach," Cleaver replied, "but the Black Panthers feel that it's a proposal black people should be polled on." From Cleaver's articles and the interview, it is hard to see just what kind of concrete, practical approach he would sympathize with.

In some ways, the Panthers have inherited the ambiguous legacy of Malcolm X. Like him, they have moved in the direction of a social rather than a purely nationalist revolution. By adding socialism to nationalism, they had to broaden their horizons to make room for whites as well as blacks, if not in their own organizations, then in some form of "alliance" and "coalition." The Panthers' position has opened them up to attacks on two sides—from those who want a pure and simple black nationalism not dependent for its ultimate success on a white social revolution and those who want a social revolution untainted by black nationalism. It has not been easy for them to maintain their uneasy equilibrium between these two camps.

[1969]

TURNING ON FOR FREEDOM

The Curious Love Affair of Sex and Socialism

by Erazim V. Kohák

My title is not a misprint. The liaison between sex and socialism, though of long standing, has always been more an affair
than a marriage. Except for occasional outbursts of passion, neither partner has been particularly eager to acknowledge the relationship. I am not thinking simply of minirevolutionaries whose
buttons proclaim MAKE LOVE NOT WAR. They are at least half in
earnest, but anyone who has ever borne arms can attest that the
two activities are by no means exclusive. Not only love but death
can be a great aphrodisiac.

There are other straws in the wind. Recently I came across an
ad in an "underground" journal, in which a self-confessed Port-
noy advertised for an "uninhibited F companion interested in
Zen, astrology, existentialism, socialism or anything mod." I
would have passed it over with a chuckle; but in the same journal the editor proclaims—quite seriously—that a silly bit of sa-
distic burlesque called *Che!* is "the *Communist Manifesto* of the
now revolution." God help the revolution and, for that matter,
sex!

There have been sexual revolutions before, as in England
under the Regency or in Germany under Weimar. Sex, it seems,
is good, wholesome fun but a bit monotonous; it needs occasional sparkling with a Cause. Yet in the past, sex has usually

come out of its excursions into Social Significance somewhat battered—though still a favorite. I am not at all sure, however, that the same can be said of social progress. Its excursions into ecstasy have been followed by Queen Victoria in one case, by Adolph Hitler in another. Historical analogies are not an argument, but our experience with *Das Kapital* suggests that it is never wise to pin social progress to any one blueprint, and it might be well to ask what the effect would be if that blueprint came from *The Amorous Drawings* of the Marquis von Bayros.

Plato included community of women among his proposals for a commune-ist society. Budding radical historians regularly supply their over-thirty-five teachers with term papers presenting Plato's *Republic* as an institutionalized sex orgy. But that is a generous misreading of the text. Plato was something of a puritan, both in his preoccupation with the passions and in his distrust of their effect on society. Like his Soviet successors, he was careful to banish all art that might arouse the passions, reserving a grudging place only for early versions of Socialist Realism and Lawrence Welk. His communal mating arrangements were certainly not designed to foster sensuous enjoyment or sexual freedom; their purpose was to protect society from passion, to restrict sex to the clinical function of assuring survival of the species. The tone is quite grim—the only thing gay about Plato was his attitude to male homosexuality. And even that was due less to any regard for sexual freedom than to his acceptance of the mores common to the Athens of his day.

Nor is Plato so unusual. In their everyday attitudes, socialist writers have regularly taken over the prevailing mores of whatever group in society was most receptive to their doctrines. In their prescriptions for the new society, however, they have usually shared Plato's distrust of passion. Marx is no exception. His Victorian contemporaries may have picked out "sexual communism" as by far the most intriguing feature of *The Communist Manifesto* and accused the Communists of having a more varied sex life than they themselves could manage but, again, the text tells a different story.

Marx, we find, does not advocate sexual communism. He accuses the bourgeoisie of having inflicted it upon the wives and daughters of the proletariat. Nor does he thank them for it as a blessing in disguise. He is indignant, and like his detractors he, too, suspects the class enemy is having far more fun in bed than is decent, seducing not only the poor working girl but each others' wives as well. A proper Victorian, Marx disapproves.

So do his followers, if they speak of the matter at all. August Bebel's *The Woman and Socialism* turns out to be anything but a ribald classic. The communes Bebel foresees are incredibly bourgeois, cooperative arrangements of proper Victorian couples, designed to bring household technology to working-class families. Accepting Marx's rather primitive version of the labor theory of value, Bebel is convinced that actual muscular exertion is the only source of value. This places a rigid upper limit on the possible increase in the productivity of labor in value terms—a man can only work so hard. Bebel concludes that *individual* workers can never create enough value to bring the marvels of modern technology within their reach. As with Plato and Marx, not individual sexual freedom but socioeconomic necessity is the basis for his commune-ism.

With the coming of the revolution, matters changed little. The puritanism of the Bolsheviks is notorious. Russian revolutionaries regarded sex as reactionary; they fitted their women into ill-shaped overalls and banned such lures of the devil as cosmetics. The U.S.S.R., Cuba, or the People's Republic of China aspire to match and surpass the capitalists in steel production, but none has the least intention of matching and surpassing even so modest a target as the *Playboy* foldout. Yet the intuitive association of sex and socialism survives all disclaimers. The relationship between sex and socialism may range from legal separation to sodomy, but it is still very much with us; and it requires explanation.

It is not particularly difficult to explain the sex phobia of some socialist theoreticians—and Communist dictators. Though willing to utilize whatever unrests are present in society, including sexual frustration, they are committed not simply to fostering change but to guiding and controlling it. They are committed to building the perfect society and, among men, perfection is never spontaneous. Society is too complex a construct for that. Perfection, as Plato already recognized, must be guided and guarded, and passions are notoriously hard to control. Philosopher kings are puritans virtually *ex officio*.

The opposite phenomenon, the common-law marriage of sex and socialism, is a converse of the Platonic considerations. Socialism and commune-ism are a response to the breakdown of community between man and man. Starting with Feuerbach's *Gesamtmensch*, radicals have sought to end the vicious isolation of individuals—caught in the productive process, joined and separated only by a cash nexus—and to establish a genuine human community. Freedom of sexual contact provides a rather facile symbol for overcoming alienation among men. Even when socialist writers and rulers chose not to use that symbol, their hearers invariably supplied it, and not without reason.

But there is a long and doubtful step between symbol and program. Against the grim background of an outdated puritanism, it may be rather easy to regard every removal of sexual restrictions as a victory for freedom, brotherhood, and enlightenment. The American Left, by and large, has yielded to this temptation. But while sexual freedom might seem an apt symbol of social freedom, it is not at all obvious that it is an adequate *program* for social action.

The sexual revolution seems to bring few of the boons promised by early pioneers who fought for progress in the darkest fifties by adopting gutter language in their classrooms. Dedicated pioneers at Berkeley or at the Grove Press may assure us that more of the same will produce something different, but their assurances grow daily less convincing. For myself, I would prefer to examine the basic premise—how valid is sex, not as personal pleasure or social symbol, but as a blueprint for progress?

I suppose we would all enjoy seeing an all-nude production of, say, Shakespeare's *Tempest*. In a fully-clad world, naked bodies do create a peculiar illusion of freedom, and it would be rather novel. But would it be progress? I doubt it. A naked *Tempest* might be fun, but an all-nude repertory theater would soon prove monotonous. Finally, skin is skin. Its initial dramatic impact might be considerable, but its dramatic possibilities would rapidly be exhausted. Costuming offers a far richer range of creative possibilities. Nudity is a possible form of costuming, and it was rather ludicrous to single it out for the Lord Chamberlain's special attention. But it is costuming which is basic and makes the richness and variety of the stage possible.

A play or, for that matter, a society may well have its roots in "nature"; but the freedom, richness, and imagination it offers its audience or its citizens are a product of art, the conventional elaboration of the natural minimum. A return to "nature" would impoverish the stage and society alike. To the extent that sexual freedom is equated with a "return to nature," it is as poverty-stricken and antihumanistic as primitivism. Freedom is a product of art, not of nature.

The appeal of nudity on stage and primitivism in society is not a function of any creative possibilities they offer, but rather of their apparent simplicity. Primitivism—the "return to nature"—in sex and society alike is an admission of inability to cope with the complexity of both society and costuming. For possibilities are always complex, and ambiguous. There is no possibility for good which does not entail the possibility of evil as well. By contrast, "nature" might offer few possibilities for genuine humanity, for freedom and imagination, but it does offer simplicity. What is natural is good, sex is natural, QED.

But how natural *is* sex? The sheer physical act of copulation may well be said to be natural, but it is also socially irrelevant. When sex becomes a symbol or is no longer a physical act but a relation between two human beings, it is no longer "natural" sex but human sexuality. As such, sex is clearly socially relevant— but it can no longer claim the innocence and simplicity of a natural phenomenon. Human sexuality, like all human activities, is highly conventional. It is socially relevant because it is a social act, and as such, it shares the ambiguity of all distinctly human acts. It can become a vehicle for *Todestrieb* as well as for *Lebenstrieb*, for the desire to dominate and destroy as well as to meet and love the other. Not by accident are love and death the two great aphrodisiacs of human sexuality.

This is the dilemma of any sexual revolution. If its program is simply sex as a physical act and its aim no more than quantitative increase in the number of individual acts of copulation per annum, then it is clear, unambiguous, but also socially irrelevant. If, on the other hand, it claims to free and foster human sexuality, it becomes socially relevant but also ethically ambiguous, a vehicle of destruction as well as of creativity.

Precisely because sex can become a vehicle of death as well as of life, we can no longer sustain the simplistic liberal illusion that drew a simple line between repression (bad) and expression (good) of the sexual impulse. Repression can, of course, become a vehicle for *Todestrieb*, for the killjoy impulse—one look at the hateful expressions in the faces of the defenders of decency is proof enough. But so can sexual expression. Not all sexual expression is necessarily the outcome of the impulse to freedom and joy. Masochism and sadism are the obvious counterinstance. In the terminology of pop revolutionism, sex can be "fascist."

I see a historical justification for this pop terminology. There was certainly nothing tepid or lifeless about the early Nazi movement. It was intense, passionate, thoroughly turned-on and existential, enough so as to satisfy Sartre's German alter ego, Martin Heidegger. The Nazi movement fairly reeked of sex. The Nazi hate sheet, *Der Stürmer*, was consummately pornographic, as crudely, openly, and inarticulately pornographic as the most underground publications of our time—and in rather the same way. The sexuality it dished out in issue after issue was of the sadistic/masochistic variety. Much as in the underground journals of our time, its aphrodisiacs were hate and death, and its pleasure was pain.

The editors of *Der Stürmer* were convinced that the orgy of destruction was justified by the nobility of the cause, an awakening, radicalizing of the German people—turning on—and that the object of its intended destruction, the German Jewry, was eminently worthy of destruction. Anyone who doubted it had sold out to the Jews. But aphrodisiacs have a way of surviving the passions they arouse. Hate remained after the sexual passions it aroused spent themselves in the Night of Long Knives, and once aroused, hate is unselective. Not only the Jews, but all of Europe, including Germany, fell victim to the sadomasochistic orgy of destruction.

The *Todestrieb*-sex of sadism and fascism does have a common basis in passion with the *Lebenstrieb*-sex of freedom and communion. But that minimal common basis does not make it any less antihumanistic, antisocial, and antisocialist. A joyless, brutal travesty like *Che!* and its journalistic counterparts have nothing to do with socialism, even though, like socialism, they are antipuritanical. They oppose puritanism with an orgy of sex as death, not with a celebration of sex as life.

The continuing hold of puritanism on American society cannot be explained simply as an arbitrary imposition on a healthy, happy society by a few vindictive puritans. The "system" sustains it, but it can sustain it only because a great many Americans choose it. Nor is their choice attributable merely to sloth or cowardice. Far more frequently, it is a rather unhappy choice of men who may not regard the tepid, lifeless propriety of bourgeois quasi sexuality as a positive good, but who still see it as a lesser evil to the death-sex orgy of *Der Stürmer* or *Che!* If the heightening of intensity in sexual passion comes to seem equivalent to a celebration of destruction, then even the choice of bourgeois propriety is not dishonorable. It may not make life free and full, but it makes it possible for the children who can laugh and play rather than die in gas chambers.

Still, the choice between not-quite-living and living-unto-death is at best a desperate choice. This is what gives an air of urgency and social significance to the quest for what, in our version of pop nomenclature, we could call "commune-ist" sex. The label has no doctrinal significance. It is at best a strained attempt to affirm the conviction that not only death but also love can be a great aphrodisiac, that intensification of sexuality does not have to mean only destruction of others, but can also mean a communion with others, a meeting of people where they live, in their bodies, a radical and free encounter.

The commune-ist sexual revolution can be found in the communes, rather reminiscent of the religious utopias, which form in the eddies of the rat race. Perhaps three or four couples, sometimes married, sometimes not, share a house, incomes, children, troubles, pleasures, bodies. Often they share a project as well, tutoring underprivileged children, housing the homeless, feeding the hungry. They are very young, though not always in years, and very earnest, and they will tell you, pleadingly, that people are never as free and together as when all clothes and inhibitions come off and that people who share common work and life share common love as well.

Theirs is a rather idyllic vision, easy to sneer at, vulnerable to ridicule. But the freedom and reality of the men and women I know who have adopted this life-style is impressive. Perhaps they have found something. They are certainly convinced of it, convinced that they are acting out the perennial dream of a Peaceable Kingdom. They are convinced they have found the freedom their contemporaries grope for, and present their love-in —or, to give it its older name, *agape*—with their ability to lock loins where most men can at best touch fingertips.

Those of us who have lived a little longer and learned how much men can cheat with their bodies, how independent the barriers among men are of their clothes, might find the symbolism apt but the hope a little naïve. Men's bodies can be naked but their souls fully clad and their daggers drawn. Yet such considerations are out of order now. Let us assume that men can in fact meet, with all barriers gone, once their clothes and sexual inhibitions are down. Let us accept for the moment the personal ideal of the commune of men completely "naked," completely open with each other. How valid is the commune-ist ideal, not as vision, but as blueprint for progress?

Oddly enough, in considering the validity of the commune-ist ideal angelology can be more useful than economics. Angelology is of little value as a descriptive science: There is a dearth of empirical evidence. But for that very reason, it has many uses as a science of pure possibilities. Since presumably neither angels nor devils exist, angelology offers a unique opportunity for projection. And since the commune-ist ideal of complete nakedness, metaphoric as well as literal, proposes nothing short of a Kingdom of Heaven on earth, angelological projection becomes singularly appropriate.

Among angels, we can say, the ideal of a complete communion, a communal existence in which all clothes and barriers to human contact are removed, would be extremely appealing. The Bible tells us that the blessed in God's presence "neither marry nor are given in marriage, but are like the angels in heaven"— presumably live in a continuous love-in, completely open, completely available, and able to meet each other without the limitations of formalized sexuality. Since by definition they are completely free, secure, and good, they need hold nothing back.

By the same token, I suppose, devils never have sex. Being totally evil, devils become incapable of sex, for sex demands a degree of mutual trust of which devils are by definition incapable.

An embrace leaves one's back exposed—and devils could not resist the opportunity. They must get their kicks by reading de Sade and by torturing each other.

Now as any angelologist can tell us, men are neither devils nor angels. They are not totally evil, and so are able to trust each other enough to lock loins and meet in love. At the same time, men are not angels, *per essentiam* and not merely *per accidens* as the Marxists would have us believe. We need not assume that they are evil, actively seeking to do harm one to another, though what we have called *Todestrieb*-sex suggests that they are also that, at least *per accidens*. But even if men are not evil, they are weak, and weakness is the *Urmutter* of cruelty. Frightened men will hurt each other, even without evil intent, simply out of fear.

Commune-ist visionaries will, to be sure, insist that their communes will change just that and produce a "new socialist man" who will be secure and free of fear. But even if, *per impossibile*, a commune were able to give its members such security that none would feel the need to strike out at the other, its members, unlike angels, would still not be omniscient. Men can hurt one another quite unwillingly, and hurt deeply. For angels, love-ins may be the *modus operandi;* for men they are at best a rather ambiguous *desideratum* precisely because in the case of men, being naked, literally and figuratively, means not only being wide open to communion but also being wide open to hurt. It takes a radical trust to be radically open, and among men there are severe limitations on trusting—not because men are unwilling to trust, but most of all because, not being omniscient, men are not unlimitedly trustworthy.

This is why, though a commune may be a symbol of a hope and even a tangible achievement of a few men and women for a very limited time, it is not an adequate model for restructuring society. Among men, clothes and inhibitions are not only barriers to communication, but also very necessary means of protection.

Not only protection against ill will, but protection against folly. Lack of omniscience survives even in Walden II or a Soviet Socialist Republic. Alienation, as Milovan Djilas pointed out recently, is not only a source of frustration, but also the barrier which protects individual freedom.

At moments, I can hear an echo of the different drummer whom my younger comrades hear in their communes. I wish them well, they are achieving something precious. I hope they keep the echo alive, and that we will not lose all ability to hear it. That deafness is what puritanism is all about, and it is death. Radical openness—commune-ism, if you wish—must remain as a perennial, insubstantial hope: the glimpse of the Kingdom. But I would hesitate to join them. Not for fear of being hurt, but for fear of hurting, because I am not all good and all wise. The ideal they are acting out is an ideal, not a blueprint for society. Man requires the protection of "clothes," barriers which not only bar but also protect.

This finally is the significance of the sexual conventions with which the young, unaware of their own capacity for hurting, are so impatient. Marriage is one such convention; so are the limitations, not imposed but formalized by society, on where, when, and with whom one can be radically open—and expect radical openness in return.

In this sense, the young are right—sex is the experimental working model for socialism. The commune-ist (and communist) vision of a society in which all "clothes" and barriers—the "bourgeois" freedoms and civil rights, the limitations of "formal" democracy—are removed and men are left entirely naked to each other is a perennial vision. Its appeal is its promise of radical commune-ion. Yet in practice the destruction of formal limitations has never created a society which could give its people bread, freedom, and justice. In every instance it has created a nightmare of men and societies broken and destroyed by well-meaning leaders who, even had they been all good, still were not omniscient. True believers may speak of these episodes as "deformations," but they are quite inevitable, a strict consequence of removing barriers which may bar men from perfect communion but also protect them from their own lack of omniscience.

Socialism for men rather than for angels, socialism with a

human face, is finally the art and the science of creating barriers between man and man which offer the maximum opportunity for communication while providing the maximum protection against human ignorance and ill will. It becomes a deeply antihumanistic nightmare when it mistakes men for angels, and sees its sole task in removing all barriers among them.

I am not a fascist because I am not a devil, and because I believe that men can communicate and meet one another. But I am not a communist because I know that men are not angels, and cannot be trusted implicitly, not even in love. I am a socialist because I believe that conventions can be replaced, that they do not have to be strained and straining relics of an irrational past but can be molded and shaped rationally, in the service of human security and human freedom. I am a socialist and a democrat because I know that a radical ideal can serve men only if it can create conventions which do this.

This, finally, applies to sexual as well as to social revolution. Radicalization, social or sexual, is not an unmitigated good. It creates opportunities, but opportunities for destruction and death as well as for love and life. If it becomes a basis for a rational restructuring of social and sexual conventions in the service of men, it offers hope. If it becomes a basis for destruction of social and sexual conventions, it no longer matters whether the ideal it invokes is love or death. The result is the same.

[1969]

ACKNOWLEDGMENTS

Many of the articles in this collection first appeared in the pages of *Dissent*. I am also grateful to the following for granting permission to reprint material:

"The Mystical Militants" by Michael Harrington. Copyright © 1966 by Harrison-Blaine of New Jersey, Inc. Reprinted by permission of *The New Republic*.

"'Confrontation Politics' Is a Dangerous Game" by Irving Howe. First published in *The New York Times Magazine*. © 1968 by The New York Times Company. Reprinted by permission.

"Unreason and Revolution" by Richard Lowenthal. Copyright © 1969 by Encounter Ltd. Reprinted by permission.

"The New Reformation" by Paul Goodman. First published in *The New York Times Magazine*. © 1969 by The New York Times Company. Reprinted by permission.

"Black Studies: Trouble Ahead" by Eugene D. Genovese. Copyright © 1969 by The Atlantic Monthly Company, Boston, Mass. Reprinted by permission.

"The Case for Professionalism" by Robert Brustein. Copyright © 1969 by Harrison-Blaine of New Jersey, Inc. Reprinted by permission of *The New Republic*.

"The Black Panthers" by Theodore Draper was first published in somewhat different form in *Commentary*. From *The Rediscovery of Black Nationalism* by Theodore Draper. Copyright © 1969, 1970 by Theodore Draper. All rights reserved. Reprinted by permission of The Viking Press, Inc.

salm 19: Lord, You Have the Words

Lord, you have the words of ev - er-last-ing life, of ev - er-last-

1. | 2.

ing life, of ev - er-last-ing life. er-last-ing life.

Text: *Lectionary for Mass*, © 1969, 1981, 1997, ICEL
Music: Kenneth W. Louis, © 2012, GIA Publications, Inc.

Verses

1. The heavens declare the glory	of	God,
2. No speech, no word, whose voice goes	un -	heeded;
3. There he has placed a tent for	the	sun;
4. At one end of the heavens is the rising of	the	sun;
5. The law of the LORD	is	perfect;
6. The precepts of the LORD	are	right;
7. The fear of the LORD	is	pure,
8. They are more to be desired	than	gold,
9. So in them your servant finds	in -	struction;
10. From presumption restrain	your	servant;
11. May the spoken words of	my	mouth,
12. Glory to the Father, and to	the	Son,

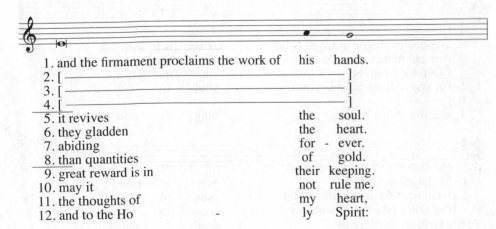

1. and the firmament proclaims the work of	his	hands.
2. [———————————————]		
3. [———————————————]		
4. [———————————————]		
5. it revives	the	soul.
6. they gladden	the	heart.
7. abiding	for -	ever.
8. than quantities	of	gold.
9. great reward is in	their	keeping.
10. may it	not	rule me.
11. the thoughts of	my	heart,
12. and to the Ho -	ly	Spirit:

Psalm 4: Have Mercy, Lord   25

Refrain

Have mer - cy, Lord. Have mer - cy, Lord.

Have mer - cy, Lord, and hear my prayer.

Text: *Liturgy of the Hours*, © 1974, ICEL
Music: Norah Duncan IV, © 2012, GIA Publications, Inc.

Verses

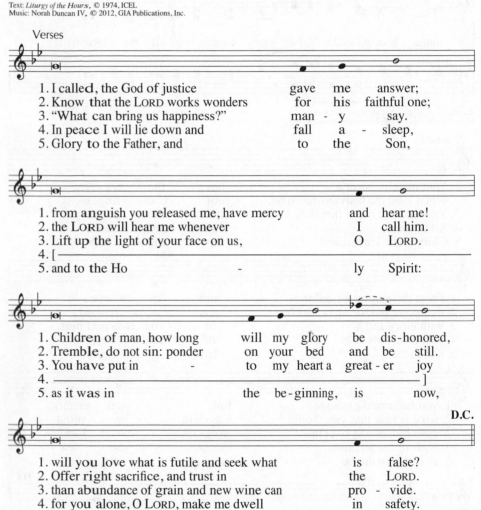

1. I called, the God of justice	gave	me	answer;
2. Know that the LORD works wonders	for	his	faithful one;
3. "What can bring us happiness?"	man - y		say.
4. In peace I will lie down and	fall	a -	sleep,
5. Glory to the Father, and	to	the	Son,

1. from anguish you released me, have mercy	and	hear me!
2. the LORD will hear me whenever	I	call him.
3. Lift up the light of your face on us,	O	LORD.
4. [		
5. and to the Ho -	ly	Spirit:

1. Children of man, how long	will	my glory	be	dis-honored,
2. Tremble, do not sin: ponder	on	your bed	and	be still.
3. You have put in -	to	my heart a	great - er	joy
4. ————————————————]				
5. as it was in	the	be - ginning,	is	now,

D.C.

1. will you love what is futile and seek what	is	false?
2. Offer right sacrifice, and trust in	the	LORD.
3. than abundance of grain and new wine can	pro -	vide.
4. for you alone, O LORD, make me dwell	in	safety.
5. and will be for ever.	A -	men.

Text: Psalm 4; *The Revised Grail Psalms*, © 2010, Conception Abbey and The Grail, admin. by GIA Publications, Inc.
Music: Rawn Harbor, © 1985, Rawn Harbor

26   Psalm 8: O Lord, Our God

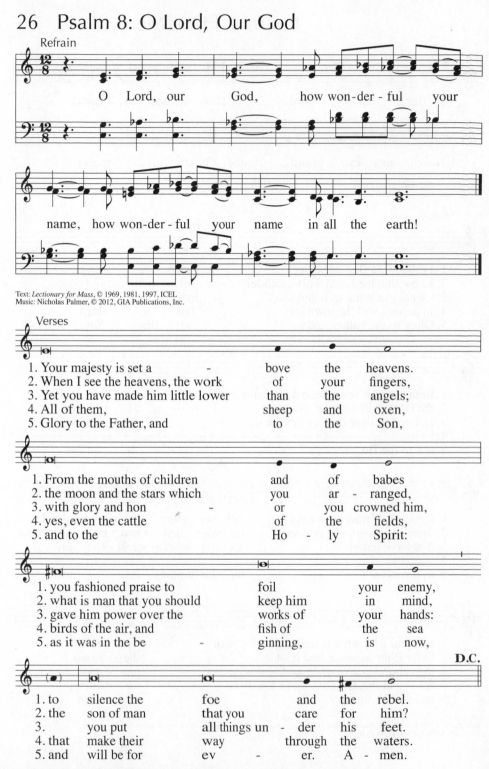

Refrain

O Lord, our God, how won-der-ful your name, how won-der-ful your name in all the earth!

Text: *Lectionary for Mass*, © 1969, 1981, 1997, ICEL
Music: Nicholas Palmer, © 2012, GIA Publications, Inc.

Verses

1. Your majesty is set a - bove the heavens.
2. When I see the heavens, the work of your fingers,
3. Yet you have made him little lower than the angels;
4. All of them, sheep and oxen,
5. Glory to the Father, and to the Son,

1. From the mouths of children and of babes
2. the moon and the stars which you ar - ranged,
3. with glory and hon - or you crowned him,
4. yes, even the cattle of the fields,
5. and to the Ho - ly Spirit:

1. you fashioned praise to foil your enemy,
2. what is man that you should keep him in mind,
3. gave him power over the works of your hands:
4. birds of the air, and fish of the sea
5. as it was in the be - ginning, is now,

D.C.

1. to silence the foe and the rebel.
2. the son of man that you care for him?
3. you put all things un - der his feet.
4. that make their way through the waters.
5. and will be for ev - er. A - men.

Text: Psalm 8; *The Revised Grail Psalms*, © 2010, Conception Abbey and The Grail, admin. by GIA Publications, Inc., agent
Music: Michel Guimont, © 1994, 1998, GIA Publications, Inc.

Psalm 16: I

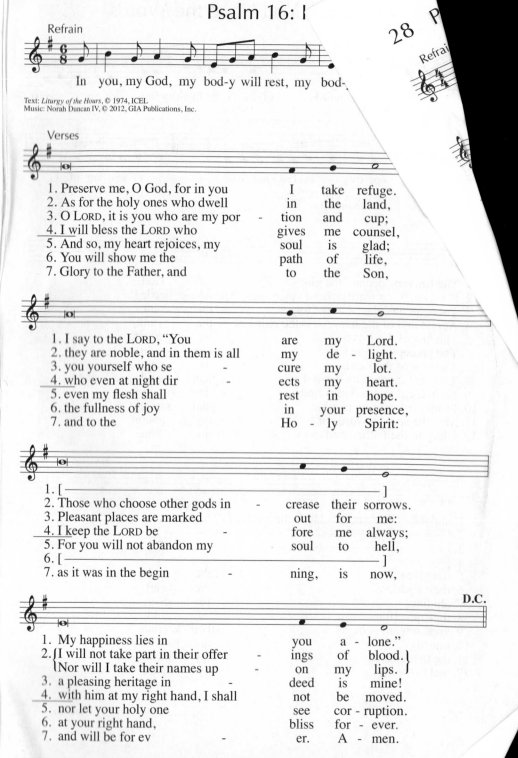

Refrain

In you, my God, my bod-y will rest, my bod-

Text: *Liturgy of the Hours*, © 1974, ICEL
Music: Norah Duncan IV, © 2012, GIA Publications, Inc.

Verses

1. Preserve me, O God, for in you I take refuge.
2. As for the holy ones who dwell in the land,
3. O Lord, it is you who are my por - tion and cup;
4. I will bless the Lord who gives me counsel,
5. And so, my heart rejoices, my soul is glad;
6. You will show me the path of life,
7. Glory to the Father, and to the Son,

1. I say to the Lord, "You are my Lord.
2. they are noble, and in them is all my de - light.
3. you yourself who se - cure my lot.
4. who even at night dir - ects my heart.
5. even my flesh shall rest in hope.
6. the fullness of joy in your presence,
7. and to the Ho - ly Spirit:

1. [———————————————————]
2. Those who choose other gods in - crease their sorrows.
3. Pleasant places are marked out for me:
4. I keep the Lord be - fore me always;
5. For you will not abandon my soul to hell,
6. [———————————————————]
7. as it was in the begin - ning, is now,

D.C.

1. My happiness lies in you a - lone."
2. {I will not take part in their offer - ings of blood.}
   {Nor will I take their names up - on my lips. }
3. a pleasing heritage in - deed is mine!
4. with him at my right hand, I shall not be moved.
5. nor let your holy one see cor - ruption.
6. at your right hand, bliss for - ever.
7. and will be for ev - er. A - men.

Text: Psalm 16: *The Revised Grail Psalms*, © 2010, Conception Abbey and The Grail, admin. by GIA Publications, Inc., agent
Music: Stanbrook Abbey, © 1984, The Benedictine Sisters of Stanbrook Abbey

28   P
Refrain

1. Day unto day conveys the · · · · · · · · · message,
2. their sound goes forth through all the · · · · earth,
3. it comes forth like a bridegroom coming from his · tent,
4. to its furthest end it runs its · · · · · · · course.
5. The decrees of the LORD are · · · · · · · · steadfast;
6. The command of the LORD is · · · · · · · · clear;
7. The judgments of the LORD are · · · · · · · true;
8. And sweeter are they than · · · · · · · · honey,
9. But who can detect their own · · · · · · · errors?
10. Then shall I be · · · · · · · · · · · blameless,
11. win favor in your sight, O · · · · · · · LORD,
12. as it was in the beginning, is · · · · · · · now,

D.C.

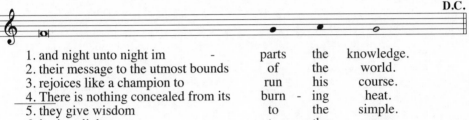

1. and night unto night im - parts the knowledge.
2. their message to the utmost bounds of the world.
3. rejoices like a champion to run his course.
4. There is nothing concealed from its burn - ing heat.
5. they give wisdom to the simple.
6. it gives light to the eyes.
7. they are, all of them, just.
8. than honey flowing from the comb.
9. From hidden faults ac - quit me.
10. clean from grave sin.
11. my rock and my re - deemer!
12. and will be for ev - er. A - men.

Text: Psalm 19; *The Revised Grail Psalms*, © 2010, Conception Abbey and The Grail, admin. by GIA Publications, Inc., agent
Music: Michel Guimont, © 1994, 1998, GIA Publications, Inc.

Psalm 31:2–6: Lord God, Be My Refuge 29

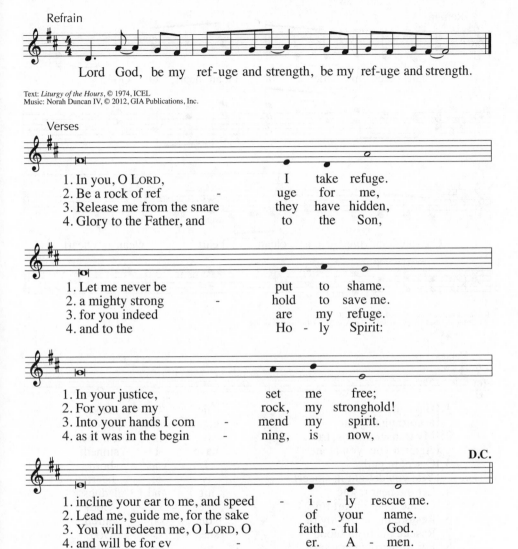

Refrain

Lord God, be my ref-uge and strength, be my ref-uge and strength.

Text: *Liturgy of the Hours*, © 1974, ICEL
Music: Norah Duncan IV, © 2012, GIA Publications, Inc.

Verses

1. In you, O LORD,   I take refuge.
2. Be a rock of ref - uge for me,
3. Release me from the snare they have hidden,
4. Glory to the Father, and to the Son,

1. Let me never be   put to shame.
2. a mighty strong - hold to save me.
3. for you indeed   are my refuge.
4. and to the   Ho - ly Spirit:

1. In your justice,   set me free;
2. For you are my   rock, my stronghold!
3. Into your hands I com - mend my spirit.
4. as it was in the begin - ning, is now,

D.C.

1. incline your ear to me, and speed - i - ly rescue me.
2. Lead me, guide me, for the sake of your name.
3. You will redeem me, O LORD, O faith - ful God.
4. and will be for ev - er. A - men.

Text: Psalm 31:2–6; *The Revised Grail Psalms*, © 2010, Conception Abbey and The Grail, admin. by GIA Publications, Inc., agent
Music: Garfield Rochard, © 1984, The Antilles Episcopal Conference

30 Psalm 51: Create in Me a Clean Heart

Refrain

Cre - ate in me a clean heart, O God.

Cre - ate in me a clean heart. clean heart.

Text: *Lectionary for Mass*, © 1969, 1981, 1997, ICEL
Music: Roderick Bell; arr. by Kenneth W. Louis, © 2012, GIA Publications, Inc.

Verses

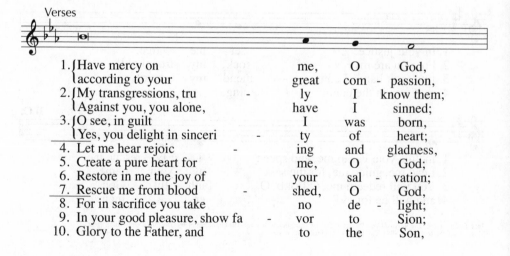

1. {Have mercy on   me,   O   God,
   {according to your   great   com - passion,
2. {My transgressions, tru - ly   I   know them;
   {Against you, you alone,   have   I   sinned;
3. {O see, in guilt   I   was   born,
   {Yes, you delight in sinceri - ty   of   heart;
4. Let me hear rejoic - ing   and   gladness,
5. Create a pure heart for   me,   O   God;
6. Restore in me the joy of   your   sal - vation;
7. Rescue me from blood - shed,   O   God,
8. For in sacrifice you take   no   de - light;
9. In your good pleasure, show fa - vor   to   Sion;
10. Glory to the Father, and   to   the   Son,

1. according to your mer - ci - ful love; ⎱
   blot out my trans - gressions. ⎰
2. my sin is al - ways be - fore me. ⎱
   what is evil in your sight I have done. ⎰
3. a sinner when my moth - er con - ceived me. ⎱
   in secret you teach me wisdom. ⎰
4. that the bones you have crushed may ex - ult.
5. renew a steadfast spir - it with - in me.
6. sustain in me a will - ing spirit.
7. God of my sal - vation,
8. burnt offering from me would not please you.
9. rebuild the walls of Je - rusalem.
10. and to the Ho - ly Spirit:

1. Wash me completely from my in - iquity,
2. So you are just in your sentence,
3. Cleanse me with hyssop, and I shall be pure;
4. Turn away your face from my sins,
5. Do not cast me away from your presence;
6. I will teach transgres - sors your ways,
7. and then my tongue shall ring out your justice.
8. My sacrifice to God, a bro - ken spirit:
9. Then you will delight in right sacrifice,
   burnt offerings whol - ly con - sumed.
10. as it was in the begin - ning, is now,

D.C.

1. and cleanse me from my sin.
2. without reproach in your judgment.
3. wash me, and I shall be whit - er than snow.
4. and blot out all my guilt.
5. take not your holy spir - it from me.
6. that sinners may re - turn to you.
7. O Lord, open my lips and my mouth shall pro - claim your praise.
8. a broken and humbled heart, O God, you will not spurn.
9. Then you will be offered young bulls on your altar.
10. and will be for ev - er. A - men.

Text: Psalm 51; *The Revised Grail Psalms*, © 2010, Conception Abbey and The Grail, admin. by GIA Publications, Inc., agent
Music: Joseph B. Smith, © 1986, GIA Publications, Inc.

31   Psalm 66: Let All the Earth

Text: *Lectionary for Mass,* © 1969, 1981, 1997, ICEL
Music: M. Roger Holland, © 2012, GIA Publications, Inc.

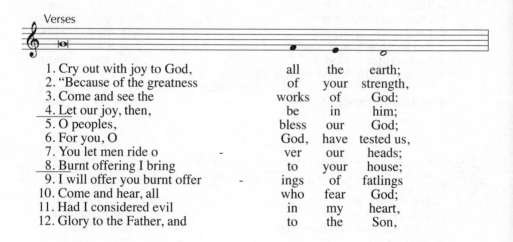

1. Cry out with joy to God,	all	the	earth;
2. "Because of the greatness	of	your	strength,
3. Come and see the	works	of	God:
4. Let our joy, then,	be	in	him;
5. O peoples,	bless	our	God;
6. For you, O	God,	have	tested us,
7. You let men ride o -	ver	our	heads;
8. Burnt offering I bring	to	your	house;
9. I will offer you burnt offer -	ings	of	fatlings
10. Come and hear, all	who	fear	God;
11. Had I considered evil	in	my	heart,
12. Glory to the Father, and	to	the	Son,

1. O sing to the glory — of his name.
2. your enemies — fawn up - on you.
3. awesome his deeds among the chil - dren of men.
4. he rules forever — by his might.
5. let the voice of his — praise re - sound,
6. you have tried us as sil - ver is tried;
7. we went through fire — and through water,
8. to you I will — pay my vows,
9. with the smoke of sacri - fi - cial rams.
10. I will tell what he did — for my soul.
11. the LORD would — not have listened.
12. and to the — Ho - ly Spirit:

1. O render him — glo - rious praise.
2. Before you all the earth — shall bow down,
3. He turned the sea — in - to dry land;
4. His eyes keep watch — on the nations:
5. of the God who gave life — to our souls
6. you led us, God, in - to the snare;
7. [————————————————————————]
8. the vows which my — lips have uttered,
9. [————————————————————————]
10. To him I — cried a - loud,
11. ⎰But truly — God has listened;
    ⎱Blest be God, who did not re - ject my prayer,
12. as it was in the begin - ning, is now,

D.C.

1. Say to God, "How awe - some your deeds!
2. shall sing to you, sing — to your name!"
3. they passed through the riv - er on foot.
4. let rebels not ex - alt them - selves.
5. and kept our — feet from stumbling.
6. you laid a heavy burden — on our backs.
7. but then you brought us to a — place of plenty.
8. which my mouth declared in — my dis - tress.
9. I will offer bul - locks and goats.
10. with exaltation ready — on my tongue.
11. he has heeded the voice — of my prayer.⎱
    nor withhold from me his mer - ci - ful love. ⎰
12. and will be for ev - er. A - men.

Text: Psalm 66; *The Revised Grail Psalms*, © 2010, Conception Abbey and The Grail, admin. by GIA Publications, Inc., agent
Music: Joseph B. Smith, © 1986, GIA Publications, Inc.

32 Psalm 84: Blessed Are They Who Dwell

Refrain

Bless-ed are they who dwell in your house,

O,   O,   O Lord.

Text: *Lectionary for Mass*, © 1969, 1981, 1997, ICEL
Music: Ray Wise, © 2012, GIA Publications, Inc.

Verses

1. How lovely is your dwelling place, O LORD	of	hosts.
2. Even the sparrow finds	a	home,
3. Blessed are they who dwell in	your	house,
4. As they go through the Ba -	ca	Valley,
5. O LORD God of hosts, hear	my	prayer;
6. One day within	your	courts
7. For the LORD God is a sun,	a	shield;
8. Glory to the Father, and to	the	Son,

1. My soul is longing and yearning for the courts	of	the	LORD.
2. and the swallow a nest	for	her -	self
3. forever sing -	ing	your	praise.
4. they make it a	place	of	springs;
5. give ear, O	God	of	Jacob.
6. is better than a	thou -	sand	elsewhere.
7. the LORD will give us his fav -	or	and	glory.
8. and to the	Ho -	ly	Spirit:

1. My heart and my flesh	cry	out
2. in which she sets her young, at	your	altars,
3. Blessed the people whose strength is	in	you,
4. the autumn rain covers it	with	pools.
5. Turn your eyes, O God,	our	shield;
6. The threshold of the house	of	God
7. { He will not withhold an -	y	good
{ O LORD of hosts,	how	blessed
8. as it was in the beginning,	is	now,

D.C.

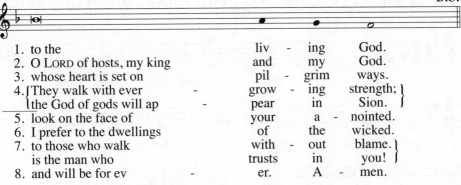

1.	to the	liv - ing	God.
2.	O LORD of hosts, my king	and my	God.
3.	whose heart is set on	pil - grim	ways.
4.	{They walk with ever -	grow - ing	strength; }
	the God of gods will ap -	pear in	Sion. }
5.	look on the face of	your a -	nointed.
6.	I prefer to the dwellings	of the	wicked.
7.	to those who walk	with - out	blame. }
	is the man who	trusts in	you! }
8.	and will be for ev -	er. A -	men.

Text: Psalm 84; *The Revised Grail Psalms*, © 2010, Conception Abbey and The Grail, admin. by GIA Publications, Inc., agent
Music: Paschal Jordan, OSB, © 1984, McCrimon Publishing Co., Ltd.

33 Psalm 86: Lord, You Are Good and Forgiving

Refrain

Lord, you are good and for - giv - ing, good and for - giv - ing.

Text: *Lectionary for Mass*, © 1969, 1981, 1997, ICEL
Music: Norah Duncan IV, © 2012, GIA Publications, Inc.

Verses

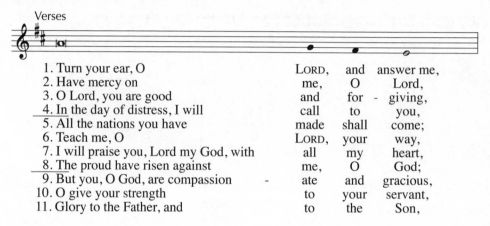

1. Turn your ear, O	LORD,	and	answer me,
2. Have mercy on	me,	O	Lord,
3. O Lord, you are good	and	for -	giving,
4. In the day of distress, I will	call	to	you,
5. All the nations you have	made	shall	come;
6. Teach me, O	LORD,	your	way,
7. I will praise you, Lord my God, with	all	my	heart,
8. The proud have risen against	me,	O	God;
9. But you, O God, are compassion -	ate	and	gracious,
10. O give your strength	to	your	servant,
11. Glory to the Father, and	to	the	Son,

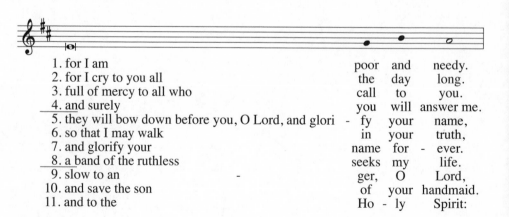

1. for I am	poor	and	needy.
2. for I cry to you all	the	day	long.
3. full of mercy to all who	call	to	you.
4. and surely	you	will	answer me.
5. they will bow down before you, O Lord, and glori -	fy	your	name,
6. so that I may walk	in	your	truth,
7. and glorify your	name	for -	ever.
8. a band of the ruthless	seeks	my	life.
9. slow to an -	ger,	O	Lord,
10. and save the son	of	your	handmaid.
11. and to the	Ho -	ly	Spirit:

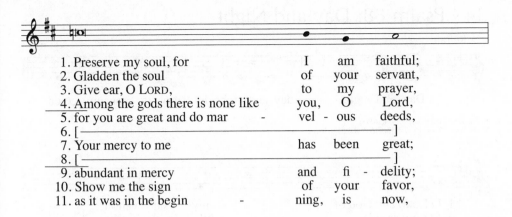

1. Preserve my soul, for — I — am — faithful;
2. Gladden the soul — of — your — servant,
3. Give ear, O LORD, — to — my — prayer,
4. Among the gods there is none like — you, — O — Lord,
5. for you are great and do mar - vel - ous — deeds,
6. [———————————————————]
7. Your mercy to me — has — been — great;
8. [———————————————————]
9. abundant in mercy — and — fi - delity;
10. Show me the sign — of — your — favor,
11. as it was in the begin - ning, — is — now,

D.C.

1. save the servant who trusts in — you, — my — God.
2. for I lift up my soul to — you, — O — Lord.
3. and attend to my voice in — sup - pli - cation.
4. nor works to com - pare — with — yours.
5. you who a - lone — are — God.
6. single-hearted to — fear — your — name.
7. you have saved me from the depths — of — the — grave.
8. To you they — pay — no — heed.
9. turn and take pit - y — on — me.
10. { that my foes may see — to — their — shame }
    { that you, O LORD, give me com - fort — and — help. }
11. and will be for ev - er. — A - men.

Text: Psalm 86; *The Revised Grail Psalms*, © 2010, Conception Abbey and The Grail, admin. by GIA Publications, Inc., agent
Music: Joseph B. Smith, © 1986, GIA Publications, Inc.

34 Psalm 88: Day and Night

Refrain

Day and night,   day and night I   cry to you, my God.

Text: *Liturgy of the Hours*, © 1974, ICEL
Music: Norah Duncan IV, © 2012, GIA Publications, Inc.

Verses

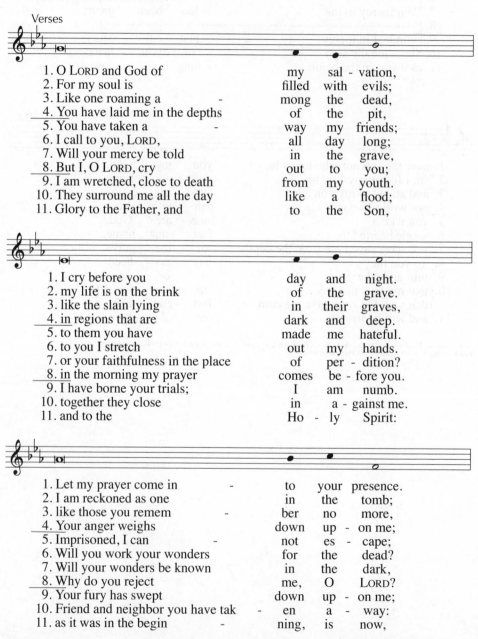

1. O LORD and God of	my	sal - vation,
2. For my soul is	filled	with evils;
3. Like one roaming a -	mong	the dead,
4. You have laid me in the depths	of	the pit,
5. You have taken a -	way	my friends;
6. I call to you, LORD,	all	day long;
7. Will your mercy be told	in	the grave,
8. But I, O LORD, cry	out	to you;
9. I am wretched, close to death	from	my youth.
10. They surround me all the day	like	a flood;
11. Glory to the Father, and	to	the Son,

1. I cry before you	day	and night.
2. my life is on the brink	of	the grave.
3. like the slain lying	in	their graves,
4. in regions that are	dark	and deep.
5. to them you have	made	me hateful.
6. to you I stretch	out	my hands.
7. or your faithfulness in the place	of	per - dition?
8. in the morning my prayer	comes	be - fore you.
9. I have borne your trials;	I	am numb.
10. together they close	in	a - gainst me.
11. and to the	Ho - ly	Spirit:

1. Let my prayer come in -	to	your presence.
2. I am reckoned as one	in	the tomb;
3. like those you remem -	ber	no more,
4. Your anger weighs	down	up - on me;
5. Imprisoned, I can -	not	es - cape;
6. Will you work your wonders	for	the dead?
7. Will your wonders be known	in	the dark,
8. Why do you reject	me,	O LORD?
9. Your fury has swept	down	up - on me;
10. Friend and neighbor you have tak - en	a -	way:
11. as it was in the begin -	ning,	is now,

D.C.

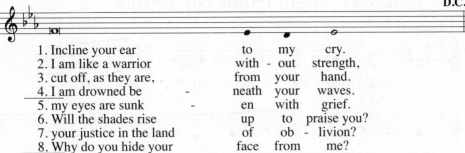

1. Incline your ear to my cry.
2. I am like a warrior with - out strength,
3. cut off, as they are, from your hand.
4. I am drowned be - neath your waves.
5. my eyes are sunk - en with grief.
6. Will the shades rise up to praise you?
7. your justice in the land of ob - livion?
8. Why do you hide your face from me?
9. your terrors have utter - ly de - stroyed me.
10. my one compan - ion is darkness.
11. and will be for ev - er. A - men.

Text: Psalm 88; *The Revised Grail Psalms*, © 2010, Conception Abbey and The Grail, admin. by GIA Publications, Inc., agent
Music: Cyril Baker, © 1984, The Antilles Episcopal Conference

35 Psalm 91: Night Holds No Terrors

Refrain I

Night holds no ter - rors for me
sleep - ing un - der God's wings.

Text: *Liturgy of the Hours*, © 1974, ICEL
Music: Norah Duncan IV, © 2012, GIA Publications, Inc.

Refrain II

Be with me, Lord, when I am in
trou - ble, be with me, Lord, I pray.

Text: Marty Haugen
Music: Marty Haugen
© 1980, GIA Publications, Inc.

Verses

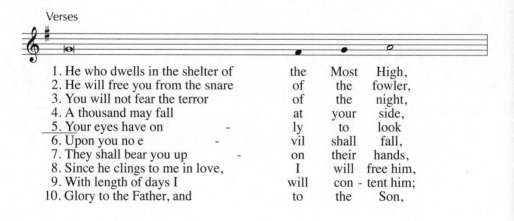

1. He who dwells in the shelter of	the	Most	High,
2. He will free you from the snare	of	the	fowler,
3. You will not fear the terror	of	the	night,
4. A thousand may fall	at	your	side,
5. Your eyes have on -	ly	to	look
6. Upon you no e -	vil	shall	fall,
7. They shall bear you up -	on	their	hands,
8. Since he clings to me in love,	I	will	free him,
9. With length of days I	will	con -	tent him;
10. Glory to the Father, and	to	the	Son,

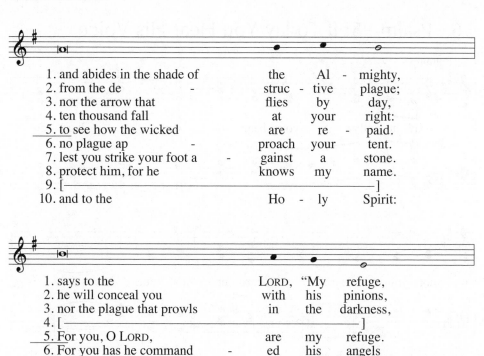

1. and abides in the shade of   the   Al - mighty,
2. from the de -   struc - tive   plague;
3. nor the arrow that   flies   by   day,
4. ten thousand fall   at   your   right:
5. to see how the wicked   are   re - paid.
6. no plague ap -   proach   your   tent.
7. lest you strike your foot a -   gainst   a   stone.
8. protect him, for he   knows   my   name.
9. [————————————————————]
10. and to the   Ho - ly   Spirit:

1. says to the   LORD, "My   refuge,
2. he will conceal you   with   his   pinions,
3. nor the plague that prowls   in   the   darkness,
4. [————————————————————]
5. For you, O LORD,   are   my   refuge.
6. For you has he command -   ed   his   angels
7. On the lion and the viper   you   will   tread,
8. When he calls on me,   I   will   answer him;
9. [————————————————————]
10. as it was in the begin -   ning,   is   now,

D.C.

1. my stronghold, my God in   whom   I   trust!"
2. {and under his wings you   will   find   refuge.}
   {His faithfulness is buck -   ler   and   shield.}
3. nor the scourge that lays   waste   at   noon.
4. you it will nev -   er   ap - proach.
5. You have made the Most   High   your   dwelling.
6. to keep you in   all   your   ways.
7. and trample the young lion   and   the   serpent.
8. {I will be with him   in   dis - tress;}
   {I will deliver him, and   give   him   glory.}
9. I will show him my   sav - ing   power.
10. and will be for ev -   er.   A - men.

Text: Psalm 88; *The Revised Grail Psalms*, © 2010, Conception Abbey and The Grail, admin. by GIA Publications, Inc., agent
Music: Stanbrook Abbey, © 1984, The Benedictine Sisters of Stanbrook Abbey

36 Psalm 95: If Today You Hear His Voice

Refrain

If to-day you hear his voice, hard-en

not your hearts, hard-en not your hearts.

Text: *Lectionary for Mass*, © 1969, 1981, 1997, ICEL
Music: Roy James Stewart, © 1993, GIA Publications, Inc.

Verses

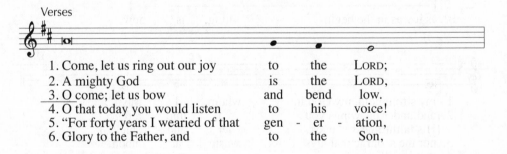

1. Come, let us ring out our joy to the LORD;
2. A mighty God is the LORD,
3. O come; let us bow and bend low.
4. O that today you would listen to his voice!
5. "For forty years I wearied of that gen - er - ation,
6. Glory to the Father, and to the Son,

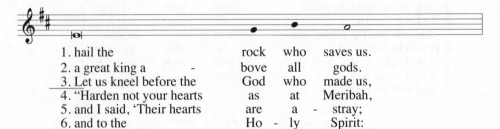

1. hail the rock who saves us.
2. a great king a - bove all gods.
3. Let us kneel before the God who made us,
4. "Harden not your hearts as at Meribah,
5. and I said, 'Their hearts are a - stray;
6. and to the Ho - ly Spirit:

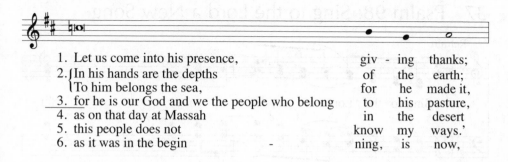

1. Let us come into his presence,   giv - ing   thanks;
2. ⌠In his hands are the depths   of   the   earth;
   ⌡To him belongs the sea,   for   he   made it,
3. for he is our God and we the people who belong   to   his   pasture,
4. as on that day at Massah   in   the   desert
5. this people does not   know   my   ways.'
6. as it was in the begin -   ning,   is   now,

D.C.

1. let us hail him with a   song of praise.
2. the heights of the moun -   tains are his. ⌉
   and the dry land that he shaped   by   his hands. ⌋
3. the flock that is led   by   his hand.
4. ⌠when your forebears put me   to   the   test; ⌉
   ⌡when they tried me, though they   saw   my   work. ⌋
5. Then I took an oath in my anger, 'Never shall they en - ter   my rest.'"
6. and will be for ev -   er.   A - men.

Text: Psalm 95; *The Revised Grail Psalms*, © 2010, Conception Abbey and The Grail, admin. by GIA Publications, Inc., agent
Music: Joseph B. Smith, © 1986, GIA Publications, Inc.

37 Psalm 98: Sing to the Lord a New Song

Refrain

Sing to the Lord a new song, for

he has done mar - vel-ous deeds.

Text: *Lectionary for Mass*, © 1969, 1981, 1997, ICEL
Music: M. Roger Holland, © 2012, GIA Publications, Inc.

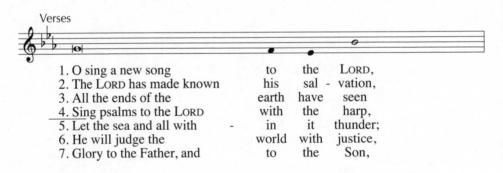

Verses

1. O sing a new song   to   the   LORD,
2. The LORD has made known his   sal - vation,
3. All the ends of the   earth have seen
4. Sing psalms to the LORD with   the   harp,
5. Let the sea and all with - in   it   thunder;
6. He will judge the   world with justice,
7. Glory to the Father, and to   the   Son,

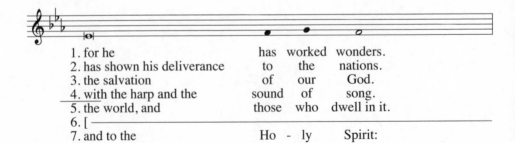

1. for he   has worked wonders.
2. has shown his deliverance to the   nations.
3. the salvation   of   our   God.
4. with the harp and the sound of   song.
5. the world, and   those who dwell in it.
6. [—
7. and to the   Ho - ly   Spirit:

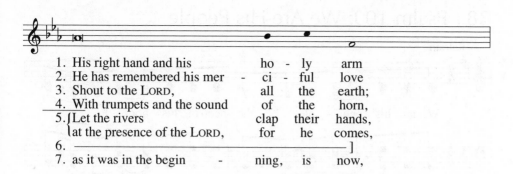

1. His right hand and his   ho - ly   arm
2. He has remembered his mer - ci - ful   love
3. Shout to the LORD,   all   the   earth;
4. With trumpets and the sound   of   the   horn,
5. {Let the rivers   clap   their   hands,
     at the presence of the LORD,   for   he   comes,
6. —————————————]
7. as it was in the begin - ning,   is   now,

D.C.

1. have   brought   sal - vation.
2. and his truth for the   house   of   Israel.
3. break forth into joyous song, and sing   out   your   praise.
4. raise a shout before the   King,   the   LORD.
5. and the hills ring   out   their   joy }
     he comes to   judge   the   earth. }
6. and the peo -   ples   with   fairness.
7. and will be for ev -   er.   A - men.

Text: Psalm 98; *The Revised Grail Psalms*, © 2010, Conception Abbey and The Grail, admin. by GIA Publications, Inc., agent
Music: Cyril Baker, © 1984, The Antilles Episcopal Conference

38 Psalm 100: We Are His People

Refrain

We are his peo - ple, the sheep of his flock,

we are his peo - ple, the sheep of his flock,

we are his peo - ple, the sheep of his flock, where he

1.
2.

leads us we will sure - ly go.

Text: *Lectionary for Mass,* © 1969, 1981, 1997, ICEL
Music: Wendell Craig Woods, © 2003, GIA Publications, Inc.

Verses

1. Cry out with joy to the LORD,   all   the   earth.
2. Know that he, the   LORD,   is   God.
3. Enter his gates   with   thanks - giving
4. Indeed, how good   is   the   LORD,
5. Glory to the Father, and to the Son, and to the   Ho   -   ly   Spirit:

1. Serve the   LORD   with   gladness.
2. He made us; we be   -   long   to   him.
3. and his courts with   songs   of   praise.
4. eternal his mer   -   ci   -   ful   love.
5. as it was in the begin   -   ning,   is   now,

D.C.

1. Come before him,   singing   for   joy.
2. We are his people,   the sheep of   his   flock.
3. Give thanks to   him, and bless   his   name.
4. He is faithful   from age   to   age.
5. and will be for   ever.   A   -   men.

Text: Psalm 100; *The Revised Grail Psalms*, © 2010, Conception Abbey and The Grail, admin. by GIA Publications, Inc., agent
Music: Michel Guimont, © 1995, GIA Publictions, Inc.

39 Psalm 121: Our Help Is from the Lord

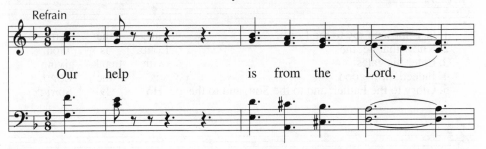

Our help is from the Lord,

who made heav - en, heav - en and earth.

Text: *Lectionary for Mass*, © 1969, 1981, 1997, ICEL
Music: Leon Roberts, © 2012, GIA Publications, Inc.

Verses

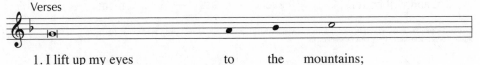

1. I lift up my eyes	to	the	mountains;
2. He will keep your	foot	from	stumbling.
3. The LORD your guard, the	LORD	your	shade
4. The LORD will guard	you	from	evil;
5. Glory to the Father, and	to	the	Son,

1. from where shall	come	my	help?
2. Your guard will	nev - er		slumber.
3. at	your	right	hand.
4. he will	guard	your	soul.
5. and to the	Ho - ly		Spirit:

1. My help shall come — from the LORD,
2. No, he sleeps — not nor slumbers,
3. By day the sun — shall not smite you,
4. The LORD will guard your go - ing and coming,
5. as it was in the begin - ning, is now,

D.C.

1. who made heav - en and earth.
2. Is - ra - el's guard.
3. nor the moon — in the night.
4. both now — and for - ever.
5. and will be for ev - er. A - men.

Text: Psalm 121; *The Revised Grail Psalms*, © 2010, Conception Abbey and The Grail, admin. by GIA Publications, Inc., agent
Music: Michel Guimont, © 1995, GIA Publictions, Inc.

40 Psalm 130: With the Lord There Is Mercy

Refrain I

With the Lord there is mer - cy and full - ness of re - demp - tion.

Text: *Lectionary for Mass*, © 1969, 1981, 1997, ICEL
Music: Leon Roberts, © 1987, GIA Publications, Inc.

Refrain II

Out of the depths I cry to you, O Lord.

Text: *Lectionary for Mass*, © 1969, 1981, 1997, ICEL
Music: Norah Duncan IV, © 2012, GIA Publications, Inc.

Verses

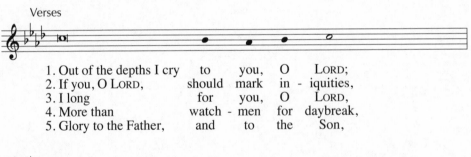

1. Out of the depths I cry   to   you,   O   LORD;
2. If you, O LORD,   should mark in - iquities,
3. I long   for   you,   O   LORD,
4. More than   watch - men   for daybreak,
5. Glory to the Father,   and   to   the Son,

1. Lord,   hear   my   voice!
2. Lord,   who   could stand?
3. my soul longs for   his   word.
4. let Israel hope for   the   LORD.
5. and to the   Ho - ly   Spirit:

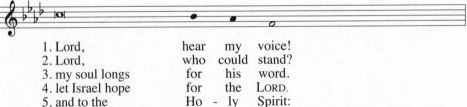

1. O let your   ears   be   at - tentive
2. But with you   is   found for - giveness,
3. My soul   hopes   in   the   Lord
4. {For with the   LORD   there is   mercy,
   {It is he who   will   re - deem Israel
5. as it was in the be - gin - ning, is   now,

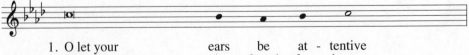

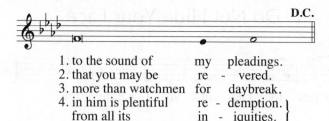

D.C.

1. to the sound of   my   pleadings.
2. that you may be   re - vered.
3. more than watchmen for daybreak.
4. in him is plentiful   re - demption. ⎤
   from all its   in - iquities. ⎦
5. and will be for ever. A - men.

Text: Psalm 130; *The Revised Grail Psalms*, © 2010, Conception Abbey and The Grail, admin. by GIA Publications, Inc., agent
Music: Rawn Harbor, © 1985, GIA Publications, Inc.

Psalm 134: In the Silent Hours of Night 41

Refrain

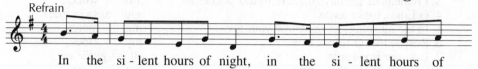

In   the si - lent hours of night, in   the si - lent hours of

night, bless the Lord,   bless the Lord.

Text: *Liturgy of the Hours*, © 1974, ICEL
Music: Norah Duncan IV, © 2012, GIA Publications, Inc.

Verses

1. O come,   bless the Lord, all you servants of the Lord,
2. Lift up your hands to the ho - ly place, and   bless the Lord.
3. Glory to the Father, and to the Son, and to the   Ho - ly Spirit:

1. who stand by night   in the courts
2. May the Lord bless   you from Sion,
3. as it was in the begin - ning, is now,

D.C.

1. of the house   of the Lord.
2. he who made both heav - en and earth.
3. and will be for ev - er. A - men.

Text: Psalm 134; *The Revised Grail Psalms*, © 2010, Conception Abbey and The Grail, admin. by GIA Publications, Inc., agent
Music: Stanbrook Abbey, © 1984, The Benedictine Sisters of Stanbrook Abbey

42 Psalm 143:1–11: Do Not Hide Your Face

Refrain

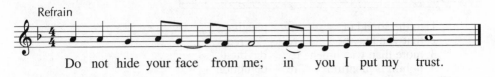

Do not hide your face from me; in you I put my trust.

Text: *Liturgy of the Hours*, © 1974, ICEL
Music: Norah Duncan IV, © 2012, GIA Publications, Inc.

Verses

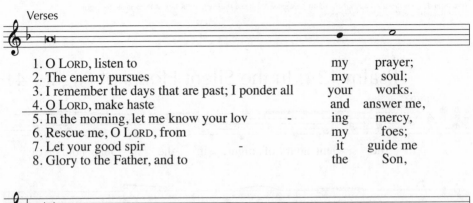

1. O Lord, listen to   my   prayer;
2. The enemy pursues   my   soul;
3. I remember the days that are past; I ponder all   your   works.
4. O Lord, make haste   and   answer me,
5. In the morning, let me know your lov - ing   mercy,
6. Rescue me, O Lord, from   my   foes;
7. Let your good spir - it   guide me
8. Glory to the Father, and to   the   Son,

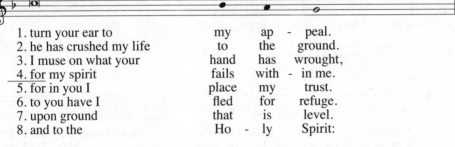

1. turn your ear to   my   ap - peal.
2. he has crushed my life   to   the   ground.
3. I muse on what your   hand   has   wrought,
4. for my spirit   fails   with - in me.
5. for in you I   place   my   trust.
6. to you have I   fled   for   refuge.
7. upon ground   that   is   level.
8. and to the   Ho - ly   Spirit:

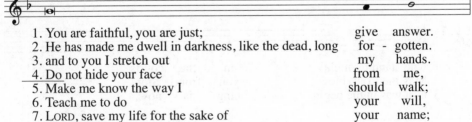

1. You are faithful, you are just;   give   answer.
2. He has made me dwell in darkness, like the dead, long   for - gotten.
3. and to you I stretch out   my   hands.
4. Do not hide your face   from   me,
5. Make me know the way I   should   walk;
6. Teach me to do   your   will,
7. Lord, save my life for the sake of   your   name;
8. as it was in the beginning,   is   now,

D.C.

1. {Do not call your ser - vant to judgment,}
   {for in your sight no one liv - ing is justified. }
2. Therefore my spirit fails; my heart is deso - late with - in me.
3. Like a parched land my soul thirsts for you.
4. lest I become like those who go down in - to the grave.
5. to you I lift up my soul.
6. for you are my God.
7. in your justice, lead my soul out of dis - tress.
8. and will be for ev - er. A - men.

Text: Psalm 143:1–11; *The Revised Grail Psalms*, © 2010, Conception Abbey and The Grail, admin. by GIA Publications, Inc., agent
Music: Paschal Jordan, OSB, © 1986, GIA Publications, Inc.

43   Psalm 145: I Will Praise Your Name

Refrain

I will praise your name for ev - er, my King and my God.

Text: *Lectionary for Mass,* © 1969, 1981, 1997, ICEL
Music: Leon Roberts, © 1987, GIA Publications, Inc.

Verses

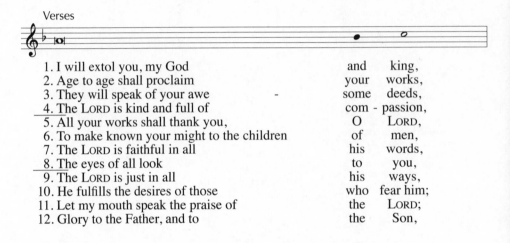

1. I will extol you, my God — and king,
2. Age to age shall proclaim — your works,
3. They will speak of your awe - some deeds,
4. The LORD is kind and full of — com - passion,
5. All your works shall thank you, — O LORD,
6. To make known your might to the children — of men,
7. The LORD is faithful in all — his words,
8. The eyes of all look — to you,
9. The LORD is just in all — his ways,
10. He fulfills the desires of those — who fear him;
11. Let my mouth speak the praise of — the LORD;
12. Glory to the Father, and to — the Son,

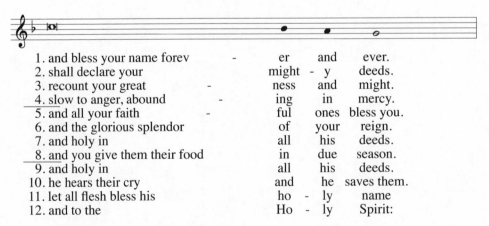

1. and bless your name forev - er and ever.
2. shall declare your might - y deeds.
3. recount your great - ness and might.
4. slow to anger, abound - ing in mercy.
5. and all your faith - ful ones bless you.
6. and the glorious splendor of your reign.
7. and holy in all his deeds.
8. and you give them their food in due season.
9. and holy in all his deeds.
10. he hears their cry and he saves them.
11. let all flesh bless his ho - ly name
12. and to the Ho - ly Spirit:

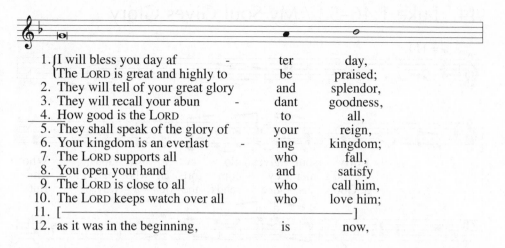

1. {I will bless you day af - ter day,
   {The LORD is great and highly to be praised;
2. They will tell of your great glory and splendor,
3. They will recall your abun - dant goodness,
4. How good is the LORD to all,
5. They shall speak of the glory of your reign,
6. Your kingdom is an everlast - ing kingdom;
7. The LORD supports all who fall,
8. You open your hand and satisfy
9. The LORD is close to all who call him,
10. The LORD keeps watch over all who love him;
11. [————————————————————]
12. as it was in the beginning, is now,

D.C.

1. and praise your name forev - er and ever. ⎱
   his greatness can - not be measured. ⎰
2. and recount your won - der - ful works.
3. and sing of your just deeds with joy.
4. compassionate to all his creatures.
5. and declare your might - y deeds,
6. your rule endures for all gen - er - ations.
7. and raises up all who are bowed down.
8. the desire of every liv - ing thing.
9. who call on him in truth.
10. the wicked he will utter - ly de - stroy.
11. forever, for a - ges un - ending.
12. and will be for ev - er. A - men.

Text: Psalm 145; *The Revised Grail Psalms*, © 2010, Conception Abbey and The Grail, admin. by GIA Publications, Inc.
Music: Paschal Jordan, OSB, © 1986, GIA Publications, Inc.

44   Luke 1:46–53 / My Soul Gives Glory

♩ = 110

1. My soul gives glo - ry to my God   Who
2. God's mer - cy   com - forts all who fear,   Em -
3. God's jus - tice   sends the rich a - way,   But

reach - es   down   with lov - ing   grace   To
brac - ing   with   a   stead - fast   arm   That
feeds   the   poor   with lav - ish   things.   Each

lift   me   from   my   low   es - state   And
casts   the   might - y   from   their   thrones,   But
hun - gry   soul   now   fills   with   joy   And

set   me   in   the high - est place.   Ma - gní - fi - cat,   ma -
keeps   the hum - ble safe from harm.   Ma - gní - fi - cat,   ma -
joins   the   song that Mar - y   sings: Ma - gní - fi - cat,   ma -

Text: *Magnificat*, Mary Louise Bringle, b.1953, © 2003, GIA Publications, Inc.
Tune: DUKTA, LMD; Norah Duncan IV, b.1952, © 2010, GIA Publications, Inc.

45 Luke 1:68–79 / Now Bless the God of Israel

♪ = 150

1. Now bless the God of Is - ra - el, Who
(2. Re -) mem - ber - ing the cov - e - nant, God
(3. In) ten - der mer - cy, God will send The

comes in love and pow'r, Who rais - es from the
res - cues us from fear, That we might serve in
day - spring from on high, Our ris - ing sun, the

roy - al house De - liv - 'rance in this hour. Through
ho - li - ness And peace from year to year; And
light of life For those who sit and sigh. God

ho - ly proph - ets God has sworn To free us from a -
you, my child, shall go be - fore To preach, to proph - e -
comes to guide our way to peace, That death shall reign no

larm, To save us from the heav - y hand Of
sy, That all may know the ten - der love, The
more. Sing prais - es to the Ho - ly One! O

1., 2.   3.

all who wish us harm. 2. Re -
grace of God most high. 3. In
wor - ship and a - dore!

Text: *Benedictus*, Ruth Duck, b.1947, © 1992, GIA Publications, Inc.
Tune: LHOTA, CMD; Norah Duncan IV, b.1952, © 2010, GIA Publications, Inc.

Luke 2:29–35 / Now Let Your Servant   46

♩ = 100

1. Now let your ser - vant go in peace;
2. Be - fore the peo - ples you pre - pare
3. Child, you are cho - sen as a sign
4. Now let us sing our Sav - ior's praise,

Let praise and bless - ing here in - crease;
Your way of life which all may share.
To test the hu - man heart and mind;
And tell God's good - ness all our days.

For in our midst your word is done And
Your sav - ing pow'r is now made known; A -
For se - crets hid - den in the night Shall
While breath is ours, let praise be heard For

you have sent your Prom - ised One.
mong the na - tions love is shown.
be re - vealed in pierc - ing light.
God's own faith - ful, sav - ing Word.

Text: *Nunc dimittis*, Ruth Duck, b.1947, © 1992, GIA Publications, Inc.
Tune: DICKSON, LM; Norah Duncan IV, b.1952, © 2010, GIA Publications, Inc.

Rites of the Church

47 Celebrating the Sacraments

Over our heads we see and hear music, singing, glory, and even trouble in the air. "There must be a God somewhere." So we sing. So we believe. Further, this God who is somewhere is made manifest in wondrous works. Creation in all its wonder is one; creation of our humankind is another. In that latter act God, bending over, fashioned us from the clay of the earth and breathed into our nostrils that divine spark that animates body and soul. And what God has created is very good indeed: flesh and bone, muscle and sinew, heart and liver, brain and breast, hand and foot.

Fearfully and wonderfully made creatures, we worship God, who created the world and all that dwells therein. We remember that in the fullness of time God stepped down from heaven, became flesh, and dwelt among us. We remember and celebrate the wonderful works God has wrought in Jesus, the Word made flesh, splendor of the Father, and we invoke the Holy Spirit, who continues to stir in our midst. We do so at dawn and dusk, day after day, but especially on Sunday, the Lord's Day, assuming a posture of thanksgiving, remembrance, and supplication. We do so at the Eucharist, which is the "source and summit of the Christian life" (*Lumen Gentium*, 11).

Flowing from and ordered to the Eucharist are other vital celebrations of the Christian faith: the six other sacraments. Through the celebration of the sacraments we engage in rites of passage in human life: birth, maturity, vocation, commitment, old age, and death. We celebrate the universal human need for communion, healing, and reconciliation. We do so celebrating the new meaning that the life, death, and resurrection of Jesus Christ gives to our lives and the lives of all people. As such, through the celebration of the sacraments the Church comes to be; and the body of Christ is built up, excited and incited to transform the world. These sacred rites are celebrations of the whole Church, invitations to the deepening of faith and praise of God, who offers salvation in Christ's name within the community of faith.

For us, both as Catholic and Black, these celebrations must be more than those to which we have become accustomed, that is, celebrations that seem to despise flesh rather than love it; celebrations that are lacking in reverence; celebrations that are haphazard, consumerist, and individualistic. On the contrary, truly Catholic and authentically Black sacramental celebrations are attentive to the expansive use of symbols, art, architecture, rhythm, pace, music, body, words, postures, gestures that are a part of the Church's longstanding repertoire and unique to our cultural genius. They are celebrations in which the faithful are full and active in their participation, fully aware of what they are doing, actively engaged in the rite and enriched by its effects (*Sacrosanctum Concilium*, 11, 14).

To celebrate the sacraments this way means realizing first what sacramentality entails. It is a vision of the world as an awesome precinct of God's presence. We tell and testify that God is at work in and through our human activity. Fearless, we draw these human realities into our remembrance of Jesus, who is our all in all. Being a sacramental people, we witness and worship in such a way that there is no competition between God's reality and ours. We are attuned to holiness, the wholly other God. Holiness is not appended to human experience or to earthly things, but drawn out of it. We know this because, as just stated, in the fullness of time God became flesh.

Jesus, Son of God and son of Mary, was indeed flesh: weeping at the death of a loved one, laughing at a wedding feast, spitting on earth and smearing mud in the eyes of a blind person, embracing the outcast, feeding the throngs, sitting at table with friends, breaking bread, bearing the pain of crucifixion, breathing on his friends. Because of our faith in Jesus, the incarnate One, we are radically convinced that God's gracious activity is actualized in and through concrete human situations. The beauty and wonder of the setting sun, the laughter of friends, the meals shared at the family dinner table, the embrace of a loved one, the welcome of a newborn baby, the fondly remembered stories of our elders—here is God made manifest. It is only natural, therefore, that we take up deceptively simple created things like water, oil, bread, and wine and deceptively simple human gestures of touching, eating, drinking, washing, and anointing when we remember the life, death, and resurrection of Jesus.

In our memory of Jesus we see that in and through our human realities God is working once more by the mighty Holy Spirit, and we are transformed. Tertullian, the learned North African layman, exclaimed:

> The flesh is the hinge on which salvation depends. When the soul is dedicated to God, it is the flesh that actually makes it capable of such dedication. For surely the flesh is washed that the soul may be cleansed. The flesh is anointed that the soul may be consecrated. The flesh is sealed that the soul may be fortified. The flesh is overshadowed by the imposition of hands that the soul may be illumined by the Spirit. The flesh feeds on the body and blood of Christ that the soul may fatten on God." (*De resurrectione carnis*, 8)

In our memory of Jesus these fleshly things are transformed to show what is to come of all creation in the Spirit: a Spirit-soaked people, glistening with God's love, reconciled to heaven and earth, and nourished beyond expectation in and through the sacraments of initiation, reconciliation, union, and anointing. In and through the visible, tangible, and audible reality that transformation becomes gripping, accessible, and operative—for the salvation of souls and God's greater glory.

48 Christian Initiation of Adults

Tertullian, a Father of the Church and our North African brother of antiquity, tells us that Christians are made, not born (*Apologetics* 18); and that making takes no little time. It's all accomplished in God's time; accomplished over an extended period of time within the community of faith. The followers of the Lamb, members of the local Church—the catechists and sponsors, the clergy and the diocesan bishop—take part in the journey from inquiry through the catechumenate to baptism, confirmation, and Eucharist. The candidates are invited by word and example to speak from heart to heart, to pray, ponder, and treasure the Scriptures, to fast and to join in the community's custom of charity. They are to learn the way of Jesus from the members of the Church—not only to talk the talk, but walk the walk, deeper, deeper.

This journey of the candidates and community is marked by rites of the Church; thus, the community acknowledges publicly, encourages mightily, and strengthens lovingly these candidates of ours.

The first of these is the rite of becoming catechumens. It concludes the sometimes lengthy period during which those who have come to ask about the way of the Church and the life of a Christian disciple have seen and heard the Gospel proclaimed and practiced. Those who then feel called by God to walk in this pilgrim way—this way of Christ's Church—ask to begin the journey toward full initiation. If the Church discerns and decides the inquirers are ready, they are accepted unreservedly into the Order of Catechumens.

Those who have entered the catechumenate are already part of the household of Christ. During this time the catechumens are to hear and reflect on God's word, to learn the teachings and practices of the Church, gradually to become accustomed to its ways of prayer and discipline, to observe and to join in the good works of Christians toward God, neighbor, and all the earth. Ordinarily the catechumens are present on Sunday for the liturgy of the word and may be sent forth after the homily— to continue prayer and study with their catechists—as we wait in joyful hope for their joining us at the liturgy of the eucharist.

Rites of exorcism and blessing may be celebrated during the catechumenate. Through these rites the gathered Church prays that the catechumens will be purified, strengthened against all evil, and thus eagerly grow in faith and good works. The very presence of the catechumens—at the table of the Word, in these special rites, and in everyday life—is itself a source of strength and blessing to all who want to be more holy, more loving, more like Jesus in their hearts.

Each year as Lent begins, the bishop, with the support of the local pastor and others involved with the catechumens, affirms what wonders God has wrought in the lives of the catechumens. He calls them forth to prepare for their more immediate preparation for baptism, confirmation, and Eucharist at the Easter Vigil. Thus the catechumens become the "elect," the chosen, and for the forty days of Lent they make ready: praying, fasting, doing good works along with all those climbing Jacob's ladder, with every rung going higher and higher. On three Sundays in Lent the rites of scrutiny take place when the assembled Church prays over the elect. Such rites are meant "to uncover, then heal all that is weak, defective, or sinful in the hearts of the elect; to bring out, then strengthen all that is upright, strong, and good . . . in order to deliver the elect from the power of sin and Satan, to protect them against temptation, and to give them strength in Christ, who is the way, the truth, and the life" (*Rite of Christian Initiation of Adults*, 141). Also during Lent the catechumens may receive publicly the words of the Church's profession of faith (Creed)—more our paean of praise than a delineation of doctrine—and the Lord's Prayer—an anchor and balm for the sin-sick soul.

Good Friday and Holy Saturday are days of prayer, fasting, and preparation for the rites of the Easter Vigil. On the night between Saturday and Easter Sunday, the Church assembles to keep vigil and listen to the old, old story—the nine prescribed readings from sacred scripture—"'cause nobody can get too much good news." Then the catechumens are called forward for baptism—that sacrament of putting on Christ, being reborn, becoming a member of the body of Christ; where the sinner sinks beneath that sacred surf that swallows up age and spits out youth. (See the inscription in the baptistery at the Cathedral of Saint John, the Lateran in Rome— translated by A. Kavanagh, *The Shape of Baptism: The Rite of Christian Initiation* [New York: Pueblo, 1978], 49). The newly baptized then experience anointing and the laying on of hands in confirmation, sealing their new life in Christ—making them radiant with the goodness of life. Made new and radiant in baptism, sealed by the Holy Spirit in confirmation, our sisters and brothers in Christ feast on the One whose death and resurrection we all share in Eucharist, saying "Amen!" to Christ and to their own identity, manifesting who and whose they are. Through it all, throughout this entire vigil, the assembled people of God who have supported those in their journey to the riverside are also revived by the sweet, sweet Spirit in that place.

The newly baptized, now called neophytes, take a special place in the Sunday Eucharist throughout the fifty days of Eastertide. This is a time to strengthen the ties that bind.

All of these stages of initiation take place in the midst of the community—those called to be unfading witnesses to Christ's presence in a world of fragile dreams and broken promises, to proclaim the gospel in word and deed, and to serve God, neighbor, and the earth with unfailing love. It is their vital concern, for in and through these various rites, the faithful affirm their support for the catechumens. Their daily discipleship shows the Christian life to the inquirers and catechumens. In turn, the faithful are strengthened and challenged in their faith by the presence of the catechumens, those, who with the world behind them, the cross before them, long to follow Jesus all the way.

In addition to the catechumens, there are others who seek to belong to the Roman Catholic Church. Already baptized, already signed up for the Christian jubilee, their names indelibly inscribed on the roll, these "candidates" are not baptized again. They are brought to full communion by pastoral discernment and personal desire; they deepen their devotion to the Church by engaging in a more profound pondering of the Church's teaching, a more intense spiritual preparation, and a more deliberate celebration of liturgical rites. Reception into full communion may be celebrated at any time. Many will choose to do so particularly during the period of enlightenment leading to the paschal vigil. This reception into full communion of the Catholic Church is accomplished simply by the profession of faith. It may include a celebration of confirmation as well. Like full Christian initiation, reception into the full communion of the Catholic Church finds its climax in the Eucharist, for it is the sacrament of sacraments, the repeatable sacrament of initiation, the pledge of our being broken and poured out for the world, our foretaste of the eternal feast, where all the baptized taste and see how good the Lord is!

49 ACCEPTANCE INTO THE ORDER OF CATECHUMENS

INTRODUCTORY RITES

The priest greets the assembly: candidates, sponsors, members of the parish. The candidates are asked what it is they seek and each replies. Before or during this rite appropriate psalms, e.g., Psalm 63, may be sung. Consult the indexes for song suggestions as well.

CANDIDATES' FIRST ACCEPTANCE OF THE GOSPEL

The priest solemnly asks if the candidates are ready to begin walking this gospel way. The sponsors and all present are asked if they stand ready to assist the candidates as they strive to know and follow Christ. All respond: **We are.**

SIGNING OF THE CANDIDATES WITH THE CROSS

The sign of the cross marks the candidates for their new way of life. The priest signs each on the forehead saying:

N., receive the cross on your forehead.
It is Christ himself who now strengthens you
with this sign of his love.
Learn now to know him and follow him.

Sponsors and others also sign the candidates. Ears and eyes and other senses may also be signed. The priest prays that the catechumens may share in the saving power of the cross.

INVITATION TO THE CELEBRATION OF THE WORD OF GOD

The assembly may go into the church for the Liturgy of the Word, singing an appropriate psalm, e.g., Psalm 34. Consult the indexes for song suggestions as well.

LITURGY OF THE WORD

There may be one or more readings from Scripture, together with a responsorial psalm. After the homily, a Bible may be given to the new catechumens for their study and prayer throughout the time of the catechumenate.

50 RITES OF THE CATECHUMENATE

DISMISSAL OF THE CATECHUMENS

When the catechumens are present at Mass, they are usually sent forth after the homily. Only when they have been baptized are they able to join the faithful in the reception of the eucharist. After their dismissal, the catechumens remain together and are joined by their catechists or others to pray and reflect on the scripture readings.

51

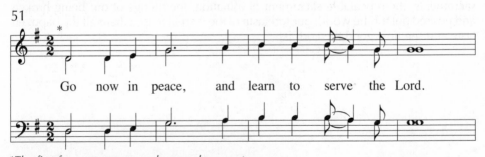

Go now in peace, and learn to serve the Lord.

*The first four measures may be sung by a cantor.

Go now in peace, and learn to fol-low his word.

Go now in peace, and seek that you may find the

the

Way, the Truth, the Life.

Text: John Edelmann
Music: John Edelmann
© 2004, John Edelmann

CELEBRATIONS OF THE WORD OF GOD

On Sundays, after the catechetical sessions, before the beginning of a new liturgical season, and at other times the catechumens and others may join for liturgy: song, reading of Scripture, psalmody, prayer and silence are normally part of such a service.

MINOR EXORCISMS

At appropriate times during the catechumenate, the catechists or other approved ministers may lead the community in prayers of exorcism over the catechumens. These prayers acknowledge the struggle against evil and ask that God strengthen the catechumens.

BLESSINGS OF THE CATECHUMENS

Prayers of blessing and the laying on of hands may take place whenever the catechumens gather for instruction or other purposes. Catechists or other approved ministers ask these blessings over the catechumens.

ANOINTINGS AND PRESENTATIONS

During the catechumenate or during Lent, the candidates may be anointed with the oil of catechumens as a sign of strength given for their struggle to live the gospel. At some point in this time they are publicly presented with the Church's treasury of prayer and faith, the Lord's Prayer and the Creed.

RITE OF ELECTION OR ENROLLMENT OF NAMES

At the beginning of Lent, it is the responsibility of the bishop to call those who are judged ready to prepare for the sacraments of initiation at Easter. The bishop is to consult first with the pastors, catechists and others. The rite of election may take place at the cathedral. If the rite takes place in the parish church, the bishop may designate the pastor to act in his place.

This rite is also called the "Enrollment of Names." Each candidate now gives his or her name, or writes it down. When all have been enrolled, the bishop says: "You have been chosen to be initiated into the sacred mysteries at the Easter Vigil." He then speaks to them and to their sponsors about their lenten preparation for baptism.

The faithful join in prayers of intercession for the elect, as the catechumens are now called. If the Eucharist is to be celebrated, the elect are first sent forth for further reflection and prayer.

SCRUTINIES

During Lent, the elect (those catechumens who have been called to prepare for baptism at Easter) are called to come before the community for exorcisms and prayers. This takes place after the Liturgy of the Word on the Third, Fourth, and Fifth Sundays of Lent. These rites are intended to purify the hearts and minds of the elect, to strengthen them against temptation, and to help them progress in the love of God.

The priest asks the assembly to pray in silence for the elect, then to join in intercessions for them. He lays hands on each of the elect and prays that the elect be delivered from the power of evil and become witnesses to the gospel. A song or psalm may be sung, then the elect are dismissed as usual, and the faithful continue with the liturgy of the eucharist.

PREPARATION RITES

Various preparation rites take place during the day on Holy Saturday. These include prayer, recitation of the Creed, and the rite of ephphetha (opening of ears and mouth).

SACRAMENTS OF INITIATION

The sacraments of initiation take place at the Easter Vigil.

PERIOD OF MYSTAGOGIA

"Mystagogia" refers to the fifty-day period of postbaptismal catechesis and celebration when the newly baptized are gradually drawn by the community into the fullness of Christian life and prayer. The newly baptized retain a special place in the assembly and are mentioned in the prayers of intercession. A special celebration, on Pentecost or just before, may mark the conclusion of the whole period of initiation.

Baptism of Children

52

Knowing that children will be faced with the glare of the conflicting lights within this or any age, parents—either by nature or nurture—bring these little ones to be baptized into the One who is the Light of the World, who saves and sets us free from sin and death. These children are baptized in the faith of the Church: of parents, godparents, the local parish, the Church throughout the world, the saints. Bringing their children for baptism, the parents profess their commitment to make a home where the gospel is loved and lived. And the godparents and all members of the community promise to support the parents in their labor of love, forming these dear ones in word and deed. Thus the children enter the waters of baptism and so are joined to this people, all baptized into the death and resurrection of Christ.

Baptism is celebrated above all at the Easter Vigil, but also on other Sundays, for Sunday is the Lord's Day, the day when the Church gathers to proclaim the paschal mystery. Baptism is always to be celebrated in an assembly of members of the Church and may take place at Sunday Mass.

RECEPTION OF THE CHILDREN

53

The parents and godparents are welcomed by all. The priest/deacon asks the names of the children and questions the parents about their own expectations and willingness to take on the responsibilities this baptism brings. The godparents are asked if they are ready to assist the parents in their responsibilities as Christian mothers and fathers.

With joy, then, the priest/deacon, the parents and godparents make the sign of the cross on the child's forehead as the priest or deacon says: "I claim you for Christ our Savior by the sign of his cross."

All then process to the place where Scripture will be read. The following antiphon, or another appropriate hymn or song, may be sung during the procession:

There is one God and Fa-ther of all.

He is o-ver all and through all.

He lives in all of us; all of us are one.

He lives in all of us; all of us are one, u-nit-ed in Christ Je-sus, u-nit-ed in Christ Je-sus.

54 LITURGY OF THE WORD

FIRST READINGS

One or more passages from Scripture are read. At the conclusion of each:

Reader: The word of the Lord.
Assembly: **Thanks be to God.**

RESPONSORIAL PSALM

The following psalm, or Psalm 23 or 34, may follow the first reading:

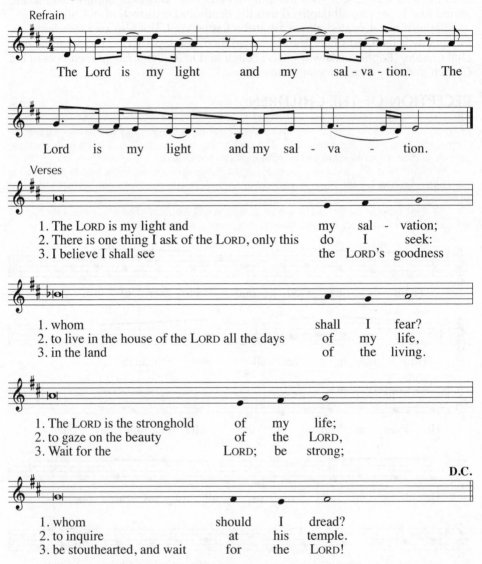

Refrain

The Lord is my light and my sal-va-tion. The

Lord is my light and my sal - va - tion.

Verses

1. The LORD is my light and   my   sal - vation;
2. There is one thing I ask of the LORD, only this   do   I   seek:
3. I believe I shall see   the LORD's goodness

1. whom   shall   I   fear?
2. to live in the house of the LORD all the days   of   my   life,
3. in the land   of   the   living.

1. The LORD is the stronghold   of   my   life;
2. to gaze on the beauty   of   the   LORD,
3. Wait for the   LORD; be   strong;

D.C.

1. whom   should   I   dread?
2. to inquire   at   his   temple.
3. be stouthearted, and wait   for   the   LORD!

Text: Psalm 27:1, 4, 13–14; *The Revised Grail Psalms*, © 2010, Conception Abbey and The Grail, GIA Publications, Inc., agent; refrain, *Lectionary for Mass*, © 1969, ICEL
Music: Norah Duncan IV, © 2012, GIA Publications, Inc.

GOSPEL

55

Before the gospel reading, an acclamation is sung:

Al - le - lu - ia! Al - le - lu - ia!

Al - le - lu - ia! Al - le - lu - ia!

Music: Norah Duncan IV, © 1987, GIA Publications, Inc.

During Lent:

Praise to you, Lord Je - sus Christ, king of end-less glo-ry!

Text: ICEL, © 1969
Music: Norah Duncan IV, © 2012, GIA Publications, Inc.

Cantor:

I am the light of the world, says the Lord;

D.C.

whoever follows me will have the light of life.

Text: ICEL, © 1969
Music: Robert J. Batastini, © 2004, GIA Publications, Inc.

Deacon (or priest): The Lord be with you.
   Assembly: **And with your spirit.**
    Deacon: A reading from the holy Gospel according to N.
   Assembly: **Glory to you, O Lord.**

After the reading:

   Deacon: The Gospel of the Lord.
   Assembly: **Praise to you, Lord Jesus Christ.**

56 INTERCESSIONS

All join in prayer for the Church, the needs of the world, the poor, the children to be baptized and their parents.

Moderately slow with rhythmic refrain

Priest:

God is a good God,
Lord of heaven and earth.
Let us humbly bring our
cares before God's throne...

Let us pray   to the Lord.

(hum)

Response

All:

O   Lord,   hear   our   prayer.

Last time

Intercessions*

Cantor:

1. For	our	Holy Father,	ʼ	for	our
2. May	God	watch over our land,	ʼ	give	our
3. May	God	water our faith,	ʼ	make	it
4. May	God	nourish the peoples of the earth,	ʼ	hun - gry
5. May	God	bring a mighty justice,	send	us	a
6. May	God	watch over our sick, dying, and dead,	ʼ	guard - ing

(hum)

Other intercessions may be interspersed and added as the occasion warrants.

shepherds — and teach - ers,
leaders — com - pas - sion,
bloom in — works of love, — let us pray to the Lord.
for the Table — and the Word,
great mercy and a — last - ing peace,
them in the shadow
of an all-em - brac - ing wing,

Text: Ray East
Music: Ray East
© 1987, GIA Publications, Inc.

This prayer concludes with the litany of the saints, which may include the patron saints of the children and of the local Church.

57

1. Holy Mary, Mother of — God, — pray for us.
2. Saint John the — Bap - tist, — pray for us.
3. Saint — Jo - seph, — pray for us.
4. Saint Peter and Saint — Paul, — pray for us.

The names of other saints may be added here. The litany concludes:

5. All holy men and women, Saints of God, — pray for us.

PRAYER OF EXORCISM AND ANOINTING   58

The priest/deacon stands before the parents with their infants and prays that God deliver these children from the power of evil. The children may be anointed with the oil of catechumens, an anointing which makes them strong for their struggle against evil in their lives. Or, the priest/deacon may lay hands on each child to show the love and concern the Church has for them. If there is a procession to the baptistry, the following may be sung:

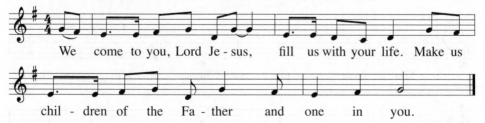

We come to you, Lord Je - sus, fill us with your life. Make us

chil - dren of the Fa - ther and one in you.

Text: *Rite of Baptism for Children,* © 1969, ICEL
Music: Norah Duncan IV, © 2012, GIA Publications, Inc.

59 SACRAMENT OF BAPTISM

BLESSING AND INVOCATION OF GOD OVER BAPTISMAL WATER
When all are gathered at the font, the priest/deacon leads a blessing of the water, unless the baptismal water has already been blessed.

RENUNCIATION OF SIN AND PROFESSION OF FAITH
The priest/deacon then questions the parents and godparents, and they make a renunciation of sin and evil and profess their faith. The assembly listens to their responses. The priest/deacon then invites all to give their assent to this profession of faith, using the following formulary, or a suitable song by which the community expresses its faith with a single voice.

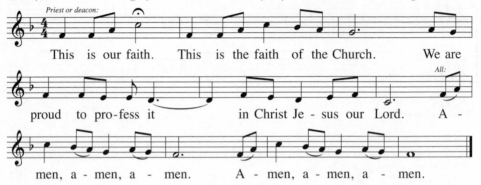

Text: *Rite of Baptism for Children*, © 1969, ICEL
Music: Norah Duncan IV, © 2012, GIA Publications, Inc.

60 BAPTISM

One by one, the infants are brought to the font by their parents. There the parents express their desire to have their child baptized in the faith of the Church which they have professed. The infant is then immersed in the water three times (or water is poured over the infant's head three times) as the priest/deacon says: "N., I baptize you in the name of the Father, and of the Son, and of the Holy Spirit." All may respond to each baptism with an acclamation.

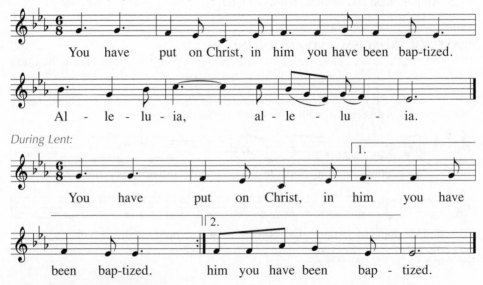

Text: *Rite of Baptism for Children*, © 1969, ICEL
Music: Norah Duncan IV, © 2012, GIA Publications, Inc.

Or, outside Lent:

You have put on Christ, in him you have been bap - tized.

Al - le - lu - ia, al - le - lu - ia.

You have put on Christ, in him you have been bap - tized.

Al - le - lu - ia, al - le - lu - ia.

May be sung in canon.

Text: *Rite of Baptism for Children*, © 1969, ICEL
Music: Howard Hughes, SM, © 1977, ICEL

ANOINTING WITH CHRISM 62

The priest/deacon anoints each child on the crown of the head with holy chrism, a mixture of oil and perfume. The word "Christ" means "anointed." The baptized child has been "Christ-ed" and the sweet smell of the anointing reminds all of this.

CLOTHING WITH THE BAPTISMAL GARMENT AND GIVING OF THE CANDLE

The infants are then clothed in baptismal garments and a candle for each of the newly bap-tized is lighted from the paschal candle.

(Optional) EPHPHETHA

The priest/deacon may touch the ears and mouth of each child: "May Jesus soon touch your ears to receive his word, and your mouth to proclaim his faith."

CONCLUSION AND BLESSING

If baptism is celebrated at Mass, the liturgy continues with the Eucharist. Otherwise, all process to the altar, carrying lighted candles. The above acclamation may be sung again dur-ing this procession. All then pray the Lord's Prayer, the parents are blessed, after which all respond: **Amen**, *and the liturgy concludes with a hymn of praise and thanksgiving.*

63 Holy Communion outside Mass

When for good reason Communion cannot be received at Mass, the faithful may share in the paschal mystery through the liturgy of the word and the reception of Holy Communion.

64 INTRODUCTORY RITES

An appropriate hymn or psalm may be sung.

GREETING

If the minister is a priest or deacon, the usual form of greeting is used:

Assembly: **And with your spirit.**

If the minister is not a priest or deacon, another form of greeting may be used:

Assembly: **Blessed be God for ever.**

PENITENTIAL ACT

The minister invites silent reflection and repentance. After some silence:

Assembly: **I confess to almighty God**
       and to you, my brothers and sisters,
       that I have greatly sinned,
       in my thoughts and in my words,
       in what I have done and in what I have failed to do,
       All strike their breast as they say:
       through my fault, through my fault,
       through my most grievous fault;
       therefore I ask blessed Mary ever-Virgin,
       all the Angels and Saints,
       and you, my brothers and sisters,
       to pray for me to the Lord our God.

The forms found at nos. 100 and 101 may also be used.

65 CELEBRATION OF THE WORD OF GOD

FIRST READINGS

One or more passages from Scripture are read. At the conclusion of each:

  Reader: The word of the Lord.
Assembly: **Thanks be to God.**

RESPONSORIAL PSALM

An appropriate psalm may follow the first reading.

GOSPEL 66

Before the gospel reading, an alleluia or Lenten acclamation is sung.

[*Deacon (or priest):* The Lord be with you.]
       Assembly: **And with your spirit.**]
        Reader: A reading from the holy Gospel according to N.
      Assembly: **Glory to you, O Lord.**

After the reading:

      Reader: The Gospel of the Lord.
     Assembly: **Praise to you, Lord Jesus Christ.**

INTERCESSIONS 67

The assembly joins in prayer for the needs of the world, of the poor, and of the Church.

HOLY COMMUNION 68

The minister invites all to join in the Lord's Prayer, then to exchange a sign of peace. The minister then raises the eucharistic bread and all respond to the invitation.

Assembly: **Lord, I am not worthy**
        that you should enter under my roof,
        but only say the word
        and my soul shall be healed.

A psalm or hymn may be sung during Communion. Afterwards, there may be a period of silence or the singing of a psalm or hymn. The minister then recites a concluding prayer.

CONCLUDING RITE

All are blessed and dismissed.

Presiding minister: Go in the peace of Christ.

    Assembly: **Thanks be to God.**

69 Eucharistic Exposition and Benediction

"Exposition of the holy eucharist . . . is intended to acknowledge Christ's marvelous presence in the sacrament. Exposition invites us to the spiritual union with him that culminates in sacramental communion. Thus it fosters very well the worship which is due to Christ in spirit and in truth.

This kind of exposition must clearly express the cult of the blessed sacrament in its relationship to the Mass. The plan of the exposition should carefully avoid anything which might somehow obscure the principal desire of Christ in instituting the eucharist, namely, to be with us as food, medicine, and comfort" (*Holy Communion and Worship of the Eucharist outside of Mass*, #82).

70 EXPOSITION

As the priest or deacon prepares the holy eucharist for adoration, the following or another suitable song is sung:

1. O sav - ing Vic - tim, o - p'ning wide The
2. To your great name be end - less praise, Im -
1. O sa - lu - tá - ris hó - sti - a, Quae
2. U - ni tri - nó - que Dó - mi - no Sit

gate of heav'n to us be - low! Our foes press on from
mor - tal God - head, One in Three; O grant us end - less
cae - li pan - dis ó - sti - um: Bel - la pre - munt ho -
sem - pi - tér - na gló - ri - a: Qui vi - tam si - ne

ev - 'ry side; Your aid sup - ply, your strength be - stow.
length of days When our true na - tive land we see.
stí - li - a, Da ro - bur fer au - xí - li - um.
tér - mi - no No - bis do - net in pá - tri - a.

Text: Thomas Aquinas, 1227–1275; tr. by Edward Caswall, 1814–1878, and John Mason Neale, 1818–1866, alt.
Music: DUGUET, LM; Dieudonné Duguet, 1794–1849

ADORATION 71

During the adoration there are prayers, songs, scripture readings, and possibly a homily to develop a better understanding of the eucharistic mystery. Silent prayer is also encouraged. If time allows, the Liturgy of the Hours may be celebrated here.

BENEDICTION 72

As the priest or deacon incenses the Blessed Sacrament, the following or another appropriate hymn or song may be sung:

1. Come a-dore this won-drous pres-ence; Bow to Christ, the source of grace! Here is kept the an-cient prom-ise Of God's earth-ly dwell-ing-place. Sight is blind be-fore God's glo-ry. Faith a-lone may see his face.

2. Glo-ry be to God the Fa-ther, Praise to his co-e-qual Son, Ad-o-ra-tion to the Spir-it, Bond of love, in God-head one. Blest be God by all cre-a-tion Joy-ous-ly while a-ges run!

1. *Tan-tum er-go Sa-cra-mén-tum Ve-ne-ré-mur cér-nu-i: Et an-tí-quum do-cu-mén-tum No-vo ce-dat rí-tu-i: Prae-stet fi-des sup-ple-mén-tum Sén-su-um de-fé-ctu-i.*

2. *Ge-ni-tó-ri, Ge-ni-tó-que Laus et ju-bi-lá-ti-o, Sa-lus, ho-nor, vir-tus quo-que Sit et be-ne-dí-cti-o: Pro-ce-dén-ti ab u-tró-que Com-par sit lau-dá-ti-o.*

Text: Thomas Aquinas, 1227–1275; tr. by James Quinn, SJ, 1919–2010, © 1969, James Quinn, SJ. Selah Publishing Co., Inc., North American agent
Music: ST. THOMAS, 8 7 8 7 8 7; John F. Wade, 1711–1786

After a prayer, the priest or deacon blesses the assembly with the Blessed Sacrament.

73 REPOSITION

As the priest or deacon replaces the Sacrament in the tabernacle, the assembly may sing or say the following acclamations:

Blessed be God.
Blessed be his holy name.
Blessed be Jesus Christ, true God and true man.
Blessed be the name of Jesus.
Blessed be his most sacred heart.
Blessed be his most precious blood.
Blessed be Jesus in the most holy sacrament of the altar.
Blessed be the Holy Spirit, the Paraclete.
Blessed be the great Mother of God, Mary most holy.
Blessed be her holy and immaculate conception.
Blessed be her glorious assumption.
Blessed be the name of Mary, virgin and mother.
Blessed be Saint Joseph, her most chaste spouse.
Blessed be God in his angels and in his saints.

The sacrament of penance, also called the sacrament of reconciliation, may be celebrated with one penitent or with many. The latter form, the communal penance service, is a gathering of a few or a large number of Christians. Together they listen to Scripture, sing psalms and hymns, pray, individually confess their sins and receive absolution, then praise God whose mercy and love are greater than our evil. In the rite of penance, the members of the Church confront the struggle that was entered at baptism. There has been failure, evil done and good undone, but the penitent Church comes again and again to name and renounce its sins and to return to the way of the Lord.

INTRODUCTORY RITES 75
An appropriate hymn or psalm may be sung (see nos. 766–777).

GREETING
The priest greets the assembly, using these or other words:

> *Priest:* Grace to you and peace from God our Father
> and the Lord Jesus Christ.
> *Assembly:* **And with your spirit.**

OPENING PRAYER
After silent prayer, the priest concludes the gathering rite with a solemn prayer.

CELEBRATION OF THE WORD OF GOD 76
The liturgy of the word is celebrated in the usual way with one or two first readings, a responsorial psalm, gospel acclamation and gospel, followed by the homily. Appropriate psalms for this rite are Psalms 13, 25, 31, 51, 90, 123, 130, or 143.

EXAMINATION OF CONSCIENCE
In silence or through some other manner all reflect on their lives with sorrow for their sins.

SACRAMENT OF PENANCE 77

GENERAL CONFESSION OF SINS
Kneeling (or with another posture that expresses sorrow), all join in confession. This form may be used:

> *Assembly:* **I confess to almighty God**
> **and to you, my brothers and sisters,**
> **that I have greatly sinned,**
> **in my thoughts and in my words,**
> **in what I have done and in what I have failed to do,**
> *All strike their breast as they say:*
> **through my fault, through my fault,**
> **through my most grievous fault;**
> **therefore I ask blessed Mary ever-Virgin,**
> **all the Angels and Saints,**
> **and you, my brothers and sisters,**
> **to pray for me to the Lord our God.**

78

Standing, all join in a litany using one of the following responses, or a song asking God's mercy. The Lord's Prayer is then recited or sung. (See no. 115)

☐ A **We pray you, hear us.**

☐ B **Lord, be merciful to me, a sinner.**

☐ C **Lord, have mercy.**

79 INDIVIDUAL CONFESSION AND ABSOLUTION

One by one the penitents approach the priest confessors. All confess their sins, accept some fitting act of satisfaction and the counsel of the confessor. Then the priest extends his hands over the penitent's head and speaks the prayer of absolution, concluding: "Through the ministry of the Church may God give you pardon and peace, and I absolve you from your sins in the name of the Father, and of the Son, and of the Holy Spirit." The penitent responds, "Amen." (Note: On those occasions when general absolution is permitted, the rest of the rite remains the same.)

PROCLAMATION OF PRAISE FOR GOD'S MERCY

The priest invites all to give thanks and to show by their lives—and in the life of the whole community—the grace of repentance. A psalm, canticle or hymn may be sung to proclaim God's mercy.

CONCLUDING PRAYER OF THANKSGIVING

This prayer is spoken by the priest.

BLESSING AND DISMISSAL

The priest blesses all present and the deacon or other minister dismisses the assembly.

All respond: **Thanks be to God.**

Anointing of the Sick

The sacrament of the anointing of the sick is celebrated when a Christian's health is seriously impaired by sickness or old age. Through the anointing with the blessed oil of the sick, the Church supports those who struggle against illness or injury and continues the healing work of Christ. The anointing is intended to bring hope and comfort to those anointed and, to the gathered assembly of family and friends, a spirit of support and sharing in the sufferings of their brothers and sisters.

The anointing may be celebrated within Mass or outside Mass. In either case a liturgy of the word precedes the anointing. Following is the rite of anointing within Mass.

INTRODUCTORY RITES 81

An appropriate hymn or psalm may be sung (see nos. 778–782).

GREETING
After all make the sign of the cross, the priest greets the assembly, using these or other words.

> *Priest:* The grace of our Lord Jesus Christ,
> and the love of God,
> and the communion of the Holy Spirit
> be with you all.

Assembly: **And with your spirit.**

The priest introduces the celebration, and the penitential act may follow (see Order of Mass, nos. 100 and 101). Then, after a period of silence, he says the opening prayer, to which all respond: **Amen**.

LITURGY OF THE WORD 82
The liturgy of the word is celebrated in the usual way with one or two first readings, a responsorial psalm, gospel acclamation and gospel, followed by the homily. Appropriate psalms for this rite are Psalms 6, 25, 27, 34, 42, 63, 71, 86, 90, 102, 103, 123, or 143.

LITURGY OF ANOINTING 83

LITANY
The assembly joins in prayers for the sick and for those who care for them. Each petition concludes with "Lord, have mercy," and all repeat:

Lord,   have   mer - cy.

LAYING ON OF HANDS
The priest silently lays hands on the head of each sick person in a gesture of prayer, healing and solidarity.

84 PRAYER OVER THE OIL

If the oil is already blessed, the priest leads a prayer of thanksgiving over it.
After each invocation:

Bless-ed be God who heals us in Christ.

Text: *Pastoral Care of the Sick: Rites of Anointing and Viaticum*, © 1982, ICEL
Music: Paul M. French, © 2011, GIA Publications, Inc.

If the oil is not blessed, the priest says the prayer of blessing.

85 ANOINTING

The priest anoints each sick person on the forehead, saying:

Through this holy anointing may the Lord in his love and mercy help you with the grace of the Holy Spirit.

Assembly: **Amen.**

The priest anoints the hands of each sick person, saying:

May the Lord who frees you from sin save you and raise you up.

Assembly: **Amen.**

The priest may anoint other parts of the body.

PRAYER AFTER ANOINTING

The priest prays for those who have been anointed. Then the liturgy of the eucharist is celebrated with special prayers for the sick (see Order of Mass, no. 108).

If the rite of anointing is celebrated outside Mass, the liturgy begins with the greeting, introduction, and penitential act (or sacrament of penance). After the scripture readings a period of silence is observed, or the priest gives a brief homily. The liturgy of anointing is celebrated as above. Then the Lord's Prayer is recited or sung, the liturgy of Holy Communion may follow, and a final blessing is given.

Marriage 86

The mutual and lifelong commitment of a man and a woman in marriage is viewed by the Church as a sacred covenant. When two Christians marry, it is also a sacrament, an effective sign of the presence of God in the world and a symbol of Christ's love for his Church. In the sacrament of matrimony God's special graces are given to the couple to live out "in mutual and lasting fidelity" the vows they make to each other and to God in the presence of the Christian community.

At their wedding the bride and groom themselves are the ministers of the sacrament to each other; the priest or deacon who presides over the wedding serves as the authorized witness of the Church and prays the nuptial blessing of the Church over the spouses.

The rite of marriage may be celebrated at Mass or outside of Mass. In either case the rite begins with a liturgy of the word: the proclamation of God's faithful love by means of readings from Scripture and a reflection on them (the homily). The following elements are included in all celebrations.

INTRODUCTORY RITES 87

An appropriate hymn or psalm may be sung during the procession or immediately after it.

GREETING

After all make the sign of the cross, the priest or deacon greets the assembly, using these or other words.

> *Priest:* The grace of our Lord Jesus Christ,
> and the love of God,
> and the communion of the Holy Spirit
> be with you all.
>
> *Assembly:* **And with your spirit.**

OPENING PRAYER

The priest or deacon introduces the celebration and, after a period of silence, says the opening prayer, to which all respond: **Amen***. All then sit.*

LITURGY OF THE WORD 88

The liturgy of the word is celebrated in the usual way with one or two first readings, a responsorial psalm, gospel acclamation and gospel, followed by the homily. Appropriate psalms for this rite are Psalms 33, 34, 103, 112, 128, 145, or 148.

RITE OF MARRIAGE 89

After the homily all stand. The priest or deacon invites the couple to declare to each other their consent to enter into marriage, and receives the couple's vows in the name of the Church. Wedding rings, a sign of love and fidelity, may be blessed and exchanged and, according to particular customs, other rituals expressing the couple's union may be added.

In the prayer of the faithful the Church prays for the needs of the world, the local community, and the newly married couple. A common response to each petition is: **Lord, hear our prayer.**

If the liturgy of the eucharist does not follow the rite of marriage, the priest or deacon prays the nuptial blessing at the end of the prayer of the faithful. The celebration concludes with the Lord's Prayer and a final blessing.

When the liturgy of the eucharist follows the rite of marriage, the nuptial blessing is given after the Lord's Prayer before Holy Communion. Everything else follows the Order of Mass, beginning with the presentation and preparation of the gifts. The bride and groom may bring the bread and wine to the altar. See Order of Mass, no. 108.

90 THE LORD'S PRAYER

Assembly: **Our Father, who art in heaven,**
hallowed be thy name;
thy kingdom come,
thy will be done
on earth as it is in heaven.
Give us this day our daily bread,
and forgive us our trespasses,
as we forgive those who trespass against us;
and lead us not into temptation,
but deliver us from evil.

BLESSING AND DISMISSAL

All respond to each part of the blessing: **Amen.**

Deacon or priest: Go in peace.
Assembly: **Thanks be to God.**

A hymn or instrumental music may follow.

Funerals 91

The rites which surround the death of a Christian extend from Viaticum (the last Holy Communion) and final prayers before death through the wake service and funeral liturgy to the burial of the body or cremated remains. In the African-American community these rites are celebrated in many and varied ways. What is common to them all is a sense of kinship that survives the grave and a hope in the eschatological future where all will be well. In all of this the community affirms its faith in the communion of saints and the resurrection of the dead. The family and friends are helped in their time of sorrow with prayer and song. Thus they express present grief even as they hold to the Church's lasting hope.

The funeral liturgy may be celebrated within Mass or outside Mass. In either case the rite begins with a liturgy of the word. The following elements are included in all celebrations.

INTRODUCTORY RITES

GREETING 92

All stand as the priest (or deacon) greets the assembly at the door, using these or other words.

> *Priest:* Grace to you and peace from God our Father
> and the Lord Jesus Christ.

Assembly: **And with your spirit.**

The body is sprinkled with holy water, a reminder of baptism. The family or pall bearers spread the pall, a garment like that which the Christian received at baptism, over the body. The funeral procession then moves into the church accompanied by an appropriate hymn or psalm.

The liturgy continues as usual with the Collect prayer and the liturgy of the word (see Order of Mass, no. 103).

The liturgy of the word consists of one or two first readings, a responsorial psalm, gospel acclamation and gospel, followed by the homily and prayer of the faithful. Appropriate psalms for this rite are Psalms 23, 25, 27, 42, 63, 103, 116, 122, 130, or 143.

FINAL COMMENDATION 93

If the funeral liturgy is celebrated within Mass, the final commendation follows the prayer after communion. When the funeral liturgy is celebrated outside Mass, the final commendation follows the prayer of the faithful. The ministers and assembly gather around the body of the deceased. After an invitation to prayer, all pray silently. The coffin may then be sprinkled with holy water and incensed, or this may take place during or after the song of farewell.

SONG OF FAREWELL 94

The following or another appropriate responsory or song may be sung.

Verses

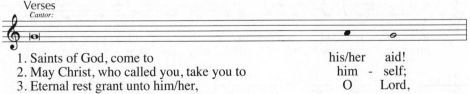

1. Saints of God, come to   his/her   aid!
2. May Christ, who called you, take you to   him - self;
3. Eternal rest grant unto him/her,   O   Lord,

Hasten to meet him/her, angels   of   the   Lord!
may angels lead you to the bos - om   of   Abraham.
and let perpetual light   shine up - on him/her.

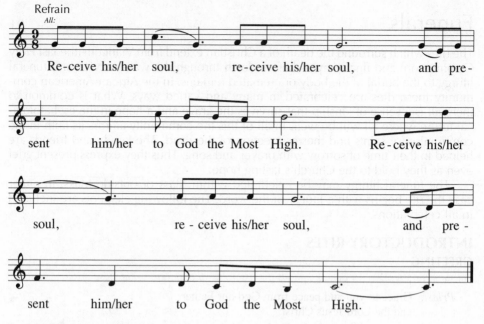

Text: *Order of Christian Funerals*, © 1985, ICEL
Music: ASSURANCE; Pheobe P. Knapp, 1839–1908; adapt. by Norah Duncan IV, © 2011, GIA Publications, Inc.

95   PRAYER OF COMMENDATION

At the conclusion of the prayer all respond: **Amen.**

PROCESSION TO THE PLACE OF COMMITTAL

The deacon or priest says: In peace let us take our brother/sister to his/her place of rest.

96   SONG

As the assembly leaves the church, one of the following, or another appropriate song may be sung.

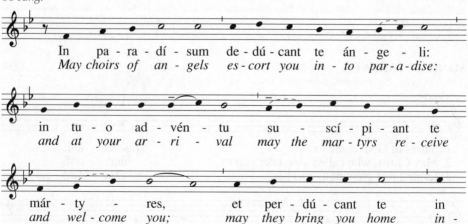

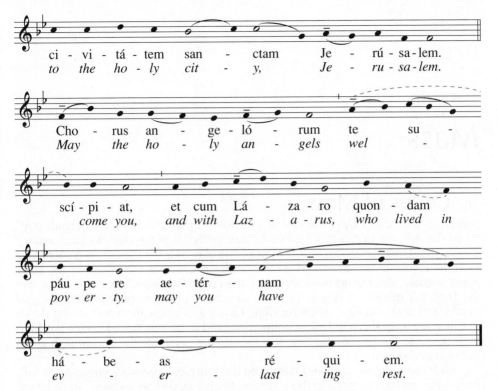

ci - vi - tá - tem san - ctam Je - rú - sa - lem.
to the ho - ly cit - y, Je - ru - sa - lem.

Cho - rus an - ge - ló - rum te su -
May the ho - ly an - gels wel -

scí - pi - at, et cum Lá - za - ro quon - dam
come you, and with Laz - a - rus, who lived in

páu - pe - re ae - tér - nam
pov - er - ty, may you have

há - be - as ré - qui - em.
ev - er - last - ing rest.

Text: *In paradísum* and *Chorus angelórum,* tr. © 1986, GIA Publications, Inc.
Tune: Mode VII; acc. by Richard Proulx, 1937–2010, © 1986, GIA Publications, Inc.

97

Je - sus, re - mem - ber me when you come in - to your King - dom.

Je - sus, re - mem - ber me when you come in - to your King - dom.

Text: Luke 23:42; Taizé Community, 1981
Tune: Jacques Berthier, 1923–1994
© 1981, Les Presses de Taizé, GIA Publications, Inc., agent

Mass

98 Order of Mass

Sunday is the Lord's Day, the day of creation and resurrection, the "eighth day" when the fullness of God's kingdom is anticipated. It is the day "to steal away"; the day the Lord "bears our spirits home." It is day that the Church is gathered by God the Father to be saved and set free by Jesus Christ in the power of the Holy Spirit, namely, the memorial of the Lord, the eucharistic sacrifice. "This is the day the Lord has made"—a day to listen to sacred scripture, to offer prayers, to give thanks and praise to God while recalling God's gifts in creation and saving deeds in Christ Jesus, to share in Holy Communion, and to be sent back into the world to transform it to God's greater glory. It is the day we celebrate the Eucharist in all its richness and power.

All those who are gathered constitute the liturgical assembly engaging in full, conscious, and active participation, willing to give as well as receive. An ordained priest or bishop, standing in the person of Christ, presides over us all, God's holy people. He gives voice to our prayers, particularly the eucharistic prayer, the high point of the entire celebration. A deacon may assist, proclaim the gospel and preach. Other members of the congregation are chosen and trained for various ministries: readers, altar servers, ushers, musicians, and extraordinary ministers of Holy Communion. All of these assist us in our prayer and praise.

The Order of Mass that follows is familiar to all who regularly join in this assembly. It is learned through repetition. Following it faithfully, attentive to the liturgical year, and with "due regard for the nature and particular circumstances of each liturgical assembly" (*General Instruction of the Roman Missal*, 18), the Order of Mass frees us to be instructed and refreshed in the Lord.

INTRODUCTORY RITES

The introductory rites serve to bring us, who come from many places both geographically and emotionally, to one place: the presence of the Lord. It is a time to remember that "in Christ there is no east or west, in him no south or north, but one great family bound by love throughout the whole wide earth." The procession and the entrance chant are ways of expressing that union of minds and hearts. For a people knowing that our arms are too short to box with God, we ask for forgiveness; and then we praise God for the mercy wrought in the redemptive death of the Savior. In the celebratory fashion of our ancestors in the faith, we acclaim: *Lord, have mercy!* (the penitential act). Remembering the triune God's promise of forgiveness we shout: *Glory to God in the highest!* Ever aware of the unfolding of God's divine drama, whether on bended knee or at play, we can never escape from standing in the need of prayer: *Let us pray!* (the collect, or opening prayer).

GREETING
All make the sign of the cross.

Priest: In the name of the Father, and of the Son, and of the Holy Spirit.

A - men.

After the sign of the cross one of the greetings is given.

A	*Priest:*	The grace of our Lord Jesus Christ,
		and the love of God,
		and the communion of the Holy Spirit
		be with you all.

B	*Priest:*	Grace to you and peace from God our Father
		and the Lord Jesus Christ.

| C | *Priest:* | The Lord be with you. (*Bishop:* Peace be with you.) |

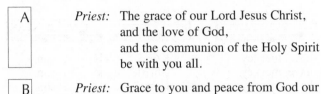

And   with   your   spir - it.

BLESSING AND SPRINKLING OF HOLY WATER   99
On Sundays, especially during the season of Easter, instead of the penitential act, the blessing and sprinkling of holy water may take place. It is a time to remember that we have waded in the water and been baptized.

PENITENTIAL ACT   100
The priest invites all to be mindful of their sins and of the great mercy of God. After a time of silence, one of the following forms is used.

A	*Assembly:*	**I confess to almighty God**
		and to you, my brothers and sisters,
		that I have greatly sinned,
		in my thoughts and in my words,
		in what I have done and in what I have failed to do,
		All strike their breast as they say:
		through my fault, through my fault,
		through my most grievous fault;
		therefore I ask blessed Mary ever-Virgin,
		all the Angels and Saints,
		and you, my brothers and sisters,
		to pray for me to the Lord our God.

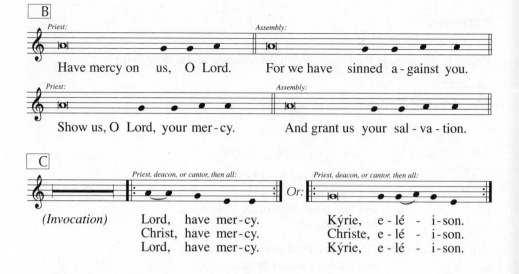

B

Priest: Have mercy on us, O Lord.

Assembly: For we have sinned a-gainst you.

Priest: Show us, O Lord, your mer-cy.

Assembly: And grant us your sal-va-tion.

C

(Invocation)

Priest, deacon, or cantor, then all:
Lord, have mer-cy.
Christ, have mer-cy.
Lord, have mer-cy.

Or:

Priest, deacon, or cantor, then all:
Kýrie, e-lé-i-son.
Christe, e-lé-i-son.
Kýrie, e-lé-i-son.

Priest: May almighty God…everlasting life.

Assembly: A - men.

101 KYRIE

Unless form C of the penitential act has been used, the Kyrie follows.

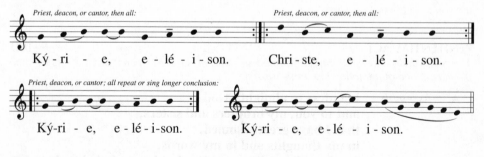

Priest, deacon, or cantor, then all:
Ký-ri-e, e-lé-i-son.

Priest, deacon, or cantor, then all:
Chri-ste, e-lé-i-son.

Priest, deacon, or cantor; all repeat or sing longer conclusion:
Ký-ri-e, e-lé-i-son.

Ký-ri-e, e-lé-i-son.

Or:

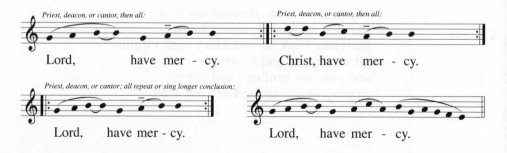

Priest, deacon, or cantor, then all:
Lord, have mer-cy.

Priest, deacon, or cantor, then all:
Christ, have mer-cy.

Priest, deacon, or cantor; all repeat or sing longer conclusion:
Lord, have mer-cy.

Lord, have mer-cy.

GLORIA

The Gloria is omitted during Advent, Lent, and most weekdays.

Glo-ry to God in the high-est, and on earth peace to peo-ple

of good will. We praise you, we bless you, we a-dore you,

we glo-ri-fy you, we give you thanks for your great glo-ry,

Lord God, heav-en-ly King, O God, al-might-y Fa-ther.

Lord Je-sus Christ, On-ly Be-got-ten Son, Lord God, Lamb of God,

Son of the Fa-ther, you take a-way the sins of the world, have mer-cy on us;

you take a-way the sins of the world, re-ceive our prayer;

you are seat-ed at the right hand of the Fa-ther, have mer-cy on us.

For you a-lone are the Ho-ly One, you a-lone are the Lord,

you a-lone are the Most High, Je-sus Christ, with the Ho-ly Spir-it,

in the glo-ry of God the Fa - ther. A - men.

COLLECT

After the invitation from the priest, all pray in silence for a while. The introductory rites conclude with the proper opening prayer to which all respond: **Amen.**

103 LITURGY OF THE WORD

It has been said that we are a people of the Book. Our Black African American bishops have stated that truth in a most compelling way: "African-American spirituality is based on the sacred Scriptures. In the dark days of slavery, reading was forbidden, but for our ancestors the Bible was never a closed book. . . . For Black people the story is our story; the Bible promise is our hope. Thus when the word of Scripture is proclaimed in the Black community, it is not a new message but a new challenge. Scripture is part of our roots; the Bible has sunk deep into our tradition; and the good news of the Gospels has been enmeshed in our past of oppression and pain" (*What We Have Seen and Heard*, 4–5).

The liturgy of the word, then, is as significant for us as it is for the entire Church. In it, the table of God's word is spread before us and the treasures of the Bible are opened for us (GIRM, 57). The first reading, proclaimed by a reader from the assigned place in the Lectionary, is normally from the Old Testament. The second reading, also proclaimed by a reader, is usually from one of the apostolic letters of the New Testament. The third reading is the gospel, normally proclaimed by the deacon from the Book of Gospels. All of this is celebrated over a three-year cycle. During the Sundays of Ordinary Time, the apostolic letters and gospels are proclaimed in order, each Sunday continuing near the place where the previous Sunday's readings ended. During Advent–Christmas and Lent–Easter, the readings are those which are traditional and appropriate to these seasons.

We listen to and—through the weeks and years—are shaped by the word of God to which we who are gathered give our full attention. A time of silence and reflection follows each of the two readings. After the first reading, this reflection continues in the singing of the responsorial psalm. The homily, bringing together the scripture readings, and the joys and hopes, the grief and anguish of those assembled, follows the gospel. The liturgy of the word concludes with the dismissal of the catechumens, followed by the profession of faith and the prayer of the faithful. In the former, we proclaim that "we've come this far by faith." In the latter, we continue the constant work of recalling and praying for the universal Church and all those in need.

This reading and hearing of the word of God—simple things that they are—are the foundation of the liturgical celebration. The public proclamation of sacred scripture and the rituals that surround this—silence and psalm and acclamation, posture and gesture, preaching and intercession—gather the Church generation after generation. They gather and sustain and gradually give us a new talk, a new walk, a new attitude; forming us once more and again in the glorious image of Christ, who is the Word made flesh, our good brother, and Lord.

FIRST READING

After the reading:

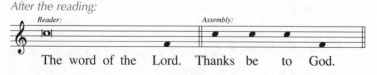

The word of the Lord. Thanks be to God.

After a period of silence, the responsorial psalm is sung.

SECOND READING

After the reading:

The word of the Lord. Thanks be to God.

A time of silence follows the reading.

GOSPEL   104

Before the gospel, an acclamation is sung.

Al - le - lú - ia, al - le - lú - ia, al - le - lú - ia.

Music: Chant Mode VI; acc. by Richard Proulx, © 1985, GIA Publications, Inc.

During Lent:

Praise and hon - or to you, O Lord Je - sus Christ.

Text: ICEL, © 1969
Music: *Kyrie Orbis Factor,* acc. by David Hurd, © 1979, GIA Publications, Inc.

Tone for verses

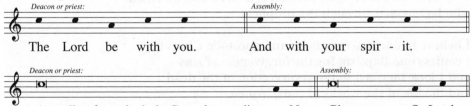

Music: Tone 6F; acc. by Robert J. Batastini, © 1986, GIA Publications, Inc.

Before the gospel:

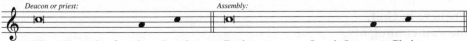

The Lord be with you. And with your spir - it.

A reading from the holy Gospel according to N. Glory to you, O Lord.

After the reading:

The Gospel of the Lord. Praise to you, Lord Je - sus Christ.

HOMILY

105 PROFESSION OF FAITH

**I believe in one God,
the Father almighty,
maker of heaven and earth,
of all things visible and invisible.**

**I believe in one Lord Jesus Christ,
the Only Begotten Son of God,
born of the Father before all ages.
God from God, Light from Light,
true God from true God,
begotten, not made, consubstantial with the Father;
through him all things were made.
For us men and for our salvation
he came down from heaven,**

All bow at the following words up to and including: and became man.

**and by the Holy Spirit was incarnate of the Virgin Mary,
and became man.**

**For our sake he was crucified under Pontius Pilate,
he suffered death and was buried,
and rose again on the third day
in accordance with the Scriptures.
He ascended into heaven
and is seated at the right hand of the Father.
He will come again in glory
to judge the living and the dead
and his kingdom will have no end.**

**I believe in the Holy Spirit, the Lord, the giver of life,
who proceeds from the Father and the Son,
who with the Father and the Son is adored and glorified,
who has spoken through the prophets.**

**I believe in one, holy, catholic and apostolic Church.
I confess one Baptism for the forgiveness of sins
and I look forward to the resurrection of the dead
and the life of the world to come. Amen.**

106 *Instead of the Nicene Creed, especially during Lent and the Easter season,
the Apostles' Creed may be used:*

**I believe in God,
the Father almighty,
Creator of heaven and earth,
and in Jesus Christ, his only Son, our Lord,**

All bow at the following words up to and including: the Virgin Mary.

who was conceived by the Holy Spirit,
born of the Virgin Mary,
suffered under Pontius Pilate,
was crucified, died and was buried;
he descended into hell;
on the third day he rose again from the dead;
he ascended into heaven,
and is seated at the right hand of God the Father almighty;
from there he will come to judge the living and the dead.

I believe in the Holy Spirit,
the holy catholic Church,
the communion of saints,
the forgiveness of sins,
the resurrection of the body,
and life everlasting. Amen.

PRAYER OF THE FAITHFUL 107
The people respond to each petition as follows, or according to local practice.

Lord, hear our prayer.

Or: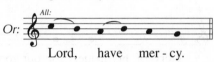

Lord, have mer-cy.

LITURGY OF THE EUCHARIST 108

The heart of the gospel message is a God who gives, waking us up in the morning, clothing us, and putting us in our right minds. From the introductory rites through the liturgy of the word we experience this reality again and again. The liturgy of the eucharist affords us an opportunity to give in return, to respond in a unique way, to give God all the glory, honor, and thanksgiving; for the very word eucharist itself means to do just that.

When the altar is prepared with the offerings of bread and wine, the priest bids us to lift our hearts on high in prayer and thanksgiving, remembering a God who sits high and looks low, remembering the wonders God has wrought in creation and beyond in saving deeds. The center of this is the paschal mystery—the paschal sacrifice—the death and resurrection of our Lord Jesus Christ, which destroyed the power of death, and brings us life to the full. That awesome and life-changing mystery into which we were baptized we proclaim each Sunday, at dawn and at dusk, year after year. It is the very shape of Christian life.

We find this mystery in the simple bread and wine, which stir our remembering and draw forth our prayer of thanksgiving addressed by the priest to God the Father through Jesus Christ in the Holy Spirit. "Fruit of the earth and work of human hands," the bread and wine become our Holy Communion in the Body and Blood of the Lord. We eat and drink and so proclaim that we belong to the Lord and one another.

We interiorly prepare ourselves even as the altar is being prepared. Again, the priest invites us to lift up our hearts and join in the eucharistic prayer. We do this by giving our full attention and by singing full-throated the acclamations from the Holy, Holy, Holy to the great Amen.

We join in the Lord's Prayer, the sign of peace, and the Lamb of God litany, which accompanies the breaking of bread. We eat and drink of the paschal banquet, singing in a union of minds and hearts, committing ourselves to the Lord and one another in good times and in bad, deciding to follow Jesus all the way. We engage in silence and prayer to become even more aware of the great gift received, its saving effects and gracious benefits. This is indeed communion, an encounter with the risen Christ, which brings health and well-being, joy and peace.

PRESENTATION AND PREPARATION OF THE GIFTS

Bread and wine are brought to the altar and the deacon or priest prepares these gifts. If there is no music, the prayers may be said aloud, and all may respond: **Blessed be God for ever.** *The priest then invites all to pray.*

Priest: **Pray, brethren (brothers and sisters),**
        that my sacrifice and yours
        may be acceptable to God, the almighty Father.

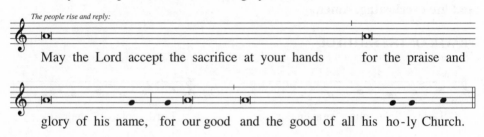

The people rise and reply:

May the Lord accept the sacrifice at your hands   for the praise and glory of his name,   for our good   and the good of all his ho-ly Church.

The priest says the prayer over the offerings and all respond: **Amen.**

109 EUCHARISTIC PRAYER

The central prayer of the Mass begins with this dialogue between priest and assembly.

Priest: The Lord be with you. *Assembly:* And with your spir - it.

Priest: Lift up your hearts. *Assembly:* We lift them up to the Lord.

Priest: Let us give thanks to the Lord our God. *Assembly:* It is right and just.

The Holy, Holy, Holy acclamation is sung to conclude the introduction to the
eucharistic prayer. **110**

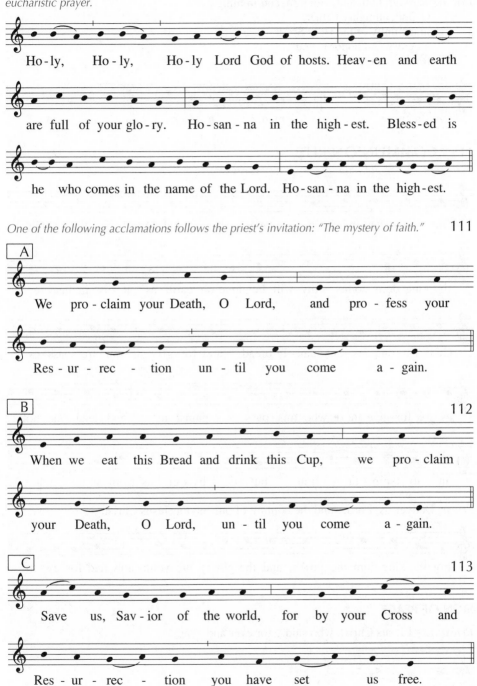

Ho-ly, Ho-ly, Ho-ly Lord God of hosts. Heav-en and earth

are full of your glo-ry. Ho-san-na in the high-est. Bless-ed is

he who comes in the name of the Lord. Ho-san-na in the high-est.

One of the following acclamations follows the priest's invitation: "The mystery of faith." **111**

A

We pro-claim your Death, O Lord, and pro-fess your

Res-ur-rec-tion un-til you come a-gain.

B **112**

When we eat this Bread and drink this Cup, we pro-claim

your Death, O Lord, un-til you come a-gain.

C **113**

Save us, Sav-ior of the world, for by your Cross and

Res-ur-rec-tion you have set us free.

114 *The eucharistic prayer concludes:*

Priest: Through him, and with him, and in him,
O God, almighty Father,
in the unity of the Holy Spirit,
all glory and honor is yours,
for ever and ever.

A - men. *Or:* A - men, a - men, a — men.

115 COMMUNION RITE

The priest invites all to join in the Lord's Prayer.

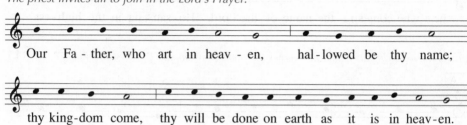

Our Fa - ther, who art in heav - en, hal - lowed be thy name;

thy king-dom come, thy will be done on earth as it is in heav-en.

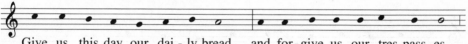

Give us this day our dai - ly bread, and for-give us our tres-pass-es,

as we for-give those who tres - pass a - gainst us; and lead us not

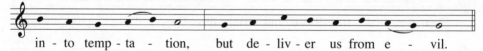

in - to temp - ta - tion, but de - liv - er us from e - vil.

Priest: Deliver us, Lord…and the coming of our Savior, Jesus Christ.

For the king-dom, the pow'r, and the glo-ry are yours now and for ev - er.

SIGN OF PEACE

Priest: Lord Jesus Christ, who said…for ever and ever.

A - men.

The peace of the Lord be with you al-ways. And with your spir - it.

Deacon or priest: Let us offer each other the sign of peace.

All exchange a sign of peace.

Then the eucharistic bread is solemnly broken and the consecrated bread and wine **116**
are prepared for Holy Communion. The litany "Lamb of God" is sung during the
breaking of the bread.

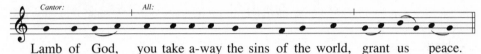

Lamb of God, you take a-way the sins of the world, have mer - cy on us.

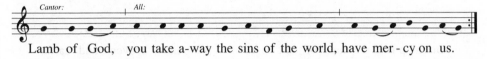

Lamb of God, you take a-way the sins of the world, grant us peace.

The priest then invites all to share in Holy Communion. **117**

Priest: Behold the Lamb of God,
behold him who takes away the sins of the world.
Blessed are those called to the supper of the Lamb.

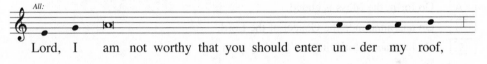

Lord, I am not worthy that you should enter un - der my roof,

but only say the word and my soul shall be healed.

Minister of communion: The Body (Blood) of Christ.
Communicant: **Amen.**

While the priest is receiving the Body of Christ, the communion song or psalm begins. After
communion, a time of silence is observed or a song of thanksgiving is sung. The rite concludes
with the prayer after communion to which all respond: **Amen.**

CONCLUDING RITES   118
From the very beginning of our wedding Christianity to our African world view, we
Black Christians have been aware that our worship of God led us to seek justice and
freedom here and now. It was our mission, a task that came from our hearing God's
word of deliverance and celebrating that deliverance in the death and resurrection
of Jesus the Lord. As it was then, so it is now.

The concluding rites consist of the priest's greeting and blessing and the dismissal of the people, which sends each member back "to do good works, praising
and blessing God" (GIRM, 90).

GREETING AND FINAL BLESSING

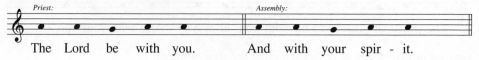

Priest: The Lord be with you.

Assembly: And with your spir - it.

When a bishop blesses the people, he adds the following:

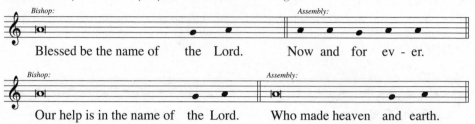

Bishop: Blessed be the name of the Lord.

Assembly: Now and for ev - er.

Bishop: Our help is in the name of the Lord.

Assembly: Who made heaven and earth.

The blessing may be in a simple or solemn form. All respond to the blessing or to each part of the blessing:

Assembly: A - men.

DISMISSAL

The deacon or priest then dismisses the assembly:

A	Go forth, the Mass is ended.
B	Go and announce the Gospel of the Lord.
C	Go in peace, glorifying the Lord by your life.

Assembly: Thanks be to God.

| D |

Deacon or priest: Go in peace.

Assembly: Thanks be to God.

EASTER DISMISSAL

The deacon or priest then dismisses the assembly:

| A | Go forth, the Mass is ended, alleluia, alleluia. |
| B | Go in peace, alleluia, alleluia. |

Assembly: Thanks be to God, al - le - lú - ia, al - le - lú - ia.

Setting One: Come, Go with Me

PENITENTIAL ACT

Priest, deacon or cantor:
You were sent to heal the con-trite of heart: Lord, have

All:
mer - cy. Lord, have mer - cy.

Priest, deacon or cantor:
You came to call sin - ners: Christ, have mer -

All:
cy. Christ, have mer - cy.

Priest, deacon or cantor:
You are seat-ed at the right hand of the Fa - ther to in-ter-cede for us: Lord, have mer - cy.

All:
Lord, have

mer - cy. May al-might-y

God have mer-cy on us, for - give us our sins, and

bring us to ev-er-last-ing life. A - men.

Text: ICEL, © 2010
Music: *Come, Go with Me,* Kenneth W. Louis, © 2012, GIA Publications, Inc.

KYRIE

121 **GLORIA**

you, we give you thanks for your great glo - ry,

Lord God, heav-en - ly King,

D.S.

O God, al - might-y Fa - ther.

Verse 2   unis.

2. Lord Je - sus Christ, On - ly Be - got - ten Son, Lord

God, Lamb of God, Son of the Fa-ther, you take a - way the

sins of the world, have mer-cy on us; you take a-way the

sins of the world, re - ceive our prayer; you are seat-ed at the

unis.

right hand of the Fa-ther, have mer - cy on us.

div.   D.S.

Verse 3

you a-lone are the Ho-ly One, you a-lone are the

Lord, you a-lone are the Most High,

Text: ICEL, © 2010
Music: *Come, Go with Me*, Kenneth W. Louis, © 2012, GIA Publications, Inc.

122 GOSPEL ACCLAMATION

Text: ICEL, © 2010
Music: *Come, Go with Me*, Kenneth W. Louis, © 2012, GIA Publications, Inc.

123 HOLY, HOLY, HOLY

Ho - ly, Ho - ly, Ho - ly Lord God of hosts.

Heav-en and earth are full of your glo-ry. Ho - san - na in the

1.
high - est.

2.
high - est.

Bless-ed is he who comes in the name of the Lord. Ho -

san - na, ho - san - na, ho - san - na, ho - san - na, ho -

san - na in the high - est.

san - na, ho - san - na, ho - san - na, ho - san - na, ho -

san - na in the high - est.

Text: ICEL, © 2010
Music: *Come, Go with Me*, Kenneth W. Louis, © 2012, GIA Publications, Inc.

124   MEMORIAL ACCLAMATION A

We pro-claim your Death, O Lord,

and pro-fess your Res - ur - rec-tion   un-til you come a-gain.

We pro-claim your Death, O Lord,   and pro-fess your

div.

Res - ur - rec-tion   un-til you come,   un-til you come,

div.

un-til you come a-gain,   un-til you come a-gain.

Text: ICEL, © 2010
Music: *Come, Go with Me*, Kenneth W. Louis, © 2012, GIA Publications, Inc.

MEMORIAL ACCLAMATION B

Text: ICEL, © 2010
Music: *Come, Go with Me*, Kenneth W. Louis, © 2012, GIA Publications, Inc.

126 MEMORIAL ACCLAMATION C

Save us, Sav-ior of the world, for by your Cross and Res - ur - rec - tion you have set us free, you have set us free, set us free.

Text: ICEL, © 2010
Music: *Come, Go with Me*, Kenneth W. Louis, © 2012, GIA Publications, Inc.

AMEN

Music: *Come, Go with Me*, Kenneth W. Louis, © 2012, GIA Publications, Inc.

128 LAMB OF GOD

Lamb of God, you take a-way, you take a-way the sins of the world, have mer-cy on us.

To repeat

Last time

world, grant us peace. *rit.*

Music: *Come, Go with Me*, Kenneth W. Louis, © 2012, GIA Publications, Inc.

Setting Two: The Sound of My People

KYRIE

Assembly sings alto part.

mer-cy,　　　　mer-cy,　　　　mer-cy.

mer-cy.　Lord, have mer-cy,　　　　mer-cy.

Music: *The Sound of My People*, M. Roger Holland II, © 2010, GIA Publications, Inc.

130 GLORIA

Glo-ry to God in the high-est, and on earth peace to peo-

ple of good will.

Choir: We praise you, we praise

We praise you,

you, we bless you, we bless

we praise you, we bless you,

to peo-ple of good will. *Choir:* Lord Je-sus Christ,

On-ly Be-got-ten Son, Lord God, Lamb of God,

Lord God, Lamb of God, Son of the Fa - ther,

Son of the Fa - ther, you take a-way the sins of the world, have mer-cy

on us; you take a - way the sins of the world, re-ceive our

prayer; you are seat-ed at the right hand of the Fa - ther,

men, a - men, a - men, a - men, a -

Assembly:

A - men, a - men, a - men, a - men,

men. We glo-ri - fy you, we glo-ri - fy you, Lord, Je - sus

a - men, a - men, a - men,

Christ. A - men, a-men.

a - men. Ah, a - men.

Text: ICEL, © 2010
Music: *The Sound of My People*, M. Roger Holland II, © 2010, GIA Publications, Inc.

131 GOSPEL ACCLAMATION

Al - le - lu - ia, al - le -

lu - ia, al - le - lu - ia,

al - le - lu - ia, al - le - lu - ia,

Last time to Coda ⊕ | *To repeat refrain* || *To verse*

al - le - lu - ia.

Verse for Ordinary Time*

Cantor:

I am the light, the light of the world, the light of the world,

*Additional verses may be found in the published edition of "The Sound of My People,"
G-7748.*

says the Lord; who-ev-er fol-lows me will have the light, the light of life.

D.S.

Coda

Al - le - lu - ia, al - le - lu - ia, al - le - lu - ia, al - le - lu - ia, al-le - lu - ia, al-le - lu - ia.

Text: ICEL, © 1969
Music: *The Sound of My People*, M. Roger Holland II, © 2010, GIA Publications, Inc.

132 LENTEN GOSPEL ACCLAMATION

Coda

Je - sus, Je - sus, Lord Je - sus,

Je - sus, Lord Je - sus, Je - sus, Lord

Je - sus, Je - sus Christ.

Text: ICEL, © 1969
Music: *The Sound of My People,* M. Roger Holland II, © 2010, GIA Publications, Inc.

133 **HOLY, HOLY, HOLY**

Ho - ly, Ho - ly, Ho - ly Lord God of hosts.

Heav-en and earth are full of your glo - ry. Ho -

san - na in the high - est. Bless-ed is he who comes

in the name of the Lord. Ho-san-

na, ho-san - na, ho-san - na in the high-

est. Ho-san - na, ho-san - na, ho-san-

na in the high - est. Ho-san - na, ho-san-

Assembly:

Ho - san-

na,   ho - san - na   in   the   high - est.

na   in   the   high - est.

Text: ICEL, © 2010
Music: *The Sound of My People*, M. Roger Holland II, © 2010, GIA Publications, Inc.

MEMORIAL ACCLAMATION A   134

The   mys - ter - y   of   faith.

We pro -

claim   your Death,   O   Lord,   and pro - fess your Res - ur - rec -

tion   un - til   you come,   un - til   you come,   un - til

1. you   come   a - gain.   We pro - **2.** you   come   a - gain,

un - til   you come,   un - til   you come,   un - til

you come   a - gain,   un - til   you come,   un - til

you come,   un - til   you come   a - gain.

Text: ICEL, © 2010
Music: *The Sound of My People*, M. Roger Holland II, © 2010, GIA Publications, Inc.

135 MEMORIAL ACCLAMATION B

The mys-ter-y of faith.

When we eat this Bread and drink this Cup, we pro-claim your Death, O Lord, un-til you come, un-til you come, un-til

1. you come a-gain. When we

2. you come a-gain, un-til you come, un-til you come, un-til

you come a-gain, un-til you come, un-til

you come, un-til you come a-gain.

Text: ICEL, © 2010
Music: *The Sound of My People*, M. Roger Holland II, © 2010, GIA Publications, Inc.

MEMORIAL ACCLAMATION C

The mys-ter-y of faith.

Save us,

Sav-ior of the world, for by your Cross and Res-ur-rec-

1.

tion you have set us, you have set us free.

2.

Save us, you have set us free,

you have set us,

you have set us free.

Text: ICEL, © 2010
Music: *The Sound of My People*, M. Roger Holland II, © 2010, GIA Publications, Inc.

137 DOXOLOGY / AMEN

Through him, and with him, and in him,

O God, al-might-y Fa - ther,

in the u - ni - ty of the Ho-ly Spir - it,

all glo-ry and hon-or is yours,

for ev - er and ev - er.

A - men, a - men,

a - men.

Text: ICEL, © 2010
Music: *The Sound of My People*, M. Roger Holland II, © 2010, GIA Publications, Inc.

138 THE LORD'S PRAYER

Our Fa - ther, who art in heav - en,

hal-low-ed be thy name; thy king - dom come, thy

will be done on earth as it is in heav - en.

Give us this day our dai - ly bread, and for -

give us our tres - pass - es, as we for - give

those who tres - pass a - gainst us;

and lead us not in-to temp-ta - tion,

but de-liv - er us from e - vil.

Deliver us, Lord, we pray,
from every evil, and gra-cious-ly grant peace in our days, that, by the

help of your mercy, we may be al - ways free from sin

and safe from all distress, as we a - wait the blessed hope and the

coming of our Savior, Jesus Christ.

For the king - dom, the pow-er

and the glo-ry   are   yours   now   and   for

ev-er   and   ev-er,   for   ev-er   and   ev-er.

A - men.

Ah,   a - men.

A - men.

LAMB OF GOD

Lamb of God, you take a-way the sins of the world,

have mer-cy on us. Lamb of God,

mer - cy on us.

Lamb of God, you take a - way the sins

of the world, grant

us peace.

Setting Three: Unity Mass

140 PENITENTIAL ACT

Text: ICEL, © 2010
Music: *Unity Mass*, Norah Duncan IV, © 2010, GIA Publications, Inc.

KYRIE

Music: *Unity Mass*, Norah Duncan IV, © 2010, GIA Publications, Inc.

142 **GLORIA**

Refrain

Glo - ry to God in the high - est, and on

Glo - ry. Glo - ry. Glo - ry to God in the high - est,

Glo - ry to God in the high - est, and on

Repeat first time only

earth peace to peo - ple, peo - ple of good will.

earth peace, peo - ple, peo - ple of good will.

earth peace to peo - ple, peo - ple of good will.

Verse 1

Cantor or S, A:

We praise you, we bless you, we a -

dore you, we glo - ri - fy you, we

give you thanks for your great glo - ry, Lord God,

heav-en-ly King, O God, al - might-y Fa - ther.

cresc.

D.S.

Verse 2

mp *Cantor or T, B:*

Lord Je - sus Christ, On - ly Be - got-ten Son,

Cantor or S, A: *mp*

Lord God, Lamb of God, Son of the Fa - ther, you

take a - way the sins of the world, have

mer - cy on us; you take a - way the sins of the world, re - ceive our prayer; you are seat - ed at the right hand, at the right hand of the Fa - ther, have mer - cy on us.

Verse 3

Cantor or S:

For you a - lone are the Ho - ly One, you a - lone are the Lord,

earth peace to peo - ple, peo - ple of good will.

earth peace, peo - ple, peo - ple of good will.

earth peace to peo - ple, peo - ple of good will.

A - men, a - men, a - men.

T, B, Assembly:

non rit.

A - men, a - men, a - men.

non rit.

*Assembly sings the Bass part.

Text: ICEL, © 2010
Music: *Unity Mass*, Norah Duncan IV, © 2010, GIA Publications, Inc.

GOSPEL ACCLAMATION

Refrain ♩ = 72

Cantor, then all (first time only):

Al - le - lu - ia, al - le - lu - ia.
Lent: O glo - ry to you, O Word of God,

Last time

Al - le - lu - ia, al - le - lu - ia.
Lord Je - sus Christ, Lord Je - sus Christ.

Last time

Verses

Cantor or choir:

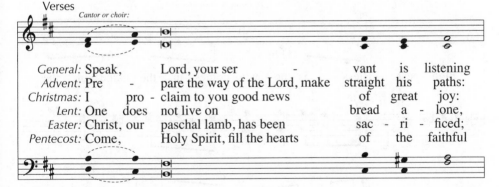

General: Speak,	Lord, your ser -	vant	is	listening
Advent: Pre -	pare the way of the Lord, make	straight	his	paths:
Christmas: I pro -	claim to you good news	of	great	joy:
Lent: One does	not live on	bread	a -	lone,
Easter: Christ, our	paschal lamb, has been	sac - ri -		ficed;
Pentecost: Come,	Holy Spirit, fill the hearts	of	the	faithful

D.C.

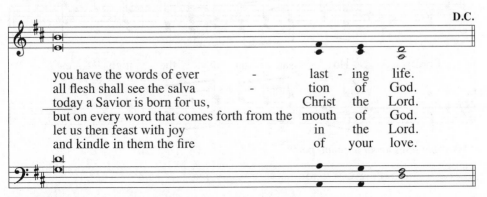

you have the words of ever - last - ing life.
all flesh shall see the salva - tion of God.
today a Savior is born for us, Christ the Lord.
but on every word that comes forth from the mouth of God.
let us then feast with joy in the Lord.
and kindle in them the fire of your love.

Text: ICEL, © 1969
Music: *Unity Mass*, Norah Duncan IV, © 2010, GIA Publications, Inc.

144 HOLY, HOLY, HOLY

♩.= 85

f

Ho - ly, Ho - ly, Ho - ly Lord God of hosts.   Heav-en and earth are

full of your glo - - ry.   Ho - san - na in   the

high - est. Bless - ed is he who comes in the name of the

Lord.   Ho - san - na in the high - est.

Assembly sings lower Soprano part.

Text: ICEL, © 2010
Music: *Unity Mass*, Norah Duncan IV, © 2010, GIA Publications, Inc.

MEMORIAL ACCLAMATION A

145

♩ = 76

The mys-ter-y of faith. We pro-claim your Death, O Lord, and pro-fess your Res-ur-rec-tion un-til you come a-gain.

*Assembly sings lower Soprano part.

Text: ICEL, © 2010
Music: *Unity Mass,* Norah Duncan IV, © 2010, GIA Publications, Inc.

MEMORIAL ACCLAMATION B

146

♩ = 76

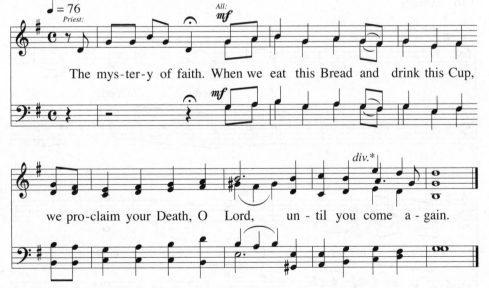

The mys-ter-y of faith. When we eat this Bread and drink this Cup, we pro-claim your Death, O Lord, un-til you come a-gain.

*Assembly sings lower Soprano part.

Text: ICEL, © 2010
Music: *Unity Mass,* Norah Duncan IV, © 2010, GIA Publications, Inc.

147 MEMORIAL ACCLAMATION C

The mys-ter-y of faith. Save us, Sav-ior of the world, for by your

Cross and Res - ur - rec - tion you have set us free.

Assembly sings lower Soprano part.

Text: ICEL, © 2010
Music: *Unity Mass,* Norah Duncan IV, © 2010, GIA Publications, Inc.

148 AMEN

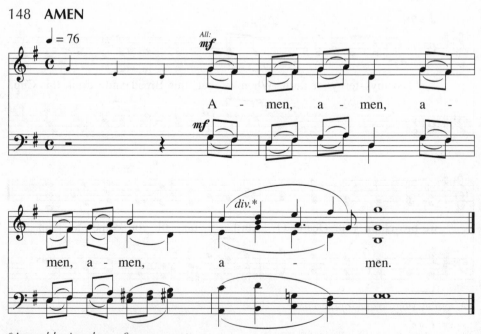

A - men, a - men, a -

men, a - men, a - men.

Assembly sings lower Soprano part.

Music: *Unity Mass,* Norah Duncan IV, © 2010, GIA Publications, Inc.

LAMB OF GOD

Lamb of God, you take a-way the sins of the world, have mer-cy on us, have mer-cy on us.

Lamb of God, you take a-way the sins, have mer-cy, have mer-cy on us.

Lamb of God, Lamb of God, have mer-cy on us, have mer-cy on us.

Lamb of God, you take a-way the sins of the world, grant us peace, grant us peace.

Lamb of God, you take a-way the sins, grant us, grant us peace.

Lamb of God, Lamb of God, grant us peace, grant us peace.

Setting Four:
Welcome Table: A Mass of Spirituals

This entire setting is unaccompanied.

150 PENITENTIAL ACT

Priest, deacon or cantor:

You were sent to heal the contrite of heart: Lord, have mer-cy.

All:

Lord, have mer - cy.

Priest, deacon or cantor:

You came to call sin - ners:

Christ, have mer - cy.

All:

Christ, have mer - cy.

Priest, deacon or cantor:

You are seated at the right hand of the Father to in - ter-cede for us:

Lord, have mer - cy.

All:

Lord, have mer - cy.

Priest:

May al - mighty God have mercy on us, forgive us our sins, and bring us to

All:

everlast - ing life. A - men.

Text: ICEL, © 2010
Music: Based on *My Soul's Been Anchored in the Lord*, *Welcome Table: A Mass of Spirituals*, Kim R. Harris, M. Roger Holland II,
© 2012, GIA Publications, Inc.

KYRIE

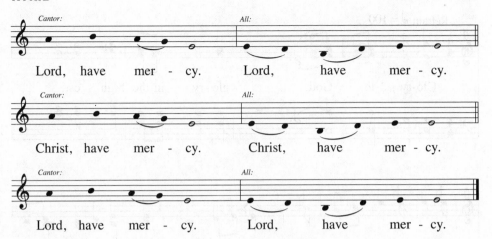

Cantor: Lord, have mer - cy. *All:* Lord, have mer - cy.

Cantor: Christ, have mer - cy. *All:* Christ, have mer - cy.

Cantor: Lord, have mer - cy. *All:* Lord, have mer - cy.

Music: Based on *My Soul's Been Anchored in the Lord*, *Welcome Table: A Mass of Spirituals*, Kim R. Harris, M. Roger Holland II, © 2012, GIA Publications, Inc.

152 **GLORIA**

Refrain ♩ = 100

Glo-ry to God, glo-ry in the high - est,

glo-ry to God in the high-est, and on earth peace to peo - ple

1.

2.

Verse 1

1. We praise you, we bless you, we a-

of good will.   of good will.   1. We praise you, bless you,

dore you, we glo-ri-fy you, we give you thanks

we

Lord God, Lamb of God, Son of the Fa-ther, you

take a-way the sins of the world, have mer-cy on us; you

take a-way the sins of the world, re-ceive our prayer;

you are seat-ed at the right hand, the right hand of the Fa-ther, have

have

Refrain

mer-cy on us. Glo-ry to God, glo-ry in the

high - est, glo-ry to God in the high-est, and on earth

will. 3. For

peace to peo - ple of good will, of good will.

Verse 3

you a - lone are the Ho - ly One, you a - lone are the

you a - lone, Ho - ly One, you a - lone,

Ho - ly, the Ho-ly One,

Ho - ly One, you a - lone,

Lord, you a - lone are the Most High,

you a - lone, Most High, Most High,

you a - lone are the Lord, a - lone, Most High,

Je-sus Christ, with the Ho-ly Spir-it, in the glo-ry of God the Fa - ther.

glo-ry,   God the Fa-ther.

a-men, a - men.

A-men, a - men,   a - men,   a - men.

A - men, a-men,   a - men,   a - men.

a-men, a - men.

A-men, a - men,   a - men.

A - men,   a - men,

a - men.

A - men, a - men.

Text: ICEL, © 2010
Music: Based on *Ride On, King Jesus*, *Welcome Table: A Mass of Spirituals*, Kim R. Harris, M. Roger Holland II, © 2012, GIA Publications, Inc.

153 GOSPEL ACCLAMATION

Refrain ♩ = 146

Cantor, then all (first time only):

Al - le - lu - ia,   al - le - lu - ia.

Al - le,   al - le - lu - ia. Al - le,   al - le - lu - ia.

Text: ICEL, © 1969
Music: Based on *Oh! What a Beautiful City, Welcome Table: A Mass of Spirituals*, Kim R. Harris, M. Roger Holland II, © 2012, GIA Publications, Inc.

154 LENTEN GOSPEL ACCLAMATION

Refrain ♩ = 60

Cantor, then all (first time only):

div.

Praise to you, Lord Je-sus Christ,   praise to you, Lord Je-sus

Je-sus.

Christ,   King of end-less glo-ry!

Christ, Lord Je-sus.

1., 3.   *2.*   *Cantor:*

Praise   to you, Lord Je-sus Christ.   Christ.   1. A

Verses

clean heart cre-ate for me, O   God;
2. If   to-day you hear his   voice,

D.C.

give me back the joy of your sal - va - tion.
hard - en not your   hearts.

Text: ICEL, © 1969
Music: Based on *Sinner, Please Don't Let This Harvest Pass, Welcome Table: A Mass of Spirituals*, Kim R. Harris, M. Roger Holland II,
© 2012, GIA Publications, Inc.

PRAYER OF THE FAITHFUL

Music: Based on *Fix Me, Jesus*, *Welcome Table: A Mass of Spirituals*, Kim R. Harris, M. Roger Holland II, © 2012, GIA Publications, Inc.

156 PREFACE DIALOGUE

The Lord be with you. And with your spir-it.

Lift up your hearts. We lift them up to the Lord.

Let us give thanks to the Lord our God. It is right and just.

Text: ICEL, © 2010
Music: Based on *Ride On, King Jesus, Welcome Table: A Mass of Spirituals*, Kim R. Harris, M. Roger Holland II, © 2012, GIA Publications, Inc.

157 HOLY, HOLY, HOLY

Ho - ly, Ho - ly, Ho - ly Lord God of hosts.

Heav-en and earth are full of your glo - ry. Ho -
san - na in the high-est. Ho - san - na in the high-est. Ho -
san - na in the high - est. Bless-ed is
he who comes in the name of the Lord. Ho -
san - na in the high - est.

Text: ICEL, © 2010
Music: Based on *Ol' Time Religion, Welcome Table: A Mass of Spirituals*, Kim R. Harris, M. Roger Holland II, © 2012, GIA Publications, Inc.

158 MEMORIAL ACCLAMATION A

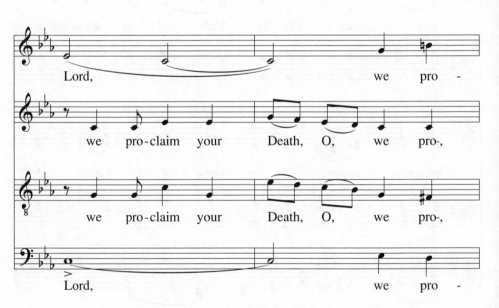

Text: ICEL, © 2010
Music: Based on *Calvary, Welcome Table: A Mass of Spirituals*, Kim R. Harris, M. Roger Holland II, © 2012, GIA Publications, Inc.

MEMORIAL ACCLAMATION B

Text: ICEL, © 2010
Music: Based on *Let Us Break Bread Together, Welcome Table: A Mass of Spirituals*, Kim R. Harris, M. Roger Holland II, © 2012, GIA Publications, Inc.

160 MEMORIAL ACCLAMATION C

Text: ICEL, © 2010
Music: Based on *Oh, Freedom, Welcome Table: A Mass of Spirituals*, Kim R. Harris, M. Roger Holland II, © 2012, GIA Publications, Inc.

AMEN

Pronounced: Ay-men

Music: Based on *He's Got the Whole World in His Hands, Welcome Table: A Mass of Spirituals*, Kim R. Harris, M. Roger Holland II,
© 2012, GIA Publications, Inc.

162 THE LORD'S PRAYER

Our Fa - ther, who art in heav-en, hal-low - ed be thy

name; thy king - dom come, thy will be done on

earth as it is in heav - en. Give us this day our

tres - pass es, as we for -

dai - ly bread, and for - give us our tres - pass - es,

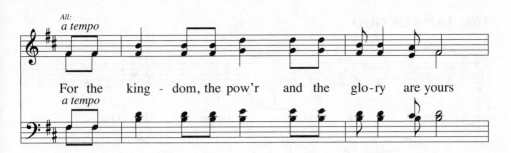

For the king-dom, the pow'r and the glo-ry are yours

now and for ev-er, now and for ev - er.

Text: Embolism, ICEL, © 2010
Music: Based on *Nobody Knows the Trouble I See, Lord, Welcome Table: A Mass of Spirituals*, Kim R. Harris, M. Roger Holland II,
   © 2012, GIA Publications, Inc.

163 LAMB OF GOD

Lamb of God, Lamb of God, you

take a-way the sins of the world, have mer - cy on us.

world, grant us peace.

Music: Based on *My Lord! What a Morning, Welcome Table: A Mass of Spirituals*, Kim R. Harris, M. Roger Holland II, © 2012, GIA Publications, Inc.

Setting Five: Mass of Saint Augustine

KYRIE

1. Lord, have mer - cy. Lord, have
2. Christ, have mer - cy. Christ, have
3. Lord, have mer - cy. Lord, have

mer - cy. Lord, have mer - cy, have
mer - cy. Christ, have mer - cy, have
mer - cy. Lord, have mer - cy, have

cresc.

1., 2. *decresc.* **3.** *decresc.*

mer - cy. mer - cy.

decresc. *decresc.*

Music: *Mass of Saint Augustine*, Leon C. Roberts, © 1981, GIA Publications, Inc.

165 GOSPEL ACCLAMATION

Al - le - lu - ia,

Al -

al - le - lu - ia,   al - le - lu - ia,   al - le - lu - ia,

le - lu - ia,

al - le - lu - ia.   ia.

Music: *Mass of Saint Augustine*; Leon C. Roberts, © 1981, GIA Publications, Inc.

166 HOLY, HOLY, HOLY

Ho - ly,   Ho - ly,   Ho - ly

Ho - ly,

Lord God of hosts. Heav-en and earth are full of your glo - ry. Ho - san - na in the high - est. Bless-ed is he who comes in the name of the Lord. Ho - san - na in the high - est.

Text: ICEL, © 2010
Music: *Mass of Saint Augustine*, Leon C. Roberts, © 1981, 2012, GIA Publications, Inc.

167   MEMORIAL ACCLAMATION A

We pro - claim your Death, O

We pro - claim your Death, O

Lord,   and pro - fess your Res - ur - rec - tion

un - til you come a - gain.

Text: ICEL, © 2010
Music: *Mass of Saint Augustine*, Leon Roberts; adapt. by Norah Duncan IV, © 2012, GIA Publications, Inc.

AMEN

A - men, a - men, a -

A - men,

men. A - men, a - men.

Music: *Mass of Saint Augustine*, Leon Roberts; adapt. by Norah Duncan IV, © 2012, GIA Publications, Inc.

169 LAMB OF GOD

Lamb of God, you take a - way the sins

of the world, have mer - cy

on us. Lamb of God,

you take a - way the sins of the

Music: *Mass of Saint Augustine*, Leon C. Roberts, © 1981, GIA Publications, Inc.

Setting Six: Mass of Saint Cyprian

170 KYRIE

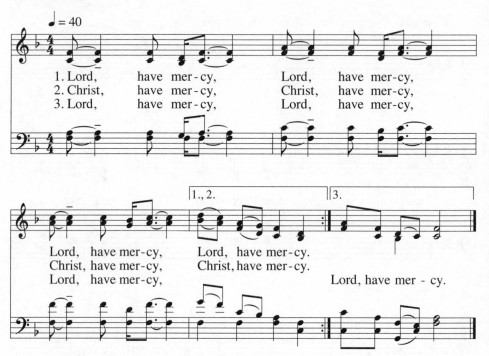

1. Lord, have mer-cy, Lord, have mer-cy,
2. Christ, have mer-cy, Christ, have mer-cy,
3. Lord, have mer-cy, Lord, have mer-cy,

Lord, have mer-cy, Lord, have mer-cy.
Christ, have mer-cy, Christ, have mer-cy.
Lord, have mer-cy, Lord, have mer - cy.

Music: *Mass of Saint Cyprian*, Kenneth W. Louis, © 2001, GIA Publications, Inc.

171 GLORIA

Refrain
Cantor, then all (first time only):

Glo - ry to God in the high - est, and on

To verses 1, 2

earth peace to peo - ple of good will.

Verse 1

Cantor:

1. We praise you, we bless you, we a -

dore you, we glo - ri - fy you, we give you thanks for

your great glo - ry, Lord God,

D.S.

heav - en - ly King, O God, al - might - y Fa - ther.

Verse 2

Cantor:

2. Lord Je - sus Christ, On - ly Be - got - ten Son,

Lord God, Lamb of God, Son of the Fa - ther, you

take a - way the sins of the world, have mer - cy on us; you

take a-way the sins of the world, re - ceive our

prayer; you are seat - ed at the right hand of the

Fa - ther, have mer - cy on us.

Refrain
All:

Glo - ry to God in the high - est, and on

earth peace to peo-ple of good will. will.

1.   2.

Verse 3
Cantor:

3. For you a - lone are the Ho - ly One, you a - lone are the

Lord, you a - lone are the

Most High, Je - sus Christ, with the Ho - ly Spir - it,

in the glo - ry of God the Fa - ther. A - men.

Final Refrain
All:

Glo - ry to God in the high - est, and on

earth peace to peo - ple of good will. will.

A - men.

Text: ICEL, © 2010
Music: *Mass of Saint Cyprian*, Kenneth W. Louis, © 2001, 2010, GIA Publications, Inc.

172 GOSPEL ACCLAMATION

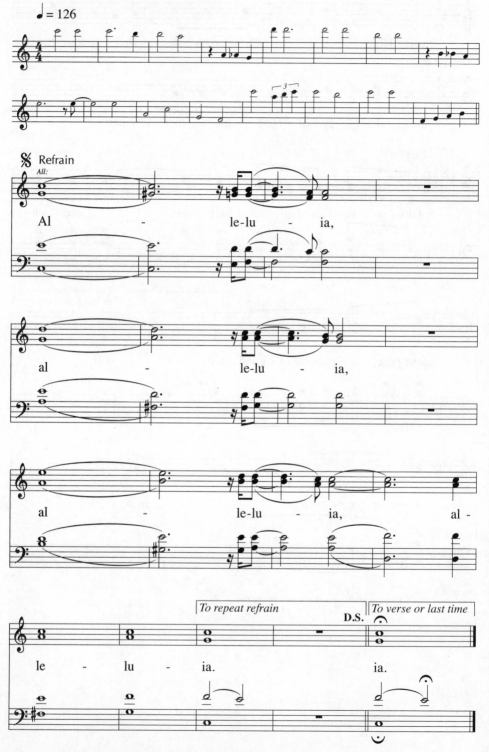

Verse

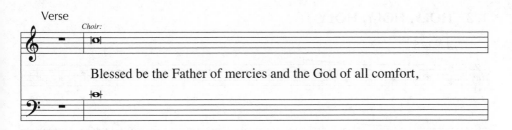

Blessed be the Father of mercies and the God of all comfort,

who con - soles us in all our af - flic-tions.

Text: ICEL, © 1969
Music: *Mass of Saint Cyprian*, Kenneth W. Louis, © 2001, GIA Publications, Inc.

173 HOLY, HOLY, HOLY

san - na in the high - est. Ho - san - na in the high-

est. Ho - san - na in the high - est.

MEMORIAL ACCLAMATION A

Text: ICEL, © 2010
Music: *Mass of Saint Cyprian*, Kenneth W. Louis, © 2001, 2010, GIA Publications, Inc.

175 MEMORIAL ACCLAMATION B

Text: ICEL, © 2010
Music: *Mass of Saint Cyprian*, Kenneth W. Louis, © 2001, 2010, GIA Publications, Inc.

MEMORIAL ACCLAMATION C

Text: ICEL, © 2010
Music: *Mass of Saint Cyprian*, Kenneth W. Louis, © 2001, 2010, GIA Publications, Inc.

177 DOXOLOGY / AMEN

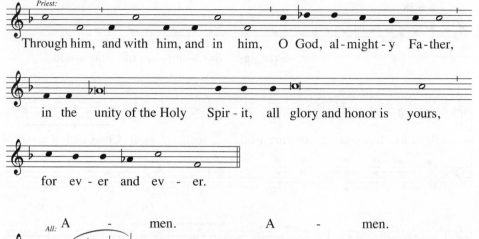

Priest: Through him, and with him, and in him, O God, al-might-y Fa-ther, in the unity of the Holy Spir-it, all glory and honor is yours, for ev-er and ev-er.

All: A - men. A - men.

A - men. A - men.

A - men. A - men.

A - men. A - men.

A - men. A - men.

A - men. A - men. A - men.

Text: ICEL, © 2010
Music: *Mass of Saint Cyprian*, Kenneth W. Louis, © 2001, 2010, GIA Publications, Inc.

THE LORD'S PRAYER

At the Savior's command and formed by divine teach-ing, we dare to say: Our Father, who art in heaven, hal-low-ed be thy name; thy king-dom come, thy will be done on earth as it is in heav-en. Give us this day our dai - ly bread, and for - give us our trespasses, as we for -

give those who tres-pass a - gainst us; and lead us not

in - to temp-ta - tion, but de - liv - er us from e - vil.

Priest:

Deliver us, Lord, we pray, from every e-vil, graciously grant peace in our days,

that, by the help of your mercy, we may be always free from sin and safe from

all dis-tress, as we await the blessed hope and the coming of our Savior,

All:

Je - sus Christ. For the king-dom, the pow-er

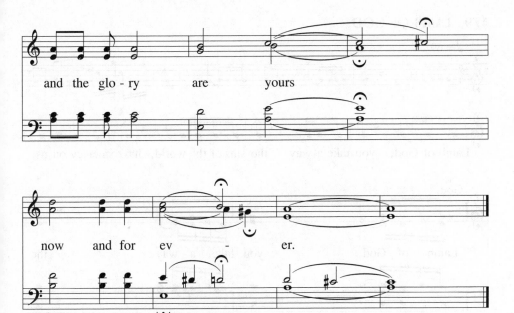

and the glo - ry   are   yours

now   and for   ev -   er.

Text: Embolism, ICEL, © 2010
Music: *Mass of Saint Cyprian*, Kenneth W. Louis, © 2001, 2010, GIA Publications, Inc.

179 LAMB OF GOD

Lamb of God, you take a-way the sins of the world, have mer-cy on us.

All:
God,

Lamb of God, you take a-way the

Cantor: *Repeat as needed*
Lamb of

sins of the world, have mer - cy on us.

Last time
All:
God,

Lamb of God, you take a-way the

sins of the world, grant us peace.

Music: *Mass of Saint Cyprian*, Kenneth W. Louis, © 2001, GIA Publications, Inc.

Setting Seven: Mass of Creation

PENITENTIAL ACT

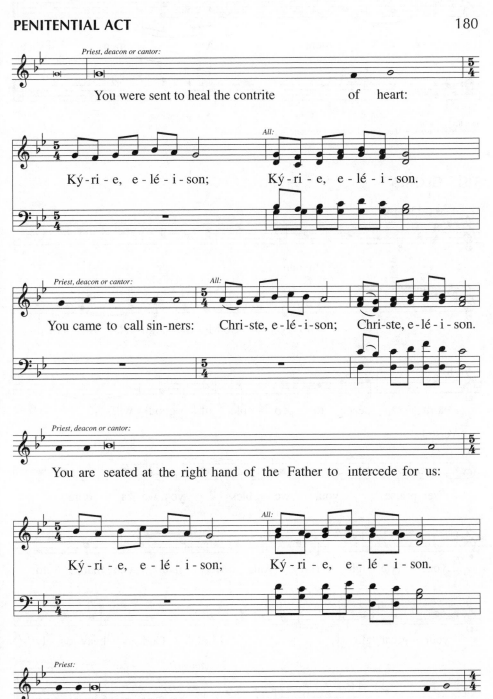

Priest, deacon or cantor:
You were sent to heal the contrite of heart:

All:
Ký - ri - e, e - lé - i - son; Ký - ri - e, e - lé - i - son.

Priest, deacon or cantor: *All:*
You came to call sin-ners: Chri - ste, e - lé - i - son; Chri - ste, e - lé - i - son.

Priest, deacon or cantor:
You are seated at the right hand of the Father to intercede for us:

All:
Ký - ri - e, e - lé - i - son; Ký - ri - e, e - lé - i - son.

Priest:
May al-mighty God have mercy on us, forgive us our sins,
and bring us to everlast - ing life.

A - men.   A - men.

Text: ICEL, © 2010
Music: *Mass of Creation,* Marty Haugen, © 1984, 1985, 2010, GIA Publications, Inc.

181 GLORIA

♩ = 134–142

Refrain
All: *f*

Glo - ry to God in the high - est,   and on earth   peace to peo - ple of   good   will.

Verse 1
mf Cantor or section:

We praise   you,   we bless   you, we a - dore you,   we glo - ri - fy you,   we give   you thanks for your   great glo - ry,   Lord   God,   heav - en - ly King,   O God,   al - might - y   Fa - ther.

poco rit.

in the glo - ry of God the Fa - ther. A - men.

in the glo - ry of the Fa - ther. A - men.

Final Refrain

poco rit.

S: *ff* Glo - ry to God,

A, Assembly: Glo-ry to God in the high-est,

poco rit. A - men.

ff

A - men.

and peace, peace to peo - ple of good

and on earth peace to peo - ple of good

div.

fff will.

non rit.

will.

fff *non rit.*

Text: ICEL, © 2010
Music: *Mass of Creation*, Marty Haugen, © 1984, 1985, 2010, GIA Publications, Inc.

182A GOSPEL ACCLAMATION

♩ = 108

℁ Refrain

ƒ *Descant (last time):*

Al-le - lu - ia, al-le - lu - ia, al-le - lu-ia, al - le - lu - ia. Al-le-

ƒ

Al-le - lu - ia, al-le - lu - ia, al-le - lu-ia, al - le - lu - ia. Al-le-

ƒ

Last time

lu - ia, al - le - lu - ia, al-le - lu-ia, al - le - lu - ia.

Last time

lu - ia, al - le - lu - ia, al-le - lu-ia, al - le - lu - ia.

Last time

Verse

Cantor or section:

O - pen our hearts, O Lord, to
Speak, O Lord, your ser - vant is list - 'ning;

D.S.

lis - ten to the words of your Son.
you have the words of ev - er-last - ing life.

Alternate Tone for Gospel Verse

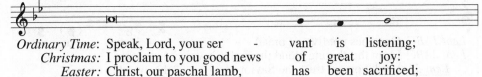

Ordinary Time:	Speak, Lord, your ser - vant is listening;
Christmas:	I proclaim to you good news of great joy:
Easter:	Christ, our paschal lamb, has been sacrificed;
Pentecost:	Come, Holy Spirit, fill the hearts of the faithful

D.S.

you have the words of   ev - er - last - ing   life.
today a Savior is born for us,   Christ   the   Lord.
let us then feast with   joy   in   the   Lord.
and kindle in them the   fire   of   your   love.

Text: ICEL, © 1969
Music: *Mass of Creation*, Marty Haugen, © 1984, 1985, 2010, GIA Publications, Inc.

LENTEN GOSPEL ACCLAMATION

182B

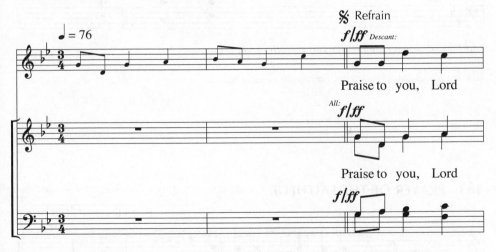

Verses*

Cantor or choir:

Lent 1ABC	One does not live on bread a - lone, but on
Lent 2ABC	From the shining cloud the Father's voice is heard:
Lent 3A	Lord, you are truly the Savior of the world;
Lent 4A	I am the light of the world, says the Lord; who -
Lent 5A	I am the resurrection and the life, says the Lord; who -

D.S.

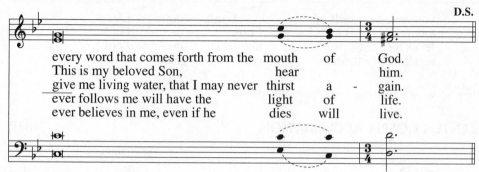

every word that comes forth from the mouth of God.
This is my beloved Son, hear him.
give me living water, that I may never thirst a - gain.
ever follows me will have the light of life.
ever believes in me, even if he dies will live.

Additional verses may be chanted with the same tone.

Text: ICEL, © 1969
Music: *Mass of Creation,* Marty Haugen, © 1984, 1985, 2010, GIA Publications, Inc.

183 PRAYER OF THE FAITHFUL

To repeat | Last time

Cantor:

For . . . . let us pray to the Lord:

All: mf

Lord, hear our prayer. prayer.

Music: *Mass of Creation,* Marty Haugen, © 1984, 1985, GIA Publications, Inc.

PREFACE DIALOGUE 184

Priest: The Lord be with you. *All:* And with your spir-it.

Priest: Lift up your hearts. *All:* We lift them up to the Lord.

Priest: Let us give thanks to the Lord our God. *All:* It is right and just.

Text: ICEL, © 2010
Music: *Mass of Creation,* Marty Haugen, © 1984, 1985, 2010, GIA Publications, Inc.

HOLY, HOLY, HOLY 185

♩ = 132–138

All: **f** Ho-ly, Ho-ly, Ho-ly

Lord God of hosts. Heav-en and earth are full of your

glo-ry. Ho-san-na in the high-est.

Bless-ed is he who comes in the name of the

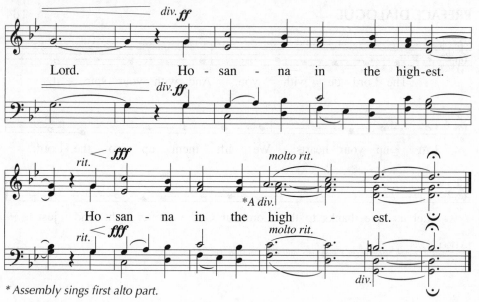

Lord. Ho - san - na in the high-est.

Ho - san - na in the high - est.

*A div.

* Assembly sings first alto part.

Text: ICEL, © 2010
Music: *Mass of Creation,* Marty Haugen, © 1984, 1985, 2010, GIA Publications, Inc.

186A MEMORIAL ACCLAMATION A

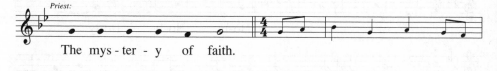

Priest:

The mys - ter - y of faith.

All:

We pro - claim your Death, O Lord, and pro-

fess your Res - ur - rec - tion un - til you come a -

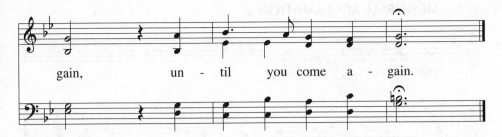

gain, un – til you come a – gain.

Text: ICEL, © 2010
Music: *Mass of Creation*, Marty Haugen, © 1984, 1985, 2010, GIA Publications, Inc.

MEMORIAL ACCLAMATION B

186B

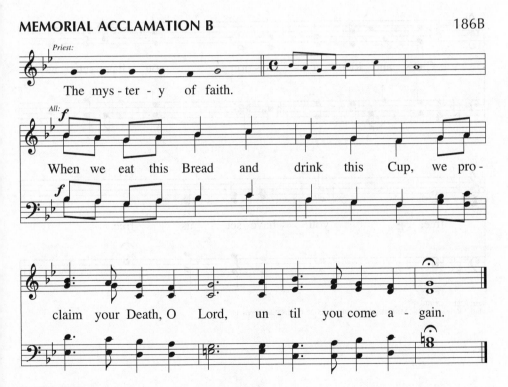

Priest: The mys - ter - y of faith.

All: When we eat this Bread and drink this Cup, we pro -

claim your Death, O Lord, un - til you come a - gain.

Text: ICEL, © 2010
Music: *Mass of Creation*, Marty Haugen, © 1984, 1985, 2010, GIA Publications, Inc.

186C MEMORIAL ACCLAMATION C

Priest: The mys - ter - y of faith.

All: **f** Save us, Sav - ior of the world, for by your

Cross and Res - ur - rec - tion you have set us

free, you have set us free.

DOXOLOGY / AMEN

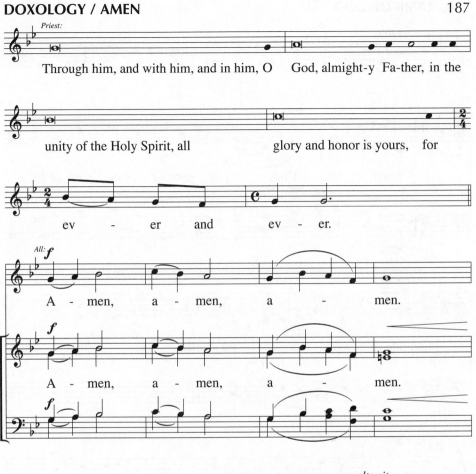

Priest:

Through him, and with him, and in him, O   God, almight-y Fa-ther, in the

unity of the Holy Spirit, all   glory and honor is yours,   for

ev - er   and   ev - er.

All: *f*

A - men,   a - men,   a - men.

f

A - men,   a - men,   a - men.

f

rit.   *molto rit.*

A - men,   a - men,   a - men.

ff   *S div.*   *rit.*   *molto rit.*   *fff*

A - men,   a - men,   a - men.   *A div.*

ff   *rit.*   *molto rit.*   *fff*

div.

Text: ICEL, © 2010
Music: *Mass of Creation*, Marty Haugen, © 1984, 1985, 2010, GIA Publications, Inc.

188 LAMB OF GOD

Lamb of God, you take a-way the sins of the

world, have mer - cy on us.

world, grant us peace.

Setting Eight: A Community Mass

KYRIE

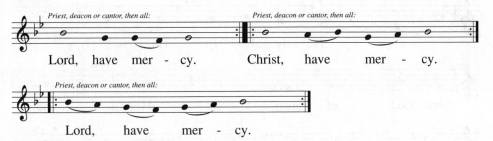

Music: *Litany of the Saints;* adapt. by Richard Proulx, © 1971, GIA Publications, Inc.

Or:

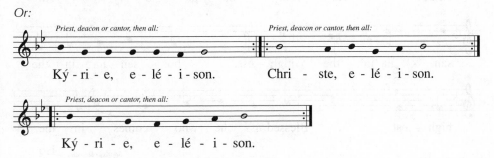

Music: *Litany of the Saints;* adapt. by Richard Proulx, © 1971, GIA Publications, Inc.

190 **HOLY, HOLY, HOLY**

Holy, Holy, Holy Lord God of hosts. Heav'n and earth are full of your glory. Hosanna in the highest, hosanna in the highest. Blessed is he who comes in the name of the Lord. Hosanna in the highest, hosanna in the highest.

Soprano Descant: Hosanna,

Text: ICEL, © 2010
Music: *A Community Mass*, Richard Proulx, © 1971, 1977, GIA Publications, Inc.

MEMORIAL ACCLAMATION B

191

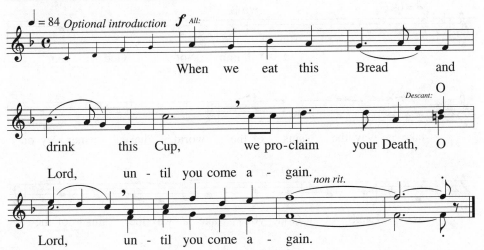

When we eat this Bread and drink this Cup, we pro-claim your Death, O Lord, un-til you come a-gain. O Lord, un-til you come a-gain.

Text: ICEL, © 2010
Music: *A Community Mass,* Richard Proulx, © 1988, 2010, GIA Publications, Inc.

AMEN

192

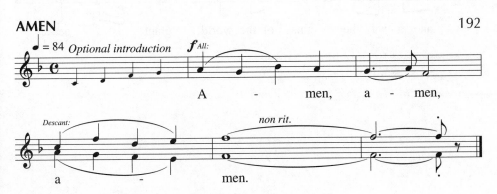

A - men, a - men, a - men.

Music: *A Community Mass,* Richard Proulx (adapt.), © 1971, 2011, GIA Publications, Inc.

193 **LAMB OF GOD**

Music: *A Community Mass,* Richard Proulx, © 1971, 1977, GIA Publications, Inc.

Setting Nine: Cantus Missae

KYRIE

Ký-ri - e, * e - lé - i-son.

Chri - ste, e - lé - i - son.

Ký-ri - e, e - lé - i - son.

Ký-ri-e, * ** e - lé-i-son.

Music: Vatican Edition VIII; acc. by Richard Proulx, © 1995, GIA Publications, Inc.

GLORIA

Gló-ri - a in ex-cél-sis De - o. Et in ter-ra pax ho-mí-ni-bus

bo - nae vo - lun - tá - tis. Lau-dá - mus te.

Be - ne - dí - ci - mus te. A - do - rá - mus te.

Glo - ri - fi - cá - mus te. Grá - ti - as á - gi - mus ti - bi

pro - pter ma - gnam gló - ri - am tu - am. Dó - mi - ne De - us,

Rex cae - lé - stis, De - us Pa - ter o - mní - po - tens.

Dó - mi - ne Fi - li u - ni - gé - ni - te, Je - su Chri - ste.

Dó - mi - ne De - us, A - gnus De - i, Fí - li - us Pa - tris.

Qui tol - lis pec - cá - ta mun - di, mi - se - ré - re no - bis.

Qui tol - lis pec - cá - ta mun - di, sú - sci - pe de - pre - ca - ti - ó -

nem no - stram. Qui se - des ad déx - te - ram Pa - tris,

mi - se - ré - re no - bis. Quó - ni - am tu so - lus San - ctus.

Tu so - lus Dó - mi - nus. Tu so - lus Al - tís - si - mus,

Je - su Chri - ste. Cum San - cto Spí - ri - tu:

in gló - ri - a De - i Pa - tris. A - men.

Music: Vatican Edition VIII, acc. by Richard Proulx, © 1995, GIA Publications, Inc.

LITURGY OF THE WORD

196 FIRST READINGS

After the first reading:

Reader: Ver - bum Dó - mi - ni. Assembly: De - o grá - ti - as.

After the second reading or if there is only one reading before the gospel:

Reader: Ver - bum Dó - mi - ni. Assembly: De - o grá - ti - as.

GOSPEL

Before the gospel reading:

Deacon or priest: — *Assembly:*

Dó - mi - nus vo - bís-cum. Et cum spí - ri - tu tu - o.

Deacon or priest:

Lé - cti - o san - cti E - van - gé - li - i se - cún - dum

Assembly:

N... Gló - ri - a ti - bi, Dó - mi - ne.

After the reading:

Deacon or priest: — *Assembly:*

Ver-bum Dó - mi-ni. Laus ti - bi, Chri - ste.

CREDO

198

Cre-do in u-num De - um, Pa - trem o - mni-po - tén-tem, fa-

ctó-rem cae - li et ter-rae, vi - si - bí - li - um ó - mni-um

et in-vi-si-bí - li-um. Et in u - num Dó - mi-num

Je - sum Chri-stum, Fí - li - um De - i U - ni-gé - ni-tum.

Et ex Pa-tre na - tum an - te ó-mni - a saé - cu-la.

De - um de De - o, lu-men de lú-mi-ne, De-um ve-rum

de De-o ve-ro. Gé-ni-tum, non fa – ctum, con-sub-stan-ti-á-lem Pa-tri: per quem ó-mni-a fa-cta sunt.

Qui pro-pter nos hó-mi-nes et pro-pter no-stram sa-lú-tem de-scén-dit de cae-lis. Et in-car-ná-tus est de Spí-ri-tu

All bow

San-cto ex Ma-rí-a Vír-gi-ne, et ho-mo fa-ctus est.

Cru-ci-fí-xus é-ti-am pro no-bis sub Pón-ti-o Pi-lá-to; pas-sus et se-púl-tus est.

Et re-sur-ré-xit tér-ti-a di-e, se-cún-dum Scri-ptú-ras.

Et a-scén-dit in cae-lum, se-det ad déx-te-ram Pa-tris.

Et í-te-rum ven-tú-rus est cum gló-ri-a, ju-di-cá-re vi-vos et mór-tu-os, cu-ius re-gni non e-rit fi-nis.

Et in Spí - ri - tum San - ctum, Dó - mi - num et vi - vi - fi - cán - tem:

qui ex Pa - tre Fi - li - ó - que pro - cé - dit.

Qui cum Pa - tre et Fí - li - o si - mul a - do - rá - tur et con - glo -

ri - fi - cá - tur: qui lo - cú - tus est per pro - phé - tas. Et u - nam,

san - ctam, ca - thó - li - cam et a - po - stó - li - cam Ec - clé - si - am.

Con - fí - te - or u - num ba - ptís - ma in re - mis - si - ó - nem pec - ca -

tó - rum. Et ex - spé - cto re - sur - re - cti - ó - nem

mor - tu - ó - rum. Et vi - tam ven - tú - ri saé - cu - li.

A - men.

Music: Vatican Edition III; acc. by Richard Proulx, © 1995, GIA Publications, Inc.

PRAYER OF THE FAITHFUL

199

Cantor: *All:*

(Petition) ex - au - dí - re di - gné - ris. Te ro - gá - mus, au - di nos.

LITURGY OF THE EUCHARIST

200 PREFACE DIALOGUE

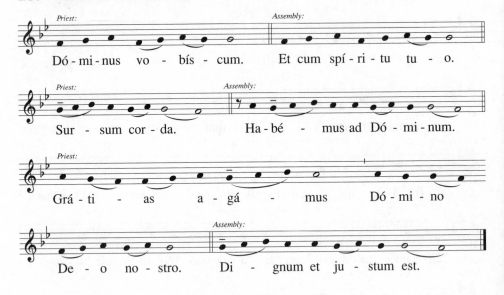

Priest: Dó-mi-nus vo-bís-cum. *Assembly:* Et cum spí-ri-tu tu-o.

Priest: Sur-sum cor-da. *Assembly:* Ha-bé-mus ad Dó-mi-num.

Priest: Grá-ti-as a-gá-mus Dó-mi-no

De-o no-stro. *Assembly:* Di-gnum et ju-stum est.

201 SANCTUS

A

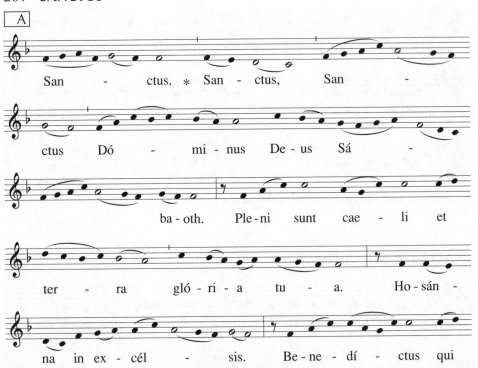

San - ctus, * San - ctus, San - ctus Dó - mi - nus De - us Sá - ba-oth. Ple-ni sunt cae - li et ter - ra gló - ri - a tu - a. Ho-sán - na in ex-cél - sis. Be-ne-dí - ctus qui

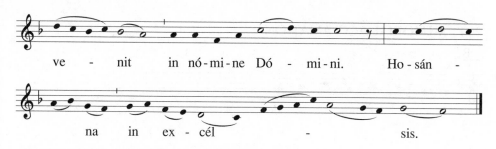

ve - nit in nó-mi-ne Dó - mi-ni. Ho - sán -

na in ex - cél - sis.

Music: Vatican Edition VIII; acc. by Richard Proulx, © 1995, GIA Publications, Inc.

SANCTUS 202

San - ctus, San - ctus, San-ctus Dó - mi - nus De - us Sá - ba-oth.

Ple - ni sunt cae - li et ter - ra gló - ri - a tu - a. Ho-sán - na

in ex - cél - sis. Be - ne - dí - ctus qui ve - nit in nó - mi - ne

Dó - mi - ni. Ho - sán - na in ex - cél - sis.

Music: Vatican Edition XVIII; acc. by Richard Proulx, © 1995, GIA Publications, Inc.

MEMORIAL ACCLAMATION 203

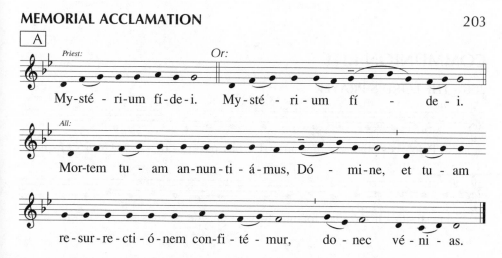

Priest: *Or:*

My - sté - ri-um fí-de-i. My - sté - ri - um fí - de - i.

All:

Mor-tem tu - am an-nun-ti - á-mus, Dó - mi-ne, et tu - am

re - sur - re - cti - ó - nem con-fi - té - mur, do - nec vé - ni - as.

Music: Vatican Edition; acc. by Richard Proulx, © 1995, GIA Publications, Inc.

204 MEMORIAL ACCLAMATION

Priest:

My - sté - ri - um fí - de - i.

All:

Mor-tem tu - am an - nun - ti - á - mus, Dó - mi - ne, et tu-am re-sur-

re - cti - ó - nem con - fi - té - mur, do - nec vé - ni - as.

Music: Vatican Edition; acc. by Richard Proulx, © 1995, GIA Publications, Inc.

205 AMEN

After the doxology:

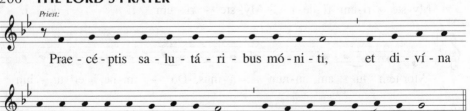

Priest:

Assembly:

...per ó - mni - a saé - cu - la sae - cu - ló - rum. A - men.

COMMUNION RITE

206 THE LORD'S PRAYER

Priest:

Prae - cé - ptis sa - lu - tá - ri - bus mó - ni - ti, et di - ví - na

in - sti - tu - ti - ó - ne for-má - ti, au - dé - mus dí - ce - re:

All:

Pa - ter no - ster, qui es in cae - lis: san - cti - fi - cé - tur no - men

tu - um; ad - vé - ni - at re - gnum tu - um; fi - at vo - lún - tas

tu - a, si - cut in cae - lo, et in ter - ra.

Pa - nem no - strum co - ti - di - á - num da no - bis hó - di - e;

et di - mít - te no - bis dé - bi - ta no - stra,

si - cut et nos di - mít - ti - mus de - bi -

tó - ri - bus no - stris. Et ne nos in - dú - cas in ten -

ta - ti - ó - nem; sed lí - be - ra nos a ma - lo.

Priest: Líbera nos...Jesu Christi.

All:

Qui - a tu - um est re - gnum, et po - té - stas,

et gló - ri - a in saé - cu - la.

207 SIGN OF PEACE

208 AGNUS DEI

Music: Vatican Edition VIII; acc. by Richard Proulx, © 1995, GIA Publications, Inc.

AGNUS DEI

209

Cantor: / All:

A-gnus De - i, qui tol-lis pec-cá-ta mun-di: mi-se-ré-re no - bis.

A-gnus De - i, qui tol-lis pec-cá-ta mun-di: mi-se-ré-re no - bis.

A-gnus De - i, qui tol-lis pec-cá-ta mun-di: do-na no-bis pa-cem.

Music: Vatican Edition XVIII; acc. by Richard Proulx, © 1995, GIA Publications, Inc.

CONCLUDING RITES

DISMISSAL

Deacon or priest, then all:

I - te, mis - sa est.
De - o grá - ti - as.

Music: Vatican Edition VIII; acc. by Richard Proulx, © 1995, GIA Publications, Inc.

Or:

Deacon or priest: / Assembly:

I - te, mis - sa est. De - o grá - ti - as.

For Easter Sunday and the octave of Easter:

Deacon or priest, then all:

I - te, mis-sa est, al - le - lú - ia, al - le - lú - ia.
De-o grá - ti - as, al - le - lú - ia, al - le - lú - ia.

Service Music

211 SPRINKLING SONG

Wash me. Wash me. Let the cleans-ing wa-ter that

flowed from your wound - ed side wash me. Oh,

wash me, Lord, wash me, and my

life will be made new a - gain.

Text: Kenneth W. Louis
Music: Kenneth W. Louis
© 2012, GIA Publications, Inc.

KYRIE 212

Lord, have mer - cy. Christ, have mer - cy.

Lord, have mer - cy, have mer - cy, O Lord.

Music: *Mass No. 1 in G,* Avon Gillespie, © 1987, GIA Publications, Inc.

KYRIE 213

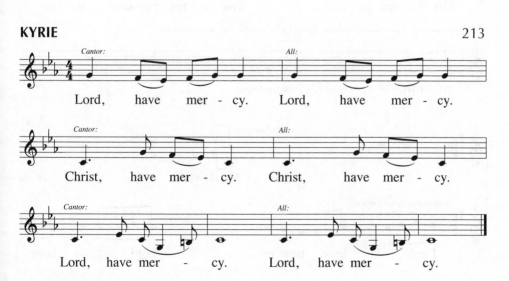

Cantor: Lord, have mer - cy. All: Lord, have mer - cy.

Cantor: Christ, have mer - cy. All: Christ, have mer - cy.

Cantor: Lord, have mer - cy. All: Lord, have mer - cy.

Music: Clarence Millard Hightower, © 1987, GIA Publications, Inc.

214 KYRIE

Priest, deacon or cantor, then all:

Ký - ri-e, e - lé-i-son. Ký - ri-e, e - lé-i-son.

Ký - ri-e, e - lé - i - son. |1. |2. son.

Priest, deacon or cantor, then all:

Cris-to, ten pie-dad, Cris-to, ten pie-dad, Cris-to, ten pie -

dad de no - so - tros. Cris-to, ten pie-dad,

Cris - to, ten pie-dad, Cris - to, ten pie - dad de no -

|1. so - tros. |2. so - tros.

Descant (2nd time only): Ký-ri - e,

Priest, deacon or cantor, then all:

Lord, have mer - cy, Lord, have

e - lé - i - son. Ký - ri - e, Ký - ri - e, e -

mer - cy. Lord, have mer -

1. 2.

lé - i - son.

cy.

Music: Norah Duncan IV, © 2011, GIA Publications, Inc.

215 GLORIA

Glo-ry to God in the high-est, and on earth peace to peo-ple of good will. We praise you, we bless you, we a-dore you, we glo-ri-fy you, we give you thanks for your great glo-ry, Lord God, heav-en-ly King, O God, al-might-y Fa-ther.

Lord Je-sus Christ, On-ly Be-got-ten Son, Lord God, Lamb of God, Son of the Fa-ther, you take a-way the sins of the world, have

mer - cy on us; you take a-way the sins of the world, re-

ceive our prayer; you are seat-ed at the right hand of the

right hand of the

Fa - ther, have mer - cy on us.

Fa - ther, have mer - cy on us.

Descant: 𝆑

Glo-ry to God. Glo - ry to

All: 𝆑

For you a-lone are the Ho-ly One, you a-lone are the

God. Glo - ry. You a - lone are the Most High, Je - sus

Lord, you a - lone are the Most High, Je - sus

Christ, Glo - ry. Glo - ry. Glo - ry of God the

Christ, with the Ho - ly Spir - it, in the glo - ry of God the

ff
Fa - ther. A - men. *rit.*

ff
Fa - ther. A - men. *rit.*

Text: ICEL, © 2010
Music: *Holy Name of Jesus Gloria*, Norah Duncan IV, © 2011, GIA Publications, Inc.

GOSPEL ACCLAMATION

Music: Norah Duncan IV, © 1987, GIA Publications, Inc.

Tone for verses

Music: Robert J. Batastini, © 2004, GIA Publications, Inc.

217 GOSPEL ACCLAMATION

1. Al - le - lu - ia, al - le - lu - ia, al - le - lu - ia, al - le - lu - ia, Oh! Al - le - lu - ia, al - le - lu - ia, al - le - lu - ia, al - le - lu - ia.

2. Je - sus is Lord, Je - sus is Lord, Je - sus is Lord, Je - sus is Lord, Je - sus is Lord, yes he is. Je - sus is Lord, Je - sus is Lord, Je - sus is Lord, Je - sus is Lord.

Music: John E. Watson, © 1985, John E. Watson

GOSPEL ACCLAMATION

*Add handclaps on beats 2 and 4 during the Refrain.

Common of the Blessed Virgin

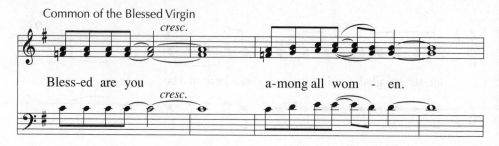

Bless-ed are you   a-mong all wom - en.

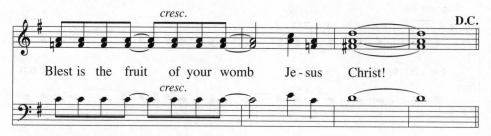

Blest is the fruit of your womb Je - sus Christ!

Text: English trans. of verses for Ordinary Time, Easter, and Pentecost from the Lectionary for Mass, © 1968, 1981, 1997, ICEL
Music: Stephen Pishner, © 2002, GIA Publications, Inc.

219 LENTEN GOSPEL ACCLAMATION

Praise   and hon - or to   you, Je - sus Christ.

Glo - ry to   your   name.

Music: Marjorie Gabriel-Burrow, © 1987, GIA Publications, Inc.

220 PRAYER OF THE FAITHFUL

Moderately slow with rhythmic refrain

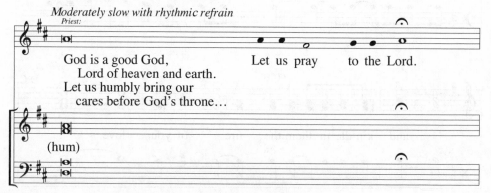

Priest:
God is a good God,   Let us pray   to the Lord.
   Lord of heaven and earth.
Let us humbly bring our
   cares before God's throne...

(hum)

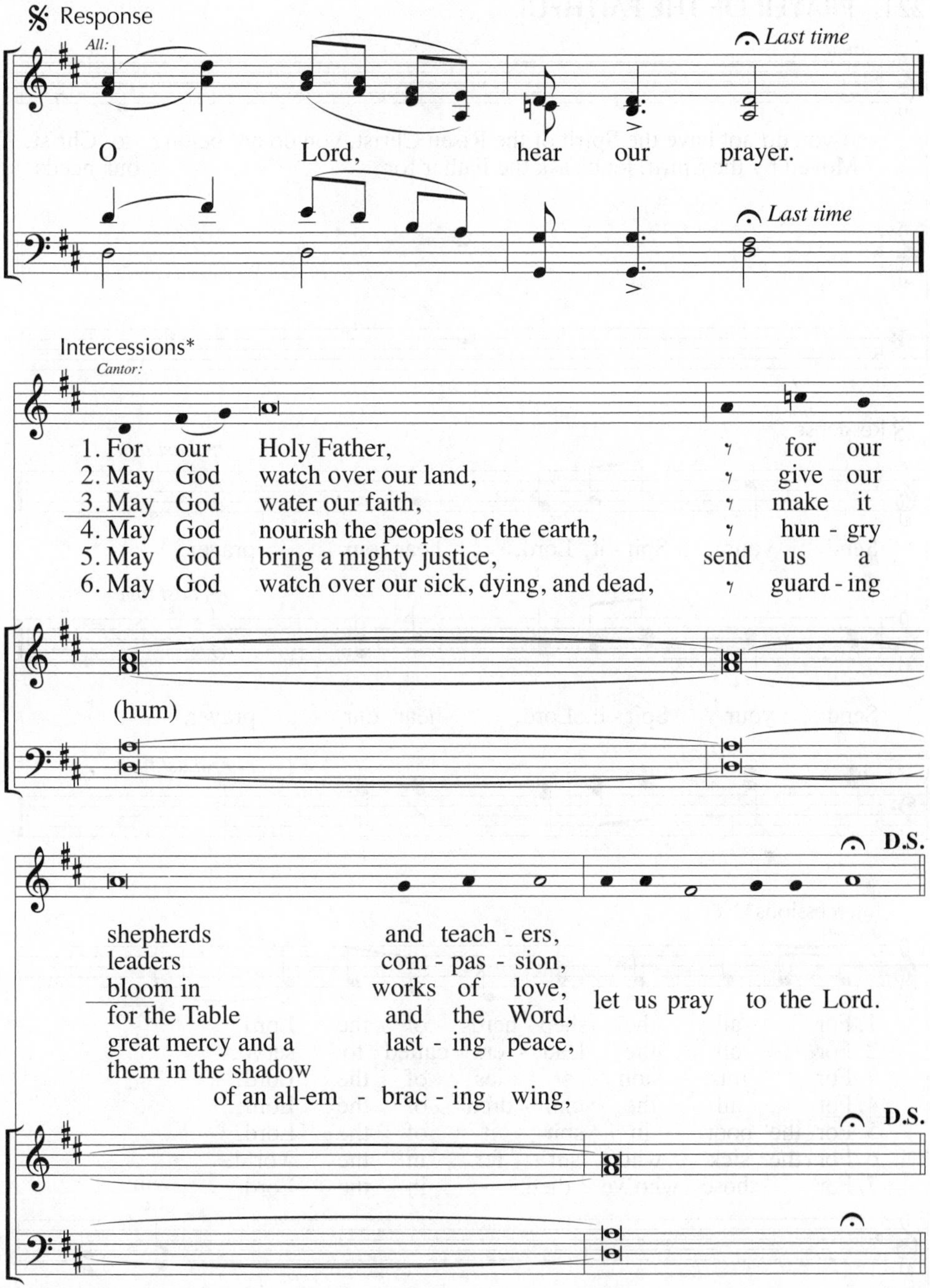
Response
All:
Last time
O Lord, hear our prayer.
Last time
Intercessions*
Cantor:
1. For our Holy Father, for our shepherds and teach - ers,
2. May God watch over our land, give our leaders com - pas - sion,
3. May God water our faith, make it bloom in works of love,
4. May God nourish the peoples of the earth, hun - gry for the Table and the Word,
5. May God bring a mighty justice, send us a great mercy and a last - ing peace,
6. May God watch over our sick, dying, and dead, guard - ing them in the shadow of an all-em - brac - ing wing,
let us pray to the Lord.
(hum)
D.S.
D.S.

*Other intercessions may be interspersed and added as the occasion warrants.

Text: Ray East
Music: Ray East
© 1987, GIA Publications, Inc.

221 PRAYER OF THE FAITHFUL

Priest:

If you do not have the Spirit of the Risen Christ, you do not belong to Christ.
Moved by the Spirit, let us ask the Father for our needs.

Response

All:

Send your Spir - it, Lord, hear our prayer.

Last time

Send your Spir - it, Lord, hear our prayer.

Last time

Intercessions*

Cantor:

1. For all the shep - herds of the Lord,
2. For all the lead - ers called to serve,
3. For mis - sion - ar - ies of the Lord,
4. For all the chil - dren of the Lord,
5. For the poor in spir - it of the Lord,
6. For the sick who suf - fer in the world,
7. For those who've died in the Lord,

A - men!

*Other intercessions may be interspersed and added as the occasion warrants.

let them love those in their care:
let the Spir - it be their guide:
let them pro - claim all God's works:
let them tes - ti - fy to God's love:
let them be a - niont - ed in God's pow'r:
let them be strength - ened in the Lord:
let them be raised up to the Lord:

A - men!

Cantor: **D.S.**

let us pray to the Lord.

Text: Ray East
Music: Ray East
© 1987, GIA Publications, Inc.

PRAYER OF THE FAITHFUL 222

Hear our prayer, O Lord; hear our prayer, O Lord. In -

cline thine ear to us, and grant us thy peace.

Text: Psalm 143:1
Music: George Whelpton, 1847–1930

PRAYER OF THE FAITHFUL 223

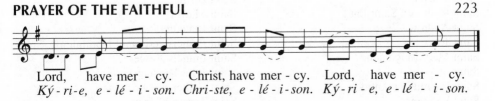

Lord, have mer - cy. Christ, have mer - cy. Lord, have mer - cy.
Ký - ri - e, e - lé - i - son. Chri - ste, e - lé - i - son. Ký - ri - e, e - lé - i - son.

Music: William B. Cooper, © 1973, Dangerfield Music Co.

224 LITANY OF THE SAINTS

It is our longstanding tradition to give thanks always and everywhere for the wondrous things that God has wrought from generation unto generation, especially in the death and resurrection of Jesus Christ, our good brother and Lord. We remember, too, what God has done in the lives of other righteous ones. We are a people who remember "those who have gone before us marked with the sign of faith." We remember, too, that "we have come over a way that with tears has been watered, we have come, treading our path thro' the blood of the slaughtered. . ." (*Lift Every Voice and Sing*). They are our saints: Felicity and Perpetua, Benedict the African, Augustine, Monica, the Ugandan Martyrs. We keep alive the memory of those who have demonstrated the continuing vitality of our traditional values and virtues. Sister Thea Bowman, FSPA, or Archbishop James Patterson Lyke, OFM, would have been voices for many a voiceless African American in our own time or whether they had lived 350 years ago. Sojourner Truth, trumpeting the call to abolish slavery, and Martin Luther King, Jr., dreaming a daring dream, were radical then and now.

These whose memories we keep alive are our "canonized" and "righteous ancestors". They are ever before us.

It is right and fitting, then, that we should often invoke our ancestors and beg for our saints to intercede on our behalf, for in their eccentricities, their persistent mortality, and their holiness, they are what we are called to be: saints to God's greater glory!

The cantor invokes the ancestor, while the people respond: **O be with us.** *The text can be adapted to most existing settings of the Litany of the Saints, including the ones that follow, and the one found within the Easter Vigil (no. 849).*

RIGHTEOUS ANCESTORS *Others may be interspersed and added.*

Daniel Rudd	Mary McLeod Bethune
Mother Mary Elizabeth Lange	Harriet Tubman
Mother Henriette DeLille	Sojourner Truth
Mother Mathilde Beasley	Frederick Douglass
Mother Theodore Williams	George Washington Carver
Father Augustine Tolton	Benjamin Banneker
Sister Thea Bowman	Reverend Doctor Martin Luther King, Jr.
Archbishop James Patterson Lyke	Medgar Evers

The cantor calls on the Saints, while the people respond: **Pray for us.** *The text can be adapted to any existing setting of the Litany of the Saints.*

SAINTS FROM THE UNIVERSAL LITANY *Other Saints may be interspersed and added.*

Holy Mary, Mother of God	Saints Perpetua and Saint Felicity
Saint Michael	Saint Agnes
Holy Angels of God	Saint Gregory
Saint John the Baptist	Saint Athanasius
Saint Joseph	Saint Basil
Saint Peter and Saint Paul	Saint Martin
Saint Andrew	Saint Benedict
Saint John	Saint Francis and Saint Dominic
Saint Mary Magdalene	Saint Francis Xavier
Saint Stephen	Saint John Vianney
Saint Ignatius of Antioch	Saint Catherine of Sienna
Saint Lawrence	Saint Teresa of Jesus

SAINTS WITH AFRICAN ROOTS

Saint Mark, Apostle and Evangelist
Saint Cyprian
Saint Apollonia
Pope Saint Victor
Pope Saint Gelasius
Pope Saint Militades
Saint Maurice
Saint Fulgentius
Saint Macarius
Saint Isidore
Saint Cyril
Saint Marcellinus
Saint Zeno
Saint Aninius
Saint Athanasius
Saint Eugenius
Saint Dionysius
Saint Anastius
Saints Monica and Augustine
Saint George
Abba Moses the African

Abba Anthony of Egypt
Saint Catherine of Alexandria
Holy Martyrs Abraham, Ethnus, Acrates,
    James and John
Saint Frumentius of Axum
Saint Elesbaan
Saint Abnodius
Saint Saint Saizana
Saint Justin de Jacobis
Saint Martin de Porres
Saint Benedict the Moor
Saints Charles Lwanga, Kizito and the
    Holy Martyrs of Uganda
Saint Josephine Bakhita of Darfur
Saint Michael Cyprian Iwene Tansi
Saint Peter Claver
Saint Katherine Drexel
Blessed Daudi Okelo and Jildo Irwa
Venerable Pierre Toussaint
All Holy Men and Women

The cantor then intercedes while the people respond: **Lord, we ask you, hear our prayer.**

O Lord our God, be merciful
Keep us from all evil
Keep us all from every sin
Keep us from everlasting death
By your Incarnation, Lord
By your death and resurrection, Lord
By your gifts of the Spirit
Have mercy on us sinners
Guide, protect your holy Church
Bring all together in trust and peace
Other intercessions may be added according to the ritual being celebrated, then finally:
Jesus, Son of the living God

225 LITANY OF THE SAINTS

Text: Grayson Warren Brown
Music: Grayson Warren Brown; arr. by Larry Adams

LITANY OF THE SAINTS

Music: Eric F. Hornsby, © 1992

227 LAMB OF GOD

Lamb of God, you take a - way the sins of the world, have mer-cy on us.

Lamb of God, you take a - way the sins of the world, have mer-cy on us.

Lamb of God, you take a - way the sins of the world, grant us peace, grant us peace.

Music: Tillis Butler, © Augsburg Fortress

228 LAMB OF GOD

Cantor:

A - gnus De - i, qui

All:

tol - lis pec-cá - ta mun - di, mi - se-ré - re

Optional 2nd cantor:

no - bis, mi - se-ré - re no - bis. Cor -

de - ro de Dios, que qui - tas el pe -

ca - do del mun - do, *All:* ten pie-dad de no -

so - tros, ten pie-dad de no - so - tros. *Repeat ad lib.*

All: Lamb of God, you take a-way the sins of the world,

Optional harmony: Cor - de-ro de Dios, que qui-tas el pe - ca - do del

grant us peace, grant us peace.

mun-do, do - na no - bis pa-cem, peace.

Music: Norah Duncan IV, © 2011, GIA Publications, Inc.

229 LAMB OF GOD

Lamb of God, you take a - way the

sins of the world, have mer - cy on us.

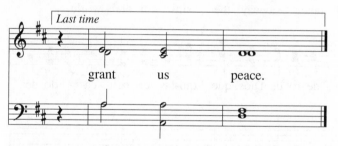

grant us peace.

Music: *Holy Cross Mass;* David Clark Isele, © 1979, GIA Publications, Inc.

230 LAMB OF GOD

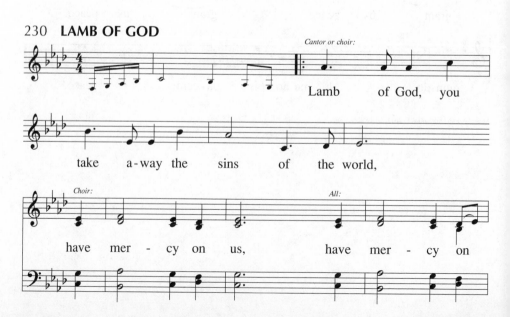

Lamb of God, you

take a - way the sins of the world,

have mer - cy on us, have mer - cy on

Music: Robert Ray, © 1984, Jensen Publications, Inc.

231 O Come, O Come, Emmanuel

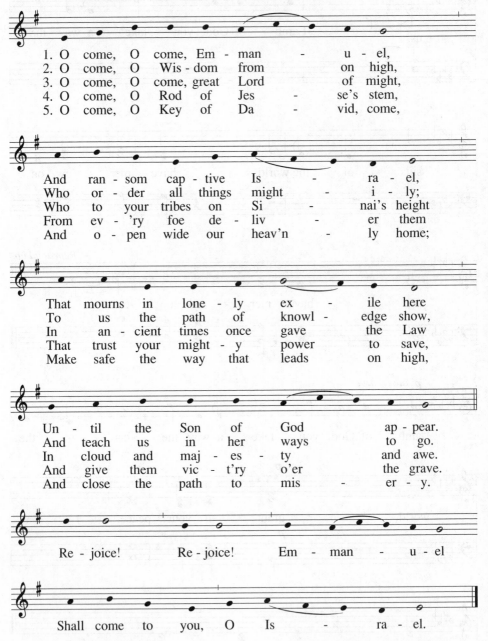

1. O come, O come, Emman - u - el,
2. O come, O Wis - dom from on high,
3. O come, O come, great Lord of might,
4. O come, O Rod of Jes - se's stem,
5. O come, O Key of Da - vid, come,

And ran - som cap - tive Is - ra - el,
Who or - der all things might - i - ly;
Who to your tribes on Si - nai's height
From ev - 'ry foe de - liv - er them
And o - pen wide our heav'n - ly home;

That mourns in lone - ly ex - ile here
To us the path of knowl - edge show,
In an - cient times once gave the Law
That trust your might - y power to save,
Make safe the way that leads on high,

Un - til the Son of God ap - pear.
And teach us in her ways to go.
In cloud and maj - es - ty and awe.
And give them vic - t'ry o'er the grave.
And close the path to mis - er - y.

Re - joice! Re - joice! Em - man - u - el

Shall come to you, O Is - ra - el.

6. O come, O Dayspring from on high,
   And cheer us by your drawing nigh;
   Disperse the gloomy clouds of night,
   And death's dark shadow put to flight.

7. O come, Desire of nations, bind
   In one the hearts of humankind;
   O bid our sad divisions cease,
   And be for us our King of Peace.

Text: *Veni, veni Emmanuel*; Latin 9th C.; tr. by John M. Neale, 1818–1866, alt.
Tune: VENI EMMANUEL, LM with refrain; Mode I; adapt. by Thomas Helmore, 1811–1890; acc. by Richard Proulx, 1937–2010, © 1975, GIA Publications, Inc.

Hail to the Lord's Anointed   232

1. Hail to the Lord's A - noint - ed, Great Da - vid's great-er Son!
2. He comes with suc - cor speed - y To those who suf - fer wrong;
3. He shall come down like show - ers Up - on the fruit - ful earth,
4. To him shall prayer un - ceas - ing And dai - ly vows as - cend;

Hail in the time ap - point - ed, His reign on earth be - gun!
To help the poor and need - y, And bid the weak be strong;
Love, joy, and hope, like flow - ers, Spring in his path to birth:
His king - dom still in - creas - ing, A king - dom with - out end:

He comes to break op - pres - sion, To set the cap - tive free;
To give them songs for sigh - ing, Their dark-ness turn to light,
Be - fore him, on the moun-tains, Shall peace, the her - ald, go,
The tide of time shall nev - er His cov - e - nant re - move,

To take a - way trans-gres - sion, And rule in eq - ui - ty.
Whose souls, con-demned and dy - ing, Are pre-cious in his sight.
And right-eous - ness, in foun-tains, From hill to val - ley flow.
His name shall stand for - ev - er; That name to us is Love.

Text: James Montgomery, 1771–1854
Tune: SHEFFIELD, 7 6 7 6 D; English melody

233 While We Are Waiting, Come

1. While we are wait - ing, come;
2. With pow'r and glo - ry, come;
3. Come, Sav - ior, quick - ly come;

While we are wait - ing, come.
With pow'r and glo - ry, come.
Come, Sav - ior, quick - ly come.

Je - sus, our Lord, Em - man - u - el,

While we are wait - ing, come.

Text: Claire Cloninger
Tune: Don Cason
© 1986, Word Music, LLC

Emmanuel, Emmanuel   234

Em-man - u - el,   Em-man - u - el,

his   name   is   called   Em - man - u - el.

God   with   us,   re-vealed   in   us,

Final ending

his   name   is   called   Em-man - u - el.

Text: Bob McGee, b.1944
Tune: McGEE, Irregular; Bob McGee, b.1944
© 1976, C. A. Music (div. of C. A. Records, Inc.) ASCAP

235 Prepare Ye the Way of the Lord!

Verse

Solo or section:

Make straight in the des-ert a high-way for our God. Pre-

All:

pare ye the way of the Lord! Bring ev-'ry hill and

Solo or section:

All:

moun - tain low. Pre-pare ye the way of the Lord! Pre-

D.S.

Text: Kenneth W. Louis, b.1956
Tune: Kenneth W. Louis, b.1956
© 2007, World Library Publications

236 The King Shall Come When Morning Dawns

1. The King shall come when morn - ing dawns And
2. Not, as of old, a lit - tle child, To
3. The King shall come when morn - ing dawns And
4. And let the end - less bliss be - gin, By
5. The King shall come when morn - ing dawns And

light tri - um - phant breaks, When beau - ty gilds the
suf - fer and to die, But crowned with glo - ry
earth's dark night is past; O haste the ris - ing
wea - ry saints fore - told, When right shall tri - umph
light and beau - ty brings. Hail, Christ, the Lord! Your

east - ern hills And life to joy a - wakes.
like the sun That lights the morn - ing sky.
of that morn Whose day shall ev - er last.
o - ver wrong, And truth shall be ex - tolled.
peo - ple pray: Come quick - ly, King of kings.

Text: John Brownlie, 1857–1925, alt.
Tune: MORNING SONG, CM; Wyeth's *Repository of Sacred Music*, 1813; arr. by Robert J. Batastini, b.1942, © 1994, GIA Publications, Inc.

Prepare Ye the Way of the Lord   237

Refrain

Pre-pare ye the way   of the   Lord.

Pre-pare ye the way   of the   Lord.

Verses

D.S.

1. Make straight in the des - ert   a high - way for   our God.
2. Fill ev - 'ry val - ley,   bring all moun-tains low.
3. Go   up   to a moun-tain   and shout with   a   loud voice.
4. Say to all peo - ple,   Here   is   your God.

Text: Isaiah 40:3–4, 9
Tune: James E. Moore, Jr., b.1951
© 1983, GIA Publications, Inc.

238 Come, O Long-Expected Jesus

1. Come, O long - ex - pect - ed Je - sus,
2. Is - rael's strength and con - so - la - tion,
3. Born your peo - ple to de - liv - er,
4. By your own e - ter - nal Spir - it

Born to set your peo - ple free; From our fears and
Hope to all the earth im - part; Dear de - sire of
Born a child, and yet a king; Born to reign in
Rule in all our hearts a - lone; By your all - suf -

sins re - lease us: Christ, in you our rest shall be.
ev - 'ry na - tion, En - ter ev - 'ry long - ing heart.
us for - ev - er, Now your grac - ious king - dom bring.
fi - cient mer - it Raise us to your glo - rious throne.

Text: Haggai 2:7; Charles Wesley, 1707–1788, alt.
Tune: STUTTGART, 8 7 8 7; *Psalmodia Sacra*, 1715; adapt. and harm. by William Henry Havergal, 1793–1870, alt.

Creator of the Stars of Night   239

1. Cre - a - tor of the stars of night,
2. In sor - row that the an - cient curse
3. When this old world drew on toward night,
4. At your great Name, O Je - sus, now
5. Come in your ho - ly might, we pray,
6. To God the Fa - ther, God the Son,

Your peo - ple's ev - er - last - ing light,
Should doom to death a u - ni - verse,
You came; but not in splen - dor bright,
All knees must bend, all hearts must bow:
Re - deem us for e - ter - nal day;
And God the Spir - it, Three in One,

O Christ, Re - deem - er of us all,
You came, O Sav - ior, to set free
Not as a mon - arch, but the child
All things on earth with one ac - cord,
De - fend us while we dwell be - low
Praise, hon - or, might, and glo - ry be

We pray you hear us when we call.
Your own in glo - rious lib - er - ty.
Of Mar - y, blame - less moth - er mild.
Like those in heav'n, shall call you Lord.
From all as - saults of our dread foe.
From age to age e - ter - nal - ly.

Text: *Creator alme siderum*, Latin 9th. C., revised 1632; tr. *The Hymnal 1982*, alt., © 1985, The Church Pension Fund
Tune: CONDITOR ALME SIDERUM, LM; Mode IV, Sarum, 9th C.; acc. by Gerard Farrell, OSB, 1919–2009, © 1986, GIA Publications, Inc.

240 On Jordan's Bank

1. On Jor - dan's bank the Bap - tist's cry An -
2. Then cleansed be ev - 'ry life from sin; Make
3. For you are our sal - va - tion, Lord, Our
4. To heal the sick stretch out your hand, And
5. All praise to you, e - ter - nal Son, Whose

noun - ces that the Lord is nigh; A - wake and heark - en,
straight the way for God with - in, And let each heart pre -
ref - uge and our great re - ward; With - out your grace we
bid the fall - en sin - ner stand; Shine forth and let your
ad - vent has our free - dom won, Whom with the Fa - ther

for he brings Glad tid - ings of the King of kings.
pare a home Where such a might - y guest may come.
waste a - way Like flow'rs that with - er and de - cay.
light re - store Earth's own true love - li - ness once more.
we a - dore, And Ho - ly Spir - it, ev - er - more.

Text: *Jordanis oras praevia;* Charles Coffin, 1676–1749; tr. by John Chandler, 1806–1876, alt.
Tune: WINCHESTER NEW, LM; adapt. from *Musikalisches Handbuch,* Hamburg, 1690

Christ Is Coming: Prepare the Way 241

mf

Christ   is com-ing: Pre - pare   the   way.

f >

Last time

Christ   is com-ing: Pre - pare   the   way.

ff

Christ is   com - ing. Christ is   com - ing.

D.C.

Text: Edward V. Bonnemère, 1921–1996
Tune: *Advent Jazz Vespers II,* Edward V. Bonnemère, 1921–1996
© 1986, Amity Music Co.

242 Come, Lord, and Tarry Not!

1. Come, Lord, and tar - ry not! Bring the long - looked - for day! O why these years of wait - ing here, These a - ges of de - lay? These a - ges of de - lay?
2. Come, for your saints still wait; Dai - ly as - cends their sigh; The Spir - it and the Bride say, "Come!" Do you not hear the cry?
3. Come, for cre - a - tion groans With long - ing for your stay, Worn out with these long years of ill, These a - ges of de - cay.
4. Come, and make all things new; Build up this ru - ined earth; Re - store our fad - ed par - a - dise, Cre - a - tion's sec - ond birth.
5. Come, and be - gin your reign Of ev - er - last - ing peace; Come, take the king - dom to your - self, Great King of Right - eous - ness!

Text: Revelation 22:17, attr. to Horatius Bonar, alt., 1808–1889
Tune: ST. BRIDE, SM; Samuel Howard, 1710–1782

Are You Ready? 243

Read - y, are you read - y for the com-ing of the Lord? Be ye al - so read - y; you know not the day. Will you be read - y when Je - sus comes?

Text: Larry E. Roberts, Sr.
Tune: Larry E. Roberts, Sr.; arr. by Kenneth W. Louis, b.1956
© 1981, Savgos Music

244 Silent Night

1. Si - lent night, ho - ly night! All is calm,
2. Si - lent night, ho - ly night! Shep - herds quake
3. Si - lent night, ho - ly night! Son of God,

all is bright Round yon vir - gin moth - er and child.
at the sight; Glo - ries stream from heav - en a - far;
love's pure light Ra - diant beams from thy ho - ly face,

Ho - ly In - fant so ten - der and mild, Sleep in heav - en - ly
Heav'n - ly hosts sing al - le - lu - ia! Christ, the Sav - ior, is
With the dawn of re - deem - ing grace, Je - sus, Lord, at thy

peace, Sleep in heav - en - ly peace.
born! Christ, the Sav - ior, is born!
birth, Je - sus, Lord, at thy birth.

Text: *Stille Nacht, heilige Nacht;* Joseph Mohr, 1792–1849; tr. by John F. Young, 1820–1885
Tune: STILLE NACHT, 66 89 66; Franz X. Gruber, 1787–1863

Night of Silence   245

1. Cold are the peo - ple, win - ter of life, We trem - ble in
2. Voice in the dis - tance, call in the night, On wind you en -
3. Spir - it a - mong us, shine like the star, Your light that guides

shad - ows this cold end - less night. Fro - zen in the snow lie
fold us, you speak of the light. Gen - tle on the ear you
shep - herds and kings from a - far. Shim - mer in the sky so

ros - es sleep-ing, Flow - ers that will ech - o the sun -
whis-per, soft - ly, Ru - mors of a dawn so em - brac -
emp - ty, lone - ly, Ris - ing in the warmth of the Son's

rise. Fire of hope is our on - ly warmth;
ing. Breath-less love a - waits dark-ened souls.
love. Star un - know - ing of night and day,

Wea - ry, its flame will be dy - ing soon.
Soon will we know of the morn - ing.
Spir - it, we wait for the lov - ing Son.

"Night of Silence" was written to be sung simultaneously with "Silent Night." It is suggested that selected voices hum "Silent Night" (in this key), while the remaining voices sing the final verse of "Night of Silence". Likewise, the song "Silent Night" may be sung by the choir and congregation as the instruments play "Night of Silence".

Text: Daniel Kantor, b.1960
Tune: Daniel Kantor, b.1960
© 1984, GIA Publications, Inc.

246 Angels We Have Heard on High

1. An - gels   we   have   heard   on   high
2. Shep - herds,   why   this   ju - bi - lee?
3. Come   to   Beth - le - hem   and   see
4. See   him   in   a   man - ger   laid

Sweet - ly   sing - ing   o'er   the   plains,
Why   your   joy - ous   strains   pro - long?
Him   whose   birth   the   an - gels   sing;
Whom   the   choirs   of   an - gels   praise;

And   the   moun - tains   in   re - ply
Say   what   may   the   tid - ings   be
Come,   a - dore   on   bend - ed   knee
Mar - y,   Jo - seph,   lend   your   aid,

Ech - o   back   their   joy - ous   strains.
Which   in - spire   your   heav'n - ly   song.
Christ   the   Lord,   the   new - born   King.
While   our   hearts   in   love   we   raise.

Gló - - - ri - a in ex - cél - sis De - o. Gló - - - ri - a in ex - cél - sis De - o.

Text: *Les anges dans nos campagnes*; French carol, c. 18th C.; tr. from *Crown of Jesus Music*, London, 1862
Tune: GLORIA, 7 7 7 7 with refrain; French carol

247 Hark! The Herald Angels Sing

1. Hark! The her - ald an - gels sing, "Glo - ry to the
2. Christ, by high - est heav'n a - dored; Christ, the ev - er -
3. Hail the heav'n - born Prince of Peace! Hail the Sun of

new - born King! Peace on earth and mer - cy mild,
last - ing Lord! Late in time be - hold him come,
Right - eous - ness! Light and life to all he brings,

God and sin - ners rec - on - ciled!" Joy - ful, all you
Off - spring of the Vir - gin's womb. Veiled in flesh the
Ris'n with heal - ing in his wings. Mild he lays his

na - tions, rise; Join the tri - umph of the skies;
God - head see; Hail the in - car - nate De - i - ty,
glo - ry by, Born that we no more may die,

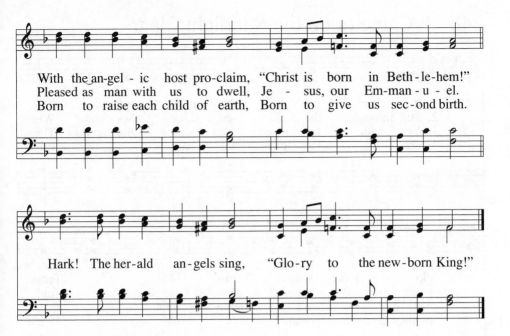

With the an-gel - ic host pro-claim, "Christ is born in Beth-le-hem!"
Pleased as man with us to dwell, Je - sus, our Em-man-u - el.
Born to raise each child of earth, Born to give us sec-ond birth.

Hark! The her-ald an-gels sing, "Glo-ry to the new-born King!"

Text: Charles Wesley, 1707–1788, alt.
Tune: MENDELSSOHN, 77 77 D with refrain; Felix Mendelssohn, 1809–1847

248 It Came upon the Midnight Clear

1. It came up - on the mid - night clear, That
2. Still through the clo - ven skies they come With
3. Yet with the woes of sin and strife The
4. For lo! The days are has - t'ning on, By

glo - rious song of old, From
peace - ful wings un - furled, And
world has suf - fered long; Be -
proph - ets seen of old, When

an - gels bend - ing near the earth To
still their heav'n - ly mu - sic floats O'er
neath the heav'n - ly hymn have rolled Two
with the ev - er - cir - cling years Shall

touch their harps of gold: "Peace
all the wea - ry world. A -
thou - sand years of wrong; And
come the time fore - told, When

on the earth, good will to all, From
bove its sad and low - ly plains They
war - ring hu - man - kind hears not The
peace shall o - ver all the earth Its

heav'n's all - gra - cious King." The
bend on hov - 'ring wing, And
tid - ings which they bring; O
an - cient splen - dors fling, And

world in sol - emn still - ness lay, To
ev - er o'er its Ba - bel sounds The
hush the noise and cease your strife And
all the world give back the song Which

hear the an - gels sing.
bless - ed an - gels sing.
hear the an - gels sing.
now the an - gels sing.

Text: Edmund H. Sears, 1810–1876, alt.
Tune: CAROL, CMD; Richard S. Willis, 1819–1900

249   Joy to the World

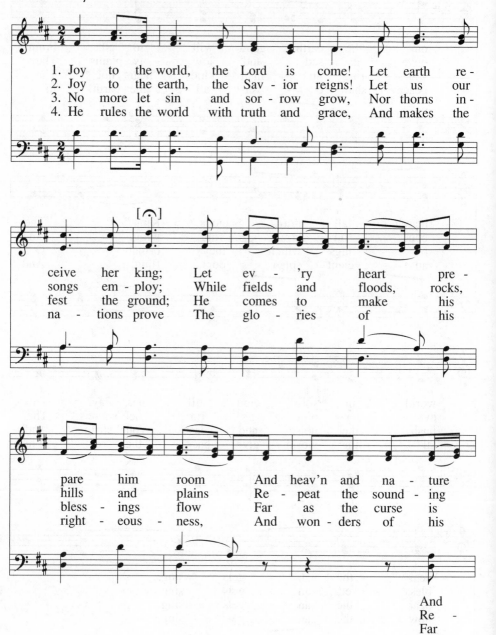

1. Joy to the world, the Lord is come! Let earth re -
2. Joy to the earth, the Sav - ior reigns! Let us our
3. No more let sin and sor - row grow, Nor thorns in -
4. He rules the world with truth and grace, And makes the

ceive her king; Let ev - 'ry heart pre -
songs em - ploy; While fields and floods, rocks,
fest the ground; He comes to make his
na - tions prove The glo - ries of his

pare him room And heav'n and na - ture
hills and plains Re - peat the sound - ing
bless - ings flow Far as the curse is
right - eous - ness, And won - ders of his

And
Re -
Far
And

sing, And heav'n and na - ture sing, And
joy, Re - peat the sound - ing joy, Re -
found, Far as the curse is found, Far
love, And won - ders of his love, And

heav'n and na - ture sing, And heav'n and na - ture
peat the sound - ing joy, Re - peat the sound - ing
as the curse is found, Far as the curse is
won - ders of his love, And won - ders of his

heav'n, and heav'n and na - ture sing.
peat, re - peat the sound - ing joy.
as, far as the curse is found.
won - ders, won - ders of his love.

sing, and heav'n and na - ture sing.
joy, re - peat the sound - ing joy.
found, far as the curse is found.
love, and won - ders of his love.

Text: Psalm 98; Isaac Watts, 1674–1748
Tune: ANTIOCH, CM; arr. from George F. Handel, 1685–1759, in T. Hawkes' *Collection of Tunes*, 1833

250   O Little Town of Bethlehem

1. O lit - tle town of Beth - le - hem, How
2. For Christ is born of Mar - y And,
3. How si - lent - ly, how si - lent - ly The
4. O ho - ly Child of Beth - le - hem, De -

still we see thee lie! A - bove thy deep and
gath - ered all a - bove While mor - tals sleep, the
won - drous gift is giv'n! So God im - parts to
scend to us, we pray; Cast out our sin and

dream - less sleep The si - lent stars go by;
an - gels keep Their watch of won - d'ring love.
hu - man hearts The bless - ings of his heav'n.
en - ter in, Be born in us to - day.

Yet in the dark streets shin - eth The
O morn - ing stars, to - geth - er Pro -
No ear may hear his com - ing, But
We hear the Christ - mas an - gels The

ev - er - last - ing Light. The hopes and fears of
claim the ho - ly birth, And prais - es sing to
in this world of sin, Where meek souls will re -
great glad tid - ings tell; O come to us, a -

all the years Are met in thee to - night.
God the King, And peace to all on earth!
ceive him, still The dear Christ en - ters in.
bide with us, Our Lord Em - man - u - el!

Text: Phillips Brooks, 1835–1893
Tune: ST. LOUIS, 8 6 8 6 7 6 8 6; Lewis H. Redner, 1831–1908

251 Messiah Now Has Come

1. From his throne a - bove The King of Love Came
2. In his life we find New hope sub - lime, His
3. In the hearts of all, Sal - va - tion's call Is

down to set us free. With his gift of life, He
King-dom will ful - fill God's man - date for peace, All
an - swered ev - er more. God's re - demp - tion tale, Em -

sac - ri - ficed From a man - ger to a tree.
con - flicts ceased, On earth on - ly good - will.
man - u - el, We wor - ship and a - dore.

So we sing, we sing, the heav - ens ring, Hail

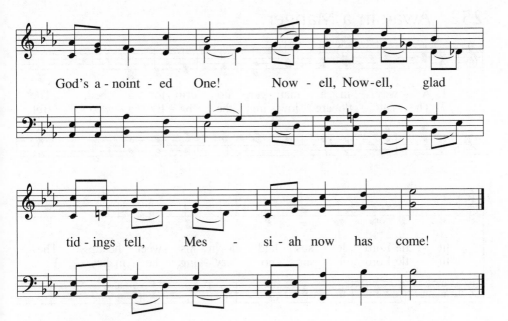

God's a - noint - ed One! Now - ell, Now-ell, glad

tid - ings tell, Mes - si - ah now has come!

Text: Nolan Williams, Jr., b.1969
Tune: MESSIAH, 54 6 D with refrain; Nolan Williams, Jr., b.1969
© 1996, NEW-J Publishing (a division of NEWorks)

252 Away in a Manger

1. A - way in a man - ger, no crib for a bed, The
2. The cat - tle are low - ing; the ba - by a - wakes, But

lit - tle Lord Je - sus laid down his sweet head; The
lit - tle Lord Je - sus, no cry - ing he makes. I

stars in the sky looked down where he
love thee, Lord Je - sus! Look down from the

lay, The lit - tle Lord Je - sus, a - sleep on the hay.
sky And stay by my cra - dle till morn - ing is nigh.

3. Be near me, Lord Je - sus; I ask thee to stay Close

by me for - ev - er, and love me, I pray. Bless

all the dear chil - dren in thy ten - der care, And

fit us for heav - en, to live with thee there.

Text: Sts. 1, 2, anonymous; st. 3, John T. McFarland, 1851–1913
Tune: MUELLER, 11 11 11 11; James R. Murray, 1841–1905; arr. by Nolan Williams, Jr., b.1969, © 2000, GIA Publications, Inc.

253 Go Tell It on the Mountain

Refrain

Go tell it on the moun-tain, O-ver the hills and ev - 'ry-where,

Go tell it on the moun - tain that Je - sus Christ is born.

Verses

1. While shep-herds kept their watch-ing O'er si - lent flocks by night,
2. The shep-herds feared and trem-bled When lo! a - bove the earth,
3. Down in a low - ly man - ger The hum - ble Christ was born,

D.C.

Be - hold, through-out the heav-ens There shone a ho - ly light.
Rang out the an - gel cho - rus That hailed our Sav - ior's birth.
And God sent us sal - va - tion That bless - ed Christ-mas morn.

Text: Negro Spiritual; adapt. by John W. Work, Jr., 1871–1925
Tune: GO TELL IT ON THE MOUNTAIN, 7 6 7 6 with refrain; Negro Spiritual; arr. by Valeria A. Foster, © 2000, GIA Publications, Inc.

He Came Down 254

He came down that we may have *love; He came down that we may have love; He came down that we may have love, Hal-le-lu-jah for ev-er-more.

Solo: Why did he come?

Substitute peace, joy, hope, life, *etc.*

Text: Cameroon traditional
Tune: Cameroon traditional; tr. and arr. by John L. Bell, b.1949, © 1990, Iona Community, GIA Publications, Inc., agent

255 O Holy Night!

1. O ho-ly night! the stars are bright-ly
2. Led by the light of faith se-rene-ly
3. Tru-ly he taught us to love one an-

shin-ing; It is the night of the dear Sav-ior's birth.
beam-ing, With glow-ing hearts by his cra-dle we stand.
oth-er; His law is love and his gos-pel is peace.

Long lay the world in sin and er-ror
So led by light of a star sweet-ly
Chains shall he break, for the slave is our

pin-ing, Till he ap-peared and the soul felt its
gleam-ing, Here came the Wise Men from O-ri-ent
broth-er, And in his name all op-pres-sion shall

worth.
land.
cease.

A thrill of hope— the
The King of kings lay
Sweet hymns of joy in

wea - ry world re - joic - es, For yon - der breaks a
thus in low - ly man - ger, In all our tri - als
grate - ful cho - rus raise we; Let all with - in us

new and glo - rious morn! Fall on your knees! O
born to be our Friend. He knows our need— to our
praise his ho - ly name. Christ is the Lord! O

hear the an - gel voic - es! O night di -
weak - ness is no stran - ger. Be - hold your
praise his name for - ev - er! His pow'r and

vine, O night when Christ was
King, be - fore him low - ly
glo - ry ev - er - more pro -

born! O night, O ho - ly
bend! Be - hold your King, be -
claim! *His pow'r and glo - ry

1., 2. **3.**

night, O night di - vine!
fore him low - ly bend!
ev - er - more pro - claim!

*Optional extended or choral ending

His pow'r and glo - ry

ev - er - more pro - claim!

Text: John S. Dwight, 1813–1893
Tune: CANTIQUE DE NOEL, Irregular; Adolphe Adam, 1803–1856

Wonderful Counselor 256

1. Oh, who do you call the won-der-ful coun-sel-or?
2. Oh, I call Je-sus the won-der-ful coun-sel-or.

Oh, glo-ry hal-le-lu-jah! Oh,

glo-ry hal-le-lu-jah! Glo-ry hal-le-lu-jah to the new-born King!

Text: Negro Spiritual
Tune: Negro Spiritual; arr. by Evelyn Simpson-Curenton, b.1953, © 2000, GIA Publications, Inc.

257 Heaven's Christmas Tree

1. I have heard of a tree, a great Christ-mas tree, It was
2. There is one I be-hold in let-ters of gold, It
3. There is one just a-bove, its ti-tle is love, It is
4. An - oth-er I see, it must be for me, The
5. There are man-y, I'm sure, but just this one more I

stall.
me.
stain.
read.
rest.

fixed in yon Beth - le - hem's, Beth - le - hem's stall. The
hangs on a limb near to, limb near to me. 'Tis
marked by a deep crim - son, deep crim-son stain. For
words "I will help you" I, "help you" I read. While
speak of a - bove all the, bove all the rest. It

bless-ings of heav-en for you and for me, A
la-beled "sal - va - tion," and Je - sus, I'm told, Has
there it was tied by the Lord when he died, And
hold-ing his hand, by faith I can stand, And
spells "hap - py home" with God near the throne, A

Christ - mas pres - ent for all.
bought that pack - age for me.
glo - ry to his dear name.
this is the pack - age I need.
place where the wea - ry shall rest.

There is a pack-age for me on that tree; A pre - cious

to - ken that some - one loves me. Oh yes, I can see on

Cal - va - ry's Tree, That there is a pack-age for me.

Text: Charles A. Tindley, 1851–1933
Tune: HEAVEN'S CHRISTMAS TREE, 11 9 11 7 with refrain, Charles A. Tindley, 1851–1933; arr. by Charles A. Tindley, Jr.

258 Rise Up, Shepherd, and Follow

Solo:

1. There's a star in the East on Christ-mas morn,
2. If you take good heed to the an-gel's words,

All:

Rise up, shep-herd, and fol-low, It will
Rise up, shep-herd, and fol-low, You'll for-

Solo:

lead to the place where the Christ was born,
get your flocks, you'll for-get your herds,

All:

Rise up, shep-herd, and fol-low.
Rise up, shep-herd, and fol-low.

Fol - low, fol - low, Rise up, shep - herd, and

fol - low, Fol - low the Star of Beth - le - hem,

Rise up, shep - herd, and fol - low.

Text: Negro Spiritual
Tune: Negro Spiritual; arr. by Joseph Joubert, b.1958, © 2000, GIA Publications, Inc.

Glória, Glória 259

Canon–*4 voices*

1. Gló - ri - a, gló - ri - a, 2. in ex - cél - sis De - o!

3. Gló - ri - a, gló - ri - a, 4. al - le - lú - ia, al - le - lú - ia!

Tune: Jacques Berthier, 1923–1994, © 1979, 1988, Les Presses de Taizé, GIA Publications, Inc., agent

260 Singing Glory Be to Jesus

Sing-ing glo - ry be to Je - sus,

O come all ye faith - ful,

Joy to the world, the Lord is come. Let

Son of God and prince of Peace. He's might-y

joy - ful and tri - um - phant, O

earth re-ceive her King.

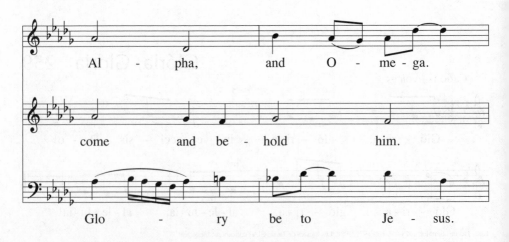

Al - pha, and O - me - ga.

come and be - hold him.

Glo - ry be to Je - sus.

Born   in our hearts   on this Christ - mas   morn.

Born   in our hearts   on this Christ - mas   morn.

Born   in our hearts   on this Christ - mas   morn.

Text: Adapted by Rawn Harbor
Tune: Rawn Harbor
© 1985, Rawn Harbor

Away in a Manger   261

1. A - way in   a   man - ger,   no   crib for   a   bed,
2. The cat - tle are low - ing; the   ba - by a - wakes,
3. Be near me, Lord Je - sus;   I   ask you to   stay

The   lit - tle Lord   Je - sus   laid down his sweet head.
But   lit - tle Lord   Je - sus,   no   cry - ing he   makes.
Close by   me for - ev - er,   and love me,   I   pray.

The   stars in   the bright sky   looked down where he   lay,
I   love you, Lord Je - sus! Look down from the   sky
Bless all   the   dear chil - dren in   your ten - der care,

The   lit - tle Lord   Je - sus,   a - sleep on   the hay.
And   stay by   my   cra - dle   till morn - ing is   nigh.
And   fit   us   for   heav - en,   to   live with you there.

Text: Sts. 1, 2, anonymous; st. 3, John T. McFarland, 1851–1913
Tune: CRADLE SONG, 11 11 11 11; William J. Kirkpatrick, 1838–1921

262 O Come, All Ye Faithful / Adéste Fidéles

1. O come, all ye faith-ful, joy - ful and tri - um - phant, O
2. God of God, Light of Light,
3. Sing, choirs of an - gels, sing in ex - ul - ta - tion,
4. Yea, Lord, we greet thee, born this hap - py morn - ing,

1. Ad - é - ste fi - dé - les, lae - ti, tri - um-phán - tes, Ve -
2. De - um de De - o, Lu - men de Lú - mi - ne
3. Can - tet nunc i - o, cho - rus an - ge - ló - rum,
4. Er - go qui na - tus Di - e ho - di - ér - na,

come ye, O come ye to Beth - le - hem;
Lo! He comes forth from the Vir - gin's womb.
Sing, all ye cit - i - zens of heav'n a - bove!
Je - sus, to thee be all glo - ry giv'n;
ní - te, ve - ní - te in Béth - le - hem.
Ge - stant pu - él - lae ví - sce - ra.
Can - tet nunc au - la cae - lé - sti - um.
Je - su ti - bi sit gló - ri - a.

Come and be - hold him, born the King of an - gels;
Our ver - y God, be - got - ten not cre - a - ted,
Glo - ry to God, all glo - ry in the high - est;
Word of the Fa - ther, now in flesh ap - pear - ing;
Na - tum vi - dé - te, Re - gem an - ge - ló - rum.
De - um ve - rum, gé - ni - tum, non fa - ctum.
Gló - ri - a, gló - ria in ex - cél - sis De - o.
Pa - tris ae - ter - nae ver - bum ca - ro fa - ctum.

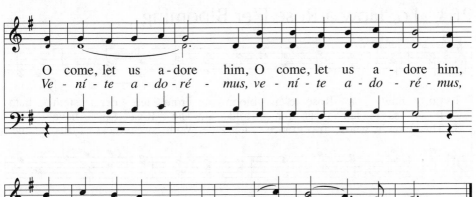

Text: *Adeste fideles;* John F. Wade, c.1711–1786; tr. by Frederick Oakeley, 1802–1880, alt.
Tune: ADESTE FIDELES, Irregular with refrain; John F. Wade, c.1711–1786

263 Lo, How a Rose E'er Blooming

1. Lo, how a Rose e'er bloom-ing From ten-der stem hath
2. I - sa - iah 'twas for - told it, The Rose I have in
3. This Flow'r, whose fra-grance ten - der With sweet-ness fills the

sprung! Of Jes-se's lin-eage com-ing, As seers of old have
mind; With Mar - y we be-hold it, The Vir-gin Moth - er
air, Dis - pels with glo-rious splen-dor The dark-ness ev - 'ry-

sung. It came, a blos-som bright, A - mid the cold of
kind. To show God's love a - right, She bore to us a
where. True man, yet ver - y God, From sin and death he

win - ter, When half spent was the night.
Sav - ior, When half spent was the night.
saves us, And light - ens ev - 'ry load.

Text: Isaiah 11:1; *Es ist ein' Ros' entsprungen;* Speyer *Gesangbuch*, 1599; tr. sts. 1–2 by Theodore Baker, 1851–1934, alt.; st. 3, Friedrich Layritz, 1808–1859; tr. by Harriet Reynolds Krauth, 1845–1925, alt.
Tune: ES IST EIN' ROS' ENSTSPRUNGEN, 7 6 7 6 6 7 6; *Geistliche Kirchengesänge*, Cologne, 1599; harm. by Michael Praetorius, 1571–1621

Angels, from the Realms of Glory 264

1. An - gels, from the realms of glo - ry,
2. Shep - herds, in the field a - bid - ing,
3. Sag - es, leave your con - tem - pla - tions,
4. Though an in - fant now we view him,

Wing your flight o'er all the earth; You who sang cre -
Watch - ing o'er your flocks by night, God on earth is
Bright - er vi - sions beam a - far; Seek the great De -
He shall fill his heav'n - ly throne, Gath - er all the

a - tion's sto - ry, Now pro - claim Mes - si - ah's birth:
now re - sid - ing, Yon - der shines the in - fant light.
sire of na - tions; You have seen his morn - ing star.
na - tions to him; Ev - 'ry knee shall then bow down.

Come and wor - ship, come and wor - ship,

Wor - ship Christ, the new - born King.

Text: Sts. 1–3, James Montgomery, 1771–1854; st. 4, *Christmas Box*, 1825
Tune: REGENT SQUARE, 8 7 8 7 with refrain; Henry Smart, 1813–1879

265 Star-Child

Last time to Coda ⊕

Verses

Descant:

5. Hope - for - peace Child,

Melody:

1. Star - Child, earth - Child,
2. Street child, beat child,
3. Grown child, old child,
4. Spared child, spoiled child,
5. Hope - for - peace Child,

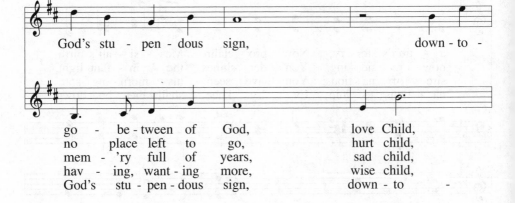

God's stu - pen - dous sign, down - to -

go - be - tween of God, love Child,
no place left to go, hurt child,
mem - 'ry full of years, sad child,
hav - ing, want - ing more, wise child,
God's stu - pen - dous sign, down - to -

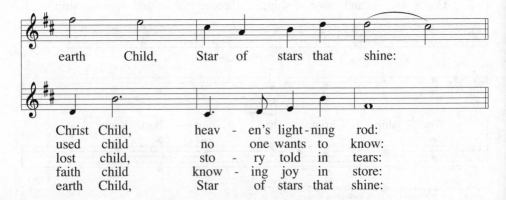

earth Child, Star of stars that shine:

Christ Child, heav - en's light - ning rod:
used child, no one wants to know:
lost child, sto - ry told in tears:
faith child, know - ing joy in store:
earth Child, Star of stars that shine:

Refrain

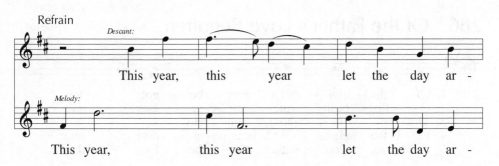

Descant:
This year, this year let the day ar -

Melody:
This year, this year let the day ar -

rive when Christ - mas comes for ev - 'ry - one,

rive when Christ - mas comes for ev - 'ry - one,

⊕ Coda

ev - 'ry - one a - live.

ev - 'ry - one a - live.

Text: Shirley Erena Murray, b.1931, © 1994, Hope Publishing Company
Tune: NOAH'S SONG, 4 5 4 5 with refrain; Ronald F. Krisman, b.1946, © 2003, GIA Publications, Inc.

266 Of the Father's Love Begotten

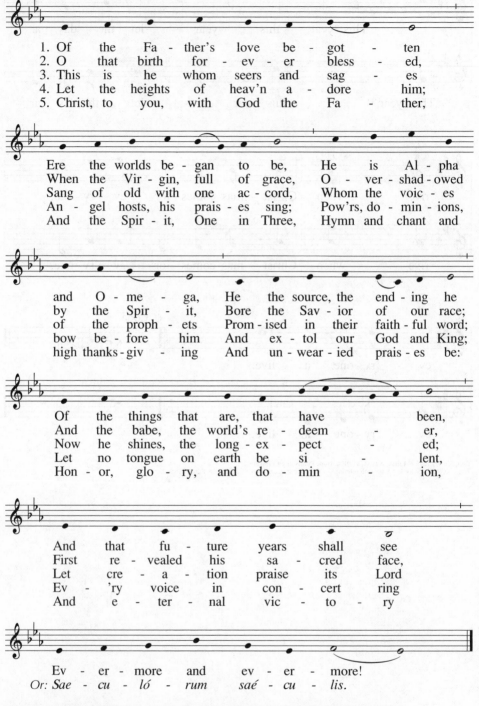

1. Of the Fa-ther's love be-got-ten
2. O that birth for-ev-er bless-ed,
3. This is he whom seers and sag-es
4. Let the heights of heav'n a-dore him;
5. Christ, to you, with God the Fa-ther,

Ere the worlds be-gan to be, He is Al-pha
When the Vir-gin, full of grace, O-ver-shad-owed
Sang of old with one ac-cord, Whom the voic-es
An-gel hosts, his prais-es sing; Pow'rs, do-min-ions,
And the Spir-it, One in Three, Hymn and chant and

and O-me-ga, He the source, the end-ing he
by the Spir-it, Bore the Sav-ior of our race;
of the proph-ets Prom-ised in their faith-ful word;
bow be-fore him And ex-tol our God and King;
high thanks-giv-ing And un-wear-ied prais-es be:

Of the things that are, that have been,
And the babe, the world's re-deem-er,
Now he shines, the long-ex-pect-ed;
Let no tongue on earth be si-lent,
Hon-or, glo-ry, and do-min-ion,

And that fu-ture years shall see
First re-vealed his sa-cred face,
Let cre-a-tion praise its Lord
Ev-'ry voice in con-cert ring
And e-ter-nal vic-to-ry

Ev-er-more and ev-er-more!
Or: Sae-cu-ló-rum saé-cu-lis.

Text: *Corde natus ex Parentis*; Aurelius Prudentius, 348–413; tr. by John M. Neale, 1818–1866 and Henry W. Baker, 1821–1877, alt.
Tune: DIVINUM MYSTERIUM, 8 7 8 7 8 7 7; 12th C.; Mode V; acc. by Richard Proulx, 1937–2010, © 1985, GIA Publications, Inc.

Alleluia! The Lord Has Come   267

Al - le - lu - ia, al - le - lu - ia, Christ has come to bring sal - va - tion, the Lord has come to bring sal - va - tion, al-le-lu - ia, al-le-lu - ia.

2. ia. Al - le - lu - ia, al - le - lu - ia, Christ has come to bring sal - va - tion, the Lord has come to bring sal - va - tion, al-le-lu - ia, al - le - lu - ia, al-le-lu - ia, al - le - lu - ia, al-le-lu - ia, al - le - lu - ia!

ia, al-le-lu - ia, al - le - lu - ia!

Text: Rawn Harbor
Music: Rawn Harbor
© 1987, Rawn Harbor

268 The Virgin Mary Had a Baby Boy

1. The vir - gin Mar-y had a ba-by boy, the vir-gin
2. The an - gels sang when the ba-by born, the an-gels
3. The wise men saw where the ba-by born, the wise men

Mar-y had a ba-by boy, the vir-gin Mar - y had a
sang when the ba-by born, the an - gels sang when the
saw where the ba-by born, the wise men went where the

ba - by boy, and they say that his name was Je-sus.
ba - by born, and they say that his name was Je-sus.
ba - by born, and they say that his name was Je-sus.

He come from the glo-ry, he come from the glo-rious king-dom.

Oh, yes! be-liev-er! Oh, yes! be-liev-er!

Oh, Oh,

He come from the glo-ry, he come from the glo-rious king-dom.

He's Here! 269

He's here! Je - sus Christ is here! Oh,

Last time to Coda ⊕ | 1.

glo - ry, glo - ry, glo - ry to his name. He's

| 2.

Born of the Vir - gin Mar - y in the

town of Beth - le - hem, the Son of God the Fa - ther, the

D.S. ⊕ Coda

Sav - ior of the world! Oh yeah! He's

Text: Anonymous
Tune: Anonymous

270 Once in Royal David's City

1. Once in roy - al Da - vid's cit - y Stood a
2. He came down to earth from heav - en Who is
3. And, through all his won - drous child - hood, He would
4. For he is our child - hood's pat - tern, Day by
5. And our eyes at last shall see him, Through his

low - ly cat - tle shed, Where a moth - er laid her
God and Lord of all, And his shel - ter was a
hon - or and o - bey, Love and watch the low - ly
day like us he grew; He was lit - tle, weak, and
own re - deem - ing love; For that child so dear and

ba - by In a man - ger for his bed.
sta - ble, And his cra - dle was a stall.
maid - en In whose gen - tle arms he lay.
help - less, Tears and smiles like us he knew.
gen - tle Is our Lord in heav'n a - bove.

Mar - y was that moth - er mild;
With the poor and meek and low - ly
Chris - tian chil - dren all should be
And he feels for all our sad - ness,
And he leads his chil - dren on

Je - sus Christ, her lit - tle child.
Lived on earth our Sav - ior ho - ly.
Kind, o - be - dient, good as he.
And he shares in all our glad - ness.
To the place where he is gone.

Text: Cecil F. Alexander, 1818–1895, alt.
Tune: IRBY, 8 7 8 7 77; Henry J. Gauntlett, 1805–1876; harm. by Arthur H. Mann, 1850–1929, © 1957, Novello & Company Limited

271 Sing of Mary, Pure and Lowly

1. Sing of Mar - y, pure and low - ly, Vir - gin Moth - er
2. Sing of Je - sus, son of Mar - y, In the home at
3. Glo - ry be to God the Fa - ther; Glo - ry be to

un - de - filed. Sing of God's own Son most ho - ly,
Naz - a - reth. Toil and la - bor can - not wea - ry
God the Son; Glo - ry be to God the Spir - it;

Who be - came her lit - tle child. Fair - est Child of
Love en - dur - ing un - to death. Con - stant was the
Glo - ry to the Three in One. From the heart of

fair - est Moth - er, God the Lord who came to earth,
love he gave her, Though he went forth from her side,
bless - ed Mar - y, From all saints the song as - cends,

Word - made - flesh, our ver - y broth - er,
Forth to preach, and heal, and suf - fer,
And the Church the strain re - ech - oes

Takes our na - ture by his birth.
Till on Cal - va - ry he died.
Un - to earth's re - mot - est ends.

Text: Roland F. Palmer, 1891–1985, © Estate of Roland Palmer
Tune: PLEADING SAVIOR, 8 7 8 7 D; *Christian Lyre*, 1830; harm. by Richard Proulx, 1937–2010, © 1986, GIA Publications, Inc.

Brightest and Best 272

1. Bright - est and best of the stars of the morn - ing,
2. Say, shall we yield him in cost - ly de - vo - tion,
3. Vain - ly we of - fer each am - ple ob - la - tion,
4. Cold on his cra - dle the dew - drops are shin - ing,

Dawn on our dark - ness and lend us your aid,
O - dors of E - dom and of - f'rings di - vine,
Vain - ly with gifts would his fa - vor se - cure;
Low lies his head with the beasts of the stall;

Star of the east, the ho - ri - zon a - dorn - ing,
Gems of the moun - tain and pearls of the o - cean,
Rich - er by far is the heart's ad - o - ra - tion,
An - gels a - dore him in slum - ber re - clin - ing,

Guide where our in - fant Re - deem - er is laid.
Myrrh from the for - est, or gold from the mine?
Dear - er to God are the prayers of the poor.
Mak - er and Mon - arch and Sav - ior of all.

Text: Reginald Heber, 1783–1826
Tune: MORNING STAR, 11 10 11 10; James P. Harding, 1850–1911

273 We Three Kings of Orient Are

1. We three kings of O - ri - ent are; Bear - ing
2. Born a King on Beth - le - hem's plain, Gold I
3. Frank - in - cense to of - fer have I; In - cense
4. Myrrh is mine: its bit - ter per - fume Breathes a
5. Glo - rious now be - hold him a - rise, King and

gifts, we trav - erse a - far Field and foun - tain,
bring to crown him a - gain; King for - ev - er,
owns a De - i - ty nigh; Prayer and prais - ing,
life of gath - er - ing gloom; Sor - rowing, sigh - ing,
God and Sac - ri - fice; "Al - le - lu - ia,

Moor and moun - tain, Fol - low - ing yon - der star.
Ceas - ing nev - er, O - ver us all to reign.
Glad - ly rais - ing, Wor - ship - ing God on high.
Bleed - ing, dy - ing, Sealed in the stone - cold tomb.
Al - le - lu - ia!" Sounds through the earth and skies.

O star of won - der, star of night, Star with

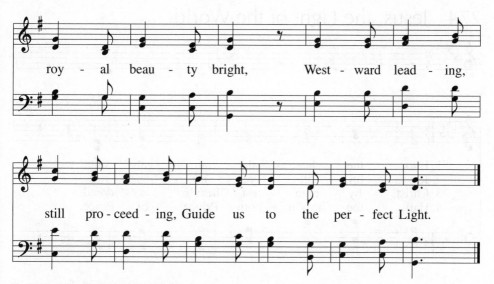

roy - al beau - ty bright, West - ward lead - ing,

still pro - ceed - ing, Guide us to the per - fect Light.

Text: Matthew 2:1–11; John H. Hopkins, Jr., 1820–1891, alt.
Tune: KINGS OF ORIENT, 88 44 6 with refrain; John H. Hopkins, Jr., 1820–1891

274 Jesus, the Light of the World

1. Hark the her - ald an - gels sing.
2. Joy - ful, all ye na - tions, rise.
3. Christ, by high - est heav'n a - dored.
4. Hail, the heav'n - born Prince of Peace.

Je - sus, the light of the world.

Glo - ry to the new - born King,
Join the tri - umph of the skies.
Christ, the ev - er - last - ing Lord,
Hail, the Sun of right - eous - ness!

Je - sus, the light of the world.

We'll walk in the light, beau - ti - ful light.

Come where the dew-drops of mer - cy shine bright. Oh,

shine all a - round us by day and by

night. Je - sus, the light of the world.

Text: George D. Elderkin; verses by Charles Wesley, 1707–1788
Tune: WE'LL WALK IN THE LIGHT, 7 7 7 7 with refrain; George D. Elderkin; arr. by Evelyn Simpson-Curenton, b.1953, © 2000,
    GIA Publications, Inc.

275 Behold the Star!

Refrain

Be-hold the star! Be-hold the star up yon-der!

Be-hold the star! It is the star of Beth-le-hem.

Verses

1. There was no room found in the inn,
2. The wise men came from the East
3. A song broke forth up-on the night.

Last time
Beth - le - hem. (ooh)

For him who was born
To wor-ship him, the
Peace on earth, good -

It is the star of Beth-le-hem. (ooh)

free from sin. Oh,
"Prince of Peace."
will to men.

It is the star of Beth-le-hem.

Text: Negro Spiritual
Tune: BEHOLD THE STAR, LM with refrain; Negro Spiritual, arr. by Nolan Williams, Jr., b.1969, © 2000, GIA Publications, Inc.

276 The First Nowell

1. The first No - well the an - gel did say Was to
2. They look - ed up and saw a star Shin - ing
3. And by the light of that same star Three
4. This star drew nigh to the north - west, O'er
5. Then en - tered in those wise men three, Full
6. Then let us all with one ac - cord Sing

cer - tain poor shep - herds in fields as they lay; In
in the east be - yond them far; And
wise men came from coun - try far; To
Beth - le - hem it took its rest; And
rev - 'rent - ly up - on their knee, And
prais - es to our heav - 'nly Lord, Who

fields where they lay keep - ing their sheep, On a
to the earth it gave great light, And
seek for a king was their in - tent, And to
there it did both stop and stay Right
of - fered there in his pres - ence Their
made the heav'ns and earth of naught, And

cold win-ter's night that was so deep.
so it con-tin-ued both day and night.
fol-low the star where-ev-er it went.
o-ver the place where Je-sus lay.
gold and myrrh and frank-in-cense.
with his blood our life has bought.

No-well, No-well, No-well, No-well!

Born is the King of Is-ra-el.

Text: English carol, 17th C.
Tune: THE FIRST NOWELL, Irregular with refrain; English carol; harm. from *Christmas Carols New and Old*, 1871

277 What Child Is This

1. What child is this, who, laid to rest, On
2. Why lies he in such mean es - tate Where
3. So bring him in - cense, gold, and myrrh; Come,

Mar - y's lap is sleep - ing, Whom an - gels greet with
ox and ass are feed - ing? Good Chris - tian, fear; for
peas - ant, king, to own him. The King of kings sal -

an - thems sweet While shep - herds watch are keep - ing?
sin - ners here The si - lent Word is plead - ing.
va - tion brings; Let lov - ing hearts en - throne him.

This, this is Christ the King, Whom shep-herds guard and an-gels sing;

Haste, haste to bring him laud, The babe, the son of Mar - y.

Text: William C. Dix, 1827–1898, alt.
Tune: GREENSLEEVES, 8 7 8 7 with refrain; English melody, 16th C.; harm. by John Stainer, 1840–1901

278 Songs of Thankfulness and Praise

1. Songs of thank - ful - ness and praise, Je - sus, Lord, to
2. Man - i - fest at Jor - dan's stream, Proph-et, Priest, and
3. Man - i - fest in mak - ing whole Pal - sied limbs and
4. Grant us grace to see you, Lord, Pres - ent in your

you we raise, Man - i - fest-ed by the star
King su - preme; And at Ca - na, wed - ding guest,
faint - ing soul; Man - i - fest in val - iant fight,
ho - ly word. By that grace which you en - dow,

To the sag - es from a - far; Branch of roy - al
In your God - head man - i - fest; Man - i - fest in
Quell - ing all the dev - il's might; Man - i - fest in
Help us im - i - tate you now, That we, pure like

Da - vid's stem In your birth at Beth - le - hem;
pow'r di - vine, Chang - ing wa - ter in - to wine;
gra - cious will, Ev - er bring - ing good from ill;
you, may be At your great e - piph - a - ny;

An - thems be to you ad-dressed, God in flesh made man - i - fest.
An - thems be to you ad-dressed, God in flesh made man - i - fest.
An - thems be to you ad-dressed, God in flesh made man - i - fest.
And may praise you, ev - er blest, God in flesh made man - i - fest.

Text: Christopher Wordsworth, 1807–1885, alt.
Tune: SALZBURG, 77 77 D; Jakob Hintze, 1622–1702, alt; harm. by J. S. Bach, 1685–1750

279 Epiphany Carol

1. Ev - 'ry na - tion sees the glo - ry
2. Ev - 'ry tongue shall sing the prais - es
3. Once a - gain may we dis - cov - er
4. Gath - er, God, the world to - geth - er

Of a star that pierced the night.
Of his birth in deep - est night.
Word made flesh sent from a - bove.
In the bright - ness of your day.

As we tell the won - drous sto - ry
He is heal - ing for the a - ges;
In our neigh - bor, sis - ter, broth - er,
Fill our hearts with joy for - ev - er;

We are bathed in ra - diant light. Star sent forth from
He is Christ, our God's de - light. He pro - claims with -
In the lone - ly and un - loved. May we touch him,
Help us walk the ho - ly way. May your jus - tice

high - est heav - en, Danc - ing light of God's de - sign,
in his be - ing All our hopes, our great de - sires.
may we hold him, May we cra - dle him with care
rule the na - tions; May all peo - ple live as one.

Shine up - on the gift that's giv - en:
He shall die to rise, re - deem - ing
As we learn to love each oth - er,
Now we see our true sal - va - tion

Word made flesh now born in time.
All who fol - low with their lives.
Bring - ing hope from out de - spair.
In the glo - ry of your Son.

Text: Francis Patrick O'Brien, b.1958, © 2002, GIA Publications, Inc.
Tune: HOLY MANNA, 8 7 8 7 D; William Moore, *Columbian Harmony*, 1825

280 Behold Your God

Oh, thou that tell-est good tid-ings to Zi-on, oh,
thou that tell-est good tid-ings to Je-ru-sa-lem;
Lift up your voice with strength. Lift it up, don't be a-fraid. Be-
hold your God. A-rise and shine, for the
light of the world is come. Be-hold your God!

Text: Isaiah 40:9
Tune: Kenneth W. Louis, b.1956, © 1985, Kenneth W. Louis

Satan, We're Gonna Tear Your Kingdom Down   281

1. Sa - tan,   we're gon - na   tear your   king-dom
2. The preach-ers   are gon - na preach your king-dom
3. The dea - cons   are gon - na   pray your   king-dom
4. The moth - ers   are gon - na   moan your king-dom

down.   Sa - tan, we're gon-na tear your king - dom
down.   The preach-ers are gon-na preach your king - dom
down.   The dea - cons are gon-na pray your king - dom
down.   The moth - ers are gon-na moan your king - dom

down.   You've been build-ing   your king-dom   all o - ver this

land.   Sa-tan, we're gon-na tear your king-dom   down.

Text: Traditional
Tune: KINGDOM DOWN, 10 10 10 12 10; traditional; arr. by James Abbington, b.1960, © 2000, GIA Publications, Inc.

282 Down at the Cross

1. Down at the cross where my Sav - ior died,
2. I am so won - drous-ly saved from sin,
3. Oh, pre-cious foun - tain that saves from sin,
4. Come to this foun - tain so rich and sweet,

Down where for cleans - ing from sin I cried,
Je - sus so sweet - ly a - bides with - in;
I am so glad I have en - tered in;
Cast thy poor soul at the Sav - ior's feet;

There to my heart was the blood ap - plied; Sing-in',
There at the cross where he took me in; Sing-in',
There Je-sus saves me and keeps me clean; Sing-in',
Plunge in to - day, and be made com - plete; Sing-in',

name! I'm sing-in'

Glo - ry to his name, his name!

name! I'm sing-in'

Glo - ry to his name, Pre-cious name.

I'm sing-in'

Glo - ry to his name, Pre-cious name.

his name.

There to my heart was the blood ap - plied; sing-in'

name.

Glo - ry to his name, his name.

name.

Text: Elisha A. Hoffman, 1839–1929
Tune: GLORY TO HIS NAME, 999 7 with refrain; John H. Stockton, 1813–1877; arr. by Evelyn Simpson-Curenton, b.1953, © 2000,
  GIA Publications, Inc.

283　Somebody's Knockin'

Some-bod - y's knock-in' at your door; Some-bod - y's

knock-in' at your door; O sin - ner, why don't you

an - swer? Some-bod - y's knock-in' at your door.

Solo: *All:*

1. Knocks like Je - sus,
2. Can't you hear him?
3. Je - sus calls you,   Some-bod - y's knock - in' at your
4. Can't you trust him?

Knocks like Je - sus,
Can't you hear him?
Je - sus calls you,
Can't you trust him?

door; Some-bod - y's knock-in' at your

door. O sin - ner, why don't you

an - swer? Some-bod - y's knock-in' at your door.

Text: Negro Spiritual
Tune: SOMEBODY'S KNOCKIN', Irregular; Negro Spiritual; harm. by Richard Proulx, 1937–2010, alt., © 1986, GIA Publications, Inc.

284 The Glory of These Forty Days

1. The glo - ry of these for - ty days
2. A - lone and fast - ing Mo - ses saw
3. So Dan - iel trained his mys - tic sight,
4. Then grant, O God, that we may, too,

We cel - e - brate with songs of praise;
The lov - ing God who gave the law;
De - liv - ered from the li - on's might;
Re - turn in fast and prayer to you.

For Christ, through whom all things were made,
And to E - li - jah, fast - ing, came
And John, the Bride - groom's friend, be - came
Our spir - its strength - en with your grace,

Him - self has fast - ed and has prayed.
The steeds and char - i - ots of flame.
The her - ald of Mes - si - ah's name.
And give us joy to see your face.

Text: *Clarum decus jejunii*; Gregory the Great, c. 540–604; tr. by Maurice F. Bell, 1862–1947, © Oxford University Press
Tune: OLD HUNDREDTH, LM; Louis Bourgeois, c.1510–1561

Lord, Who throughout These Forty Days   285

1. Lord, who through-out these for-ty days For
2. As you with Sa-tan did con-tend And
3. As you did hun-ger and did thirst, So
4. And through these days of pen-i-tence, And
5. A-bide with us that, when this life Of

us did fast and pray, Teach us to o-ver-
did the vic-t'ry win, O give us strength in
teach us, gra-cious Lord, To die to self, and
through your Pas-sion-tide, For ev-er-more, in
suf-fer-ing is past, An East-er of un-

come our sins, And close by you to stay.
you to fight, In you to con-quer sin.
on-ly live By your most ho-ly word.
life and death, O Lord, with us a-bide.
end-ing joy We may at-tain at last!

Text: Claudia F. Hernaman, 1838–1898, alt.
Tune: ST. FLAVIAN, CM; John Day's *Psalter*, 1562

286 At the Cross Her Station Keeping

Verses 1–8

1. At the cross her sta - tion keep - ing, Mar - y stood in
2. While she wait - ed in her an - guish, See - ing Christ in
3. With what pain and des - o - la - tion, With what no - ble
4. Ev - er pa - tient in her yearn - ing, Though her tear - filled
5. Who, that sor - row con - tem - plat - ing, On that pas - sion
6. Christ she saw, for our sal - va - tion, Scourged with cru - el
7. Christ she saw with life-blood fail - ing, All her an - guish
8. Mar - y, fount of love's de - vo - tion, Let me share with

sor - row, weep - ing, When her Son was cru - ci - fied.
tor - ment lan - guish, Bit - ter sor - row pierced her heart.
res - ig - na - tion, Mar - y watched her dy - ing Son.
eyes were burn - ing, Mar - y gazed up - on her Son.
med - i - tat - ing, Would not share the Vir - gin's grief?
ac - cla - ma - tion, Bruised and beat - en by the rod.
un - a - vail - ing, Saw him breathe his ver - y last.
true e - mo - tion All the sor - row you en - dured.

Verses 9–15

9. Vir - gin, ev - er in - ter - ced - ing, Hear me in my
10. Moth - er, may this prayer be grant - ed: That Christ's love may
11. At the cross, your sor - row shar - ing, All your grief and
12. Fair - est maid of all cre - a - tion, Queen of hope and
13. Vir - gin, in your love be - friend me, At the Judg - ment
14. Sav - ior, when my life shall leave me, Through your moth - er's
15. Let me to your love be tak - en, Let my soul in

fer - vent plead - ing:	Fire	me	with	your	love	of	Christ.
be im - plant - ed	In	the	depths	of	my	poor	soul.
tor - ment bear - ing,	Let	me	stand	and	mourn with		you.
con - so - la - tion,	Let	me	feel	your	grief	sub - lime.
Day de - fend me.	Help	me	by	your	con - stant		prayer.
prayers re - ceive me	With	the	fruits	of	vic - to -		ry.
death a - wak - en	To	the	joys	of	Par - a -		dise.

Text: *Stabat mater dolorosa;* Jacopone da Todi, 1230–1306; trans. by Anthony G. Petti, 1932–1985, © 1971, Faber Music, Ltd.
Tune: STABAT MATER, 88 7; Mainz *Gesangbuch,* 1661; harm. by Richard Proulx, 1937–2010, © 1986, GIA Publications, Inc.

287 Remember You Are Dust

Refrain *Melody:*

Turn a-way from sin and be faith-ful to the Gos-pel. Re-

Counter melody (optional):

For thy gra-cious bless-ing we give thanks, O Lord.

mem-ber you are dust, and to dust you will re-turn.

For thy lov-ing kind-ness we give thanks, O Lord.

To verses *Cantor:* | *Last time*

1.–4. Re-

Verses

pent, the king-dom is at hand. Re-pent, the king-dom is at

Cantor:

hand.
1. Rend your hearts, not your gar-ments.
2. Blow the trum-pet in Zi-on.
3. For - give one an-oth-er.
4. Now, the day of sal-va-tion.

Now, the ac-cept-a-ble

All: **D.C.**

time. Now, the ac-cept-a-ble time.

Additional verses for the season of Lent:

Seek the God of compassion...
Live in kindness and mercy...
Trust in God and be faithful...
Praise the God of salvation...
Let us bow down in worship...

Text: Joel 2:12–18, 2 Corinthians 5:20—6:2; Paul A. Tate, b.1968, © 2003, GIA Publications, Inc.; refrain from the *Sacramentary*, © 1973, ICEL
Tune: Paul A. Tate, b.1968, © 2003, GIA Publications, Inc.

Forty Days and Forty Nights   288

1. For - ty days and for - ty nights You were fast - ing
2. Shall not we your sor - row share And from world - ly
3. Then, if Sa - tan on us press, Flesh or spir - it
4. So shall we have peace di - vine; Ho - lier glad - ness
5. Keep, O keep us, Sav - ior dear, Ev - er con - stant

in the wild; For - ty days and for - ty nights
joys ab - stain, Fast - ing with un - ceas - ing prayer,
to as - sail, Vic - tor in the wil - der - ness,
ours shall be. 'Round us, too, shall an - gels shine,
by your side, That with you we may ap - pear

Tempt - ed, and yet un - de - filed.
Strong with you to suf - fer pain?
Grant we may not faint nor fail!
Such as served you faith - ful - ly.
At the e - ter - nal East - er - tide.

Text: George H. Smyttan, 1822–1870, alt.
Tune: HEINLEIN, 7 7 7 7; attr. to Martin Herbst, 1654–1681, *Nürnbergisches Gesangbuch*, 1676

289 Stations of the Cross

* Kneel - ing in the gar - den grass, Je - sus
1. While the court and priests con - spire How to
2. When the mas - sive cross of wood Bends and
3. Je - sus falls be - neath the weight Of the

groans a - gainst his death, Let this cup of sor - row
slant the ev - i - dence Je - sus calm - ly bears their
bruis - es Je - sus' frame Hear him seek e - ter - nal
cross he's forced to bear Yet its load of sin and

pass, While he prays in that same breath:
ire As his prayer grows more in - tense:
good As he prays in Heav - en's name:
hate Do not crush his hope and prayer:

Not my will but yours be done, Not my will but yours be done.

1. Jesus is condemned to death

2. Jesus carries his Cross

3. Jesus falls the first time

4. Jesus meets his afflicted mother
Jesus reads in Mary's eyes
All the sorrow mothers bear,
And he prays his friend supplies
Grace to strengthen her own prayer:
    Not my will but yours be done.

**5. Simon of Cyrene helps Jesus to
    carry his Cross**
We with Simon of Cyrene
Help the Savior bear the cross.
Step by step we slowly glean
What true faith and prayer will cost:
    Not my will but yours be done.

6. Veronica wipes the face of Jesus
Seek the courage and the grace
That Veronica displays
When she wipes the bleeding face
Of the one who bravely prays:
    Not my will but yours be done.

7. Jesus falls the second time
Jesus trips and falls again
As he struggles through the street
Where the mob's unceasing din
Mocks the prayer his lips repeat:
    Not my will but yours be done.

8. Jesus meets the women of Jerusalem
Christ directs the women's tears
Toward the coming judgment day
When God weighs our faithless years
With our willingness to pray:
    Not my will but yours be done.

*This stanza begins the devotions. Stanzas 1–14 accompany each station.

9. Jesus falls a third time
Jesus stumbles one last time
Nearly broken by the load
Yet by prayer finds strength to climb
Calvary's final stretch of road:
    Not my will but yours be done.

10. Jesus is stripped of his clothes
Naked to the sun and clouds
And the jeers and gawking stare
Of the soldiers and the crowds
Christ countinues with his prayer:
    Not my will but yours be done.

11. Jesus is nailed to the Cross
While the soldiers throw their dice
They ignore their victim's groans,
Lost to them the sacrifice
And the prayer that Jesus moans:
    Not my will but yours be done.

12. Jesus dies on the Cross
Jesus gives one loud last cry
At the moment of his death
While his prayer moves heaven's sky
With his final, parting breath:
    Not my will but yours be done.

**13. The body of Jesus is taken
    down from the Cross**
As they take the body down
And they wrap it in a sheet
In their hearts they hear the sound
That his lips no more repeat:
    Not my will but yours be done.

14. Jesus is laid in the tomb
Quiet is the hollowed cave.
Peace and tears and grief descend.
Mourners offer at the grave
What they learned from Christ their friend:
    Not my will but yours be done.

Text: Thomas H. Troeger, b.1945, © 1993, Oxford University Press
Tune: RULAND, 7 7 7 7 with refrain; Norah Duncan IV, © 2012, GIA Publications, Inc.

290 Jesus, Tempted in the Desert

1. Je - sus, tempt - ed in the des - ert,
2. Je - sus, tempt - ed at the tem - ple,
3. Je - sus, tempt - ed on the moun - tain
4. When we face temp - ta - tion's pow - er,

Lone - ly, hun - gry, filled with dread:
High a - bove its an - cient wall:
By the lure of vast do - main:
Lone - ly, strug - gling, filled with dread,

"Use your pow'r," the tempt - er tells him;
"Throw your - self from loft - y tur - ret;
"Fall be - fore me! Be my ser - vant!
Christ, who knew the tempt - er's ho - ur,

"Turn these bar - ren rocks to bread!"
An - gels wait to break your fall!"
Glo - ry, fame, you're sure to gain!"
Come and be our liv - ing bread.

"Not a - lone by bread," he an - swers,
Je - sus shuns such emp - ty mar - vels,
Je - sus sees the daz - zling vi - sion,
By your grace, pro - tect, pre - serve us

"Can the hu - man heart be filled.
Feats that fick - le crowds re - quest:
Turns his eyes an - oth - er way:
Lest we fall, your trust be - tray.

On - ly by the Word that calls us
"God, whose grace pro - tects, pre - serves us,
"God a - lone de - serves our hom - age!
Yours, a - bove all oth - er voic - es,

Is our deep - est hun - ger stilled!"
We must nev - er vain - ly test."
God a - lone will I o - bey!"
Be the Word we hear, o - bey.

Text: Matthew 4:1–11, Luke 4:1–13; Herman G. Stuempfle, Jr., 1923–2007, © 1993, GIA Publications, Inc.
Tune: EBENEZER, 8 7 8 7 D; Thomas J. Williams, 1869–1944

291 Hold Us in Your Mercy: Penitential Litany

Hold us in your mer - cy. Hold us in your mer - cy.

Hold us in your mer - cy. Hold us in your mer - cy.

Verses 1–3

1. Mak - er's love poured out from heav - en.
2. Born as one of home - less pil - grims. Hold us in your mer - cy.
3. You who shared the sin - ner's ta - ble.

Mer - cy's word - made - flesh a - mong us.
Sent to bring the poor good news. Hold us in your mer - cy.
You who cleansed the lep - er's flesh.

Verses 4–7

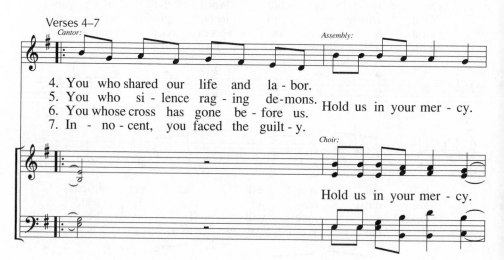

4. You who shared our life and la - bor.
5. You who si - lence rag - ing de - mons. Hold us in your mer - cy.
6. You whose cross has gone be - fore us.
7. In - no - cent, you faced the guilt - y.

Hold us in your mer - cy.

You who chose to walk our roads.
You who bid the storm be si-lent.
You who bear our cross with us,
One in death with us for - ev-er.

Hold us in your mer - cy.

Hold us in your mer - cy.

Verses 8–11

8. Come and break the chains that bind us.
9. Break the pow-er of the dark-ness.
10. Ky - ri - e e - le - i - son!
11. Ky - ri - e e - le - i - son!

Hold us in your mer - cy.

Hold us in your mer - cy.

Free us from ad - dic-tion's pris-on.
Let us rise to life with you.
Chri - ste e - le - i - son!
Ky - ri - e e - le - i - son!

Hold us in your mer - cy.

Hold us in your mer - cy.

Text: Rory Cooney, b.1952
Tune: Based on PARCE DOMINE; Gary Daigle, b.1957
© 1993, GIA Publications, Inc.

All Glory, Laud, and Honor 292

Refrain

All glo-ry, laud, and hon - or To you, Re-deem-er, King!

To whom the lips of chil - dren Made sweet ho - san - nas ring.

Verses

1. You are the King of Is - ra - el And Da - vid's roy - al Son,
2. The com-pa - ny of an - gels Are prais - ing you on high;
3. The peo-ple of the He - brews With palms be - fore you went;
4. To you, be - fore your pas - sion, They sang their hymns of praise.
5. Their prais-es you ac - cept - ed; Ac - cept the prayers we bring,

D.C.

Now in the Lord's Name com - ing, Our King and Bless-ed One.
And we, with all cre - a - tion, In cho-rus make re - ply.
Our praise and prayers and an - thems Be - fore you we pre - sent.
To you, now high ex - alt - ed, Our mel - o - dy we raise.
Great source of love and good - ness, Our Sav - ior and our King.

Text: *Gloria, laus et honor;* Theodulph of Orléans, c.760–821; tr. by John M. Neale, 1818–1866, alt.
Tune: ST. THEODULPH, 7 6 7 6 with refrain; Melchior Teschner, 1584–1635

293 Ride On, Jesus, Ride

Ride on, Je - sus, ride. Ride on, Je - sus, ride.

Ride on, Je - sus, con-quering King, Ride on, Je - sus ride.

1. King Je - sus rides on a milk white horse. Ride on, Je - sus,
2. My Je - sus lift - ed his throne a - bove. Ride on, Je - sus,
3. The chil - dren of Je - ru - sa - lem, Ride on, Je - sus,
4. ＇ "Bless - ings on the Ho - ly One!" Ride on, Je - sus,
5. ＇ Ride so hum - ble, ride so true, Ride on, Je - sus,
6. ＇ Ride to set your peo - ple free, Ride on, Je - sus,
7. ＇ Ride o - be - dient un - to death, Ride on, Je - sus,
8. ＇ Ride a - gain in the hearts of us, Ride on, Je - sus,
9. ＇ Now be - yond all time and space, Ride on, Je - sus,

ride. The riv - er Jor - dan he did cross.
ride. ＇ See his mer - cy and his love.
ride, ＇ strewed their branch - es on his way.
ride. ＇ "Bless - ings on the Sav - ing One!"
ride. ＇ Ride to bring the world to you, Ride on, Je - sus,
ride. ＇ Ride the road to Cal - va - ry,
ride. ＇ Ride to break the chains of death,
ride. ＇ Ride a - gain in the hands of us,
ride. ＇ Now in ev - 'ry land and race,

ride. Ride on, Je - sus, con-quering King. Ride on, Je - sus ride.

Text: Negro Spiritual; verses 3–9, Marty Haugen, b.1950, © 1991, GIA Publications, Inc.
Tune: Negro Spiritual; harm. by Barbara Jackson Martin, b.1947, © 1987, GIA Publications, Inc.

Jesu, Jesu, Fill Us with Your Love   294

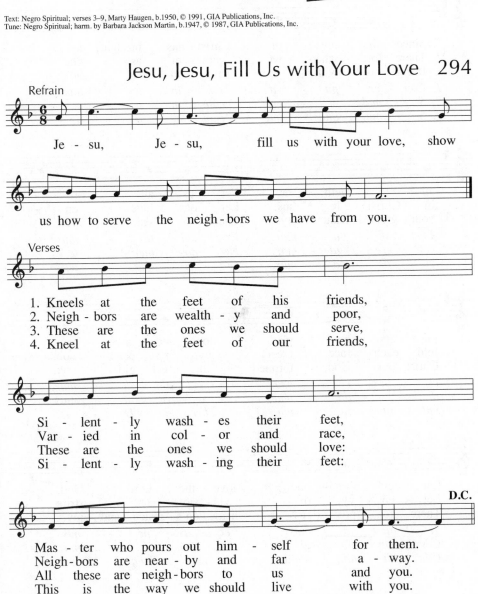

Refrain

Je - su,   Je - su,   fill us with your love,   show

us how to serve   the neigh-bors   we have   from you.

Verses

1. Kneels at   the   feet   of   his   friends,
2. Neigh - bors   are   wealth - y   and   poor,
3. These   are   the   ones   we   should   serve,
4. Kneel   at   the   feet   of   our   friends,

Si - lent - ly   wash - es   their   feet,
Var - ied   in   col - or   and   race,
These   are   the   ones   we   should   love:
Si - lent - ly   wash - ing   their   feet:

D.C.

Mas - ter   who pours out   him - self   for   them.
Neigh-bors   are   near - by   and   far   a - way.
All   these   are   neigh-bors   to   us   and   you.
This   is   the   way   we should   live   with   you.

Text: Tom Colvin, 1925–2000, alt.
Tune: CHEREPONI, 7 7 9 with refrain; Ghana folk song; adapt. by Tom Colvin, 1925–2000, alt.; acc. by Jane M. Marshall, b.1924
© 1969, and arr. © 1982, Hope Publishing Company

295 Where True Love and Charity Are Found / Ubi Cáritas

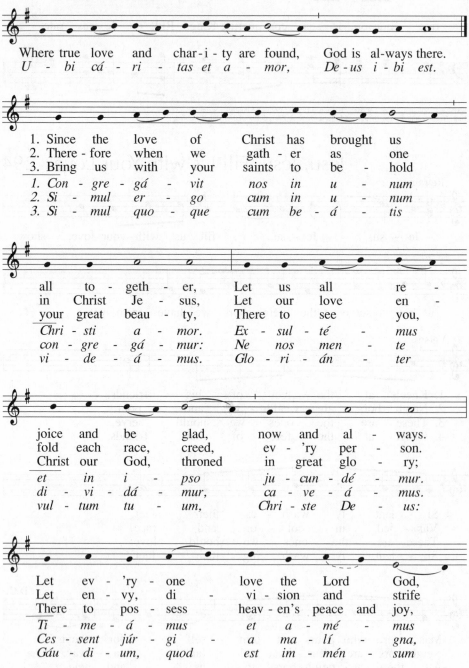

Where true love and char-i-ty are found, God is al-ways there.
U - bi cá - ri - tas et a - mor, De-us i - bi est.

1. Since the love of Christ has brought us
2. There - fore when we gath - er as one
3. Bring us with your saints to be - hold
1. *Con - gre - gá - vit nos in u - num*
2. *Si - mul er - go cum in u - num*
3. *Si - mul quo - que cum be - á - tis*

all to - geth - er, Let us all re -
in Christ Je - sus, Let our love en -
your great beau - ty, There to see you,
Chri - sti a - mor. Ex - sul - té - mus
con - gre - gá - mur: Ne nos men - te
vi - de - á - mus. Glo - ri - án - ter

joice and be glad, now and al - ways.
fold each race, creed, ev - 'ry per - son.
Christ our God, throned in great glo - ry;
et in i - pso ju - cun - dé - mur.
di - vi - dá - mur, ca - ve - á - mus.
vul - tum tu - um, Chri - ste De - us:

Let ev - 'ry - one love the Lord God,
Let en - vy, di - vi - sion and strife
There to pos - sess heav - en's peace and joy,
Ti - me - á - mus et a - mé - mus
Ces - sent júr - gi - a ma - lí - gna,
Gáu - di - um, quod est im - mén - sum

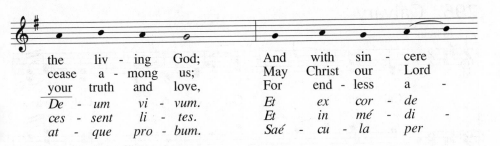

the	liv - ing	God;	And	with	sin - cere
cease	a - mong	us;	May	Christ	our	Lord
your	truth and	love,	For	end - less	a -
De - um	*vi - vum.*	*Et*	*ex*	*cor - de*
ces - sent	*li - tes.*	*Et*	*in*	*mé - di -*
at - que	*pro - bum.*	*Saé - cu - la*	*per*

D.C.

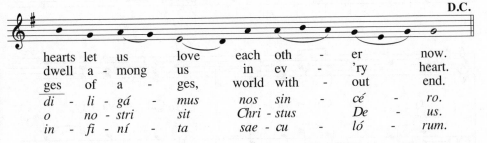

hearts let us	love	each oth - er	now.
dwell a - mong	us	in ev - 'ry	heart.
ges of a -	ges,	world with - out	end.
di - li - gá - mus	*nos sin - cé - ro.*
o no - stri	*sit*	*Chri - stus*	*De - us.*
in - fi - ní - ta	*sae - cu - ló - rum.*

Text: *Ubi caritas et amor*, Latin, 9th C.; tr. by Richard Proulx, 1937–2010, © 1975, 1986, GIA Publications, Inc.
Tune: UBI CARITAS, 12 12 12 12 with refrain; Mode VI; acc. by Richard Proulx, 1937–2010, © 1986, GIA Publications, Inc.

296 Calvary

Refrain

Cal - va - ry, Cal - va - ry, Cal - va -

ry, Cal - va - ry, Cal - va - ry,

Cal - va - ry, Sure - ly he died on Cal - va - ry.

Verses

1. Ev - 'ry time I think a - bout Je - sus, Ev - 'ry
2. Sin - ner, do you love my Je - sus? Sin - ner,
3. We are climb - ing Ja - cob's lad - der, We are
4. Ev - 'ry round goes high - er and high - er, Ev - 'ry

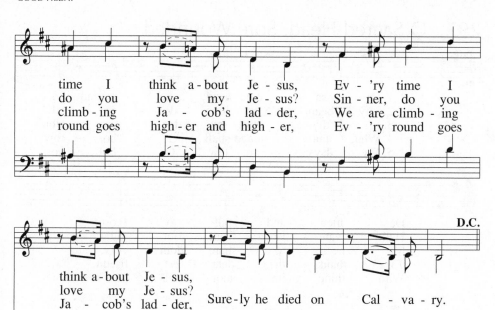

time   I   think a-bout Je - sus,   Ev - 'ry time   I
do   you   love   my   Je - sus?   Sin - ner, do   you
climb - ing   Ja - cob's lad - der,   We   are climb - ing
round goes   high - er and high - er,   Ev - 'ry round goes

think a - bout Je - sus,
love   my   Je - sus?   Sure - ly he died on   Cal - va - ry.
Ja - cob's lad - der,
high-er and high - er,

Text: Negro Spiritual
Tune: CALVARY, LM with refrain; Negro Spiritual

297 O Sacred Head, Sore Wounded

1. O sa - cred head, sore wound - ed,
2. Thy beau - ty, long de - sir - ed,
3. In thy most bit - ter pas - sion
4. What lan - guage shall I bor - row
5. My days are few, O fail not,

De - filed and put to scorn;
Hath van - ished from our sight;
My heart to share doth cry,
To thank thee, dear - est friend,
With thine im - mor - tal pow'r,

O king - ly head, sur - round - ed
Thy pow'r is all ex - pir - ed,
With thee for my sal - va - tion
For this thy dy - ing sor - row,
To hold me that I quail not

With mock - ing crown of thorn;
And quenched the light of light.
Up - on the cross to die.
Thy pit - y with - out end?
In death's most fear - ful hour:

What sor - row mars thy grand - eur?
Ah me! for whom thou di - est,
Ah, keep my heart thus mov - ed
Oh, make me thine for - ev - er!
That I may fight be - friend - ed,

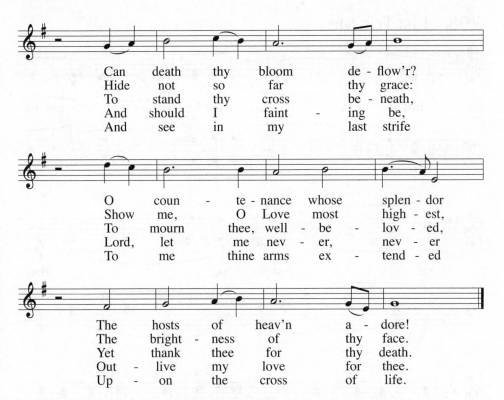

Can death thy bloom de - flow'r?
Hide not so far thy grace:
To stand thy cross be - neath,
And should I faint - ing be,
And see in my last strife

O coun - te - nance whose splen - dor
Show me, O Love most high - est,
To mourn thee, well - be - lov - ed,
Lord, let me nev - er, nev - er
To me thine arms ex - tend - ed

The hosts of heav'n a - dore!
The bright - ness of thy face.
Yet thank thee for thy death.
Out - live my love for thee.
Up - on the cross of life.

Text: Paulus Gerhardt, 1607–1676, sts. 1–3, 5, tr. by Robert S. Bridges, 1844–1930; st. 4, tr. by James W. Alexander, 1804–1859, alt.
Tune: REDDING, 7 6 7 6 D; David Hurd, b.1950, © 1983, GIA Publications, Inc.

298 Just For Me

Just for me, just for me, just for me, just for me. They pierced him in his side. He hung his head and died. He did all that just for me.

Optional Solo:

Oh, what a shame to kill him, as he hung on that rug - ged cross. His death was sure - ly need - ed to save this world from be - ing lost. My blind - ed eyes were o - pen so that I might see. He did all *Choir:* that just for me.

299 O Sacred Head, Surrounded

1. O sa-cred head, sur-round-ed By crown of pierc-ing
2. I see your strength and vig - or All fad-ing in the
3. In this, your bit-ter pas - sion, Good Shep-herd, think of

thorn! O bleed-ing head, so wound-ed, Re -
strife, And death with cru - el rig - or, Be -
me With your most sweet com - pas - sion, Un -

viled and put to scorn! The pow'r of death comes
reav - ing you of life. O ag - o - ny and
worth - y though I be: Be - neath your cross a -

o'er you, The glow of life de - cays, Yet
dy - ing! O love to sin - ners free! Je -
bid - ing For - ev - er would I rest, In

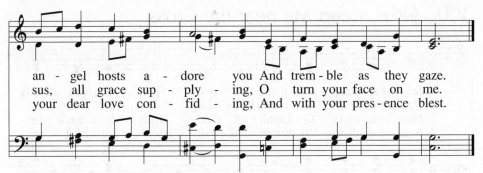

an - gel hosts a - dore you And trem - ble as they gaze.
sus, all grace sup - ply - ing, O turn your face on me.
your dear love con - fid - ing, And with your pres - ence blest.

Text: *Salve caput cruentatum;* ascr. to Bernard of Clairvaux, 1091–1153; tr. by Henry Baker, 1821–1877
Tune: PASSION CHORALE, 7 6 7 6 D; Hans Leo Hassler, 1564–1612; harm. by J. S. Bach, 1685–1750

300 Jesus, Keep Me near the Cross

1. Je - sus, keep me near the cross; There's a pre - cious
2. Near the cross, a trem - bling soul, Love and mer - cy
3. Near the cross! O Lamb of God, Bring its scenes be -
4. Near the cross I'll watch and wait, Hop - ing, trust - ing

foun - tain, Free to all, a heal - ing stream, Flows from Cal - v'ry's
found me; There the bright and morn - ing star Sheds its beams a -
fore me; Help me walk from day to day With its shad - ows
ev - er, Till I reach the gold - en strand Just be - yond the

moun - tain.
round me.
o'er me. In the cross, in the cross, Be my glo - ry
riv - er.

ev - er, Till my rap - tured soul shall find Rest be - yond the riv - er.

Text: Fanny J. Crosby, 1820–1915
Tune: NEAR THE CROSS, 7 6 7 6 with refrain; William H. Doane, 1832–1915; harm. by J. Jefferson Cleveland, 1937–1988, and Verolga Nix-Allen, b.1933, © 1981, Abingdon Press, admin. by The Copyright Company

Were You There 301

1. Were you there when they cru - ci - fied my Lord? Were you
2. Were you there when they nailed him to the tree? Were you
3. Were you there when they pierced him in the side? Were you
4. Were you there when the sun re - fused to shine? Were you
5. Were you there when they laid him in the tomb? Were you
6. Were you there when they rolled the stone a - way? Were you

there when they cru - ci - fied my Lord?
there when they nailed him to the tree?
there when they pierced him in the side? Oh!
there when the sun re - fused to shine?
there when they laid him in the tomb?
there when they rolled the stone a - way?

Some-times it caus - es me to trem-ble, trem-ble, trem-ble,

Were you there when they cru - ci - fied my Lord?
Were you there when they nailed him to the tree?
Were you there when they pierced him in the side?
Were you there when the sun re - fused to shine?
Were you there when they laid him in the tomb?
Were you there when they rolled the stone a - way?

Text: Negro Spiritual
Tune: WERE YOU THERE, 10 10 with refrain; Negro Spiritual; harm. by C. Winfred Douglas, 1867-1944, © 1940, 1943, 1961, Church Pension Fund

302 Only Love

Refrain

On - ly love held him there on the cross.

On - ly love held him there on the cross.

He could have called ten thou - sand an - gels to

come to his res - cue. On - ly love held him there

Last time

on the cross.

1. On a

Verses

hill far a - way stood an old rug - ged
(2.) cross, at the cross where I first saw the

cross, the em - blem of suf - f'ring and
light, and the bur - den of my heart rolled a -

shame.
way.

It was there on the cross Je - sus

died in my place On - ly love held him there

1.
on the cross.

2. At the

2.
On - ly love,

D.S.

Text: Patrick D. Bradley, © 1998
Tune: Patrick D. Bradley, © 1998; arr. by Kenneth W. Louis, b.1956, © 2012, GIA Publications, Inc.

303 Because He Lives

1. God sent his Son, they called him Je - sus,
2. How sweet to hold a new - born ba - by,
3. And then one day I'll cross the riv - er,

He came to love, heal, and for - give;
And feel the pride and joy he gives;
I'll fight life's fi - nal war with pain;

He lived and died to buy my par - don, An
But great - er still the calm as - sur - ance, This
And then as death gives way to vic - t'ry, I'll

emp - ty grave is there to prove my Sav - ior lives.
child can face un - cer - tain days be - cause he lives.
see the lights of glo - ry and I'll know he lives.

Be-cause he lives I can face to-mor - row,

Be-cause he lives all fear is gone;

Be-cause I know he holds the fu - ture.

Last time to Coda ⊕   **D.C.**

And life is worth the liv-ing just be-cause he lives.

⊕ Coda (Optional Chorus)

lives.

Melody:

Be - cause he

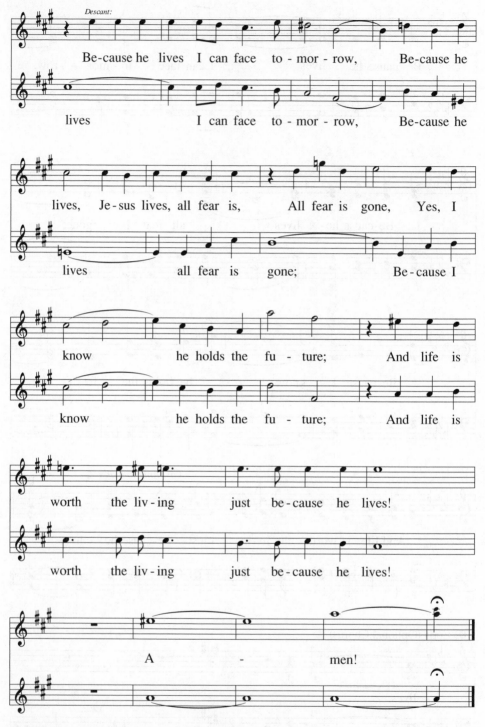

Text: Gloria Gaither, and William J. Gaither
Tune: RESURRECTION, 9 8 9 12 with refrain; William J. Gaither; arr. by Nolan Williams, Jr., b.1969

He Is Lord 304

He is Lord, He is Lord! He is ris - en from the
dead and he is Lord! Ev - 'ry knee shall bow, ev - 'ry
tongue con - fess That Je - sus Christ is Lord.

Text: Based on Philippians 2:11
Tune: HE IS LORD, 6 11 10 6; traditional

305 This Is the Day

This is the day, this is the day that the Lord has made, that the Lord has made. I will re-joice, I will re-joice and be glad in it, and be glad in it. This is the day that the Lord has made. I will re-joice and be glad in it. This is the day, this is the day that the Lord has made.

Text: Psalm 118:24
Tune: Les Garrett, b.1944, © 1967, Scripture in Song, admin. by Music Services; arr. by Stephen Key

Go and Tell Mary and Martha   306

1. Go and tell Mar - y and Mar-tha, Go and
(2.) tell John and Pe - ter, Go and
(3.) tell all the a - pos-tles, Go and
(4.) tell ev - 'ry - bod - y, Go and

tell Mar - y and Mar - tha, Go and
tell John and Pe - ter, Go and
tell all the a - pos-tles, Go and
tell ev - 'ry - bod - y, Go and

tell Mar - y and Mar - tha:
tell John and Pe - ter:
tell all the a - pos - tles: "Yes,
tell ev - 'ry - bod - y:

Je-sus is ris - en from the dead!"
2. Go
3. Go from the dead!"
4. Go

Text: Negro Spiritual
Tune: Negro Spiritual; arr. by Charlene Moore Cooper, © 2000, GIA Publications, Inc.

307 He Arose

1. They cru - ci - fied my Sav - ior And nailed him to the cross. They
2. ⁊ Jo - seph begged his bod - y And laid it in the tomb. ⁊
3. ⁊ Mar - y, she came run - ning, A - look - ing for my Lord. ⁊
4. An an - gel came from heav - en And rolled the stone a - way. An

cru - ci - fied my Sav - ior And nailed him to the cross. They
Jo - seph begged his bod - y And laid it in the tomb. ⁊
Mar - y, she came run - ning, A - look - ing for my Lord. ⁊
an - gel came from heav - en And rolled the stone a - way. An

cru - ci - fied my Sav - ior And nailed him to the cross.
Jo - seph begged his bod - y And laid it in the tomb.
Mar - y, she came run - ning, A - look - ing for my Lord.
an - gel came from heav - en And rolled the stone a - way.

And the Lord will bear my spir - it home.

He 'rose, he 'rose, he 'rose from the dead, He
He 'rose, he 'rose, he

'rose, he 'rose, he 'rose from the dead. He
he 'rose, he 'rose, he

'rose, he 'rose, he 'rose from the dead, And the
he 'rose, he 'rose, he

Lord will bear my spir - it home.

Text: Negro Spiritual
Tune: HE AROSE, 7 6 7 6 7 6 9 with refrain; Negro Spiritual; arr. by Valeria A. Foster, © 2000, GIA Publications, Inc.

308 The Strife Is O'er

Refrain

Al - le - lu - ia, al - le - lu - ia, al - le - lu - ia!

Verses

1. The strife is o'er, the bat - tle done;
2. The pow'rs of death have done their worst;
3. On the third day Christ rose a - gain,
4. He closed the yawn - ing gates of hell;
5. Lord, by the stripes which wound - ed you,

Now is the Vic - tor's tri - umph won! Songs of re -
But Christ their le - gions has dis - persed. Let shouts of
Glo - rious in maj - es - ty to reign. O let us
The bars from heav'n's high por - tals fell. Let hymns of
Free from death's sting your ser - vants too, That we may

D.C.

joic - ing have be - gun. Al - le - lu - ia!
ho - ly joy out - burst. Al - le - lu - ia!
swell the joy - ful strain. Al - le - lu - ia!
praise his tri - umph tell. Al - le - lu - ia!
live and sing to you. Al - le - lu - ia!

Text: *Finita jam sunt praelia;* Latin, 12th C.; tr. by Francis Pott, 1832–1909, alt.
Tune: VICTORY, 888 with alleluia and refrain; Giovanni da Palestrina, 1525–1594; adapt. by William H. Monk, 1823–1889

I Know That My Redeemer Lives!   309

1. I know that my Redeemer lives!
2. He lives to bless me with his love;
3. He lives and grants me daily breath;
4. He lives, all glory to his name;

What joy this blest assurance gives!
He lives to plead for me above;
He lives, and I shall conquer death;
He lives, my Savior, still the same;

He lives, he lives who once was dead;
He lives my hungry soul to feed;
He lives my mansion to prepare;
What joy this blest assurance gives:

He lives, my everlasting Head!
He lives to help in time of need.
He lives to bring me safely there.
I know that my Redeemer lives!

Text: Samuel Medley, 1738–1799
Tune: DUKE STREET, LM; John Hatton, c.1710–1793

310 Rejoice!

Refrain ♩ = 120

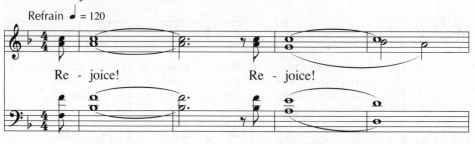

Re - joice! Re - joice!

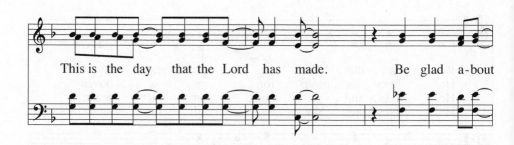

This is the day that the Lord has made. Be glad a-bout

it. Ev - 'ry-bod - y re - joice! Re -

joice! This is the day that he's made.

Be glad!

Verse

This is the day that the Lord has made, let us re - joice and be glad! Stop your com - plain-ing and be - lieve on God's word, this is the day that he's made. Be glad!

Text: Based on Psalm 118, Kenneth W. Louis, b.1956
Tune: Kenneth W. Louis, b.1956
© 1986, Kenneth W. Louis

311 Christ the Lord Is Risen Today

1. Christ the Lord is ris'n to-day; Chris-tians, haste your
2. Christ, the Vic-tim un-de-filed, God and sin-ners
3. Say, O won-d'ring Mar-y, say What you saw a-
4. Christ, who once for sin-ners bled, Now the first-born

vows to pay; Make your joy and prais-es known
rec-on-ciled, When in fierce and blood-y strife
long your way. "I be-held the glo-ry bright
from the dead, Throned in end-less might and pow'r,

At the Pas-chal Vic-tim's throne. For the sheep the
Met to-geth-er death and life. Chris-tians, on this
Of the ris-en Lord of light, Emp-ty tomb and
Lives and reigns for-ev-er-more. Hail, e-ter-nal

Lamb has bled, Sin-less in the sin-ner's stead.
hap-py day Raise your hearts with joy and say:
an-gels seen Where Christ's bod-y once had been.
Hope on high! Hail, O King of vic-to-ry!

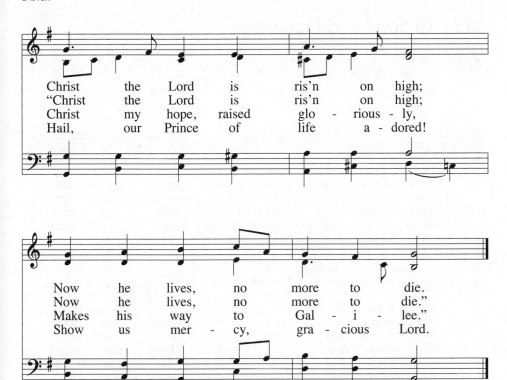

Christ   the   Lord   is   ris'n   on   high;
"Christ   the   Lord   is   ris'n   on   high;
Christ   my   hope,   raised   glo - rious - ly,
Hail,   our   Prince   of   life   a - dored!

Now   he   lives,   no   more   to   die.
Now   he   lives,   no   more   to   die."
Makes   his   way   to   Gal - i - lee."
Show   us   mer - cy,   gra - cious   Lord.

Text: *Victimae paschali laudes;* ascr. to Wipo of Burgundy, d.1048; tr. by Jane E. Leeson, 1809–1881, alt.
Tune: VICTIMAE PASCHALI, 77 77 D; Wirth's *Katholisches Gesangbuch*, 1859; revised in *Catholic Youth's Hymn Book*, 1871

312 O Sons and Daughters

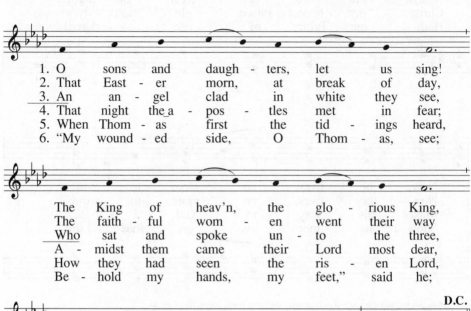

Al - le - lu - ia, al - le - lu - ia, al - le - lu - ia.

1. O	sons	and	daugh - ters,	let	us	sing!
2. That	East - er	morn,	at	break	of	day,
3. An	an - gel	clad	in	white	they	see,
4. That	night the a - pos - tles	met	in	fear;
5. When	Thom - as	first	the	tid - ings	heard,
6. "My	wound - ed	side,	O	Thom - as,	see;

The	King	of	heav'n,	the	glo - rious	King,
The	faith - ful	wom - en	went	their	way
Who	sat	and	spoke	un - to	the	three,
A -	midst	them	came	their	Lord	most	dear,
How	they	had	seen	the	ris - en	Lord,
Be -	hold	my	hands,	my	feet,"	said	he;

D.C.

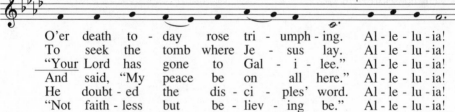

O'er	death	to - day	rose	tri - umph - ing.	Al - le - lu - ia!
To	seek	the	tomb	where Je - sus	lay.	Al - le - lu - ia!
"Your	Lord	has	gone	to	Gal - i - lee."	Al - le - lu - ia!
And	said,	"My	peace	be	on	all here."	Al - le - lu - ia!
He	doubt - ed	the	dis - ci - ples'	word.	Al - le - lu - ia!
"Not	faith - less	but	be - liev - ing	be."	Al - le - lu - ia!

7. No longer Thomas then denied;
   He saw the feet, the hands, the side;
   "You are my Lord and God," he cried. Alleluia!

8. How blest are they who have not seen,
   And yet whose faith has constant been,
   For they eternal life shall win. Alleluia!

9. On this most holy day of days,
   To God your hearts and voices raise,
   In laud and jubilee and praise. Alleluia!

Text: *O filii et filiae;* Jean Tisserand, d.1494; tr. by John M. Neale, 1818–1866, alt.
Tune: O FILII ET FILIAE, 888 with alleluia and refrain; Mode II, French carol, 15th C.; acc. by Richard Proulx, 1937–2010,
© 1975, GIA Publications, Inc.

Goodness Is Stronger than Evil   313

Good-ness is strong-er than e - vil; love is strong-er than

hate; light is strong-er than dark - ness;

Vic-t'ry is ours, vic-t'ry is

life is strong-er than death.

Oh, vic-t'ry is ours,

ours through him who loved us. us.

vic-t'ry is ours through him who loved us. us.

Text: Desmond Tutu, b.1931, ©; adapt. by John L. Bell, b.1949
Tune: GOODNESS IS STRONGER, Irregular; John L. Bell, b.1949, © 1996, Iona Community, GIA Publications, Inc., agent

314 Christ Has Arisen, Alleluia / Mfurahini, Haleluya

1. Christ has a - ris - en, Al - le - lu - ia! Re - joice and praise him, Al - le - lu - ia! For our Re - deem - er burst from the tomb, E - ven from death dis - pel - ling its gloom.
2. For three long days the grave did its worst, Un - til its strength by God was dis - persed. He who gives life did death un - der - go, And in its con - quest his might did show.
3. The an - gel said to them, "Do not fear, You look for Je - sus who is not here. See for your - selves, the tomb is all bare. On - ly the grave cloths are ly - ing there."
4. "Go spread the news, he's not in the grave." He has a - ris - en, all folk to save. Je - sus' re - deem - ing la - bors are done. E - ven the bat - tle with sin is won.
5. He has a - ris - en to set us free. Al - le - lu - ia, to him prais - es be. The pow'r of Sa - tan no long - er binds, Nor can en - slave the thoughts of our minds.
6. Je - sus is liv - ing, let us all sing. He reigns tri - um - phant, e - ter - nal King. And he has prom - ised those who be - lieve In - to his king - dom he will re - ceive.

M - fu - ra - hi - ni, Ha - le - lu - ya, M - ko - mbo - zi a - me - fu - fu - ka. A - me - fu - fu - ka, Ha - le - lu - ya, M - si - fu - ni sa - sa yu ha - i.

African phonetics:

Mm-foo-rah-hee-nee, Hah-lay-loo-yah, Mm-koh-mboh-zee ah-may-foo-foo-kah.
Ah-may-foo-foo-kah, Hah-lay-loo-yah, Mm-see-foo-nee sah-sah yoo hah-ee.

Too-mwee-mbee-ay soh-tay kwah foo-rah-hah.
Yay-soo ah-may-toh-kah kah-boo-ree-nee.
Kah-shee-ndah kee-foh, Hah-lay-loo-yah, Hah-lay-loo-yah, Yay-soo yoo hah-ee.

Let us sing praise to him with end - less joy.
Tu - mwi - mbi - e so - te kwa fu - ra - ha.

Let's sing

Death's fear - ful sting he has come to de - stroy,
Ye - su a - me - to - ka ka - bu - ri - ni.

Death he's

Descant:

our sins for - giv - ing, Al - le - lu - ia!
Ka - shi - nda ki - fo, Ha - le - lu - ya,

liv - ing, Je - sus lives.

Je - sus is liv - ing, Al - le - lu - ia!
Ha - le - lu - ya, Ye - su yu ha - i.

Text: Swahili; Bernard Kyamanywa; tr. by Howard S. Olson, 1922–2010, © 1977, Augsburg Publishing House
Tune: MFURAHINI, HALELUYA, 99 99 with refrain; Haya tune; arr. by Svein Rustad and Anne Rustad, © Svein and Anne Rustad,
    admin. Augsburg Publishing House

315 Jesus Christ Is Risen Today

Descant:

4. Sing we to our God a - bove, Al - le - lu - ia!

1. Je - sus Christ is ris'n to - day, Al - le - lu - ia!
2. Hymns of praise then let us sing, Al - le - lu - ia!
3. But the pains which he en - dured, Al - le - lu - ia!
4. Sing we to our God a - bove, Al - le - lu - ia!

Praise e - ter - nal, as his love; Al - le - lu - ia!

Our tri - um - phant ho - ly day, Al - le - lu - ia!
Un - to Christ, our heav'n - ly King, Al - le - lu - ia!
Our sal - va - tion have pro - cured; Al - le - lu - ia!
Praise e - ter - nal, as his love; Al - le - lu - ia!

Praise him, now his might con-fess, Al - le - lu - ia!

Who did once up - on the cross, Al - le - lu - ia!
Who en-dured the cross and grave, Al - le - lu - ia!
Now a - bove the sky he's King, Al - le - lu - ia!
Praise him, now his might con-fess, Al - le - lu - ia!

Fa - ther, Son, and Spir - it blest. Al - le - lu - ia!

Suf - fer to re - deem our loss. Al - le - lu - ia!
Sin - ners to re - deem and save. Al - le - lu - ia!
Where the an - gels ev - er sing. Al - le - lu - ia!
Fa - ther, Son, and Spir - it blest. Al - le - lu - ia!

Text: St. 1, *Surrexit Christus hodie*, Latin, 14th C.; para. in *Lyra Davidica*, 1708, alt.; sts. 2, 3, *The Compleat Psalmodist*, c.1750, alt.; st. 4, Charles
    Wesley, 1707–1788, alt.
Tune: EASTER HYMN, 77 77 with alleluias; *Lyra Davidica*, 1708

316 At the Lamb's High Feast We Sing

1. At the Lamb's high feast we sing Praise to our vic-
2. Where the Pas-chal blood is poured, Death's dark an-gel
3. Might-y vic-tim from on high, Hell's fierce pow'rs be-
4. East-er tri-umph, East-er joy, This a-lone can

to-rious King, Who has washed us in the tide
sheathes his sword; Is-rael's hosts tri-umph-ant go
neath you lie; You have con-quered in the fight,
sin de-stroy; From sin's pow'r, Lord, set us free,

Flow-ing from his pierc-ed side. Praise we him, whose
Through the wave that drowns the foe. Praise we Christ, whose
You have brought us life and light. Now no more can
New-born souls in you to be. Fa-ther, who the

love di-vine Gives his sa-cred Blood for wine,
blood was shed, Pas-chal vic-tim, Pas-chal bread;
death ap-pall, Now no more the grave en-thrall;
crown shall give, Sav-ior, by whose death we live,

Gives his Bod - y for the feast:
With sin - cer - i - ty and love
You have o - pened par - a - dise,
Spir - it, guide through all our days:

Christ the vic - tim, Christ the priest.
Eat we man - na from a - bove.
And in you your saints shall rise.
Three in One, your name we praise.

Text: *Ad regias agni dapes;* Latin, 4th C.; tr. by Robert Campbell, 1814–1868, alt.
Tune: SALZBURG, 77 77 D; Jakob Hintze, 1622–1702; harm. by J. S. Bach, 1685–1750

317 Sing with All the Saints in Glory

1. Sing with all the saints in glo - ry, Sing the res - ur -
2. O what glo - ry, far ex - ceed - ing All that eye has
3. Life e - ter - nal! heav'n re - joic - es: Je - sus lives who
4. Life e - ter - nal! O what won - ders Crowd on faith; what

rec - tion song! Death and sor - row, earth's dark sto - ry,
yet per-ceived! Ho - liest hearts, for a - ges plead-ing,
once was dead. Shout with joy, O death - less voic - es!
joy un-known, When, a - mid earth's clos - ing thun - ders,

To the for - mer days be - long. All a - round the
Nev - er that full joy con-ceived. God has prom-ised,
Child of God, lift up your head! Pa - tri - archs from
Saints shall stand be - fore the throne! Oh, to en - ter

clouds are break - ing, Soon the storms of time shall cease;
Christ pre - pares it, There on high our wel - come waits.
dis - tant a - ges, Saints all long - ing for their heav'n,
that bright por - tal, See that glow-ing fir - ma - ment,

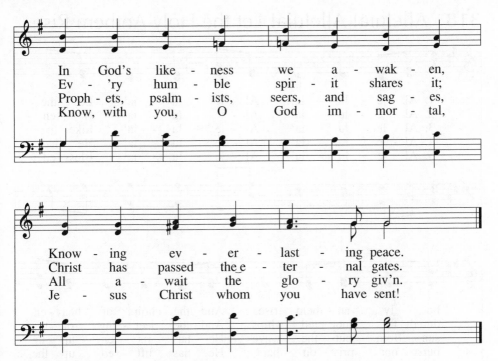

In God's like - ness we a - wak - en,
Ev - 'ry hum - ble spir - it shares it;
Proph - ets, psalm - ists, seers, and sag - es,
Know, with you, O God im - mor - tal,

Know - ing ev - er - last - ing peace.
Christ has passed the e - ter - nal gates.
All a - wait the glo - ry giv'n.
Je - sus Christ whom you have sent!

Text: 1 Corinthians 15:20; William J. Irons, 1812–1883, alt.
Tune: HYMN TO JOY, 8 7 8 7 D; arr. from Ludwig van Beethoven, 1770–1827, by Edward Hodges, 1796–1867

318 Alleluia! Alleluia! Let the Holy Anthem Rise

1. Al - le - lu - ia! Al - le - lu - ia! Let the
2. Al - le - lu - ia! Al - le - lu - ia! He en -
3. Al - le - lu - ia! Al - le - lu - ia! Like the
4. Al - le - lu - ia! Al - le - lu - ia! He has
5. Al - le - lu - ia! Al - le - lu - ia! Bless - ed

ho - ly an - them rise, And the choirs of heav - en
dured the knot - ted whips, And the jeer - ing of the
sun from out the wave He has ris - en up in
burst our pris - on bars; He has lift - ed up the
Je - sus, make us rise From the life of this cor -

chant it In the tem - ple of the skies; Let the
rab - ble, And the scorn of mock - ing lips, And the
tri - umph From the dark - ness of the grave. He's the
por - tals Of our home be - yond the stars; He has
rup - tion To the life that nev - er dies. May we

moun - tains skip with glad - ness And the
ter - rors of the gib - bet Up - on
splen - dor of the na - tions; He's the
won for us our free - dom— 'Neath his
share with you your glo - ry When the

joy - ful val - leys ring With ho - san - nas in the
which he would be slain, But his death was on - ly
lamp of end - less day; He's the ver - y Lord of
feet our foes are trod; He has pur - chased back our
days of time are past, And the dead shall be a -

high - est To our Sav - ior and our King!
slum - ber; He is ris - en up a - gain!
glo - ry Who is ris - en up to - day!
birth - right To the king - dom of our God!
wak - ened By the trum - pet's might-y blast!

Text: Edward Caswall, 1814–1878
Tune: NETTLETON, 8 7 8 7 D; Wyeth's *Repository of Sacred Music,* 1813

319 We Walk His Way / Ewe, Thina

Refrain

We walk his way. We walk
E - we, thi - na. E - we,

We walk his way. We walk his way.
E - we, thi - na. E - we, thi - na.

1.

his way. We walk
thi - na. E - we,

We walk his way. We walk his way.
E - we, thi - na. E - we, thi - na.

2. To verses | Last time

1. Un - armed, he
2. He breaks the
3. The tree of
1. Si - zo - wa

We walk his way. We walk his way.
E - we, thi - na. E - we, thi - na.

Verses

(1.) fac - es forc - es of de - mons and death. We walk
(2.) bonds of hell, dy - ing on the cross. E - we,
(3.) free - dom blooms by his emp - ty grave.
(1.) nya - the - la a - ma - di - mo - ni.

(1.) fac - es forc - es of de - mons and death.
(2.) bonds of hell, dy - ing on the cross.
(3.) free - dom blooms by his emp - ty grave.
(1.) nya - the - la a - ma - di - mo - ni.

We walk his way.
E - we, thi - na.

We walk his way.
E - we, thi - na.

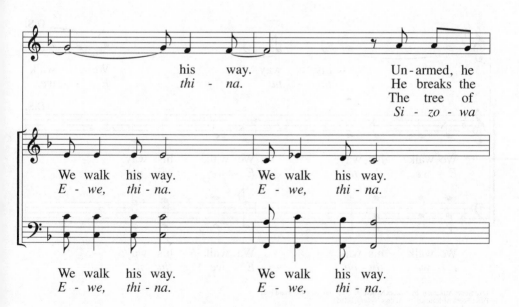

his way.
thi - na.

Un - armed, he
He breaks the
The tree of
Si - zo - wa

We walk his way.
E - we, thi - na.

We walk his way.
E - we, thi - na.

We walk his way.
E - we, thi - na.

We walk his way.
E - we, thi - na.

African phonetics:
Ay-way, thee-nah.
See-zow-wah nyah-thay-lah ah-mah-dee-mow-nee.

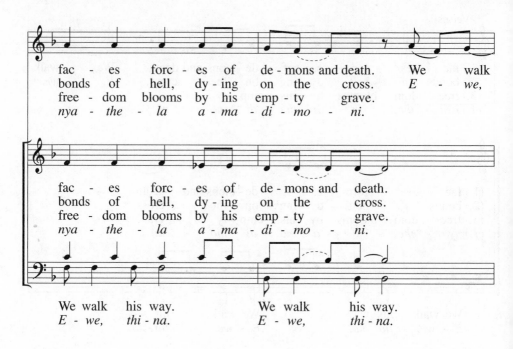

fac - es forc - es of de - mons and death. We walk
bonds of hell, dy - ing on the cross. E - we,
free - dom blooms by his emp - ty grave.
nya - the - la a - ma - di - mo - ni.

fac - es forc - es of de - mons and death.
bonds of hell, dy - ing on the cross.
free - dom blooms by his emp - ty grave.
nya - the - la a - ma - di - mo - ni.

We walk his way.
E - we, thi - na.
We walk his way.
E - we, thi - na.

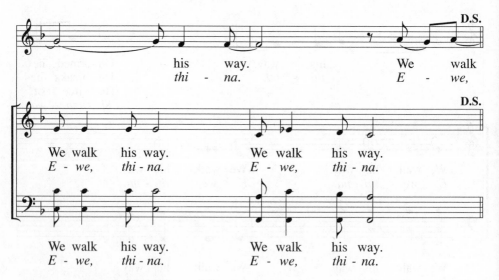

his way.
thi - na.
We walk
E - we,

We walk his way.
E - we, thi - na.
We walk his way.
E - we, thi - na.

We walk his way.
E - we, thi - na.
We walk his way.
E - we, thi - na.

Text: South African; tr. by Anders Nyberg, b.1955, and Sven-Bernhard Fast
Tune: South African; arr. by Anders Nyberg, b.1955

Go 320

1. Go ye there-fore and teach all na - tions, go,
2. If you love me, real - ly love me, feed

go, go. Go ye there-fore and teach all
my sheep. If you love me, real - ly

na - tions, go, go, go.
love me, feed my sheep. And

Bap - tiz - ing them in the name of the Fa - ther and
lo, I'll be with you for ev - er and ev - er un -

Son and Ho - ly Ghost. Go,
til the ends of the world, go,

Last time

go, go.
go, go.

Text: Leon Patillo, b.1947
Tune: Leon Patillo, b.1947
© 1981, 1982, Word Music, Inc.

321 Go to the World!

1. Go to the world! Go in-to all the earth. Go preach the cross where Christ re-news life's worth, Bap-tiz - ing as the sign of our re-birth. Al - le-lu - ia! Al - le-lu - ia!

2. Go to the world! Go in-to ev - 'ry place. Go live the Word of God's re-deem - ing grace. Go seek God's pres - ence in each time and space. Al - le-lu - ia! Al - le-lu - ia!

3. Go to the world! Go strug - gle, bless and pray. The nights of tears give way to joy - ous day. As ser - vant Church, you fol - low Christ's own way. Al - le-lu - ia! Al - le-lu - ia!

4. Go to the world! Go as the ones I send, For I am with you till the age shall end, When all the hosts of glo - ry cry "A - men!" Al - le-lu - ia! Al - le-lu - ia!

Text: Sylvia G. Dunstan, 1955–1993, © 1991, GIA Publications, Inc.
Tune: SINE NOMINE, 10 10 10 with alleluias; Ralph Vaughan Williams, 1872–1958

Go Ye Therefore 322

Go ye there-fore and teach ev-e-ry na - tion.

Don't be a - fraid, don't be a - fraid! Christ said,

"I will be with you al - ways and for-ev - er, un -

1. 2. *Last time*

til the end of the world.

Don't be a - fraid! Don't be a - fraid!

D.C.

Don't be a - fraid! Don't be a - fraid!

Text: Kenneth W. Louis, b.1956
Tune: Kenneth W. Louis, b.1956
© 2012, GIA Publications, Inc.

323 Spirit of God, Descend upon My Heart

1. Spir - it of God, de - scend up - on my heart;
2. I ask no dream, no proph - et ec - sta - sies,
3. Teach me to feel that thou art al - ways nigh;
4. Teach me to love thee as thine an - gels love,

Wean it from earth; through all its puls - es move;
No sud - den rend - ing of the veil of clay,
Teach me the strug - gles of the soul to bear,
One ho - ly pas - sion fill - ing all my frame;

Stoop to my weak - ness, might - y as thou art,
No an - gel vis - i - tant, no o - p'ning skies;
To check the ris - ing doubt, the reb - el sigh;
The kin - dling of the heav'n - de - scend - ed Dove,

And make me love thee as I ought to love.
But take the dim - ness of my soul a - way.
Teach me the pa - tience of un - an - swered prayer.
My heart an al - tar, and thy love the flame.

Text: George Croly, 1780–1860
Tune: MORECAMBE, 10 10 10 10; Frederick C. Atkinson, 1841–1897

Come, Holy Ghost 324

1. Come, Ho-ly Ghost, Cre-a-tor blest, And in our hearts take up thy rest; Come with thy grace and heav'n-ly aid To fill the hearts which thou hast made, To fill the hearts which thou hast made.

2. O Com-fort-er, to thee we cry, Thou heav'n-ly gift of God most high, Thou fount of life, And sweet a-noint-ing from a-bove, And sweet a-noint-ing from a-bove.

3. O Ho-ly Ghost, through thee a-lone Know we the Fa-ther and the Son; Be this our firm un-chang-ing creed, That thou dost from them both pro-ceed, That thou dost from them both pro-ceed.

4. Praise we the Lord, Fa-ther and Son, And Ho-ly Spir-it with them one; And may the Son on us be-stow All gifts that from the Spir-it flow, All gifts that from the Spir-it flow.

Text: *Veni Creator Spiritus;* attr. to Rabanus Maurus, 776–856; tr. by Edward Caswall, 1814–1878, alt.
Tune: LAMBILLOTTE, LM with repeat; Louis Lambillotte, SJ, 1796–1855, harm. by Richard Proulx, 1937–2010, © 1986, GIA Publications, Inc.

325 Spirit of the Living God

Text: Daniel Iverson, 1890–1977
Tune: IVERSON, Irregular; Daniel Iverson, 1890–1977
© 1935, Birdwing Music, admin. at EMICMGPublishing.com

Veni Sancte Spíritus 326

Ostinato Refrain

Ve - ni San - cte Spí - ri - tus.

Ve - ni San - cte Spí - ri - tus.

As the ostinato continues, vocal and instrumental verses are sung or played as desired with some space always left between the verses (after the cantor's "Veni Sancte Spiritus").

Verses

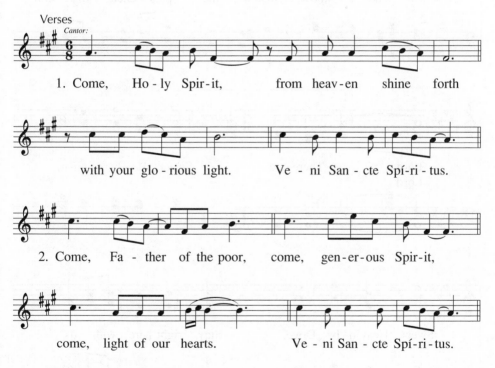

1. Come, Ho - ly Spir - it, from heav - en shine forth with your glo - rious light. Ve - ni San - cte Spí - ri - tus.

2. Come, Fa - ther of the poor, come, gen - er - ous Spir - it, come, light of our hearts. Ve - ni San - cte Spí - ri - tus.

Text: *Come Holy Spirit;* verses drawn from the Pentecost Sequence; Taizé Community, 1978
Tune: Jacques Berthier, 1923–1994
© 1979, Les Presses de Taizé, GIA Publications, Inc., agent

327 Sweet, Sweet Spirit

There's a sweet, sweet spir - it in this place,
sweet ex - pres - sions on each face,

And I know that it's the spir - it of the
And I know that it's the pres - ence of the

Lord. There are
Lord.

Sweet Ho - ly Spir-it,

Sweet Heav'n - ly Dove, Stay right here with us

Fill-ing us with your love. And for those bless-ings We lift our hearts with praise; With-out a doubt we'll know that we have been re-vived, when we shall leave this place.

Text: Doris Akers, 1922–1995
Tune: MANNA, Irregular; Doris Akers, 1922–1995

328 Veni Creátor Spíritus

1. Ve - ni Cre - á - tor Spí - ri - tus,
2. Qui dí - ce - ris Pa - rá - cli - tus,
3. Tu se - pti - fór - mis mú - ne - re,
4. Ac - cén - de lu - men sén - si - bus,
5. Ho - stem re - pél - las lón - gi - us,
6. Per te sci - á - mus da Pa - trem,
7. De - o Pa - tri sit gló - ri - a,

Men - tes tu - ó - rum ví - si - ta:
Al - tís - si - mi do - num De - i,
Dí - gi - tus pa - tér - nae déx - te - rae,
In - fún - de a - mó - rem cór - di - bus,
Pa - cém - que do - nes pró - ti - nus:
No - scá - mus at - que Fí - li - um
Et Fí - li - o, qui a mór - tu - is

Im - ple su - pér - na grá - ti - a
Fons vi - vus, i - gnis, cá - ri - tas,
Tu ri - te pro - mís - sum Pa - tris,
In - fír - ma no - stri cór - po - ris
Du - ctó - re sic te práe - vi - o,
Te - que u - tri - ús - que Spí - ri - tum
Sur - ré - xit, ac Pa - rá - cli - to,

Quae tu cre - á - sti pé - cto - ra.
Et spi - ri - tá - lis ún - cti - o.
Ser - mó - ne di - tans gút - tu - ra.
Vir - tú - te fir - mans pér - pe - ti.
Vi - té - mus o - mne nó - xi - um.
Cre - dá - mus o - mni tém - po - re.
In sae - cu - ló - rum saé - cu - la. A - men.

Text: *Veni Creator Spiritus*, attr. to Rabanus Maurus, 776–856
Tune: VENI CREATOR SPIRITUS, LM; Mode VIII; acc. by Richard Proulx, 1937–2010, © 1975, GIA Publications, Inc.

Holy Spirit, Flow through Me 329

1. Ho - ly Spir - it, flow through me,
2. Ho - ly Spir - it, rest on me,
3. Ho - ly Spir - it, flow out from me,

Ho - ly Spir - it, flow through me, And
Ho - ly Spir - it, rest on me, And
Ho - ly Spir - it, flow out through me, That

make my life what it ought to be,
use me, Lord, win the lost to thee,
oth - ers, Lord, may see you in me,

Ho - ly Spir - it, flow through me.
Ho - ly Spir - it, rest on me.
Ho - ly Spir - it, flow out through me.

Text: Walt Mills, b.1936
Tune: Walt Mills b.1936
© 1974, Heartwarming Music Co./BMI

330 Holy Spirit, Come and Fill

Ho-ly Spir-it, come and fill this place, bring us

heal-ing and your warm em - brace; show your pow-er, make your

pres - ence known. Ho-ly Spir - it, come fill this place.

Breath of God, we need a touch from you, shine down

on us with the light of truth; stir our hearts and set our

spir-its free, Ho-ly Spir-it, come fill this place,

Ho-ly Spir-it, come fill this place.

Text: Marty Hennis and Babbie Mason, © 1996, Word Music, Inc. and May Sun Music
Tune: Marty Hennis and Babbie Mason, © 1996, Word Music, Inc. and May Sun Music; arr. by Kenneth W. Louis, b.1956, © 2012, GIA Publications, Inc.

Wa Wa Wa Emimimo / Come, O Holy Spirit 331

Wa wa wa E-mi-mi-mo.   Wa wa wa A-lag-ba-
Come, O Ho-ly Spir-it, come.   *Come, Al-might-y Spir-it,*

E - mi - o - lo - ye.
Ho-ly Spir-it, come.

ra.   Wa-o, wa-o, wa-o.
come.   *Come, come, come.*

A - lag-ba-ra-me-ta.
Al-might-y Spir-it, come.

E - mi - mi - mo.
O Spir-it, come.

Text: Nigerian traditional
Tune: As taught by Samuel Solanke; transcription and paraphrase © 1990, Iona Community, GIA Publications, Inc., agent

332 Come Down, O Love Divine

1. Come down, O Love divine, Seek now this soul of mine, And visit it with your own ardor glowing; O Comforter, draw near, Within my heart appear, And kindle it, your holy flame bestowing.

2. O let it freely burn, Till earthly passions turn To dust and ashes in its heat consuming; And let your glorious light Shine ever on my sight, And clothe me round, the while my path illuming.

3. And so the yearning strong, With which the soul will long, Shall far out-pass the pow'r of human telling; No soul can guess Love's grace Till it become the place Wherein the Holy Spirit makes a dwelling.

Text: *Discendi, Amor Santo;* Bianco da Siena, d. 1434; tr. by Richard F. Littledale, 1833–1890, alt.
Tune: DOWN AMPNEY, 66 11 D; Ralph Vaughan Williams, 1872–1958

God Sends Us His Spirit 333

1. God sends us his Spir-it to be-friend and help us.
2. Dark-ened roads are clear-er, heav-y bur-dens light-er,
3. Now we are God's peo-ple, bond-ed by God's pres-ence,

Re-cre-ate and guide us, Spir-it-Friend.
When we're walk-ing with our Spir-it-Friend.
A-gents of God's pur-pose, Spir-it-Friend.

Spir-it who en-liv-ens, sanc-ti-fies, en-light-ens,
Now we need not fear the pow-ers of the dark-ness.
Lead us for-ward ev-er, slip-ping back-ward nev-er,

Sets us free, is now our Spir-it - Friend.
None can o-ver-come our Spir-it - Friend.
To your re-made world, our Spir-it - Friend.

Spir-it of our Mak-er, Spir-it-Friend.
Spir-it of our Je-su, Spir-it-Friend.

Last time

Spir-it of God's peo-ple, Spir-it-Friend.

*Hand claps

Text: Tom Colvin, 1925–2000
Tune: NATOMAH, 12 9 12 9 with refrain; Gonja folk song; adapt. by Tom Colvin, 1925–2000
© 1969, Hope Publishing Company

334 Come Now, Almighty King

1. Come now, al - might - y King, Help us your
2. Come now, in - car - nate Word, Mer - ci - ful,
3. Come, ho - ly Com - fort - er, Your sa - cred
4. To the great One in Three, E - ter - nal

name to sing, Help us to praise.
might - y Lord, Our prayer at - tend.
wit - ness bear In this glad hour.
prais - es be For - ev - er - more!

Fa - ther all glo - ri - ous, Ev - er vic - to - ri - ous,
Come and your peo - ple bless, And give your word suc - cess,
Your grace to us im - part, Now rule in ev - 'ry heart,
Your sov - 'reign maj - es - ty May we in glo - ry see

Come and reign o - ver us, An - cient of Days.
Grant us your ho - li - ness, Sav - ior and Friend.
Nev - er from us de - part, Spir - it of pow'r.
And, to e - ter - ni - ty, Love and a - dore.

Text: Anon.; *Collection of Hymns for Social Worship*, 1757, alt.
Tune: ITALIAN HYMN, 66 4 666 4; Felice de Giardini, 1716–1796

Holy, Holy, Holy! Lord God Almighty! 335

1. Ho - ly, Ho - ly, Ho - ly! Lord God Al - might - y!
2. Ho - ly, Ho - ly, Ho - ly! All the saints a - dore thee,
3. Ho - ly, Ho - ly, Ho - ly! Though the dark - ness hide thee,

Ear - ly in the morn - ing our song shall rise to thee.
Cast - ing down their gold - en crowns a - round the glass - y sea;
Though the eye made blind by sin thy glo - ry may not see,

Ho - ly, Ho - ly, Ho - ly, mer - ci - ful and might - y!
Cher - u - bim and ser - a - phim fall - ing down be - fore thee,
On - ly thou art ho - ly; there is none be - side thee,

God in three Per - sons, bless - ed Trin - i - ty.
God ev - er - last - ing through e - ter - ni - ty.
Per - fect in pow'r, in love, and pu - ri - ty.

Descant:

4. Ho - ly,   Ho - ly!   Lord, God Al - might - y!

4. Ho - ly, Ho - ly, Ho - ly!   Lord   God Al - might - y!

All   thy works shall praise thy Name in   earth and sky and sea.

All   thy works shall praise thy Name in   earth and sky and sea.

Ho - ly,   Ho - ly,   mer - ci - ful and might - y!

Ho - ly, Ho - ly,   Ho - ly,   mer - ci - ful and might - y!

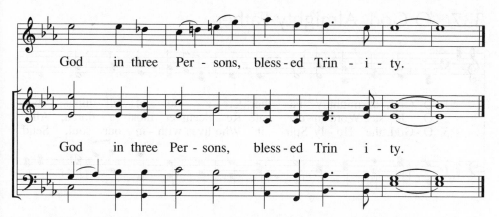

God in three Per - sons, bless - ed Trin - i - ty.

God in three Per - sons, bless - ed Trin - i - ty.

Text: Reginald Heber, 1783–1826, alt.
Tune: NICAEA, 11 12 12 10; John Bacchus Dykes, 1823–1876; arr. by Nolan Williams, Jr., b.1969, © 2000, GIA Publications, Inc.

Father, I Adore You 336

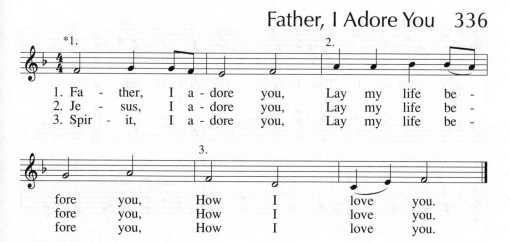

1. Fa - ther, I a - dore you, Lay my life be -
2. Je - sus, I a - dore you, Lay my life be -
3. Spir - it, I a - dore you, Lay my life be -

fore you, How I love you.
fore you, How I love you.
fore you, How I love you.

May be sung as a 3-part round.

Text: Terrye Coelho-Strom, b.1952
Tune: MARANATHA, 6 6 4; Terrye Coelho-Strom, b.1952
© 1972, Maranatha! Music

337 O God, Almighty Father

1. O God, al-might-y Fa - ther, Cre - a - tor of all things, The
2. O Je - sus, Word in - car - nate, Re - deem-er most a - dored, All
3. O God, the Ho - ly Spir - it, Who lives with - in our soul, Send

heav-ens stand in won - der, While earth your glo - ry sings.
glo - ry, praise, and hon - or Be yours, O sov-'reign Lord.
forth your light and lead us To our e - ter - nal goal.

O most ho - ly Trin - i - ty, Un - di - vid - ed u - ni - ty,

Ho-ly God, might - y God, God im - mor-tal be a - dored!

Text: *Gott Vater sei gepriesen*; anon; tr. by Irvin Udulutsch, OFM Cap., 1920–2010, alt. © 1959, 1977, Order of Saint Benedict, admin. Liturgical Press
Tune: GOTT VATER SEI GEPRIESEN, 7 6 7 6 with refrain; Limburg *Gesangbuch*, 1838; harm. by Healey Willan, 1880–1968, © 1958,
Ralph Jusko Publications, Inc.

O Dawn of All Creation 338

1. O Dawn of all cre - a - tion And
(2. O) Light of in - car - na - tion, The
(3. O) Flame of trans - for - ma - tion And
(4. O) Dawn of all the liv - ing, What

Mys - ter - y un - known, Whose ways are not as
face of Love here known, Whose ways were not as
Pow - er yet un - known, Whose ways are not as
is and what shall be, O Light and Flame of

our ways, Whose thoughts are not our own: In
our ways, Whose thoughts were not our own: In
our ways, Whose thoughts are not our own: In
lov - ing, Tran - scen - dent Mys - ter - y: You

grace you made and blessed us; In mer - cy you for - gave;
fol - ly was your wis - dom; Your wealth, in pov - er - ty;
per - il you are fear - less; In hu - man weak - ness, strong;
dwell where none can fol - low, In worlds be - yond our own,

In ten - der - ness and long - ing, In faith - ful - ness you
A cross, your ex - al - ta - tion; De - feat, your vic - to -
In bond - age you are free - dom; In griev - ing hearts, a
Yet all who seek may find you In flesh and blood and

1.–3. | 4. 3

save. | 2. O
ry. | 3. O
song. | 4. O
bone.

Text: Delores Dufner, OSB, b.1939, © 1999, 2003, GIA Publications, Inc.
Tune: ANDÚJAR, 7 6 7 6 D; David Hurd, b.1950, © 1984, GIA Publications, Inc.

339 Hidden Here before Me / Adóro Te Devóte

1. Hid - den here be - fore me, Lord, I wor - ship you,
2. See - ing, touch - ing, tast - ing: these are all de - ceived;
3. On - ly God was hid - den when you came to die;
4. I am not like Thom - as, who could see and touch;
5. Re - cord of the Pas - sion when the Lamb was slain,
6. Once a nest - ing pel - i - can gashed her - self to blood
7. Je - sus, for the pres - ent seen as through a mask,

1. A - dó - ro te de - vó - te, la - tens Dé - i - tas,
2. Vi - sus, ta - ctus, gu - stus in te fál - li - tur,
3. In cru - ce la - te - bat so - la Dé - i - tas,
4. Pla - gas, si - cut Tho - mas, non in - tú - e - or,
5. O me - mo - ri - á - le mor - tis Dó - mi - ni,
6. Pi - e pel - li - cá - ne, Je - su Dó - mi - ne,
7. Je - su, quem ve - lá - tum nunc a - spí - ci - o,

Hid - den in these sym - bols, yet com - plete - ly true.
On - ly through the hear - ing can it be be - lieved.
Hu - man na - ture al - so here es - capes the eye.
Though your wounds are hid - den, I be - lieve as much.
Liv - ing bread that brings us back to life a - gain:
For the pres - er - va - tion of her starv - ing brood.
Give me what I thirst for, give me what I ask:

Quae sub his fi - gú - ris ve - re lá - ti - tas:
Sed au - dí - tu so - lo tu - to cré - di - tur:
At hic la - tet si - mul et hu - má - ni - tas:
De - um ta - men me - um te con - fí - te - or:
Pa - nis vi - vus vi - tam prae - stans hó - mi - ni,
Me im - mún - dum mun - da tu - o sán - gui - ne,
O - ro fi - at il - lud quod tam sí - ti - o:

Lord, my soul sur - ren - ders, long - ing to o - bey,
Noth - ing is more cer - tain: Christ has told me so;
Both are my pro - fes - sion, both are my be - lief;
Let me say so bold - ly, mean - ing what I say,
Feed me with your pres - ence, make me live on you;
Now heal me with your blood, take a - way my guilt:
Let me see your glo - ry in a blaze of light,

Ti - bi se cor me - um to - tum súb - ji - cit,
Cre - do quid-quid di - xit De - i Fí - li - us:
Am - bo ta - men cre - dens at - que cón - fi - tens
Fac me ti - bi sem - per ma - gis cré - de - re,
Prae - sta me - ae men - ti de te ví - ve - re,
Cu - ius u - na stil - la sal - vum fá - ce - re,
Ut te re - ve - lá - ta cer - nens fá - ci - e,

And in con - tem - pla - tion whol - ly faints a - way.
What the Truth has ut - tered, I be - lieve and know.
Bring me to your King - dom, like the dy - ing thief.
Lov - ing you and trust - ing, now and ev - 'ry day.
Let that love - ly fra - grance fill me through and through.
All the world is ran - somed if one drop is spilt.
And in - stead of blind - ness give me, Lord, my sight.

Qui - a te con - tém - plans to - tum dé - fi - cit.
Nil hoc ver - bo ve - ri - tá - tis vé - ri - us.
Pe - to quod pe - tí - vit la - tro paé - ni - tens.
In te spem ha - bé - re, te di - lí - ge - re.
Et ti il - li sem - per dul - ce sá - pe - re.
To - tum mun - dum quit ab o - mni scé - le - re.
Vi - su sim be - á - tus tu - ae gló - ri - ae.

Text: *Adoro te devote*, attr. to St. Thomas Aquinas, c.1225–1274; English tr. from *A Book of Prayers*, © 1982, ICEL
Tune: ADORO TE DEVOTE, 11 11 11 11; Mode V, *Processionale*, Paris, 1697; acc. by Richard Proulx, 1937–2010, © 1986, GIA Publications, Inc.

340 We Will Glorify

1. We will glo - ri - fy the King of kings, We will glo - ri - fy the Lamb; We will glo - ri - fy the Lord of lords, Who is the great I Am.

2. Lord Je - ho - vah reigns in maj - es - ty, We will bow be - fore his throne; We will wor-ship him in right-eous - ness, We will wor-ship him a - lone.

3. He is Lord of heav - en, Lord of earth, He is Lord of all who live; He is Lord a - bove the u - ni - verse— All praise to him we give.

4. Hal - le - lu - jah to the King of kings, Hal - le - lu - jah to the Lamb; Hal - le - lu - jah to the Lord of lords, Who is the great I Am.

Text: Twila Paris, b.1958
Tune: WE WILL GLORIFY, 9 7 9 6; Twila Paris, b.1958
© 1982, Singspiration Music (ASCAP)

The King of Glory 341

Refrain

The King of glo - ry comes, the na - tion re - joic - es.

1.–5. *To verses* 6.

O - pen the gates be - fore him, lift up your voic - es. lift up your voic - es.

Verses

1. Who is the king of glo - ry; how shall we call him?
2. In all of Gal - i - lee, in cit - y or vil - lage,
3. Sing then of Da - vid's Son, our Sav - ior and broth - er;
4. He gave his life for us, the pledge of sal - va - tion,
5. He con - quered sin and death; he tru - ly has ris - en.

D.C.

He is Em - man - u - el, the prom - ised of a - ges.
He goes a - mong his peo - ple cur - ing their ill - ness.
In all of Gal - i - lee was nev - er an - oth - er.
He took up - on him - self the sins of the na - tion.
And he will share with us his heav - en - ly vi - sion.

Text: Willard F. Jabusch, b.1930, © 1966, 1982, Willard F. Jabusch. Administered by OCP.
Tune: KING OF GLORY, 12 12 with refrain; Israeli; harm. by Richard Proulx, 1937–2010, © 1986, GIA Publications, Inc.

342   All Hail the Power of Jesus' Name!

1. All hail the pow'r of Je - sus' name!
2. Ye cho - sen seed of Is - rael's race,
3. Let ev - 'ry kin - dred, ev - 'ry tribe,
4. Oh, that with yon - der sa - cred throng

Let an - gels pros - trate fall, Let an - gels pros - trate
Ye ran - somed from the fall, Ye ran - somed from the
On this ter - res - trial ball, On this ter - res - trial
We at his feet may fall, We at his feet may

fall. Bring forth the roy - al di - a - dem,
fall, Hail him who saves you by his grace,
ball, To him all maj - es - ty as - cribe,
fall! We'll join the ev - er - last - ing song,

Text: Edward Perronet, 1726–1792
Tune: DIADEM, CM with refrain; James Ellor, 1819–1899

343 All Hail the Power of Jesus' Name!

1. All hail the pow'r of Je-sus' name! Let an-gels pros-trate
2. Ye cho-sen seed of Is-rael's race, Ye ran-somed from the
3. Let ev-'ry kin-dred, ev-'ry tribe, On this ter-res-trial
*4. O that with yon-der sa-cred throng, We at his feet may

fall. Bring forth the roy-al di-a-dem, And crown him
fall, Hail him who saves you by his grace, And crown him
ball, To him all maj-es-ty as-cribe, And crown him
fall! We'll join the ev-er-last-ing song, And crown him

Lord of all; Bring forth the roy-al di-a-dem, And
Lord of all; Hail him who saves you by his grace, And
Lord of all; To him all maj-es-ty as-cribe, And
Lord of all; We'll join the ev-er-last-ing song, And

1., 2. **3.**

crown him Lord of all!
crown him Lord of all!
crown him Lord of all!
crown him Lord of all!

Sing this 4th verse if no key change is desired.

Text: Edward Perronet, 1726–1792, alt. by John Rippon, 1751–1836
Tune: CORONATION, 8 6 8 6 8 6; Oliver Holden, 1765–1844; arr. by Nolan Williams, Jr., b.1969, © 2000, GIA Publications, Inc.

344 Crown Him with Many Crowns

1. Crown him with man - y crowns, The Lamb up - on his
2. Crown him the Lord of life, Who tri - umphed o'er the
3. Crown him the Lord of love— Be - hold his hands and
4. Crown him the Lord of peace, Whose pow'r a scep - ter
5. Crown him the Lord of years, The mas - ter of all

throne. Hark! How the heav'n - ly an - them drowns All
grave, And rose vic - to - rious in the strife For
side, Rich wounds, yet vis - i - ble a - bove, In
sways From pole to pole, that wars may cease, Ab -
time, Cre - a - tor of the roll - ing spheres, And

mu - sic but its own. A - wake, my soul, and sing Of
those he came to save. His glo - ries now we sing, Who
beau - ty glo - ri - fied. No an - gel in the sky Can
sorbed by prayer and praise. His reign shall know no end, And
ris - en Lord sub - lime. All hail, Re - deem - er, hail! For

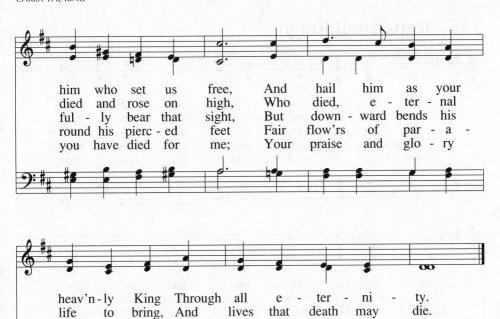

him   who   set   us   free,   And   hail   him   as   your
died   and   rose   on   high,   Who   died,   e - ter - nal
ful - ly bear   that   sight,   But   down - ward bends his
round   his   pierc - ed   feet   Fair   flow'rs of   par - a -
you   have   died   for   me;   Your   praise and   glo - ry

heav'n - ly King   Through all   e - ter - ni - ty.
life   to   bring, And   lives that death may   die.
burn - ing   eye   At   mys - ter - ies   so   bright.
dise   ex - tend   Their fra - grance ev - er   sweet.
shall   not   fail   Through - out e - ter - ni - ty.

Text: Revelation 19:12; st. 1, 3–5, Matthew Bridges, 1800–1894; st. 2, Godfrey Thring, 1823–1903
Tune: DIADEMATA, SMD; George J. Elvey, 1816–1893

345 Jesus Shall Reign

1. Je - sus shall reign wher - e'er the sun
2. To him shall end - less prayer be made,
3. Peo - ple and realms of ev - 'ry tongue
4. Bless - ings a - bound wher - e'er he reigns:
5. Let ev - 'ry crea - ture rise and bring

Does its suc - ces - sive jour - neys run;
And prais - es throng to crown his head;
Dwell on his love with sweet - est song;
The pris - 'ners leap to lose their chains,
Bless - ing and hon - or to our King,

His king - dom stretch from shore to shore,
His name like sweet per - fume shall rise
And in - fant voic - es shall pro - claim
The wea - ry find e - ter - nal rest,
An - gels de - scend with songs a - gain,

Till moons shall wax and wane no more.
With ev - 'ry morn - ing sac - ri - fice.
Their ear - ly bless - ings on his name.
And all who suf - fer want are blest.
And earth re - peat the loud A - men.

Text: Isaac Watts, 1674–1748, alt.
Tune: DUKE STREET, LM; John Hatton, c.1710–1793

He Is King of Kings   346

Refrain

He is King of kings, he is Lord of lords.

Je-sus Christ, the first and last, no one works like him.

Verses

Solo:

1. He built his throne up in the air,
2. He pitched his tents on Ca-naan's ground,

All: No one works like him.

Solo:

And called his saints from ev - 'ry - where,
And broke the Ro - man king-dom down,

All: No one works like him.

D.C.

Text: Negro Spiritual, ed. by John W. Work, III, 1901–1967
Tune: HE IS KING, Irregular; Negro Spiritual, ed. by John W. Work, III, 1901–1967

347 To Jesus Christ, Our Sovereign King

1. To Je - sus Christ, our sov - 'reign King, Who
2. Your reign ex - tend, O King be - nign, To
3. To you and to your Church, great King, We

is the world's sal - va - tion, All praise and hom - age
ev - 'ry land and na - tion; For in your king - dom,
pledge our hearts' ob - la - tion Un - til be - fore your

do we bring And thanks and ad - o - ra - tion.
Lord di - vine, A - lone we find sal - va - tion.
throne we sing In end - less ju - bi - la - tion.

Christ Je - sus, Vic - tor! Christ Je - sus, Rul - er!

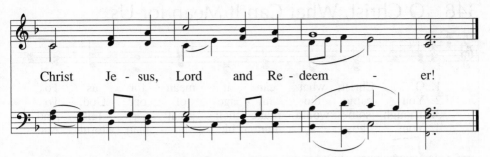

Christ Je - sus, Lord and Re - deem - er!

Text: Martin B. Hellriegel, 1890–1981, alt., © 1941, Irene C. Mueller
Tune: ICH GLAUB AN GOTT, 8 7 8 7 with refrain; Mainz *Gesangbuch*, 1870; harm. by Richard Proulx, 1937–2010, © 1986, GIA Publications, Inc.

348 O Christ, What Can It Mean for Us

1. O Christ, what can it mean for us To
2. You came, the im - age of our God, To
3. Though some would make their great - ness felt And
4. You chose a hum - ble hu - man form And

claim you as our king? What roy - al face have
heal and to for - give, To shed your blood for
lord it o - ver all, You said the first must
shunned the world's re - nown; You died for us up -

you re - vealed Whose praise the Church would sing? As -
sin - ners' sake That we might rise and live. To
be the last And serv - ice be our call. O
on a cross With thorns your on - ly crown. But

pir - ing not to glo - ry's height, To
break the law of death you came, The
Christ, in work - place, church, and home Let
still, be - yond the span of years, Our

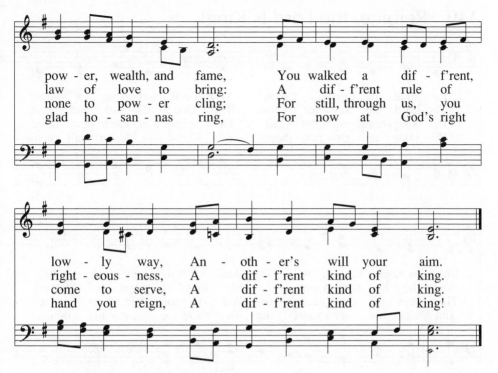

pow - er, wealth, and fame, You walked a dif - f'rent,
law of love to bring: A dif - f'rent rule of
none to pow - er cling; For still, through us, you
glad ho - san - nas ring, For now at God's right

low - ly way, An - oth - er's will your aim.
right - eous - ness, A dif - f'rent kind of king.
come to serve, A dif - f'rent kind of king.
hand you reign, A dif - f'rent kind of king!

Text: Delores Dufner, OSB, b.1939, © 2001, 2003, GIA Publications, Inc.
Tune: KINGSFOLD, CMD; English; harm. by Ralph Vaughan Williams, 1872–1958

349 Rejoice, the Lord Is King!

1. Re - joice, the Lord is King! Your Lord and King a - dore!
2. The Lord, our Sav - ior, reigns, The God of truth and love.
3. His king - dom can - not fail, He rules o'er earth and heav'n.
4. Re - joice in glo - rious hope! For Christ the Judge shall come

Re - joice, give thanks, and sing, And tri - umph ev - er - more.
When he had purged our sins, He took his seat a - bove.
The keys of death and hell Are to our Je - sus giv'n.
And take his ser - vants up To their e - ter - nal home.

Lift up your heart, lift up your voice!

Re - joice, a - gain I say, re - joice!

Text: Charles Wesley, 1707–1788, alt.
Tune: DARWALL'S 148TH, 6 6 6 6 with refrain; John Darwall, 1731–1789; harm. from *The Hymnal 1940*

Give Me Jesus 350

1. I heard my moth-er say, I heard my moth-er say,
2. Dark mid-night was my cry, Dark mid-night was my cry,
3. Oh, when I come to die, Oh, when I come to die,

I heard my moth-er say, Give me Je - sus.
Dark mid-night was my cry, Give me Je - sus.
Oh, when I come to die, Give me Je - sus.

Give me Je - sus. Give me Je - sus,

You may have all this world, Give me Je - sus.

Text: Negro Spiritual
Tune: GIVE ME JESUS, 666 4 with refrain; Negro Spiritual; arr. by Nolan Williams, Jr., b.1969, © 2000, GIA Publications, Inc.

351 No, Not One!

1. There's not a friend like the low - ly Je - sus—
2. No friend like him is so high and ho - ly—
3. There's not an hour that he is not near us—
4. Was e'er a gift like the Sav - ior giv - en?

No, not one! no, not one! None else could heal all our
No, not one! no, not one! And yet no friend is so
No, not one! no, not one! No night so dark but his
No, not one! no, not one! Will he re - fuse us a

soul's dis - eas - es— No, not one! no, not one!
meek and low - ly— No, not one! no, not one!
love can cheer us— No, not one! no, not one!
home in heav - en? No, not one! no, not one!

Je - sus knows all a - bout our strug - gles, He will guide till the

day is done; There's not a friend like the

low - ly Je - sus— No, not one! no, not one!

Text: Johnson Oatman, Jr., 1856–1922
Tune: HARPER MEMORIAL, 10 6 10 6 with refrain; George C. Hugg, 1848–1907

Oh, It Is Jesus 352

Chorus

Oh, it is Je - sus. Yes, it is Je - sus. It's

Je - sus in my soul. For I have touched the hem of his

gar - ment and his blood has made me whole.

Text: Andraé Crouch, b.1942
Tune: Andraé Crouch, b.1942; arr. by Stephen Key
© Crouch Music, admin. at EMICMGPublishing.com

353 O Holy Savior!

1. O ho - ly Sav - ior! Friend un -
2. What though the world de - ceit - ful
3. Though faith and hope a - while be

seen, Since on thine arm thou bid'st me
prove, And earth - ly friends and joys re -
tried, I ask not, need not aught be -

lean, Help me, through - out life's chang - ing
move? With pa - tient, un - com - plain - ing
side: How safe, how calm, how sat - is -

scene, By faith to cling to thee!
love Still I would cling to thee.
fied, The souls that cling to thee.

Text: Charlotte Elliot, 1789–1871
Tune: HOLY SAVIOR, 888 6; Ulysses Elam; arr. by Robert Nathaniel Dett, 1882–1943, © 1936, (renewed), Paul A. Schmitt Music Co., c/o
Belwin-Mills Publishing Corp.

He's So Real 354

Refrain

He's so real, real in my soul to-day! He has

washed all of my sins a-way. Je - sus' love just

bub - bles o - ver in my soul, in my soul.

Verses

1. Some peo-ple doubt the Lord.
2. He's done so much for me.

They don't be - lieve in his word;
One day he set me free. And,

They

D.C.

try to make you think that God is dead.
and now I want the world to know.

Text: Charles H. Nicks, Jr., 1941–1988, © 1975, Bridgeport Music, Inc.
Tune: Charles H. Nicks, Jr., 1941–1988, © 1975, Bridgeport Music, Inc.; arr. by Kenneth W. Louis, b.1956, © 2006, GIA Publications, Inc.

355 Jesus Is a Rock in a Weary Land

Refrain

Je - sus is a rock in a wea - ry land, a wea - ry land, a wea - ry land; My Je - sus is a rock in a wea - ry land, a shel - ter in the time of storm.

Verses

1. No   man   can   do   like   Je - sus,   Not a
2. When   Je - sus   was   on   earth,   The
3. Yon - der   comes   my   Sav - ior,   Him

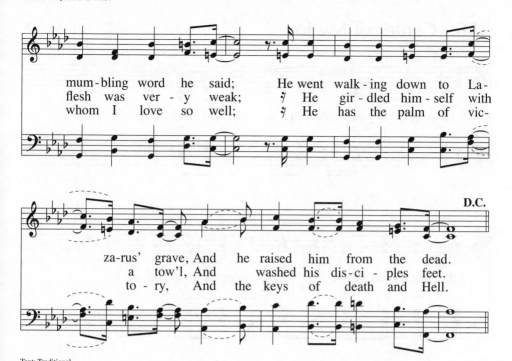

mum-bling word he said; He went walk-ing down to La-
flesh was ver - y weak; 𝄍 He gir - dled him - self with
whom I love so well; 𝄍 He has the palm of vic-

D.C.

za-rus' grave, And he raised him from the dead.
a tow'l, And washed his dis-ci - ples feet.
to - ry, And the keys of death and Hell.

Text: Traditional
Tune: WEARY LAND, 6 6 8 6 with refrain; traditional, arr. by Dr. Wyatt Tee Walker, b.1929, ©; administered by GIA Publications, Inc.

356 Center of My Joy

Refrain

Je - sus, you're the cen - ter of my joy.

All that's good and per - fect comes from you.

You're the heart of my con - tent - ment, hope for all I do.

Last time

Je - sus, you're the cen - ter of my joy.

1. When I've lost my di - rec - tion, you're the com-pass for my way,
2. You are why I find pleas-ure in the sim - ple things in life,

you're the fire and light when nights are long and cold;
you're the mu - sic in the mead-ows and the streams;

3

Through the sad-ness, you are the laugh-ter that shad-ows all my
You're in the voic - es of my chil-dren, in my fam - 'ly and my

3

D.C.

fears, when I'm down and out your hand is there to hold.
home, you're the source and fin - ish - er of my high-est dreams.

Text: Gloria Gaither
Tune: Richard Smallwood, William Gaither; arr. by Nolan Williams, Jr., b.1969
© 1987, Hanna Street Music and Century Oak /Richwood Music

357 Jesus Is Real to Me

Chorus

Real, real, Jesus is real to me.

Oh yes, he gives me the victory.

So many people doubt him. I can't live without him.

That is why I love him so, he's so real to me.

Text: Beatrice Brown, © 1963, Beatrice Brown's Music House
Tune: Beatrice Brown, © 1963, Beatrice Brown's Music House; arr. by Stephen Key, © 2000, GIA Publications, Inc.

I Know Jesus 358

Chorus: I know Je - sus, he's my guid - ing light.
1. I need Je - sus, each and ev - 'ry day.
2. Share with oth - ers as you share with him,
3. I found Je - sus in my broth - er's eye,

I know Je - sus, he's the light that shines.
I need Je - sus to show me the way.
Let him en - ter your heart with - in,
I found Je - sus in my sis - ter's eye.

I know Je - sus, he's my guid - ing light.
I need Je - sus, each and ev - 'ry day.
Share with oth - ers as you share with him.
I found Je - sus, he is by my side.

Let it shine, let it shine, let it shine.
I need Je - sus, each and ev - 'ry day.
Share with oth - ers as you share with him.
I found Je - sus, he is by my side.

Text: Edward V. Bonnemère, 1921–1996
Tune: Edward V. Bonnemère, 1921–1996
© 1983, Amity Music Co.

359 You, Lord, Are Both Lamb and Shepherd

1. You, Lord, are both Lamb and Shep - herd.
2. Clothed in light up - on the moun - tain,
3. You, who walk each day be - side us,
4. Wor - thy is our earth - ly Je - sus!

You, Lord, are both prince and slave.
Stripped of might up - on the cross,
Sit in pow - er at God's side.
Wor - thy is our cos - mic Christ!

You, peace - mak - er and sword - bring - er
Shin - ing in e - ter - nal glo - ry,
You, who preach a way that's nar - row,
Wor - thy your de - feat and vic - t'ry.

Of the way you took and gave.
Beg - gar'd by a sol - dier's toss.
Have a love that reach - es wide.
Wor - thy still your peace and strife.

You, the ev - er - last - ing in - stant;
You, the ev - er - last - ing in - stant;
You, the ev - er - last - ing in - stant;
You, the ev - er - last - ing in - stant;

You, whom we both scorn and crave.
You, who are both gift and cost.
You, who are our pil - grim guide.
You, who are our death and life.

Text: *Christus Paradox*, Sylvia G. Dunstan, 1955–1993, © 1991, GIA Publications, Inc.
Tune: PICARDY, 8 7 8 7 8 7; French carol; harm. by Richard Proulx, 1937–2010, © 1986, GIA Publications, Inc.

He's Sweet, I Know 360

Refrain: He's sweet, I know. He's sweet, I know.
1. I can't for-get when I was sad.
2. I have my tick-et here in my hand.

Storm clouds may rise, strong winds may blow.
Head hang-ing down, soul feel-ing bad.
I'm go-ing to that beau-ti-ful land.

I'll tell the world wher-ev-er I go.
All I could say was Lord take my heart.
Some-time I weep and some-time I moan.

That I've found a Sav-ior, and he's sweet, I know.
Je-sus heard and saved me, and gave me a start.
But I'm bound for glo-ry, and I'm go-ing on.

Text: Traditional Gospel hymn
Tune: HE'S SWEET, 88 9 11; traditional Gospel hymn; arr. by Kenneth W. Louis b.1956, and Nolan Williams, Jr., b.1969, © 2000, GIA Publications, Inc.

361 What a Friend We Have in Jesus

1. What a Friend we have in Je - sus, All our
2. Have we tri - als and temp - ta - tions? Is there
3. Are we weak and heav - y - la - den, Cum - bered

sins and griefs to bear! What a priv - i - lege to
trou - ble an - y - where? We should nev - er be dis -
with a load of care? Pre - cious Sav - ior, still our

car - ry Ev - 'ry-thing to God in prayer! O what
cour - aged— Take it to the Lord in prayer. Can we
ref - uge— Take it to the Lord in prayer. Do thy

peace we of - ten for - feit, O what need-less pain we
find a friend so faith - ful Who will all our sor - rows
friends de-spise, for - sake thee? Take it to the Lord in

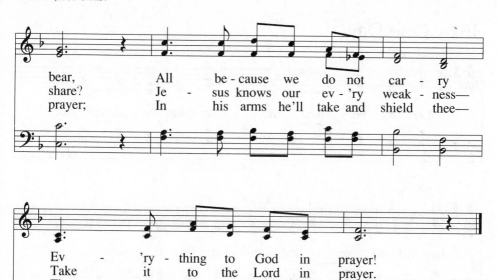

bear,
share?
prayer;

All
Je - sus knows our
In his arms he'll

be - cause we do not car - ry
ev - 'ry weak - ness—
take and shield thee—

Ev - 'ry - thing to God in prayer!
Take it to the Lord in prayer.
Thou wilt find a sol - ace there.

Text: Joseph M. Scriven, 1819–1866
Tune: CONVERSE, 8 7 8 7 D; Charles C. Converse, 1832–1918

362 One Day

Chorus

Living he loved me, dying he saved me,
buried he carried my sins far away.
Rising he justified, freed me for heaven.
One day he's coming back, glorious day.

Text: J. Wilbur Chapman, 1859–1918
Tune: Charles H. Marsh, 1886–1956; arr. by Evelyn Simpson-Curenton, b.1953, © 2000, GIA Publications, Inc.

More Love to Thee 363

1. More love to thee, O Christ, More love to thee!
2. Once earth-ly joy I craved, Sought peace and rest;
3. Then shall my lat-est breath Whis-per thy praise;

Hear thou the prayer I make On bend-ed knee;
Now thee a-lone I seek, Give what is best;
This be the part-ing cry My heart shall raise;

This is my ear-nest plea:
This all my prayer shall be; More love, O Christ, to thee,
This still its prayer shall be;

More love to thee, More love to thee!

Text: Elizabeth Prentiss, 1818–1878
Tune: MORE LOVE TO THEE, 6 4 6 4 66 44; William H. Doane, 1832–1915

364 My Jesus, I Love Thee

1. My Je - sus, I love thee, I know thou art mine— For
2. I love thee be - cause thou hast first lov - ed me And
3. I'll love thee in life, I will love thee in death, And
4. In man - sions of glo - ry and end - less de - light, I'll

thee all the fol - lies of sin I re - sign; My
pur - chased my par - don on Cal - va - ry's tree; I
praise thee as long as thou lend - est me breath; And
ev - er a - dore thee in heav - en so bright; I'll

gra - cious Re - deem - er, my Sav - ior art thou: If
love thee for wear - ing the thorns on thy brow: If
say when the death - dew lies cold on my brow, "If
sing with the glit - ter - ing crown on my brow, "If

ev - er I loved thee, my Je - sus, 'tis now.
ev - er I loved thee, my Je - sus, 'tis now.
ev - er I loved thee, my Je - sus, 'tis now."
ev - er I loved thee, my Je - sus, 'tis now."

Text: William R. Featherston, 1846–1873
Tune: GORDON, 11 11 11 11; Adoniram J. Gordon, 1836–1895

O How I Love Jesus   365

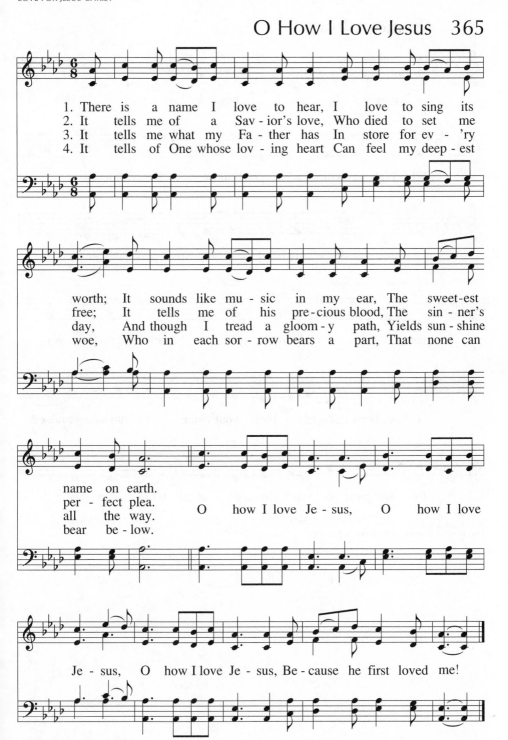

1. There is a name I love to hear, I love to sing its
2. It tells me of a Sav - ior's love, Who died to set me
3. It tells me what my Fa - ther has In store for ev - 'ry
4. It tells of One whose lov - ing heart Can feel my deep - est

worth; It sounds like mu - sic in my ear, The sweet-est
free; It tells me of his pre - cious blood, The sin - ner's
day, And though I tread a gloom - y path, Yields sun - shine
woe, Who in each sor - row bears a part, That none can

name on earth.
per - fect plea.
all the way.
bear be - low.

O how I love Je - sus, O how I love

Je - sus, O how I love Je - sus, Be - cause he first loved me!

Text: Frederick Whitfield, 1829–1904
Tune: HOW I LOVE JESUS, CM with refrain; American melody

366 Precious Jesus

Pre - cious Je - sus, how I love you. How I
lift high my voice with your praise. Ho-ly Spir - it, I im-
plore thee, drench my heart as my lips part your grace.

grace. I am per-suad - ed, Lord, to love you.
I have been changed to bless your name. I am con - strained
by this great gos - pel, for ev - er to wor - ship thee.

Text: Thomas A. Whitfield
Tune: Thomas A. Whitfield; arr. by Thomas W. Jefferson

I Really Love the Lord! 367

Chorus

I real-ly love the Lord! I real-ly love the Lord! You don't know what he's done for me. *Faith is the vic - to - ry. I love him, I love him; I real-ly love the Lord!

*Alternate text: Gave me the victory.

368 Is There Anybody Here Who Loves My Jesus?

Refrain

Is there an-y-bod-y here who loves my Je-sus? An-y-bod-y here who loves the Lord? I want to know if you love my Je-sus; I want to know if you love the Lord?

Verses
unis.

1. ⁝ Hap - py day, oh, hap - py day.
2. ⁝ He taught me how to watch and pray.
3. I went to the val - ley but I did-n't go to stay.

unis.

I want to know if you love the Lord.

When Je - sus washed my sins a - way.
And live re - joic - ing ev - 'ry day.
My soul got hap - py and I stayed all day.

I want to know if you love the Lord.

Text: Jubilee Song
Tune: ANYBODY HERE, Irregular with refrain; Jubilee Song; arr. by Jeffrey P. Radford, 1953–2002, © 2000, GIA Publications, Inc.

369   Lamb of God

1. Your on - ly Son,   no sin   to hide,   But   you have
2. Your gift of love   they cru - ci - fied,   They laughed and
3. I   was so lost,   I should have died,   But   you have

sent   him from your side   To walk up - on   this guilt - y
scorned   him as   he died: The hum - ble King   they named a
brought   me   to your side   To be led by   your staff and

sod,   And to be - come the Lamb   of   God. *(To verse 2)*
fraud, And sac - ri - ficed the Lamb of   God. *(To refrain)*
rod,   And to be called a lamb   of   God. *(To refrain)*

O Lamb of   God,   sweet Lamb of God,   I love the

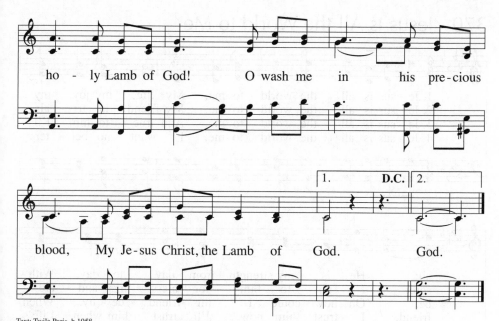

ho - ly Lamb of God! O wash me in his pre-cious

blood, My Je-sus Christ, the Lamb of God. God.

Text: Twila Paris, b.1958
Tune: LAMB OF GOD, LM with refrain; Twila Paris, b.1958
© 1985, Mountain Spring Music/Straightway Music, admin. at EMICMGPublishing.com

370 Jesus Is All the World to Me

1. Je - sus is all the world to me, My life, my joy, my
2. Je - sus is all the world to me, My friend in tri - als
3. Je - sus is all the world to me, And true to him I'll
4. Je - sus is all the world to me, I want no bet - ter

all; He is my strength from day to day, With-
sore; I go to him for bless - ings, and He
be; Oh, how could I this friend de - ny, When
friend; I trust him now, I'll trust him when Life's

out him I would fall: When I am sad, to
gives them o'er and o'er: He sends the sun - shine
he's so true to me? Fol - low-ing him I
fleet - ing days shall end: Beau-ti - ful life with

him I go, No oth - er one can cheer me so;
and the rain, He sends the har - vest's gold - en grain;
know I'm right, He watch-es o'er me day and night;
such a friend, Beau-ti - ful life that has no end;

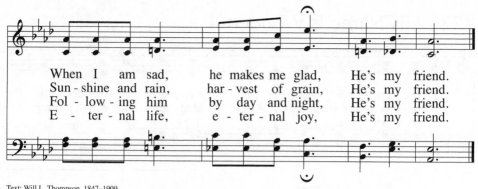

When I am sad, he makes me glad, He's my friend.
Sun - shine and rain, har - vest of grain, He's my friend.
Fol - low - ing him by day and night, He's my friend.
E - ter - nal life, e - ter - nal joy, He's my friend.

Text: Will L. Thompson, 1847–1909
Tune: ALL THE WORLD, 8 6 8 6 88 8 3; Will L. Thompson, 1847–1909

Now Behold the Lamb 371

1. Now be - hold the Lamb, the pre - cious Lamb
2. Ho - ly is the Lamb, the pre - cious Lamb
3. Thank you for the Lamb, the pre - cious Lamb

of God. Born in - to sin, that I may
of God. Why you love me so, Lord, I shall
of God. Be - cause of your grace I can fin -

live a - gain: the pre - cious Lamb of God.
nev - er know; the pre - cious Lamb of God.
ish the race: the pre - cious Lamb of God.

Text: Kirk Franklin, b.1970
Tune: Kirk Franklin, b.1970

372   His Name Is Wonderful

1. His name is Won-der-ful, His name is Won-der-ful,
2. He is the might-y King, Mas-ter of ev-'ry-thing,

His name is Won-der-ful, Je-sus, my Lord;

Je-sus, my Lord. He's the great Shep-herd, the Rock of all

a-ges, Al-might-y God is he; Bow down be-fore him,

Love and a-dore him, His name is Won-der-ful, Je-sus my Lord.

Text: Audrey Mieir, 1916–1996
Tune: Audrey Mieir, 1916–1996
© 1959, 1987, Manna Music, Inc. (admin. by ClearBox Rights)

Bless That Wonderful Name of Jesus 373

Refrain: Bless that won-der-ful name of Je - sus.
1. There's pow - er in the name of Je - sus.
2. There's heal - ing in the name of Je - sus.

Bless that won-der-ful name of Je - sus.
Pow - er in the name of Je - sus.
Heal - ing in the name of Je - sus.

Bless that won - der - ful name of Je - sus,
Pow - er in the name of Je - sus,
Heal - ing in the name of Je - sus,

no oth - er name I know.

Text: Congregational Praise Song
Tune: Congregational Praise Song; arr. by Stephen Key, © 2000, GIA Publications, Inc.

374 Glorious Is the Name of Jesus

Glo - rious is the name of Je-sus, prais - es to his name. Oh,

glo - rious and right - eous and ho - ly is his

name, Oh, glo - ri - ous is his name.

I feel his pres-ence in this place, his Spir - it has con -

trol. Can't you feel his warm em - brace and all the

joy with-in your soul? Oh, glo - ri - ous is his

name, Oh, glo - ri - ous is his name.

Text: Robert J. Fryson, 1944–1994
Tune: Robert J. Fryson, 1944–1994

375 Take the Name of Jesus with You

1. Take the name of Je - sus with you, Child of sor - row and of woe.
2. Take the name of Je - sus ev - er As pro - tec - tion ev - 'ry - where.
3. At the name of Je - sus bow - ing, When in heav - en we shall meet,

1. It will joy and com - fort give you, Take it then wher - e'er you go.
2. If temp - ta - tions 'round you gath - er, Breathe that ho - ly name in prayer.
3. King of kings, we'll glad - ly crown him When our jour - ney is com - plete.

Pre - cious name, O how sweet! Hope of pre - cious name, O how sweet!

earth and joy   of heav-en;   Pre-cious name,   O how

pre - cious name,

sweet!   Hope of   earth   and   joy   of   heav-en.

O how sweet!

Text: Lydia Baxter, 1809–1874
Tune: PRECIOUS NAME, 8 7 8 7 with refrain; William H. Doane, 1832–1915

376 In the Name of Jesus

In the name of Je - sus, in the name of Je - sus,

we have the vic - to - ry. In the name of Je - sus,

in the name of Je - sus, Sa - tan, you have to flee.

Oh, what can ev - er stand be - fore us
(Tell me who can)

when we call on that great name? Je - sus, Je - sus,

Optional Chorus

pre - cious Je - sus, we have the vic - to - ry.

Vic - to - ry, oh, vic - to - ry, we have the vic - to - ry.

Vic - to - ry, oh, vic - to - ry, we have the vic - to - ry.

Text: Congregational Praise Song
Tune: Congregational Praise Song; arr. by Walter Owens, Jr., © 2000, GIA Publications, Inc.

377 Perfect Praise

Oh Lord, how ex-cel-lent, how ex-cel-lent, how

ex-cel-lent, how ex-cel-lent is thy

is thy

is thy

name! Oh There is

is thy

none like you, none like you, none like you,

Je - sus, ex-cel-lent is

is thy

is thy

*Special Chorus

*Begin with tenor line, repeat adding alto, soprano and bass lines respectively.

name!

In all the

Text: Brenda Joyce Moore, © 1989
Tune: Brenda Joyce Moore, © 1989; arr. by Nolan Williams, Jr., b.1969, © 2000, GIA Publications, Inc.

378 Praise the Name of Jesus

Praise the name of Je - sus; praise the name of

Je - sus. He's my Rock, he's my For - tress,

he's my De-liv-er - er, in him will I trust.

Praise the name of Je - sus.

Text: Psalm 18:1; Roy Hicks, Jr., b.1943
Tune: Roy Hicks, Jr., b.1943; arr. by Joseph Joubert, b.1958
© 1976, Latter Rain Music, admin. at EMICMGPublishing.com

So Glad I'm Here 379

1. So glad I'm here in Je - sus' name;
2. Pray* while I'm here in Je - sus' name;

Oh Lord, I'm
Oh Lord, I'll

So glad I'm here in Je - sus' name!
Pray while I'm here in Je - sus' name!

I don't know what you've come to do,

I've come to praise his name,

I've come to praise his name!

*3. Sing while..., 4. Shout while....

Text: Praise and Worship Song
Tune: Praise and Worship Song; arr. by Nolan Williams, Jr., b.1969, © 2000, GIA Publications, Inc.

380 There's Something about That Name

Je - sus, Je - sus, Je - sus! There's just

some - thing a - bout that name!

Mas - ter, Sav - ior, Je - sus! Like the

fra - grance af - ter the rain;

Je - sus, Je - sus, Je - sus! Let all

heav-en   and earth   pro - claim:

Kings   and   king-doms   will   all   pass a - way,   But there's

some-thing   a - bout   that   name!

Text: William J. Gaither and Gloria Gaither
Tune: THAT NAME, 6 8 6 8 6 8 9 8; William J. Gaither
© 1970, Hanna Street Music

381 There Is a Fountain

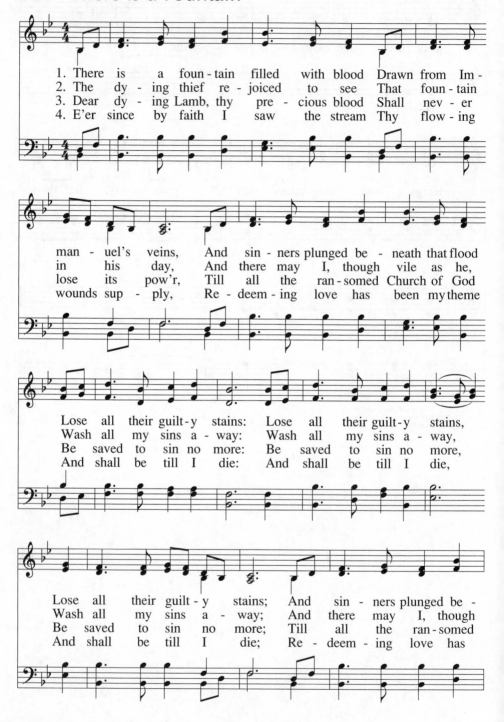

1. There is a foun-tain filled with blood Drawn from Im-
2. The dy-ing thief re-joiced to see That foun-tain
3. Dear dy-ing Lamb, thy pre-cious blood Shall nev-er
4. E'er since by faith I saw the stream Thy flow-ing

man-uel's veins, And sin-ners plunged be-neath that flood
in his day, And there may I, though vile as he,
lose its pow'r, Till all the ran-somed Church of God
wounds sup-ply, Re-deem-ing love has been my theme

Lose all their guilt-y stains: Lose all their guilt-y stains,
Wash all my sins a-way: Wash all my sins a-way,
Be saved to sin no more: Be saved to sin no more,
And shall be till I die: And shall be till I die,

Lose all their guilt-y stains; And sin-ners plunged be-
Wash all my sins a-way; And there may I, though
Be saved to sin no more; Till all the ran-somed
And shall be till I die; Re-deem-ing love has

SAVING BLOOD OF CHRIST

neath   that flood   Lose   all   their guilt - y   stains.
vile   as   he,   Wash   all   my   sins   a - way.
Church   of   God   Be   saved   to   sin   no   more.
been   my theme   And   shall   be   till   I   die.

Text: William Cowper, 1731–1800
Tune: CLEANSING FOUNTAIN, 8 6 8 66 6 8 6; Early American melody

382 I Know It Was the Blood

1. I know it was the blood, I
2. They whipped him all day long, They
3. They pierced him in his side, They
4. He nev-er said a mum - blin' word, He nev-er
5. He hung his head and died, He
6. He's com - ing back a - gain, He's

know it was the blood, I
whipped him all day long, They
pierced him in his side, They
said a mum - blin' word, He nev-er
hung his head and died, He
com - ing back a - gain, He's

know it was the blood for me.
whipped him all day long for me.
pierced him in his side for me.
said a mum - blin' word for me.
hung his head and died for me.
com - ing back a - gain for me.

One day when I was lost   He died up-on the cross.

I know it was the blood   for me.

Text: African American traditional
Tune: IT WAS THE BLOOD, 66 8 with refrain; African American traditional; arr. by Evelyn Simpson-Curenton, b.1953, © 2000, GIA Publications, Inc.

383 The Blood Will Never Lose Its Power

1. The blood that Je - sus shed for me,
2. It soothes my doubts and calms my fears,

Way back on Cal - va - ry,
And it dries all my tears; The

blood that gives me strength from day to day, It will

nev - er lose its pow'r.

It reach-es from the high - est moun - tain.

(moun - tain) And it flows to the low - est val - ley.

(val - ley) The blood that gives me strength from day to

day, It will nev - er lose its pow'r.

Text: Andraé Crouch, b.1942
Tune: THE BLOOD, 86 10 7 with refrain; Andraé Crouch, b.1942; arr. by Nolan Williams, Jr., b.1969
© 1966, renewed 1994, Manna Music, Inc./ASCAP (admin. by ClearBox Rights)

384 I've Got the Joy, Joy, Joy

1. I've got the joy, joy, joy, joy,
2. I've got the peace that pass - eth un - der - stand - ing,
3. I've got the love of Je - sus, love of Je - sus,
4. For there is there - fore now no con - dem - na - tion,

Down in my heart, Down in my heart, Down in my heart;

I've got the joy, joy, joy, joy,
I've got the peace that pass - eth un - der - stand - ing,
I've got the love of Je - sus, love of Je - sus,
For there is there - fore now no con - dem - na - tion,

Down in my heart, Down in my heart to stay.

Text: George W. Cooke, 1848–1923
Tune: I'VE GOT THE JOY, Irregular; George W. Cooke, 1848–1923

Certainly, Lord! 385

1. Have you got good re - lig - ion, Have you got good re - lig - ion,
2. Do you love ev - 'ry - bod - y, Do you love ev - 'ry - bod - y,
3. Have you been con - vert - ed, Have you been con - vert - ed,
4. Have you been to the wa - ter, Have you been to the wa - ter,
5. Have you been bap - tized, Have you been bap - tized,

Cert - 'n - ly, Lord!

got good re - lig - ion, Have you got good re - lig - ion?
love ev - 'ry - bod - y, Do you love ev - 'ry - bod - y?
been con - vert - ed, Have you been con - vert - ed?
been to the wa - ter, Have you been to the wa - ter?
been bap - tized, Have you been bap - tized?

Cert - 'n - ly, Lord!

Last time

Cert - 'n - ly, Lord! Cert - 'n - ly, cert - 'n - ly, cert - 'n - ly, Lord!

Last time

Text: Negro Spiritual
Tune: CERTAINLY LORD, 7 4 7 4 7 4 10; Negro Spiritual; arr. by Evelyn Simpson-Curenton, b.1953, © 2000, GIA Publications, Inc.

386 I've Been 'Buked

1. I've been 'buked an' I've been scorned,
2. Dere is trou-ble all o-ver dis worl',
3. Ain' gwine lay my 'li-gion down,

I've been 'buked an' I've been scorned, chil - dren;
Dere is trou-ble all o-ver dis worl', chil - dren;
Ain' gwine lay my 'li-gion down, chil - dren;

I've been 'buked an' I've been scorned,
Dere is trou-ble all o-ver dis worl',
Ain' gwine lay my 'li-gion down,

I've been talked a-bout sho's you' born.
Dere is trou-ble all o-ver dis worl'.
Ain' gwine lay my 'li-gion down.

Text: Traditional
Tune: I'VE BEEN 'BUKED, 7 9 7 8; Negro Spiritual; arr. by Carl Haywood, b.1949, from *The Haywood Collection of Negro Spirituals,* © 1992

Lord, I Want to Be a Christian 387

1. Lord, I want to be a Chris-tian In my heart, in my
2. Lord, I want to be more lov-ing In my heart, in my
3. Lord, I want to be more ho-ly In my heart, in my
4. Lord, I want to be like Je-sus In my heart, in my

heart; Lord, I want to be a Chris-tian In my heart,
heart; Lord, I want to be more lov-ing In my heart,
heart; Lord, I want to be more ho-ly In my heart,
heart; Lord, I want to be like Je-sus In my heart,

In my heart, In my heart,

Lord, I want to be a Chris-tian In my heart.
Lord, I want to be more lov-ing In my heart.
Lord, I want to be more ho-ly In my heart.
Lord, I want to be like Je-sus In my heart.

Text: Negro Spiritual; adapt. by John W. Work, Jr., 1872–1925, and Frederick J. Work, 1879–1942
Tune: I WANT TO BE A CHRISTIAN, 8 6 8 3 6 8 3; Negro Spiritual; adapt. by Frederick J. Work, 1879–1942

388 I Want Jesus to Walk with Me

1. I want Je - sus to walk with me,
2. In my tri - als, Lord, walk with me,

I want Je - sus to walk with me,
In my tri - als, Lord, walk with me,

All a - long my pil - grim jour - ney,
When the shades of life are fall - ing,

Lord, I want

Je - sus to walk with me.

Text: Negro Spiritual
Tune: WALK WITH ME, 88 8 9; Negro Spiritual; arr. by Nolan Williams, Jr., b.1969, © 2000, GIA Publications, Inc.

Glory, Glory, Hallelujah! 389

1. Glo - ry, glo - ry, hal - le -
2. Friends don't treat me like they
3. I'm goin' home to live with

lu - jah! Since I laid my bur-dens down.
used to Since I laid my bur-dens down.
Je - sus Since I laid my bur-dens down.

Glo - ry, glo - ry, hal - le - lu - jah!
Friends don't treat me like they used to
I'm goin' home to live with Je - sus

1., 2. | **3.**

Since I laid my bur-dens down!
Since I laid my bur-dens down!
Since I laid my bur-dens down!

Text: Negro Spiritual
Tune: GLORY, 15 15; Negro Spiritual; arr. by Nolan Williams, Jr., b.1969, © 2000, GIA Publications, Inc.

390 I Don't Feel No Ways Tired

I don't feel no ways tired

I've come too far from where I've start-ed from.

No-bod-y told me that the road would be eas-y. I

1.
don't be-lieve he brought me this far to leave me.

2.
repeat ad lib.
don't be-lieve he brought me this far I

Last time

don't be - lieve he brought me this far to leave me.

Text: Curtis Burrell
Tune: Curtis Burrell; arr. by Stephen Key and Nolan Williams, Jr., b.1969
© 1978, 1984, Savgos Music, Inc.

Jesus in the Morning 391

1. Je - sus, Je - sus, Je - sus in the morn - ing,
2. Praise him, praise him, praise him in the morn - ing,

Je - sus in the noon - time; Je - sus,
praise him in the noon - time; praise him,

Je - sus, Je - sus when the sun goes down!
praise him, praise him when the sun goes down!

3. Love him...
4. Serve him...

Text: African American folk song
Tune: African American folk song; arr. by Kenneth W. Louis, b.1956, © 2012, GIA Publications, Inc.

392 God Is

Chorus

God is the joy and the strength of my life. He

moves all pain, mis-er-y, and strife. He

prom-ised to keep me, nev-er to leave me, He's

nev-er, ev-er come short of his word. I've got to

fast and pray, stay in the nar-row way. I'll keep my life clean

ev - 'ry day. I want to go with him when he comes back.

I've come too far and I'll nev-er turn back.

God is, God is, God is, God is.

To repeat **D.C.**

God is my all and all.

Final ending

God is my all and all.

Text: Robert J. Fryson, 1944–1994, © 1976
Tune: Robert J. Fryson, 1944–1994, © 1976; arr. by Evelyn Simpson-Curenton, b.1953, and Nolan Williams, Jr., b.1969, © 2000, GIA Publications, Inc.

393 'Tis the Ol' Ship of Zion

Verse 1
rubato

1. 'Tis the ol' ship of Zi - on, 'Tis the ol' ship of Zi - on, 'Tis the ol' ship of Zi - on; Get on board, get on board!

Verses 2-4

2. It has land - ed man-y a thou-sand, It has
3. King Je - sus is the cap - tain, King
4. Hum

land-ed man-y a thou-sand, It has land-ed man-y a
Je - sus is the cap - tain, King Je - sus is the
(hum)

thou-sand; Get on board, get on board!
cap - tain; Get on board, get on board!
Get on board, get on board!

Text: Negro Spiritual
Tune: OL' SHIP OF ZION, 7 7 7 6; Negro Spiritual; arr. by Stanley Thurston, © 2000, GIA Publications, Inc.

394 The Lord Is Blessing Me Right Now

The Lord is bless-ing me right now, Oh, right now! The Lord is now, bless-ing me right now, Oh, right now! He now, woke me up this morn - ing, And start-ed me on my way; The Lord is bless-ing me right

1.

now!   The

2.   *rit.*

now!

Text: Gospel Song
Tune: Gospel Song; arr. by Nolan Williams, Jr., b.1969, © 2000, GIA Publications, Inc.

If You Live Right   395

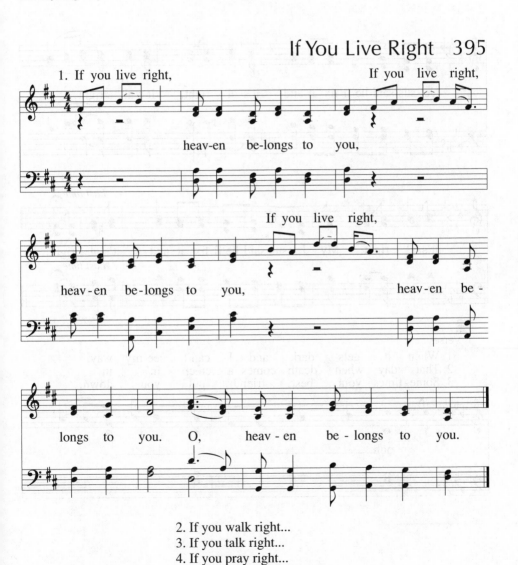

1. If you live right,   If you live right,

heav-en be-longs to you,

If you live right,

heav-en be-longs to you,   heav-en be-

longs to you.   O,   heav-en be-longs to you.

2. If you walk right...
3. If you talk right...
4. If you pray right...
5. Treat your neighbor right...

Text: Congregational Praise Song
Tune: Congregational Praise Song; arr. by James Abbington, b.1960, © 2000, GIA Publications, Inc.

396 It's Alright

Refrain

It's al - right, it's al - right. My

Je - sus said he'll fix it and it's al - right. It's al - right,

it's al - right. My Je - sus said he'll fix it and it's al - right.

Last time

Verses

1. When it gets dark and I can't see my way,
2. That day when death comes a creep - in' in,
3. Some - times your best friend put you down,

ooh

I
I
just

Je - sus said he'll fix it and it's al - right.

know he's gon - na send me a bright - er day.
know you've fought a good fight to the end.
keep your eye on the heav-en - ly crown.

ooh

D.C.

Je - sus said he'll fix it and it's al - right.

Text: Negro Spiritual
Tune: Negro Spiritual; arr. by Bill Cummings, © 2000, GIA Publications, Inc.

397 The Master's Love

1. Car - ing, shar - ing, lov - ing his peo - ple. That's what our
2. Pray - ing, o - bey - ing, lis - t'ning to Je - sus. He is the
3. Bless - ed Sav - ior, we a - dore you. We glo - ri -

Mas - ter does both day and night. Teach - ing, reach - ing,
One who will pro - tect us all. Where he leads us
fy your ho - ly name from a - bove. Let all things be done de - cent -

Last time to Coda

spread - ing the gos - pel. Help - ing his chil - dren learn to
we will fol - low. With hand in hand we know we'll
ly and in or - der. These are the words that show the

1.
do what's right. Ah Ooh

2.
nev - er fall. Lord, we wor - ship you. We pray to you, too.

D.S.
We want to do all the things you've taught us.

Coda
Mas - ter's love. Ah These are the words that show the Mas - ter's love!

Text: Geraldine Woods, ©
Tune: Geraldine Woods, ©; adapt. from Pachelbel's *Canon in D* by Nolan Williams, Jr., b.1969, © 2000, GIA Publications, Inc.

Lord, Be Glorified   398

Text: Bob Kilpatrick, b.1952
Tune: Bob Kilpatrick, b.1952
© 1978, Bob Kilpatrick Music. Assigned 1998 to The Lorenz Corporation.

399 Walk Together, Children

*Walk to-geth - er, chil - dren, don't you get wea - ry,

walk to-geth - er, chil - dren, don't you get wea - ry,

walk to - geth - er, chil - dren, don't you get wea - ry,

there's a great camp meet - ing in the prom - ised land.

We're gon - na walk and nev - er tire,

*Sing, Pray, Work

walk and nev-er tire, walk and

nev-er tire, there's a

great camp meet-ing in the prom-ised land.

Text: Traditional
Tune: Negro Spiritual, arr. Evelyn Simpson-Curenton, b.1953, © 2000, GIA Publications, Inc.

400 Bambelela / Never Give Up

bam - ba, bam - be - le - la. Si - zo bam - be - le - la,
nev - er, nev - er give up. You must nev - er give up,

bam - ba, bam - be - le - la.
nev - er, nev - er give up.

Text: Traditional South African
Tune: Traditional South African; tr. by Mairi Munro and Martine Stemerick; adapt. by Mairi Munro and Philip Jakob
© 2002, JL Zwane Memorial Congregation

Lord, Keep Me Day by Day 401

1. Lord, keep me day by day
2. Lord, keep my bod - y strong
3. I'm just a stran - ger here,

in a pure and per - fect way.
so that I can do no wrong.
trav - 'ling through this bar - ren land.

I want to live ... I want to
Lord, give me grace ... just to run this Chris - tian
Lord, I know ... there's a build - ing some-

live on in a build - ing not made by hand.
race to a build - ing not made by hand.
where, a build - ing not made by hand.

Text: Eddie Williams
Tune: Eddie Williams; arr. by Valeria Foster
© 1959 (renewed), Martin and Morris, Inc., admin. by Unichappell Music, Inc.

402 Great Change Since I've Been Born

Refrain

Great change since I've been born. Great change

since I've been born. Great change since I've been born.

There's been a great change since I've been born.

Verses

Leader: *Choir:*

1. Plac-es I used to go,   I don't go   no more.
2. Things I used to do,   I don't do   no more.
3. Com-pa-ny I used to keep, I don't keep no more.

Plac - es I used to go, I don't go no more.
Things I used to do, I don't do no more.
Com - pa - ny I used to keep, I don't keep no more.

Plac - es I used to go, I don't go no more.
Things I used to do, I don't do no more.
Com - pa - ny I used to keep, I don't keep no more.

D.C.

There's been a great change since I've been born.

Text: African American Prayer and Praise Hymn, c.1900; adapt. by C. Eugene Cooper
Tune: African American Prayer and Praise Hymn, c.1900; adapt. by C. Eugene Cooper
© 1987, 1988, 1991, GIA Publications, Inc.

403 Something on the Inside

1. Some - thing on the in - side, work - ing on the out-
2. Love on the in - side, work - ing on the out-
3. Ho - ly Ghost on the in - side, work - ing on the out-

side,
side, I feel a change in my life.
side,

Some - thing on the in - side, work - ing on the out-
Love on the in - side, work - ing on the out-
Ho - ly Ghost on the in - side, work - ing on the out-

side,
side, I feel a change in my life.
side,

Some - thing on the in - side, work - ing on the out -
Love on the in - side, work - ing on the out -
Ho - ly Ghost on the in - side, work - ing on the out -

side,
side, I feel a change in my life.
side,

I feel a change in my life.

Text: African American Prayer and Praise Hymn, c.1900; adapt. by C. Eugene Cooper
Tune: African American Prayer and Praise Hymn, c.1900; adapt. by C. Eugene Cooper

404 Glory, Glory, Hallelujah!

Refrain

Glo - ry, glo - ry, hal - le - lu - jah! since I laid my, my
Friends don't treat me like they used to, since I laid my, my

bur - dens down. Glo - ry, glo - ry hal - le - lu - jah,
bur - dens down. Friends don't treat me like they used to,

since I laid my, my bur - dens down.
since I laid my, my bur - dens down.

Verses

1. I feel bet - ter,
2. Ev-'ry sit - u - a - tion,
3. Je - sus can han - dle it,
4. All of my prob - lems,

bet - ter, so much

bet - ter,
I   feel   bet - ter,
Ev - 'ry sit - u - a - tion,
Je - sus can han - dle it,
All of my prob - lems,

bet - ter, so much bet - ter.

Text: Negro Spiritual; additional text by Patrick D. Bradley, © 2003, Patrick D. Bradley
Tune: Negro Spiritual; arr. by Patrick D. Bradley, © 2003, Patrick D. Bradley; acc. by Kenneth W. Louis, b.1956, © 2012, GIA Publications, Inc.

405 How Great Thou Art

1. O Lord my God, when I in awe-some
2. When through the woods and for - est glades I
3. And when I think that God, his Son not
4. When Christ shall come with shout of ac - cla -

won - der Con - sid - er all the works thy hands have
wan - der And hear the birds sing sweet - ly in the
spar - ing, Sent him to die, I scarce can take it
ma - tion And take me home, what joy shall fill my

made, I see the stars, I hear the roll - ing
trees, When I look down from loft - y moun-tain
in That on the cross, my bur - den glad - ly
heart! Then I shall bow in hum - ble ad - o -

thun - der, Thy pow'r through-out the un - i - verse dis - played!
gran - deur And hear the brook and feel the gen - tle breeze,
bear - ing, He bled and died to take a - way my sin!
ra - tion And there pro - claim, "My God, how great thou art!"

Then sings my soul, my Sav - ior God, to thee: How great thou art, how great thou art! Then sings my soul, my Sav - ior God, to thee: How great thou art, how great thou art!

Text: Stuart K. Hine, 1899–1989
Tune: HOW GREAT THOU ART, 11 10 11 10 with refrain; Stuart K. Hine, 1899–1989

406 This Is My Father's World

1. This is my Fa-ther's world, And to my list-'ning
2. This is my Fa-ther's world— The birds their car-ols
3. This is my Fa-ther's world— O let me ne'er for -

ears All na - ture sings, and round me rings The
raise; The morn - ing light, sun shin - ing bright, De -
get That tho' the wrong seems oft so strong God

mu - sic of the spheres. This is my Fa-ther's world! I
clares its Mak - er's praise. This is my Fa-ther's world! He
is the Rul - er yet. This is my Fa-ther's world! The

rest me in the thought Of rocks and trees, of
shines in all that's fair; In the rus - tling grass I
bat - tle is not done; Je - sus who died shall be

skies and seas— His hand the won - ders wrought.
hear him pass— He speaks to me ev - 'ry - where.
sat - is - fied, And earth and heav'n be one.

Text: Maltbie D. Babcock, 1858–1901
Tune: TERRA BEATA, SMD; Franklin L. Sheppard, 1852–1930; harm. by Norman Johnson, 1928–1983, © 1966, Singspiration Music (ASCAP)

407 All Creatures of Our God and King

1. All crea-tures of our God and King, Lift
2. O rush-ing wind and breez-es soft, O
3. O flow-ing wa-ter, pure and clear, Make
4. Dear moth-er earth, who day by day Un -
5. And ev-'ry one of ten-der heart, For -

up your voice and with us sing: Al-le-lu-ia!
clouds that ride the winds a-loft, Sing your prais-es!
mu-sic for your Lord to hear. Sing your prais-es!
fold rich bless-ings on our way, Sing your prais-es!
giv-ing oth-ers, take your part, Sing your prais-es!

Al-le-lu-ia! O burn-ing sun with gold-en beam
Al-le-lu-ia! O ris-ing morn, in praise re-joice,
Al-le-lu-ia! O fire so mas-ter-ful and bright,
Al-le-lu-ia! The flow'rs and fruits that in you grow,
Al-le-lu-ia! All you who pain and sor-row bear,

And sil-ver moon with soft-er gleam,
O lights of eve-ning, find a voice.
Pro-vid-ing us with warmth and light,
Let them God's glo-ry al-so show.
Praise God and cast on him your care.

Sing your prais-es! Al-le-lu-ia! Al-le-lu-ia,

al-le-lu-ia, al-le-lu - ia!

6. And you, most kind and gentle death,
   Waiting to hush our final breath,
   Sing your praises! Alleluia!
   You lead to heav'n the child of God,
   Where Christ our Lord the way has trod.
   Sing your praises! Alleluia!
   Alleluia, alleluia, alleluia!

7. Let all things their Creator bless,
   And worship God in humbleness,
   Sing your praises! Alleluia!
   Praise God the Father, God the Son,
   And God the Spirit, Three in One!
   Sing your praises! Alleluia!
   Alleluia, alleluia, alleluia!

Text: *Altissimu, onnipotente bon Signore*; St. Francis of Assisi, 1182–1226; tr. by William H. Draper, 1855–1933, alt.
Tune: LASST UNS ERFREUEN, LM with alleluias; *Geistliche Kirchengesänge*, Cologne, 1623; harm. by Ralph Vaughan Williams, 1872–1958

God Is a Good God 408

Chorus

God is a good God. He's a great God. He can do an-y-thing but fail. He has moved so man-y moun-tains out of my way. God is a won-der-ful God.

Text: Keith Hunter, © 1989, Bridgeport Music, Inc.
Tune: Keith Hunter, © 1989, Bridgeport Music, Inc.; arr. by Stephen Key and Nolan Williams, Jr., b.1969, © 2000, GIA Publications, Inc.

409 God Will Take Care of You

1. Be not dis - mayed what - e'er be - tide,
2. Through days of toil when heart does fail,
3. All you may need he will pro - vide,
4. No mat - ter what may be the test,

God will take care of you; Be - neath his wings of
God will take care of you; When dan - gers fierce your
God will take care of you; Noth - ing you ask will
God will take care of you; Lean, wea - ry one, up -

love a - bide, God will take care of you.
path as - sail, God will take care of you.
be de - nied, God will take care of you.
on his breast, God will take care of you.

God will take care of you, Through ev - 'ry day,

O'er all the way; He will take care of you,

of you.

God will take care take care of you.

of you.

Text: Civilla D. Martin, 1869–1948
Tune: GOD CARES, CM with refrain; W. Stillman Martin, 1862–1935

410 All the Way My Savior Leads Me

1. All the way my Sav-ior leads me— What have I to
2. All the way my Sav-ior leads me— Cheers each wind - ing
3. All the way my Sav-ior leads me— O the full - ness

ask be - side? Can I doubt his ten-der mer - cy, Who through
path I tread, Gives me grace for ev - 'ry tri - al, Feeds me
of his love! Per - fect rest to me is prom - ised In my

life has been my guide? Heav'n - ly peace, di - vin - est com - fort,
with the liv - ing bread. Though my wea - ry steps may fal - ter
Fa - ther's house a - bove. When my spir - it, clothed im - mor - tal,

Here by faith in him to dwell! For I know, what -
And my soul a - thirst may be, Gush-ing from the
Wings its flight to realms of day, This my song through

e'er be - fall me, Je - sus do - eth all things well; well.
rock be - fore me, Lo! a spring of joy I see; see.
end - less a - ges: Je - sus led me all the way; way.

Text: Fanny J. Crosby, 1820–1915
Tune: ALL THE WAY, 8 7 8 7 D; Robert Lowry, 1826–1899

He's Got the Whole World in His Hand 411

1. He's got the whole world
2. He's got the sun and the moon
3. He's got the wind and the rain
4. He's got the lit - tle bit - ty ba - by
5. He's got you and me, broth - er,

in his hand, He's got the whole world
in his hand, He's got the sun and the moon
in his hand, He's got the wind and the rain
in his hand, He's got the lit - tle bit - ty ba - by
in his hand, He's got you and me, sis - ter,

in his hand, He's got the whole world
in his hand, He's got the sun and the moon
in his hand, He's got the wind and the rain
in his hand, He's got the lit - tle bit - ty ba - by
in his hand, He's got ev - 'ry - bod - y here

in his hand, He's got the whole world in his hand.

Text: Traditional
Tune: WHOLE WORLD, Irregular; Negro Spiritual; arr. by Hezekiah Brinson, Jr., b.1958, © 1990

412 Over My Head

1. O - ver my head   I see trou - ble in the
2. O - ver my head   I hear mu - sic in the
3. O - ver my head   I hear sing - ing in the
4. O - ver my head   I see glo - ry in the

air. O - ver my head   I see trou - ble in the
air. O - ver my head   I hear mu - sic in the
air. O - ver my head   I hear sing - ing in the
air. O - ver my head   I see glo - ry in the

air. O - ver my head   I see trou - ble in the
air. O - ver my head   I hear mu - sic in the
air. O - ver my head   I hear sing - ing in the
air. O - ver my head   I see glo - ry in the

air;
air;   There must be a God some - where!
air;
air;

Text: Traditional
Tune: OVER MY HEAD, 11 11 11 7; traditional; arr. by Nolan Williams, Jr., b.1969, © 2000, GIA Publications, Inc.

Awesome God 413

414 Be Still, God Will Fight Your Battles

Verse 1

Leader:

Percussion*
Hand-claps:

1. Be still, God will fight your bat - tles. Be

Bass drum/foot stomps:

All:

1. Be still, God will fight your bat - tles.

still, God will fight your bat - tles. Be

Be still, God will fight your bat - tles.

still, God will fight your bat - tles. God

Be still, God will fight your bat - tles. God

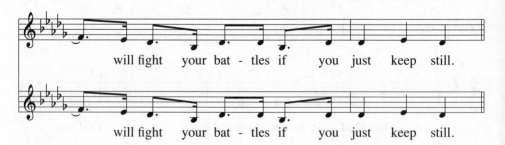

will fight your bat - tles if you just keep still.

will fight your bat - tles if you just keep still.

*Percussion is to be used throughout the piece.

Verse 2

2. *Keep a pray-in', God will fight your bat-tles. Keep a

2. *Keep a pray-in', God will fight your bat-tles.

pray-in', God will fight your bat-tles. Keep a

Keep a pray-in', God will fight your bat-tles.

pray-in', God will fight your bat-tles. God

Keep a pray-in' God will fight your bat-tles. God

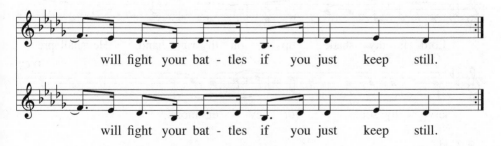

will fight your bat-tles if you just keep still.

will fight your bat-tles if you just keep still.

*3. Keep a waitin', God will fight your battles…
4. Keep a singin', God will fight your battles…
5. I'm a witness, God will fight your battles…

Text: African American traditional
Tune: African American traditional; arr. by Nolan Williams, Jr., b.1969, © 2000, GIA Publications, Inc.

415 My Help Cometh from the Lord

I will look to the hills from whence com-eth my help.

My help com-eth from the Lord. I will look to the hills

from whence com-eth my help. My help com-eth from the

Last time to Coda ⊕ | 1. | 2.

Lord. My help com-eth from the Lord. Lord.

Optional solo:

He will not suf - fer thy foot to be moved. He that

keep - eth thee shall nei-ther slum-ber nor sleep. The

Lord is thy shade up - on thy right hand. He shall pre -

D.C.

serve thy soul for ev - er-more.

⊕ Coda

help com-eth from the Lord. My help com-eth from the Lord.

Text: Psalm 121; Geraldine Woods, ©
Tune: Geraldine Woods; arr. by Nolan Williams, Jr., b.1969, © 2000, GIA Publications, Inc.

For God So Loved the World   416

For God so loved the world that he gave his on-ly be-got-ten Son, that who - so - ev - er be - liev-eth on him should not per-ish, should not per - ish, but they shall have, they shall have ev - er - last - ing life.

Text: Lanny Wolfe, b.1942
Tune: Lanny Wolfe, b.1942; arr. by Evelyn Simpson-Curenton, b.1953
© 1982, Lanny Wolfe Music

417 He Knows Just What I Need

1. There are times when I want to do wrong, so I
2. Some - times in his per - mis - sive will he

go to God in prayer. He com - forts me and he
lets me have my way. When I've fouled up and

guides me a-long. He knows just what I need.
can't re - treat he's there to guard my stay.

He knows just what I need, he a - lone de-cides for

me. Tho' temp-ta - tions come, he is al - ways there, he knows
just what I need. He knows just what I
need, he knows just what I need.

Text: Robert J. Fryson, 1944–1994
Tune: HE KNOWS, Irregular with refrain; Robert J. Fryson, 1944–1994
© 1984, Bob Jay Music Co.

418 He's So Freely Passing Out Blessings

1. He's so free-ly pass-ing out bless-ings each day.
2. He's so free-ly pass-ing out bless-ings each day.
3. He's so free-ly pass-ing out bless-ings each day.

Faith-ful-ly he's send-ing a bless-ing my way;
Touch-ing all he sees a - long his way;
An - sw'ring prayers to him that I have prayed;

More than I have room for, more than I can see.
Al - ways think-ing of me, al - ways bless-ing me.
He knows I'm not wor-thy, yet he bless-es me.

1., 2.

He's so free-ly pass-ing out bless-ings for me.

me. Ev-'ry day he's bless-ing me. He's

bless-ing me. He's bless-ing me. bless-ing me.

He's so free - ly pass-ing out bless-ings for me.

419 Siyahamba / We Are Marching

Si - ya - hamb' e - ku - kha - nyen' kwen - khos',
We are march - ing* in the light of God,

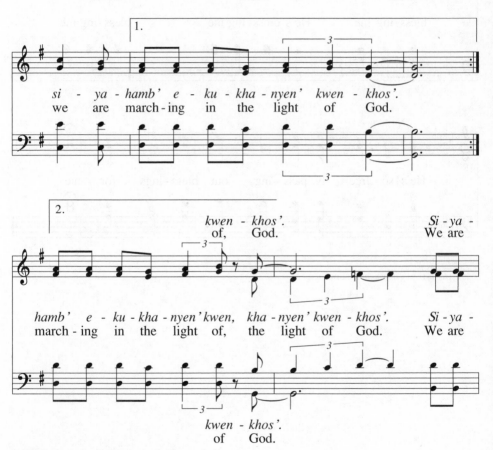

1.

si - ya - hamb' e - ku - kha - nyen' kwen - khos'.
we are march - ing in the light of God.

2.

kwen - khos'.   *Si - ya -*
of, God.   We are

hamb' e - ku - kha - nyen' kwen, kha - nyen' kwen - khos'.   *Si - ya -*
march - ing in the light of, the light of God.   We are

kwen - khos'.
of God.

Alternate text: dancing, singing, praying...

African phonetics:
See-yah-hahmb eh-koo-kah-nyen kwen-kose
See-yah-hahm-bah

Text: South African folk song
Tune: South African folk song
© 1984, Peace of Music Publishing AB, admin. by Walton Music Corp.

420 I Want to Walk as a Child of the Light

1. I want to walk as a child of the light.
2. I want to see the bright-ness of God.
3. I'm look - ing for the com - ing of Christ.

I want to fol - low Je - sus.
I want to look at Je - sus.
I want to be with Je - sus.

God set the stars to give light to the world. The
Clear sun of right - eous - ness shine on my path And
When we have run with pa - tience the race, We

star of my life is Je - sus.
show me the way to the Fa - ther.
shall know the joy of Je - sus.

In him there is no dark - ness at all. The

night and the day are both a - like. The

Lamb is the light of the cit - y of God.

Shine in my heart, Lord Je - sus.

Text: Ephesians 5:8–10, Revelation 21:23, John 12:46, 1 John 1:5, Hebrews 12:1; Kathleen Thomerson, b.1934, © 1970, 1975, Celebration
Tune: HOUSTON, 10 7 10 8 9 9 10 7; Kathleen Thomerson, b.1934, © 1970, 1975, Celebration; acc. by Robert J. Batastini, b.1942, © 1987, GIA
Publications, Inc.

The Word 421

Verse 1

1. The Lord has called us his chil-dren, to gath-er in his name. To cel - e - brate his vic - to - rious Word, to - geth-er as one bod - y in Christ. 2. His

Verse 2

word will al - ways be with us, wheth-er near or far a - way. We hear his call deep in our hearts, as we lis - ten to his word. 3. His

Verse 3

word is our great sal - va-tion. Food for our ver - y be - ing. Oh, lis-ten, oh, lis-ten to his call as his word grows in our hearts.

Text: Llewellyn Gill
Tune: Llewellyn Gill; arr. by Paschal Jordan, OSB, b.1944
© 1998, Antilles Episcopal Conference

422 Is There a Word from the Lord?

Is there a word   from the Lord? Send your Word,   send your Word.

We need a word   from the Lord. Send your Word,   send your Word.

There is heal-ing in   your Word,   de-liv-er-ance in your Word, sal-

va-tion in   your Word.   Send your Word,   send your Word.

send your Word. Your Word can save sin-ners,

re - claim back - slid - ers, en - cour - age be -

1.

2. *Last time*

liev - ers. Send your Word. Your Word can

Last time

Text: Based on Jeremiah 37:17 and Psalm 107:20; Glenn E. Burleigh, 1949–2007
Tune: Glenn E. Burleigh, 1949–2007
© 1998, GIA Publications, Inc.

423 From the Dawning of Creation

1. From the
2. Light ap -
3. Hu - man

dawn - ing of cre - a - tion God was pres - ent in the
peared in deep - est dark - ness. Night was end - ed; morn - ing
eyes have seen God's glo - ry; Hu - man hands have touched God's

Word. And the Word was God e - ter - nal, Will - ing
dawned. And that light is ev - er burn - ing, Bright - ness
own. In our like - ness, here a - mong us, Dwells the

all that came to be. Je - sus is that Word e -
nev - er o - ver-come. Je - sus is that Light e -
Word, in - car - nate God. Je - sus is that Word in -

ter - nal. Je - sus is the Word of life.
ter - nal. Je - sus is the Word of life.
car - nate. Je - sus is the Word of life.

Coda

Text: Delores Dufner, OSB, b.1939, © 1988, 2003, GIA Publications, Inc.
Tune: JULION, 8 7 8 7 8 7; David Hurd, b.1950, © 1983, GIA Publications, Inc.

Oh, the Glory of Your Presence 424

Oh, the glo-ry of your pres-ence;

we, your tem-ple, give you rev-'rence.

Come and rise to your rest, and be blest by our

praise as we glo-ry in your em-brace,

as your pres-ence now fills this place.

Text: Steve Fry, b.1954
Tune: Steve Fry, b.1954
© 1983, Birdwing Music/BMG Songs, admin. at EMICMGPublishing.com

425 In the Garden

1. I come to the gar-den a - lone, While the
2. He speaks, and the sound of his voice Is so
3. I'd stay in the gar-den with him Though the

dew is still on the ros - es; And the voice I hear
sweet the birds hush their sing - ing; And the mel - o - dy
night a - round me be fall - ing; But he bids me go—

fall - ing on my ear, The Son of God dis - clos - es.
that he gave to me With - in my heart is ring - ing.
through the voice of woe, His voice to me is call - ing.

And he walks with me, and he talks with me,

And he tells me I am his own, And the joy we share

as we tar - ry there, None oth-er has ev - er known.

Text: C. Austin Miles, 1868–1946
Tune: GARDEN, 8 9 10 7 with refrain; C. Austin Miles, 1868–1946

426 We Are Standing on Holy Ground

We are stand - ing on Ho - ly Ground,

and I know that there are an - gels all a - round;

Let us praise Je - sus now. We are

stand - ing in his pres-ence on Ho - ly Ground.

Text: Geron Davis, b.1960
Tune: Geron Davis, b.1960; arr. by Nolan Williams, Jr., b.1969
© 1983, Meadowgreen Music Co./Songchannel Music Co.

Something Within 427

1. Preach-ers and teach — ers would make their ap - peal,
2. Have you that some - thing, that burn-ing de - sire?
3. I met God one morn', my soul feel-ing bad,
Refrain: *Some - thing with - in me that hold-eth the reins,*

Fight-ing as sol - diers on great bat - tle-fields;
Have you that some - thing, that nev - er doth tire?
Heart heav-y la - den with a bowed down head.
Some-thing with - in me that ban - ish - es pain;

When to their plead - ings my poor heart did yield,
Oh, if you have it— that Heav - en - ly Fire!
He lift - ed my bur - den, made me so glad,
Some-thing with - in me I can - not ex - plain,

All I can say, there is some - thing with - in.
Then let the world know there is some - thing with - in.
All that I know there is some - thing with - in.
All that I know there is some - thing with - in.

Text: Lucie E. Campbell, 1885–1963
Tune: SOMETHING WITHIN, 10 10 10 10; Lucie E. Campbell, 1885–1963; arr. by James Abbington, b.1960, © 2000, GIA Publications, Inc.

428 He's Blessing Me

Refrain

He's bless-ing me   o-ver and o - ver a-gain.

He's bless-ing me   right here   where   I   stand.

Ev - 'ry time I   turn   a - round he's

mak-ing a way some - how.   O-ver and o - ver a-gain

Last time

he's bless-ing   me.

Verses

Solo:

1. The Lord is   bless-ing me,   bless-ing me right   now.
2. He's in   my   walk, oh yes,   the   Lord is bless-ing   me.

The Lord is   bless - ing me,
He's in   my   talk,   oh   yes,   the

mak-ing a way some - how.   You may not be a - ble, be
Lord   is bless - ing   me.   I   looked at my hands and

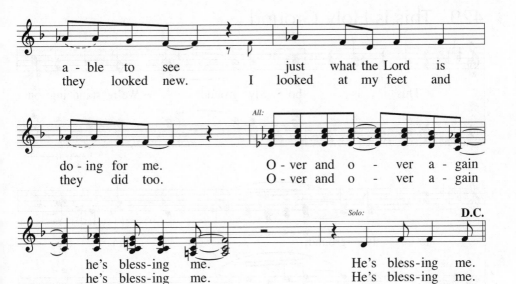

a - ble to see just what the Lord is
they looked new. I looked at my feet and

do - ing for me. O - ver and o - ver a - gain
they did too. O - ver and o - ver a - gain

All:

Solo: **D.C.**

he's bless-ing me. He's bless-ing me.
he's bless-ing me. He's bless-ing me.

Text: Norris O. Garner
Tune: Norris O. Garner
© 1999, Norris Garner/BMI

429 This Is Holy Ground

This is ho - ly ground. We're stand-ing on

ho - ly ground. For the

Lord is pres-ent and where he is it's ho - ly!

This is ho - ly ground. We're stand-ing on

ho - ly ground. For the

Lord is pres-ent and where he is it's ho - ly!

Text: Christopher Beatty, b.1944
Tune: Christopher Beatty, b.1944; arr. by Kenneth W. Louis, b.1956
© Birdwing Music, admin. at EMICMGPublishing.com

O Come, Let Us Adore Him   430

1. O come, let us a - dore him, O
come, let us a - dore him, O come, let
us a - dore him, Christ the Lord.

2. For he alone is worthy,
3. Let's praise his name together,
4. We'll give him all the glory,

Text: St. 1, John F. Wade, c.1711–1786; tr. by Frederick Oakeley, 1802–1880, alt.
Tune: ADESTE FIDELES, 7 7 7 3; John F. Wade, c.1711–1786; arr. by Stephen Key, © 2000, GIA Publications, Inc.

431 Blessed Assurance, Jesus Is Mine!

1. Bless-ed as - sur - ance, Je - sus is mine! O what a
2. Per - fect sub - mis - sion, per-fect de - light, Vi-sions of
3. Per - fect sub - mis - sion, all is at rest, I in my

fore - taste of glo-ry di - vine! Heir of sal - va - tion,
rap - ture now burst on my sight; An - gels de - scend - ing
Sav - ior am hap-py and blest; Watch-ing and wait - ing,

pur - chase of God, Born of his Spir - it, washed in his blood.
bring from a - bove Ech - oes of mer - cy, whis-pers of love.
look - ing a - bove, Filled with his good-ness, lost in his love.

This is my sto - ry, this is my song, Prais-ing my

Sav - ior all the day long; This is my sto - ry, this is my

song, Prais-ing my Sav - ior all the day long.

Text: Fanny J. Crosby, 1820–1915
Tune: ASSURANCE, 9 10 9 9 with refrain; Phoebe P. Knapp, 1839–1908

God Is So Good   432

1. God   is   so   good,   God   is   so   good,
2. He   saved   my   soul,   He   saved   my   soul,
3. I'll   praise   his   name,   I'll   praise   his   name,

God   is   so   good—   O   so   good   to   me.
He   saved   my   soul—   God's   so   good   to   me.
I'll   praise   his   name—   God's   so   good   to   me.

Text: Traditional
Tune: SO GOOD, 4 4 4 5; traditional

433 Come, Thou Fount of Every Blessing

1. Come, thou Fount of ev-'ry bless - ing, Tune my heart to
2. Here I raise mine *Eb-en - e - zer; Hith - er by thy
3. O to grace how great a debt - or Dai - ly I'm con -

sing thy grace; Streams of mer - cy, nev - er ceas - ing, Call for
help I'm come; And I hope, by thy good pleas - ure, Safe - ly
strained to be! Let thy grace, Lord, like a fet - ter, Bind my

songs of loud - est praise: Teach me some me - lo - dious
to ar - rive at home: Je - sus sought me when a
wan - d'ring heart to thee: Prone to wan - der, Lord, I

son - net, Sung by flam - ing tongues a - bove; Praise the
stran - ger, Wan - d'ring from the fold of God; He, to
feel it, Prone to leave the God I love; Here's my

*I Samuel 7:12

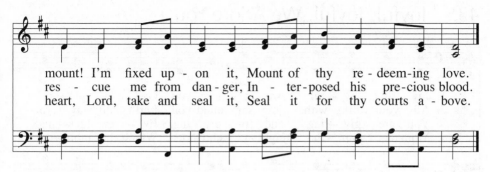

mount! I'm fixed up - on it, Mount of thy re - deem-ing love.
res - cue me from dan - ger, In - ter-posed his pre-cious blood.
heart, Lord, take and seal it, Seal it for thy courts a - bove.

Text: Robert Robinson, 1735–1790
Tune: NETTLETON, 8 7 8 7 D; Wyeth's *Repository of Sacred Music,* 1813

Worship Him 434

Wor - ship him.   Wor - ship him.

Je - sus   Christ   our   Lord.

Wor - ship him.   Wor - ship him.

Je - sus Christ   our   Lord.

Text: Leslie Parker Barnes, © 1991
Tune: Leslie Parker Barnes, © 1991; arr. by Bernadette Blount Salley

435 Joyful, Joyful, We Adore You

1. Joy - ful, joy - ful, we a - dore you, God of glo - ry,
2. All your works with joy sur - round you, Earth and heav'n re -
3. You are giv - ing and for - giv - ing, Ev - er bless - ing,
4. Mor - tals, join the might - y cho - rus, Which the morn - ing

Lord of love; Hearts un - fold like flow'rs be - fore you,
flect your rays, Stars and an - gels sing a - round you,
ev - er blest, Well - spring of the joy of liv - ing,
stars be - gan; God's own love is reign - ing o'er us,

O - p'ning to the sun a - bove. Melt the clouds of
Cen - ter of un - bro - ken praise. Field and for - est,
O - cean-depth of hap - py rest! God our Fa - ther,
Join - ing peo - ple hand in hand. Ev - er sing - ing,

sin and sad - ness; Drive the dark of doubt a - way;
vale and moun - tain, Flow - 'ry mead - ow, flash - ing sea,
Christ our broth - er, Let your light up - on us shine;
march we on - ward, Vic - tors in the midst of strife;

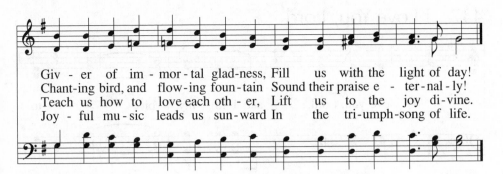

Giv - er of im - mor - tal glad-ness, Fill us with the light of day!
Chant-ing bird, and flow-ing foun-tain Sound their praise e - ter-nal-ly!
Teach us how to love each oth - er, Lift us to the joy di-vine.
Joy - ful mu - sic leads us sun-ward In the tri-umph-song of life.

Text: Henry van Dyke, 1852–1933, alt.
Tune: HYMN TO JOY, 8 7 8 7 D; arr. from Ludwig van Beethoven, 1770–1827, by Edward Hodges, 1796–1867

Praise Him, All Ye Little Children   436

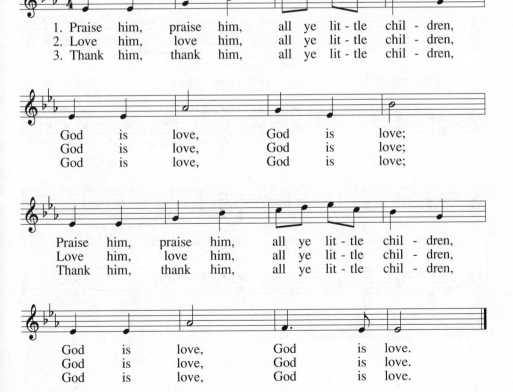

1. Praise him, praise him, all ye lit - tle chil - dren,
2. Love him, love him, all ye lit - tle chil - dren,
3. Thank him, thank him, all ye lit - tle chil - dren,

God is love, God is love;
God is love, God is love;
God is love, God is love;

Praise him, praise him, all ye lit - tle chil - dren,
Love him, love him, all ye lit - tle chil - dren,
Thank him, thank him, all ye lit - tle chil - dren,

God is love, God is love.
God is love, God is love.
God is love, God is love.

Text: Anonymous
Tune: BONNER, 10 6 10 6; Carey Bonner, 1859–1938

437 I Love You, Lord

I love you, Lord, and I lift my voice to wor - ship you, O my soul, re - joice! Take joy, my King, in what you hear: may it be a sweet, sweet sound in your ear.

Text: Laurie Klein, b.1950
Tune: Laurie Klein, b.1950; arr. by Nolan Williams, Jr., b.1969
© 1978, House of Mercy Music, admin. by Music Services

O for a Thousand Tongues to Sing 438

1. O for a thou - sand tongues to sing My
2. My gra - cious Mas - ter and my God, As -
3. Je - sus! the name that charms our fears, That
4. He breaks the pow'r of can - celed sin, He
5. He speaks, and lis - t'ning to his voice, New
*6. Hear him, ye deaf; his praise, ye dumb, Your
7. In Christ, your head, you then shall know, Shall

great Re - deem - er's praise, The glo - ries of my
sist me to pro - claim, To spread through all the
bids our sor - rows cease, 'Tis mu - sic in the
sets the pris - 'ner free; His blood can make the
life the dead re - ceive; The mourn - ful, bro - ken
loos - ened tongues em - ploy; Ye blind, be - hold your
feel your sins for - giv'n; An - tic - i - pate your

God and King, The tri - umphs of his grace!
earth a - broad The hon - ors of thy name.
sin - ner's ears, 'Tis life, and health, and peace.
foul - est clean; His blood a - vailed for me.
hearts re - joice; The hum - ble poor, be - lieve.
Sav - ior come, And leap, ye lame, for joy.
heav'n be - low, And own that love is heav'n.

May be omitted.

Text: Charles Wesley, 1707–1788
Tune: AZMON, CM; Carl G. Glaser, 1784–1829; harm. by Lowell Mason, 1792–1872

439 Praise to the Lord, the Almighty

1. Praise to the Lord, the Al - might - y, the King of cre -
2. Praise to the Lord, who o'er all things is won - drous - ly
3. Praise to the Lord, who will pros - per your work and de -
4. Praise to the Lord! O let all that is in me a -

a - tion! O my soul, praise him, for
reign - ing And, as on wings of an
fend you; Sure - ly his good - ness and
dore him! All that has life and breath,

he is your health and sal - va - tion!
ea - gle, up - lift - ing, sus - tain - ing.
mer - cy shall dai - ly at - tend you.
come now with prais - es be - fore him!

All you who hear, Now to his tem - ple draw near.
Have you not seen All you have need - ed has been
Pon - der a - new What the Al - might - y can do,
Let the "A - men" Sound from his peo - ple a - gain!

Praise him in glad ad - o - ra - tion!
Met by his gra - cious or - dain - ing?
Who with his love does be - friend you.
Glad - ly with praise we a - dore him!

Text: *Lobe den Herren, den mächtigen König;* Joachim Neander, 1650–1680; tr. by Catherine Winkworth, 1827–1878, alt.
Tune: LOBE DEN HERREN, 14 14 47 8; *Straslund Gesangbuch,* 1665

Psalm 8: O Lord, How Excellent   440

O Lord, our Lord, how ex-cel-lent is thy name.

O Lord, our Lord, how ex-cel-lent is thy name.

Text: Psalm 8:1
Tune: Richard Smallwood, b.1948; arr. by Stephen Key, © 2000, GIA Publications, Inc.

441 Praise Him! Praise Him!

1. Praise him! praise him! Je-sus, our bless-ed Re-deem-er!
2. Praise him! praise him! Je-sus, our bless-ed Re-deem-er!
3. Praise him! praise him! Je-sus, our bless-ed Re-deem-er!

Sing, O earth— his won-der-ful love pro-claim!
For our sins he suf-fered and bled and died;
Heav'n-ly por-tals loud with ho-san-nas ring!

Hail him! hail him! high-est arch-an-gels in glo-ry,
He our Rock, our hope of e-ter-nal sal-va-tion,
Je-sus, Sav-ior, reign-eth for ev-er and ev-er,

Strength and hon-or give to his ho-ly name!
Hail him! hail him! Je-sus the Cru-ci-fied.
Crown him! crown him! Proph-et and Priest and King!

Like a shep - herd Je - sus will guard his chil - dren—
Sound his prais - es— Je - sus who bore our sor - rows—
Christ is com - ing, o - ver the world vic - to - rious—

In his arms he car - ries them all day long:
Love un - bound - ed, won - der - ful, deep and strong:
Pow'r and glo - ry un - to the Lord be - long:

Praise him! praise him! tell of his ex - cel - lent great - ness!

Praise him! praise him! ev - er in joy - ful song!

Text: Fanny J. Crosby, 1820–1915
Tune: JOYFUL SONG, 12 10 12 10 11 10 with refrain; Chester G. Allen, 1838–1878

442 To God Be the Glory

1. To God be the glo-ry— great things he hath
2. O per - fect re - demp - tion, the pur - chase of
3. Great things he hath taught us, great things he hath

done! So loved he the world that he gave us his
blood! To ev - 'ry be - liev - er, the prom - ise of
done, And great our re - joic - ing through Je - sus the

Son, Who yield - ed his life, an a - tone - ment for
God; The vil - est of - fend - er who tru - ly be -
Son; But pur - er and high - er and great - er will

sin, And o - pened the life - gate that all may go in.
lieves, That mo - ment from Je - sus a par - don re - ceives.
be Our won - der, our trans-port, when Je - sus we see.

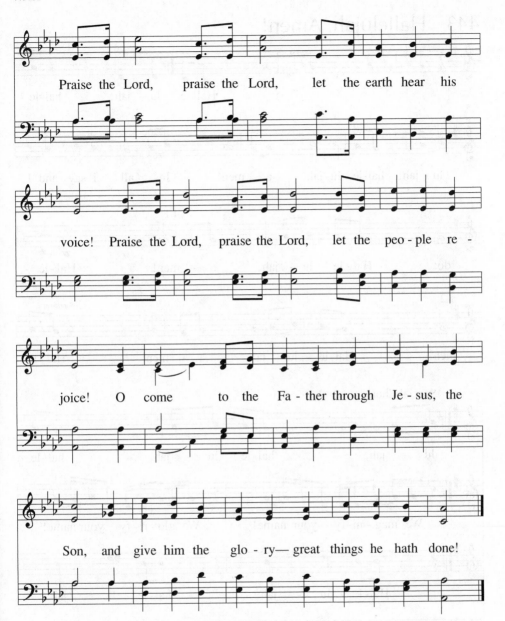

Praise the Lord, praise the Lord, let the earth hear his

voice! Praise the Lord, praise the Lord, let the peo - ple re -

joice! O come to the Fa - ther through Je - sus, the

Son, and give him the glo - ry— great things he hath done!

Text: Fanny J. Crosby, 1820–1915
Tune: TO GOD BE THE GLORY, 11 11 11 11 with refrain; William H. Doane, 1832–1915

443 Hallelujah, Amen!

Hal-le - lu - jah, hal-le -

lu - jah, hal-le - lu-jah, a - men! In all I say and I

do: Hal - le - lu - jah, a - men! Hal-le -

| 1.

| 2.

men! Hal - le - lu - jah, a - men! Hal - le -

Sopranos:

*Special Chorus

lu - jah, hal-le - lu - jah, hal-le -

We mag - ni - fy your name! We glo - ri - fy your name!

Hal-le - lu - jah, hal-le - lu - jah.

Hal - le -

* *Begin with soprano line, then add each part one at a time, increasing in volume and intensity.*

lu - jah, hal - le - lu - jah, hal - le -

For you are wor - thy of the praise!

You are wor - thy of the praise. Oh!

lu - jah!

Sopranos only: *All:*

lu - jah, a - men! Hal - le - lu - jah, a -

men! Hal - le - lu - jah, a - men!

Text: Nolan Williams, Jr., b.1969
Tune: Nolan Williams, Jr., b.1969
© 1994, NEW-J Publishing (a division of NEWorks)

444 Revive Us Again

1. We praise thee, O God, for the Son of thy love, For
2. We praise thee, O God, for thy Spir - it of light, Who has
3. All glo - ry and praise to the Lamb that was slain, Who has
4. Re - vive us a - gain— fill each heart with thy love; May each

Je - sus who died and is now gone a - bove.
shown us our Sav - ior and scat - tered our night.
borne all our sins and has cleansed ev - 'ry stain.
soul be re - kin - dled with fire from a - bove.

Hal - le - lu - jah, thine the glo - ry! Hal - le - lu - jah, A -

men! Hal - le - lu - jah, thine the glo - ry! Re - vive us a - gain.

Text: William P. Mackay, 1837–1885
Tune: REVIVE US AGAIN, 11 11 with refrain; John J. Husband, 1760–1825

I Will Bless the Lord 445

I will bless the Lord at all times. His
praise shall con-tin - u - al - ly be in my mouth.
be in my mouth. In my mouth, in my mouth,
His praise shall con-tin - u - al - ly be in my mouth.

Text: Psalm 34:1
Tune: Shirley M. K. Berkeley; arr. by Valeria A. Foster, © 2000, GIA Publications, Inc.

446 Praise Him!

Refrain

Praise him! Praise him! Praise him! Praise him!
Glo - ry! Glo - ry! In all things give him glo - ry.

Je - sus, bless-ed Sav - ior, he's wor-thy to be praised.

Verse 1

1. From the ris - ing of the sun un - til the go - ing down of the same, he's wor-thy, Je-sus is wor-thy, he's wor-thy to be praised.

D.C.

Verse 2

2. God is our rock, hope of sal - va - tion; A

strong de - liv-er - er   in him will I al-ways trust.

Text: Donnie Harper
Tune: Donnie Harper; arr. by Stephen Key
© 1986, Bud John Tunes, admin. at EMICMGPublishing.com

Jesus   447

1. Je - sus,   Je - sus,
2. I   wor - ship you,   I   wor - ship you,
3. I   love you, Lord,   I   love you, Lord,

Je - sus, Je - sus, Je - sus.

Coda

Je - sus,   Je - sus.

Text: Glen Woodward
Tune: Glen Woodward; arr. by Valeria A. Foster, © 2000, GIA Publications, Inc.

448 Praise God from Whom All Blessings Flow

Praise God from whom all bless - ings flow,

Praise him all crea - tures here be - low.

Praise him a - bove ye heav - en - ly host,

Praise Fa - ther, Son and Ho - ly Ghost.

Peo - ple and realms of ev - 'ry tongue
Sing to the Lord with cheer - ful voice,

Dwell on his love with sweet - est song,
Come ye be - fore him and re - joice,

To him shall end - less prayer be made,
All peo - ple that on earth do dwell,

And end - less prais - es crown his head.
Serve him with mirth, his prais - es tell.

A - men, A - men.

Text: Isaac Watts, 1675–1748, and William Kethe, d.1593; adapt. by Thomas Ken, 1637–1711
Tune: John Hatton, c.1710–1793; adapt. by George Coles, 1792–1858; arr. by Roberta Martin, 1912–1969, © 1968, alt.

We Bring the Sacrifice of Praise   449

We bring the sac-ri-fice of praise in-to the house of the Lord. We bring the sac-ri-fice of praise in-to the house of the Lord. And we of-fer up to you the sac-ri-fic - es of thanks-giv-ing, and we of-fer up to you the sac-ri-fic - es of praise.

450 How Majestic Is Your Name

O Lord, our Lord, how ma-jes-tic is your

name in all the earth. O earth. O Lord,

we praise your name. O Lord, we

mag-ni-fy your name: Prince of Peace, Might-y God; O

Lord God Al-might - y. O y.

Text: Michael W. Smith, b.1957
Tune: HOW MAJESTIC, Irregular; Michael W. Smith, b.1957
© 1981, Meadowgreen Music Co., admin. at EMICMGPublishing.com

Bless the Lord 451

Refrain

Bless the Lord, O my soul, and all that is with-in me, bless his ho - ly

1. name! 2. name! *To verse* 3. name!

Verse

He has done great things, he has done great things,

D.C.

he has done great things, bless his ho - ly name!

Text: Psalm 103:1
Tune: Andraé Crouch, b.1942, © 1973, Bud John Songs, admin. at EMICMGPublishing.com; arr. by Nolan Williams, Jr., b.1969

452 Halleluya! Pelo Tsa Rona / Halleluya! We Sing Your Praises

Refrain

Ha - le - lu - ya! Pe - lo tsa ro - na, di tha-
Hal - le - lu - ya! We sing your prais - es, all our

bi - le ka - o - fe - la. Ha - le - lu - ya! Pe - lo tsa
hearts are filled with glad - ness. Hal - le - lu - ya! We sing your

ro - na, di tha - bi - le ka - o - fe - la.
prais - es, all our hearts are filled with glad - ness.

Verses

1. Ke Mo - re - na Je - so, ya re
2. O na na le bo mang? Le ba -
1. Christ the Lord to us said: I am
2. Now he sends us all out, strong in

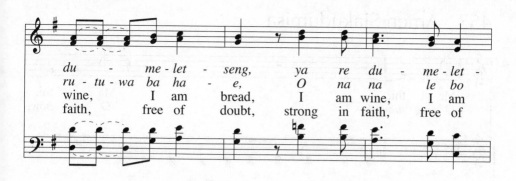

du -		me - let -	seng,		ya	re	du -	me - let -
ru - tu - wa	ba	ha -	e,		O	na	na	le bo
wine,	I	am	bread,		I	am	wine,	I am
faith,	free	of	doubt,	strong	in	faith,		free of

seng	ho	tsa - mai - sa	e - van - ge -	di.
mang?	Le	ba - ru - tu - wa	ba	ha - e.
bread,	give	to all who thirst	and hun -	ger.
doubt,	to	pro - claim the joy -	ful Gos -	pel.

African phonetics:

Refrain

Hah-lay-loo-yah! Pay-loh tsah roh-nah, dee tah-bil-lay kah-oh-fay-lah. (2x)

Verses

1. Lay Mow-ray-nah Jay-zoh, yah ray doo-may-layt-sang, yah ray doo-may-layt-sang,
   hoh tsah-mah-sah ay-vahn-heh-dee.

2. Oh nah nah lay boh mahng? Lay bah-roo-too-wah bah hah-ay. (2x)

Text: South African spiritual (Sotho)
Tune: South African spiritual
© 1984, Peace of Music Publishing AB, admin. by Walton Music Corp.

453 Amen Siakudumisa

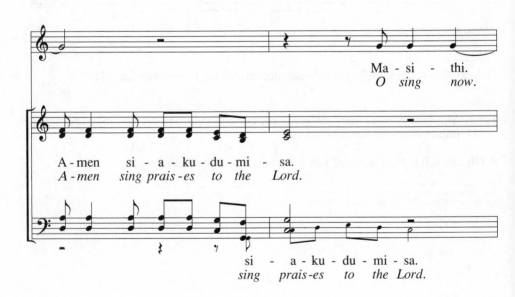

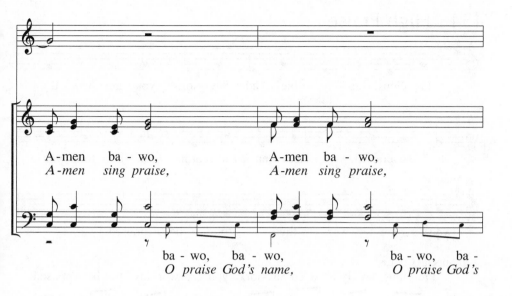

A-men ba - wo,   A-men ba - wo,
A-men sing praise,   *A-men sing praise,*

ba - wo,   ba - wo,   ba - wo,   ba -
O praise God's name,   *O praise God's*

(Omit last time)

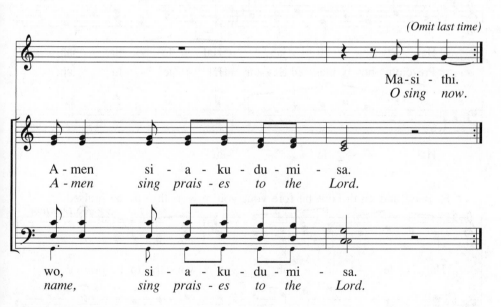

Ma - si - thi.
O sing now.

A - men   si - a - ku - du - mi - sa.
A - men sing prais - es to the Lord.

wo,   si - a - ku - du - mi - sa.
name,   *sing prais - es to the Lord.*

African phonetics:
Mah-see-tee
Amen see-ah-koo-doo-mee-sah

Text: *Amen. Praise the name of the Lord.* South African Traditional (Xhosa); English text, *Hymnal Version*
Tune: Attr. to Stephen C. Molefe, c.1915–1987, as taught by George Mxadana; arr. by John L. Bell, b.1949, © 1990, Iona Community,
    GIA Publications, Inc., agent

454 High Praise

Pre-cious, ho-ly bless-ed Sav-ior, you are wor-thy
to be praised. Heav-en and earth bow be-fore you,
you are wor-thy to be praised.

Special Chorus*
Pre-cious, ho-ly bless-ed Sav-ior, you are wor-thy to be praised.

Hal - le - lu - jah, Hal - le - lu - jah,
Pre-cious, ho-ly bless-ed Sav-ior, Hal - le - lu - jah,

Hal - le - lu - jah,

Heav-en and earth bow be-fore you, you're wor-thy to be praised.
Last time

Hal - le - lu - jah, you're wor-thy to be praised.
Last time

Begin with soprano line, then add each part one at a time.

Text: Margaret Pleasant Douroux, b.1941, © 1989, Rev. Earl Pleasant Publishing
Tune: Margaret Pleasant Douroux, b.1941, © 1989, Rev. Earl Pleasant Publishing; arr. by Nolan Williams, Jr., b.1969, © 2000, GIA Publications, Inc.

Praise You   455

Praise you,

Praise you, praise you, praise you, Let my

life praise you; Praise you, praise you, praise

you, Let my life, O Lord, praise you. Praise

Praise you,

1.

2.

you. Let my life, O Lord, praise you!

Text: Elizabeth Goodine, b.1962
Tune: Elizabeth Goodine, b.1962

456 In the Beauty of Holiness

Come let us wor-ship the Lord in the beau-ty of

ho - li - ness. Come let us wor - ship the Lord

in the beau-ty of ho - li - ness. Give him the hon-

or. Give him the praise.

Come let us wor-ship the Lord; Let's give him the praise.

Text: Nettie L. Sawyer Lester, © 1992, Joy Publishing Co. (SESAC)
Tune: Nettie L. Sawyer Lester, © 1992, Joy Publishing Co. (SESAC); arr. by Stephen Key, © 2000, GIA Publications, Inc.

457 Total Praise

Lord, I will lift mine eyes to the hills

know - ing my help is com - ing from you.

Your peace you give me in time of the storm.

You are the source of my strength.

You are the strength of my life.

I lift my hands in to-tal praise to you.

you. A - men, a - men. A - men.

A - men, a - men. A -

men, a - men. A - men, a -

men, a - men. A - men.

men. A - men.

men. A - men, a - men.

men. A - men, a - men.

458 I Will Call upon the Lord

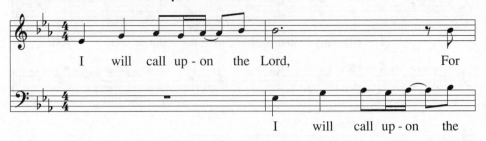

I will call up-on the Lord, For

I will call up-on the

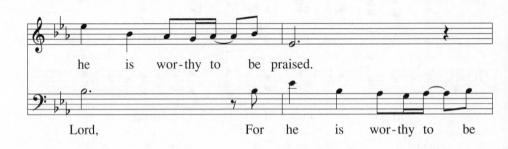

he is wor-thy to be praised.

Lord, For he is wor-thy to be

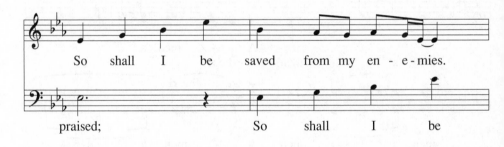

So shall I be saved from my en - e - mies.

praised; So shall I be

div.

The Lord liv - eth, and

div.

saved from my en - e - mies.

bless-ed be the Rock; And let the God of my sal-va - tion be ex -

alt - ed. The Lord liv-eth, and bless-ed be the Rock;

And let the God of my sal-va - tion be ex - alt - ed.

Text: Psalm 18:2, 2 Samuel 22:47; Michael O'Shields, b.1948, © 1981, Sound III, Inc.
Tune: Michael O'Shields, b.1948, © 1981, Sound III, Inc.; arr. by Joseph Joubert, b.1958, © 2000, GIA Publications, Inc.

459 I Love You, Lord, Today

1. I love you. I love you. I love you, Lord, to-day
2. My heart, my mind, my soul be-long to you.

be-cause you care for me in
You paid the price for me way

such a spe - cial way. And yes I praise you. I
back on Cal - va - ry.

lift you up. I mag - ni - fy your name.

That's why my heart is filled with praise.

Text: William F. Hubbard
Tune: William F. Hubbard
© 1985, Chinwah Songs (SESAC)

460 When in Our Music God Is Glorified

1. When in our mu - sic God is glo - ri - fied,
2. How of - ten, mak - ing mu - sic, we have found
3. So has the Church, in lit - ur - gy and song,
4. And did not Je - sus sing a psalm that night
5. Let ev - 'ry in - stru-ment be tuned for praise!

And ad - o - ra - tion leaves no room for pride,
A new di - men - sion in the world of sound,
In faith and love, through cen - tu - ries of wrong,
When ut - most e - vil strove a - gainst the light?
Let all re - joice who have a voice to raise!

It is as though the whole cre - a - tion cried:
As wor - ship moved us to a more pro - found
Borne wit - ness to the truth in ev - 'ry tongue:
Then let us sing, for whom he won the fight:
And may God give us faith to sing al - ways:

Al - le - lu - ia!

Text: Fred Pratt Green, 1903–2000, © 1972, Hope Publishing Company
Tune: ENGELBERG, 10 10 10 with alleluia; Charles V. Stanford, 1852–1924

Know That God Is Good / Mungu Ni Mwema   461

Know that   God is   good.   Know that
Hal - le,   hal - le - lu - jah.   Hal - le,
Mun - gu   *ni   mwe - ma.*   *Mun - gu*

God is   good.   Know that   God is   good,
hal - le - lu - jah.   Hal - le,   hal - le - lu - jah,
ni   mwe - ma.   *Mun - gu*   *ni   mwe - ma,*

God is   good,   God is   good.
hal - le - lu - jah,   hal - le - lu - jah.
ni   mwe - ma,   *ni   mwe - ma.*

African phonetics: Moon-goo nee mway-mah.

Text: Anonymous
Tune: Anonymous; arr. by John L. Bell, b.1949, Iona Community, GIA Publications, Inc., agent

462 How Excellent Is Thy Name

Verses 1, 3

1., 3. Lord how ex - cel - lent is thy name

in all the earth. I will sing prais-

D.S.

Verses 2, 4

2., 4. Let ev - 'ry-thing that has breath, that has breath,

praise the Lord. O Lord, how ex -

cel - lent is thy name in all the earth, how

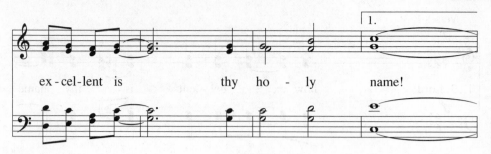

ex-cel-lent is thy ho-ly name!

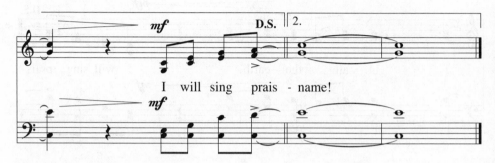

I will sing prais - name!

Text: John W. Higdon
Tune: John W. Higdon; arr. by Joseph Joubert, b.1958
© 1997, 2003, GIA Publications, Inc.

463 Jubiláte, Sérvite / Raise a Song of Gladness

Canon —2 voices

Ju - bi - lá - te   De - o   o - mnis ter - ra.
Raise a song of   glad-ness,   peo-ples of the earth.

Sér - vi - te   Dó - mi - no   in lae - tí - ti - a.
Christ has come,   bring-ing peace,   joy to ev - 'ry heart.

Al - le - lú - ia,   al - le - lú - ia,   in lae - tí - ti - a!
Al - le - lu - ia,   al - le - lu - ia,   joy to ev - 'ry heart!

Al - le - lú - ia,   al - le - lú - ia,   in lae - tí - ti - a!
Al - le - lu - ia,   al - le - lu - ia,   joy to ev - 'ry heart!

Text: Psalm 100, *Rejoice in God, all the earth, Serve the Lord with gladness;* Taizé Community, 1978
Tune: Jacques Berthier, 1923–1994
© 1979, Les Presses de Taizé, GIA Publications, Inc., agent

Praise, My Soul, the King of Heaven   464

1. Praise, my soul, the King of heav - en; To his
2. Praise him for his grace and fa - vor To his
3. Fa - ther - like he tends and spares us; Well our
4. Frail as sum - mer's flow'r we flour - ish, Blows the
5. An - gels, help us to a - dore him; You be -

feet your trib - ute bring. Ran - somed, healed, re - stored, for -
peo - ple in dis - tress. Praise him, still the same as
fee - ble frame he knows. In his hands he gen - tly
wind and it is gone. But while mor - tals rise and
hold him face to face. Sun and moon, bow down be -

giv - en, Ev - er - more his prais - es sing. Al - le - lu - ia!
ev - er, Slow to chide and swift to bless. Al - le - lu - ia!
bears us, Res - cues us from all our foes. Al - le - lu - ia!
per - ish, God en - dures un - chang - ing on. Al - le - lu - ia!
fore him, Dwell - ers all in time and space. Al - le - lu - ia!

Al - le - lu - ia! Praise the ev - er - last - ing King.
Al - le - lu - ia! Glo - rious in his faith - ful - ness.
Al - le - lu - ia! Wide - ly yet his mer - cy flows.
Al - le - lu - ia! Praise the high e - ter - nal one.
Al - le - lu - ia! Praise with us the God of grace.

Text: Psalm 103; Henry F. Lyte, 1793–1847, alt.
Tune: LAUDA ANIMA, 8 7 8 7 8 7; John Goss, 1800–1880

465 Holy God, We Praise Thy Name

1. Ho - ly God, we praise thy name;
2. Hark! the loud ce - les - tial hymn
3. Lo, the ap - os - tol - ic train
4. Ho - ly Fa - ther, Ho - ly Son,

Lord of all, we bow be - fore thee!
An - gel choirs a - bove are rais - ing;
Joins, the sa - cred name to hal - low;
Ho - ly Spir - it, Three we name thee;

All on earth thy scep - ter claim,
Cher - u - bim and Ser - a - phim,
Proph - ets swell the loud re - frain,
While in es - sence on - ly One,

All in heav'n a - bove a - dore thee;
In un - ceas - ing cho - rus prais - ing,
And the white - robed mar - tyrs fol - low;
Un - di - vid - ed God we claim thee;

In - fi - nite thy vast do - main,
Fill the heav'ns with sweet ac - cord:
And from morn to set - ting sun,
And a - dor - ing bend the knee,

Ev - er - last - ing is thy reign.
"Ho - ly, ho - ly, ho - ly Lord!"
Through the Church the song goes on.
While we own the mys - ter - y.

⌐Optional repeat of last eight measures

In - fi - nite thy vast do - main,
Fill the heav'ns with sweet ac - cord:
And from morn to set - ting sun,
And a - dor - ing bend the knee,

Ev - er - last - ing is thy reign.
"Ho - ly, ho - ly, ho - ly Lord!"
Through the Church the song goes on.
While we own the mys - ter - y.

Text: *Grosser Gott, wir loben dich;* ascr. to Ignaz Franz, 1719–1790; tr. by Clarence Walworth, 1820–1900, alt.
Tune: GROSSER GOTT, 7 8 7 8 77; *Katholisches Gesangbuch,* Vienna, c.1774

466 Praise to the Lord

% Refrain

Praise to the Lord, praise him! Praise to the Lord!

Praise to the Lord, praise him! Praise to the Lord!

Verses

1. Shout to God, all you heav - ens, and
2. Know that God is our Fa - ther; he
3. Mer - ci - ful to us sin - ners, com -
4. Praise him, then, with full voic - es and
5. Praise the Lord with the trum - pet, O

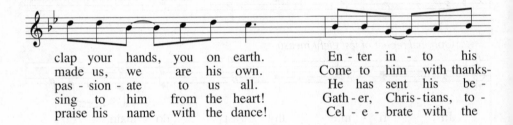

clap your hands, you on earth. En - ter in - to his
made us, we are his own. Come to him with thanks-
pas - sion - ate to us all. He has sent his be -
sing to him from the heart! Gath - er, Chris - tians, to -
praise his name with the dance! Cel - e - brate with the

D.S.

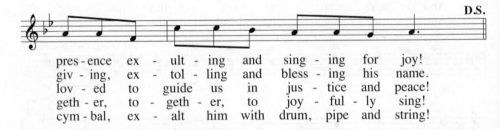

pres - ence ex - ult - ing and sing - ing for joy!
giv - ing, ex - tol - ling and bless - ing his name.
lov - ed to guide us in jus - tice and peace!
geth - er, to - geth - er, to joy - ful - ly sing!
cym - bal, ex - alt him with drum, pipe and string!

Text: Paschal Jordan, OSB, b.1944
Tune: Refrain, anonymous; verses by Paschal Jordan, OSB, b.1944; arr. by Robert J. Batastini, b.1942
© 2012, GIA Publications, Inc.

He's Worthy   467

He's wor-thy of the glo - ry, he's wor-thy of the hon-

or, he's wor-thy of the hon - or, and the praise.

Let ev-'ry knee bow be-fore him, let all the saints a - dore

him. He's wor-thy, wor-thy, wor - thy of the praise.

Text: Robert J. Fryson, 1944–1994
Tune: Robert J. Fryson, 1944–1994
© 1982, Bob Jay Music Co.

468 Come, Magnify the Lord with Me

Verses

1. I will bless the Lord at all times; his praise
2. Glo-ri-fy the Lord with me, to - geth-er
3. Look towards God and be ra - diant, and your fac - es

shall be on my lips. My soul will boast in the
let us praise his name. I sought the Lord and was
may not blush with shame. When the poor cry out the Lord

Lord; the hum - ble will hear and be glad.
heard: from all my ter - rors was set free.
hears them; and res - cues them from all their dis - tress.

Refrain

Come, mag - ni - fy the Lord with me; let us ex -

alt his name to - geth - er. Come, mag - ni - fy the

Lord with me; let us ex - alt his name to - geth - er.

3. geth - er.

A - men, a - men.
A - men, a - men.
A - men, a - men.

A - men, a - men.
men.
A - men, a - men. A - men, a -
A - men, a - men.
A - men, a -

men.
men.
men. A - men, a - men.

Text: Psalm 34; W. Clifford Petty, b.1967
Tune: W. Clifford Petty, b.1967; acc. by Thomas W. Jefferson
© 2002, World Library Publications

469 Holy Is the Lord

Ho - ly, ho - ly, ho - ly is the Lord,

wor - thy of glo - ry, hon-or, and praise. Ho - ly is the

Lord, ho - ly is the Lord. Lord. You are

ho - ly, a ho - ly God. You are Ho - ly, a

ho - ly God. You are ho - ly, a ho - ly God.

Ho - ly is the Lord. Ho - ly is the Lord.

Blessing and Honor and Glory and Power   470

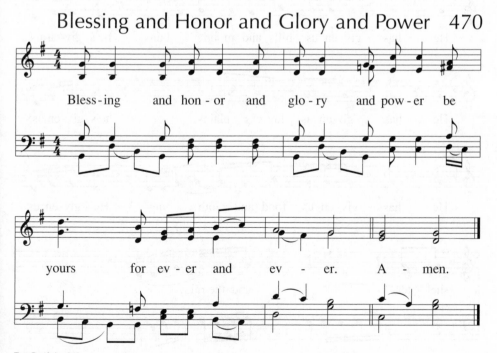

Bless-ing and hon - or and glo - ry and pow-er be

yours for ev - er and ev - er. A - men.

471 I Will Sing Hallelujah

I will sing hal-le-lu-jah, I will sing, O Lord. I will

sing hal-le-lu-jah, O Lord. For you are the source

of my sup-ply; Lord, I lift your name on high. I will

1.
sing hal-le-lu-jah, O Lord. I will
2.
He's giv-en us:

T, B:
He has giv-en us hills and moun - tains, he's giv-en us:

S, A:
He has giv-en us lev-el plains, he's giv-en us:

T, B:
He has giv-en us food and cloth - ing. He's giv-en us

S, A:
shel - ter and the rain.

T, B:
from the storm and the rain.

Text: Donnie Harper
Tune: Donnie Harper; arr. by Kenneth W. Louis, b.1956, © 2012, GIA Publications, Inc.

472 I Worship Thee

Oh Lord, I wor-ship thee;

oh Lord, I wor-ship thee. Lord,

just for who you are, just for keep-ing me this far;

you've been good to me and I do wor-ship thee.

1.   2.

Lord,

just for who you are, just for keep-ing me this far;

you've been good to me and I do wor-ship thee.

To repeat   *Last time*

Lord,

Bless the Lord   473

Cantor:

1. My sis‑ters,   my sis‑ters,   my sis‑ters,

Bless   the Lord,   bless   the Lord,

2. My broth‑ers,

bless   the   Lord: there is   no   oth‑er   God.

2. My brothers...   3. You children...   4. You elders...   5. Together...

Text: Kenyan Folk Song
Tune: Kenyan Folk Song

474 With Hands Lifted Up

Verse 1

1. Praise, you ser-vants of the Lord,
praise the name of the Lord.
Blest be the name, blest be the name,
both now and for - ev - er.

D.C.

Verse 2

2. High a - bove all na - tions is the
Lord; a - bove the heav - ens is God's glo -
ry. Who is like the Lord, our God,
who is en - throned on high, and looks up - on the heav - ens
and the earth be - low?

D.C.

Text: Verses, Psalm 113:1–2, 4–6; refrain by Leon C. Roberts, 1950–1999
Tune: Leon C. Roberts, 1950–1999
© 1998, Leon Roberts. Published by OCP.

475 Let All the People Praise Thee

1. Oh, mag - ni - fy the Lord with me, Ye
2. Oh, praise him for his ho - li - ness, His
3. Had I a thou - sand tongues to sing, The

peo - ple of his choice, Let all to whom he
wis - dom and his grace; Sing prais - es for the
half could ne'er be told Of love so rich, so

lend - eth breath Now in his name re - joice; For
pre - cious blood Which ran - somed all our race; In
full and free, Of bless - ings man - i - fold; Of

love's blest rev - e - la - tion, For rest from con - dem -
ten - der - ness he sought us, From depths of sin he
grace that fail - eth nev - er, Peace flow - ing like a

na - tion, For ut - ter - most sal -
brought us, The way of life then
riv - er, From God the glo - rious

To him give thanks.

va - tion
taught us, To him, to him give thanks.
Giv - er,

Let all the peo - ple praise thee, Let all the peo-ple
Let all, let all Let all, let all

praise thee! Let all the peo - ple praise thy name For -
Let all, let all

ev - er and for-ev - er-more, for - ev - er-more, O Lord! Let more.

Text: Leila N. Morris, 1862–1929
Tune: Leila N. Morris, 1862–1929

476 My Tribute

How can I say thanks for the things you have
done for me— Things so un-de-served, Yet you
give to prove your love for me? The voic-es of a mil-lion
an-gels could not ex-press my grat-i-tude— All that I
am and ev-er hope to be, I owe it all to thee.

Just let me live my life— Let it be pleas-ing, Lord, to thee; And should I gain an-y praise, Let it go to Cal - va - ry. With his

D.S.

Text: Andraé Crouch, b.1942
Tune: MY TRIBUTE; Andraé Crouch, b.1942

Thank You, Lord   477

Chorus

Thank you, Lord, for sav - ing my soul,

Thank you, Lord, for mak - ing me whole;

Thank you, Lord, for giv - ing to me

Thy great sal - va - tion so rich and free.

Text: Seth Sykes, 1892–1950
Tune Seth Sykes, 1892–1950, and Bessie Sykes, 1905–1982
© 1940, Singspiration Music (ASCAP)

478 Count Your Blessings

1. When up-on life's bil-lows you are tem-pest-tossed,
2. Are you ev-er bur-dened with a load of care?
3. When you look at oth-ers with their lands and gold,
4. So, a-mid the con-flict, wheth-er great or small,

When you are dis-cour-aged think-ing all is lost,
Does the cross seem heav-y you are called to bear?
Think that Christ has prom-ised you his wealth un-told;
Do not be dis-cour-aged, God is o-ver all;

Count your man-y bless-ings, name them one by one,
Count your man-y bless-ings, ev-'ry doubt will fly,
Count your man-y bless-ings, mon-ey can-not buy,
Count your man-y bless-ings, an-gels will at-tend,

And it will sur-prise you what the Lord has done.
And you will be sing-ing as the days go by.
Your re-ward in heav-en, nor your home on high.
Help and com-fort give you to your jour-ney's end.

Count your bless-ings, Name them one by one;

Count your bless-ings, See what God has done.

Count your bless-ings, Name them one by one;

Count your man - y bless-ings, See what God has done.

Text: Johnson Oatman, Jr., 1856–1922
Tune: BLESSINGS, 11 11 11 11 with refrain; Edwin O. Excell, 1851–1921; arr. by Evelyn Simpson-Curenton, b.1953, © 2000, GIA Publications, Inc.

479   I Will Bless Thee, O Lord

I will bless thee,   O   Lord!
                     up,
I will bless thee, O
And my mouth filled with

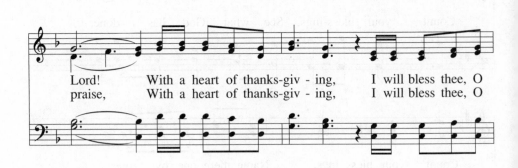

Lord!   With a heart of thanks-giv - ing,   I will bless thee, O
praise,   With a heart of thanks-giv - ing,   I will bless thee, O

1.
Lord!   With my hands lift-ed

2.
Lord!

Text: Esther Watanabe, © 1970, New Song Music
Tune: Esther Watanabe, © 1970, New Song Music; arr. by Nolan Williams, Jr., b.1969, © 2000, GIA Publications, Inc.

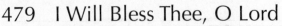

For the Beauty of the Earth   480

1. For the beau - ty of the earth, For the glo - ry
2. For the beau - ty of each hour Of the day and
3. For the joy of ear and eye, For the heart and
4. For the joy of hu - man love, Broth - er, sis - ter,
5. For your Church that ev - er - more Lifts its ho - ly
6. For your - self, best Gift Di - vine, To this world so

of the skies, For the love which from our birth
of the night, Hill and vale, and tree and flow'r,
mind's de - light, For the mys - tic har - mo - ny
par - ent, child, Friends on earth, and friends a - bove;
hands a - bove, Of - f'ring up on ev - 'ry shore
free - ly giv'n; Word In - car - nate, God's de - sign,

O - ver and a - round us lies:
Sun and moon, and stars of light:
Link - ing sense to sound and sight:
For all gen - tle thoughts and mild:
Its pure sac - ri - fice of love:
Peace on earth and joy in heav'n: Lord of all, to

you we raise This our hymn of grate - ful praise.

Text: Folliot S. Pierpont, 1835–1917, alt.
Tune: DIX, 7 7 7 7 with refrain; arr. from Conrad Kocher, 1786–1872, by William H. Monk, 1823–1889

481 Come, You Thankful People, Come

1. Come, you thank-ful peo-ple, come; Raise the song of
2. All the world is God's own field, Fruit un-to his
3. For the Lord our God shall come And shall take his
4. E - ven so, Lord, quick-ly come To your fi - nal

har - vest home. All is safe-ly gath-ered in
praise to yield; Wheat and tares to-geth-er sown,
har - vest home; From his field shall in that day
har - vest home. Gath - er all your peo-ple in,

Ere the win-ter storms be-gin. God, our Mak-er,
Un - to joy or sor-row grown. First the blade, and
All of-fens-es purge a-way, Giv - ing an-gels
Free from sor-row, free from sin, There, for ev - er

does pro-vide For our wants to be sup-plied.
then the ear, Then the full corn shall ap-pear.
charge at last In the fire the tares to cast,
pu - ri-fied, In your pres-ence to a - bide.

Come to God's own tem - ple, come.
Lord of har - vest, grant that we
But the fruit - ful ears to store
Come with all your an - gels, come!

Raise the song of har - vest home.
Whole - some grain and pure may be.
In God's gar - ner ev - er - more.
Raise the glo - rious har - vest home.

Text: Henry Alford, 1810–1871
Tune: ST. GEORGE'S WINDSOR, 77 77 D; George J. Elvey, 1816–1893

Tino Tenda Jesu / Thank You, Jesus, Amen! 482

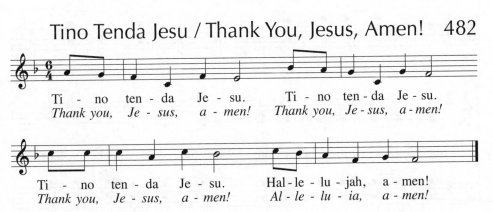

Ti - no ten - da Je - su. Ti - no ten - da Je - su.
Thank you, Je - sus, a - men! *Thank you, Je - sus, a - men!*

Ti - no ten - da Je - su. Hal - le - lu - jah, a - men!
Thank you, Je - sus, a - men! *Al - le - lu - ia, a - men!*

African phonetics: Tee-noe tayn-dah Yay-zoo.

Text: Shona Traditional; tr. by Patrick Matsikenyiri
Tune: Shona Traditional; arr. by Patrick Matsikenyiri
© 1996, GBGMusik

483 I Thank You, Jesus

Text: Kenneth Morris, 1917-1988
Tune: Kenneth Morris, 1917-1988; arr. by Joseph Joubert, b.1958
© 1948 (renewed), arr. © 2011, Martin and Morris Studio, Inc.; admin. by Unichappell Music, Inc.

484 Thank You, Jesus

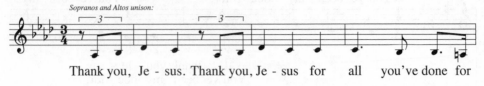

Sopranos and Altos unison:

Thank you, Je - sus. Thank you, Je - sus for all you've done for

me; Thank you, Je - sus. Thank you, Je - sus for Cal - va-ry.

All:

The pain you bore to set me free. All this and

more you have done for me. Thank you, Je - sus. Thank you

Je - sus, I thank you, Je - sus, my Lord and King.

Text: Bernadette Blount Salley
Tune: Bernadette Blount Salley
© 1984, Bernadette Blount Salley. Administered by GIA Publications, Inc.

One More Day   485

1. One more day, one more day, I thank God just for
2. One more chance, one more chance, I thank God just for

one more day. One more day, the Lord has made a
one more chance. One more chance to do the best I

way, I thank God just for one more day.
can, I thank God just for one more chance.

Text: Margaret Pleasant Douroux, b.1941, © Rev. Earl Pleasant Publishing
Tune: ONE MORE DAY, 6 8 9 9; Margaret Pleasant Douroux, b.1941, © Rev. Earl Pleasant Publishing; arr. by Nolan Williams, Jr., b.1969,
    © 2000, GIA Publications, Inc.

486 Let All Things Now Living

Unison

1. Let all things now liv-ing A song of thanks-giv-ing
2. God rules all the forc-es: The stars in their cours-es

To God the Cre - a - tor tri - um-phant-ly raise,
And sun in its or - bit o - be-dient-ly shine;

Who fash-ioned and made us, Pro - tect - ed and stayed us,
The hills and the moun-tains, The riv - ers and foun-tains,

And guides us with care to the end of our days.
The deeps of the o - cean pro - claim God di - vine.

Harmony

God's ban - ners are o'er us, God's light goes be -
We too should be voic - ing Our love and re -

fore us, A pil - lar of fire shin-ing forth in the night,
joic-ing; With glad ad - o - ra - tion a song let us raise

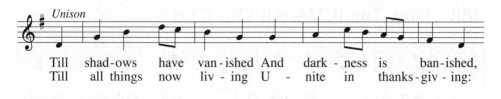

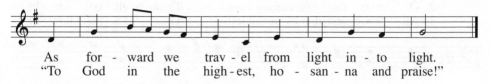

Till shad-ows have van-ished And dark-ness is ban-ished,
Till all things now liv-ing U – nite in thanks-giv-ing:

As for – ward we trav-el from light in – to light.
"To God in the high-est, ho – san - na and praise!"

Text: Katherine K. Davis, 1892–1980, alt., © 1939, 1966, E. C. Schirmer Music Co.
Tune: ASH GROVE, 66 11 66 11 D; Welsh melody; harm. by Gerald H. Knight, 1908–1979, © The Royal School of Church Music

Imela / We Thank You, God 487

I - me - la, i - me - la, i - me - la, O - ka - ka.
We thank you, thank you, God, we thank you for who you are.

I - me - la, Chi - ne - ke. I - me - la, On - y'o - ma.
You have been good to us; we thank you, O great God.

African phonetics:
Ee-may-lah, Ee-may-lah, Ee-may-lah, Oh-kah-kah.
Ee-may-lah, Chee-nay-kay. Ee-may-lah, Oh-nyo-mah.

Text: Nigerian traditional; English adapt. by Nolan Williams, Jr., b.1969, © 2000, GIA Publications, Inc.
Tune: Nigerian traditional, © 1990, Christ Church Gospel Band, Uwani-Engu; arr. by John L. Bell, b.1949, © 1990, Iona Community,
    GIA Publications, Inc., agent

488 Now Thank We All Our God

1. Now thank we all our God With hearts and hands and
2. O may this boun-teous God Through all our life be
3. All praise and thanks to God The Fa - ther now be

voic - es, Who won - drous things has done, In
near us, With ev - er joy - ful hearts And
giv - en, The Son, and him who reigns With

whom his world re - joic - es; Who from our moth-ers'
bless - ed peace to cheer us; Pre - serve us in his
them in high - est heav - en— The one e - ter - nal

arms Has blessed us on our way With
grace, And guide us in dis - tress, And
God, Whom earth and heav'n a - dore— For

count-less gifts of love, And still is ours to - day.
free us from all harm Till heav - en we pos - sess.
thus it was, is now, And shall be ev - er - more.

Text: *Nun danket alle Gott;* Martin Rinkhart, 1586–1649; tr. by Catherine Winkworth, 1827–1878, alt.
Tune: NUN DANKET, 6 7 6 7 6 6 6; Johann Crüger, 1598–1662; harm. by A. Gregory Murray, OSB, 1905–1992

Thank You, Lord 489

1. Thank you, Lord, thank you, Lord,
2. Been so good, been so good,

thank you, Lord, I just want to thank you, Lord.
been so good,

Text: Traditional
Tune: Negro Spiritual; arr. by Stephen Key, © 2000, GIA Publications, Inc.

490 Every Day Is a Day of Thanksgiving

Refrain

Ev - 'ry day   is a   day   of   thanks-giv-ing.

God's been so good to me;   Ev'ry day he's bless-ing me.

Last time to Coda

Take the time to

Ev - 'ry day   is a   day   of   thanks-giv-ing;

glo - ri-fy   the Lord   to-day.

Verse 1

Solo:

1. I thank God for the mo - ments when I wor-ship in his name. I

thank him for the sac - ri - fice of praise. It's no

mys - ter-y to say how my God is ev - 'ry day

mak - ing my way through clouds so dark,

D.C.

bring-ing his light in - to my heart.

⊕ Coda

Glo - ri - fy the Lord to - day. He keeps bless-ing me,

bless-ing me. He o-pens the door that I might see he's

bless-ing me. He keeps bless-ing me,

Take the time to

bless-ing me. glo-ri-fy the Lord,

glo - ri - fy the Lord to - day.

Verse 2

2. Yes, there are pressures all around me
   When fighting Satan's descending powers
   That never cease from trying to bring me down;
   But I just lift my hands to glory
   Believing in God's redemption story;
   Thanking him for his saving grace
   As God gives me power to win this race.

Text: Leonard Burks
Tune: Leonard Burks
© Legré Publishing Co. (BMI)

Jesus Loves Me 491

1. Je - sus loves me! this I know, For the Bi - ble
2. Je - sus loves me! he who died Heav-en's gates to
3. Je - sus loves me! loves me still, Tho' I'm ver - y
4. Je - sus loves me! he will stay Close be - side me

tells me so; Lit - tle ones to him be - long,
o - pen wide! He will wash a - way my sin,
weak and ill; From his shin - ing throne on high,
all the way; If I love him when I die,

They are weak, but he is strong.
Let his lit - tle child come in.
Comes to watch me where I lie. Yes, Je - sus loves me.
He will take me home on high.

Yes, Je-sus loves me. Yes, Je-sus loves me, for the Bi-ble tells me so.

Text: Anna B. Warner, 1820–1915
Tune: CHINA, 77 77 with refrain; William B. Bradbury, 1816–1868

492 Great Is Thy Faithfulness

1. Great is thy faith - ful - ness, O God my Fa - ther,
2. Sum - mer and win - ter, and spring-time and har - vest,
3. Par - don for sin and a peace that en - dur - eth,

There is no shad - ow of turn - ing with thee;
Sun, moon and stars in their cours - es a - bove,
Thine own dear pres - ence to cheer and to guide;

Thou chang - est not, thy com - pas - sions, they fail not,
Join with all na - ture in man - i - fold wit - ness,
Strength for to - day and bright hope for to - mor - row,

As thou has been thou for ev - er wilt be.
To thy great faith - ful - ness, mer - cy and love.
Bless - ings all mine, with ten thou-sand be - side!

Great is thy faith-ful-ness! Great is thy faith-ful-ness!

Morn-ing by morn-ing new mer-cies I see;

All I have need-ed thy hand hath pro-vid-ed,

Great is thy faith-ful-ness, Lord un-to me!

Text: Thomas O. Chisholm, 1866–1960
Tune: FAITHFULNESS, 11 10 11 10 with refrain; William M. Runyan, 1870–1957
© 1923, 1951, Hope Publishing Company

493 He Looked beyond My Fault

A - maz - ing grace shall al - ways be my song of praise,

For it was grace that bought my lib - er - ty;

I do not know just why Christ came to love me so,

He looked be - yond my fault and saw my need.

I shall for - ev - er lift mine eyes to Cal - va - ry,

To view the cross where Je - sus died for me;

How mar - vel - ous the grace that caught my fall - ing soul,

He looked be - yond my fault and saw my need.

Text: Dottie Rambo, b.1934, © 1968, John T. Benson Publishing Co. (ASCAP)
Tune: LONDONDERRY AIRE, 11 10 11 10 D; traditional

494   Love Divine, All Loves Excelling

1. Love di - vine, all loves ex - cel - ling, Joy of
2. Come, Al - might - y, to de - liv - er, Let us
3. Fin - ish then your new cre - a - tion, Pure and

heav'n, to earth come down! Fix in us your
all your life re - ceive; Sud - den - ly re -
spot - less, gra - cious Lord. Let us see your

hum - ble dwell - ing, All your faith - ful mer - cies crown.
turn and nev - er, Nev - er - more your tem - ples leave.
great sal - va - tion Per - fect - ly in you re - stored.

Je - sus, source of all com - pas - sion, Love un -
You we would be al - ways bless - ing, Serve you
Changed from glo - ry in - to glo - ry, Till in

bound - ed, love all pure; Vis - it us with
as your hosts a - bove, Pray, and praise you
heav'n we take our place, Till we sing be -

your sal - va - tion, Let your love in us en - dure.
with - out ceas - ing, Glo - ry in your pre - cious love.
fore the Al - might - y, Lost in won - der, love, and praise.

Text: Charles Wesley, 1707–1788, alt.
Tune: HYFRYDOL, 8 7 8 7 D; Rowland H. Prichard, 1811–1887

495 Amazing Grace!

1. A - maz - ing grace! how sweet the sound
2. 'Twas grace that taught my heart to fear,
3. The Lord has prom - ised good to me,
4. Through man - y dan - gers, toils and snares,
5. When we've been there ten thou - sand years,

That saved a wretch like me!
And grace my fears re - lieved;
His word my hope se - cures;
I have al - read - y come;
Bright shin - ing as the sun,

I once was lost but now I'm found,
How pre - cious did that grace ap - pear
He will my shield and por - tion be
'Twas grace hath brought me safe thus far,
We've no less days to sing God's praise

Was blind but now I see.
The hour I first be - lieved.
As long as life en - dures.
And grace will lead me home.
Than when we'd first be - gun.

Text: St. 1–3, John Newton, 1725–1807, st. 4, attr. to John Rees, fl.1859
Tune: NEW BRITAIN, CM; *Virginia Harmony,* 1831; arr. by Evelyn Simpson-Curenton, b.1953, © 2000, GIA Publications, Inc.

Amazing Grace! 496

1. A - maz - ing grace! How sweet the sound, A -
2. I once was lost, but now am found, I
3. (hum throughout)

maz - ing grace!
once was lost,

How sweet the sound, That
but now am found. Twas

saved a wretch like me! That saved
blind, but now I see. Twas blind,

a wretch like me!
but now I see.

Text: John Newton, 1725–1807
Tune: Meter hymn; arr. by Evelyn Simpson-Curenton, b.1953, © 2000, GIA Publications, Inc.

497 O How He Loves You and Me

1. O how he loves you and me, O how he
2. Je - sus to Cal - v'ry did go, His love for

loves you and me, He gave his life, what
all he did show; What he did there brought

more could he give; O how he loves you, O how he
hope from de - spair: O how he loves you, O how he

loves you, O how he loves you and me.
loves you, O how he loves you and me.

Text: Kurt Kaiser, b.1934
Tune: PATRICIA, 77 4 5 5 5 7; Kurt Kaiser, b.1934; arr. by Nolan Williams, Jr., b.1969, Evelyn Simpson-Curenton, b.1953, and Robert J. Fryson, 1944–1994
© 1975, Word Music, Inc. (ASCAP), admin. by Warner/Chappell

I'm So Glad   498

1. I'm so glad Je-sus lift-ed me. I'm so glad
Je-sus lift-ed me. I'm so glad Je-sus lift-ed me,
I'm glad that
sing-in' Glo-ry, Hal-le-lu-jah, Je-sus lift-ed me!

2. Satan had me bound; Jesus lifted me…
3. When I was in trouble, Jesus lifted me…

Text: African American traditional
Tune: African American traditional; arr. by Evelyn Simpson-Curenton, b.1953, © 2000, GIA Publications, Inc.

499　God Has Smiled on Me

Refrain

God has smiled on me, he has set me free. God has

smiled on me, he's been good to me.

1.

2. Last time

Last time

Verses

1. He is the source of all my joy, He
2. A light un-to my path is he, My

fills me with his love. The grace that I em-ploy,
strength when I would fall. He guides each day for me,

D.S.

He sends down from a - bove.
God is my all and all.

Text: Isaiah Jones, Jr.
Tune: SMILED ON ME, 8 6 6 6 with refrain; Isaiah Jones, Jr.; arr. by Nolan Williams, Jr., b.1969
© 1973, 2000, Davike Music Co./Fricon Music Co.

What Wondrous Love Is This   500

1. What won-drous love is this, O my soul, O my soul!
2. To God and to the Lamb I will sing, I will sing;
3. And when from death I'm free, I'll sing on, I'll sing on;

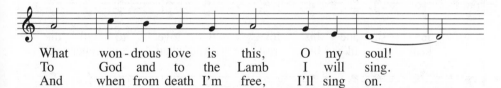

What won-drous love is this, O my soul!
To God and to the Lamb I will sing.
And when from death I'm free, I'll sing on.

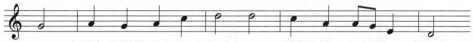

What won-drous love is this that caused the Lord of bliss
To God and to the Lamb, who is the great I AM,
And when from death I'm free, I'll sing and joy - ful be,

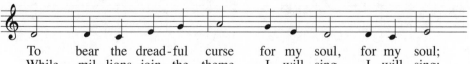

To bear the dread-ful curse for my soul, for my soul;
While mil - lions join the theme, I will sing, I will sing;
And through e - ter - ni - ty I'll sing on, I'll sing on;

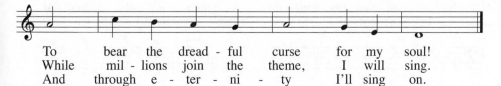

To bear the dread - ful curse for my soul!
While mil - lions join the theme, I will sing.
And through e - ter - ni - ty I'll sing on.

Text: Alexander Means, 1801–1883
Tune: WONDROUS LOVE, 12 9 12 12 9; *Southern Harmony*, 1835; harm. by Richard Proulx, 1937–2010, © 1975, GIA Publications, Inc.

501   I Love to Tell the Story

1. I love to tell the story Of un - seen things a -
2. I love to tell the story, For those who know it

bove, Of Je - sus and his glo - ry, Of
best Seem hun - ger - ing and thirst - ing To

Je - sus and his love. I love to tell the
hear it, like the rest. And when, in scenes of

sto - ry, Be - cause I know it's true; It
glo - ry, I sing the new, new song, 'Twill

sat - is - fies my long-ings As noth - ing else would do.
be the old, old sto - ry That I have loved so long.

I love to tell the sto-ry; 'Twill be my theme in glo-ry.

To tell the old, old sto-ry Of Je-sus and his love.

Text: A. Katherine Hankey, 1831–1911
Tune: HANKEY, 7 6 7 6 D with refrain; William G. Fischer, 1835–1912

502 There Is a Balm in Gilead

Refrain

There is a balm in Gil-e-ad To make the wound-ed whole;

There is a balm in Gil-e-ad To heal the sin-sick soul.

Verses

1. Some - times I feel dis - cour - aged And think my work's in vain, But then the Ho - ly
2. Don't ev - er be dis - cour - aged, For Je - sus is your friend; And if you lack for
3. If you can - not preach like Pe - ter, If you can - not pray like Paul, You can tell the love of

D.S.

Spir - it   Re - vives   my soul   a - gain.   There   is   a
knowl - edge,   He'll ne'er   re - fuse   to   lend.   There   is   a
Je - sus,   And   say,   "He died   for   all!"   There   is   a

Text: Negro Spiritual
Tune: BALM IN GILEAD, 7 6 7 6 with refrain; Negro Spiritual; arr. by Nolan Williams, Jr., b.1969, © 2000, GIA Publications, Inc.

503   Rock of Ages

1. Rock of a - ges, cleft for me, Let me
2. Could my tears for ev - er flow, Could my
3. While I draw this fleet - ing breath, When my

hide my - self in thee; Let the wa - ter and the
zeal no lan-guish know, These for sin could not a -
eyes shall close in death, When I rise to worlds un -

blood, From thy wound - ed side which flowed, Be of
tone— Thou must save, and thou a - lone: In my
known And be - hold thee on thy throne, Rock of

sin the dou - ble cure, Save from wrath and make me pure.
hand no price I bring, Sim - ply to thy cross I cling.
A - ges, cleft for me, Let me hide my - self in thee.

Text: Augustus M. Toplady, 1740–1778
Tune: TOPLADY, 77 77 77; Thomas Hastings, 1784–1872

Your Grace and Mercy 504

Your grace and mer - cy brought me through, I'm liv-ing this mo - ment be - cause of you; I want to thank you, and praise you too: your grace and mer - cy brought me through.

Last time to Coda

D.C.

Coda

mer - cy, your grace and mer - cy brought me through.

Text: Franklin D. Williams
Tune: Franklin D. Williams; arr. by Nolan Williams, Jr., b.1969
© 1993, Malaco, Inc.

505 Can't Nobody Do Me Like Jesus

1. Can't no - bod - y do me like Je - sus. Can't no - bod - y do me like the Lord.
2. Healed my bod - y; told me to run on. Healed my bod - y; told me to run.
3. Picked me up and turned me a - round. Oh, Picked me up and turned me a - round.

Can't no - bod - y do me like Je - sus.
Healed my bod - y; told me to run on.
Picked me up and turned me a - round. Oh,

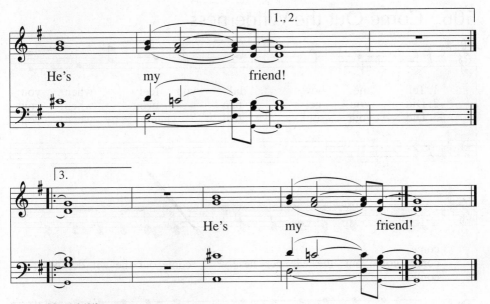

He's my friend!

He's my friend!

Text: Andraé Crouch, b.1942
Tune: HEALING, 9 9 9 3; Andraé Crouch, b.1942; arr. by Nolan Williams, Jr., b.1969

506 Come Out the Wilderness

Solo:

1. Tell me, how did you feel when you
2. Did you get bap - tized when you
3. Did your soul feel hap - py when you

All:

come,
come, come out the wil - der - ness, come out the wil - der - ness,
come,

Tell me,
Did you
Did your

Solo:

come out the wil - der - ness? get how did you feel when you
bap - tized when you
soul feel hap - py when you

All:

come,
come, come out the wil - der - ness, lean - ing on the Lord.
come,

leaning on the Lord, I am leaning on his word. I am

leaning on the Lord who died on Cal-va-ry.

Text: Negro Spiritual
Tune: Negro Spiritual; arr. by Kenneth W. Louis, b.1956, © 2012, GIA Publications, Inc.

507 He's Done So Much for Me

1. He's done so much for me, I can-not tell it all,
2. He washed my sins a-way; I can-not tell it all,
3. He walks and talks with me; I can-not tell it all,
4. He gave me vic-to-ry; I can-not tell it all,

I can-not tell it all, I can-not tell it all.
I can-not tell it all, I can-not tell it all.
I can-not tell it all, I can-not tell it all.
I can-not tell it all, I can-not tell it all.

He's done so much for me, I can-not tell it all.
He washed my sins a-way; I can-not tell it all.
He walks and talks with me; I can-not tell it all.
He gave me vic-to-ry; I can-not tell it all.

I can - not tell it all.

Text: Theodore R. Frye and Lillian Bowles, c.1884–1949
Tune: DONE SO MUCH, 12 12 12 6; Theodore R. Frye and Lillian Bowles, c.1884–1949; arr. by Nolan Williams, Jr., b.1969,
© 2000, GIA Publications, Inc.

We Won't Leave Here Like We Came 508

*We won't leave here like *we came, in Je-sus' name.

Bound, op-pressed, af-flict-ed, sick or lame.

For the Spir-it of the Lord is still the same.

We won't leave here like we came, in Je-sus' name.

*You, I

Text: Rev. Maceo Woods, ©
Tune: Rev. Maceo Woods, ©; arr. by Nolan Williams, Jr., b.1969, © 2000, GIA Publications, Inc.
Administered by GIA Publications, Inc.

509 I Am Redeemed

Chorus

I am re-deemed, bought with a price; Je-sus has changed my whole life. If an-y-bod-y asks you just who I am, tell them I am re-deemed!

Text: Jessy Dixon, 1938-2011, © 1993, Jessy Dixon Music Co., admin. Larry Spier Music LLC
Tune: Jessy Dixon, 1938-2011, © 1993, Jessy Dixon Music Co., admin. Larry Spier Music LLC; arr. by Nolan Williams, Jr., b.1969,
    © 2000, GIA Publications, Inc.

Oh, What He's Done for Me   510

1. Oh, what he's done for me.

Oh, what he's done for me.

Oh, what he's done for me. I

nev-er shall for-get what he's done for me.

2. He took my feet out the miry clay, that's...
3. He feeds me when I'm hungry, that's...
4. He picked me up and turned me around, that's...
5. He gave me a home in glory, that's...

Text: Congregational Praise Song
Tune: Congregational Praise Song; arr. by James Abbington, b.1960, © 2000, GIA Publications, Inc.

511 There's a Wideness in God's Mercy

1. There's a wide-ness in God's mer-cy Like the wide-ness
2. For the love of God is broad-er Than the meas-ures
3. Trou - bled souls, why will you scat-ter Like a crowd of

of the sea; There's a kind-ness in God's jus-tice
of the mind; And the heart of the E - ter-nal
fright - ened sheep? Fool - ish hearts, why will you wan-der

Which is more than lib - er - ty. There is plen - ti -
Is most won - der - ful - ly kind. If our love were
From a love so true and deep? There is wel - come

ful re - demp - tion In the blood that has been shed;
but more faith - ful, We should rest up - on God's word;
for the sin - ner, And more grac - es for the good;

There is joy for all the mem - bers
And our lives would be thanks - giv - ing
There is mer - cy with the Sav - ior,

In the sor - rows of the Head.
For the good - ness of our Lord.
There is heal - ing in his blood.

Text: Frederick W. Faber, 1814–1863, alt.
Tune: IN BABILONE, 8 7 8 7 D; *Oude en Nieuwe Hollantse Boerenlieties en Contredansen*, c.1710

512 Taste and See

Refrain

Taste and see the good-ness of the Lord.

Taste and see the good-ness of the Lord. He's

o-pened doors for me, doors that I just could-n't see.

Oh, taste and see the good-ness of the Lord.

I will bless the Lord at all times. His
praise shall al - ways be on my lips. My
soul shall glo-ry in the Lord, for he's been good to me.
Oh, taste and see the good-ness of the Lord.

Text: Psalm 34; Kenneth W. Louis, b.1956
Tune: Kenneth W. Louis, b.1956
© 2001, GIA Publications, Inc.

513 Have Thine Own Way, Lord!

1. Have thine own way, Lord! Have thine own way! Thou art the pot - ter, I am the clay! Mold me and make me Af - ter thy will, While I am wait - ing, Yield-ed and still.

2. Have thine own way, Lord! Have thine own way! Search me and try me, Mas - ter, to - day! Bright - er than snow, Lord, Wash me just now, As in thy pres - ence Hum - bly I bow.

3. Have thine own way, Lord! Have thine own way! Wound - ed and wea - ry, Help me, I pray! Pow - er all pow - er Sure - ly is thine! Touch me and heal me, Sav - ior di - vine!

4. Have thine own way, Lord! Have thine own way! Hold o'er my be - ing Ab - so - lute sway! Fill with thy Spir - it 'Til all shall see Christ on - ly, al - ways, Liv - ing in me!

Text: Adelaide A. Pollard, 1862–1934
Tune: ADELAIDE, 5 4 5 4 D; George C. Stebbins, 1846–1945

My Faith Looks Up to Thee 514

1. My faith looks up to thee, Thou Lamb of
2. May thy rich grace im - part Strength to my
3. While life's dark maze I tread, And griefs a -
4. When ends life's tran - sient dream, When death's cold,

Cal - va - ry, Sav - ior di - vine! Now hear me
faint - ing heart, My zeal in - spire; As thou hast
round me spread, Be thou my guide; Bid dark - ness
sul - len stream Shall o'er me roll; Blest Sav - ior,

while I pray, Take all my guilt a - way,
died for me, O may my love to thee
turn to day, Wipe sor - row's tears a - way,
then, in love, Fear and dis - trust re - move;

O let me from this day Be whol - ly thine!
Pure, warm and change - less be, A liv - ing fire!
Nor let me ev - er stray From thee a - side.
O bear me safe a - bove, A ran - somed soul!

Text: Ray Palmer, 1808–1887
Tune: OLIVET, 66 4 666 4; Lowell Mason, 1792–1872

515 Keep Me Every Day

1. Lord, I want to live for thee, Ev - 'ry
2. In my weak - ness be my strength; In my
3. Leave me not to walk a - lone, Lest I

day and hour; Let thy Spir - it be with
tri - als all, Be thou near me all the
faint and die; Let thy Spir - it go with

me, In its sav - ing pow'r!
day, Hear my ev - 'ry call!
me, And at - tend my cry!

Keep my heart, and keep my hand,

Keep my soul, I pray! Keep my tongue to speak thy praise, Keep me all the way!

Text: Franklin L. Eiland, 1860–1909
Tune: EVERY DAY, 7 5 7 5 with refrain; Emmet S. Dean, 1876–1936

516 Standin' in the Need of Prayer

1. Not my broth-er, not my sis-ter, but it's me, O Lord,
2. Not the preach-er, not the dea-con, but it's me, O Lord,
3. Not my fa-ther, not my moth-er, but it's me, O Lord,
4. Not the stran-ger, not my neigh-bor, but it's me, O Lord,

Stand-in' in the need of prayer; Not my
Stand-in' in the need of prayer; Not the
Stand-in' in the need of prayer; Not my
Stand-in' in the need of prayer; Not the

broth-er, not my sis-ter, but it's me, O Lord,
preach-er, not the dea-con, but it's me, O Lord,
fa-ther, not my moth-er, but it's me, O Lord,
stran-ger, not my neigh-bor, but it's me, O Lord,

Stand-in' in the need of prayer.
Stand-in' in the need of prayer.
Stand-in' in the need of prayer.
Stand-in' in the need of prayer.

It's me,

It's me, it's me, O Lord,

It's me,

Stand-in' in the need of prayer; It's me, it's

me, O Lord, Stand-in' in the need of prayer.

Text: Negro Spiritual
Tune: STANDIN' IN THE NEED; 13 7 13 7 with refrain; Negro Spiritual

517 Sweet Hour of Prayer

1. Sweet hour of prayer, sweet hour of prayer, That calls me
2. Sweet hour of prayer, sweet hour of prayer, Thy wings shall
3. Sweet hour of prayer, sweet hour of prayer, May I thy

from a world of care And bids me at my
my pe - ti - tion bear To him whose truth and
con - so - la - tion share, Till from Mount Pis - gah's

Fa - ther's throne Make all my wants and wish - es known!
faith - ful - ness En - gage the wait - ing soul to bless;
loft - y height I view my home and take my flight:

In sea - sons of dis - tress and grief My soul has of - ten
And since he bids me seek his face, Be - lieve his word and
This robe of flesh I'll drop, and rise To seize the ev - er -

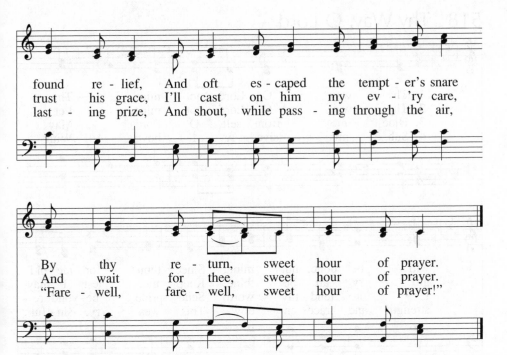

found   re - lief,   And   oft   es - caped   the   tempt - er's snare
trust   his   grace,   I'll   cast   on   him   my   ev - 'ry   care,
last - ing   prize,   And   shout,   while   pass - ing through   the   air,

By   thy   re - turn,   sweet   hour   of   prayer.
And   wait   for   thee,   sweet   hour   of   prayer.
"Fare - well,   fare - well,   sweet   hour   of   prayer!"

Text: William W. Walford, 1772–1850
Tune: SWEET HOUR, LMD; William B. Bradbury, 1816–1868

518 Thy Way, O Lord

1. Thy way, O Lord, not mine, Thy will be done, not mine; Since thou for me did bleed, And now do in-ter-cede, Each day I sim-ply plead, Thy will be done.

2. Thy way, O Lord, not mine, Let glo-ry all be thine; Keep me, lest I may stray, Near thee from day to day; Teach me to watch and pray, Thy will be done.

3. Hide me from self, O Lord, May I at-tend thy word; Send pride be-yond re-call, Let each as-sail-er fall, Be thou my all in all, Thy will be done.

4. Sub-mis-sive-ly I bow; With strength and grace en-dow This wea-ry, sin-ful heart; Shield from each cru-el dart; May I from thee ne'er part, Thy will be done.

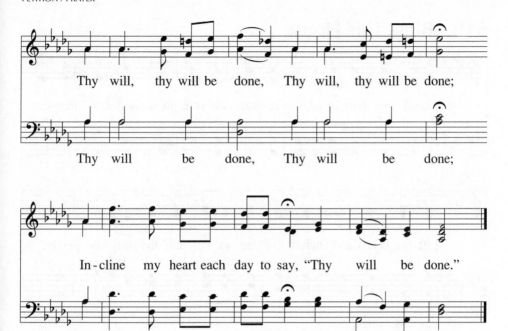

Thy will, thy will be done, Thy will, thy will be done;

Thy will be done, Thy will be done;

In-cline my heart each day to say, "Thy will be done."

Text: Nina B. Jackson
Tune: THY WAY, 66 666 4 with refrain; Edward C. Deas

519 Bless This House

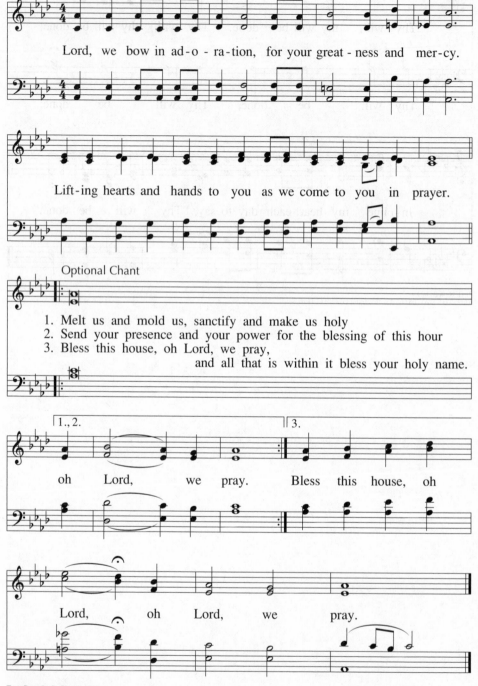

Lord, we bow in ad-o-ra-tion, for your great-ness and mer-cy.

Lift-ing hearts and hands to you as we come to you in prayer.

Optional Chant

1. Melt us and mold us, sanctify and make us holy
2. Send your presence and your power for the blessing of this hour
3. Bless this house, oh Lord, we pray,
   and all that is within it bless your holy name.

1., 2.

oh Lord, we pray.

3.

Bless this house, oh

Lord, oh Lord, we pray.

Text: Betty D. Gadling, b.1921
Tune: Betty D. Gadling, b.1921
© 1994, Betty D. Gadling. Administered by GIA Publications, Inc.

I Need Thee Every Hour   520

1. I need thee ev-'ry hour, Most gra - cious Lord;
2. I need thee ev-'ry hour, Stay thou near - by;
3. I need thee ev-'ry hour, In joy or pain;
4. I need thee ev-'ry hour, Teach me thy will;

No ten - der voice like thine Can peace af - ford.
Temp - ta - tions lose their pow'r When thou art nigh.
Come quick - ly and a - bide, Or life is vain.
And thy rich prom - is - es In me ful - fill.

I need thee, O I need thee; Ev - 'ry hour I need thee;

O bless me now, my Sav - ior, I come to thee.

Text: Annie S. Hawkes, 1835–1918
Tune: NEED, 6 4 6 4 with refrain; Robert Lowry, 1826–1899

521 Acceptable to You

Let the words of my mouth and the med-i-ta-tion of my

heart be ac-cept-a-ble in thy sight. Let the

cept-a-ble Lord, to thee. Here I am, Lord,

at your feet, Lord, My soul looks up to

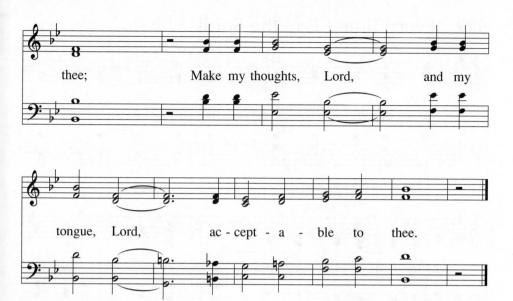

thee; Make my thoughts, Lord, and my

tongue, Lord, ac - cept - a - ble to thee.

Text: Eli Wilson, Jr.
Tune: Eli Wilson, Jr.
© 1989, Chenaniah Publications, Inc.

522 Every Time I Feel the Spirit

Refrain

Ev - 'ry time I feel the Spir - it mov - ing in my heart, I will pray. Ev - 'ry time I feel the Spir - it mov - ing in my heart, I will pray.

Verses

1. Up - on the moun - tain when my God spoke,
   All a - round me, it looked so shine,
2. 'Ol Jor - dan Riv - er, chill - y and cold,
   There ain't but one train that's on this track,

D.C.

Out of God's mouth came fire and smoke.
I asked my Lord if all was mine.
It chills the bod - y, but not the soul.
It runs to heav - en and runs right back.

Text: Negro Spiritual
Tune: FEEL THE SPIRIT, 98 98 with refrain; Negro Spiritual; arr. by Nolan Williams, Jr., b.1969, © 2000, GIA Publications, Inc.

Sanctuary 523

Lord, pre - pare me to be a sanc-tu - ar - y, pure and

ho - ly, tried and true; with thanks-giv - ing, I'll be a

liv - ing sanc-tu - ar - y for you.

Text: John Thompson, b.1950 and Randy Scruggs
Tune: John Thompson, b.1950 and Randy Scruggs
© 1982, Full Armor Music and Whole Armor Music

524   This Day

Give us this day our dai - ly bread. You said you would sup - ply all my needs ac - cord - ing to your rich - es. I have but to ask and I shall re - ceive. To go from here and share this love you gave to me, to show some - one who's lost and help them find their

way, the way to truth and faith so they can be free like

me, free like me. Lord, we need your love.

Lord, we need your peace. Lord, we need your joy this

day. Thank you for this day. Lord, we thank you for this day.

day.

Text: Edwin Hawkins, b.1943
Tune: Edwin Hawkins, b.1943; arr. by Stephen Key, © 2000, GIA Publications, Inc.

525 I Am Thine

1. I am thine, O Lord, I have heard thy voice, And it
2. Con - se - crate me now to thy serv - ice, Lord, By the
3. O, the pure de - light of a sin - gle hour That be -
4. There are depths of love that I can - not know Till I

told thy love to me; But I long to rise in the
pow'r of grace di - vine; Let my soul look up with a
fore thy throne I spend, When I kneel in prayer, and with
cross the nar - row sea; There are heights of joy that I

arms of faith, And be clos - er drawn to thee.
stead - fast hope, And my will be lost in thine.
thee, my God, I com - mune as friend with friend!
may not reach Till I rest in peace with thee.

near - er,

Draw me near - er, near - er, near - er, bless-ed Lord, To the

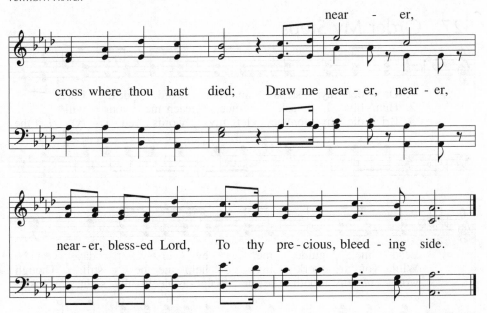

near - er,

cross where thou hast died; Draw me near - er, near - er,

near - er, bless-ed Lord, To thy pre - cious, bleed - ing side.

Text: Fanny J. Crosby, 1820–1915
Tune: I AM THINE, 10 7 10 7 with refrain; William H. Doane, 1832–1915

Remember Me 526

freely

1. Re - mem - ber me, re - mem - ber
2. Fa - ther I stretch my hands to
3. If thou with - draw thy - self from

me, Oh Lord, re - mem - ber me.
thee, no oth - er help I know.
me, Oh whith - er shall I go?

Text: Congregational Praise Song
Tune: Congregational Praise Song; harm. by Leon C. Roberts, 1950–1999, from *Mass of St. Augustine,* © 1981, GIA Publications, Inc.

527 Order My Steps

1. Or - der my steps in your word, dear Lord,
2. Hum - bly I ask thee, teach me your will.
3. Bri - dle my tongue, let my words ed - i - fy, Let the

Lead me, guide me, ev - er - y day.
While you are work - ing, help me be still. Though
words of my mouth be ac - cept - a - ble in thy sight. Take

Send your a - noint - ing, Fa - ther, I pray.
Sa - tan is bus - y, God is real!
charge of my thoughts, both day and night.

Or - der my steps in your word. Please,

or - der my steps in your word. word. I want to walk

wor - thy.   My   call - ing   to ful - fill.

Please or-der my   steps,   Lord,   And I'll

do   your bless - ed will,   The world is ev - er

chang - ing,   but   you are still   the same.

If you or-der my   steps,   I'll   praise   your

1.

name.   I want to walk

2.

528 Come by Here, My Lord

1. Come by here, my Lord, come by here. Come by here, my Lord, come by here. Oh Lord, come by here.
2. Some-one needs you, Lord, come by here. Some-one needs you, Lord, come by here. Oh Lord, come by here.
3. Some-one's pray - in', Lord, come by here. Some-one's pray - in', Lord, come by here. Oh Lord, come by here.
4. Kum Ba Yah, my Lord, come by here. Kum Ba Yah, my Lord, come by here. Oh Lord, come by here.

Text: Negro Spiritual
Tune: DESMOND, 8885; Negro Spiritual; arr. by Evelyn Simpson-Curenton, b.1953, © 2000, GIA Publications, Inc.

Lord, Make Me More Holy 529

1. Lord, make me more ho - ly, Lord, make me more ho - ly, Lord, make me more ho - ly, un - til we meet a - gain. Ho - ly, ho - ly, ho - ly, un - til we meet a - gain.
2. Lord, make me more faith - ful, Lord, make me more faith - ful, Lord, make me more faith - ful, un - til we meet a - gain. Faith - ful, faith - ful, faith - ful, un - til we meet a - gain.
3. Lord, make me more hum - ble, Lord, make me more hum - ble, Lord, make me more hum - ble, un - til we meet a - gain. Hum - ble, hum - ble, hum - ble, un - til we meet a - gain.
4. Lord, make me more right - eous, Lord, make me more right - eous, Lord, make me more right - eous, un - til we meet a - gain. Right - eous, right - eous, right - eous, un - til we meet a - gain.

Text: African American traditional
Tune: African American traditional

530 Lead Me, Lord

Lead me, Lord, lead me in thy right-eous-ness,

Make thy way plain be - fore my face.

Optional Ending

For it is thou, Lord, thou, Lord on - ly, that

mak - est me dwell in safe - ty.

Text: Psalm 5:8
Tune: Samuel Sebastian Wesley, 1810–1876

Oh Lord, Have Mercy 531

1. Oh Lord, have mer - cy. Oh Lord, have
2. While I am pray - ing, While I am
3. While I am wait - ing, While I am
4. When I'm in trou - ble, When I'm in
5. I am your child, I am your

mer - cy. Oh Lord, have mer - cy,
pray - ing, While I am pray - ing,
wait - ing, While I am wait - ing, Have
trou - ble, When I'm in trou - ble,
child, I am your child,

mer - cy on me.

Text: Traditional
Tune: HAVE MERCY ON ME, 5 5 5 5; traditional; arr. by Joseph Joubert, b.1958, © 2000, GIA Publications, Inc.

532 Until I Found the Lord

1. Lord, I prayed and I prayed, prayed all night long,
Oh Lord, I prayed and I prayed, un-til I found the Lord,
Oh Lord, I
My Lord
My soul My soul
just could-n't rest con-tent-ed,
My soul
just could-n't rest con-tent-ed,
Lord, I

just could-n't rest con-tent-ed, un-til I found the Lord.

2. Lord, I cried and I cried,...
3. Lord, I moaned and I moaned,...

O Lord, Hear My Prayer 533

Ostinato Refrain

O Lord, hear my prayer, O Lord, hear my prayer:

when I call an-swer me. O Lord, hear my prayer, O

Last time

Lord, hear my prayer. Come and lis-ten to me. O

Last time

534 Come Here, Jesus, If You Please

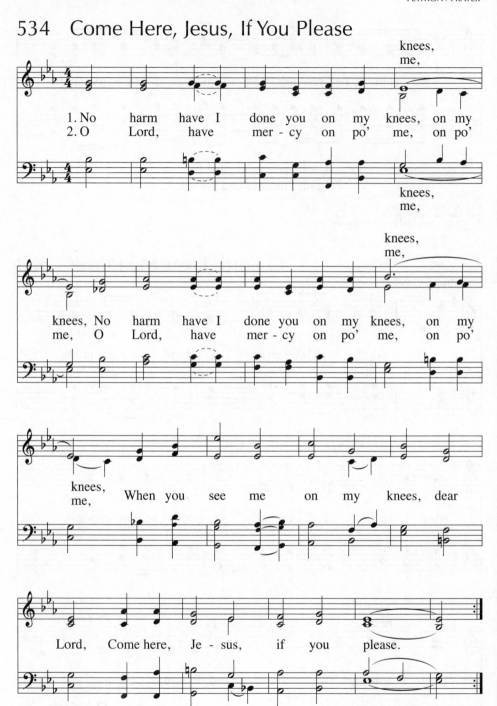

1. No harm have I done you on my knees, on my
2. O Lord, have mer-cy on po' me, on po'

knees, No harm have I done you on my knees, on my
me, O Lord, have mer-cy on po' me, on po'

knees, When you see me on my knees, dear
me,

Lord, Come here, Je-sus, if you please.

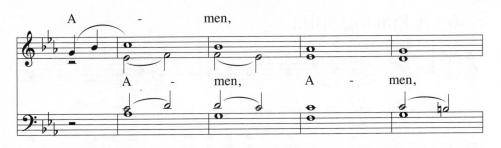

A - men,

A - men, A - men,

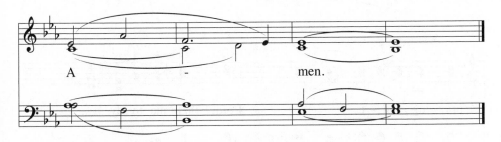

A - men.

Text: African American traditional; adapt. by Roland M. Carter, b.1942, © 1978, Mar-Vel
Tune: COME HERE JESUS, 99 9 7 with amen; African American traditional; arr. by Roland M. Carter, b.1942, © 1978, Mar-Vel

I Will Do a New Thing 535

"I will do a new thing in you; I will do a

new thing in you; What - ev - er you ask for, what-

ev - er you pray for, noth - ing shall be de-

nied," sa-ith the Lord; sa-ith the Lord! Lord!

Text: Audrey Byrd
Tune: Audrey Byrd; arr. by Nolan Williams, Jr., b.1969, © 2000, GIA Publications, Inc.

536 A Praying Spirit

Lord, give me a pray - ing spir - it, a pray - ing spir - it. Lord, help me to say yes, yes, yes, Lord; yes, yes, Lord. Lord, when I'm pray - ing tell me

what   to   say!   what   to   say!   Yes!   Yes!

Yes!   Yes, Lord!   Yes,   yes, Lord!

Text: Elbernita "Twinkie" Clark Terrell, © 1980, Bridgeport Music, Inc.
Tune: Elbernita "Twinkie" Clark Terrell, © 1980, Bridgeport Music, Inc.; arr. by Nolan Williams, Jr., b.1969, © 2000, GIA Publications, Inc.

537 Guide My Feet

1. Guide my feet
2. Hold my hand
3. Stand by me
4. I'm your child

while I run this race,

Oh, Lord,

Guide my feet
Hold my hand
Stand by me
I'm your child

while I run this race,

Oh, Lord,

Guide my feet
Hold my hand
Stand by me
I'm your child

while I run this race, For I

vain.

don't want to run this race in vain, race in vain.

vain.

Text: Negro Spiritual
Tune: GUIDE MY FEET, 888 10; Negro Spiritual; harm. by Dr. Wendell P. Whalum, 1931–1987, © Estate of Wendell Whalum

Lead Me, Guide Me 538

Refrain

Lead me, guide me, a-long the way,

For if you lead me, I can-not stray.

Lord, let me walk each day with thee.

Lead me, O Lord, lead me.

Verses

1. I am weak and I need thy strength and
2. Help me tread in the paths of right - eous -
3. I am lost if you take your hand from

pow'r To help me o - ver my weak - est
ness. Be my aid when Sa - tan and sin op -
me, I am blind with - out thy Light to

hour. Help me through the dark - ness thy face to
press. I am put - ting all my trust in
see. Lord, just al - ways let me thy ser - vant

D.C.

see. Lead me, O Lord, lead me.
thee. Lead me, O Lord, lead me.
be. Lead me, O Lord, lead me.

Text: Doris M. Akers, 1922–1995
Tune: LEAD ME, GUIDE ME, Irregular with refrain; Doris M. Akers, 1922–1995; harm. by Richard Smallwood, b.1948
© 1953, ren., arr. © 2011, Doris M. Akers, Admin. Chappell & Co., Inc.

539 Eternal Father, Strong to Save

1. E - ter - nal Fa - ther, strong to save, Whose arm has bound the
2. O Sav - ior, whose al - might - y word The wind and waves sub -
3. O Ho - ly Spir - it, who did brood Up - on the cha - os
4. O Trin - i - ty of love and pow'r, All   trav -'lers guard in

rest - less wave, Who bade   the might - y   o - cean deep Its
mis - sive heard, Who walked up - on the   foam - ing deep, And
wild and rude, And bade   its an - gry tu - mult cease, And
dan - ger's hour; From rock   and tem - pest, fire   and foe, Pro -

own ap - point - ed   lim - its keep: O   hear   us when we
calm a - mid its   rage did sleep: O   hear   us when we
gave, for fierce con - fu - sion, peace: O   hear   us when we
tect them where - so - e'er they go; Thus ev - er - more shall

cry   to thee For those in per - il on the sea.
cry   to thee For those in per - il on the sea.
cry   to thee For those in per - il on the sea.
rise   to thee Glad praise from air and land and sea.

Text: William Whiting, 1825–1878
Tune: MELITA, 88 88 88; John Bacchus Dykes, 1823–1876

Jesus on the Main Line 540

Je-sus on the main line, Tell him what you want.

Je-sus on the main line, Tell him what you want.

Je-sus on the main line, Tell him what you want.

now!

Je-sus on the main line now, the main line now!

now!

Text: African American Prayer and Praise Hymn, c.1900; adapt. by C. Eugene Cooper
Tune: African American Prayer and Praise Hymn, c.1900; adapt. by C. Eugene Cooper
© 1987, 1988, 1991, GIA Publications, Inc.

541   Call Him Up

1. If you con-fess the Lord, call him up.
2. When dark-ness comes your way,

If you con-fess the Lord, call him up.
He'll bright-en up your day,

If you be-lieve on the Fa-ther, the Son, and the Ho-

ly Ghost, call him up and

tell him what you want.

De - light your-self in the Lord

and he will give you the de - sires of your heart

unis.

Je - sus knows some - times we stum-

ble, Je - sus knows some-times we fall. Call him up

div.

and tell him what you want.

sus.   Hal-le-lu - jah,   Je - sus.

Je - sus.   Je - sus.

Prais - ing his name,

Text: Ricky R. Grundy and Herman Netter
Tune: Ricky R. Grundy and Herman Netter; arr. by Kenneth W. Louis, b.1956

542 Hamba Nathi / Come, Walk with Us

mku - lu - lu we - thu,
The jour-ney is long.

lu - lu we - thu,
jour-ney is long,

mku - lu - lu, mku - lu - lu, mku -
the jour-ney, the jour-ney, the

1.

mku - lu - lu we - thu.
The jour - ney is long.

2.

1.

lu - lu we - thu,
jour - ney is long.

2.

mku - lu - lu we - thu.
The jour-ney is long.

Additional English Verses

Listen to us, our sorrow is great.
Come talk with us, give meaning in life.
Come eat with us, and share in our bread.
Come stay with us, for evening is nigh.

African phonetics:
Hahm-bah nah-tee mkoo-loo-loo way-too.

Text: South African traditional; tr. by Gerhard M. Cartford, b.1923, © Lutheran World Federation
Tune: South African traditional; arr. by Anders Nyberg, © Peace of Music Publishing AB, admin. by Walton Music Corp.

543 Mayenziwe / Your Will Be Done

Ma - ye - (Ma - ye) nzi - we 'nta - ndo ya - kho. Ma - ye
Your will (Your will) be done on earth, O Lord. Your

ye - (Ma - ye) nzi - we 'nta - ndo ya - kho. Ma - ye - nzi -
will (Your will) be done on earth, O Lord. Your will be

we 'nta - ndo ya - kho. Ma - ye - nzi - we 'nta -
done on earth, O Lord. Your will be done on

ndo ya - kho. Ma - ye - nzi - we 'nta - ndo ya - kho.
earth, O Lord. Your will be done on earth, O Lord.

African phonetics:
My-yen-zee-way tahn-doe yah-koe.

Text: from the Lord's Prayer, South African (Xhosa)
Tune: South African traditional, as taught by George Mxadana; transcribed by John L. Bell, b.1949; © 1990, Iona Community,
   GIA Publications, Inc., agent

Sing Praise to God for Friends   544

1. Sing praise to God for friends who bring Our needs to Christ the Lord, Who pray that he will bend to us And speak his heal - ing Word.

2. We may not see their fold - ed hands Nor know what prayers they raise, But Christ will al - ways hear the voice That for an - oth - er prays.

3. And so those clouds of wit - ness - es Whose race has now been run Still lift their prayers by day and night For us be - fore God's throne.

4. Sing praise for that great com - pa - ny Of all who in - ter - cede, Who by the hid - den hand of prayer Sup - port us in our need.

Text: Herman G. Stuempfle, Jr., 1923–2007, © 1997, GIA Publications, Inc.
Tune: AZMON, CM; Carl G. Gläser, 1784–1829; harm. by Lowell Mason, 1792–1872

545 God Be with You Till We Meet Again

1. God be with you till we meet a - gain; By God's
2. God be with you till we meet a - gain; 'Neath God's
3. God be with you till we meet a - gain; When life's
4. God be with you till we meet a - gain; Keep love's

coun - sels guide, up - hold you, With God's sheep se - cure - ly
wings pro - tect - ing hide you, Dai - ly man - na still proper - ils thick con - found you, Put God's arms un - fail - ing
ban - ner float - ing o'er you, Smite death's threat-'ning wave be-

fold you: God be with you till we meet a - gain.
vide you: God be with you till we meet a - gain.
round you: God be with you till we meet a - gain.
fore you: God be with you till we meet a - gain.

Till we meet, till we meet, Till we

meet   at   Je - sus'   feet,   Till we meet,   till we

till we meet,

meet,   God be with you   till we meet   a - gain.

Text: Jeremiah E. Rankin, 1828–1904
Tune: GOD BE WITH YOU, 9 8 8 9 with refrain; William G. Tomer, 1832–1896

546 God Be with You

God be with you, God be with you,

God be with you, un-til we meet a - gain;

God be with you, God be with you,

God be with you, un-til we meet a - gain.

Text: Thomas A. Dorsey, 1899–1993
Tune: Thomas A. Dorsey, 1899–1993; arr. by Horace Clarence Boyer, 1935–2009
© 1940 (renewed), arr. © 2011, Warner-Tamerlane Publishing Co., Inc.

Till We Gather Again 547

Till we gath-er a-gain, God be with you. Till we gath-er a-gain, God be with you. May he give you his love, give you his kind-ness, keep you in per-fect peace. God be with you till we meet a-gain.

Text: Stephen Key
Tune: Stephen Key
© StepKey Music

548 We've Come This Far by Faith

We've come this far by faith, Lean-ing on the Lord; Trust-ing in his ho-ly word, He's nev-er failed me yet. Oh, can't turn a - round, We've come this far by faith.

Verse 1

1. Don't be dis-cour-aged when trou-ble's in your life, He'll bear your bur - dens and move all mis-er-y and strife.

That's why we've

D.S.

2. Just the other day I heard someone say
   He didn't believe in God's word;
   But I can truly say that God had made a way,
   And he's never failed me yet.
   That's why we've...

Text: Albert A. Goodson, b.1933
Tune: Albert A. Goodson, b.1933; arr. by James Abbington, b.1960

549 Yes, God Is Real

1. There are some things I may not know,
2. Some folks may doubt, some folks may scorn,
3. I can not tell just how you felt

There are some plac - es I can - not go,
All can de - sert and leave me a - lone,
When Je - sus took your sins a - way,

But I am sure of this one thing,
But as for me I'll take God's part,
But since that day, yes, since that hour,

That God is real for I can feel him deep with - in.
For God is real and I can feel him in my heart.
God has been real for I can feel his ho - ly pow'r.

Solo:

Yes, God is real, he's real in my soul; Yes, God is

Yes, God is yes, God is real, real in my soul;

real for he has washed and made me whole; His love for

real for he has washed and made me whole;

me is like pure gold. Yes, God is

His love for me is like pure gold. Yes, God is

real   for I can feel   him in my   soul.

real   for I can feel   him in my, him   in   my soul.

Text: Kenneth Morris, 1917–1988
Tune: GOD IS REAL, 8 9 8 12 with refrain; Kenneth Morris, 1917–1988; arr. by Evelyn Simpson-Curenton, b.1953
© 1944, (renewed), arr. © 2011, Martin and Morris Inc., admin. by Unichappell Music, Inc.

550   We Walk by Faith

1., 5. We   walk   by   faith,   and   not   by   sight;   No
2. We   may   not   touch   his   hands and   side,   Nor
3. Help then, O   Lord,   our un - be - lief;   And
4. That, when our   life   of   faith is   done,   In

gra - cious words   we   hear   From him who spoke   as
fol - low where   he   trod;   But   in   his prom - ise
may our faith   a - bound   To   call on   you when
realms of clear - er   light   We   may be - hold you

none e'er spoke; But we be - lieve him   near.
we   re - joice, And cry, "My Lord and   God!"
you are near,   And seek where you are found:
as   you are,   With full and end - less sight.

Text: Henry Alford, 1810–1871, alt.
Tune: SHANTI, CM; Marty Haugen, b.1950, © 1984, GIA Publications, Inc.

Old Time Religion 551

Refrain: Give me that old time re - lig - ion, Give me that
1. It was good for Paul and Si - las, It was
2. It was good for the He - brew chil - dren, It was
3. It was good for our moth - ers, It was
4. Makes me love ev - 'ry - bod - y, Makes me

old time re - lig - ion, Give me that
good for Paul and Si - las, It was
good for the He - brew chil - dren, It was
good for our moth - ers, It was
love ev - 'ry - bod - y, Makes me

old time re - lig - ion,
good for Paul and Si - las,
good for the He - brew chil - dren, It's good e - nough for me.
good for our moth - ers,
love ev - 'ry - bod - y,

Text: Traditional
Tune: OLD TIME RELIGION, Irregular; traditional; arr. by Joseph Joubert, b.1958, © 2000, GIA Publications, Inc.

552   A Living Faith

1. Faith of our fa - thers, liv - ing still
2. Faith of our moth - ers, dar - ing faith,
3. Faith of our broth - ers, sis - ters too,
4. Faith born of God, O call us yet;

In spite of dun - geon, fire and sword;
Your work for Christ is love re - vealed,
Who still must bear op - pres - sion's might,
Bind us with all who fol - low you,

O how our hearts beat high with joy,
Spread - ing God's word from pole to pole,
Rais - ing on high, in pris - ons dark,
Shar - ing the strug - gle of your cross

When - e'er we hear that glo - rious word:
Mak - ing love known and free - dom real:
The cross of Christ still burn - ing bright:
Un - til the world is made a - new,

Faith of our fa - thers, ho - ly faith,
Faith of our moth - ers, ho - ly faith,
Faith for to - day, O liv - ing faith,
Faith born of God, O liv - ing faith,

We will be true to you till death.

Text: St. 1, Frederick W. Faber, 1814–1863, alt.; sts. 2–4, Joseph R. Alfred, b.1947, © 1981, alt.
Tune: ST. CATHERINE, LM with refrain; Henry F. Hemy, 1818–1888; adapt. by James G. Walton, 1821–1905

553   I Say "Yes," Lord / Digo "Sí," Señor

Verses

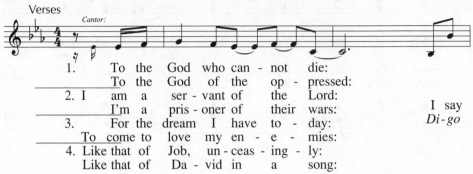

1. To the God who can - not die:
   To the God of the op - pressed:
2. I am a ser - vant of the Lord:
   I'm a pris - oner of their wars:
3. For the dream I have to - day:
   To come to love my en - e - mies:
4. Like that of Job, un - ceas - ing - ly:
   Like that of Da - vid in a song:

I say
Di - go

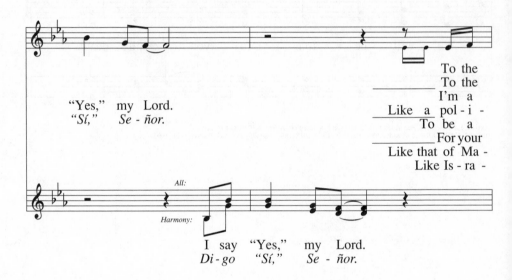

"Yes," my Lord.
"Sí," Se - ñor.

To the
To the
I'm a
Like a pol - i -
To be a
For your
Like that of Ma -
Like Is - ra -

I say "Yes," my Lord.
Di - go "Sí," Se - ñor.

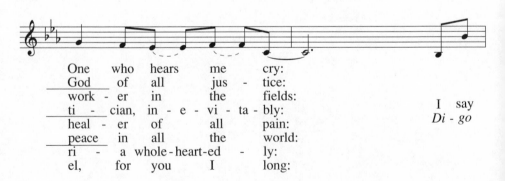

One who hears me cry:
God of all jus - tice:
work - er in the fields:
ti - cian, in - e - vi - ta - bly:
heal - er of all pain:
peace in all the world:
ri - a whole - heart - ed - ly:
el, for you I long:

I say
Di - go

"Yes," my Lord.
"Sí," Se - ñor.

All:
Harmony:
I say "Yes," my Lord. "Yes," my Lord.
Di - go "Sí," Se - ñor. "Sí," Se - ñor.

Refrain
Descant:
I say "Yes," my Lord, in all the good times, through
Di - go "Sí," Se - ñor, en tiem - pos ma - los, en

Melody:
I say "Yes," my Lord, in all the good times, through
Di - go "Sí," Se - ñor, en tiem - pos ma - los, en

all the bad times, I say "Yes," my Lord, to
tiem - pos bue - nos, Di - go "Sí," Se - ñor, a

all the bad times, I say "Yes," my Lord, to
tiem - pos bue - nos, Di - go "Sí," Se - ñor, a

To verses D.C. | **Last time**

ev - 'ry word you speak.
to - do lo que_ha - blas.

ev - 'ry word you speak.
to - do lo que_ha - blas.

Text: Donna Peña, b.1955
Tune: Donna Peña, b.1955; arr. by Marty Haugen, b.1950
© 1989, GIA Publications, Inc.

554 You Can't Make Me Doubt Him

You can't make me doubt him, you can't make me doubt him,

you can't make me doubt him in my heart.

You can't make me doubt him, you can't make me doubt him,

you can't make me doubt him in my heart.

Text: African American Prayer and Praise Hymn, c.1900; adapt. by C. Eugene Cooper
Tune: African American Prayer and Praise Hymn, c.1900; adapt. by C. Eugene Cooper

How Firm a Foundation 555

1. How firm a foun - da - tion, you saints of the
2. "Fear not, I am with you, O be not dis -
3. "When through the deep wa - ters I call you to
4. "The soul that on Je - sus still leans for re -

Lord, Is laid for your faith in Christ Je - sus, the
mayed, For I am your God, and will still give you
go, The riv - ers of woe shall not you o - ver -
pose, I will not, I will not de - sert to its

Word! What more can God say than to you has been
aid; I'll strength - en you, help you, and cause you to
flow; For I will be with you, your trou - bles to
foes; That soul, though all hell should en - deav - or to

said, To you who for ref - uge to Je - sus have fled?
stand, Up - held by my right - eous, om - nip - o - tent hand.
bless, And sanc - ti - fy to you your deep - est dis - tress.
shake, I'll nev - er, no nev - er, no nev - er for - sake!"

Text: 2 Peter 1:4; "K" in Rippon's *A Selection of Hymns*, 1787, alt.
Tune: FOUNDATION, 11 11 11 11; Funk's *Compilation of Genuine Church Music*, 1832

556 A Mighty Fortress Is Our God

1. A might - y for - tress is our God,
2. No strength of ours can match his might!
3. Though hordes of dev - ils fill the land
4. God's Word for - ev - er shall a - bide,

A sword and shield vic - to - rious, Who breaks the
We would be lost, re - ject - ed. But now a
All threat-'ning to de - vour us, We trem - ble
No thanks to foes, who fear it; For God, our

cruel op - pres - sor's rod And wins sal - va - tion
cham - pion comes to fight, Whom God a - lone e -
not, un - moved we stand; They can - not o - ver -
Lord, fights by our side With weap - ons of the

glo - rious. The old sa - tan - ic foe
lect - ed. You ask who this may be?
pow'r us. Let this world's ty - rant rage;
Spir - it. Were they to take our house,

Has sworn to work us woe!
The Lord of hosts is he!
In bat - tle we'll en - gage!
Goods, hon - or, child, or spouse,

With craft and
Christ Je - sus,
His might is
Though life be

dread - ful might
might - y Lord,
doomed to fail;
wrenched a - way,

He arms him - self to fight.
God's on - ly Son, a - dored.
God's judg - ment must pre - vail!
They can - not win the day.

On earth he has no e - qual.
He holds the field vic - to - rious.
One lit - tle word sub - dues him.
The King - dom's ours for - ev - er!

Text: Psalm 46; *Ein' feste Burg ist unser Gott*; Martin Luther, 1483–1546; tr. © 1978, *Lutheran Book of Worship*, alt., admin. by Augsburg Fortress
Tune: EIN' FESTE BURG, 8 7 8 7 66 66 7; Martin Luther, 1483–1546; harm by J. S. Bach, 1685–1750

557 His Eye Is on the Sparrow

1. Why should I feel dis-cour-aged, Why should the shad-ows come, Why should my heart be lone-ly, And long for heav'n and home; When Je-sus is my por-tion? My con-stant friend is he:

2. "Let not your heart be trou-bled," His ten-der word I hear, And rest-ing on his good-ness, I lose my doubts and fears; Though by the path he lead-eth, But one step I may see; His

3. When ev-er I am tempt-ed, When ev-er clouds a-rise, When songs give place to sigh-ing When hope with-in me dies, I draw the clos-er to him, From care he sets me free;

Text: Civilla D. Martin, 1860–1948
Tune: SPARROW, 7 6 7 6 7 6 7 7 7 7 with refrain; Charles H. Gabriel, 1865–1932; arr. by Horace Clarence Boyer, 1935–2009, © 1992

558 I Must Tell Jesus

1. I must tell Je - sus all of my tri - als,
2. I must tell Je - sus all of my trou - bles,
3. Tempt-ed and tried, I need a great Sav - ior,
4. O how the world to e - vil al - lures me!

I can-not bear these bur-dens a - lone;
He is a kind, com - pas-sion-ate Friend;
One who can help my bur-dens to bear;
O how my heart is tempt-ed to sin!

In my dis - tress he kind-ly will help me,
If I but ask him, he will de - liv - er,
I must tell Je - sus, I must tell Je - sus,
I must tell Je - sus, and he will help me

He ev - er loves and cares for his own.
Make of my trou - bles quick-ly an end.
He all my cares and sor - rows will share.
O - ver the world the vic-t'ry to win.

I must tell Je - sus! I must tell Je - sus! I can-not bear my bur-dens a - lone; I must tell Je - sus! I must tell Je - sus! Je - sus can help me, Je-sus a - lone.

Text: Elisha A. Hoffman, 1839–1929
Tune: ORWIGSBURG, 10 9 10 9 with refrain; Elisha A. Hoffman, 1839–1929

559 Just a Little Talk with Jesus

1. I once was lost in sin But Je-sus took me in,
2. Some-times my path seems drear, With-out a ray of cheer,
3. I may have doubts and fears, My eyes be filled with tears,

And then a lit-tle light from heav-en filled my soul;
And then a cloud of doubt may hide the light of day;
But Je-sus is a friend who watch-es day and night;

It bathed my heart in love And wrote my name a-bove,
The mists of sin may rise And hide the star-ry skies,
I go to him in prayer, He knows my ev-'ry care,

And just a lit-tle talk with Je-sus made me whole.
But just a lit-tle talk with Je-sus clears the way.
And just a lit-tle talk with Je-sus makes it right.

Have a lit-tle talk with Je - sus, tell him all a-bout our
Now let us let us

trou - bles, Hear our faint - est cry,
he will and he will

an - swer by and by; Feel a lit - tle prayer wheel
Now when you

turn - ing, know a lit - tle fire is burn - ing,
and you you will

right.
Find a lit - tle talk with Je - sus makes it right, makes it right.

Text: Cleavant Derricks, b.1937
Tune: JUST A LITTLE TALK, 66 12 66 12 with refrain; Cleavant Derricks, b.1937
© 1937, Stamps-Baxter Music (BMI)

560 O God, Our Help in Ages Past

1. O God, our help in a - ges past, Our
2. Un - der the shad - ow of your throne Your
3. Be - fore the hills in or - der stood, Or
4. A thou - sand a - ges in your sight Are
5. Time, like an ev - er - roll - ing stream, Bears
6. O God, our help in a - ges past, Our

hope for years to come, Our shel - ter from the
saints have dwelt se - cure; Suf - fi - cient is your
earth re - ceived its frame, From ev - er - last - ing
like an eve - ning gone, Short as the watch that
all our years a - way; They fly for - got - ten,
hope for years to come, Still be our guard while

storm - y blast, And our e - ter - nal home.
arm a - lone, And our de - fense is sure.
you are God, To end - less years the same.
ends the night Be - fore the ris - ing sun.
as a dream Dies at the o - p'ning day.
trou - bles last, And our e - ter - nal home.

Text: Psalm 90; Isaac Watts, 1674–1748, alt.
Tune: ST. ANNE, CM; attr. to William Croft, 1678–1727; harm. composite from 18th C. versions

The Solid Rock 561

1. My hope is built on noth-ing less Than Je - sus' blood and
2. When dark-ness veils his love - ly face, I rest on his un -
3. His oath, his cov - e - nant, his blood Sup - port me in o'er -
4. When he shall come with trum-pet sound, O may I then in

right - eous-ness; I dare not trust the sweet-est frame, But
chang - ing grace; In ev - 'ry high and storm - y gale My
whelm-ing floods; When all a - round my soul gives way, He
him be found, Dressed in his right - eous - ness a - lone, Fault -

whol-ly lean on Je - sus' name.
an - chor holds with - in the veil.
then is all my hope and stay.
less to stand be - fore the throne.

On Christ, the sol - id Rock, I stand—

All oth-er ground is sink-ing sand, All oth-er ground is sink-ing sand.

Text: Edward Mote, 1797–1874
Tune: SOLID ROCK, LM with refrain; William B. Bradbury, 1816–1868

562 Standing on the Promises

1. Stand - ing on the prom - is - es of Christ, my King,
2. Stand - ing on the prom - is - es that can - not fail.
3. Stand - ing on the prom - is - es of Christ, the Lord,
4. Stand - ing on the prom - is - es I can - not fall,

Through e - ter - nal a - ges let his prais - es ring;
When the howl - ing storms of doubt and fear as - sail,
Bound to him e - ter - nal - ly by love's strong cord,
Lis - t'ning ev - 'ry mo - ment to the Spir - it's call,

Glo - ry in the high - est, I will shout and sing,
By the liv - ing word of God I shall pre - vail,
O - ver-com - ing dai - ly with the Spir - it's sword,
Rest - ing in my Sav - ior, as my all in all,

Stand - ing on the prom - is - es of God.

Text: R. Kelso Carter, 1849–1928
Tune: PROMISES, 11 11 11 9 with refrain; R. Kelso Carter, 1849–1928

563 Father, I Stretch My Hands to Thee

1. Fa - ther, I stretch my hands to thee;
2. What did thine on - ly Son en - dure,
3. Sure - ly thou canst not let me die;
4. Au - thor of faith! to thee I lift

No oth - er help I know.
Be - fore I drew my breath!
O speak and I shall live;
My wea - ry, long - ing eyes;

If thou with - draw thy - self from me,
What pain, what la - bor to se - cure
And here I will un - wea - ried lie,
O let me now re - ceive that gift!

O! whith - er shall I go?
My soul from end - less death!
Till thou thy Spir - it give.
My soul with - out it dies.

Text: Charles Wesley, 1707–1788
Tune: MARTYRDOM, CM; Hugh Wilson, 1766–1824; arr. by Nolan Williams, Jr., b.1969, © 2000, GIA Publications, Inc.

Father, I Stretch My Hands to Thee 564

Text: Charles Wesley, 1707–1788
Tune: Meter hymn, lined out and arr. by Evelyn Simpson-Curenton, b.1953, © 2000, GIA Publications, Inc.

565 Trust and Obey

1. When we walk with the Lord In the light of his
2. Not a shad-ow can rise, Not a cloud in the
3. Not a bur-den we bear, Not a sor-row we
4. But we nev-er can prove The de-lights of his
5. Then in fel-low-ship sweet We will sit at his

Word, What a glo-ry he sheds on our way! While we
skies, But his smile quick-ly drives it a-way; Not a
share, But our toil he doth rich-ly re-pay; Not a
love Un-til all on the al-tar we lay, For the
feet, Or we'll walk by his side in the way; What he

do his good will He a-bides with us
doubt nor a fear, Not a sigh nor a
grief nor a loss, Not a frown nor a
fa-vor he shows And the joy he be-
says we will do, Where he sends we will

still, And with all who will trust and o-bey.
tear, Can a-bide while we trust and o-bey.
cross, But is blest if we trust and o-bey.
stows Are for those who will trust and o-bey.
go— Nev-er fear, on-ly trust and o-bey.

Trust and o - bey— For there's no oth - er way To be

hap - py in Je - sus But to trust and o - bey.

Text: John H. Sammis, 1846–1919
Tune: TRUST AND OBEY, 66 9 D with refrain, Daniel B. Towner, 1850–1919

566 Hold Back the Night

Chorus

Hold back the night. Give me strength to fight. I'll do your will if you just say to my soul: peace, be still. O Lord, I love your name. Ev-'ry day you're just the same. I'll be all right if you hold back the night.

Text: Charles H. Nicks, Jr., 1941–1988
Tune: Charles H. Nicks, Jr., 1941–1988; arr. by Stephen Key, © 2000, GIA Publications, Inc.

Keep Hope Alive! 567

Keep hope a - live!

Keep hope a - live! Keep hope a - live!

Keep hope a - live!

Don't let the dream die!

Got to keep hope a - live!

Text: Donald Vails, ©
Tune: Donald Vails, ©; arr. by Nolan Williams, Jr., b.1969, © 2000, GIA Publications, Inc.

568 Lord, Help Me to Hold Out

Lord, help me to hold out,

Lord, help me to hold out,

Lord, help me to hold out un -

1. and to Coda ⊕ ‖ 2.

til my change comes.

My way may not be eas-y You did not say that it would

be. But if it gets dark, I can't see my way, you

D.C.

told me to put my trust in thee, that's why I'm ask-ing you.

Text: James Cleveland, b.1932
Tune: James Cleveland, b.1932; arr. by Kenneth Morris, 1917–1988
© 1974, Planemar Music Co.

569 It Is Well with My Soul

1. When peace, like a riv - er, at - tend - eth my
2. Though Sa - tan should buf - fet, though tri - als should
3. My sin— oh, the bliss of this glo - ri - ous
4. And Lord, haste the day when my faith shall be

way, When sor - rows, like sea bil - lows, roll; What -
come, Let this blest as - sur - ance con - trol, That
thought: My sin, not in part but the whole, Is
sight, The clouds be rolled back as a scroll, The

ev - er my lot, thou hast taught me to say,
Christ has re - gard - ed my help - less es - tate,
nailed to the cross, and I bear it no more,
trump shall re - sound, and the Lord shall de - scend,

It is well, it is well with my soul.
And hath shed his own blood for my soul.
Praise the Lord, praise the Lord, O my soul!
"E - ven so," it is well with my soul.

It is well with my soul,

It is well with my soul,

It is well, it is well with my soul.

Text: Horatio G. Spafford, 1828–1888
Tune: VILLE DU HAVRE, 11 8 11 9 with refrain; Philip P. Bliss, 1838–1876

People Need the Lord 570

Chorus

Peo-ple need the Lord, peo-ple need the Lord;

1.
At the end of bro-ken dreams, He's the o-pen door.

2.
When will we re-al-ize that peo-ple need the Lord?

Text: Greg Nelson, b.1948, and Phill McHugh, b.1951
Tune: Greg Nelson, b.1948, and Phill McHugh, b.1951
© 1983, Shepherd's Fold Music/River Oaks Music Co., admin. at EMICMGPublishing.com

571 I've Got a Feelin'

Verse 1

1. I've got a feel-in' ev-'ry-thing's gon-na be al - right.

I've got a feel-in' ev-'ry-thing's gon-na be al - right.

Oh,

I've got a feel-in' ev-'ry-thing's gon-na be al - right,

be al - right, be al - right, be al - right.

Verse 2

2. The Ho-ly Ghost done told me ev-'ry-thing's gon-na be al - right.

Text: Congregational Praise Song
Tune: Congregational Praise Song; arr. by Kenneth W. Louis, b.1956, and Nolan Williams, Jr., b.1969, © 2000, GIA Publications, Inc.

572 The Lord Is My Light

Verse 1

1. The Lord is my light and my sal - va - tion, the Lord is my light and my sal - va-tion, the Lord is my light and my sal - va - tion. Whom shall I fear?

Refrain

Whom shall I fear? Whom shall I fear? The Lord is the strength of my life. Whom shall I fear?

Last time to Coda

Verse 2

2. In the time of trou - ble he shall hide me,

in the time of trou - ble he shall hide me,

D.S.

in the time of trou-ble he shall hide me. Whom shall I fear?

Coda

fear.

Verse 3

3. Wait on the Lord and

be of good cour - age, wait on the Lord and

be of good cour - age, wait on the Lord and

be of good cour - age. Whom shall I fear?

Refrain

Whom shall I fear? Whom shall I fear? The

Lord is the strength of my life. Whom shall I fear?

Text: Lillian Bouknight
Tune: Lillian Bouknight; arr. by Stephen Key
© 1981, Peermusic III, Ltd. and Savgos Music, Inc.

Be Strong! 573

Be strong! Do not be a-fraid. Our God will come,

will come to save us. Be strong! Do not be a-fraid.

Our God will come, will come to save us.

Tell those who are fright-ened, Be strong!

Tell those who are fright-ened, Do not be a-fraid.

Tell those who are fright-ened, Do not be a-fraid.

Our God will come, will come to save us.

Text: Robert J. Ledogar
Tune: *Advent Mass,* Edward V. Bonnemère, 1921–1996
© 1967, 1986, Amity Music Co.

574 We'll Understand It Better By and By

1. We are of-ten tossed and driv'n On the rest-less
2. We are of-ten des-ti-tute Of the things that
3. Tri-als dark on ev-'ry hand, And we can-not
4. Temp-ta-tions, hid-den snares Of-ten take us

sea of time. Som-ber skies and howl-ing tem-pests oft suc-
life de-mands. Want of food and want of shel-ter, thirst-y
un-der-stand, All the ways that God would lead us to that
un-a-wares. And our hearts are made to bleed for some

ceed a bright sun-shine. In that land of per-fect day, When the
hills and bar-ren lands. We are trust-ing in the Lord, And ac-
bless-ed Prom-ised Land. But he guides us with his eye And we'll
thought-less word or deed. And we won-der why the test When we

mists have rolled a-way, We will un-der-stand it bet-ter by and
cord-ing to his Word, We will un-der-stand it bet-ter by and
fol-low till we die. For we'll un-der-stand it bet-ter by and
try to do our best, But we'll un-der-stand it bet-ter by and

By. By and by when the morn-ing comes,

When the saints of God are gath-ered home, We will

tell the sto - ry how we've o - ver-come; For we'll

un - der - stand it bet - ter by and by.

Text: Charles A. Tindley, 1851–1933
Tune: BY AND BY, 7 7 15 7 7 11 with refrain; Charles A. Tindley, 1851–1933; arr. by Nolan Williams, Jr., b.1969, © 2000, GIA Publications, Inc.

575 Savior, Lead Me Lest I Stray

1. Sav - ior, lead me lest I, lead me lest I stray,
2. Thou the ref - uge of my, ref - uge of my soul,
3. Sav - ior, lead me, then at, lead me, then at last,

Gen - tly lead me all the, lead me all the way;
When life's storm - y bil - lows, storm - y bil - lows roll;
When the storm of life is, storm of life is past;

I am safe when by thy, safe when by thy side,
I am safe when thou art, safe when thou art nigh,
To the land of end-less, land of end-less day,

I would in thy love a-bide.
All my hopes on thee re-ly.
Where all tears are wiped a-way.

Lead me, lead me. Sav - ior, lead me lest I stray;

Gen - tly down the stream of, down the stream of time,

time,

Lead me, Sav - ior, all the, lead me all the way.

way.

Text: Frank M. Davis, 1839–1897
Tune: LEAD ME, 77 77 with refrain; Frank M. Davis, 1839–1897; arr. by Kenneth W. Louis, b.1956, © 2012, GIA Publications, Inc.

576 I Will Trust in the Lord

1. I will trust in the Lord, I will trust in the Lord, I will trust in the Lord till I die.
2. I'm gon-na treat ev-'ry-bod-y right, I'm gon-na treat ev-'ry-bod-y right, I'm gon-na treat ev-'ry-bod-y right till I die.
3. I'm gon-na stay on the bat-tle-field, I'm gon-na stay on the bat-tle-field, I'm gon-na stay on the bat-tle-field till I die.
4. I'm gon-na stay on bend-ed knee, I'm gon-na stay on bend-ed knee, I'm gon-na stay on bend-ed knee till I die.

Alternate lyrics:
Father, I stretch my hands to thee;
No other help I know.
If thou withdraw thyself from me,
O whither shall I go?

Text: Negro Spiritual
Tune: TRUST IN THE LORD, Irregular; Negro Spiritual; arr. by Jeffrey Radford, 1953–2002, and Nolan Williams, Jr., b.1969, © 2000,
   GIA Publications, Inc.

577 All My Help Comes from the Lord

Verses

1. Fa - ther I stretch my hands to thee.
2. When I am weak he gives my strength.

1. Fa - ther I stretch, I stretch my hands to thee.
2. When I am weak, when I'm weak he gives me strength.

I know that you re-mem-ber me.
When I am lone - ly he com-forts me.

I know that you, on-ly you, re-mem-ber me. When
When I am lone - ly he com-forts me.

oth - ers for - get, when oth-ers for - get and leave me a - lone,
When I am tired of the load that I am bear - ing,

D.C.

I know that Je - sus, Je - sus, Je - sus will hear my groan.
He gives me cour-age, cour-age, cour-age to bear my share.

Text: Rev. Cleophus Robinson, © 1964, Lion Publishing Co.
Tune: Rev. Cleophus Robinson, © 1964, Lion Publishing Co.; arr. by Evelyn Simpson-Curenton, b.1953, © 2000, GIA Publications, Inc.

578 God Never Fails

Refrain

God nev-er fails. God nev-er fails. He a-bides in me. He gives me vic-to-ry. No, God nev-er fails! Just keep the faith, and nev-er cease to pray; just walk up-right, call him noon, day, or night. He'll be there. He'll be there. There's

no need to wor-ry, for God nev-er fails!

Verses

1. I nev-er wor-ry, I nev-er fret;
2. No need to wor-ry, no need to cry;

For God Al-might-y has nev-er failed me yet.
I've got my Lord, I know he is on my side.

Though 'buked and scorned, I know that I've been re-
Dai-ly I trust. I nev-er shall doubt

D.C.

born, for God nev-er fails.
him, for God nev-er fails.

Text: George Jordan, © 1968, Greater Detroit Music and Record Mart
Tune: George Jordan, © 1968, Greater Detroit Music and Record Mart; arr. by Jeffrey P. Radford, 1953–2002, © 2000, GIA Publications, Inc.

579 My Heavenly Father Watches over Me

1. I trust in God wher-ev-er I may be, Up-on the land or on the roll-ing sea; For come what may, from day to day, My heav'n-ly Fa-ther watch-es o-ver me.

2. He makes the rose an ob-ject of his care, He guides the ea-gle through the path-less air; And sure-ly he re-mem-bers me,

3. I trust in God, for, in the li-on's den, On bat-tle-field, or in the pris-on pen; Through praise or blame, through flood or flame,

4. The val-ley may be dark, the shad-ows deep, But oh, the shep-herd guards his lone-ly sheep; And through the gloom, he'll lead me home,

I trust in God, I know he cares for me, On moun-tain bleak or on the storm-y sea; Though bil-lows roll, he keeps my soul, My heav'n-ly Fa-ther watch-es o - ver me.

Text: W. C. Martin
Tune: HEAVENLY FATHER, 10 10 8 10 with refrain; Charles H. Gabriel, 1856–1932; arr. by J. Jefferson Cleveland, 1937–1988 and
   Verolga Nix-Allen, b.1933

580 There's a Bright Side Somewhere

Chorus

There's a bright side some - where, there's a bright side some - where. Don't you rest un - til you find it. There's a bright side some - where.

Special Chorus

When your way seems dark and drear, don't have to wor - ry cause

God is near. If in your heart there is no song,

just keep the faith and keep hold - ing on.

Turn your plate down, fast and pray. Je - sus will al - ways make a

way. There's a bright side some - where.

Text: Margaret Jenkins, ©
Tune: Margaret Jenkins, ©; arr. by Joseph Joubert, b.1958, © 2000, GIA Publications, Inc.

581 Hold to God's Unchanging Hand

1. Time is filled with swift tran - si - tion.
2. Trust in him who will not leave you.
3. Cov - et not this world's vain rich - es
4. When your jour - ney is com - plet - ed,

Naught of earth un - moved can stand.
What - so - ev - er years may bring.
That so rap - id - ly de - cay.
If to God you have been true,

Build your hopes on things e - ter - nal.
If by earth - ly friends for - sak - en,
Seek to gain the heav'n - ly treas - ures.
Fair and bright the home in Glo - ry

Hold to God's un - chang - ing hand.
Still more close - ly to him cling.
They will nev - er pass a - way.
Your en - rap - tured soul will view.

Text: Jennie Wilson
Tune: UNCHANGING HAND, 8 7 8 7 with refrain; Franklin L. Eiland, 1860–1909; arr. by Stephen Key, © 2000, GIA Publications, Inc.

582 I Can Do All Things through Christ

I can do all things through Christ who strength-ens
who
me. I can do all things through
Christ who strength-ens me. I can
do all things through Christ, I can do all things through
Christ, I can do all things through Christ who strength-ens

me, strength - ens me.

Text: Elbernita "Twinkie" Clark Terrell
Tune: Elbernita "Twinkie" Clark Terrell
© 1980, Bridgeport Music, Inc.

Be Not Afraid 583

Verse 1

1. You shall cross the bar-ren des-ert, but you shall not die of thirst. You shall wan-der far in safe-ty though you do not know the way. You shall speak your words in for-eign lands and all will un-der-stand. You shall see the face of God and live.

Refrain

Be not a - fraid. I go be -

Be not a - fraid. I go be -

fore you al - ways. Come, fol - low me, and

fore you al - ways. Come, fol - low me,

I will give you rest.

I will give you rest.

Verse 2

2. If you pass through rag - ing wa - ters in the

sea, you shall not drown. If you walk a - mid the

burn - ing flames, you shall not be harmed. If you

stand be - fore the pow'r of hell and death is at your side,

D.S.

know that I am with you through it all.

Verse 3

Descant:

Ooh ___ king - dom shall be

3. Bless - ed are your poor, for the king - dom shall be

theirs. Bless - ed are the

theirs. Blest are you that weep and mourn, for

ones who mourn. If they

one day you shall laugh. And if wick - ed tongues in -

hate you all be - cause of me,

sult and hate you all be - cause of me,

D.S.

bless - ed, bless - ed are you!

bless - ed, bless - ed are you!

Text: Isaiah 43:2–3, Luke 6:20ff; Bob Dufford, SJ, b.1943
Tune: Bob Dufford, SJ, b.1943; acc. by Theophane Hytrek, OSF, 1915–1992
© 1975, 1978, Robert J. Dufford, SJ, and OCP

584 Through It All

1. I've had man-y tears and sor-rows, I've had
2. I've been to lots of plac-es, And I've
3. I thank God for the moun-tains, And I

ques-tions for to-mor-row, There have been times I did-n't know
seen a lot of fac-es, There have been times I felt so
thank him for the val-leys, I thank him for the storms he

right from wrong; But in ev-'ry sit-u-
all a-lone; But in my lone-ly
brought me through; For if I'd nev-er

a-tion God gave bless-ed con-so-la-tion that my
hours, yes, those pre-cious lone-ly hours, Je-sus
had a prob-lem I would-n't know that he could solve them, I'd

tri - als come to on - ly make me strong.
let me know that I was his own.
nev - er know what faith in God could do.

Through it all, through it all, I've

learned to trust in Je - sus, I've learned to trust in

God; Through it all, through it all,

I've learned to de - pend up - on his word.

Text: Andraé Crouch, b.1942
Tune: Andraé Crouch, b.1942

585 On Eagle's Wings

Verse 1

1. You who dwell in the shel-ter of the Lord, who a-
bide in his shad-ow for life, say to the Lord: "My
ref-uge, my rock in whom I trust!"

Refrain

Descant:

Melody:

And he will raise you up on ea-gle's wings, bear you on the
breath of dawn, make you to shine like the sun, and

Last time to Coda

of his hand.

To verses

hold you in the palm of his hand. 2. The

Verse 2

snare of the fowl-er will nev-er cap-ture you, and fam-ine will bring you no

D.S.

fear: un-der his wings your ref-uge, his faith-ful-ness your shield.

Verse 3

3. You need not fear the ter-ror of the night, nor the ar-row that flies by day; though thou-sands fall a-bout you, near you it shall not come.

D.S.

Verse 4

4. For to his an-gels he's giv-en a com-mand to guard you in all of your ways; up-on their hands they will bear you up, lest you dash your foot a-gainst a stone.

D.S.

Coda

And hold you, hold you in the palm of his hand.

Text: Psalm 91; Michael Joncas, b.1951
Tune: Michael Joncas, b.1951
© 1979, OCP

586 Into Your Hands

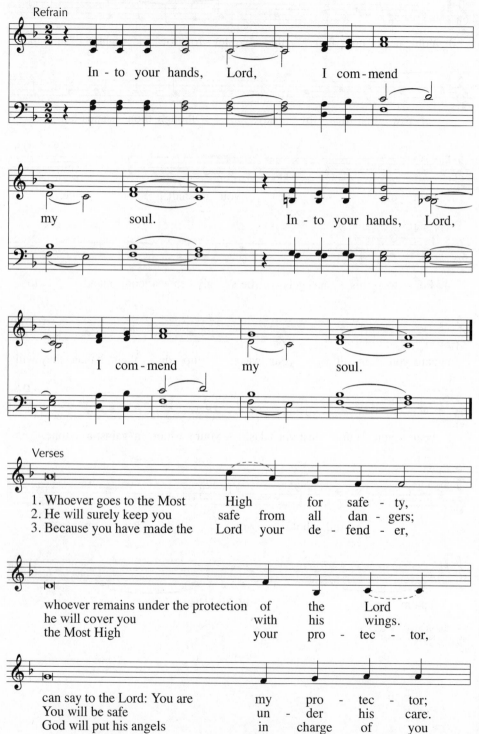

Refrain

In - to your hands, Lord, I com-mend my soul. In - to your hands, Lord, I com-mend my soul.

Verses

1. Whoever goes to the Most High for safe - ty,
2. He will surely keep you safe from all dan - gers;
3. Because you have made the Lord your de - fend - er,

whoever remains under the protection of the Lord
he will cover you with his wings.
the Most High your pro - tec - tor,

can say to the Lord: You are my pro - tec - tor;
You will be safe un - der his care.
God will put his angels in charge of you

D.C.

you are my	God,	in	you	I	trust.
His faithful - ness		will pro - tect	and de -	fend you.
to protect	you	wher - ev -	er you	go.

Text: Based on Psalm 91; Grayson Warren Brown, b.1948
Tune: Grayson Warren Brown, b.1948; arr. by Grayson Warren Brown, Val Parker, and Larry Adams
© 1992, Grayson Warren Brown. Published by OCP.

God Hears Me When I Pray 587

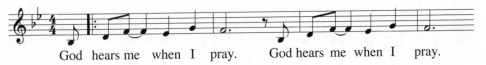

God hears me when I pray. God hears me when I pray.

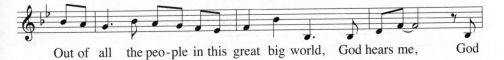

Out of all the peo-ple in this great big world, God hears me, God

knows my voice, and he hears me when I pray. God pray.

Text: Cynthia Gowens
Tune: Cynthia Gowens; arr. by Mark Lomax, II
© 2002, Gowens Music

588 I Love the Lord, He Heard My Cry

I love the Lord, he heard my cry;
And pit-ied ev-'ry groan. Long as I live,
while trou-bles rise, I'll has-ten to
his throne. throne. I'll
has-ten to his throne. I'll has-ten to his throne.

Text: Richard Smallwood, b.1948
Tune: Richard Smallwood, b.1948; arr. by Nolan Williams, Jr., b.1969
© 1990, Century Oak/Richwood Music (BMI), admin. by Conexion Media Group, Inc.

The Gift of Love 589

1. Though I may speak with brav-est fire,
2. Though I may give all I pos-sess,
3. Come, Spir-it, come, our hearts con-trol,

And have the gift to all in-spire,
And striv-ing so my love pro-fess,
Our spir-its long to be made whole.

And have not love, my words are vain,
But not be giv'n by love with-in,
Let in-ward love guide ev-'ry deed;

As sound-ing brass, and hope-less gain.
The prof-it soon turns strange-ly thin.
By this we wor - ship, and are freed.

Text: Hal H. Hopson, b.1933
Tune: GIFT OF LOVE, LM; Hal H. Hopson, b.1933
© 1972, Hope Publishing Company

590 Come, Ye Disconsolate

1. Come, ye dis-con-so-late, wher-e'er ye lan-guish—
2. Joy of the des-o-late, light of the stray-ing,
3. Here see the Bread of Life, see wa-ters flow-ing

Come to the mer-cy-seat, fer-vent-ly kneel;
Hope of the pen-i-tent, fade-less and pure!
Forth from the throne of God, pure from a-bove;

Here bring your wound-ed hearts, here tell your an-guish:
Here speaks the Com-fort-er, ten-der-ly say-ing,
Come to the feast of love— come ev-er know-ing

Earth has no sor-row that heav'n can-not heal.
"Earth has no sor-row that heav'n can-not cure."
Earth has no sor-row but heav'n can re-move.

Text: Sts. 1, 2, Thomas Moore, 1779–1852; st. 3, Thomas Hastings, 1784–1872
Tune: CONSOLATOR, 11 10 11 10; Samuel Webbe, 1740–1816

The Joy of the Lord   591

1. The joy of the Lord is my strength; The
2. If you want joy you must pray for it, If
3. He giv-eth liv-ing wa-ter and I thirst no more, He
4. He heals the bro-ken heart-ed and they cry no more, He

joy of the Lord is my strength; The
you want joy you must pray for it, If
giv-eth liv-ing wa-ter and I thirst no more, He
heals the bro-ken heart-ed and they cry no more, He

joy of the Lord is my strength; The
you want joy you must pray for it, The
giv-eth liv-ing wa-ter and I thirst no more, The
heals the bro-ken heart-ed and they cry no more, The

joy of the Lord is my strength.
joy of the Lord is my strength.
joy of the Lord is my strength.
joy of the Lord is my strength.

Text: Nehemiah 8:10, Alliene G. Vale, b.1918
Tune: JOY OF THE LORD, Irregular; Alliene G. Vale, b.1918
© 1971, Multisongs/His Eye Music/Joy of the Lord Publishing, admin. at EMICMGPublishing.com

592 Leaning on the Everlasting Arms

1. What a fel-low-ship, what a joy di-vine,
2. O how sweet to walk in this pil-grim way,
3. What have I to dread, what have I to fear,

Lean - ing on the ev - er - last - ing arms;
Lean - ing on the ev - er - last - ing arms;
Lean - ing on the ev - er - last - ing arms?

What a bless - ed - ness, what a peace is mine,
O how bright the path grows from day to day,
I have bless - ed peace with my Lord so near,

Lean - ing on the ev - er - last - ing arms.

Lean - ing, lean - ing,

Lean - ing on Je - sus Christ, my Sav - ior,

Safe and se - cure from all a - larms;

Lean - ing, lean - ing,

Lean - ing on Je - sus Christ, my Sav - ior,

Lean - ing on the ev - er - last - ing arms.

Text: Elisha A. Hoffman, 1839–1929
Tune: SHOWALTER, 10 9 10 9 with refrain; Anthony J. Showalter, 1858–1924; arr. by Nolan Williams, Jr., b.1969, © 2000, GIA Publications, Inc.

593 Leave It There

1. If the world from you with-hold of its sil - ver and its gold,
2. If your bod - y suf - fers pain and your health you can't re-gain,
3. When your en - e - mies as - sail and your heart be - gins to fail,
4. When your youth-ful days are gone and old age is steal-ing on,

And you have to get a - long with mea - ger fare,
And your soul is al - most sink - ing in de - spair,
Don't for - get that God in heav - en an - swers prayer;
And your bod - y bends be - neath the weight of care,

Just re - mem-ber, in his Word, how he feeds the lit - tle bird—
Je - sus knows the pain you feel, he can save and he can heal—
He will make a way for you and will lead you safe-ly through—
He will nev - er leave you then, he'll go with you to the end—

Take your bur - den to the Lord and leave it there.

Leave it there, leave it there, Take your
Leave it there, leave it there, leave it there, leave it there, Take your
bur - den to the Lord and leave it there; If you
leave it there;
trust and nev - er doubt, he will sure - ly bring you out. Take your
bur - den to the Lord and leave it there.

Text: Charles A. Tindley, 1851–1933
Tune: LEAVE IT THERE, 14 11 14 11 with refrain; Charles A. Tindley, 1851–1933; arr. by Nolan Williams, Jr., b.1969, © 2000, GIA Publications, Inc.

594 Blessed Quietness

1. Joys are flow-ing like a riv-er, Since the Com-fort-er has come; He a-bides with us for ev-er, Makes the trust-ing heart his home.

2. Bring-ing life and health and glad-ness All a-round this heav'n-ly Guest, Con-quered un-be-lief and sad-ness, Changed our wea-ri-ness to rest.

3. Like the rain that falls from heav-en, Like the sun-light from the sky, So the Ho-ly Spir-it's giv-en, Com-ing on us from on high.

4. See, a fruit-ful field is grow-ing, Bless-ed fruit of right-eous-ness; And the streams of life are flow-ing In the lone-ly wil-der-ness.

5. What a won-der-ful sal-va-tion, When we al-ways see his face, What a per-fect hab-i-ta-tion, What a qui-et rest-ing place.

Bless-ed qui-et-ness, Ho-ly qui-et-ness, What as-

sur - ance in my soul; On the storm-y sea, Je - sus

speaks to me, And the bil - lows cease to roll.

Text: Marie P. Ferguson, c.1897
Tune: BLESSED QUIETNESS, 8 7 8 7 with refrain; W. S. Marshall, c.1897; arr. by Nolan Williams, Jr., b.1969, © 2000, GIA Publications, Inc.

595 The Storm Is Passing Over

Take cour-age my soul and let us jour-ney on,

tho' the night is dark and

I am far from home. Thanks be to God,

the morn-ing light ap-pears. The

storm is pass-ing o - ver, the storm is pass-ing o -

Text: Charles A. Tindley, 1851–1933, and Donald Vails, ©
Tune: Donald Vails, ©; arr. by Evelyn Simpson-Curenton, b.1953, © 2000, GIA Publications, Inc.

596 The Angels Keep A-Watchin'

All night, all day, the an-gels keep a-watch-in' o-ver me, my Lord!

All night, all day, the an-gels keep a-watch-in' o-ver me!

Text: Negro Spiritual
Tune: Negro Spiritual; arr. by Nolan Williams, Jr., b.1969, © 2000, GIA Publications, Inc.

Shine on Me 597

1. I heard the voice of Je - sus
2. With pit - y - ing eyes the Prince of

say, "Come un - to me and rest.
Peace Be - held our help - less grief;

Lay down thou wea - ry one, lay
He saw, and O a - maz - ing

down Thy head up - on my breast."
love! He came to our re - lief.

Shine on me, Shine on me. Let the

light from the light-house, Shine on me.

Shine on me. Shine on me. Let the

light from the light-house Shine on me.

Text: Negro Spiritual
Tune: SHINE ON ME, CM with refrain; Negro Spiritual; arr. by James Abbington, b.1960, © 2000, GIA Publications, Inc.

598 I Heard the Voice of Jesus Say

1. I heard the voice of Je - sus say, "Come un - to me and
2. I heard the voice of Je - sus say, "Be - hold, I free - ly
3. I heard the voice of Je - sus say, "I am this dark world's

rest;   Lay down, thou wea - ry   one,   lay   down   Thy
give   The liv - ing wa - ter; thirst - y   one,   Stoop
Light;   Look un - to me; thy   morn   shall   rise,   And

head   up - on   my   breast."   I   came to Je - sus
down, and drink, and   live."   I   came to Je - sus,
all   thy day   be   bright."   I   looked to Je - sus,

as   I was, So wea - ry, worn, and sad;
and   I drank Of that life - giv - ing stream;
and   I found In him   my   star, my   sun;

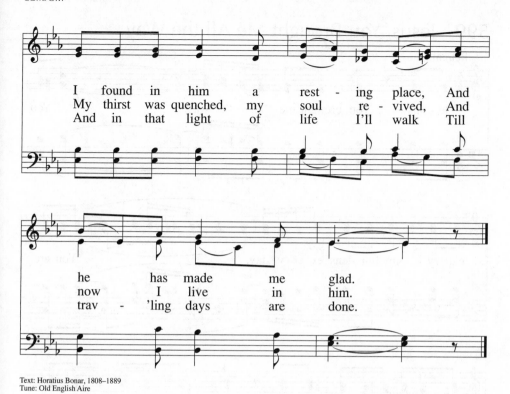

I found in him a rest - ing place, And
My thirst was quenched, my soul re - vived, And
And in that light of life I'll walk Till

he has made me glad.
now I live in him.
trav - 'ling days are done.

Text: Horatius Bonar, 1808–1889
Tune: Old English Aire

599 Jesus, You Brought Me All the Way

Refrain

Je - sus, you brought me all the way. You carry my bur-dens ev-er-y day. You are such a won-der-ful Sav-ior, I've nev-er known you to fail me yet. 'Cause you brought me, 'cause you brought me, thank God, all of the way, 'cause you brought me, thank God, all of the way, thank God,

'cause you brought me.

all of the way, thank God, all of the way.

Je - sus, you brought me all of the way.

Last time

Verses

Solo (very freely):

1. Trou - bles and tri - als, they seem to block my way.
2. Went to the val - ley one day to pray.

Some - times I find it so dif - fi - cult to pray.
My soul got hap - py and I stayed there all day.

Oh, but there's one thing I can tru - ly say: that you've brought

D.C.

me, thank God, all the way.

Text: Kenneth W. Louis, b.1956
Tune: Kenneth W. Louis, b.1956
© 2001, GIA Publications, Inc.

600 Come, Bring Your Burdens to God / Woza Nomthwalo Wakho

Solo:
Come, bring your bur-dens, oh,

Come, bring your bur-dens to God, come, bring your
Wo - za nom - thwa - lo wa-kho, wo - za nom-

come, bring your bur - dens, oh, come, bring your bur-dens,

bur - dens to God, come, bring your bur - dens to God for
thwa - lo wa-kho, wo - za nom-thwa - lo wa-kho U-

To repeat | *Last time*

Je-sus will nev-er say no.

Je-sus will nev-er say no. Come, bring your no.
ye-s's-ka-so-za-thi hayi. Wo - za nom-hayi.

African phonetics:
Woh-zah nohm-thwah-loh wah-khoh, U-yehs skah-soh-zah-thee hahyee

Text: South African; tr. by Barbara Clark, Mairi Munro, and Martine Stemerick, © 2008, Iona Community, GIA Publications, Inc., agent
Tune: South African melody; arr. by Welile Sigabi, © 2008, Iona Community, GIA Publications, Inc., agent

The King of Love My Shepherd Is   601

1. The King of love my shep - herd is, Whose
2. Where streams of liv - ing wa - ter flow, My
3. Con - fused and fool - ish oft I strayed, But
4. In death's dark vale I fear no ill With
5. You spread a ta - ble in my sight, Your
6. And so, through all the length of days Your

good - ness fails me nev - er; I noth - ing lack if
ran - somed soul he's lead - ing, And, where the ver - dant
yet in love he sought me, And on his shoul - der
you, dear Lord, be - side me, Your rod and staff my
sav - ing grace be - stow - ing; And, oh, what trans - port
good - ness fails me nev - er; Good Shep - herd, may I

I am his And he is mine for - ev - er.
pas - tures grow, With food ce - les - tial feed - ing.
gent - ly laid, And home, re - joic - ing, brought me.
com - fort still, Your cross be - fore to guide me.
of de - light From your pure chal - ice flow - ing!
sing your praise With - in your house for - ev - er.

Text: Psalm 23; Henry W. Baker, 1821–1877, alt.
Tune: ST. COLUMBA, 8 7 8 7; Irish melody; harm. by A. Gregory Murray, OSB, 1905–1992, © Downside Abbey

602 Blest Are They

Verses 1–3

1. Blest are they, the poor in spir - it;
2. Blest are they, the low - ly ones;
3. Blest are they who show mer - cy;

theirs is the king - dom of God.
they shall in - her - it the earth.
mer - cy shall be theirs.

Blest are they, full of sor - row;
Blest are they who hun - ger and thirst;
Blest are they, the pure of heart;

they shall be con - soled.
they shall have their fill.
they shall see God.

Refrain

Descant:

Re - joice and be glad!

Melody:

Re - joice and be glad!

Men's voices:

Re - joice and be glad!

Verses 4, 5

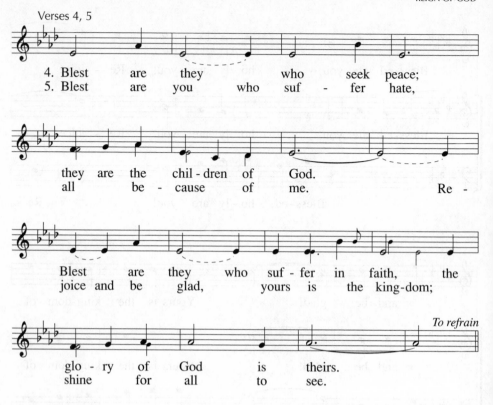

4. Blest are they who seek peace;
5. Blest are you who suf - fer hate,

they are the chil - dren of God.
all be - cause of me. Re -

Blest are they who suf - fer in faith, the
joice and be glad, yours is the king-dom;

To refrain

glo - ry of God is theirs.
shine for all to see.

Text: Matthew 5:3-12; David Haas, b.1957
Tune: David Haas, b.1957; vocal arr. by David Haas and Michael Joncas, b.1951
© 1985, GIA Publications, Inc.

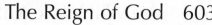

The Reign of God 603

1. The reign of God, like farm - er's field, Bears
2. The reign of God can - not be found In
3. The reign of God is like a pearl On
4. Though hid - den now, the reign of God May,
5. Like mus - tard tree, the reign of God From
6. The reign of God is come in Christ; The

weeds a - long with wheat; The good and bad are
far - off, for - eign land Till in fa - mil - iar
bar - ren land con - cealed. If once you find that
yet un - no - ticed, grow; From deep with - in it
ti - ny seed will spread, Till birds of ev - 'ry
reign of God is near. A - blaze a - mong us,

in - ter - twined Till har - vest is com - plete.
face and place We find it close at hand.
pre - cious pearl, Go out and buy that field.
ris - es up, Like yeast in swell - ing dough.
feath - er come To nest, and there be fed.
kin - dling hearts, The reign of God is here!

Text: Delores Dufner, OSB, b.1939, © 1995, 2003, GIA Publications, Inc.
Tune: McKEE, CM; African American; adapt. by Harry T. Burleigh, 1866–1949

604 We Will Walk with God / Sizohamba

We will walk   with God, my broth-ers,   we will walk   with God.
We will walk   with God, my sis-ters,   we will walk   with God.
Si - zo-ham-ba na - ye,   wo wo wo,   si-zo-ham-ba na - ye.

We will walk   with God, my broth-ers,   we will walk   with God.
We will walk   with God, my sis - ters,   we will walk   with God.
Si - zo - ham-ba na - ye,   wo wo wo,   si - zo - ham - ba na - ye.

We   will go re - joic - ing   till the king-dom has come.
Ngom-hla wen - ja - bu - la,   si - zo - ham - ba na - ye.

We   will go re - joic - ing   till the king - dom has come.
Ngom-hla wen - ja - bu - la,   si - zo - ham - ba na - ye.

African phonetics:
See-zoh-hahm-bah nah-yay, woh woh woh, see-zoh-hahm-bah nah-yay.
Ngahm-hlah wen-jah-boo-lah, see-zoh-hahm-bah nah-yay.

Text: Swaziland traditional; transcribed by Swedish Youth Exchange Project, ©; tr. by John L. Bell, b.1949, © 2002, Iona Community,
   GIA Publications, Inc., agent
Tune: Swaziland traditional; transcribed by Swedish Youth Exchange Project, ©

Blest Be the Tie That Binds 605

1. Blest be the tie that binds Our hearts in Chris - tian love; The fel - low - ship of kin - dred minds Is like to that a - bove.
2. Be - fore our Fa - ther's throne We pour our ar - dent prayers; Our fears, our hopes, our aims are one, Our com - forts and our cares.
3. We share each oth - er's woes, Each oth - er's bur - dens bear; And of - ten for each oth - er flows The sym - pa - thiz - ing tear.
4. From sor - row, toil, and pain, And sin we shall be free; And per - fect love and joy shall reign Through all e - ter - ni - ty.

Text: John Fawcett, 1740–1817
Tune: DENNIS, SM; John G. Nägeli, 1773–1836; arr. by Lowell Mason, 1792–1872

606 The Church's One Foundation

1. The Chur-ch's one foun - da - tion Is Je - sus Christ, her
2. E - lect from ev - 'ry na - tion, Yet one o'er all the
3. Through toil and trib - u - la - tion And tu - mult of her
4. Yet she on earth has u - nion With God, the Three in

Lord; She is his new cre - a - tion By wa - ter and the
earth; Her char - ter of sal - va - tion: One Lord, one faith, one
war She waits the con - sum - ma - tion Of peace for - ev - er -
One, And mys - tic sweet com - mun - ion With those whose rest is

Word. From heav'n he came and sought her To
birth. One ho - ly name she bless - es, Par -
more Till with the vi - sion glo - rious Her
won. O bless - ed heav'n - ly cho - rus! Lord,

be his ho - ly bride; With his own blood he
takes one ho - ly food, And to one hope she
long - ing eyes are blessed, And the great Church vic -
save us by your grace That we, like saints be -

bought her, And for her life he died.
press - es With ev - 'ry grace en - dued.
to - rious Shall be the Church at rest.
fore us, May see you face to face.

Text: Samuel J. Stone, 1839–1900, alt.
Tune: AURELIA, 7 6 7 6 D; Samuel S. Wesley, 1810–1876

607 The Glory of the Lord

When the glo-ry of the Lord fills this ho-ly tem-ple, he will lift us high. And on an-gels' wings we'll rise to the pure and ho-ly, when his Spir-it fills this place. *When his glo - ry, when his glo - ry, when his glo-ry fills this place. When his glo - ry, when his glo - ry, when his glo-ry fills this place.

*Alternate text: Let thy glory... Let thy glory fill this place...

Text: Gloria Gaither, William Gaither, and Richard Smallwood, b.1948
Tune: Gloria Gaither, William Gaither, and Richard Smallwood, b.1948; arr. by Nolan Williams, Jr., b.1969

Somebody Prayed for Me   608

1. Some-bod-y prayed for me, had me on their mind,

took the time and prayed for me.

I'm so glad they prayed.   I'm so glad they prayed.

I'm so glad they prayed for me.

2. The preacher prayed for me...
3. My mother prayed for me...
4. Jesus prayed for me...

Text: Dorothy Norwood and Alvin Darling
Tune: Dorothy Norwood and Alvin Darling; arr. by Nolan Williams, Jr., b.1969, and Stephen Key
© 1994, Malaco Music, Inc.

609 Renew Thy Church, Her Ministries Restore

1. Re - new thy church, her min - is - tries re - store:
2. Teach us thy Word, re - veal its truth di - vine;
3. Teach us to pray, for thou art ev - er near;
4. Teach us to love, with strength of heart and mind,

Both to serve and a - dore. Make her a - gain as
On our path let it shine. Tell of thy works, thy
Thy still voice let us hear. Our souls are rest - less
Ev - 'ry - one, all man - kind. Break down old walls of

salt through-out the land, And as light from a stand.
might - y acts of grace; From each page show thy face.
till they rest in thee: This our glad des - ti - ny.
prej - u - dice and hate; Leave us not to our fate.

'Mid som - ber shad - ows of the night Where
As thou hast loved us, sent thy Son, And
Be - fore thy pres - ence keep us still, That
As thou hast loved and giv'n thy life To

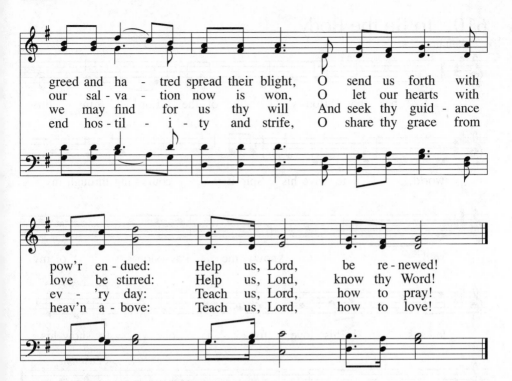

greed and ha - tred spread their blight, O send us forth with
our sal - va - tion now is won, O let our hearts with
we may find for us thy will And seek thy guid - ance
end hos - til - i - ty and strife, O share thy grace from

pow'r en - dued: Help us, Lord, be re - newed!
love be stirred: Help us, Lord, know thy Word!
ev - 'ry day: Teach us, Lord, how to pray!
heav'n a - bove: Teach us, Lord, how to love!

Text: Kenneth L. Cober, 1902–1993, © 1960, Kenneth L. Cober, renewed 1985, Judson Press
Tune: ALL IS WELL, 10 6 10 6 88 86; J. T. White's *Sacred Harp*

610 To Be the Body

Refrain

To be the Bod-y of the Lord in this
world, to have his Spir-it cours-ing through my
soul, to know the Pas-sion of my
Je-sus in his love for ev-'ry one, to show his

Last time

mer-cy in the shad-ows of this land.

Verses

1. Come, walk with me; come, share my
2. No eyes have I, no ears to
3. O - pen your eyes, see what I
4. I am the Vine, branch - es are
5. One bread, one cup; one heart and

life. You must know the shad-ows
hear. You must be my Bod-y
see. For this world how I suf-fer.
you. Life for me e - ter-nal
mind. One great hu - man peo-ple

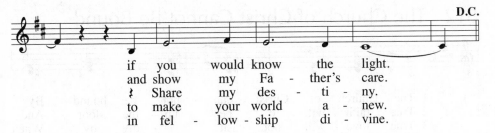

D.C.

if you would know the light.
and show my Fa - ther's care.
℟ Share my des - ti - ny.
to make your world a - new.
in fel - low - ship di - vine.

Text: Clyde Harvey
Tune: Clyde Harvey; arr. by Paschal Jordan, OSB, b.1944
© 1998, Antilles Episcopal Conference

Make of Our Life a House of Praise 611

1. Make of our life a house of praise Where
2. Here may we find our prayers are heard, And
3. May such a house of calm and peace The
4. Teach us our house of life to share, That
5. So may our doors be o - pen wide, And

all, with one ac - cord, U - nite to walk in
grow in truth and grace, Re - ceive from Christ his
Spir - it strive to build; Where kind - li - ness and
all who will may come, The lost be dou - bly
life to - geth - er prove A house where God is

Je - sus' ways, The tem - ple of the Lord.
ho - ly word And know his love's em - brace.
faith in - crease, The storms of life are stilled.
wel - come there, The wan - d'rer find a home.
glo - ri - fied, And a house of praise and love.

Text: Timothy Dudley-Smith, b.1926, © 2009, Hope Publishing Company
Tune: RICHMOND, CM; Thomas Haweis, 1734–1820; adapt. by Samuel Webbe, 1770–1843

612 The Church of Christ Cannot Be Bound

1. The Church of Christ can - not be bound By
2. True faith will o - pen up the door And
3. True love will not sit i - dly by When
4. If what we have we free - ly share To
5. The Church of Christ can - not be bound By

walls of wood or stone. Where char - i - ty and
step in - to the street. True serv - ice will seek
jus - tice is de - nied. True mer - cy hears the
meet our neigh - bor's need, Then we ex - tend the
walls of wood or stone. Where char - i - ty and

love are found, There can the Church be known.
out the poor And ask to wash their feet.
home - less cry And wel - comes them in - side.
Spir - it's care Through ev - 'ry self - less deed.
love are found, There can the Church be known.

Text: Adam M. L. Tice, b.1979, © 2005, GIA Publications, Inc.
Tune: McKEE, CM; African American; adapt. by Harry T. Burleigh, 1866–1949

I Have Decided to Follow Jesus 613

1. I have de-cid - ed to fol-low Je - sus,
2. Though no one join me, still I will fol - low,
3. The world be - hind me, the cross be - fore me,

I have de-cid - ed to fol-low Je - sus,
Though no one join me, still I will fol - low,
The world be - hind me, the cross be - fore me,

I have de-cid - ed to fol-low Je - sus—
Though no one join me, still I will fol - low—
The world be - hind me, the cross be - fore me—

No turn-ing back, no turn-ing back!
no turn-ing back,

Text: Ascribed to an Indian prince; as sung in Garo, Assam
Tune: ASSAM, 10 10 10 8; Indian Folk melody, Paul B. Smith; harm. by Norman Johnson, 1928–1983
© 1963, Singspiration Music (ASCAP)

614 Lead Me to Calvary

1. King of my life I crown thee now— Thine shall the
2. Show me the tomb where thou wast laid, Ten - der - ly
3. Let me like Mar - y, thru the gloom, Come with a
4. May I be will - ing, Lord, to bear Dai - ly my

glo - ry be; Lest I for - get thy thorn - crowned brow,
mourned and wept; An - gels in robes of light ar - rayed
gift to thee; Show to me now the emp - ty tomb—
cross for thee; E - ven thy cup of grief to share—

Lead me to Cal - va - ry.
Guard - ed thee whilst thou slept.
Lead me to Cal - va - ry.
Thou hast borne all for me.

Lest I for - get Geth -

sem - a - ne, Lest I for - get thine ag - o - ny,

Lest I for-get thy love for me, Lead me to Cal-va-ry.

Text: Jennie E. Hussey, 1874–1958
Tune: DUNCANNON, CM with refrain; William J. Kirkpatrick, 1838–1921

Must Jesus Bear the Cross Alone 615

1. Must Je - sus bear the cross a - lone And
2. The con - se - crat - ed cross I'll bear Till
3. Up - on the crys - tal pave - ment, down At
4. O pre - cious cross! O glo - rious crown! O

all the world go free? No, there's a cross for
death shall set me free, And then go home my
Je - sus' pierc - ed feet, Joy - ful, I'll cast my
res - ur - rec - tion day! Ye an - gels, from the

ev - 'ry one, And there's a cross for me.
crown to wear, For there's a crown for me.
gold - en crown And his dear name re - peat.
stars come down And bear my soul a - way.

Text: Thomas Shepherd, 1665–1739
Tune: MAITLAND, CM; George N. Allen, 1812–1877

616   I Surrender All

1. All to Je - sus I sur - ren - der,
I will ev - er love and trust him,
2. All to Je - sus I sur - ren - der,
World - ly pleas - ures all for - sak - en,
3. All to Je - sus I sur - ren - der,
Fill me with thy Ho - ly Spir - it—
4. All to Je - sus I sur - ren - der,
Fill me with thy love and pow - er,

All to him I free - ly give;
In his pres - ence dai - ly live.
Hum - bly at his feet I bow;
Take me, Je - sus, take me now.
Make me, Sav - ior, whol - ly thine;
Tru - ly know that thou art mine.
Lord, I give my - self to thee;
Let thy bless - ings fall on me.

I sur-ren-der all,   I sur-ren-der all.

I sur-ren-der all,   I sur-ren-der all.

All to thee, my bless - ed Sav-ior, I sur-ren-der all.

Text: Judson W. Van De Venter, 1855–1939
Tune: SURRENDER, 8 7 8 7 with refrain; Winfield S. Weeden, 1847–1908

We Are Climbing Jacob's Ladder   617

1. We are climb-ing Ja-cob's lad - der, We are climb-ing Ja-cob's lad - der, We are climb-ing Ja-cob's lad - der, Sol-diers of the cross.
2. Ev - 'ry round goes high - er, high - er, Ev - 'ry round goes high - er, high - er, high - er, high - er, Sol-diers of the cross.
3. Chil-dren, do you love my Je - sus? Chil-dren, do you love my Je - sus? love my Je - sus? Sol-diers of the cross.
4. If you love him, why not serve him? If you love him, why not serve him? why not serve him? Sol-diers of the cross.
5. Rise, shine, give God glo - ry, Rise, shine, give God glo - ry, give God glo - ry, Sol-diers of the cross.

Text: Negro Spiritual
Tune: JACOB'S LADDER, 8 8 8 5; Negro Spiritual

618 Close to Thee

1. Thou my ev - er - last - ing por - tion, More than
2. Not for ease or world - ly pleas - ure, Nor for
3. Lead me through the vale of shad - ows, Bear me

friend or life to me, All a - long my pil - grim
fame my prayer shall be; Glad - ly will I toil and
o'er life's fit - ful sea; Then the gate of life e -

jour - ney, Sav - ior, let me walk with thee.
suf - fer, On - ly let me walk with thee.
ter - nal May I en - ter, Lord, with thee.

Close to thee, Close to thee, Close to thee, Close to thee;

All a-long my pil-grim jour-ney, Sav-ior, let me walk with thee.
Glad-ly will I toil and suf-fer, On-ly let me walk with thee.
Then the gate of life e-ter-nal May I en-ter, Lord, with thee.

Text: Fanny J. Crosby, 1820–1915
Tune: CLOSE TO THEE, 8 7 8 7 with refrain; Silas J. Vail, 1818–1884; arr. by Nolan Williams, Jr., b.1969, © 2000, GIA Publications, Inc.

Take, O Take Me As I Am 619

Ostinato Refrain

Take, O take me as I am; sum-mon out what I shall be;

set your seal up-on my heart and live in me.

Text: John L. Bell, b.1949
Tune: John L. Bell, b.1949
© 1995, Iona Community, GIA Publications, Inc., agent

620 I'll Be Somewhere Listening for My Name

1. When he calls me I will an - swer, When he
2. With a glad heart I will an - swer, With a
3. When he calls you, will you an - swer? When he

calls me I will an - swer, When he calls me I will
glad heart I will an - swer, With a glad heart I will
calls you, will you an - swer? When he calls you, will you

an - swer; I'll be some-where list-'ning for my name.
an - swer; I'll be some-where list-'ning for my name.
an - swer? Some-where list - 'ning, list-'ning for your name.

1., 2. I'll be some-where list-'ning, I'll be some-where list-'ning,
3. You'll be some-where list-'ning, You'll be some-where list-'ning,

I'll be some-where list-'ning for my name. Oh,
You'll be some-where list-'ning for your name. Oh,

I'll be some-where list-'ning, I'll be some-where
you'll be some-where list-'ning, You'll be some-where

list-'ning, I'll be some-where list-'ning for my name.
list-'ning, You'll be some-where list-'ning for your name.

Text: Eduardo J. Lango
Tune: SOMEWHERE LISTENING, 888 9 66 9 76 9; Eduardo J. Lango; adapt. by Louis Sykes, © 2000, GIA Publications, Inc.

621 Where He Leads Me

1. I can hear my Sav-ior call-ing, I can hear my Sav-ior call-ing, I can hear my Sav-ior call-ing, "Take thy cross and fol-low, fol-low me."
2. I'll go with him through the gar-den, I'll go with him through the gar-den, I'll go with him through the gar-den, I'll go with him, with him all the way.
3. I'll go with him through the judg-ment, I'll go with him through the judg-ment, I'll go with him through the judg-ment, I'll go with him, with him all the way.
4. He will give me grace and glo-ry, He will give me grace and glo-ry, He will give me grace and glo-ry, And go with me, with me all the way.

Refrain: Where he leads me I will fol-low, Where he leads me I will fol-low, Where he leads me I will fol-low, I'll go with him, with him all the way.

Text: E. W. Blandy, c.1890
Tune: NORRIS, 888 9 with refrain; John S. Norris, 1844–1907

The Summons 622

1. Will you come and fol - low me If I but
2. Will you leave your - self be - hind If I but
3. Will you let the blind - ed see If I but
4. Will you love the "you" you hide If I but
5. Lord, your sum - mons ech - oes true When you but

call your name? Will you go where
call your name? Will you care for
call your name? Will you set the
call your name? Will you quell the
call my name. Let me turn and

you don't know And nev - er be the same?
cruel and kind And nev - er be the same?
pris - 'ners free And nev - er be the same?
fear in - side And nev - er be the same?
fol - low you And nev - er be the same.

Will you let my love be shown, Will you
Will you risk the hos - tile stare Should your
Will you kiss the lep - er clean, And do
Will you use the faith you've found To re -
In your com - pa - ny I'll go Where your

let my name be known, Will you let my
life at - tract or scare? Will you let me
such as this un - seen, And ad - mit to
shape the world a - round, Through my sight and
love and foot - steps show. Thus I'll move and

life be grown In you and you in me?
an - swer prayer In you and you in me?
what I mean In you and you in me?
touch and sound In you and you in me?
live and grow In you and you in me.

Text: John L. Bell, b.1949, © 1987, Iona Community, GIA Publications, Inc., agent
Tune: KELVINGROVE, 7 6 7 6 777 6; Scottish melody; arr. by John L. Bell, b.1949, © 1987, Iona Community, GIA Publications, Inc., agent

623 Completely Yes

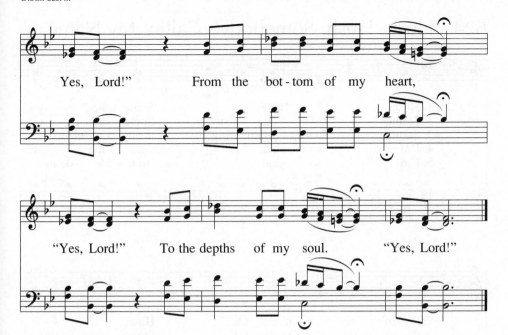

Yes, Lord!" From the bot-tom of my heart,

"Yes, Lord!" To the depths of my soul. "Yes, Lord!"

Text: Sandra Crouch, b.1942
Tune: Sandra Crouch, b.1942; arr. by Stephen Key
© 1985, Sanabella Music/Bud John Songs, admin. at EMICMGPublishing.com

624 Hush, Hush, Somebody's Callin' My Name

1. Hush. Hush. Some-bod-y's
2. Sounds like Je-sus. Some-bod-y's
3. Soon one morn-ing, death come creep-in'
4. I'm so glad, got me re-
5. I'm so glad trou-ble don't

call-in' my name. Oh, Hush.
call-in' my name. Oh, Sounds like
in my room. Oh, Soon one
lig-ion on time. Oh, I'm so
last al-ways. Oh, I'm so

Hush. Some-bod-y's call-in' my name.
Je-sus. Some-bod-y's call-in' my name.
morn-ing, death come creep-in' in my room.
glad, got me re-lig-ion on time.
glad trou-ble don't last al-ways.

Hush. Hush. Some-bod - y's call-in' my
Sounds like Je - sus. Some-bod - y's call-in' my
Soon one morn-ing, death come creep-in' in my
I'm so glad, got me re - lig-ion on
I'm so glad trou-ble don't last al -

name.
name.
room. Oh, my Lord, Oh, my Lord, what shall I do?
time.
ways.

1.-4.   5.

what shall I do?

Text: Traditional
Tune: SOMEBODY'S CALLIN', Irregular; Negro Spiritual; arr. by Nolan Williams, Jr., b.1969, © 2000, GIA Publications, Inc.

625 Give Me a Clean Heart

Refrain

Give me a clean heart so I may serve thee. Lord, fix my heart so that I may be used by thee. For I'm not wor - thy of all these bless - ings.

Last time

Give me a clean heart, and I'll fol-low thee.

Last time

Verses

1. I'm not ask - ing for the rich - es of the land.
2. Some-times I am up and some-times I am down.

I'm not ask - ing for the proud to know my name.
Some-times I am al - most lev - el to the ground.

Please give me, Lord, a clean heart, that

I may fol - low thee. Give me a clean heart

1.   2.   D.C.

and I'll fol - low thee.

Text: Margaret Pleasant Douroux, b.1941, © 1970, Rev. Earl Pleasant Publishing
Tune: Margaret Pleasant Douroux, b.1941, © 1970, Rev. Earl Pleasant Publishing; arr. by Albert Dennis Tessier and Nolan Williams, Jr., b.1969,
© 2000, GIA Publications, Inc.

626 I've Decided to Make Jesus My Choice

1. Some folk would rath-er have hous-es and land.
2. These clothes may be rag-ged that I'm wear - ing.

Some folk choose sil - ver and gold.
Heav - y is the load that I'm bear - ing.

These things they treas - ure and for-get a-bout their souls;
These old bur - dens that I'm car - rying

I've de - cid - ed to make Je - sus my choice.

The road is rough; the go-ing gets tough, and the
hills are hard to climb. I've start-ed out a
long time a-go, there's no doubt in my mind; I've de-
cid - ed to make Je - sus my choice.

Text: Harrison Johnson
Tune: Harrison Johnson

627 Lord, When You Came /
Pescador de Hombres

Verses

1. Lord, when you came to the sea - shore
2. Lord, you knew what my boat car - ried:
3. Lord, have you need of my la - bor,
4. Lord, send me where you would have me,

1. Tú has ve - ni - do_a la_o - ri - lla,
2. Tú sa - bes bien lo que ten - go;
3. Tú ne - ce - si - tas mis ma - nos,
4. Tú, pes - ca - dor de_o - tros la - gos,

You weren't seek - ing the wise or the
Nei - ther mon - ey nor weap - ons for
Hands for serv - ice, a heart made for
To a vil - lage, or heart of the

No_has bus - ca - do ni_a sa - bios, ni_a
En mi bar - ca no_hay o - ro ni_es -
Mi can - san - cio que_a o - tros des -
An - sia_e - ter - na de al - mas que_es-

wealth - y, But on - ly ask - ing
fight - ing, But nets for fish - ing,
lov - ing, My arms for lift - ing
cit - y; I will re - mem - ber

ri - cos; Tan só - lo quie - res
pa - das, Tan só - lo re - des
can - se, A - mor que quie - ra
pe - ran; A - mi - go bue - no,

that I might fol - low.
my dai - ly la - bor.
the poor and bro - ken?
that you are with me.

que yo te si - ga.
y mi tra - ba - jo.
se - guir a - man - do.
que_a - sí me lla - mas.

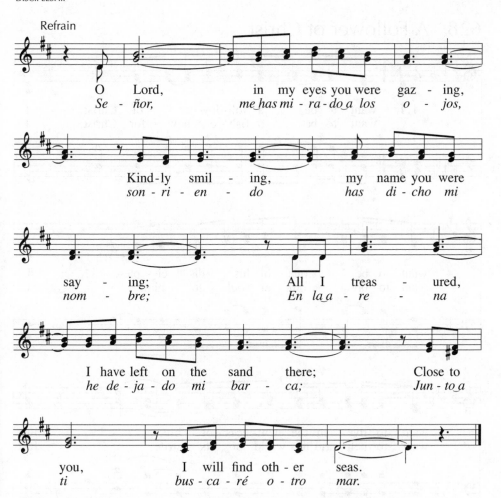

Refrain

O Lord, in my eyes you were gaz - ing,
Se - ñor, me has mi - ra - do a los o - jos,

Kind - ly smil - ing, my name you were
son - ri - en - do has di - cho mi

say - ing; All I treas - ured,
nom - bre; En la a - re - na

I have left on the sand there; Close to
he de - ja - do mi bar - ca; Jun - to a

you, I will find oth - er seas.
ti bus - ca - ré o - tro mar.

Text: *Pescador de Hombres,* Cesáreo Gabaráin, 1936–1991, © 1979, published by OCP; tr. by Willard F. Jabusch, b.1930, © 1982, administered by OCP
Tune: PESCADOR DE HOMBRES, 8 10 10 with refrain; Cesáreo Gabaráin, 1936–1991, © 1979, published by OCP; acc. by Diana Kodner, b.1957

628 A Follower of Christ

1. I want to be a fol - low - er of Christ. I
   want to be a fish - er, now for Christ. I

want to be one of his dis - ci - ples. I
want to bring oth - er souls to him, I

want to live in the new - ness of life, Just
want to help rid this world of its strife, Just

let me be a fol - low - er of Christ. 2. I
let me be a fol - low - er of

Christ. What do I have to do? What do I have to say? How do I have to walk each and ev-'ry day? Tell me what does it cost if I car-ry the cross? Just let me be a fol-low-er of Christ.

Text: J. W. Harris, alt.
Tune: J. W. Harris; arr. by Kenneth W. Louis, b.1956, © 2012, GIA Publications, Inc.

629 Done Made My Vow to the Lord

Refrain

Done made my vow to the Lord, and I

Oh, I

nev - er will turn back, will go, I

shall go to see what the end will be.

Verses
1. Some - times I'm up, some - times I'm down;
2. When I was a mourn - er just like you;

(hum)

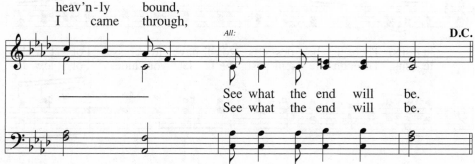

Text: Negro Spiritual
Tune: Negro Spiritual; arr. by Evelyn Davidson White, 1921–2007

630 Follow Jesus

1. Fol - low Je - sus, take no chance get - ting lost. Fol - low
2. Fol - low Je - sus, he will lead, he will guide. Fol-low

Je - sus, There'll be des - erts you'll have to cross. Fol - low Je -
Je - sus, Through life's tem - pest he'll let you hide. Fol - low Je -

sus. He's got a safe moun - tain plan;
sus. Reach out and touch, hold his hand; and if

he can't take you to the top, there's no - bod - y else who can.

Don't wor-ry if you can-not see, learn to trust him and to fol-low his lead. Don't wor-ry if it's day or night. He is bright-er than the bright-est light. And if he can't take you to the top, there's no-bod-y else who can.

631 You Walk along Our Shoreline

1. You walk a - long our shore - line, Where land meets un-known sea.
2. You call us, Christ, to gath - er The peo - ple of the earth.
3. We cast our net, O Je - sus; We cry the king-dom's name;

We hear your voice of pow - er, "Now come and fol - low me.
We can - not fish for on - ly Those lives we think have worth.
We work for love and jus - tice; We learn to hope through pain.

And if you still will fol - low Through storm and wave and shoal,
We spread your net of gos - pel A - cross the wa - ter's face,
You call us, Lord, to gath - er God's daugh-ters and God's sons,

Then I will make you fish - ers, But of the hu - man soul."
Our boat a com-mon shel - ter For all found by your grace.
To let your judg-ment heal us So that all may be one.

Text: Sylvia Dunstan, 1955–1993, © 1991, GIA Publications, Inc.
Tune: AURELIA, 7 6 7 6 D; Samuel Sebastian Wesley, 1810–1876

Just As I Am   632

1. Just as I am, with - out one plea,
2. Just as I am, and wait - ing not
3. Just as I am, though tossed a - bout
4. Just as I am— poor, wretch - ed, blind;
5. Just as I am— thou wilt re - ceive,

But that thy blood was shed for me,
To rid my soul of one deep blot,
With man - y a con - flict, man - y a doubt,
Sight, rich - es, heal - ing of the mind,
Wilt wel - come, par - don, cleanse, re - lieve,

And that thou bidd'st me come to thee,
To thee whose blood can cleanse each spot,
Fight - ings and fears with - in, with - out,
Yea, all I need in thee to find,
Be - cause thy prom - ise I be - lieve,

O Lamb of God, I come! I come!

Text: Charlotte Elliott, 1789–1871
Tune: WOODWORTH, LM; William B. Bradbury, 1816–1868

633   Lift Him Up

1. How to reach the mass - es, *men of ev - 'ry birth,
2. Oh! the world is hun - gry for the Liv - ing Bread,
3. Don't ex - alt the preach-er, don't ex - alt the pew,
4. Lift him up by liv - ing as a Chris - tian ought,

For an an - swer Je - sus gave the key: "And
Lift the Sav - ior up for them to see; Trust
Preach the Gos - pel sim - ple, full and free; Prove
Let the world in you the Sav - ior see; Then

I, if I be lift - ed up from the earth,
him, and do not doubt the words that he said,
him and you will find that prom - ise is true,
men will glad - ly fol - low him who once taught,

Will draw all men un - to me."
"I'll draw all men un - to me."
"I'll draw all men un - to me."
"I'll draw all men un - to me."

*Saints *can be substituted for* men *throughout this text.*

Lift him up, Lift him up,
Lift the pre-cious Sav-ior up, Lift the pre-cious Sav-ior up,

Still he speaks from e - ter - ni - ty: "And I, if I be lift-ed

up from the earth, Will draw all men un - to me."

Text: Johnson Oatman, Jr., 1856–1922
Tune: LIFT HIM UP, 11 9 11 7 with refrain; B. B. Beall; adapt. by Nolan Williams, Jr., b.1969, Evelyn Simpson-Curenton, b.1953,
    and Robert J. Fryson, 1944–1994, © 2000, GIA Publications, Inc.

634 What a Mighty God We Serve

up your weap-ons and flee, for the Lord has giv-en me au-

thor - i - ty to walk all o - ver thee.

Text: Traditional
Tune: Traditional; arr. by Stephen Key, © 2000, GIA Publications, Inc.

He Has Done Great Things for Me   635

1. He has done great things for me. Great things,
2. He has made a way for me. Made a way,
3. He will give you vic - to - ry. Vic - to - ry,
4. I'm gonna be a wit - ness for him. Wit - ness,
5. I'm gonna let my lit - tle light shine. Shine,

great things. He has done great things for me.
made a way. He has made a way for me.
vic - to - ry. He will give you vic - to - ry.
wit - ness. I'm gonna be a wit - ness for him.
shine. I'm gonna let my lit - tle light shine.

Text: Jessy Dixon, b.1938, © Dixon Music, Inc.
Tune: GREAT THINGS, 7 4 7; Jessy Dixon, b.1938, © Dixon Music, Inc.; arr. by Stephen Key, © 2000, GIA Publications, Inc.

636 Here Am I

1. God has no hands but those that strive to mend
2. God has no eyes but those a - lert to see
3. God's call is now for us to build and keep

The bro - ken hearts of wound - ed kin,
Some-one dis - tressed, some soul in need,
The liv - ing Church, Christ's Bride to be,

God has no feet but those that stride to win
God has no voice un - less we yield to be
So we must work the work and sow the seeds,

An - oth - er soul to en - ter in!
A ves - sel willed to bold - ly sing!
And trust God's prom - is - es to reap!

Here am I, Lord, send me. Here am I,

I'll heed your voice, o - bey your will.

Here am I, Lord, send me. Here am I:

Last time to Coda ✛ **D.S.**

I will glad - ly do your bid!

✛ Coda

I will glad - ly do your bid!

Text: Nolan Williams, Jr., b.1969
Tune: HERE AM I, 10 8 10 8 with refrain; Nolan Williams, Jr., b.1969
© NEW-J Publishing (a division of NEWorks)

637 This Little Light of Mine

1. This lit-tle light of mine, I'm gon-na let it shine.
2. Ev - 'ry - where I go, I'm gon-na let it shine.
3. Je - sus gave it to me, I'm gon-na let it shine.

oh

This lit - tle light of mine, I'm gon-na let it shine.
Ev - 'ry - where I go, I'm gon-na let it shine.
Je - sus gave it to me, I'm gon-na let it shine.

oh

This lit - tle light of mine, I'm gon-na let it shine.
Ev - 'ry - where I go, I'm gon-na let it shine.
Je - sus gave it to me, I'm gon-na let it shine.

oh   oh

Let it shine, let it shine, let it shine.

4. Shine, shine, shine, I'm gonna let it shine....
5. All in my home, I'm gonna let it shine....

Text: Harry Dixon Loes, 1895–1965
Tune: LIGHT OF MINE, 12 12 12 9; Harry Dixon Loes, 1895–1965; arr. by Nolan Williams, Jr., b.1969, © 2000, GIA Publications, Inc.

Thuma Mina / Send Me, Jesus   638

1. Thu - ma mi -na.

1. Thu -ma mi -na, Thu -ma mi - na, Thu - ma mi - na So -man - dla.
Je-sus, send me, Je - sus, Send me, Je - sus, send me, Lord.
Je-sus, lead me, Je - sus, Lead me, Je - sus, lead me, Lord.
Je-sus, fill me, Je - sus Fill me, Je - sus, fill me,

1.–3.
2. Send me, Lord.
3. Lead me, Lord.
4. Fill me, Lord.

4.
2. Send me,
3. Lead me,
4. Fill me,
Lord.

African phonetics:
Too-mah mee-nah, So-mahn-dlah

Text: South African Spiritual (Zulu)
Tune: THUMA MINA, 8 7; South African
© 1984, Peace of Music Publishing AB, admin. by Walton Music Corp.

639 I Shall Not Be Moved

1. I shall not be, I shall not be moved. I shall not be, I shall not be moved; Like a tree plant-ed by the wa - ter, I shall not be moved, be moved. moved. moved.

2. When my cross is heav - y, I shall not be moved,
3. The church of God is march-ing, I shall not be moved, The
4. King Je - sus is our Cap - tain, I shall not be moved, King
5. Come on and join the ar - my, I shall not be moved, Come
6. Fight-ing sin and Sa - tan, I shall not be moved,
7. When my bur - den's heav - y, I shall not be moved,
8. Don't let the world de - ceive you, I shall not be moved, Don't
9. If my friends for - sake me, I shall not be moved,

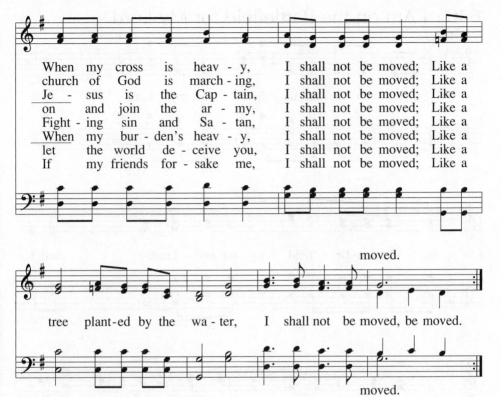

When my cross is heav - y, I shall not be moved; Like a
church of God is march - ing, I shall not be moved; Like a
Je - sus is the Cap - tain, I shall not be moved; Like a
on and join the ar - my, I shall not be moved; Like a
Fight - ing sin and Sa - tan, I shall not be moved; Like a
When my bur - den's heav - y, I shall not be moved; Like a
let the world de - ceive you, I shall not be moved; Like a
If my friends for - sake me, I shall not be moved; Like a

moved.

tree plant-ed by the wa - ter, I shall not be moved, be moved.

moved.

Text: Traditional
Tune: I SHALL NOT BE MOVED, Irregular; Negro Spiritual

640   I Am on the Battlefield for My Lord

I am on the bat-tle - field for my Lord, I'm

on the bat-tle - field for my Lord; And I

prom-ised him that I would serve him till I die. I am

on the bat-tle - field for my Lord.

Verses

1. I was a - lone and i - dle, I was a
2. I left my friends and kin - dred Bound for the
3. Now when I met my Sav - ior, I met him

sin - ner too, I heard a voice from heav - en Say
Prom - ised Land, The grace of God up - on me, The
with a smile, He healed my wound - ed spir - it, And

there is work to do, I took the Mas - ter's hand, And I
Bi - ble in my hand, In dis - tant lands I trod, Cry - ing
owned me as his child, A - round the throne of grace, He ap -

D.C.

joined the Chris - tian band, I'm on the bat - tle - field for my Lord.
sin - ner come to God, I'm on the bat - tle - field for my Lord.
points my soul a place, I'm on the bat - tle - field for my Lord.

Text: Sylvana Bell and E. V. Banks
Tune: BATTLEFIELD, 7 6 7 6 67 9 with refrain; Gospel Hymn; arr. by Joseph Joubert, b.1958, © 2000, GIA Publications, Inc.

641 Children, Go Where I Send Thee

*Three by three, four by four, etc…
**These two measures get repeated in countdown fashion using the following verses.

Verses

3. three   are   the   He - brew   chil - dren,
4. four   are   the   gos - pel   writ - ers,

5. five   are   the   five   that   dressed   so   fine,

6. six   are   the   six   that   could - n't get   fixed,

7. sev - en   are   the   sev - en came   down   from heav - en,

8. eight   are   the   eight that   stood   at   the   gate,

9. nine   are   the   nine   that   dressed   so   fine,

10. ten   are   the   ten   com -   mand - ments,

11. e - lev - en are the 'lev - en came down   from   heav - en,

12. twelve   are   the   twelve dis -   ci - ples,

Text: African American traditional
Tune: African American traditional; arr. by Evelyn Simpson-Curenton, b.1953, © 2000, GIA Publications, Inc.

We Must Work 642

We must work while it is day, Spread-ing the Word of God as we go a-long the way. We must be will - ing to do God's will, Spread - ing the Word of God till it reach - es through-out the hills. We must wit-ness to ev - 'ry-one we meet, in ev - 'ry song we sing. We must tell them of a soon - com - ing King!

Text: Keith C. Laws, © KCL Music
Tune: Keith C. Laws, © KCL Music; arr. by Nolan Williams, Jr., b.1969, © 2000, GIA Publications, Inc.

643 Here I Am, Lord

Verses

Descant:
3. Ah _____ Ah _____

_____ Ah _____

Melody:

1. I, the Lord of sea and sky, I have heard my
2. I, the Lord of snow and rain, I have borne my
3. I, the Lord of wind and flame, I will tend the

peo-ple cry. All who dwell in dark and sin
peo-ple's pain. I have wept for love of them.
poor and lame. I will set a feast for them.

My hand will save. Fin - est bread I

My hand will save. I, who made the
They turn a - way. I will break their
My hand will save. Fin-est bread I

will pro - vide Till their hearts be

stars of night, I will make their
hearts of stone, Give them hearts for
will pro - vide Till their hearts be

sat - is - fied. I will give my

dark - ness bright. Who will bear my
love a - lone. I will speak my
sat - is - fied. I will give my

life to them. Whom shall I send?

light to them? Whom shall I send?
word to them. Whom shall I send?
life to them. Whom shall I send?

Refrain

Here I am, Lord. Is it I, Lord?

I have heard you call-ing in the night. I will

go, Lord, if you lead me. I will hold your

1., 2.   3.

peo - ple in my heart.   heart.

Text: Isaiah 6; Dan Schutte, b.1947
Tune: HERE I AM, LORD, 77 7 4 D with refrain; Dan Schutte, b.1947; arr. by Michael Pope, SJ, and John Weissrock
© 1981, OCP

644 I'm Available to You

Verses 1, 2

1. You gave me my hands to reach out to man, to
2. You gave me my voice to speak your word, to

show him your love and your per - fect plan. You
sing all your prais - es to those who nev - er heard. But

gave me my ears, I can hear your voice so clear. I can
with my eyes I see a need for more a - vail - a - bil - i - ty. I see

hear the cries of sin - ners but can I wipe a - way their tears?
hearts that have been bro - ken so man - y peo - ple to be free.

Refrain

Lord, I'm a - vail - a - ble to you. My will I give to you. I'll

do what you say do. Use me, Lord, to show some - one the way,

and en - a - ble me to say, my

stor - age is emp - ty, and I am a - vail - a - ble to

1., 2. *To verses* 3.

you.

Verse 3

3. Now I'm giv-ing back to you all the tools you gave to me. My hands,

my ears, my voice, my eyes, so you can use them as you please. I have

emp - tied out my cup so that you can fill it up.

D.S.

Now I'm free, I just want to be more a - vail - a - ble to you.

Text: Carlis Moody, Jr.
Tune: Carlis Moody, Jr.
© 1988, Moodeasy Music and Word Music

645 Lord, Whose Love in Humble Service

1. Lord, whose love in hum-ble serv - ice Bore the weight of hu - man need, Who up - on the cross, for - sak - en, Of - fered mer - cy's per - fect deed: We, your ser - vants, bring the wor - ship Not of
2. Still the chil - dren wan-der home - less, Still the hun - gry cry for bread. Still the cap - tives long for free - dom, Still in grief we mourn our dead. As you, Lord, in deep com - pas - sion,
3. As we wor - ship, grant us vi - sion, Till your love's re - veal - ing light In its height and depth and great-ness Dawns up - on our hu - man sight, Mak - ing known the needs and bur - dens Your com -
4. Called from wor - ship in - to serv - ice, Forth in your great name we go To the child, the youth, the a - ged, Love in liv - ing deeds to show. Hope and health, good - will and com - fort, Coun - sel,

voice a - lone, but heart, Con - se - crat - ing
sick and freed the soul, Use the love your
pas - sion bids us bear, Stir - ring us to
aid, and peace we give That your chil - dren,

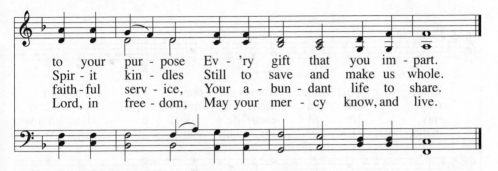

to your pur - pose Ev - 'ry gift that you im - part.
Spir - it kin - dles Still to save and make us whole.
faith - ful serv - ice, Your a - bun - dant life to share.
Lord, in free - dom, May your mer - cy know, and live.

Text: Albert F. Bayly, 1901–1984, © Oxford University Press, Inc.
Tune: BEACH SPRING, 8 7 8 7 D; *The Sacred Harp*, 1844; harm. by Ronald A. Nelson, b.1927, © 1978, *Lutheran Book of Worship*,
    admin. by Augsburg Fortress

646 Go Make of All Disciples

1. "Go make of all dis - ci - ples." We hear the call, O
2. "Go make of all dis - ci - ples," Bap - tiz - ing in the
3. "Go make of all dis - ci - ples." We at your feet would
4. "Go make of all dis - ci - ples." We wel-come your com -

Lord, That comes from you, our Fa - ther, In
name Of Fa - ther, Son, and Spir - it— From
stay Un - til each life's vo - ca - tion Shows
mand. "Lo, I am with you al - ways." We

your e - ter - nal Word. In - spire our ways of
age to age the same. We call each new dis -
forth your ho - ly way. We cul - ti - vate the
take your guid - ing hand. The task looms large be -

learn - ing Through earn - est, fer - vent prayer, And
ci - ple To fol - low you, O Lord, Re -
na - ture God plants in ev - 'ry heart, Re -
fore us— We fol - low with - out fear. In

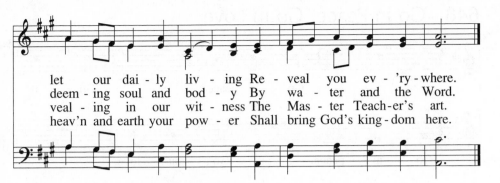

let our dai - ly liv - ing Re - veal you ev - 'ry - where.
deem - ing soul and bod - y By wa - ter and the Word.
veal - ing in our wit - ness The Mas - ter Teach - er's art.
heav'n and earth your pow - er Shall bring God's king - dom here.

Text: Matthew 28:19–20; Leon M. Adkins, 1896–1986, alt. © 1964, Abingdon Press
Tune: ELLACOMBE, 7 6 7 6 D; *Gesangbuch der Herzogl,* Wirtemberg, 1784

Till I Die, Till I Die 647

Till I die, till I die, till I die,

till I die, I'm gon - na keep on serv - ing my

Last time

Je - sus till I die, till I die. Till I die.

Last time

Text: African American Prayer and Praise Hymn, c.1900; adapt. by C. Eugene Cooper
Tune: African American Prayer and Praise Hymn, c.1900; adapt. by C. Eugene Cooper
© 1987, 1988, 1991, GIA Publications, Inc.

648 Go in Peace, Go in Love

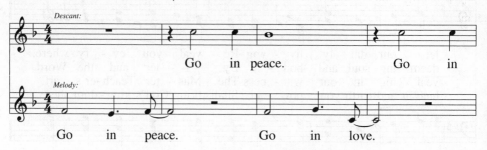

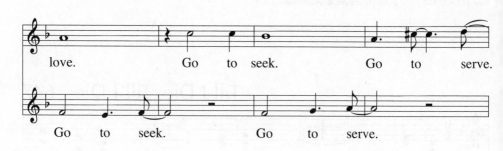

And God goes with you, and God goes with

And God goes with

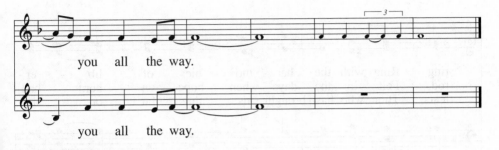

you all the way.

you all the way.

Text: Mary Louise Bringle, b.1953
Tune: GIPGIL; Sally Ann Morris, b.1952
© 2011, GIA Publications, Inc.

649 Lift Every Voice and Sing

1. Lift ev - 'ry voice and sing, Till earth and heav - en
2. Ston - y the road we trod, Bit - ter the chas - t'ning
3. God of our wea - ry years, God of our si - lent

ring, Ring with the har - mo - nies of lib - er -
rod, Felt in the days when hope un - born had
tears, Thou who hast brought us thus far on the

ty; Let our re - joic - ing rise High as the lis - t'ning
died; Yet with a stead - y beat, Have not our wea - ry
way; Thou who hast by thy might Led us in - to the

skies, Let it re - sound loud as the roll - ing sea.
feet Come to the place for which our peo - ple sighed?
light, Keep us for - ev - er in the path, we pray.

Sing a song full of the faith that the dark past has taught us;
We have come o - ver a way that with tears has been wa - tered;
Lest our feet stray from the plac - es, our God, where we met thee;

Sing a song full of the hope that the pres - ent has
We have come, tread - ing our path through the blood of the
Lest our hearts, drunk with the wine of the world, we for -

brought us; Fac - ing the ris - ing sun Of our new
slaugh - tered; Out from the gloom - y past, Till now we
get thee; Shad - owed be - neath thy hand, May we for -

day be - gun, Let us march on till vic - to - ry is won.
stand at last Where the bright gleam of our bright star is cast.
ev - er stand, True to our God, true to our na - tive land.

Text: James W. Johnson, 1871–1938
Tune: ANTHEM, 66 10 66 10 14 14 66 10; J. Rosamund Johnson, 1873–1954

650 Go Down, Moses

1. When Is - rael was in E - gypt's land,
2. The Lord told Mo - ses what to do,
3. As Is - rael stood by the wa - ter side,
4. When they had reached the oth - er shore,
5. Oh, let us all from bon - dage flee,

Let my peo - ple go;

Op - pressed so hard they
To lead the chil - dren of
At God's com - mand it
They sang the song of
And let us all in

could not stand,
Is - rael through,
did di - vide,
tri - umph o'er,
Christ be free,

Let my peo - ple go.

Go down, Mo - ses, Way down in E - gypt land,
Go down, go down, Mo - ses, Way down in E - gypt land,

Go down, go down, Mo - ses,

Tell ol' Phar-aoh, let my peo-ple go.

Text: Negro spiritual
Tune: GO DOWN MOSES, 8 5 8 5 with refrain; Negro spiritual

Oh, Freedom 651

1. Oh, free-dom, Oh, free-dom,
2. No more moan-ing, no more moan-ing,
3. There'll be sing-ing, there'll be sing-ing,

oh, free-dom o - ver me.
no more moan-ing o - ver me.
there'll be sing-ing o - ver me.

And be -

O - ver me.

fore I'd be a slave I'll be bur-ied in my grave,

and go home to my Lord and be free.

Text: Traditional
Tune: OH FREEDOM, Irregular; Negro Spiritual, arr. by Valeria A. Foster, © 2000, GIA Publications, Inc.

652 We Shall Overcome

1. We shall o - ver - come. We shall o - ver -
2. We'll walk hand in hand. We'll walk hand in
3. We shall live in peace. We shall live in
4. We are not a - fraid. We are not a -
5. God will see us through. God will see us

come. We shall o - ver - come some - day.
hand. We'll walk hand in hand some - day.
peace. We shall live in peace some - day.
fraid. We are not a - fraid to - day.
through. God will see us through to - day.

Oh, deep in my heart I do be -

lieve. We shall o - ver - come some - day.

Text: Negro Spiritual
Tune: WE SHALL OVERCOME, 5 5 7 9 7; Negro Spiritual; arr. by Nolan Williams, Jr., b.1969, © 2000, GIA Publications, Inc.

If You Believe and I Believe   653

If you be-lieve and I be-lieve And we to-geth-er

pray, The Ho-ly Spir-it must come down And

set God's peo-ple free, And set God's peo-ple

free, And set God's peo-ple free; The

Ho-ly Spir-it must come down And set God's peo-ple free.

Text: Zimbabwean traditional
Tune: Zimbabwean traditional; adapt. of English traditional; as taught by Tarasai; arr. by John L. Bell, b.1949, © 1991, Iona Community,
    GIA Publications, Inc., agent

654 Free at Last

Refrain

Free at   last,   free at   last,   I thank God I'm

free at last;   Free at   last,   free at   last,

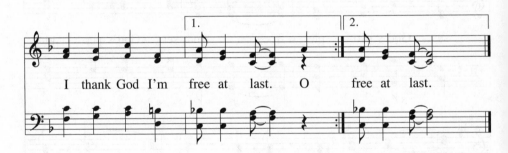

I thank God I'm   free at   last.   O   free at   last.

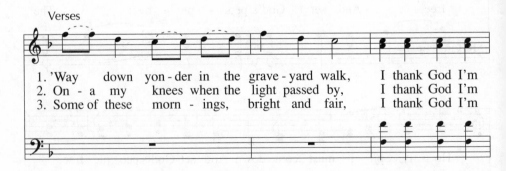

Verses

1. 'Way   down   yon-der in   the grave-yard walk,   I thank God I'm
2. On-a my   knees when the light passed by,   I thank God I'm
3. Some of these   morn-ings,   bright and fair,   I thank God I'm

FREEDOM

free   at   last.   Me   and   my   Je - sus goin' to
free   at   last.   Thought my   soul   would
free   at   last.   Goin'   meet   King   Je -   sus

D.C.

meet   and   talk,   I thank God I'm   free at   last.   O
rise   and   fly,
in   the   air,

Text: Negro Spiritual
Tune: Negro Spiritual; arr. by Kenneth W. Louis, b.1956, © 2012, GIA Publications, Inc.

655 We've Come a Long Way, Lord

Refrain

We've come a long way, Lord, a might-y long way.

We've come a long way, Lord,

a might-y long way. We've borne our

bur-dens in the heat of the day, but we know the

Lord has made the way. We've come a long

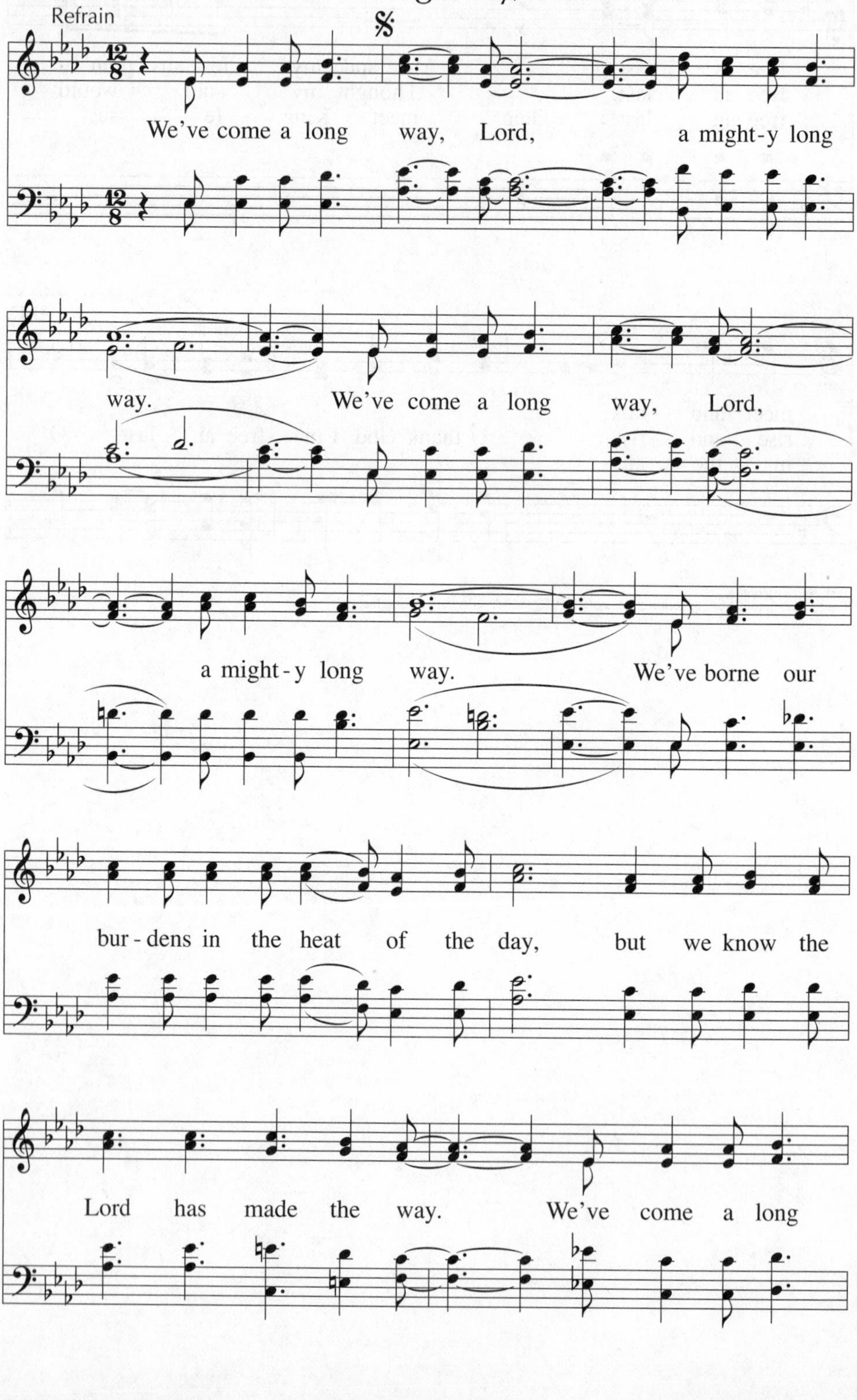

way, Lord, a might-y long way.

Verses

1. I've been in the val - ley and I prayed night and
   tri - als each and ev - 'ry

day. I've been in the val - ley
day. I've had hard tri - als

and I prayed night and day. I've been in the
each and ev - 'ry day. I've had hard

val - ley and I prayed night and day, And I know the
tri - als each and ev - 'ry day, But I know the

Lord   has   made   the   way.
Lord   has   made   the   way.   We've come   a   long

way,   a might-y   long   way.

1.
2. I've had   hard   We've come   a   long

D.S.

Text: Negro Spiritual
Tune: Negro Spiritual; arr. by Kenneth W. Louis, b.1956, © 2012, GIA Publications, Inc.

656   Keep the Dream Alive

1. Mar - tin's dream for   all   of   us   so   set   his   soul a -
2. In   our   land   let   free - dom ring was   Mar - tin's great   de -
3. Those   so   filled with   in - ner light, so   filled with   no - ble

fire And lift - ed him to soar - ing heights that
sire And as he marched a - mong the poor so
dreams, Must feel the wrath of Sa - tan's might to

he might with his God con - spire to change the course of
man - y did his dream in - spire to self es - teem and
teth - er and to slay. It seems the Christ a - gain is

his - to - ry that all be fam - 'ly, all be free.
dig - ni - ty in strug - gle for our lib - er - ty.
cru - ci - fied. Let Mar - tin's dream not be de - nied.

Keep the dream a - live. Keep the dream a - live.

We will have the vic - to - ry, Just keep the dream a - live.

Text: Robert Manuel
Tune: Robert Manuel
© 1986, Robert Manuel

657 Freedom Is Coming

FREEDOM

Text: South African
Tune: South African
© 1984, Peace of Music Publishing AB, admin. by Walton Music Corp.

658 He Had a Dream

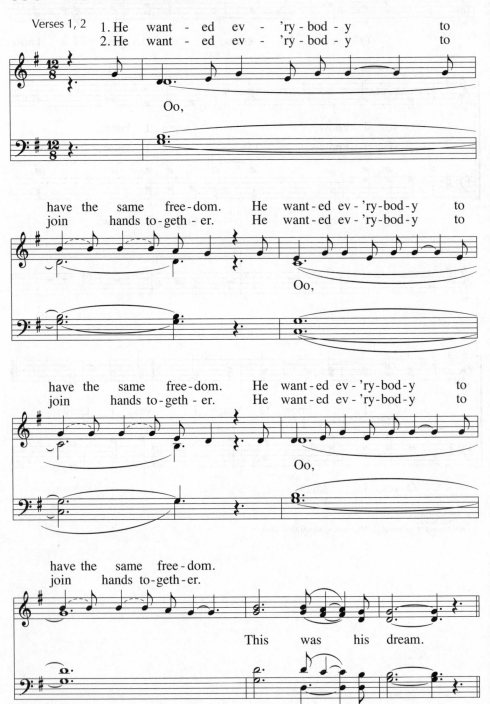

Verses 1, 2

1. He want-ed ev-'ry-bod-y to have the same free-dom. He want-ed ev-'ry-bod-y to have the same free-dom. He want-ed ev-'ry-bod-y to have the same free-dom. This was his dream.

2. He want-ed ev-'ry-bod-y to join hands to-geth-er. He want-ed ev-'ry-bod-y to join hands to-geth-er. He want-ed ev-'ry-bod-y to join hands to-geth-er.

Oo,

𝄋 Refrain

Doc - tor King, Doc - tor King, Doc - tor King was a

civ - il rights lead - er. Doc - tor King,

Doc - tor King, he had a dream.

Verse 3

Love,

3. Let's all love each oth - er and

Love,

Text: Ruth Manier, © 1978
Tune: Ruth Manier, © 1978; arr. by Jeffry Mickus, b.1962, © 2012, GIA Publications, Inc.

659 What Shall I Render

1. What shall I ren-der un-to God for all his
2. All I can ren-der is my bod-y and my

bless-ings? What shall I ren-der, Tell me
soul. That's all I can ren-der. That's

what shall I give? God has ev-'ry-thing;
all I can give.

Ev-'ry-thing be-longs to him. God has ev-'ry-thing;

Ev-'ry-thing be-longs to him. What shall I
All I can

ren-der, Tell me what shall I give?
ren-der, That's all I can give.

Text: Margaret Pleasant Douroux, b.1941, © 1975, Rev. Earl Pleasant Publishing
Tune: Margaret Pleasant Douroux, b.1941, © 1975, Rev. Earl Pleasant Publishing; arr. by Stephen Key, © 2000, GIA Publications, Inc.

660 Is Your All on the Altar

1. You have longed for sweet peace, And for faith to in-
2. Would you walk with the Lord In the light of his
3. O we nev - er can know What the Lord will be-
4. Who can tell all the love He will send from a -

crease, And have ear - nest - ly, fer - vent - ly prayed.
Word, And have peace and con - tent - ment al - way?
stow Of the bless - ings for which we have prayed,
bove, And how hap - py our hearts will be made,

But you can - not have rest, Or be per - fect - ly
You must do his sweet will To be free from all
Till our bod - y and soul He doth ful - ly con -
Of the fel - low-ship sweet We shall share at his

blest, Un - til all on the al - tar is laid.
ill— On the al - tar your all you must lay.
trol, And our all on the al - tar is laid.
feet When our all on the al - tar is laid!

Is your all on the al - tar of sac - ri - fice laid? Your heart does the Spir - it con - trol? You can on - ly be blest, And have peace and sweet rest, As you yield him your bod - y and soul.

Text: Elisha A. Hoffman, 1839–1929
Tune: YOUR ALL, 66 9 66 9 with refrain; Elisha A. Hoffman, 1839–1929; arr. by Nolan Williams, Jr., b.1969, © 2000, GIA Publications, Inc.

661 I've Got Peace Like a River

1. I've got peace like a riv-er, I've got peace like a
2. I've got joy like a foun-tain, I've got joy like a
3. I've got love like an o-cean, I've got love like an

riv-er, I've got peace like a riv-er in my
foun-tain, I've got joy like a foun-tain in my
o-cean, I've got love like an o-cean in my

soul.   I've got riv-er in my soul.
soul.   I've got foun-tain in my soul.
soul.   I've got o-cean in my soul.

Text: Congregational Praise Song
Tune: PEACE LIKE A RIVER, 7 7 10, Congregational Praise Song

Let There Be Peace on Earth   662

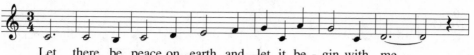

Let there be peace on earth, and let it be-gin with me.

Let there be peace on earth, the peace that was meant to be. With

God our cre-a-tor, broth-ers all are we. / fam-'ly all are we.

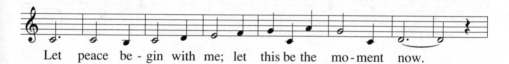

Let me walk with my broth-er in per-fect har-mo-ny. / us each oth-er

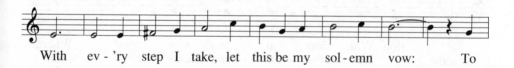

Let peace be-gin with me; let this be the mo-ment now.

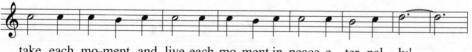

With ev-'ry step I take, let this be my sol-emn vow: To

take each mo-ment, and live each mo-ment in peace e-ter-nal-ly!

Let there be peace on earth, and let it be-gin with me.

Text: Jill Jackson, 1913–1995, © 1955, 1983, Jan-Lee Music
Tune: Sy Miller, 1908-1941, © 1955, 1983, Jan-Lee Music; acc. by Diana Kodner, b.1957, © 1993, GIA Publications, Inc.

663 O God of Every Nation

1. O God of ev - 'ry na - tion, Of
2. From search for wealth and pow - er And
3. Lord, strength - en those who la - bor That
4. Keep bright in us the vi - sion Of

ev - 'ry race and land, Re - deem the whole cre -
scorn of truth and right, From trust in bombs that
all may find re - lease From fear of rat - tling
days when wars shall cease, When ha - tred and di -

a - tion With your al - might - y hand. Where
show - er De - struc - tion through the night, From
sa - ber, From dread of war's in - crease. When
vi - sion Give way to love and peace, Till

hate and fear di - vide us And
pride of race and sta - tion And
hope and cour - age fal - ter, Lord,
dawns the morn - ing glo - rious When

bit - ter threats are hurled, In love and mer - cy
blind - ness to your way, De - liv - er ev - 'ry
let your voice be heard; With faith that none can
truth and jus - tice reign, And Christ shall rule vic -

guide us And heal our strife - torn world.
na - tion, E - ter - nal God, we pray.
al - ter, Your ser - vants un - der - gird.
to - rious O'er all the world's do - main.

Text: William W. Reid, Jr., b.1923, alt., © 1958, 1986, The Hymn Society (admin. by Hope Publishing Company)
Tune: PASSION CHORALE, 7 6 7 6 D; Hans Leo Hassler, 1564–1612; harm. by J. S. Bach, 1685–1750

664 In Christ There Is No East or West

1. In Christ there is no east or west, In
2. In him shall true hearts ev-'ry-where Their
3. Join hands, dis-ci-ples in the faith, What-
4. In Christ now meet both east and west, In

him no south or north, But one great fam-'ly
high com-mun-ion find; His serv-ice is the
e'er your race may be! Who serve each oth-er
him meet south and north; All Christ-ly souls are

bound by love Through-out the whole wide earth.
gold-en cord Close bind-ing hu-man-kind.
in Christ's love Are sure-ly kin to me.
one in him Through-out the whole wide earth.

Text: Galatians 3:28; William A. Dunkerley, 1852–1941, alt.
Tune: McKEE, CM; African American; adapt. by Harry T. Burleigh, 1866–1949

We Are One 665

We are one, we are one. We are
one in the Spir - it, we are one. Hal - le -
lu - jah, Hal - le - lu - jah, we are
one in the Spir - it, we are one.

Text: Timothy Wright, 1947–2009, ©
Tune: Congregational Praise Song, arr. Valeria A. Foster, © 2000, GIA Publications, Inc.

666 Unity (Psalm 133:1)

Be-hold how good and how pleas - ant it is for

kin - dred to dwell to-geth-er in u - ni-ty. Be -

hold how good and how pleas - ant it is for kin - dred to

1. dwell to-geth-er in u - ni-ty. 2. u-ni-ty.

U - ni-ty, u - ni-ty, Lord, we pray for

u - ni-ty. U - ni - ty,

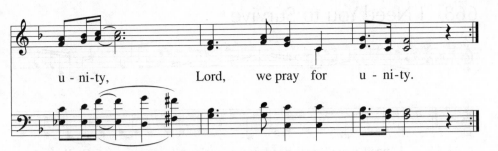

u - ni-ty,   Lord,   we pray   for   u - ni-ty.

Text: Psalm 133:1, Glorraine Moone, © 1989. Published by Professionals for Christ Publications (BMI)
Tune: Glorraine Moone, © 1989; arr. by Dr. Daniel Mario Cason II. Published by Professionals for Christ Publications (BMI); adapt. by Valeria A. Foster,
    © 2000, GIA Publications, Inc.

Jesus Loves the Little Children   667

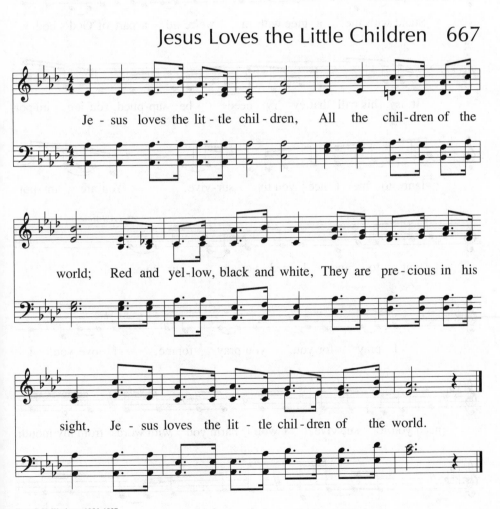

Je - sus loves the lit - tle chil - dren,   All   the   chil-dren of the

world;   Red and yel-low, black and white, They are pre - cious in his

sight,   Je - sus loves   the lit - tle chil-dren of   the world.

Text: C. H. Woolston, 1856–1927
Tune: CHILDREN, 8 7 77 11; George F. Root, 1820–1895

668 I Need You to Survive

I need you, you need me, we're all a part of God's bod-y.

Stand with me, a-gree with me, we're all a part of God's bod-y.

It is his will that ev-'ry need be sup-plied. You are im-por-tant to me. I need you to sur-vive. You are im-por-

Last time

tant to me. I need you to sur-vive.

I pray for you, you pray for me, I love you, I

need you to sur-vive. I won't harm you with words from my mouth,

D.S.

I love you, I need you to sur-vive.

Text: David Frazier
Tune: David Frazier
© God's Music, Inc.

We Gather Together 669

1. We gath-er to-geth-er to ask the Lord's bless-ing;
2. Be-side us to guide us, our God with us join-ing,
3. We all do ex-tol you our lead-er tri-um-phant,

He chas-tens and has-tens his will to make known;
Whose king-dom calls all to the love which en-dures.
And pray that you still our de-fend-er will be.

The wick-ed op-press-ing now cease from dis-tress-ing:
So from the be-gin-ning the fight we were win-ning:
Let your con-gre-ga-tion es-cape trib-u-la-tion:

Sing prais-es to his name; he for-gets not his own.
You, Lord, were at our side; all glo-ry be yours!
Your name be ev-er praised! O Lord, make us free!

Text: *Wilt heden nu treden,* Netherlands folk hymn; English tr. by Theodore Baker, 1851–1934, alt.
Tune: KREMSER, 12 11 12 11; Valerius' *Nederlandtsch Gedenckclanck,* 1626; harm. by Edward Kremser, 1838–1914

670 We Have Come into This House

1. We have come in - to this house to
2. So, for - get a - bout your - self,
3. Let us lift up ho - ly hands,

gath - er in his name and wor - ship him. We have
con - cen-trate on him and wor - ship him. So, for -
mag - ni - fy his name and wor - ship him. Let us

come in - to this house to gath - er in his name and
get a - bout your - self, con - cen-trate on him and
lift up ho - ly hands, mag - ni - fy his name and

wor - ship him. We have come in - to this house to
wor - ship him. So, for - get a - bout your - self,
wor - ship him. Let us lift up ho - ly hands,

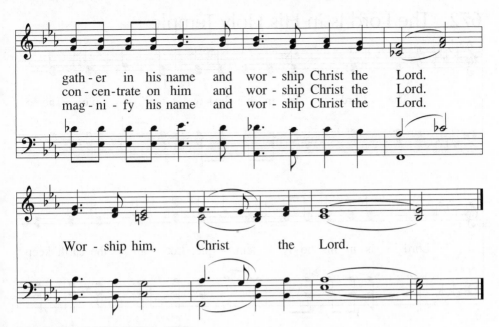

gath-er in his name and wor-ship Christ the Lord.
con-cen-trate on him and wor-ship Christ the Lord.
mag-ni-fy his name and wor-ship Christ the Lord.

Wor-ship him, Christ the Lord.

Text: Bruce Ballinger, b.1945, alt., © 1976, Sound III, Inc.
Tune: WORSHIP HIM, 16 16 18 6; Bruce Ballinger, b.1945, © 1976, Sound III, Inc.; arr. by Stephen Key, © 2000, GIA Publications, Inc.

Jesu Tawa Pano / Jesus, We Are Here   671

Je - su   ta - wa pa - no;   Je - su   ta - wa pa - no;
Je - sus,   we are here;   Je - sus,   we are here;

Solo:
*Mam-bo Je-su.

Je - su   ta - wa pa - no;   ta - wa pa - no, mu zi - ta re - nyu.
Je - sus,   we are here;   we are here   for   you.

*Omit last time

African Phonetics:
Yay-zoo tah-wah pah-no
tah-wah pah-no, moo zee-tah ray-noo

Text: Zimbabwean; Patrick Matsikenyiri
Tune: Patrick Matsikenyiri
© 1990, Patrick Matsikenyiri

672 The Lord Is in His Holy Temple

The Lord is in his ho-ly tem - ple, The

Lord is in his ho-ly tem - ple: Let all the earth keep

si-lence, Let all the earth keep si - lence be - fore

him— Keep si-lence, keep si-lence be - fore him.

Text: Habakkuk 2:20
Tune: George F. Root, 1820–1895

We've Come to Worship You   673

1. Lord, we've come to wor - ship you.
2. Lord, we've come to give you thanks.
3. Lord, we've come to give you praise.

Lord, we've come to wor - ship you, for we
Lord, we've come to give you thanks, for we
Lord, we've come to give you praise, for we

know that your name is wor - thy, oh Lord, and we've
know that your name is wor - thy, oh Lord, and we've
know that your name is wor - thy, oh Lord, and we've

come to wor - ship you.
come to give you thanks.
come to give you praise.

Text: Stephen Key
Tune: Stephen Key
© 1993, StepKey Music

674 All People That on Earth Do Dwell

1. All peo - ple that on earth do dwell,
2. Know that the Lord is God in - deed;
3. O en - ter then his gates with praise;
4. For why? The Lord our God is good:
5. To Fa - ther, Son, and Ho - ly Ghost,
 * Praise God, from whom all bless - ings flow;

Sing to the Lord with cheer - ful voice;
With - out our aid he did us make.
Ap - proach with joy his courts un - to;
His mer - cy is for ev - er sure;
The God whom heaven and earth a - dore,
Praise him, all crea - tures here be - low;

Him serve with mirth, his praise forth tell;
We are his folk, he does us feed,
Praise, laud, and bless his Name al - ways,
His truth at all times firm - ly stood,
From us and from the an - gel host
Praise him a - bove, you heav'n - ly host:

*May be sung alone or as an alternate to stanza 5.

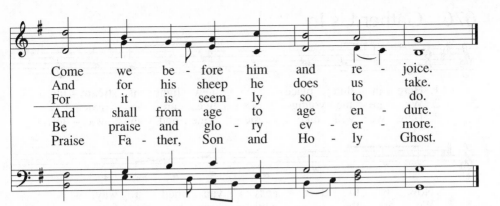

Come we be - fore him and re - joice.
And for his sheep he does us take.
For it is seem - ly so to do.
And shall from age to age en - dure.
Be praise and glo - ry ev - er - more.
Praise Fa - ther, Son and Ho - ly Ghost.

Text: Psalm 100; William Kethe, d. c.1593; Doxology, Thomas Ken, 1637–1711
Tune: OLD HUNDREDTH, LM; Louis Bourgeois, c.1510–1561

I Just Came to Praise the Lord 675

1. I just came to praise the Lord, I just came to praise the
2. I just came to thank the Lord, I just came to thank the
3. I just came to love the Lord, I just came to love the

Lord; I just came to praise his ho - ly name,
Lord; I just came to praise his ho - ly name,
Lord; I just came to praise his ho - ly name,

I just came to praise the Lord.
I just came to thank the Lord.
I just came to love the Lord.

Text: Wayne Romero, b.1950
Tune: Wayne Romero, b.1950
© 1975, Paragon Music

676 Gather Us In

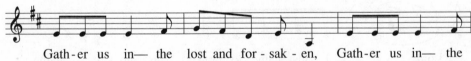

1. Here in this place new light is stream-ing,
2. We are the young— our lives are a mys-t'ry,
3. Here we will take the wine and the wa-ter,

Now is the dark-ness van-ished a-way,
We are the old— who yearn for your face,
Here we will take the bread of new birth,

See in this space our fears and our dream-ings,
We have been sung through-out all of his-t'ry,
Here you shall call your sons and your daugh-ters,

Brought here to you in the light of this day.
Called to be light to the whole hu-man race.
Call us a-new to be salt for the earth.

Gath-er us in— the lost and for-sak-en, Gath-er us in— the
Gath-er us in— the rich and the haugh-ty, Gath-er us in— the
Give us to drink the wine of com-pas-sion, Give us to eat the

blind and the lame; Call to us now, and we shall a-wak-en,
proud and the strong; Give us a heart so meek and so low-ly,
bread that is you; Nour-ish us well, and teach us to fash-ion

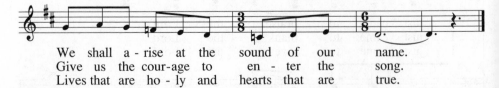

We shall a-rise at the sound of our name.
Give us the cour-age to en-ter the song.
Lives that are ho-ly and hearts that are true.

Text: Marty Haugen, b.1950
Tune: GATHER US IN, 10 9 10 10 D; Marty Haugen, b.1950
© 1982, GIA Publications, Inc.

Gather, Christians 677

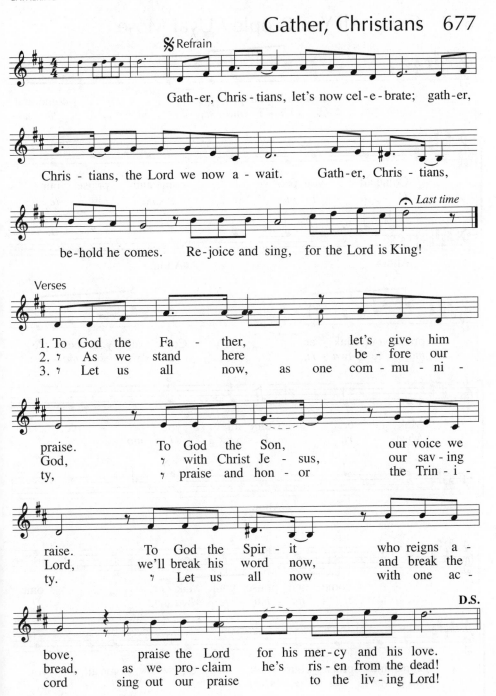

Refrain

Gath-er, Chris-tians, let's now cel-e-brate; gath-er, Chris-tians, the Lord we now a-wait. Gath-er, Chris-tians, be-hold he comes. Re-joice and sing, for the Lord is King!

Last time

Verses

1. To God the Fa - ther, let's give him praise. To God the Son, our voice we raise. To God the Spir - it who reigns a - bove, praise the Lord for his mer-cy and his love.

2. ₇ As we stand here be - fore our God, ₇ with Christ Je - sus, our sav - ing Lord, ₇ we'll break his word now, and break the bread, as we pro-claim he's ris - en from the dead!

3. ₇ Let us all now, as one com - mu - ni - ty, ₇ praise and hon - or the Trin - i - ty. ₇ Let us all now with one ac - cord sing out our praise to the liv - ing Lord!

D.S.

Text: Garfield Rochard
Tune: Garfield Rochard; arr. by P. E. P.
© 1998, Antilles Episcopal Conference

678 Come All You People / Uyai Mose

Solo:

Come all you peo - ple,   come and
U - ya - i mo - se,   *ti - na-*

Come all you peo - ple,   come and praise your
U - ya - i mo - se,   *ti - na - ma - te*

Ahom   Ahom

praise your Mak - er;   Come all you peo - ple,
ma - te Mwa - ri,   *U - ya - i mo - se,*

Mak - er;   Come all you peo - ple,
Mwa - ri,   *U - ya - i mo - se,*

Ahom

come and praise your Mak - er;   Come
ti - na - ma - te Mwa - ri,   *U -*

come and praise your Mak - er;   Come all you
ti - na - ma - te Mwa - ri,   *U - ya - i*

Ahom   Ahom

all you peo - ple, come and praise your Mak - er;
ya - i mo - se, ti - na - ma - te Mwa - ri,

peo - ple, come and praise your Mak - er;
mo - se, ti - na - ma - te Mwa - ri,

Ahom

Come now and wor-ship the Lord. Come and praise your Mak-er.
U - ya - i mo - se zvi - no. Ti - na - ma - te Mwa-ri.

Last time

Come now and wor-ship the Lord.
U - ya - i mo - se zvi - no.

Last time

Ahom Ahom Ahom

Last time

African phonetics:
Oo-yah-ee mo-say, tee-nah-mah-tay Mwah-ree...
Oo-yah-ee mo-say zvee-no.

Text: Alexander Gondo, b.1936
Tune: Alexander Gondo, b.1936; arr. by John L. Bell, b.1949; © 1994, Iona Community, GIA Publications, Inc., agent

679 Enter into Jerusalem

1. En-ter in-to Je-ru-sa-lem, let us go to God's house With the
2. En-ter in-to Je-ru-sa-lem, *mek we walk a-down there, With the
3. En-ter in-to Je-ru-sa-lem, let us go to God's house With your

health-y and the sick, with the work-er and the weak,
young and the old, with the lit-tle and the large,
pa - pa and your ma-ma, with your un-cle and your aunt,

Let us go to God's house. En-ter in-to Je-ru-sa-lem,
Mek we walk a-down there. En-ter in-to Je-ru-sa-lem,
Let us go to God's house. En-ter in-to Je-ru-sa-lem,

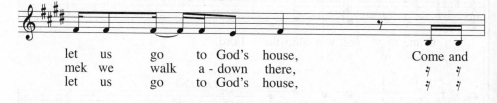

let us go to God's house, Come and
mek we walk a-down there,
let us go to God's house,

run with the wind and the God who reigns in peace,
Sway-ing to the breeze with the God who reigns in peace,
Run and catch the breeze with the God who reigns in peace,

let us go to God's house.
Mek we walk a-down there. We go cel-e-brate, we go cel-e-
Let us go to God's house.

brate, we go cel-e-brate, oh, Is-ra-el!

*mek = make

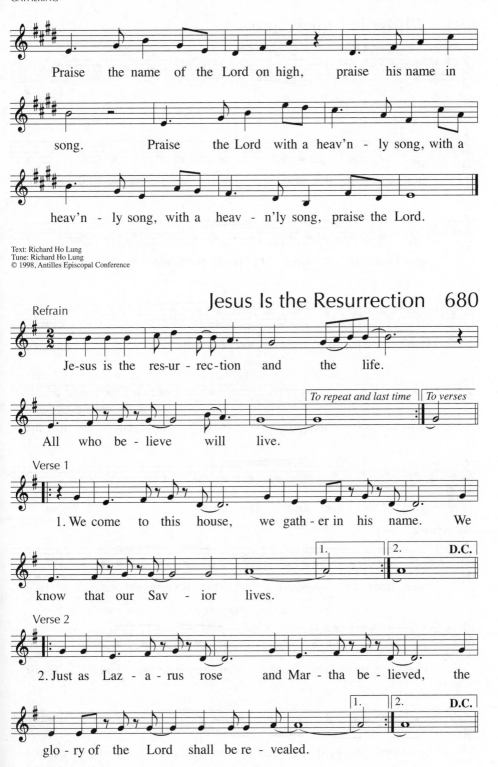

Praise the name of the Lord on high, praise his name in song. Praise the Lord with a heav'n - ly song, with a heav'n - ly song, with a heav - n'ly song, praise the Lord.

Text: Richard Ho Lung
Tune: Richard Ho Lung
© 1998, Antilles Episcopal Conference

Jesus Is the Resurrection   680

Refrain

Je-sus is the res-ur - rec-tion and the life. All who be - lieve will live.

To repeat and last time | *To verses*

Verse 1

1. We come to this house, we gath-er in his name. We know that our Sav - ior lives.

Verse 2

2. Just as Laz - a - rus rose and Mar - tha be - lieved, the glo - ry of the Lord shall be re - vealed.

Text: Derek Campbell, 1963–2004
Tune: Derek Campbell, 1963–2004
© 2002, GIA Publications, Inc.

681 Christ Is Our Peace

1. We've

Verse 1

gath - ered in this place to be on one ac - cord, to

bless God's ho - ly name for all the things he has done. We

know not what the Lord has in store but we

know all things work to - geth - er for the

good of them that love the Lord. 2. We've

Verse 2

come from ev - 'ry - where to u - nite in prayer, so let's

med - i - tate on him and con - cen - trate on him. Christ

prom - ised us he'd be with us al - ways be - cause

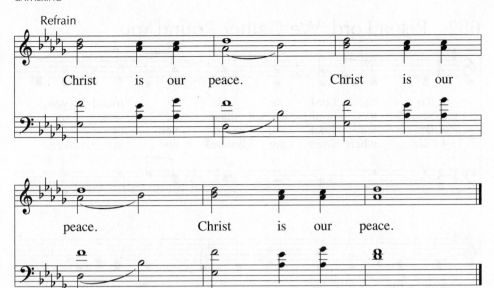

Refrain

Christ is our peace. Christ is our peace. Christ is our peace.

Text: Kenneth W. Louis, b.1956
Tune: Kenneth W. Louis, b.1956
© 1999, Kenneth W. Louis

682 Risen Lord, We Gather Round You

1. Ris - en Lord, we gath - er round you,
2. Sis - ters, broth - ers, stand be - side us,
*3. By the Loaf and Cup you of - fer,
4. "Go where lives are bruised and bro - ken;

Drawn by words for - ev - er new: "Come, my peo - ple,
Called from ev - 'ry land and race. One the Bread of
Strength - en us to fol - low you. By your Bod - y,
Go where chil - dren waste and blight. Go a - mong the

all are wel - come; Share the feast pre - pared for you!"
Life that feeds us, One the Cup of brim-ming grace.
ris - en, giv - en, Heal us, Christ, and make us new.
lost, for - got - ten; Be for them my heal - ing Light.

Emp - ty hands and hearts that hun - ger, Christ, we bring to
Form us, Lord, a sin - gle bod - y, Free from en - mi -
Help us hear your ur - gent sum-mons, Cut - ting through our
Take the Bread of Life I give you; Share it with a

*This stanza may be replaced by an appropriate stanza taken from the following page.

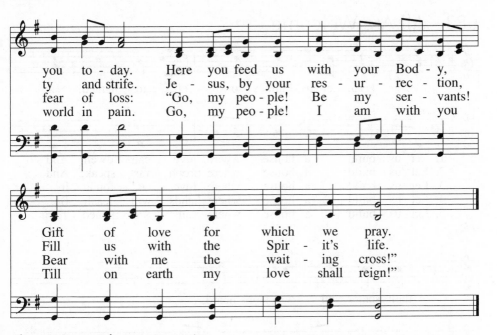

you to - day. Here you feed us with your Bod - y,
ty and strife. Je - sus, by your res - ur - rec - tion,
fear of loss: "Go, my peo - ple! Be my ser - vants!
world in pain. Go, my peo - ple! I am with you

Gift of love for which we pray.
Fill us with the Spir - it's life.
Bear with me the wait - ing cross!"
Till on earth my love shall reign!"

Alternate Stanza 3 for various occasions:

Feasts of the Blessed Virgin Mary
3. God, you made your servant Mary
Chosen vessel of your Word,
Bearer of the Christ among us,
Mother of our Risen Lord!
We would also be your servants,
Human vessels that you claim.
May we be Christ's present bearers;
Help us magnify your name!

Sacraments of Initiation
3. Christ, our Shepherd, still you lead us
Where baptismal waters flow.
There by grace you bless and claim us;
There the Spirit's gifts bestow.
Through your Church you call and
feed us
With the Bread by which we live.
Grant that, as your chosen people,
We may bread to others give.

Evening Mass of the Lord's Supper
3. With your friends this night you gathered,
Gave them bread you blessed to eat.
Though their Lord, you moved among them
Washing weary, dusty feet.
Jesus, by your great example,
Teach our hearts humility.
Help us take the towel and basin,
Serve in selfless charity.

Ordination
3. Loaves you blessed along the lakeside
By your grace were multiplied.
When disciples took and shared them,
Hungry folk were satisfied.
Christ, you still ordain your servants
For the Breaking of the Bread.
Through these empty hands we offer,
Let your Church again be fed.

Chrism Mass
3. Risen Lord, we bring before you
Precious oil for you to bless.
May it bear your living presence,
Oil of gladness, sign of grace.
Heal the sick, restore the fallen,
Show the poor compassion's face.
Let it be your benediction,
Binding all in love's embrace.

Text: Herman G. Stuempfle, Jr., 1923–2007, © 2006, GIA Publications, Inc.
Tune: HOLY MANNA, 8 7 8 7 D; William Moore, *Columbian Harmony*, 1825

683 All Are Welcome

Descant:

5. Let us build   so   all   are   named,

Melody:

1. Let us build   a house   where love   can   dwell   And
2. Let us build   a house   where proph - ets   speak,   And
3. Let us build   a house   where love   is   found   In
4. Let us build   a house   where hands   will   reach   Be -
5. Let us build   a house   where all   are   named,   Their

their songs and   vi - sions heard,

all   can safe - ly   live,   A   place   where saints and
words are strong   and   true,   Where all   God's   chil - dren
wa - ter,   wine   and wheat: A   ban - quet hall   on
yond the   wood   and stone   To   heal   and strength - en,
songs and   vi - sions heard   And   loved   and   treas - ured,

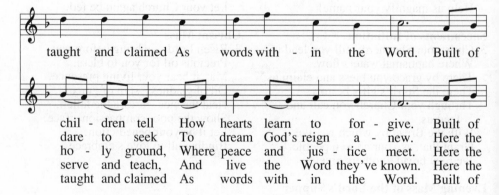

taught and claimed As   words with - in   the   Word. Built of

chil - dren tell   How   hearts learn   to   for - give.   Built of
dare   to   seek   To   dream God's reign   a - new.   Here the
ho - ly ground,   Where peace   and   jus - tice   meet.   Here the
serve and teach,   And   live   the   Word they've known.   Here the
taught and claimed As   words with - in   the   Word. Built of

tears and cries and laugh - ter, Prayers and songs of

hopes and dreams and vi - sions, Rock of faith and vault of
cross shall stand as wit - ness And as sym - bol of God's
love of God, through Je - sus, Is re-vealed in time and
out - cast and the stran - ger Bear the im - age of God's
tears and cries and laugh - ter, Prayers of faith and songs of

grace, Let this house pro - claim from floor to raft - er:

grace; Here the love of Christ shall end di - vi - sions:
grace; Here as one we claim the faith of Je - sus:
space; As we share in Christ the feast that frees us:
face; Let us bring an end to fear and dan - ger:
grace, Let this house pro - claim from floor to raft - er:

All are wel-come, all are wel - come, wel - come

All are wel-come, all are wel-come, all are wel - come

in this place.

in this place.

Text: Marty Haugen, b.1950
Tune: TWO OAKS, 9 6 8 6 8 7 10 with refrain; Marty Haugen, b.1950
© 1994, GIA Publications, Inc.

684 Come to the Feast

Refrain

Come to the feast, come hear the Word, come to the ta-ble of the Lord. O come to the feast, come sing your song, come, let us join and be one.

D.C. 2.–7. one. *To verses* 8. one.

Verses

1. On this moun - tain the Lord will pro - vide for his
2. On this moun - tain tears will be gone for -
3. On this moun - tain the Lord speaks to his
4. On this moun - tain we break bread to -
5. On this moun - tain the Lord hears the cry of his
6. On this moun - tain a new, clean heart is cre-

peo - ple. On this moun - tain
ev - er. On this moun - tain
peo - ple. On this moun - tain we
geth - er. On this moun - tain we
peo - ple. On this moun - tain
a - ted. On this moun - tain we

D.C.

death will be wiped a - way.
here is our God and King.
see our God, our King.
wor - ship our God and King.
we are on Ho - ly Ground.
come and we join as one!

Text: Verses based on Isaiah 25:6a, 7–9; James E. Moore, Jr., b.1951
Tune: James E. Moore, Jr., b.1951
© 2002, GIA Publications, Inc.

685 As We Gather at Your Table

1. As we gath - er at your Ta - ble,
2. Turn our wor - ship in - to wit - ness
3. Gra - cious Spir - it, help us sum - mon

As we lis - ten to your Word,
In the sac - ra - ment of life;
Oth - er guests to share that feast

Help us know, O God, your pres - ence:
Send us forth to love and serve you,
Where tri - um - phant Love will wel - come

Let our hearts and minds be stirred.
Bring - ing peace where there is strife.
Those who had been last and least.

Nour - ish us with
Give us, Christ, your
There no more will

sa - cred sto - ry   Till   we claim it   as   our own;
great com - pas - sion To   for - give as   you   for - gave;
en - vy   blind us   Nor will pride our   peace de - stroy,

Teach   us   through this   ho - ly   ban - quet
May   we   still   be - hold   your   im - age
As   we   join   with   saints and   an - gels

How   to   make   Love's   vic - t'ry   known.
In   the world   you   died   to   save.
To   re - peat   the   sound - ing   joy.

Text: Carl P. Daw, Jr., b.1944, © 1989, Hope Publishing Company
Tune: HOLY MANNA, 8 7 8 7 D; William Moore, *Columbian Harmony*, 1825

686 We Gather in Memory

1. We gath - er in mem - 'ry, in hope, and in praise,
2. We thank you for stead - fast com - pan - ions and friends:
3. To - geth - er in wor - ship, in prayer and in song,
4. We join in the wit - ness of ones gone be - fore

To hon - or the Light that en - light - ens our days:
For neigh - bors and part - ners whose love nev - er ends;
We find in your house - hold a place to be - long:
Who stand at the thresh - old of Christ's o - pen door:

The dec - ades of serv - ice and e - ons of grace;
For broth - ers and sis - ters, for hus - bands and wives,
In preach - ing that voic - es a truth to be heard,
Your saints, like the stars, who now bril - liant - ly shine

Your faith - ful-ness reach - ing through time and through space.
For par - ents and chil - dren, en - rich - ing our lives.
And calls us to jus - tice and joy in your Word.
And draw us to full - ness, re - deem - ing the time!

Text: Mary Louise Bringle, b.1953, © 2006, GIA Publications, Inc.
Tune: FOUNDATION, 11 11 11 11; Funk's *Compilation of Genuine Church Music*, 1832

When Morning Gilds the Sky   687

1. When morn-ing gilds the sky, Let hearts a-
2. To God the Word, on high The hosts of
3. In heav'n's e-ter-nal bliss The love-liest
4. Then let us join to sing To Christ, our

wak-ing cry: May Je-sus Christ be praised! In
an-gels cry: May Je-sus Christ be praised! Let
strain is this: May Je-sus Christ be praised! Let
lov-ing King: May Je-sus Christ be praised! Be

work and prayer re-joice To sing with grate-ful
mor-tals, too, em-ploy Their hymns of end-less
earth and sea and sky, From depth to height, re-
this the e-ter-nal song Through all the a-ges

voice: May Je-sus Christ be praised!
joy: May Je-sus Christ be praised!
ply: May Je-sus Christ be praised!
long: May Je-sus Christ be praised!

Text: *Wach ich früh Morgens auf; Katholisches Gesangbuch*, Würzburg, 1828; tr. by Edward Caswall, 1814–1878, alt.
Tune: LAUDES DOMINI, 66 6 D; Joseph Barnby, 1838–1896

688 Day Is Done

1. Day is done, but Love un-fail-ing Dwells ev - er
2. Dark de-scends, but Light un-end-ing Shines through our
3. Eyes will close, but you un-sleep-ing Watch by our

here; Shad - ows fall, but hope, pre - vail - ing,
night; You are with us, ev - er lend - ing
side; Death may come, in Love's safe-keep - ing

Calms ev - 'ry fear. God, our Mak - er, none for - sak - ing,
New strength to sight. One in love, your truth con - fess - ing,
Still we a - bide. God of love, all e - vil quell-ing,

Take our hearts, of Love's own mak - ing; Watch our sleep - ing,
One in hope of heav - en's bless - ing, May we see, in
Sin for - giv - ing, fear dis - pel - ling, Stay with us, our

guard   our wak - ing,   Be   al - ways near.
love's   pos - sess - ing,   Love's   end - less light!
hearts   in - dwell - ing,   This   e - ven - tide.

Text: James Quinn, SJ, 1919–2010, © 1969, Used by permission of Selah Publishing Co., Inc.
Tune: AR HYD Y NOS, 8 4 8 4 888 4; Welsh melody

689 Mary's Canticle

Refrain ♩ = 54

My be-ing pro-claims the great-ness of the Lord,

my spir-it finds joy in God my Sav - ior.

Verse 1

1. For he has looked up-on his ser-vant in her low-li-ness; all a-ges to come shall

D.C.

call me, call me bless - ed.

Verse 2

2. God who is might-y has done great

things for me, great things God has

done for me, ho-ly is his name.

D.C.

Verse 3

3. His mer-cy is from age to age on those who

fear him. He has shown might with his arm.

D.C.

He has con-fused the proud in their in-most thoughts.

Verse 4

4. He has de-posed the might-y from their thrones

and raised the low-ly to high plac-es.

The hun-gry he has giv-en ev-'ry good thing, while the

D.C.

rich he has sent emp-ty a-way.

Verse 5

5. He has up-held Is - ra - el his ser-vant,

ev - er mind - ful of his mer-cy; E-ven as he

prom-ised our fa - thers, prom - ised A - bra-ham and his de -

D.C.

scen - dants for - ev - er.

Text: Luke 1:46–55; Leon C. Roberts, 1950–1999
Tune: Leon C. Roberts, 1950–1999
© 1993, GIA Publications, Inc.

God of Day and God of Darkness   690

1. God of day and God of dark - ness, Now we
2. Still the na - tions curse the dark - ness, Still the
3. You shall be the path that guides us, You the
4. Praise to you in day and dark - ness, You our

stand be - fore the night; As the shad - ows stretch and
rich op - press the poor; Still the earth is bruised and
light that in us burns; Shin - ing deep with - in all
source and you our end; Praise to you who love and

deep - en, Come and make our dark - ness bright. All cre -
bro - ken By the ones who still want more. Come and
peo - ple, Yours the love that we must learn. For our
nur - ture As a fa - ther, moth - er, friend. Grant us

a - tion still is groan - ing For the dawn - ing of your
wake us from our sleep - ing, So our hearts can - not ig -
hearts shall wan - der rest - less 'Til they safe to you re -
all a peace - ful rest - ing, Let each mind and bod - y

might, When the Sun of peace and jus - tice
nore All your peo - ple lost and bro - ken,
turn; Find - ing you in one an - oth - er,
mend, So we rise re - freshed to - mor - row,

Fills the earth with ra - diant light.
All your chil - dren at our door.
We shall all your face dis - cern.
Hearts re - newed to king - dom tend.

Text: Marty Haugen, b.1950, © 1985, 1994, GIA Publications, Inc.
Tune: BEACH SPRING, 8 7 8 7 D; *The Sacred Harp*, 1844; harm. by Marty Haugen, b.1950, © 1985, GIA Publications, Inc.

691 Soon and Very Soon

1. Soon and ver - y soon we are goin' to see the King,
2. No more cry - in' there we are goin' to see the King,
3. No more dy - in' there we are goin' to see the King,
4. Soon and ver - y soon we are goin' to see the King,

Soon and ver - y soon we are goin' to see the King,
No more cry - in' there we are goin' to see the King,
No more dy - in' there we are goin' to see the King,
Soon and ver - y soon we are goin' to see the King,

Soon and ver - y soon we are goin' to see the King,
No more cry - in' there we are goin' to see the King,
No more dy - in' there we are goin' to see the King,
Soon and ver - y soon we are goin' to see the King,

Hal - le - lu - jah, Hal - le - lu - jah, we're

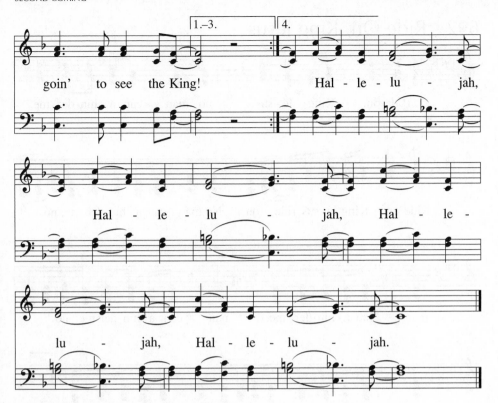

goin' to see the King! Hal - le - lu - jah,

Hal - le - lu - jah, Hal - le -

lu - jah, Hal - le - lu - jah.

Text: Andraé Crouch, b.1942
Tune: SOON AND VERY SOON, 12 12 12 14; Andraé Crouch, b.1942
© 1976, Crouch Music/Bud John Songs, admin. at EMICMGPublishing.com

692 Ride On, King Jesus

Ride on, King Je-sus, no man can a-hin-der me.

Ride on, King Je-sus, ride on. No man can a-hin-der me, no

1.

2.

man can a-hin-der me. man can a-hin-der me, no

man can a-hin-der me, no man can a-hin-der me. In that

great get-tin' up morn-ing, fare ye well, fare ye well. In that

Repeat ad lib.

great get-tin' up morn-ing, fare ye well, fare ye well. In that

Last time

well, fare ye well. No man can a-hin-der me, no

man   can a-hin-der me,   no   man   can a-hin-der me,   no

man   can a - hin -der me.   Ride on,   King Je - sus.

Text: Traditional
Tune: Negro Spiritual; arr. by Stephen Key, from a version by Ernest Davis, © 2000, GIA Publications, Inc.

693 My Lord, What a Morning

D.C.

hand   When the   stars   be - gin   to   fall.

Text: Negro Spiritual
Tune: WHAT A MORNING, 7 8 7 7 with refrain; Negro Spiritual; arr. by Melva Costen, © 1990

694 Mine Eyes Have Seen the Glory

1. Mine eyes have seen the glo - ry of the
2. I have seen him in the watch - fires of a
3. He has sound - ed forth the trum - pet that shall
4. In the beau - ty of the lil - ies Christ was

com - ing of the Lord; He is tram - pling out the
hun - dred cir - cling camps; They have build - ed him an
nev - er call re - treat; He is sift - ing out all
born a - cross the sea, With a glo - ry in his

vin - tage where the grapes of wrath are stored; He has
al - tar in the eve - ning dews and damps. I can
hu - man hearts be - fore his judg - ment seat. O be
bos - om that trans - fig - ures you and me. As he

loosed the fate - ful light - ning of his ter - ri - ble swift sword:
read the right - eous sen - tence by the dim and flar - ing lamps;
swift, my soul, to an - swer him; be ju - bi - lant, my feet!
died to make us ho - ly, let us live to make all free

His truth is march - ing on.
His day is march - ing on.
Our God is march - ing on.
While God is march - ing on.

Glo - ry, glo - ry! Hal - le - lu - jah! Glo - ry,

glo - ry! Hal - le - lu - jah! Glo - ry, glo - ry! Hal - le -

lu - jah! His truth is march - ing on.

Text: Julia W. Howe, 1819–1910, alt.
Tune: BATTLE HYMN OF THE REPUBLIC, 15 15 15 6 with refrain; attr. to William Steffe, d.1911

695 In That Great Gittin' Up Mornin'

Refrain

In that great git-tin' up morn-in', fare ye well, fare ye well, In that

great git-tin' up morn-in', fare ye well, fare ye well. In that

great git-tin' up morn-in', fare ye well, fare ye well. Oh, in a that

great git-tin' up morn-in', fare ye well, fare ye well.

Verses

1. There's a bet - ter day a com-in', fare ye well, fare ye well. There's a
2. There'll be no more dy - in', fare ye well, fare ye well. There'll be
3. Oh, saints will be a ris - in', fare ye well, fare ye well. Oh,

bet - ter day a com - in', fare ye well, fare ye well. When I
no more dy - in', fare ye well, fare ye well. There'll be
saints will be a ris - in', fare ye well, fare ye well. There'll be

see King Je - sus, fare ye well, fare ye well. When I
no more cry - in', fare ye well, fare ye well. There'll be
no more striv - in', fare ye well, fare ye well. There'll be

see King Je - sus, fare ye well, fare ye well.
no more cry - in', fare ye well, fare ye well.
no more striv - in', fare ye well, fare ye well.

Text: Negro Spiritual
Tune: FARE YE WELL, 14 14 12 12 with refrain; Negro Spiritual; arr. by Joseph Joubert, b.1958, © 2000, GIA Publications, Inc.

696 Sign Me Up

Sign me up for the Chris-tian ju-bi-lee,

Write my name on the roll.

I've been changed since the Lord has lift-ed me.

I want to be read-y when Je-sus comes.

When Je-sus comes, oh, the trum-pet will sound

loud, When my Sav - ior comes, all the

saints in Christ shall rise, Oh, I've been

changed since the Lord has lift - ed me, I

want to be read-y when Je - sus comes.

Text: Kevin Yancy and Jerome Metcalfe
Tune: Kevin Yancy and Jerome Metcalfe; arr. by James Abbington, b.1960
© 1979, 2000, GIA Publications, Inc.

697 Where Shall I Be?

1. When judg-ment day is draw-ing nigh, Where shall I be?
2. When wick-ed men his wrath shall see, Where shall I be?
3. When heav'n and earth as some great scroll, Where shall I be?
4. All trou-ble done, all con-flict past, Where shall I be?

When God the works of men shall try, Where shall I be?
And to the rocks and moun-tains flee, Where shall I be?
Shall from God's an-gry pres-ence roll, Where shall I be?
And old *A-pol-yon bound at last, Where shall I be?

When east and west the fire shall roll, Where shall I be?
When hills and moun-tains flee a-way, Where shall I be?
When all the saints re-deemed shall stand, Where shall I be?
When Christ shall reign from shore to shore, Where shall I be?

How will it be with my poor soul; Where shall I be?
When all the works of men de-cay, Where shall I be?
For-ev-er blest at God's right hand, Where shall I be?
And peace a-bide for-ev-er-more, Where shall I be?

*A place of the destruction, Sheol, the depths of Hell.

where shall I be when the first trum - pet sounds,

where shall I be when it sounds so loud? When it sounds so loud as to

wake up the dead? where shall I be when it sounds?

Text: Charles P. Jones, 1865–1949
Tune: JUDGMENT DAY, 8 4 8 4 with refrain; Charles P. Jones, 1865–1949

698 We Shall Behold Him

1. The sky shall un - fold, pre - par-ing his en - trance;
2. The an - gel shall sound the shout of his com-ing;

The stars shall ap - plaud him with
The sleep-ing shall rise from their

thun-ders of praise. The sweet light in his eyes,
slum-ber-ing place, And those who re - main,

(his eyes) shall en - hance those a - wait - ing; And
(re - main) shall be changed in a mo - ment; And

we shall be-hold him then face to face.
we shall be-hold him then face to face.

And we shall be - hold him, We shall be -
hold him Face to face in all of his
glo - ry. O we shall be - hold him,
(glo - ry.)
Yes, we shall be - hold him Face to
face, our Sav - ior and Lord.

Text: Dottie Rambo, b.1934
Tune: WE SHALL BEHOLD HIM, 11 11 15 10 with refrain; Dottie Rambo, b.1934; arr. by Nolan Williams, Jr., b.1969
© 1980, John T. Benson Publishing Co.

699 Keep Your Lamps Trimmed and Burning

1. Keep your lamps trimmed and burn - ing, Keep your
   jour - ney soon be o - ver, Chris - tian

lamps trimmed and burn - ing, Keep your lamps trimmed and burn-
jour - ney soon be o - ver, Chris - tian jour - ney soon be o -

Last time

ing, The time is draw-ing nigh. 2. Chris-tian   Chil-dren
ver.

don't get wea - ry, Chil-dren don't get wea - ry, Chil-dren

D.S.

don't get wea - ry, 'Til your work is done. Keep your

Text: African American Prayer and Praise Hymn, c.1900; adapt. by C. Eugene Cooper
Tune: African American Prayer and Praise Hymn, c.1900; adapt. by C. Eugene Cooper

700 Jesus Christ Is the Way

Verses

1. When I think a-bout the hour
2. No one knows the day nor the hour,

then I know what I must do,
may be morn, night or noon,

when I think a-bout what God
but just rest as-sured time will be no more,

has done for me;
he is com - ing soon.

Refrain

I will o-pen up my heart to ev-'ry-one I

see, and say "Je-sus Christ is the Way."

Text: Walter Hawkins
Tune: Walter Hawkins
© 1977, Bud John Music, admin. at EMICMGPublishing.com

Steal Away to Jesus 701

Refrain

Steal a-way, steal a-way, steal a-way to Je - sus!

Steal a-way, steal a-way home, I ain't got long to stay here.

Verses

Unison

1. My Lord, he calls me, He calls me by the thun - der;
2. Green trees are bend-ing, Poor sin - ners stand a trem-bling;
3. My Lord, he calls me, He calls me by the light-ning;

div. D.C.

The trum-pet sounds with - in my soul; I ain't got long to stay here.

Text: Negro Spiritual
Tune: STEAL AWAY, 5 7 8 7 with refrain; Negro Spiritual

702 Deep River

Deep riv-er, my home is o-ver Jor-dan,

Deep riv-er, Lord, I want to cross o-ver in-to

camp-ground. Oh, don't you want to go to that

gos-pel feast, That prom-ised land where

all   is   peace?   Oh,   deep

riv - er, Lord,   I   want to cross   o - ver in - to camp-ground.

Text: Traditional
Tune: DEEP RIVER, Irregular; Negro spiritual; arr. Carl Haywood, b.1949, © 1992

703 Soon-a Will Be Done

Refrain

Soon - a will be done - a with the trou - bles of the world,

Trou - bles of the world, The trou - bles of the world.

Goin'

Soon - a will be done - a with the trou - bles of the world.

home to live with God.

Verses

1. No more weep-ing and a-wail-ing, No more
2. I want to meet my moth-er, I want to
3. I want to meet my Je-sus, I want to

weep-ing and a-wail-ing, No more
meet my moth-er, I want to
meet my Je-sus, I want to

D.C.

weep-ing and a-wail-ing, I'm goin' to live with God.
meet my moth-er, I'm goin' to live with God.
meet my Je-sus, I'm goin' to live with God.

Text: Traditional
Tune: SOON-A WILL BE DONE, 888 6 with refrain; traditional

704 Swing Low, Sweet Chariot

Refrain

Swing low, sweet char - i - ot, Com-ing for to car-ry me home.

Swing low, sweet char - i - ot, Com-ing for to car-ry me home.

Verses

1. I looked o - ver Jor - dan, and what did I see
2. If you get there be - fore I do,
3. The bright - est day that ev - er I saw
4. I'm some - times up and some - times down,

Com-ing for to car - ry me home. A band of an - gels
Com-ing for to car - ry me home. Tell all my friends I'm
Com-ing for to car - ry me home. When Je - sus washed my
Com-ing for to car - ry me home. But still my soul feels

D.C.

com-ing af-ter me,	Com-ing for to car-ry me home.	O,
com - ing too,	Com-ing for to car-ry me home.	O,
sins a - way,	Com-ing for to car-ry me home.	O,
heav'n - ly bound,	Com-ing for to car-ry me home.	O,

Text: Traditional
Tune: SWING LOW, LM with refrain; Negro Spiritual; arr. by Robert Nathaniel Dett, 1882–1943, © 1936 (renewed), Paul A. Schmitt Music Co.,
c/o Belwin-Mills Publishing Corp.

705　The Sweet By and By

1. There's a land that is fair-er than day, And by
2. We shall sing on that beau-ti-ful shore The me-
3. To our boun-ti-ful Fa-ther a-bove We will

faith we can see it a-far, For the Fa-ther waits o-ver the
lo-di-ous songs of the blest; And our spir-its shall sor-row no
of-fer our trib-ute of praise For the glo-ri-ous gift of his

way To pre-pare us a dwell-ing place there.
more— Not a sigh for the bless-ing of rest.
love And the bless-ings that hal-low our days.

In the sweet by and by, We shall

In the sweet by and by, by and by,

meet on that beau - ti - ful shore; In the

by and by,

sweet by and by, We shall

In the sweet by and by, by and by,

meet on that beau - ti - ful shore.

Text: Sanford F. Bennett, 1836–1889
Tune: SWEET BY AND BY, 9 9 9 9 with refrain; Joseph P. Webster, 1819–1875

706 We're Marching to Zion

1. Come, we that love the Lord, And let our joys be
2. Let those re - fuse to sing Who nev - er knew our
3. The hill of Zi - on yields A thou - sand sa - cred
4. Then let our songs a - bound, And ev - 'ry tear be

known, Join in a song with sweet ac - cord, Join
God; But chil - dren of the heav'n - ly King, But
sweets Be - fore we reach the heav'n - ly fields, Be -
dry; We're march - ing through Im - man - uel's ground, We're

in a song with sweet ac - cord, And thus sur -
chil - dren of the heav'n - ly King, May speak their
fore we reach the heav'n - ly fields, Or walk the
march - ing through Im - man - uel's ground, To fair - er

1. And thus sur - round the
2. May speak their joys a -
3. Or walk the gold - en
4. To fair - er worlds on

round the throne, And thus sur-round the throne.
joys a - broad, May speak their joys a - broad.
gold - en streets, Or walk the gold - en streets.
worlds on high, To fair - er worlds on high.

throne, And thus sur - round the throne.
broad, May speak their joys a - broad.
streets, Or walk the gold - en streets.
high, To fair - er worlds on high.

We're march - ing to Zi - on, Beau - ti - ful,

We're march - ing on to Zi - on,

beau - ti - ful Zi - on; We're march - ing up - ward to

Zi - on, The beau - ti - ful cit - y of God.

Zi - on, Zi - on,

Text: Isaac Watts, 1674–1748
Tune: MARCHING TO ZION, 6 6 88 66 with refrain; Robert Lowry, 1826–1899

707 Ain't-a That Good News!

1. I got a crown up in - a that king-dom,
2. I got a robe up in - a that king-dom, Ain't-a that
3. I got a Sav - ior in - a that king-dom,

good news!
              I got a crown up in - a that
              I got a robe up in - a that
              I got a Sav - ior in - a that

king-dom,
king-dom, Ain't-a that good news!   I'm-a gon-na lay down this
king-dom,

world,   gon-na shoul - der up - a my cross.   Gon-na

take it home-a to my Je - sus, Ain't-a that good news!

Text: Negro Spiritual
Tune: GOOD NEWS, 10 5 10 5 16 10 5; Negro Spiritual; arr. by Robert J. Fryson, 1944–1994, © 2000, GIA Publications, Inc., alt.

New Name in Glory 708

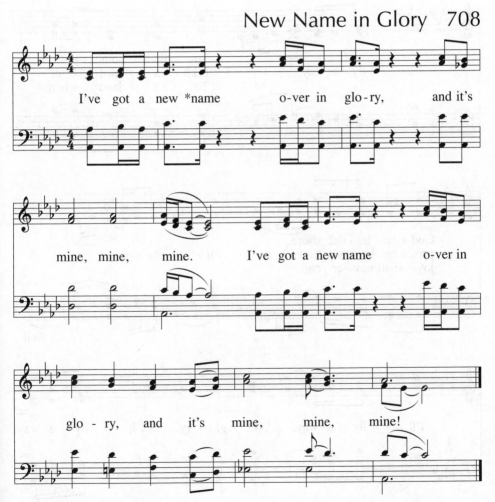

I've got a new *name o-ver in glo-ry, and it's

mine, mine, mine. I've got a new name o-ver in

glo - ry, and it's mine, mine, mine!

*Substitute song, shout, etc.

Text: African American traditional
Tune: African American traditional; arr. by Robert J. Fryson, 1944–1994, © 1982, Bob Jay Music Co.

709 I'll Fly Away

1. Some glad morn-ing   when this life is o'er,
2. When the shad-ows   of this life have gone,
3. Just a few more   wea - ry days and then,

I'll   fly a - way;   To   that   home   on
Like   a   bird   from
To   a   land   where

God's ce - les - tial shore,   I'll   fly a-way.
pris - on bars has flown,
joys shall nev - er end,

Well

I'll   fly   a - way,   O glo - ry,   I'll   fly   a - way;

When I die, Hal - le - lu - jah, by and by, I'll fly a - way.

Text: Albert E. Brumley, 1905–1977
Tune: I'LL FLY AWAY, 9 4 9 4 with refrain; Albert E. Brumley, 1905–1977; arr. by Evelyn Simpson-Curenton, b.1953

710 Fix Me, Jesus

Refrain

Oh,   fix me;   Oh,   fix me;

Je - sus   Je - sus

fix me.

Oh,   fix me, Lord.   Fix me, Je - sus,   fix me.

fix me.

fix me, Lord.

Verses

1. Fix me for my long, white robe;   Fix me, Je - sus, fix me.
2. Fix me for my jour - ney home;   Fix me, Je - sus, fix me.

D.C.

Fix me for my star - ry crown;   Fix me, Je - sus, fix me.
Fix me for my dy - ing bed;   Fix me, Je - sus, fix me.

Text: Traditional
Tune: FIX ME, 7 6 7 6 with refrain; Negro Spiritual; arr. by Nolan Williams, Jr., b.1969, © 2000, GIA Publications, Inc.

Come and Go with Me 711

1. Come and go with me to my Fa-ther's house,
2. Peace and love a - bide in my Fa-ther's house,
3. Peace and hap-pi - ness in my Fa-ther's house,

To my Fa-ther's house, to my Fa-ther's house.
In my Fa-ther's house, in my Fa-ther's house.
In my Fa-ther's house, in my Fa-ther's house.

Come and go with me to my Fa-ther's house;
Peace and love a - bide in my Fa-ther's house;
Peace and hap-pi - ness in my Fa-ther's house;

There is joy, joy, joy!

4. No more dyin' there, in my Father's house...
5. Sweet communion up there, in my Father's house...

Text: Congregational Praise Song
Tune: COME AND GO WITH ME, 10 10 10 5; Congregational Praise Song; arr. by Kenneth W. Louis, b.1956, © 2000, GIA Publications, Inc.

712 I Wanna Be Ready

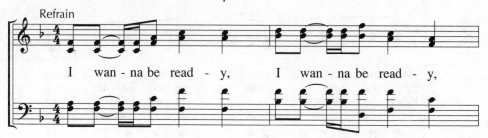

Refrain

I wan - na be read - y, I wan - na be read - y,

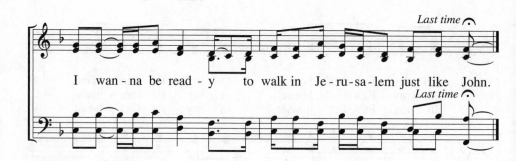

I wan - na be read - y to walk in Je - ru - sa - lem just like John.

Last time

Verses
Solo:

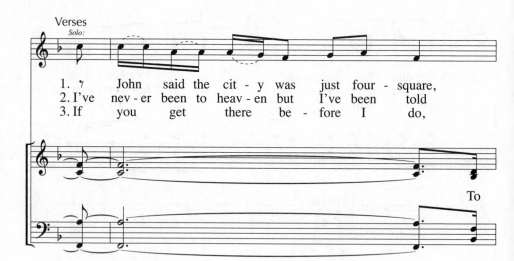

1. John said the cit - y was just four - square,
2. I've nev - er been to heav - en but I've been told
3. If you get there be - fore I do,

To

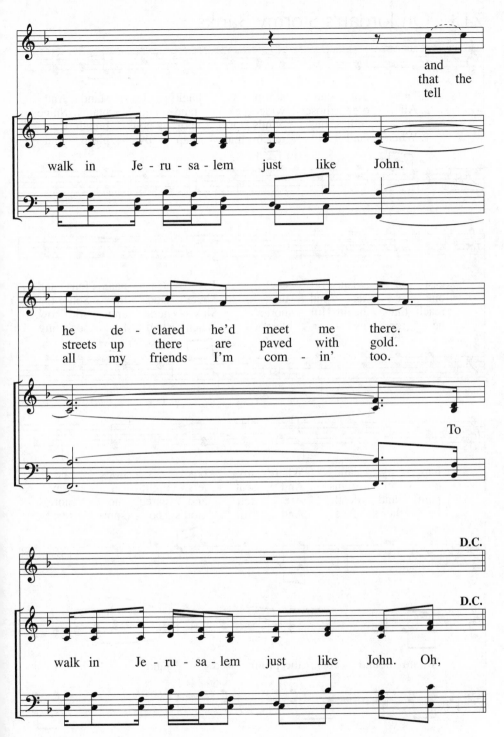

Text: Negro Spiritual
Tune: BE READY, 8 10 8 10 with refrain; Negro Spiritual; arr. by Evelyn Simpson-Curenton, b.1953, © 2000, GIA Publications, Inc., alt.

713 On Jordan's Stormy Banks

1. On Jor-dan's storm-y banks I stand, And
2. All o'er those wide-ex-tend-ed plains, Shines
3. No chill-ing winds or poi-s'nous breath Can
4. When shall I reach that hap-py place And

cast a wish-ful eye; To Ca-naan's fair and
one e-ter-nal day; There God the Son for-
reach that health-ful shore; Sick-ness and sor-row,
be for-ev-er blest? When shall I see my

hap-py land, Where my pos-ses-sions lie.
ev-er reigns, And scat-ters night a-way.
pain and death, Are felt and feared no more.
Fa-ther's face, And in God's bo-som rest?

I am bound for the prom-ised land, I am

bound for the prom-ised land; Oh, who will come and

go with me? I am bound for the prom-ised land.

Text: Samuel Stennett, 1727–1795
Tune: STORMY BANKS, CM with refrain; American melody; adapt by Rigdon McCoy McIntosh, 1836–1899; arr. by Norman Johnson, 1928–1983,
   © 1968, Singspiration Music (ASCAP)

714 Plenty Good Room

Refrain

Plen-ty good room, plen-ty good room, plen-ty good room in my Fa-ther's king-dom,

Plen-ty good room, plen-ty good room, just choose your seat and sit down.

Verses

1. I would not be a sin - ner,
2. I would not be a li - ar,   I'll
3. I would not be a back - slid - er,

tell you the rea - son why;   cause

if my Lord should call on me   I

D.C.

would-n't be read - y to die.

Text: Negro Spiritual
Tune: Negro Spiritual; arr. by Joseph Joubert, b.1958, © 2000, GIA Publications, Inc.

715 When We All Get to Heaven

1. Sing the won-drous love of Je-sus, Sing his
2. While we walk the pil-grim path-way Clouds will
3. Let us then be true and faith-ful, Trust-ing,
4. On-ward to the prize be-fore us! Soon his

mer-cy and his grace; In the man-sions
o-ver-spread the sky; But when trav-'ling
serv-ing ev-'ry day; Just one glimpse of
beau-ty we'll be-hold; Soon the pearl-y

bright and bless-ed He'll pre-pare for us a place.
days are o-ver Not a shad-ow, not a sigh.
him in glo-ry Will the toils of life re-pay.
gates will o-pen— We shall tread the streets of gold.

When we all get to heav - en, what a

When we all get to heav - en,

day of re-joic-ing that will be! When we

what a day of re-joic-ing that will be!

all see Je - sus, we'll

When we all see Je - sus, we'll

sing and shout the vic - to - ry!

sing and shout, and shout the vic - to - ry!

Text: Eliza E. Hewitt, 1851–1920
Tune: HEAVEN, 8 7 8 7 with refrain; Emily D. Wilson, 1865–1942; arr. by Valeria A. Foster, © 2000, GIA Publications, Inc.

716 Shall We Gather at the River

1. Shall we gath - er at the riv - er,
2. On the mar - gin of the riv - er,
3. Ere we reach the shin - ing riv - er,
4. Soon we'll reach the shin - ing riv - er,

Where bright an - gel feet have trod,
Wash - ing up its sil - ver spray,
Lay we ev - 'ry bur - den down;
Soon our pil - grim-age will cease,

With its crys - tal tide for ev - er Flow - ing
We will walk and wor - ship ev - er, All the
Grace our spir - its will de - liv - er, And pro -
Soon our hap - py hearts will quiv - er With the

by the throne of God?
hap - py gold - en day.
vide a robe and crown.
mel - o - dy of peace.

Yes, we'll gath - er at the riv - er, The
beau - ti - ful, the beau - ti - ful riv - er;
Gath - er with the saints at the riv - er That
flows by the throne of God.

Text: Robert Lowry, 1826–1899
Tune: HANSON PLACE, 8 7 8 7 with refrain; Robert Lowry, 1826–1899

717 I'll Be Singing Up There

Refrain

there,

I'll be sing-ing up, sing-ing up there, I'll be sing-ing up,

yes,

there.   Oh,

sing-ing   up   there.   come on   up   to bright

sing-ing   up   there.   Oh,

glo - ry,   I'll   be   sing - ing up   there.

Verses

1. If   you miss me *sing-ing down here,   If you miss me

*2. praying...
  3. walking...
  4. shouting...

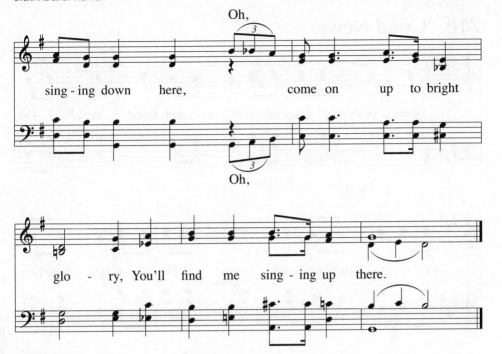

sing-ing down here, come on up to bright

Oh,

glo - ry, You'll find me sing-ing up there.

Text: Negro Spiritual
Tune: Negro Spiritual; arr. by W. O. Hoyle, Lillian Bowles, and W. Webb

718 Good News!

*2. pair of wings...
 3. pair of shoes...
 4. starry crown...
 5. golden harp...

long white robe in the heav-en, I know. There's a

long white robe in the heav-en, I know.

long white robe in the heav-en, I know, And I

don't want it to leave me be-hind.

Text: Negro Spiritual
Tune: Negro Spiritual

719 We Shall Rise Again

1. Come to me, all you wea - ry,
2. Though we walk through the dark - ness,
3. We de - pend on God's mer - cy,
4. Do not fear death's do - min - ion,
5. At the door there to greet us,

with your bur - dens and pain. Take my yoke on your
e - vil we do not fear. You are walk - ing be -
mer - cy which nev - er fades. We re - mem - ber our
look be - yond earth and grave. See the bright - ness of
mar - tyrs, an - gels, and saints, And our fam - 'ly and

shoul - ders and learn from
side us with your rod and your
cov - e - nant and the prom - ise Je - sus
Je - sus shin - ing out to light our
loved ones, ev - 'ry - one freed from their

me: I am gen - tle and hum - ble,
staff. On - ly good - ness and kind - ness
made: If we die with Christ Je - sus,
way. Lov - ing Fa - ther and Spir - it,
chains. We shall feel their ac - cep - tance,

and your soul will find rest, For my yoke is
fol - low us all our lives. We shall dwell in the
we shall live with him, And if we are
lov - ing Je - sus the Son, All God's peo - ple to -
and the joy of new life. We shall join in the

eas - y and my bur - den is light.
Lord's house for so man - y years to come!
faith - ful, we shall reign with him!
geth - er, we shall live on as one!
gath - er - ing, re - u - nit - ed in God's love!

We shall rise a-gain on the last day with the

with the

faith - ful, rich and poor. Com - ing

Com - ing

faith - ful, rich and poor, Com - ing

to the house of Lord Je - sus, we will find an o - pen

to the house of Je - sus,

door there, we will find an o - pen door.

1.–4.   5.

Text: Matthew 11:29–30, Psalm 23, John 11, 2 Timothy 2; Jeremy Young, b.1948
Tune: RESURRECTION; Irregular with refrain; Jeremy Young, b.1948
© 1987, GIA Publications, Inc.

720 Talkin' 'bout a Good Time

Verse 1

(1.) nev-er been to Heav-en, but I been told that the

D.C.

gates are pearl - y and the streets are gold.

Verse 2

2. When I get to Heav-en, I'm gon-na walk a - round,

D.C.

gon-na ask my Lord for my star - ry crown.

Verse 3

(3.) star - ry crown gon-na fit me well, 'cause I

D.C.

tried it on at the gates of Hell.

Text: African American Prayer and Praise Hymn, c.1900; adapt. by C. Eugene Cooper
Tune: African American Prayer and Praise Hymn, c.1900; adapt. by C. Eugene Cooper
© 1987, 1988, 1991, GIA Publications, Inc.

721 You Better Run

Refrain

You bet-ter run, bet-ter run, bet-ter run. You bet-ter run,

bet-ter run, bet-ter run. You bet-ter run to the cit-y of

1.
ref - uge, you bet - ter run.

2., 3. *Last time*
run.

Verse 1
Solo:

1. If you don't be - lieve that I'm sing-ing it right, just

pick up your Bi - ble and read it to - night. Just

read in Gen - e - sis, you un - der - stand, that Me -

"Mo-ses, don't you leave my chil - dren be - hind. I want

you to lead them to the Prom - ised Land, All you

D.S.

have to do is fol-low my com - mand." He had to

Verse 3   *Solo:*

3. God sent Jo - nah to Nin - e - veh land, He

did - n't o - bey my Lord's com - mand. Wind blew

the ship from shore to shore, the whale

D.S.

swal - lowed Jo - nah and he was no more. He had to

Text: African American Prayer and Praise Hymn, c.1900; adapt. by C. Eugene Cooper
Tune: African American Prayer and Praise Hymn, c.1900; adapt. by C. Eugene Cooper
© 1987, 1988, 1991, GIA Publications, Inc.

Transform Us   722

1. Trans - form   us   as   you,   trans - fig - ured,
2. Trans - form   us   as   you,   trans - fig - ured,
3. Trans - form   us   as   you,   trans - fig - ured,

Stood   a - part   on   Ta - bor's   height.
Once   spoke   with   those   ho - ly   ones.
Would   not   stay   with - in   a   shrine.

Lead   us   up   our   sa - cred   moun - tains,
We,   sur - round - ed   by   the   wit - ness
Keep   us   from   our   great   temp - ta - tion—

Search   us   with   re - veal - ing   light.
Of   those   saints   whose   work   is   done,
Time   and   truth   we   quick - ly   bind.

Lift   us   from   where   we   have   fall - en,
Live   in   this   world   as   your   Bod - y,
Lead   us   down   those   dai - ly   path - ways

Full   of   ques - tions,   filled   with   fright.
Cho - sen   daugh - ters,   cho - sen   sons.
Where   our   love   is   not   con - fined.

Text: Sylvia Dunstan, 1955–1993, © 1993, GIA Publications, Inc.
Tune: PICARDY, 8 7 8 7 8 7; French Carol; harm. by Richard Proulx, 1937–2010, © 1986, GIA Publications, Inc.

723 Salve Regína / Hail, Queen of Heaven

Sal - ve Re - gí - na, ma - ter mi - se - ri - cór - di - ae:
Hail, Queen of Heav-en, hail, our Moth-er com-pas-sion-ate,

Vi - ta, dul - cé - do et spes no - stra sal - ve.
True life and com - fort and our hope, we greet you!

Ad te cla - má - mus, éx - su - les fí - li - i He - vae.
To you we ex - iles, chil-dren of Eve, raise our voic - es.

Ad te sus - pi - rá - mus, ge - mén - tes et flen - tes
We send up sighs to you, as mourn-ing and weep-ing,

in hac la - cri - má - rum val - le. E - ia er - go,
we pass through this vale of sor - row. Then turn to us,

ad - vo - cá - ta no - stra, il - los tu - os
O most gra - cious Wom - an, those eyes of yours,

mi - se - ri - cór - des ó - cu - los ad nos con - vér - te.
so full of love and ten - der-ness, so full of pit - y.

Et Je - sum, be - ne - dí - ctum fru - ctum ven - tris tu - i,
And grant us af - ter these, our days of lone - ly ex - ile,

no - bis post hoc ex - sí - li - um o - stén - de.
the sight of your blest Son and Lord, Christ Je - sus.

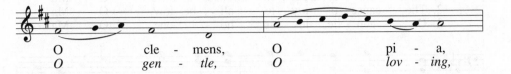

O cle - mens, O pi - a,
O gen - tle, O lov - ing,

O dul - cis Vir - go Ma - rí - a.
O ho - ly, sweet Vir - gin Mar - y.

Text: *Salve Regina, mater misericordiae*, c.1080, tr. by John C. Selner, SS, 1904–1992, © 1954, GIA Publications, Inc.
Tune: SALVE REGINA, Irregular; Mode V; acc. by Gerard Farrell, OSB, 1919–2009, alt., © 1986, GIA Publications, Inc.

724 Hail, Holy Queen Enthroned Above

1. Hail, ho - ly Queen en - throned a - bove, O Ma -
2. The cause of joy to all be - low, O Ma -
3. O gen - tle, lov - ing, ho - ly one, O Ma -

rí - a. Hail, Queen of mer - cy and of love,
rí - a. The spring through which all grac - es flow,
rí - a. The God of light be - came your Son,

O Ma - rí - a. Tri - umph, all ye
O Ma - rí - a. An - gels, all your
O Ma - rí - a. Tri - umph, all ye

Cher - u - bim; Sing with us, ye Ser - a - phim.
prais - es bring; Earth and heav - en, with us sing;
Cher - u - bim; Sing with us, ye Ser - a - phim.

Heav'n and earth re - sound the hymn: Sal - ve,
All cre - a - tion ech - o - ing: Sal - ve,
Heav'n and earth re - sound the hymn: Sal - ve,

Sal - ve, Sal - ve Re - gí - na.
Sal - ve, Sal - ve Re - gí - na.
Sal - ve, Sal - ve Re - gí - na.

Text: *Salve, Regina, mater misericordia*; c.1080; tr. *Roman Hymnal*, 1884; st. 2–3, adapt. by M. Owen Lee, CSB, b.1930
Tune: SALVE REGINA COELITUM, 8 4 8 4 777 4 5; *Choralmelodien zum Heiligen Gesänge*, 1808; harm. by Healey Willan, 1880–1968,
© Willis Music Co.

725 When I Survey the Wondrous Cross

1. When I sur - vey the won - drous cross
2. For - bid it, Lord, that I should boast,
3. See, from his head, his hands, his feet,
4. Were the whole realm of na - ture mine,

On which the Prince of glo - ry died,
Save in the death of Christ, my God;
Sor - row and love flow min - gled down;
That were a pres - ent far too small:

My rich - est gain I count but loss,
All the vain things that charm me most—
Did e'er such love and sor - row meet,
Love so a - maz - ing, so di - vine,

And pour con - tempt on all my pride.
I sac - ri - fice them to his blood.
Or thorns com - pose so rich a crown?
De - mands my soul, my life, my all.

Text: Isaac Watts, 1674–1748
Tune: HAMBURG, LM; Gregorian Chant; arr. by Lowell Mason, 1792–1872

Lift High the Cross 726

Lift high the cross, the love of Christ pro-claim till
all the world a-dore his sa-cred name.

Harmony:

1. Come, Chris-tians, fol-low where our Sav-ior trod, Our
2. Led on their way by this tri-um-phant sign, The
3. Each new-born ser-vant of the Cru-ci-fied Bears
4. O Lord, once lift-ed on the glo-rious tree, Your
5. So shall our song of tri-umph ev-er be: Praise

King vic-to-rious, Christ, the Son of God.
hosts of God in con-quering ranks com-bine.
on the brow the seal of him who died.
death has bought us life e-ter-nal-ly.
to the Cru-ci-fied for vic-to-ry!

D.C.

Text: 1 Corinthians 1:18; George W. Kitchin, 1827-1912, and Michael R. Newbolt, 1874-1956, alt.
Tune: CRUCIFER, 10 10 with refrain; Sydney H. Nicholson, 1875-1947
© 1974, Hope Publishing Company

727　The Old Rugged Cross

1. On a hill far a - way stood an old rug - ged cross,
2. O that old rug - ged cross, so de - spised by the world,
3. In the old rug - ged cross, stained with blood so di - vine,
4. To the old rug - ged cross I will ev - er be true,

The em - blem of suf - f'ring and shame;
Has a won - drous at - trac - tion for me;
A won - drous beau - ty I see;
Its shame and re - proach glad - ly bear;

And I love that old cross where the dear - est and best
For the dear Lamb of God left his glo - ry a - bove
For 'twas on that old cross Je - sus suf - fered and died
Then he'll call me some day to my home far a - way,

For a world of lost sin - ners was slain.
To bear it to dark Cal - va - ry.
To par - don and sanc - ti - fy me.
Where his glo - ry for ev - er I'll share.

old rug - ged cross,

So I'll cher - ish the cross, the old rug - ged cross, Till my

old rug - ged

tro - phies at last I lay down; I will cling to the cross, the

cross,

old rug - ged cross, And ex - change it some day for a crown.

Text: George Bennard, 1873–1958
Tune: OLD RUGGED CROSS, 12 8 12 8 with refrain; George Bennard, 1873–1958

728 For All the Saints

1. For all the saints, who from their la - bors
2. You were their rock, their for - tress and their
3. O may your sol - diers, faith - ful, true, and
7. But then there breaks a yet more glo - rious
8. From earth's wide bounds, from o - cean's far - thest

rest, Who to the world their
might; You, Lord, their Cap - tain
bold, Fight as the saints who
day; The saints tri - um - phant
coast, Through gates of pearl streams

faith in you con - fessed; Your name, O
in the well - fought fight; You, in the
no - bly fought of old, And win with
rise in bright ar - ray; The King of
in the count - less host, Sing - ing to

Je - sus, be for - ev - er blest.
dark - ness drear, their one true light.
them the vic - tor's crown of gold.
glo - ry pass - es on his way.
Fa - ther, Son, and Ho - ly Ghost:

Al - le - lu - ia! Al - le - lu - ia!

4. O blest com - mun - ion, fel - low - ship di - vine!
5. And when the strife is fierce, the war - fare long,
6. The gold - en eve - ning bright - ens in the west;

We fee - bly strug - gle, they in glo - ry shine;
Steals on the ear the dis - tant tri - umph song,
Soon, soon to faith - ful war - riors comes their rest;

Yet all are one with - in your great de - sign.
And hearts are brave a - gain, and arms are strong.
Sweet is the calm of par - a - dise the blest.

Al - le - lu - ia!
Al - le - lu - ia! Al - le - lu - ia!

Text: William W. How, 1823–1897, alt.
Tune: SINE NOMINE, 10 10 10 with alleluias; Ralph Vaughan Williams, 1872–1958

729 When the Saints Go Marching In

1. O when the saints go march-ing in, O when the
2. O when the sun re-fused to shine, O when the
3. O when they crown him Lord of all, O when they

saints go march - ing in, O Lord, I want to be in that
sun re - fused to shine,
crown him Lord of all,

num-ber when the saints go march - ing in.
when the sun re - fused to shine.
when they crown him Lord of all.

Text: Negro Spiritual
Tune: WHEN THE SAINTS, 88 10 7; Negro Spiritual; arr. by Stephen Key, © 2000, GIA Publications, Inc.

Ye Watchers and Ye Holy Ones 730

1. Ye watch-ers and ye ho-ly ones, Bright
2. O high-er than the cher-u-bim, More
3. Re-spond, ye souls in end-less rest, Ye
4. O friends, in glad-ness let us sing, Su -

ser-aphs, cher-u-bim, and thrones, Raise the
glo-rious than the ser-a-phim, Lead their
pa-tri-archs and proph-ets blest: "Al - le -
per-nal an-thems ech-o-ing: "Al - le -

[⌢]

glad strain: "Al-le-lu-ia!" Cry out, do-min-ions, prince-doms,
prais-es: "Al-le-lu-ia!" O bear-er of the e-ter-nal
lu-ia, Al-le-lu-ia!" Ye ho-ly twelve, ye mar-tyrs
lu-ia, Al-le-lu-ia!" To God the Fa-ther, God the

pow'rs, Vir - tues, arch-an-gels, an-gels' choirs:
Word, Most gra-cious, mag-ni-fy the Lord:
strong, All saints tri-um-phant, raise the song:
Son, And God the Spir-it, Three in One:

"Al-le-lu-ia! Al-le-lu-ia!" Al-le-lu-ia,

al-le-lu-ia, al-le-lu-ia!

Text: John A. Riley, 1858–1945
Tune: LASST UNS ERFREUEN, LM with alleluias; *Geistliche Kirchengesänge*, Cologne, 1623; harm. by Ralph Vaughan Williams, 1872–1958

731 Stand Firm

Cantor(s):

with Mar - y,
with John the Bap - tist,
with Mar - y Mag-da-lene,
with Paul,
with Ag - nes,
with Law - rence,
with Joan of Arc,
with Ro - mer - o,

All:

Stand, O stand firm, stand, O

with Mi - chael,
with Jo - seph,
with Per-pet - u - a,
with Ste - phen,
with Cath-er-ine,
with Greg-or - y,
with Hil - de-gard,
with King,

with the an - gels,
with Pe - ter,
with Fe - li - ci - ty,
with Ig - na - tius,
with Te - re - sa,
with Be - ne - dict,
with Ju - lia,
with Thom-as Mer - ton,

stand firm, stand, O stand firm and see what the

O my sis - ters,
O my broth - ers, Stand ver - y firm.
O God's peo - ple,

Lord can do.

Text: Litany of the Saints and Exodus 14:13
Tune: Cameroon traditional; arr. by John L. Bell, b.1949; adapt. by Marty Haugen, b.1952, © 1998, Iona Community, GIA Publications, Inc., agent

732 Immaculate Mary

1. Im - mac - u - late Mar - y, your prais - es we sing;
2. Pre - des - tined for Christ by e - ter - nal de - cree,
3. To you by an an - gel, the Lord God made known
4. Most blest of all wom - en, you heard and be - lieved;
5. The an - gels re - joiced when you brought forth God's Son;
6. Your child is the Sav - ior, all hope lies in him:
7. In glo - ry for ev - er now close to your Son,

You reign now in splen - dor with Je - sus our King.
God willed you both vir - gin and moth - er to be.
The grace of the Spir - it, the gift of the Son.
Most blest is the fruit of your womb then con - ceived.
Your joy is the joy of all a - ges to come.
He gives us new life and re - deems us from sin.
All a - ges will praise you for all God has done.

A - ve, a - ve, a - ve, Ma - rí - a.

A - ve, a - ve, Ma - rí - a.

Text: St. 1, Jeremiah Cummings, 1814–1866, alt.; sts. 2–7, Brian Foley, 1919–2000, © 1971, Faber Music Ltd.
Tune: LOURDES HYMN, 11 11 with refrain; French melody, Grenoble, 1882

Ave María 733

A - ve Ma - rí - a, grá - ti - a ple - na,

Dó - mi - nus te - cum, be - ne - dí - cta tu in mu - li - é -

ri - bus, et be - ne - dí - ctus fru - ctus ven-tris tu - i, Je - sus.

San-cta Ma - rí - a, Ma-ter De - i, o - ra pro no - bis pec - ca -

tó - ri - bus, nunc et in ho - ra mor-tis no - strae. A - men.

Text: *Hail, Mary, full of grace,* Luke 1:29; Latin, 13th C.
Tune: AVE MARIA, Irregular; Mode I; acc. by Robert LeBlanc, b.1948, © 1986, GIA Publications, Inc.

734 O Sanctíssima / O Most Holy One

1. O san - ctís - si - ma, O pi - ís - si - ma,
2. Tu so - lá - ti - um Et re - fú - gi - um,
3. Ec - ce dé - bi - les, Per quam flé - bi - les,
4. Vir - go ré - spi - ce, Ma - ter, á - spi - ce,

1. *O most ho - ly one, O most low - ly one,*
2. *Com - fort in our tears, Ref - uge in our fears,*
3. *See us pow - er - less. In our hope - less - ness*
4. *Maid - en, look on us, Moth - er, care for us.*

Dul - cis vir - go Ma - rí - a!
Vir - go ma - ter Ma - rí - a!
Sal - va nos, O Ma - rí - a!
Au - di nos, O Ma - rí - a!

Praise to you, vir - gin Mar - y!
Vir - gin moth - er, sweet Mar - y!
Save us! Aid us, O Mar - y!
Hear our plead - ing, O Mar - y!

Ma - ter a - má - ta, In - te - me - rá - ta,
Quid - quid o - ptá - mus, Per te spe - rá - mus,
Tol - le lan - guó - res, Sa - na do - ló - res,
Tu me - di - cí - nam, Por - tas di - ví - nam;

Kind, lov - ing Moth - er, Graced like no oth - er,
What - e'er our souls need Grant us, as we plead:
Come, take our sad - ness; Fill us with glad - ness.
You bring us heal - ing, God's love re - veal - ing.

BLESSED VIRGIN MARY

O - ra, o - ra pro no - bis.
O - ra, o - ra pro no - bis.
O - ra, o - ra pro no - bis.
O - ra, o - ra pro no - bis.
Pray, O pray for us, Mar - y!
Pray, O pray for us, Mar - y!
Pray, O pray for us, Mar - y!
Pray, O pray for us, Mar - y!

Text: St. 1, *Stimmen der Völker in Liedern,* 1807; st. 2, *Arundel Hymnal,* 1902; tr. Neil Borgstrom, b.1953, © 1994, 2011, GIA Publications, Inc.
Tune: O DU FRÖLICHE, 55 7 55 7; Tattersall's *Improved Psalmody,* 1794

735 Anointing

A - noint - ing fall on me.

A - noint - ing fall on me.

Let the pow-er of the Ho - ly Ghost fall on me.

A - noint - ing fall on me.

Text: Donn C. Thomas, b.1949, © Paragon Music Corp.
Tune: Donn C. Thomas, b.1949, © Paragon Music Corp.; arr. by Evelyn Simpson-Curenton, b.1953, © 2000, GIA Publications, Inc.

Take Me to the Water 736

1. Take me to the wa - ter,
2. None but the right - eous,
3. I love Je - sus,
4. In the name of Je - sus,
5. I know I got re - lig - ion, I
6. Glo - ry, hal - le - lu - jah,

Take me to the wa - ter, Take me to the
None but the right - eous, None but the
I love Je - sus, I love
In the name of Je - sus, In the name of
know I got re - lig - ion, I know I got re -
Glo - ry, hal - le - lu - jah, Glo - ry, hal - le -

wa - ter to be bap - tized.
right - eous shall see God.
Je - sus. Yes, I do.
Je - sus we shall be saved.
lig - ion. Yes, I do.
lu - jah, to be bap - tized.

Text: Negro Spiritual
Tune: TO THE WATER, Irregular; Negro Spiritual; arr. by Valeria A. Foster, © 2000, GIA Publications, Inc.

737 Wash, O God, Our Sons and Daughters

1. Wash, O God, our sons and daugh - ters, Where your cleans - ing wa - ters flow. Num-ber them a - mong your peo - ple; Bless as Christ blessed long a - go. Weave them gar - ments bright and spar - kling; Com - pass

2. We who bring them long for nur - ture; By your milk may we be fed. Let us join your feast, par - tak - ing Cup of bless - ing, liv - ing bread. God, re - new us, guide our foot - steps; Free from

3. O how deep your ho - ly wis - dom! Un - i - mag - ined, all your ways! To your name be glo - ry, hon - or! With our lives we wor - ship, praise! We your peo - ple stand be - fore you, Wa - ter -

them   with   love   and   light.   Fill,   a - noint   them;
sin   and   all   its   snares,   One   with   Christ   in
washed and   Spir - it - born.   By   your   grace,   our

send   your   Spir - it,   Ho - ly   dove   and   heart's de - light.
liv - ing, dy - ing,   By   your   Spir - it,   chil - dren, heirs.
lives   we   of - fer.   Re - cre - ate   us;   God,   trans - form!

Text: Ruth Duck, b.1947, © 1989, The United Methodist Publishing House
Tune: BEACH SPRING, 8 7 8 7 D, *The Sacred Harp*; harm. by Ronald A. Nelson, b.1927, © 1978, *Lutheran Book of Worship*,
    admin. by Augsburg Fortress

738   Wade in the Water

Refrain

Wade in the wa - ter, wade in the wa - ter, chil - dren,

Wade in the wa - ter, God's gon-na trou-ble the wa - ter.

Verses

1. See that host all dressed in white,
2. See that band all dressed in red,
3. Look o - ver yon-der, what do I see?
3. If you don't be - lieve I've been re - deemed,

God's gon-na trou-ble the wa - ter.

The lead - er looks like the Is - rael - ite,
Looks like the band that Mo - ses led,
The Ho - ly Ghost a com-in' on me,
Just fol-low me down to Jor - dan's stream,

D.C.

God's gon - na trou - ble the wa - ter.

Text: Negro Spiritual
Tune: WADE IN THE WATER, 7 8 8 8 with refrain; Negro Spiritual; arr. by James Abbington, b.1960, © 2000, GIA Publications, Inc.

We Offer Christ 739

We of-fer Christ to you, oh, my broth-er, We

of - fer Christ to you, oh, my sis - ter. He will

give you brand new life Through life a-bun - dant-ly; Oh

come, come on to Christ.

Text: Joel Britton, © 1995, Mo'Berries Music (ASCAP) / Y'Shua Publishing (ASCAP)
Tune: Joel Britton, © 1995, Mo'Berries Music (ASCAP) / Y'Shua Publishing (ASCAP); arr. by Valeria A. Foster, © 2000, GIA Publications, Inc.

740   I've Just Come from the Fountain

I've just come from the foun-tain, I've just come from the foun-tain,

Lord, I've just come from the foun-tain, his name's so sweet. Oh

*broth-er, do you love Je - sus? "Yes, yes, I do love my Je-sus."

*Broth-er, do you love Je - sus? His name's so sweet. Oh Lord, I've

*Sister, sinner, preacher

Text: Negro Spiritual
Tune: Negro Spiritual; arr. by Evelyn Simpson-Curenton, b.1953, © 2012, GIA Publications, Inc.

I Know My Name Is Written There   741

1. I know, I know, I know, I know, my name, my name, is there. is there. is there. I know, I know, I know, I know, my name is writ - ten there.
2. On high, on high, on high, on high, my name, my name, is there. is there. is there. On high, on high, on high, on high, my name is writ - ten there.
3. Be sure, be sure, be sure, be sure, your name, your name, is there. is there. is there. Be sure, be sure, be sure, be sure, your name is writ - ten there.
4. Thank God, thank God, thank God, thank God, our name, our name, is there. is there. is there. Thank God, thank God, thank God, thank God, our name is writ - ten there.

Text: African American Prayer and Praise Hymn, c.1900; adapt. by C. Eugene Cooper
Tune: African American Prayer and Praise Hymn, c.1900; adapt. by C. Eugene Cooper
© 1987, 1988, 1991, GIA Publications, Inc.

742 Mold Me, Lord

Descant:

1. Mold me, Lord. Shape me, Lord. Make me ac-
2. Save us, Lord. Keep us, Lord. Guide us ac-
3. Cleanse us, Lord. Purge us, Lord. Heal us ac-
4. Use us, Lord. Lead us, Lord. Send us ac-

Melody:

cord - ing to your will all a - new.
cord - ing to your will with your hand.
cord - ing to your will by your grace.
cord - ing to your will in your strength.

My thoughts ac - cord - ing to your will all a - new.
In time of tri - al, guide us, Lord, with your hand.
From sin and e - vil, heal us, Lord, by your grace.
To those in suf - f'ring, send us, Lord, in your strength.

My words ac - cord - ing to your will all a - new.
In joy and sor - row, guide us, Lord, with your hand.
From pride and en - vy, heal us, Lord, by your grace.
To those in dark - ness, send us, Lord, in your strength.

My deeds ac-cord - ing to your will all a - new.
Lest we for-get you, guide us, Lord, with your hand.
From guilt and ter - ror, heal us, Lord, by your grace.
To those un-heed - ing, send us, Lord, in your strength.

Text: Howard S. Olson, 1922–2010
Tune: Nyaturu Tune
© 1977, Augsburg Publishing House

Come to Jesus 743

1. Come to Je - sus, Come to Je - sus, Come to
Je - sus just now, just now. Come to
Je - sus, Come to Je - sus just now!

2. Only trust him,...
3. He is able,...
4. He will save you,...

Text: Traditional
Tune: COME TO JESUS, 4 4 8 4 6; traditional; arr. by Evelyn Simpson-Curenton, b.1953, © 2000, GIA Publications, Inc.

744 Changed Mah Name

1. Ah tol' Je - sus it would be all right if he
2. Je - sus tol' me ah would have to live hum - ble if he
3. Je - sus tol' me that the world would be 'gainst me if he
4. But ah tol' Je - sus it would be all right if he

changed mah name.
changed mah name.
changed mah name.
changed mah name.

(Changed mah name.)

Ah tol' Je - sus it would be all right if he
Je - sus tol' me ah would have to live hum - ble if he
Je - sus tol' me that the world would be 'gainst me if he
But ah tol' Je - sus it would be all right if he

changed mah name.
changed mah name.
changed mah name.
changed mah name.

(If he changed mah name.)

Ah tol' Je - sus it would be all right,
Je - sus tol' me ah would have to live hum - ble,
Je - sus tol' me that the world would be 'gainst me,
But ah tol' Je - sus it would be all right,

Ah tol' Je - sus it would be all right,
Je - sus tol' me ah would have to live hum - ble,
Je - sus tol' me that the world would be 'gainst me,
But ah tol' Je - sus it would be all right,

Ah tol' Je - sus it would be all right if he
Je - sus tol' me ah would have to live hum - ble if he
Je - sus tol' me that the world would be 'gainst me if he
But ah tol' Je - sus it would be all right if he

changed mah name.
changed mah name.
changed mah name.   (If he changed mah name.)
changed man name.

Text: Negro Spiritual
Tune: Negro Spiritual; arr. by Evelyn Simpson-Curenton, b.1953, © 2012, GIA Publications, Inc.

745 There Is One Lord

Ostinato Refrain

There is one Lord, one faith, one bap - tis-m,

There is one God who is Fa - ther of all.

Verses

Cantor:

1. Bear with one an - oth - er in love and char - i - ty, be

hum - ble, be pa - tient, be self - less, be as one.

2. There is one bod - y, there is one Spir - it,

there is one hope to which we are called.

3. We are all to come to u - ni - ty, in our

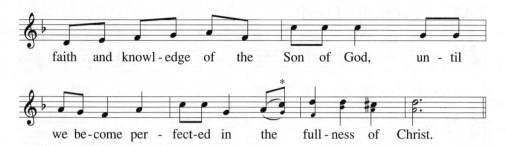

faith and knowl-edge of the Son of God, un - til

we be-come per - fect-ed in the full - ness of Christ.

*Choose either part

Text: Ephesians 4, adapt. by Robert J. Batastini, b.1942, and the Taizé Community, 1984
Tune: Jacques Berthier, 1923–1994
© 1984, Les Presses de Taizé, GIA Publications, Inc., agent

Baptized in Water 746

1. Bap - tized in wa - ter, Sealed by the Spir - it, Cleansed by the
2. Bap - tized in wa - ter, Sealed by the Spir - it, Dead in the
3. Bap - tized in wa - ter, Sealed by the Spir - it, Marked with the

blood of Christ our King: Heirs of sal - va - tion, Trust-ing his
tomb with Christ our King: One with his ris - ing, Freed and for-
sign of Christ our King: Born of one Fa - ther, We are his

prom - ise, Faith - ful - ly now God's praise we sing.
giv - en, Thank-ful - ly now God's praise we sing.
chil - dren, Joy - ful - ly now God's praise we sing.

Text: Michael Saward, b.1932, © 1982, The Jubilate Group (admin. by Hope Publishing Company)
Tune: BUNESSAN, 5 5 8 D; Gaelic melody; acc. by Robert J. Batastini, b.1942, © 1999, GIA Publications, Inc.

747 Certainly, Lord!

Cantor (freely):

1. Do you re-ject old Sa-tan and all

Cert - 'n-ly, Lord!

his works and all his emp-ty prom-is-es?

Cert-'n-ly, Lord!

Cert-'n-ly, Lord! Cert-'n-ly, cert-'n-ly, cert-'n-ly, Lord!

2. He is the Father of Sin, *Cert'nly, Lord!*
   he is the Prince of Darkness. *Cert'nly, Lord!*
   Do you reject old Satan? *Cert'nly, Lord!*

3. Do you believe in God
   the Father Almighty
   who created heaven and earth?

4. Do you believe in Jesus
   his only Son,
   born of the Virgin Mary?

5. He was crucified
   bowed his head and died!
   But he rose on Easter!

6. He is seated at the right hand
   of the Father!
   Do you believe in Jesus?

7. Do you believe in God's Spirit?
   The holy cath'lic Church?
   In the communion of saints?

8. Can God forgive sin?
   Can God raise the dead?
   Can God give life everlasting?

9. Church, this is our faith!
   We are proud to profess it!
   In Jesus Christ!

10. Oh, cert'nly, cert'nly.
    Oh, cert'nly, cert'nly.
    This is our faith!

Text: Negro Spiritual; verses from *Renunciation of Sin and Renewal of Baptismal Promises*, adapt. by Ray East, © 2012, GIA Publications, Inc.
Tune: CERTAINLY LORD, 7 4 7 4 7 4 10; Negro Spiritual; arr. by Evelyn Simpson-Curenton, b.1953, © 2000, 2012, GIA Publications, Inc.

748 Holy Spirit

Text: Richard Smallwood, b.1948
Tune: Richard Smallwood, b.1948; arr. by Nolan Williams, Jr., b.1969
© Century Oak Publishing Group/Richwood Music (BMI), admin. by Conexion Media Group, Inc.

This Is My Body 749

Text: Edward V. Bonnemère, 1921–1996, © 1985, 1987, Amity Music Co.
Tune: Edward V. Bonnemère, 1921–1996, © 1985, 1987, Amity Music Co.; arr. by Kenneth W. Louis, b.1956, © 2012, GIA Publications, Inc.

750 Taste and See

Refrain

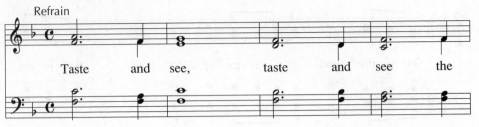

Taste and see, taste and see the

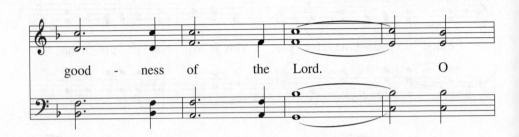

good - ness of the Lord. O

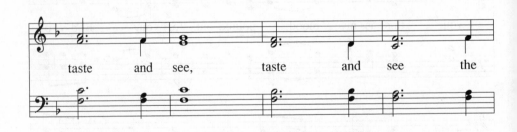

taste and see, taste and see the

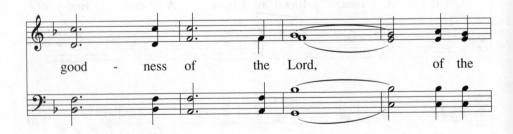

good - ness of the Lord, of the

Lord.   Lord.

Verses

1. I will bless the Lord at all times.
2. Glo-ri-fy the Lord with me. To-
3. Wor-ship the Lord, all you peo-ple.

Praise shall al-ways be on my lips; my
geth-er let us all praise God's name. I
You'll want for noth-ing if you ask.

soul shall glo-ry in the Lord for
called the Lord who an-swered me; from
Taste and see that the Lord is good; in

God has been so good to me.
all my trou-bles I was set free.
God we need put all our trust.

751 Jesus Is Here Right Now

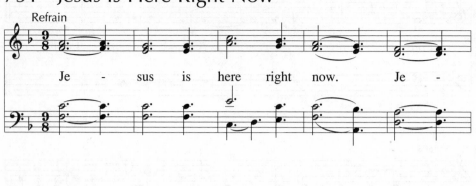

Refrain

Je - sus is here right now. Je -

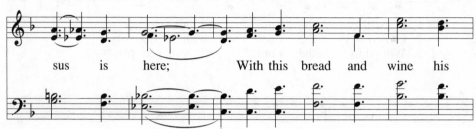

sus is here; With this bread and wine his

peace you'll find, Christ Je - sus is here right

now. | *To verses* | *Last time*

now, right now. now.

Verse 1

1. Do not let your old hearts be trou-bled.

Have faith in God and have faith in me.

In my Fa-ther's house there are man-y man-sions;

oth-er-wise, how could I have told you so?

Verse 2

2. I am in-deed go-ing to pre-pare a place for you,

and then I shall come back to take you with me;

that where I am you al-so may be.

For you know the way that leads to where I go.

Text: Leon C. Roberts, 1950–1999; verses, John 14:1–4
Tune: Leon C. Roberts, 1950–1999
© 1986, GIA Publications, Inc.

752 Alleluia! Sing to Jesus

1. Al - le - lu - ia! Sing to Je - sus!
2. Al - le - lu - ia! Not as or - phans
3. Al - le - lu - ia! Bread of an - gels,
4. Al - le - lu - ia! King e - ter - nal,

His the scep - ter, his the throne.
Are we left in sor - row now;
Here on earth our food, our stay!
You the Lord of lords we own;

Al - le - lu - ia! His the tri - umph,
Al - le - lu - ia! He is near us;
Al - le - lu - ia! Here the sin - ful
Al - le - lu - ia! Born of Mar - y,

His the vic - to - ry a - lone.
Faith be - lieves, nor ques - tions how.
Flee to you from day to day.
Earth your foot - stool, heav'n your throne.

Hark! The songs of peace - ful Zi - on
Though the cloud from sight re - ceived him
In - ter - ces - sor, friend of sin - ners,
You with - in the veil have en - tered,

Thun - der like a might - y flood:
When the for - ty days were o'er,
Earth's re - deem - er, plead for me,
Robed in flesh, our great high priest;

"Je - sus out of ev - 'ry na - tion
Shall our hearts for - get his prom - ise:
Where the songs of all the sin - less
Here on earth both priest and vic - tim

Has re - deemed us by his blood."
"I am with you ev - er - more"?
Sweep a - cross the crys - tal sea.
In the eu - cha - ris - tic feast.

Text: Revelation 5:9; William C. Dix, 1837–1898
Tune: HYFRYDOL, 8 7 8 7 D; Rowland H. Prichard, 1811–1887

753 Eat This Bread

Refrain

Eat this bread, drink this cup, come to him and nev-er be hun-gry.

Eat this bread, drink this cup, trust in him and you will not thirst.

Verse 1

1. Christ is the bread of life, the true bread sent from the Fa - ther.

Verse 2

2. Our an - ces - tors ate man - na in the des - ert, but this is the bread come down from heav - en.

Verse 3

3. Eat his flesh and drink his blood, and Christ will raise you up on the last day.

Verse 4

4. An - y - one who eats this bread, will live for ev - er.

*Choose either part

Verse 5

D.C.

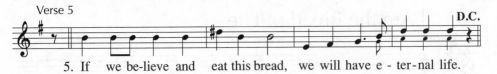

5. If we be-lieve and eat this bread, we will have e - ter-nal life.

Text: John 6; adapt. by Robert J. Batastini, b.1942
Tune: Jacques Berthier, 1923–1994
© 1984, Les Presses de Taizé, GIA Publications, Inc., agent

I Come with Joy 754

1. I come with joy, a child of God, For -
2. I come with Chris - tians far and near To
3. As Christ breaks bread, and bids us share, Each
4. The Spir - it of the ris - en Christ, Un -
5. To - geth - er met, to - geth - er bound By

giv - en, loved, and free, The life of Je - sus
find, as all are fed, The new com - mu - ni -
proud di - vi - sion ends. The love that made us,
seen, but ev - er near, Is in such friend - ship
all that God has done, We'll go with joy, to

to re - call, In love laid down for me.
ty of love In Christ's com - mu - nion bread.
makes us one, And strang - ers now are friends.
bet - ter known, A - live a - mong us here.
give the world The love that makes us one.

Text: Brian Wren, b.1936, © 1971, rev. 1995, Hope Publishing Company
Tune: LAND OF REST, CM; American; adapt. by Annabel M. Buchanan, 1888–1983, © 1938 (renewed), this arr. © 2011, The H.W. Gray Company

755 I Am the Bread of Life

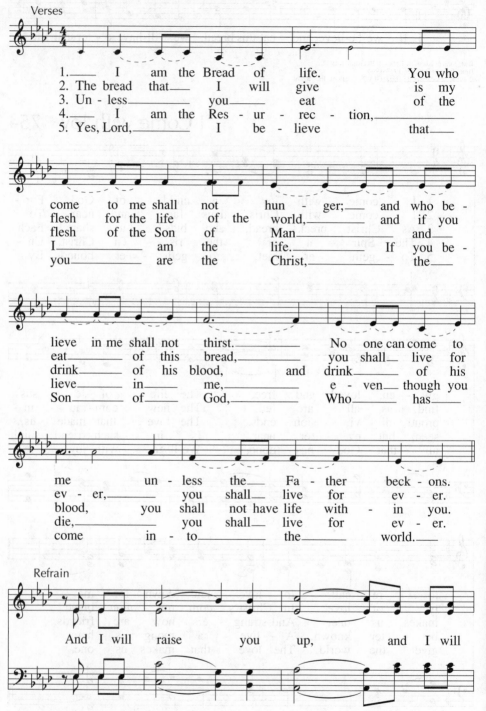

Verses

1. ____ I am the Bread of life. You who
2. The bread that____ I will give is my
3. Un - less____ you____ eat of the
4. ____ I am the Res - ur - rec - tion,____
5. Yes, Lord,____ I be - lieve that____

come to me shall not hun - ger;____ and who be -
flesh for the life of the world,____ and if you
flesh of the Son of Man____ and____
I____ am the life.____ If you be -
you____ are the Christ,____ the____

lieve in me shall not thirst.____ No one can come to
eat____ of this bread,____ you shall__ live for
drink____ of his blood, and drink____ of his
lieve____ in____ me,____ e - ven__ though you
Son____ of____ God,____ Who____ has____

me un - less the__ Fa - ther beck - ons.
ev - er,____ you shall__ live for ev - er.
blood, you shall not have life with - in you.
die,____ you shall__ live for ev - er.
come in - to____ the____ world.__

Refrain

And I will raise you up, and I will

raise you up, and I will raise you

up on the last day.

Text: John 6; Suzanne Toolan, RSM, b.1927
Tune: BREAD OF LIFE, Irregular with refrain; Suzanne Toolan, RSM, b.1927
© 1966, 1970, 1986, 1993, GIA Publications, Inc.

756 Lord, Who at Your First Eucharist

1. Lord, who at your first Eu - cha - rist did pray
2. For all your Church, O Lord, we in - ter - cede;
3. We pray for those who wan - der from your fold;
4. So, Lord, at length when sac - ra - ments shall cease,

That all your Church might be for - ev - er one,
O make our lack of char - i - ty to cease.
O bring them back, Good Shep - herd of the sheep,
May we be one with all your Church a - bove,

Help us at ev - 'ry Eu - cha - rist to say
Draw us the near - er each to each, we plead,
Back to the faith which saints be - lieved of old,
One with your saints in one un - bro - ken peace,

With long - ing heart and soul, "Your will be done."
By draw - ing all to you, O Prince of Peace.
Back to the Church which still that faith does keep.
One with your saints in one un - bound - ed love.

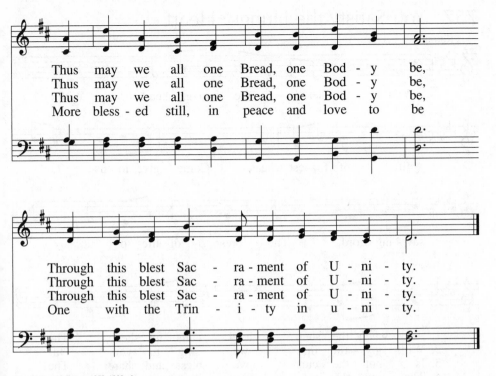

Thus may we all one Bread, one Bod - y be,
Thus may we all one Bread, one Bod - y be,
Thus may we all one Bread, one Bod - y be,
More bless - ed still, in peace and love to be

Through this blest Sac - ra - ment of U - ni - ty.
Through this blest Sac - ra - ment of U - ni - ty.
Through this blest Sac - ra - ment of U - ni - ty.
One with the Trin - i - ty in u - ni - ty.

Text: William H. Turton, 1859–1938, alt.
Tune: UNDE ET MEMORES, 10 10 10 10 10 10; William H. Monk, 1823–1889, alt.

757 You Satisfy the Hungry Heart

Refrain

You sat-is-fy the hun-gry heart With
gift of fin-est wheat; Come give to us, O
sav-ing Lord, The bread of life to eat.

Verses

1. As when the shep - herd calls his sheep, They
2. With joy-ful lips we sing to you Our
3. Is not the cup we bless and share The
4. The mys-t'ry of your pres-ence, Lord, No
5. You give your-self to us, O Lord; Then

know and heed his voice; So when you call your
praise and grat-i-tude, That you should count us
blood of Christ out-poured? Do not one cup, one
mor - tal tongue can tell: Whom all the world can-
self - less let us be, To serve each oth - er

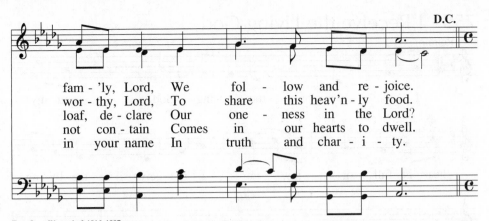

D.C.

fam - 'ly, Lord, We fol - low and re - joice.
wor - thy, Lord, To share this heav'n - ly food.
loaf, de - clare Our one - ness in the Lord?
not con - tain Comes in our hearts to dwell.
in your name In truth and char - i - ty.

Text: Omer Westendorf, 1916–1997
Tune: BICENTENNIAL, CM with refrain; Robert E. Kreutz, 1922–1996
© 1977, Archdiocese of Philadelphia. Published by International Liturgy Publications

Let Us Talents and Tongues Employ 758

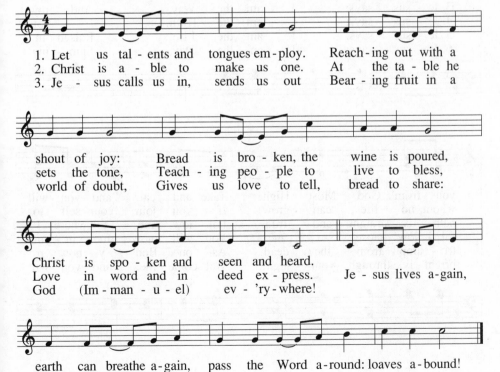

1. Let us tal - ents and tongues em - ploy. Reach - ing out with a
2. Christ is a - ble to make us one. At the ta - ble he
3. Je - sus calls us in, sends us out Bear - ing fruit in a

shout of joy: Bread is bro - ken, the wine is poured,
sets the tone, Teach - ing peo - ple to live to bless,
world of doubt, Gives us love to tell, bread to share:

Christ is spo - ken and seen and heard.
Love in word and in deed ex - press. Je - sus lives a - gain,
God (Im - man - u - el) ev - 'ry - where!

earth can breathe a - gain, pass the Word a - round: loaves a - bound!

Text: Fred Kaan, 1929–2009
Tune: LINSTEAD, LM with refrain; Jamaican folk melody; adapt. by Doreen Potter, 1925–1980
© 1975, Hope Publishing Company

759 I Receive the Living God

Refrain

I re - ceive the liv - ing God, and my

heart is full of joy. I re - ceive the liv-ing

God, and my heart is full of joy.

Verses

1. Je - sus says: I am the Bread Sent to
2. Je - sus says: I am the Vine, Far from
3. Je - sus says: I am the Way, And my
4. Je - sus says: I am the Truth. If you
5. Je - sus says: I am the Life, Raised in
6. Je - sus says: I am the Day, Shin - ing

you from God Most High. Take and eat, and you will
whom no life can grow. If you join your - self to
path is straight and true. Fol - low me to where I
fol - low close to me, You will know me in your
tri - umph from the dead. As one Bod - y now re -
bright - ly through your night. Wel - come me, and you will

D.C.

live;   You need nev - er fear to die.
me,   A rich har - vest you will know.
lead;   There my Fa - ther waits for you.
heart,   And my word will make you free.
main,   Mem - bers joined to me, the Head.
walk   By the Spir - it's guid - ing light.

7. Jesus says: I am the Love
   Which can bind you close to me.
   Those who know this gift I bring
   Will find true community.

8. Jesus says: I am the Peace
   Which the world cannot bestow.
   Learn to love and live in me,
   And in you my Reign will grow.

9. Jesus says: I am the Lamb,
   And my death set sinners free.
   Those who drink the cup I drink
   Must take up this work with me.

Text: Vss. 1–3, 5–9, Bernard Geoffroy, b.1946; tr. by Ronald F. Krisman, b.1946, © 2011, GIA Publications, Inc.; vs. 4, anonymous
Tune: LIVING GOD, 7 7 7 7 with refrain; Dom Clément Jacob, OSB, 1906–1977, adapt.; harm. by Richard Proulx, 1937–2010, © 1986,
   GIA Publications, Inc.

760 One Bread, One Body

Refrain

Descant:

One bread, one bod-y, one Lord of

Melody:

One bread, one bod-y, one Lord of

all, one cup of bless - ing which we

all, one cup of bless - ing which we

bless. And we, though man-y,

bless. And we, though man-y,

through-out the earth, we are one

through-out the earth, we are one

Last time to Coda

bod - y in this one Lord.

bod - y in this one Lord.

Verses

1. Gen - tile or Jew, ser - vant or
2. Man - y the gifts, man - y the
3. Grain for the fields, scat - tered and

free, wom - an or man
works, one in the Lord
grown, gath - ered to one

D.C.

no more.
of all.
for all.

Coda

Lord.

Lord.

Text: 1 Corinthians 10:16–17, 12:4, 12–13, 20; Galatians 3:28; Ephesians 4:46; the *Didache* 9; John Foley, SJ, b.1939
Tune: ONE BREAD, ONE BODY, 4 4 6 with refrain; John Foley, SJ, b.1939
© 1978, John B. Foley, SJ, and OCP

761 Your Sacrifice

Verses

1. Lord, we praise you for your sac-ri-fice, your ex-am-ple of a per-fect life. Be-cause of you we can have e-ter-nal life. We re-mem-ber your sac-ri-fice. We re-

2. As we drink this cup and eat this bread, we re-mem-ber the thou-sand souls you fed. Bless us Lord, let our hun-gry souls be fed. We re-mem-ber your sac-ri-fice. We re-

3. There is heal-ing pow'r in the Eu-cha-rist, it makes us one in the bod-y of Je-sus Christ, Lord, we thank you for this gift of life. We re-mem-ber your sac-ri-fice. We re-

mem - ber your sac - ri - fice.
mem - ber your sac - ri - fice.
mem - ber your sac - ri - fice.

Refrain

Lord, feed us with your bod - y and blood, and

we'll be made whole. U - nite us, ed - i -

fy us; we re - mem - ber your sac - ri - fice.

We re - mem - ber your sac - ri - fice.

Text: Thomas Lucas
Tune: Thomas Lucas; acc. by Thomas W. Jefferson
© 2000, World Library Publications

762 Let Us Enter into Covenant

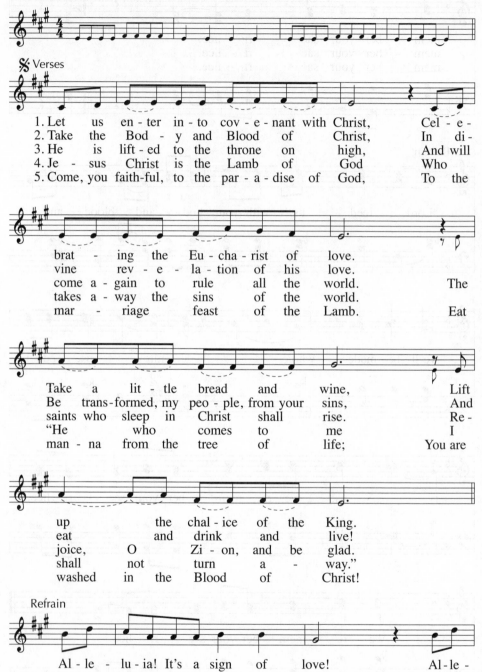

Verses

1. Let us en-ter in-to cov-e-nant with Christ, Cel-e-
2. Take the Bod-y and Blood of Christ, In di-
3. He is lift-ed to the throne on high, And will
4. Je-sus Christ is the Lamb of God Who
5. Come, you faith-ful, to the par-a-dise of God, To the

brat - ing the Eu-cha-rist of love.
vine rev-e-la-tion of his love.
come a-gain to rule all the world. The
takes a-way the sins of the world. The
mar - riage feast of the Lamb. Eat

Take a lit-tle bread and wine, Lift
Be trans-formed, my peo-ple, from your sins, And
saints who sleep in Christ shall rise. Re-
"He who comes to me I
man-na from the tree of life; You are

up the chal-ice of the King.
eat and drink and live!
joice, O Zi-on, and be glad.
shall not turn a - way."
washed in the Blood of Christ!

Refrain

Al-le-lu-ia! It's a sign of love! Al-le-

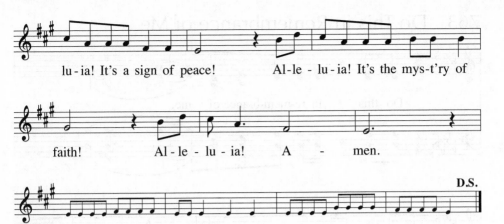

lu - ia! It's a sign of peace! Al - le - lu - ia! It's the mys-t'ry of faith! Al - le - lu - ia! A - men.

D.S.

Text: Norbert Farrell
Tune: Norbert Farrell; arr. by Paschal Jordan, OSB, b.1944
© 1998, Antilles Episcopal Conference

763 Do This in Remembrance of Me

Do this   in re-mem-brance of   me.

Do this   in re-mem-brance of   me.   I hung out on   a   tree

for thee,   for thee.   Do this   in re-mem-brance of   me.

| 1. | 2. |

Eat   this bread,   drink this cup

Last time to Coda

to show forth my suf-fer-ing till I come.

I hung out on a tree called Cal-va-ry, oh,

do this in re-mem-brance of me. Eat this bread,

Coda

Do this in re-mem-brance of me. Oh,

Do this in re-mem-brance of me.

Text: Based on 1 Corinthians 11:24–26; Glenn E. Burleigh, 1949–2007
Tune: Glenn E. Burleigh, 1949–2007

764 Pan de Vida

Refrain

*Bread of Life, body of the Lord,
**power is for service, because God is Love.

Verses

1. We are the dwell-ing of God,
***2. *Us - te - des me lla - man "Se - ñor,"* me_in -
3. There is no Jew or Greek,

fra - gile and wound - ed and weak. We are the
cli - no_a la - var - les los pies. Ha - gan lo
there is no slave or free; there is no

bod - y of Christ, called to be
mis - mo, hu - mil - des, sir - vién -
wom - an or man; on - ly heirs

D.C.

the com - pas - sion of God.
do - se u - nos a o - tros.
of the prom - ise of God.

***You call me "Lord", and I bow to wash your feet:
you must do the same, humbly serving each other.*

Text: John 13:13–14, Galatians 3:28–29; Bob Hurd, b.1950, and Pia Moriarty, b.1948
Tune: Bob Hurd, b.1950; acc. by Craig S. Kingsbury, b.1952
© 1988, Bob Hurd and Pia Moriarty. Published by OCP.

765 Take and Eat

Take and eat; take and eat: this is my bod - y giv-en up for you. Take and drink; take and drink: this is my blood giv - en up for you.

Verses

1. I am the Word that spoke and light was made;
2. I am the way that leads the ex - ile home;
3. I am the Lamb that takes a - way your sin;
4. I am the cor - ner - stone that God has laid;
5. I am the light that came in - to the world;
6. I am the first and last, the Liv - ing One;

I am the seed that died to be re-born;
I am the truth that sets the cap-tive free;
I am the gate that guards you night and day;
A cho-sen stone and pre-cious in his eyes;
I am the light that dark-ness can-not hide;
I am the Lord who died that you might live;

I am the bread that comes from heav'n a-bove;
I am the life that rais-es up the dead;
You are my flock: you know the shep-herd's voice;
You are God's dwell-ing place, on me you rest;
I am the morn-ing star that nev-er sets;
I am the bride-groom, this my wed-ding song;

D.C.

I am the vine that fills your cup with joy.
I am your peace, true peace my gift to you.
You are my own: your ran-som is my blood.
Like liv-ing stones, a tem-ple for God's praise.
Lift up your face, in you my light will shine.
You are my bride, come to the mar-riage feast.

Text: Verse text, James Quinn, SJ, 1919–2010, © 1989. Used by permission of Selah Publishing Co., Inc.; refrain text, Michael Joncas, b.1951,
© 1989, GIA Publications, Inc.
Tune: CORPUS DOMINI, 10 10 10 10 with refrain; Michael Joncas, b.1951, © 1989, GIA Publications, Inc.

766 I Will Arise

1. Come, you sin - ners, poor and need - y,
2. Come, you thirst - y, come, and wel - come,
3. Come, you wea - ry, heav - y lad - en,

Weak and wound - ed, sick and sore, Je - sus, Son of
God's free boun - ty glo - ri - fy: True be - lief and
Lost and ru - ined by the fall; If you tar - ry

God, will save you, Full of pit - y, love, and pow'r.
true re - pen - tance, Ev - 'ry grace that brings you nigh.
till you're bet - ter, You will nev - er come at all.

I will a - rise and go to Je - sus, He will em - brace me

in his arms; In the arms of my dear

Sav - ior, Oh, there are ten thou - sand charms.

Text: Verses, Joseph Hart, 1712–1768, *Hymns Composed on Various Subjects*, 1759, alt.; refrain anonymous
Tune: RESTORATION, 8 7 8 7 with refrain; *Southern Harmony*, 1835; harm. by George E. Mims, b.1938, © 1979, George E. Mims

767 Pass Me Not, O Gentle Savior

1. Pass me not, O gen - tle Sav - ior,
2. Let me at a throne of mer - cy
3. Trust - ing on - ly in thy mer - it,
4. Thou the Spring of all my com - fort,

Hear my hum - ble cry, While on oth - ers thou art
Find a sweet re - lief; Kneel - ing there in deep con -
Would I seek thy face; Heal my wound - ed, bro - ken
More than life to me, Whom have I on earth be -

Solo:
I'm call - ing

call - ing, Do not pass me by.
tri - tion, Help my un - be - lief.
spir - it, Save me by thy grace.
side thee? Whom in heav'n but thee?

Sav - ior, Sav - ior, Hear my hum - ble cry;

While on oth - ers thou art call - ing, Do not pass me by.

Text: Fanny J. Crosby, 1820–1915
Tune: PASS ME NOT, 8 5 8 5 with refrain; William H. Doane, 1832–1915

Dear Lord, Forgive! 768

1. If I have wound - ed an - y soul to - day,
2. If I have ut - tered i - dle words or vain,
3. If I have been per - verse, or hard, or cold,
4. For - give the sins I have con - fessed to thee;

If I have caused one foot to go a - stray,
If I have turned a - side from want or pain,
If I have longed for shel - ter in the fold,
For - give the se - cret sins I do not see;

If I have walked in my own will - ful way,
Lest I of - fend some oth - er through the strain,
When thou hast giv - en me some fort to hold,
O guide me, love me, and my keep - er be.

1.–3.
Dear Lord, for - give! (For - give!)

4.
A - men. (A - men.)

Text: *An Evening Prayer*, C. Maud Battersby
Tune: EVENING, 10 10 10 4; Charles Gabriel, 1856–1932

769 Softly and Tenderly Jesus Is Calling

1. Soft - ly and ten - der - ly Je - sus is call - ing,
2. Why should we tar - ry when Je - sus is plead - ing,
3. Time is now fleet - ing, the mo - ments are pass - ing,
4. O for the won - der - ful love he has prom - ised,

Call - ing for you and for me; See, on the
Plead - ing for you and for me? Why should we
Pass - ing from you and from me; Shad - ows are
Prom - ised for you and for me; Though we have

por - tals he's wait - ing and watch - ing,
lin - ger and heed not his mer - cies,
gath - er - ing, death - beds are com - ing,
sinned he has mer - cy and par - don,

Watch - ing for you and for me.
Mer - cies for you and for me?
Com - ing for you and for me.
Par - don for you and for me.

Come home, come home, come home, come home,

Come home, come home, come home,

Ye who are wea-ry, come home;

Ear - nest-ly, ten - der - ly, Je - sus is call - ing—

Call-ing, "O sin - ner, come home!"

Text: Will L. Thompson, 1847–1909
Tune: THOMPSON, 11 7 11 7 with refrain; Will L. Thompson, 1847–1909

770 Yield Not to Temptation

1. Yield not to temp - ta - tion, For yield - ing is sin;
2. Shun e - vil com - pan - ions, Bad lan - guage dis - dain;
3. To him that o'er - com - eth, God giv - eth a crown;

Each vic - t'ry will help you, Some oth - er to win;
God's name hold in rev -'rence, Nor take it in vain;
Through faith we will con - quer, Though of - ten cast down;

Fight val - iant - ly on - ward, E - vil pas - sions sub - due;
Be thought-ful and ear - nest, Kind - heart - ed and true;
He who is our Sav - ior, Our strength will re - new;

Look ev - er to Je - sus, He will car - ry you through.

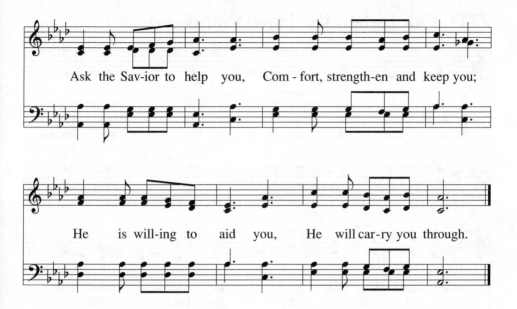

Ask the Sav-ior to help you, Com - fort, strength-en and keep you;

He is will-ing to aid you, He will car-ry you through.

Text: Horatio R. Palmer, 1834–1907
Tune: YIELD NOT, 6 5 6 5 6 6 6 6 with refrain; Horatio R. Palmer, 1834–1907; harm. by Carl Haywood, b.1949, from *Songs of Praise,* © 1992

771 Our Father, We Have Wandered

1. Our Fa - ther, we have wan - dered And
2. And now at length dis - cern - ing The
3. O Lord of all the liv - ing, Both

hid - den from your face; In fool - ish - ness have
e - vil that we do, Be - hold us, Lord, re -
ban - ished and re - stored, Com - pas - sion - ate, for -

squan - dered Your leg - a - cy of grace. But
turn - ing With hope and trust to you. In
giv - ing, And ev - er - car - ing Lord, Grant

now, in ex - ile dwell - ing, We
haste you come to meet us And
now that our trans - gress - ing, Our

rise with fear and shame, As, dis - tant but com -
home re - joic - ing bring, In glad - ness there to
faith - less - ness may cease. Stretch out your hand in

pel - ling, We hear you call our name.
greet us With calf and robe and ring.
bless - ing, In par - don, and in peace.

Text: Kevin Nichols, 1929–2006, © 1980, ICEL
Tune: PASSION CHORALE, 7 6 7 6 D; Hans Leo Hassler, 1564–1612; harm. by J. S. Bach, 1685–1750

772 Oh, Happy Day

washed, he washed my sins a - way.

when Je - sus washed,

oh, hap-py day, oh, hap-py day.

He taught me how to watch,

fight, and pray, fight, and pray,

and live re - joic - ing ev - 'ry day,

Oh, hap-py day,

ev-'ry day.

oh, hap-py day,

Oh, hap-py day,

oh, hap-py day,

oh, hap-py day.

oh, hap-py day.

Text: Philip Doddridge, 1702–1751
Tune: Edwin Hawkins, b.1943; arr. by Kenneth W. Louis, b.1956, © 2012, GIA Publications, Inc.

Just Let Him In   773

He'll take a - way   all of your heart-aches,   He'll take a -
way   all of your sins,   He'll help you to bear   all of your
bur - dens   if you will   on - ly   let him in.   When sin and
grief   have filled your soul,   just tell my   Je - sus,   He'll make you
whole.   He'll take a - way   all, all of your bur - dens,   just let him in.

Text: S. Boddie, ©
Tune: S. Boddie, ©; arr. by Bill Cummings, © 2000, GIA Publications, Inc.

774 Sinner, Please Don't Let This Harvest Pass

Refrain

Sin-ner, please don't let this har-vest pass; Sin-ner,

please don't let this har-vest pass; Sin-ner,

please don't let this har - vest pass, and

die and lose your soul at last.

Text: Negro Spiritual
Tune: Negro Spiritual; arr. by Kenneth W. Louis, b.1956, © 2012, GIA Publications, Inc.

775 Anoint Us

Cre - ate in me a clean heart, O God,

and re - new in me a right spir - it.

A - noint us. A - noint us.

Wash us with the wa - ter of your Word.

776 Cast Down, O God, the Idols

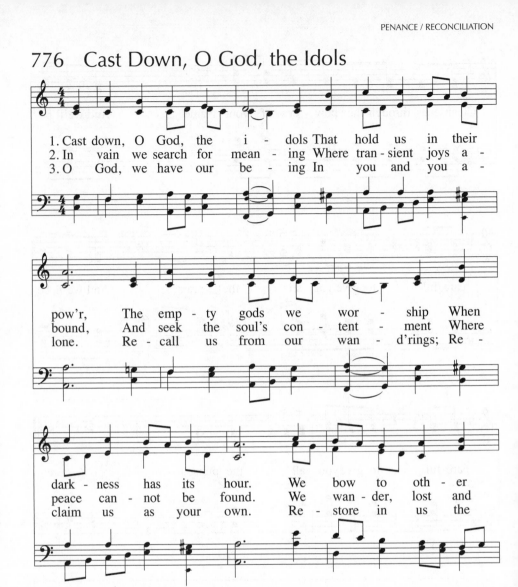

1. Cast down, O God, the i - dols That hold us in their pow'r, The emp - ty gods we wor - ship When dark - ness has its hour. We bow to oth - er mas - ters And by their prom - ise live. Re -

2. In vain we search for mean - ing Where tran - sient joys a - bound, And seek the soul's con - tent - ment Where peace can - not be found. We wan - der, lost and home - less, In end - less, aim - less quest, Our

3. O God, we have our be - ing In you and you a - lone. Re - call us from our wan - d'rings; Re - claim us as your own. Re - store in us the im - age Re - vealed in Christ, your Word, Till

deem our way-ward pas - sions; Our re - bel wills for - give.
hearts for - ev - er rest - less Un - til in you they rest.
heart and will pay hom - age To him, our God and Lord.

Text: Herman G. Stuempfle, Jr., 1923–2007, © 1997, GIA Publications, Inc.
Tune: PASSION CHORALE, 7 6 7 6 D; Hans Leo Hassler, 1564–1612; harm. by J. S. Bach, 1685–1750

Victory Is Mine 777

The melody is in the alto part.

1. Vic - to - ry is mine. Vic - to - ry is mine.
2. Joy is mine. Joy is mine.
3. Hap - pi - ness is mine. Hap - pi - ness is mine.

Vic - to - ry to-day is mine. I told Sa - tan
Joy to-day is mine. I told Sa - tan
Hap - pi - ness to-day is mine. I told Sa - tan

get thee be - hind. Vic - to - ry to-day is mine.
get thee be - hind. Joy to-day is mine.
get thee be - hind. Hap - pi - ness to-day is mine.

Text: Dorothy Norwood and Alvin Darling
Tune: VICTORY, 5 5 7 8 7; Dorothy Norwood and Alvin Darling; arr. by Stephen Key
© 1994, Malaco Music, Inc.

778 Be Still, My Soul

1. Be still, my soul: the Lord is on your side.
2. Be still, my soul: your God will un - der - take
3. Be still, my soul: the hour is has - t'ning on

Bear pa - tient - ly the cross of grief or pain;
To guide the fu - ture, as in a - ges past.
When we shall be for ev - er with the Lord,

Leave to your God to or - der and pro - vide;
Your hope, your con - fi - dence let noth - ing shake;
When dis - ap - point - ment, grief, and fear are gone,

In ev - 'ry change God faith - ful will re - main.
All now mys - te - rious shall be bright at last.
Sor - row for - got, love's pur - est joys re - stored.

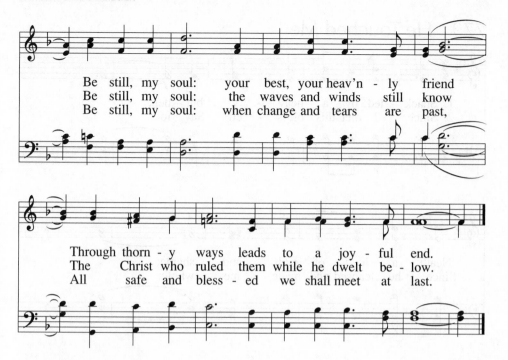

Be still, my soul: your best, your heav'n - ly friend
Be still, my soul: the waves and winds still know
Be still, my soul: when change and tears are past,

Through thorn - y ways leads to a joy - ful end.
The Christ who ruled them while he dwelt be - low.
All safe and bless - ed we shall meet at last.

Text: Katharina von Schlegel, 1697–1768; tr. by Jane L. Borthwick, 1813–1897. alt.
Tune: FINLANDIA, 10 10 10 10 10 10; Jean Sibelius, 1865–1957

779 He Touched Me

1. Shack - led by a heav - y bur - den,
2. Since I met this bless - ed Sav - ior,

'Neath a load of guilt and shame;
Since he cleansed and made me whole;

Then the hand of Je - sus touched me, And
I will nev - er cease to praise him, I'll

now I am no long - er the same.
shout it while e - ter - ni - ty rolls.

He touched me, O, he touched me, and O, the joy that floods my soul; Some-thing hap-pened, and now I know, He touched me and made me whole.

Text: William J. Gaither
Tune: HE TOUCHED ME, 8 7 8 9 with refrain; William J. Gaither
© 1963, Hanna Street Music

780 Precious Lord, Take My Hand

Verses 1–3

1. Pre - cious Lord, take my hand, Lead me on, help me
2. When my way grows drear, Pre - cious Lord, lin - ger
3. When the dark - ness ap - pears And the night draws

stand; I am tired, I am weak, I am worn;
near; When my life is al - most gone,
near, And the day is past and gone;

Through the storm, through the night, Lead me on to the
Hear my cry, hear my call, Hold my hand lest I
At the riv - er I stand, Guide my feet, hold my

light, Take my hand, pre-cious Lord, lead me home.
fall; Take my hand, pre-cious Lord, lead me home.
hand; Take my hand, pre-cious Lord, lead me home.

Verse 4

4. Pre - cious Lord, I love your name, When I look back from whence I came; Some-times stumb-ling, some-times fall - ing, some-times a - lone. Friends and loved ones I love so dear, Man-y are gone, but still I'm here; Take my hand, pre-cious Lord, and lead me on.

Text: Thomas A. Dorsey, 1899–1993
Tune: PRECIOUS LORD, Irregular; George N. Allen, 1812–1877; adapt. by Thomas A. Dorsey, 1899–1993

781 I Know the Lord Has Laid His Hands on Me

Oh, I know the Lord, I know the Lord,
I know the Lord has laid his hands on me. Oh,
I know the Lord, I know the Lord,
I know the Lord has laid his hands on me.

Verses

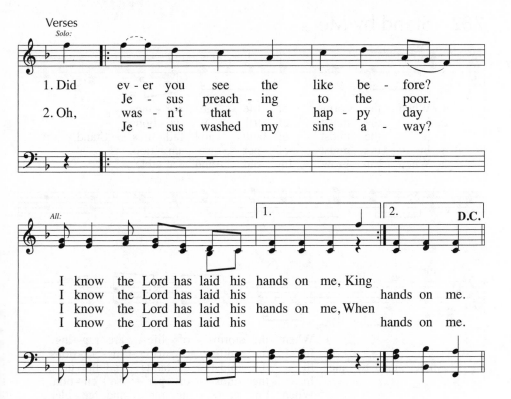

1. Did ev - er you see the like be - fore?
   Je - sus preach - ing to the poor.
2. Oh, was - n't that a hap - py day
   Je - sus washed my sins a - way?

I know the Lord has laid his hands on me, King
I know the Lord has laid his hands on me.
I know the Lord has laid his hands on me, When
I know the Lord has laid his hands on me.

Text: Negro Spiritual
Tune: HANDS ON ME, Irregular with refrain; Negro Spiritual; arr. by Valeria A. Foster, © 2000, GIA Publications, Inc.

782 Stand by Me

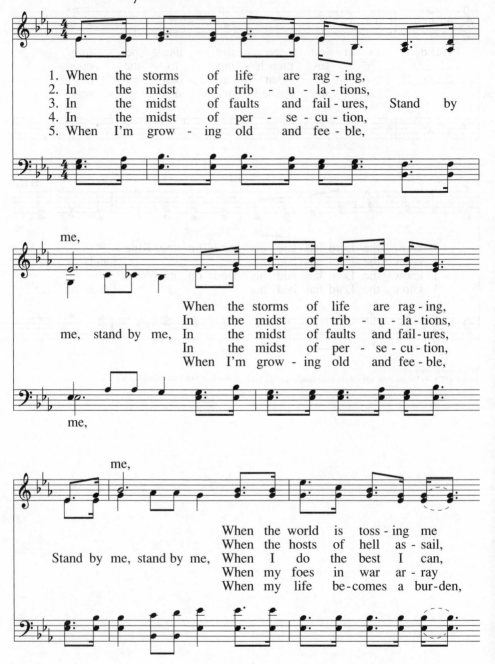

1. When the storms of life are rag - ing,
2. In the midst of trib - u - la - tions,
3. In the midst of faults and fail - ures, Stand by
4. In the midst of per - se - cu - tion,
5. When I'm grow - ing old and fee - ble,

me,

When the storms of life are rag - ing,
In the midst of trib - u - la - tions,
me, stand by me, In the midst of faults and fail - ures,
In the midst of per - se - cu - tion,
When I'm grow - ing old and fee - ble,

me,

me,

Stand by me, stand by me,
When the world is toss - ing me
When the hosts of hell as - sail,
When I do the best I can,
When my foes in war ar - ray
When my life be - comes a bur - den,

Like a ship up - on the sea; Thou who
And my strength be - gins to fail, Thou who
And my friends mis - un - der - stand, Thou who
Un - der - take to stop my way, Thou who
And I'm near - ing chill - y Jor - dan, O thou

me.

rul - est wind and wa - ter,
nev - er lost a bat - tle,
know - est all a - bout me, Stand by me, stand by me.
saved Paul and Si - las,
"Lil - y of the Val - ley,"

me.

Text: Charles A. Tindley, 1851–1933
Tune: STAND BY ME, 8 3 8 3 77 8 3; Charles A. Tindley, 1851–1933; harm. by Francis A. Clark, 1851–1933

783 Just a Closer Walk with Thee

1. I am weak but thou art strong;
2. Through this world of toil and snares,
3. When my fee-ble life is o'er,

Refrain: Just a clos-er walk with thee,

Je - sus, keep me from all wrong;
If I fal - ter, Lord, who cares?
Time for me will be no more;
Grant it, Je-sus, is my plea;

I'll be sat-is-fied as long
Who with me my bur-den shares?
Guide me gen-tly, safe-ly o'er
Dai - ly walk-ing close to thee,

As I walk, let me walk close to thee.
None but thee, dear Lord, none but thee.
To thy king - dom shore, to thy shore.
Let it be, dear Lord, let it be.

Text: Anonymous
Tune: CLOSER WALK, 777 8; anonymous

Nearer, My God, to Thee 784

1. Near - er, my God, to thee, Near - er to thee!
2. Though like the wan - der - er, The sun gone down,
3. There let the way ap - pear, Steps un - to heav'n;
4. Then, with my wak - ing thoughts Bright with thy praise,
5. Or if, on joy - ful wing Cleav - ing the sky,

E'en though it be a cross That rais - eth me,
Dark - ness be o - ver me, My rest a stone;
All that thou send - est me, In mer - cy giv'n;
Out of my ston - y griefs Beth - el I'll raise;
Sun, moon, and stars for - got, Up - ward I fly,

Still all my song shall be, Near - er, my God, to thee;
Yet in my dreams I'd be Near - er, my God, to thee;
An - gels to beck - on me Near - er, my God, to thee;
So by my woes to be Near - er, my God, to thee;
Still all my song shall be, Near - er, my God, to thee;

Near - er, my God, to thee, Near - er to thee!

Text: Sarah F. Adams, 1805–1848
Tune: BETHANY, 6 4 6 4 66 6 4; Lowell Mason, 1792–1872

785 He Understands; He'll Say, "Well Done"

1. If when you give the best of your serv - ice,
2. Mis - un - der - stood, the Sav - ior of sin - ners,
3. If when this life of la - bor is end - ed,
4. But if you try and fail in your try - ing,

Tell - ing the world that the Sav - ior is come;
Hung on the cross; he was God's on - ly Son;
And the re - ward of the race you have run;
Hands sore and scarred from the work you've be - gun;

Be not dis - mayed when friends don't be - lieve you;
Oh! hear him call - ing his Fa - ther in heav'n,
Oh! the sweet rest pre - pared for the faith - ful,
Take up your cross, run quick - ly to meet him;

He un - der - stands; he'll say, "Well done."
"Not my will, but thine be done."
Will be his blest and fi - nal "Well done."
He'll un - der - stand; he'll say, "Well done."

Oh, when I come to the end of my jour-ney, Wea-ry of life and the bat-tle is won; Car-rying the staff and cross of re-demp-tion, He'll un-der-stand, and say, "Well done."

Text: Lucie E. Campbell, 1885–1963
Tune: WELL DONE, 10 10 10 8 with refrain; Lucie E. Campbell, 1885–1963

786 I Call You to My Father's House

1. I call you to my Fa - ther's
2. Lay down your sor - row, calm your
3. Al - though the way be hard and
4. I have pre - pared a wed - ding
5. I call you to my Fa - ther's

house, A love - ly dwell - ing place.
fear; The Fa - ther bids you come.
long In - to the prom - ised land,
feast Of fin - est food and wine.
house, A love - ly dwell - ing place.

He comes to meet you on the
With o - pen arms he wel - comes
Be not a - fraid to walk with
O join us at this ban - quet
Be not a - fraid to trav - el

road, Arms read - y to em - brace.
you To your e - ter - nal home.
me: I hold you by the hand.
where My friends, the saints, now dine.
there And meet him face to face.

Text: Delores Dufner, OSB, b.1939, © 1983, 2003, GIA Publications, Inc.
Tune: NEW BRITAIN, CM; *Virginia Harmony,* 1831; arr. by Evelyn Simpson-Curenton, b.1953, © 2000, GIA Publications, Inc.

God of Our Fathers 787

Trumpets before each stanza (optional)

1. God of our fa - thers, whose al - might - y
2. Your love di - vine has led us in the
3. From war's a - larms, from dead - ly pes - ti -
4. Re - fresh your peo - ple on their toil - some

hand Leads forth in beau - ty all the star - ry
past, In this free land by you our lot is
lence, Be your strong arm our ev - er sure de -
way, Lead us from night to nev - er - end - ing

band Of shin - ing worlds in splen - dor through the
cast; Be our strong rul - er, guard - ian, guide, and
fense; Your true re - li - gion in our hearts in -
day; Fill all our lives with heav'n - born love and

skies, Our grate - ful songs be - fore your throne a - rise.
stay, Your word our law, your paths our cho - sen way.
crease, Your boun - teous good - ness nour - ish us in peace.
grace, Un - til at last, we meet be - fore your face.

Text: Daniel C. Roberts, 1841–1907, alt.
Tune: NATIONAL HYMN, 10 10 10 10; George W. Warren, 1828–1902

788 America the Beautiful

1. O beau - ti - ful for spa - cious skies, For
2. O beau - ti - ful for pil - grim feet, Whose
3. O beau - ti - ful for he - roes proved In
4. O beau - ti - ful for pa - triot dream That

am - ber waves of grain, For pur - ple moun - tain
stern, im - pas-sioned stress A thor - ough - fare for
lib - er - at - ing strife, Who more than self their
sees be - yond the years Thine al - a - bas - ter

maj - es - ties A - bove the fruit - ed plain! A -
free - dom beat A - cross the wil - der - ness! A -
coun - try loved, And mer - cy more than life! A -
cit - ies gleam, Un - dimmed by hu - man tears! A -

mer - i - ca! A - mer - i - ca! God
mer - i - ca! A - mer - i - ca! God
mer - i - ca! A - mer - i - ca! May
mer - i - ca! A - mer - i - ca! God

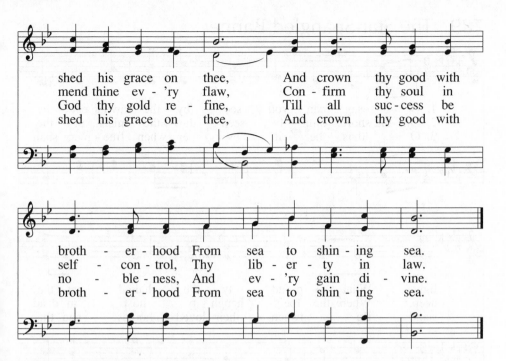

shed his grace on thee, And crown thy good with
mend thine ev - 'ry flaw, Con - firm thy soul in
God thy gold re - fine, Till all suc - cess be
shed his grace on thee, And crown thy good with

broth - er - hood From sea to shin - ing sea.
self - con - trol, Thy lib - er - ty in law.
no - ble - ness, And ev - 'ry gain di - vine.
broth - er - hood From sea to shin - ing sea.

Text: Katherine L. Bates, 1859–1929
Tune: MATERNA, CMD; Samuel A. Ward, 1848–1903

789 The Star-Spangled Banner

1. O say can you see by the dawn's ear-ly
2. On the shore, dim-ly seen thro' the mists of the
3. O thus be it ev-er when free-men shall

light, What so proud-ly we hailed at the
deep, Where the foe's haugh-ty host in dead
stand Be-tween their loved homes and the

twi-light's last gleam-ing, Whose broad stripes and bright
si-lence re-pos-es, What is that which the
war's des-o-la-tion! Blest with vic-t'ry and

stars, through the per-il-ous fight, O'er the ram-parts we
breeze, o'er the tow-er-ing steep, As it fit-ful-ly
peace, may the heav'n-res-cued land Praise the Pow'r that hath

Star - Span - gled   Ban - ner   yet   wave   O'er the
Ban - ner   O   long   may   it   wave   O'er the
Ban - ner   in   tri - umph shall   wave   O'er the

land   of the   free   and the home   of   the   brave?
land   of the   free   and the home   of   the   brave!
land   of the   free   and the home   of   the   brave!

Text: Francis S. Key, 1779–1843
Tune: STAR SPANGLED BANNER, Irregular; John S. Smith, 1750–1836

790   The Right Hand of God

1. The   right   hand   of   God   is   writ-ing   in   our   land,
2. The   right   hand   of   God   is   point-ing   in   our   land,
3. The   right   hand   of   God   is   strik-ing   in   our   land,
4. The   right   hand   of   God   is   lift-ing   in   our   land,
5. The   right   hand   of   God   is   heal-ing   in   our   land,

Writ - ing with pow - er and with love.
Point - ing the way we must go.
Strik-ing out at en - vy, hate and greed.
Lift - ing the fal - len one by one.
Heal-ing bro - ken bod - ies, minds and souls.

Our con - flicts and our fears, our tri-umphs and our
So cloud - ed is the way, so eas - i - ly we
Our self - ish - ness and lust, our pride and deeds un -
Each one is known by name, and res - cued now from
So won-d'rous is its touch with love that means so

tears Are re - cord-ed by the right hand of God.
stray, But we're guid-ed by the right hand of God.
just Are de - stroyed by the right hand of God.
shame By the lift-ing of the right hand of God.
much, When we're healed by the right hand of God.

Text: Patrick Prescod
Tune: Noel Dexter
© 1998, Antilles Episcopal Conference

Lectionary

791 First Sunday of Advent A, Ps. 122

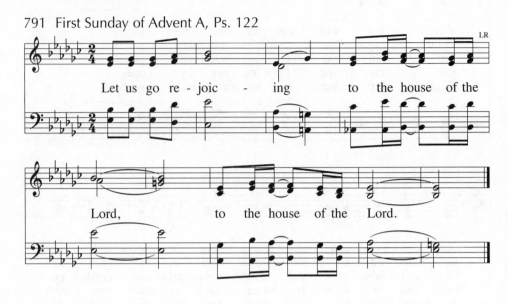

Let us go re - joic - ing to the house of the Lord, to the house of the Lord.

792 First Sunday of Advent B, Ps. 80

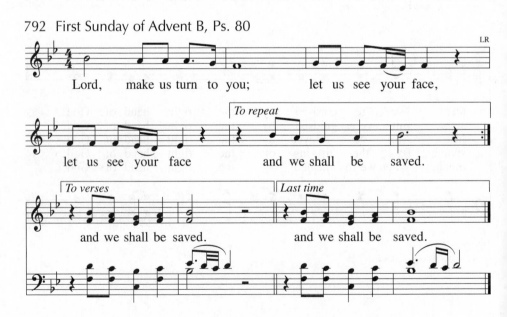

Lord, make us turn to you; let us see your face,

To repeat

let us see your face and we shall be saved.

To verses

and we shall be saved.

Last time

and we shall be saved.

First Sunday of Advent C, Ps. 25 793

To you, O Lord, I lift my soul.

To you, O Lord, I lift my soul.

Second Sunday of Advent A, Ps. 72 794

Jus-tice shall flour - ish in his time and full-ness of peace for

ev-er. Jus-tice shall flour-ish, shall flour-ish in his time.

shall flour-ish in his time.

Second Sunday of Advent B, Ps. 85 795

O Lord, let us see your kind-ness. O Lord, let us see your

Last time

truth. O Lord, let us see your kind-ness, and grant us your sal - va-tion.

796 Second Sunday of Advent C, Ps. 126

MRH

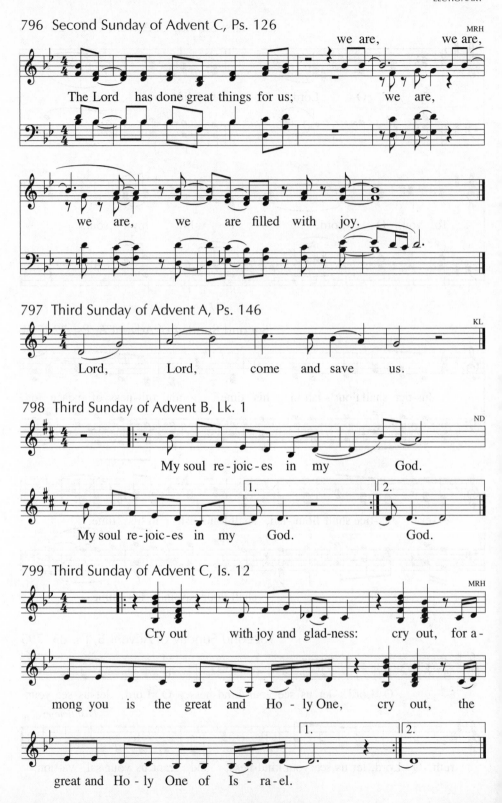

The Lord has done great things for us; we are, we are, we are, we are filled with joy.

797 Third Sunday of Advent A, Ps. 146

KL

Lord, Lord, come and save us.

798 Third Sunday of Advent B, Lk. 1

ND

My soul re-joic-es in my God.

1. My soul re-joic-es in my God.

2. God.

799 Third Sunday of Advent C, Is. 12

MRH

Cry out with joy and glad-ness: cry out, for a-
mong you is the great and Ho-ly One, cry out, the
great and Ho-ly One of Is-ra-el.

Fourth Sunday of Advent A, Ps. 24   800

Let the Lord en - ter, let the Lord en - ter,

let the Lord en - ter; he is king of glo - ry.

Fourth Sunday of Advent B, Ps. 89   801

For ev-er I will sing the good-ness of the Lord, the good-ness of the Lord.

Fourth Sunday of Advent C   *See no. 792*   802

December 25: Christmas–Vigil Mass ABC   *See no. 801*   803

December 25: Christmas–Mass During the Night ABC, Ps. 96   804

To - day   is born our Sav-ior,   Christ   the Lord.

December 25: Christmas–Mass at Dawn ABC, Ps. 97   805

A light will shine   on us   this day: the   Lord

is born   for us.   The   Lord   is born   for us.

December 25: Christmas–Mass During the Day ABC, Ps. 98   806

All   the   ends   of   the   earth   have

seen   the   sav - ing   pow'r   of   God.

807 Holy Family of Jesus, Mary and Joseph ABC, Ps. 128

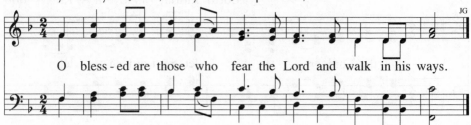

O bless-ed are those who fear the Lord and walk in his ways.

808 Holy Family of Jesus, Mary and Joseph B, Ps. 105

The Lord re-mem-bers his cov - e-nant for ev - er.

809 Holy Family of Jesus, Mary and Joseph C, Ps. 84

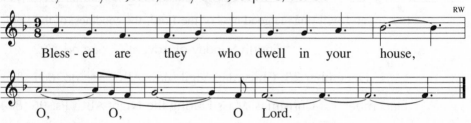

Bless - ed are they who dwell in your house,

O, O, O Lord.

810 Jan. 1: Solemnity of Mary, Holy Mother of God ABC, Ps. 67

May God bless us in his mer-cy. Bless us in his mer-cy.

811 Epiphany of the Lord ABC, Ps. 72

Lord, ev-'ry na-tion on earth will a - dore you, ev-'ry

na-tion on earth will a - dore you.

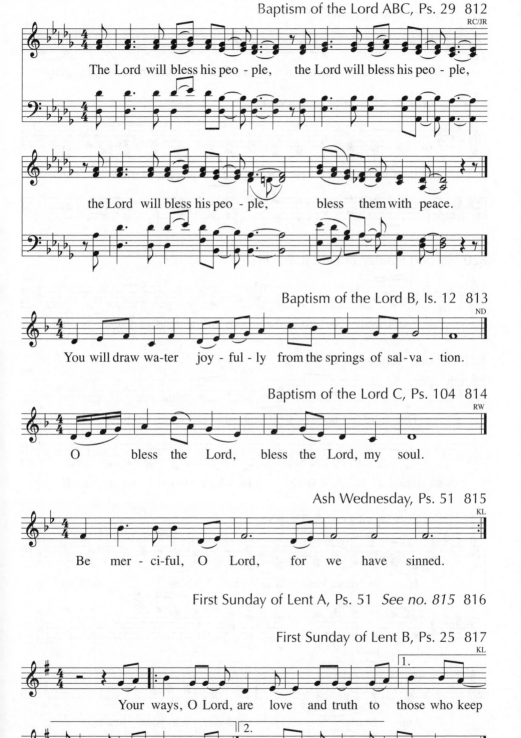

Baptism of the Lord ABC, Ps. 29 812

RC/JR

The Lord will bless his peo - ple, the Lord will bless his peo - ple,

the Lord will bless his peo - ple, bless them with peace.

Baptism of the Lord B, Is. 12 813

ND

You will draw wa-ter joy - ful - ly from the springs of sal-va - tion.

Baptism of the Lord C, Ps. 104 814

RW

O bless the Lord, bless the Lord, my soul.

Ash Wednesday, Ps. 51 815

KL

Be mer - ci-ful, O Lord, for we have sinned.

First Sunday of Lent A, Ps. 51 *See no. 815* 816

First Sunday of Lent B, Ps. 25 817

KL

1.

Your ways, O Lord, are love and truth to those who keep

2.

your cov - e - nant. Your those who keep your cov - e - nant.

818 First Sunday of Lent C, Ps. 91

MH

Be with me, Lord, when I am in trou-ble, be with me, Lord, I   pray.

819 Second Sunday of Lent A, Ps. 33

RJS

Lord, let your mer-cy   be   on us, as we place our trust in   you.

820 Second Sunday of Lent B, Ps. 116

KL

I   will walk   be - fore the   Lord in the land of the liv - ing.

821 Second Sunday of Lent C, Ps. 27

DH

The Lord   is   my light and my   sal - va - tion,   of

whom should I   be   a - fraid,   of whom should I   be   a - fraid?

822 Third Sunday of Lent A, Ps. 95

NP

1.

If   to - day you   hear   his   voice,   hard-en   not

2.

your   hearts.   hard-en   not your   hearts.

Third Sunday of Lent B, Ps. 19 823

KL

Lord, you have the words of ev - er - last - ing life, of ev-

er - last - ing life, of ev - er - last - ing life.

Third Sunday of Lent C, Ps. 103 824

KL

The Lord is kind, the Lord is kind and mer - ci - ful.

Fourth Sunday of Lent A, Ps. 23 825

LR

The Lord is my shep - herd; there is noth-ing I shall want.

Fourth Sunday of Lent B, Ps. 137 826

NP

Let my tongue be si - lenced, if ev - er I for - get you!

Fourth Sunday of Lent C, Ps. 34 827

JM

Taste and see, taste and see the good - ness

of the Lord. O Lord, of the Lord.

828 Fifth Sunday of Lent A, Ps. 130

With the Lord there is mer-cy and full-ness of re-demp-tion.

829 Fifth Sunday of Lent B, Ps. 51

Cre - ate in me a clean heart, O God.

1. Cre-ate in me a clean heart.
2. clean heart.

830 Fifth Sunday of Lent C *See no. 796*

831 Palm Sunday of the Passion of the Lord / Opening Antiphon

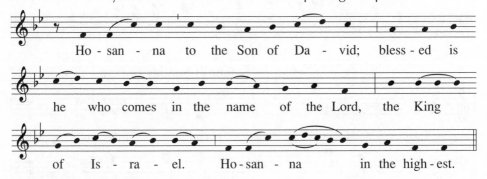

Ho - san - na to the Son of Da - vid; bless - ed is he who comes in the name of the Lord, the King of Is - ra - el. Ho-san - na in the high - est.

Text: ICEL, © 2010
Music: ICEL, © 2010; acc. by Richard Proulx, © 1985, 2011, GIA Publications, Inc.

832 Palm Sunday of the Passion of the Lord / Procession

Priest, deacon, or other minister:
Let us go forth in peace.

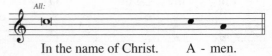

All:

In the name of Christ. A - men.

Palm Sunday of the Passion of the Lord, Ps. 22 833

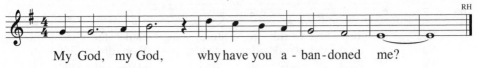

My God, my God, why have you a - ban-doned me?

Thursday of the Lord's Supper: Evening Mass, Ps. 116 834

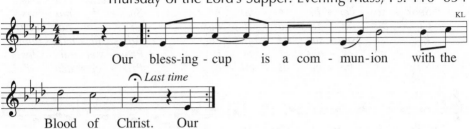

Our bless-ing - cup is a com - mun-ion with the

Last time

Blood of Christ. Our

Thursday of the Lord's Supper / 835
Transfer of the Most Blessed Sacrament

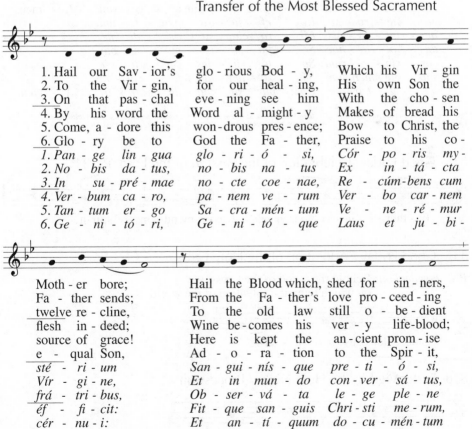

1. Hail our Sav - ior's glo - rious Bod - y, Which his Vir - gin
2. To the Vir - gin, for our heal - ing, His own Son the
3. On that pas - chal eve - ning see him With the cho - sen
4. By his word the Word al - might - y Makes of bread his
5. Come, a - dore this won-drous pres - ence; Bow to Christ, the
6. Glo - ry be to God the Fa - ther, Praise to his co -

1. Pan - ge lin - gua glo - ri - ó - si, Cór - po - ris my -
2. No - bis da - tus, no - bis na - tus Ex in - tá - cta
3. In su - pré - mae no - cte coe - nae, Re - cúm-bens cum
4. Ver - bum ca - ro, pa - nem ve - rum Ver - bo car - nem
5. Tan - tum er - go Sa - cra - mén - tum Ve - ne - ré - mur
6. Ge - ni - tó - ri, Ge - ni - tó - que Laus et ju - bi -

Moth - er bore; Hail the Blood which, shed for sin - ners,
Fa - ther sends; From the Fa - ther's love pro - ceed - ing
twelve re - cline, To the old law still o - be - dient
flesh in - deed; Wine be - comes his ver - y life-blood;
source of grace! Here is kept the an - cient prom - ise
e - qual Son, Ad - o - ra - tion to the Spir - it,

sté - ri - um San - gui - nís - que pre - ti - ó - si,
Vír - gi - ne, Et in mun - do con - ver - sá - tus,
frá - tri - bus, Ob - ser - vá - ta le - ge ple - ne
éf - fi - cit: Fit - que san - guis Chri - sti me - rum,
cér - nu - i: Et an - tí - quum do - cu - mén - tum
lá - ti - o, Sa - lus, ho - nor, vir - tus quo - que

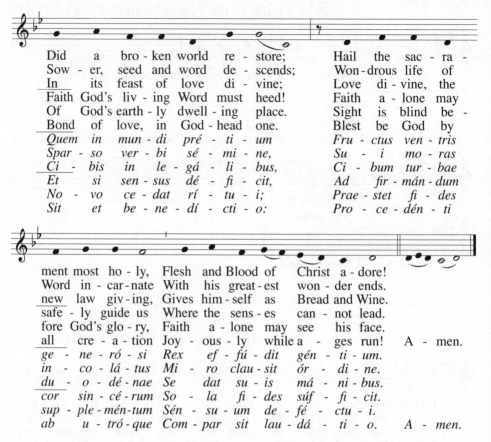

Did	a	bro - ken	world	re -	store;	Hail	the	sac - ra -
Sow - er,	seed and	word	de -	scends;	Won - drous	life	of
In	its	feast of	love	di -	vine;	Love	di - vine,	the
Faith	God's	liv - ing	Word must	heed!	Faith	a - lone	may
Of	God's	earth - ly	dwell - ing	place.	Sight	is	blind	be -
Bond	of	love, in	God - head	one.	Blest	be	God	by
Quem	*in*	*mun - di*	*pré - ti - um*	*Fru - ctus*	*ven - tris*
Spar - so	*ver - bi*	*sé - mi - ne,*	*Su - i*	*mo - ras*
Ci - bis	*in*	*le - gá - li - bus,*	*Ci - bum*	*tur - bae*
Et	*si*	*sen - sus*	*dé - fi - cit,*	*Ad*	*fir - mán - dum*
No - vo	*ce - dat*	*rí - tu - i;*	*Prae - stet*	*fi - des*
Sit	*et*	*be - ne - dí - cti - o:*	*Pro - ce - dén - ti*

ment most	ho - ly,	Flesh	and Blood of	Christ	a - dore!
Word in - car - nate	With	his great - est	won - der ends.
new	law	giv - ing,	Gives him - self	as	Bread and Wine.
safe - ly	guide us	Where the	sens - es	can - not lead.
fore	God's	glo - ry,	Faith	a - lone	may see	his face.
all	cre - a - tion	Joy - ous - ly	while a - ges run!	A - men.
ge - ne - ró - si	*Rex*	*ef - fú - dit*	*gén - ti - um.*
in - co - lá - tus	*Mi - ro*	*clau - sit*	*ór - di - ne.*
du - o - dé - nae	*Se*	*dat*	*su - is*	*má - ni - bus.*
cor	*sin - cé - rum*	*So - la*	*fi - des*	*súf - fi - cit.*
sup - ple - mén - tum	*Sén - su - um*	*de - fé - ctu - i.*
ab	*u - tró - que*	*Com - par sit*	*lau - dá - ti - o.*	A - men.

Text: *Pange lingua*, Thomas Aquinas, 1227–1274; tr. by James Quinn, SJ, 1919–2010, © 1969. Used by permission of Selah Publishing, Inc.
Tune: PANGE LINGUA GLORIOSI, 8 7 8 7; Mode III; acc. by Eugene Lapierre, 1899–1970, © 1964, GIA Publications, Inc.

836 Good Friday: Celebration of the Passion of the Lord, Ps. 31

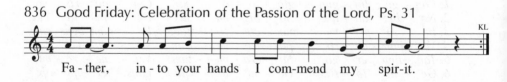

Fa - ther, in - to your hands I com - mend my spir - it.

837 Good Friday / Adoration of the Holy Cross

Priest or deacon: Behold the wood of the Cross,
on which hung the salvation of the world.

Come, let us a - dore.

838 Easter Vigil in the Holy Night / Procession

The Light of Christ. Thanks be to God.

842 Easter Vigil IV, Ps. 30

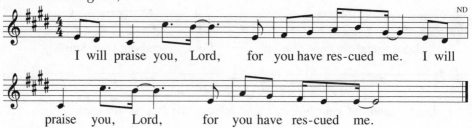

I will praise you, Lord, for you have res-cued me. I will

praise you, Lord, for you have res-cued me.

843 Easter Vigil V *See no. 813*

844 Easter Vigil VI *See no. 823*

845 Easter Vigil VII, Ps. 42

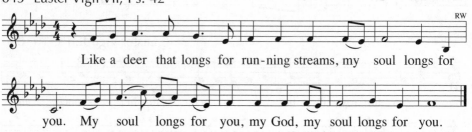

Like a deer that longs for run-ning streams, my soul longs for

you. My soul longs for you, my God, my soul longs for you.

846 *Or:* Is. 12 *See no. 813*

847 *Or:* Ps. 51 *See no. 829*

848 Easter Vigil / Alleluia and Ps. 118

Al - le - lu - ia, al - le - lu - ia, al - le - lu - ia,

al - le - lu - ia, al - le - lu - ia.

849 Easter Vigil / Litany of the Saints

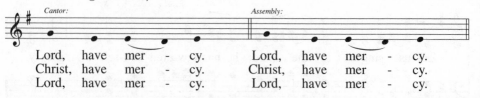

Cantor: *Assembly:*

Lord, have mer - cy. Lord, have mer - cy.
Christ, have mer - cy. Christ, have mer - cy.
Lord, have mer - cy. Lord, have mer - cy.

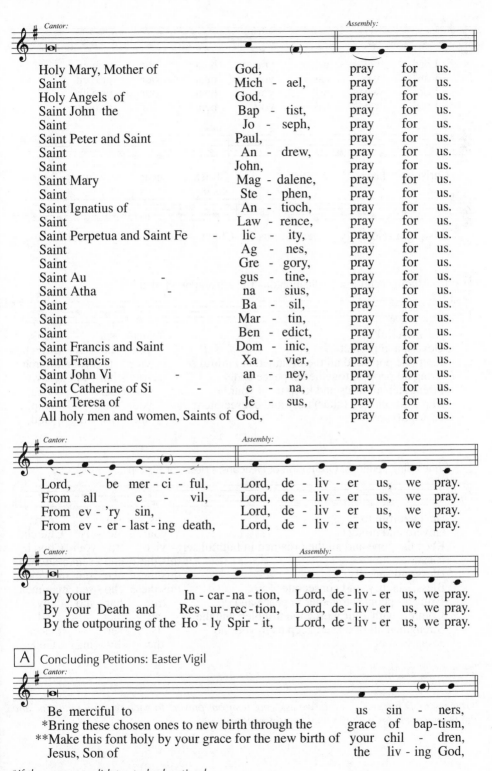

Cantor: Assembly:

Holy Mary, Mother of	God,	pray	for	us.
Saint	Mich - ael,	pray	for	us.
Holy Angels of	God,	pray	for	us.
Saint John the	Bap - tist,	pray	for	us.
Saint	Jo - seph,	pray	for	us.
Saint Peter and Saint	Paul,	pray	for	us.
Saint	An - drew,	pray	for	us.
Saint	John,	pray	for	us.
Saint Mary	Mag - dalene,	pray	for	us.
Saint	Ste - phen,	pray	for	us.
Saint Ignatius of	An - tioch,	pray	for	us.
Saint	Law - rence,	pray	for	us.
Saint Perpetua and Saint Fe -	lic - ity,	pray	for	us.
Saint	Ag - nes,	pray	for	us.
Saint	Gre - gory,	pray	for	us.
Saint Au -	gus - tine,	pray	for	us.
Saint Atha -	na - sius,	pray	for	us.
Saint	Ba - sil,	pray	for	us.
Saint	Mar - tin,	pray	for	us.
Saint	Ben - edict,	pray	for	us.
Saint Francis and Saint	Dom - inic,	pray	for	us.
Saint Francis	Xa - vier,	pray	for	us.
Saint John Vi -	an - ney,	pray	for	us.
Saint Catherine of Si -	e - na,	pray	for	us.
Saint Teresa of	Je - sus,	pray	for	us.
All holy men and women, Saints of God,		pray	for	us.

Cantor: Assembly:

Lord, be mer - ci - ful,	Lord, de - liv - er us, we pray.
From all e - vil,	Lord, de - liv - er us, we pray.
From ev - 'ry sin,	Lord, de - liv - er us, we pray.
From ev - er - last - ing death,	Lord, de - liv - er us, we pray.

Cantor: Assembly:

By your In - car - na - tion,	Lord, de - liv - er us, we pray.
By your Death and Res - ur - rec - tion,	Lord, de - liv - er us, we pray.
By the outpouring of the Ho - ly Spir - it,	Lord, de - liv - er us, we pray.

A Concluding Petitions: Easter Vigil

Cantor:

Be merciful to	us sin - ners,
*Bring these chosen ones to new birth through the	grace of bap - tism,
**Make this font holy by your grace for the new birth of	your chil - dren,
Jesus, Son of	the liv - ing God,

*If there are candidates to be baptized.
**If there are no candidates to be baptized.

Assembly:

Lord, we ask you, hear our prayer.
Lord, we ask you, hear our prayer.
Lord, we ask you, hear our prayer.
Lord, we ask you, hear our prayer.

Cantor: ... Assembly:

Christ, hear us. Christ, hear us.

Cantor: ... Assembly:

Christ, gra-cious-ly hear us. Christ, gra-cious-ly hear us.

B Concluding Petitions: Dedication of a Church and/or an Altar*

Cantor:

Be merciful to us sin - ners,
Govern and protect your ho - ly Church,
Keep the pope and all the ordained in faithful ser - vice to your Church,
Bring all peoples together in peace and true har - mo - ny,
Strengthen all of us and keep us in your ho - ly ser - vice,
Make this church (altar) holy and consecrate it to your wor - ship,
Jesus, Son of the liv - ing God,

C Concluding Petitions: Ordination of Deacons, Priests, or Bishops*

Cantor:

Be merciful to us sin - ners,
Govern and protect your ho - ly Church,
Keep the pope and all the ordained in faithful ser - vice to your Church,
Bless this/these cho - sen man/men,
Bless and sanctify this/these cho - sen man/men,
Bless, sanctify, and consecrate this/these cho - sen man/men,
Bring all peoples together in peace and true har - mo - ny,
Comfort with your mercy the troubled and the af - flict - ed,
Strengthen all of us and keep us in your ho - ly ser - vice,
Jesus, Son of the liv - ing God,

Text: *Litany of the Saints, Roman Missal*
Music: *Litany of the Saints, Roman Missal*
© 2010, ICEL

*The assembly responds, "Lord, we ask you, hear our prayer" to each of these petitions, and the litany concludes with the final two lines above.

Easter Vigil / Blessing of Water 850

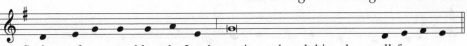

Springs of wa-ter, bless the Lord; praise and exalt him above all for ev-er.

Text: *Roman Missal*
Music: *Roman Missal*
© 2010, ICEL

Easter Vigil / The Baptisms *See no. 60* 851

Easter Vigil / Dismissal 852

Assembly:

Thanks be to God, al-le-lú - ia, al-le - lú - ia.

Easter Sunday ABC, Ps. 118 853

LR

This is the day the Lord has made; let us re-joice and be

glad in it! let us be glad, be glad, be glad, be glad

To repeat 2nd ending

and re-joice in it!

854 Easter Sunday ABC / Sequence

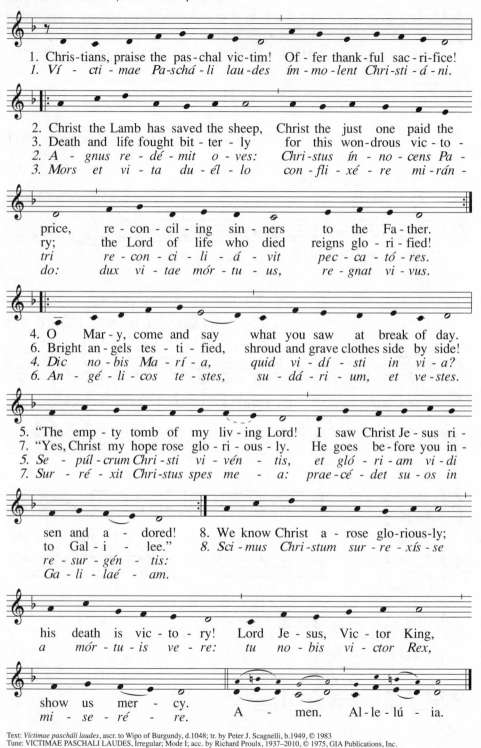

1. Chris-tians, praise the pas-chal vic-tim! Of - fer thank-ful sac-ri-fice!
1. *Ví - cti - mae Pa-schá - li lau -des ím - mo -lent Chri -sti - á - ni.*

2. Christ the Lamb has saved the sheep, Christ the just one paid the
3. Death and life fought bit - ter - ly for this won-drous vic - to -
2. *A - gnus re - dé - mit o - ves: Chri -stus ín - no - cens Pa -*
3. *Mors et vi - ta du - él - lo con - fli - xé - re mi -rán -*

price, re - con - cil - ing sin - ners to the Fa - ther.
ry; the Lord of life who died reigns glo - ri - fied!
tri re - con - ci - li - á - vit pec - ca - tó - res.
do: dux vi - tae mór - tu - us, re - gnat vi - vus.

4. O Mar - y, come and say what you saw at break of day.
6. Bright an - gels tes - ti - fied, shroud and grave clothes side by side!
4. *Dic no - bis Ma - rí - a, quid vi - dí - sti in vi - a?*
6. *An - gé - li - cos te - stes, su - dá - ri - um, et ve -stes.*

5. "The emp - ty tomb of my liv - ing Lord! I saw Christ Je - sus ri -
7. "Yes, Christ my hope rose glo - ri - ous - ly. He goes be -fore you in -
5. *Se - púl - crum Christi vi - vén - tis, et gló - ri - am vi - di*
7. *Sur - ré - xit Christus spes me - a: prae -cé - det su - os in*

sen and a - dored! 8. We know Christ a - rose glo-rious-ly;
to Gal - i - lee." 8. *Sci - mus Chri -stum sur - re - xís - se*
re - sur - gén - tis: Ga - li - laé - am.

his death is vic - to - ry! Lord Je - sus, Vic - tor King,
a mór - tu - is ve - re: tu no - bis vi - ctor Rex,

show us mer - cy. A - men. Al - le - lú - ia.
mi - se - ré - re.

Text: *Victimae pascháli laudes,* ascr. to Wipo of Burgundy, d.1048; tr. by Peter J. Scagnelli, b.1949, © 1983
Tune: VICTIMAE PASCHALI LAUDES, Irregular; Mode I; acc. by Richard Proulx, 1937–2010, © 1975, GIA Publications, Inc.

Second Sunday of Easter ABC, Ps. 118 855
WCP

Give thanks to the Lord for he is good, his love is ev - er - last - ing.

Third Sunday of Easter A, Ps. 16 856
MRH
Last time to Coda

Lord, you will show us the path of life.

Coda

The path of life. The path of life, the path of life.

Third Sunday of Easter B, Ps. 4 857
NP

Lord, let your face shine on us, let your face shine on us.

Third Sunday of Easter C, Ps. 30 858
KL

I will praise you, Lord. I will praise you, Lord.

I will praise you, Lord, for you have res - cued me.

859 Fourth Sunday of Easter A, Ps. 23

The Lord is my shep-herd; there is noth-ing I shall want.

860 Fourth Sunday of Easter B, Ps. 118

The stone re-ject-ed by the build-ers has be-

To repeat refrain   *To verses*

come the cor-ner-stone. The

861 Fourth Sunday of Easter C, Ps. 100

We are his peo - ple, the sheep of his flock,

we are his peo - ple, the sheep of his flock,

we are his peo - ple, the sheep of his flock, where he

leads us we will sure - ly go.

Fifth Sunday of Easter A *See no. 819* 862

Fifth Sunday of Easter B, Ps. 22 863

ND

I will praise you, Lord, in the as - sem - bly of your peo-

ple, in the as - sem - bly of your peo - ple.

Fifth Sunday of Easter C, Ps. 145 864

KL

I will praise your name for ev - er,

my king and my God.

Sixth Sunday of Easter A, Ps. 66 865

MRH

Let all the earth, let all the earth, let all

the earth cry out to God with joy. Let all

Optional repeat

866 Sixth Sunday of Easter B, Ps. 98

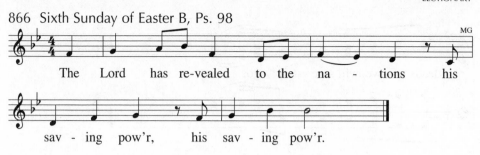

The Lord has re-vealed to the na - tions his
sav - ing pow'r, his sav - ing pow'r.

867 Sixth Sunday of Easter C, Ps. 67

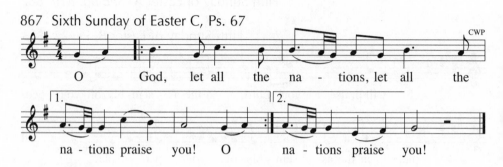

O God, let all the na - tions, let all the
1. na - tions praise you! O 2. na - tions praise you!

868 Ascension of the Lord ABC, Ps. 47

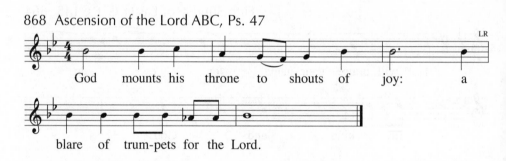

God mounts his throne to shouts of joy: a
blare of trum-pets for the Lord.

869 Seventh Sunday of Easter A, Ps. 27

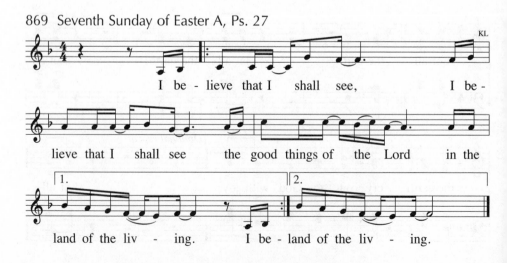

I be - lieve that I shall see, I be -
lieve that I shall see the good things of the Lord in the
1. land of the liv - ing. 2. I be - land of the liv - ing.

Seventh Sunday of Easter B, Ps. 103 870

The Lord has set his throne in heav - en.

Seventh Sunday of Easter C, Ps. 97 871

The Lord is king, the Most High o - ver all the earth.

The Lord is king, the Most High o - ver all the earth.

Pentecost Sunday—Vigil Mass *See no. 839A* 872

Pentecost Sunday—Mass during the Day *See no. 839A* 873

Pentecost Sunday—Mass during the Day ABC / Sequence 874

1. Ho - ly Spir - it, Lord di - vine, Come, from heights of
2. Come, O Fa - ther of the poor, Come, whose treas - ured

heav'n and shine, Come with bless - ed ra - diance bright!
gifts en - dure, Come, our heart's un - fail - ing light!

3. Of con - sol - ers, wis - est, best, And our soul's most
4. In our la - bor rest most sweet, Pleas - ant cool - ness

wel - come guest, Sweet re - fresh - ment, sweet re - pose.
in the heat, Con - so - la - tion in our woes.

5. Light most bless - ed, shine with grace In our heart's most
6. Left with - out your pres - ence here, Life it - self would

se - cret place, Fill your faith - ful through and through.
dis - ap - pear, Noth - ing thrives a - part from you!

7. Cleanse our soil - ed hearts of sin, Ar - id souls re -
8. Bend the stub - born heart and will, Melt the fro - zen,

fresh with - in, Wound - ed lives to health re - store.
warm the chill, Guide the way - ward home once more!

9. On the faith - ful who are true And pro - fess their
10. Give us vir - tue's sure re - ward, Give us your sal -

faith in you, In your sev'n - fold gift de - scend!
va - tion, Lord, Give us joys that nev - er end!

A - men. Al - le - lú - ia.

Text: *Veni Sancte Spiritus*; attr. to Stephen Langston, ca. 1150–1228, et al.; tr. by Peter J. Scagnelli, b.1949, after Edward Caswall, 1814–1878, © 1983
Tune: VENI SANCTE SPIRITUS, 7 7 7; Dublin *Troper*, ca. 1360; Mode I; acc. by Adriaan Engels, 1906–2003, © Interkerkelijke Stichting voor het
Kerklied Den Haag

875 Most Holy Trinity A, Dan. 3

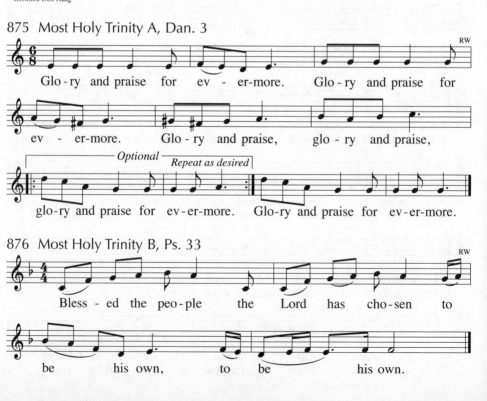

RW

Glo - ry and praise for ev - er-more. Glo - ry and praise for

ev - er-more. Glo - ry and praise, glo - ry and praise,

Optional — *Repeat as desired*

glo - ry and praise for ev - er-more. Glo - ry and praise for ev - er-more.

876 Most Holy Trinity B, Ps. 33

RW

Bless - ed the peo - ple the Lord has cho - sen to

be his own, to be his own.

Most Holy Trinity C, Ps. 8 877

NP

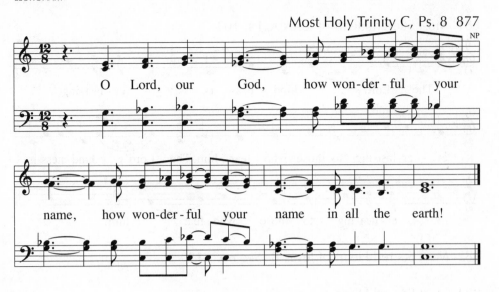

O Lord, our God, how won-der-ful your name, how won-der-ful your name in all the earth!

Most Holy Body and Blood of Christ A, Ps. 147 878

MW

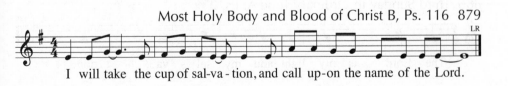

Descant:
Praise the Lord. Praise the Lord, Je-ru-sa-lem.

Melody:
Praise the Lord, Je-ru-sa-lem. Praise the Lord, Je-ru-sa-lem.

Most Holy Body and Blood of Christ B, Ps. 116 879

LR

I will take the cup of sal-va-tion, and call up-on the name of the Lord.

Most Holy Body and Blood of Christ C, Ps. 110 880

ND

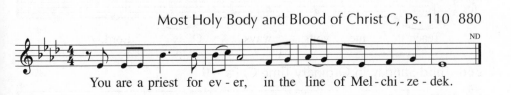

You are a priest for ev-er, in the line of Mel-chi-ze-dek.

881 Most Sacred Heart of Jesus A, Ps. 103

The Lord's kind - ness is ev - er - last-ing,

ev - er-last-ing to those who fear him. The Lord's kind-ness is

ev - er - last-ing to those who fear him.

882 Most Sacred Heart of Jesus B *See no. 813*

883 Most Sacred Heart of Jesus C *See no. 825*

884 Second Sunday in Ordinary Time AB, Ps. 40

Here am I, Lord; here am I, Lord; I come to do your will.

885 Second Sunday in Ordinary Time C, Ps. 96

Pro-claim his mar-vel-ous deeds to the na - tions.

886 Third Sunday in Ordinary Time A, Ps. 27

The Lord is my light and my sal - va - tion.

887 Third Sunday in Ordinary Time B, Ps. 25

Teach me your ways, O Lord.

888 Third Sunday in Ordinary Time C, Ps. 19

Your words, O Lord, are Spir - it and life.

Fourth Sunday in Ordinary Time A, Ps. 146 889

MRH

Bless-ed the poor in spir-it; the king-dom of heav-en is theirs.

Fourth Sunday in Ordinary Time B, Ps. 95 890

RJS

If to-day you hear his voice, hard-en

not your hearts, hard-en not your hearts.

Fourth Sunday in Ordinary Time C, Ps. 71 891

MRH

I will sing, I will sing of your sal-va-tion.

Fifth Sunday in Ordinary Time A, Ps. 112 892

RP

The just man is a light in dark-ness to the up-right.

Fifth Sunday in Ordinary Time B, Ps. 147 893

MRH

Praise the Lord, praise the Lord, who heals the bro-ken-heart-ed.

894 Fifth Sunday in Ordinary Time C, Ps. 138

MRH

In the sight of the an-gels, I will sing your prais-es,

To repeat

To verses
Last time

sing your prais - es, Lord. In the Lord.

Last time

Lord, prais - es,

895 Sixth Sunday in Ordinary Time A, Ps. 119

WCP

Bless - ed are they who fol - low the law,

fol - low the law of the Lord!

896 Sixth Sunday in Ordinary Time B, Ps. 32

RJS

I turn to you, Lord, in time of trou-ble, and you fill me

To repeat

To verses
Last time

with the joy of sal - va - tion. I tion.

Last time

Sixth Sunday in Ordinary Time C, Ps. 1 897

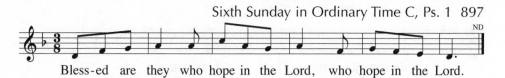

Bless-ed are they who hope in the Lord, who hope in the Lord.

Seventh Sunday in Ordinary Time A *See no. 824* 898

Seventh Sunday in Ordinary Time B, Ps. 41 899

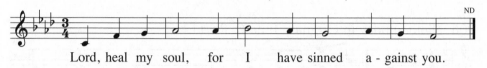

Lord, heal my soul, for I have sinned a - gainst you.

Seventh Sunday in Ordinary Time C *See no. 824* 900

Eighth Sunday in Ordinary Time A, Ps. 62 901

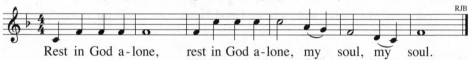

Rest in God a-lone, rest in God a-lone, my soul, my soul.

Eighth Sunday in Ordinary Time B *See no. 824* 902

Eighth Sunday in Ordinary Time C, Ps. 92 903

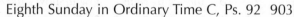

Lord, it is good, good, good to give thanks,

thanks, thanks, to give thanks to you.

Ninth Sunday in Ordinary Time A, Ps. 31 904

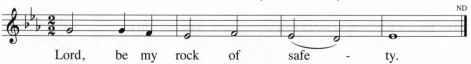

Lord, be my rock of safe - ty.

905 Ninth Sunday in Ordinary Time B, Ps. 81

RW

Sing with joy to God! Sing with joy to God!

Sing with joy to God, to God our help!

906 Ninth Sunday in Ordinary Time C, Ps. 117

RW

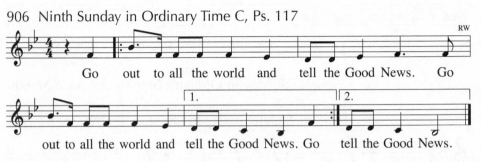

Go out to all the world and tell the Good News. Go

out to all the world and tell the Good News. Go tell the Good News.

907 Tenth Sunday in Ordinary Time A, Ps. 50

WCP

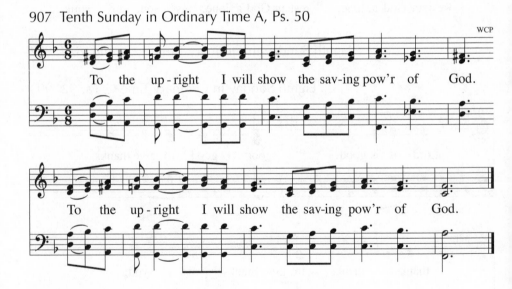

To the up-right I will show the sav-ing pow'r of God.

To the up-right I will show the sav-ing pow'r of God.

908 Tenth Sunday in Ordinary Time B *See no. 828*

909 Tenth Sunday in Ordinary Time C *See no. 842*

910 Eleventh Sunday in Ordinary Time A *See no. 861*

Eleventh Sunday in Ordinary Time B, Ps. 92 911

KL

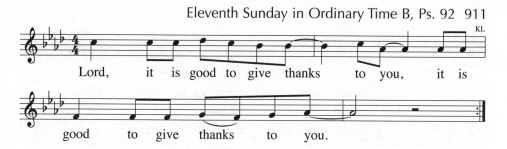

Lord, it is good to give thanks to you, it is good to give thanks to you.

Eleventh Sunday in Ordinary Time C, Ps. 32 912

KL

Lord, for-give the wrong I have done. Please,

Last time

Lord, for-give the wrong I have done.

Twelfth Sunday in Ordinary Time A, Ps. 69 913

NP

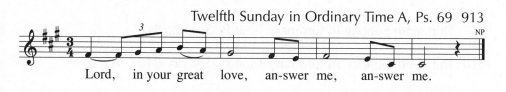

Lord, in your great love, an-swer me, an-swer me.

Twelfth Sunday in Ordinary Time B, Ps. 107 914

RJS

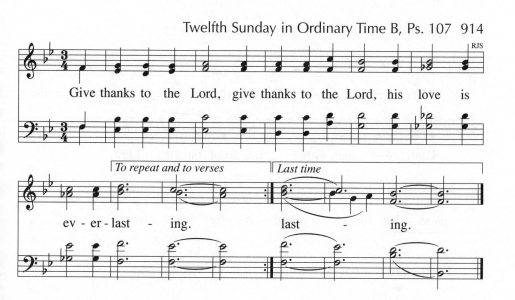

Give thanks to the Lord, give thanks to the Lord, his love is

To repeat and to verses | *Last time*

ev-er-last - ing. last - ing.

915 Twelfth Sunday in Ordinary Time C, Ps. 63

My soul is thirst-ing for you, O Lord,

To repeat *To verses* *Last time*

thirst-ing for you, my God. My

Last time

This phrase is sung after every verse.

916 Thirteenth Sunday in Ordinary Time A *See no. 801*

917 Thirteenth Sunday in Ordinary Time B *See no. 842*

918 Thirteenth Sunday in Ordinary Time C *See no. 840*

919 Fourteenth Sunday in Ordinary Time A *See no. 864*

920 Fourteenth Sunday in Ordinary Time B, Ps. 123

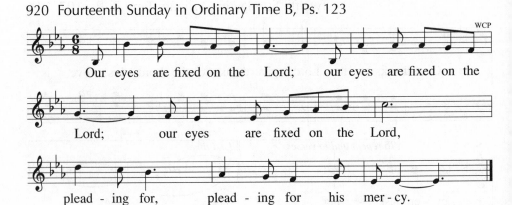

Our eyes are fixed on the Lord; our eyes are fixed on the

Lord; our eyes are fixed on the Lord,

plead - ing for, plead - ing for his mer - cy.

921 Fourteenth Sunday in Ordinary Time C *See no. 865*

Fifteenth Sunday in Ordinary Time A, Ps. 65 922

RC/JR

Good ground, Good ground, good ground, the seed that falls on

Good, good ground,

good ground good ground, good ground will yield a fruit-ful har-vest.

good, good ground

2. har-vest. Good ground.

Fifteenth Sunday in Ordinary Time B *See no. 795* 923

Fifteenth Sunday in Ordinary Time C, Ps. 69 924

ND

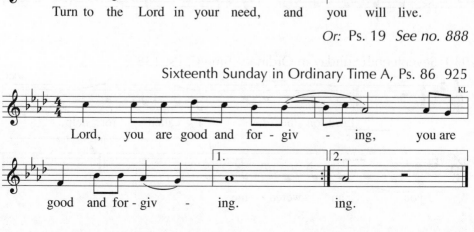

Turn to the Lord in your need, and you will live.

Or: Ps. 19 See no. 888

Sixteenth Sunday in Ordinary Time A, Ps. 86 925

KL

Lord, you are good and for-giv - ing, you are

1. good and for-giv - ing.   2. ing.

926 Sixteenth Sunday in Ordinary Time B *See no. 825*

927 Sixteenth Sunday in Ordinary Time C, Ps. 15

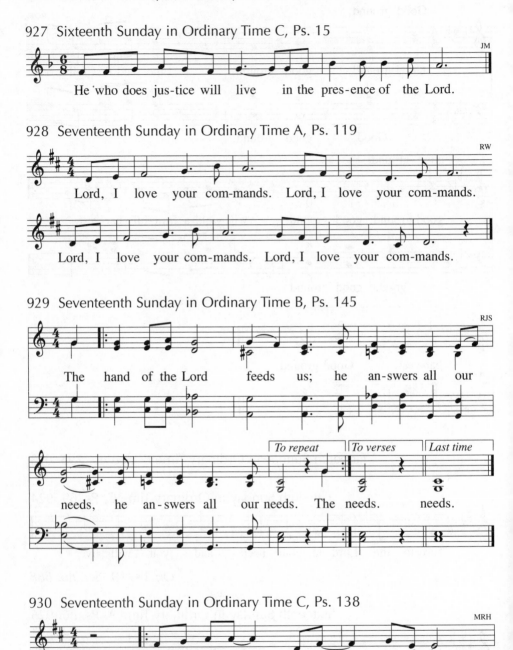

He 'who does jus-tice will live in the pres-ence of the Lord.

928 Seventeenth Sunday in Ordinary Time A, Ps. 119

Lord, I love your com-mands. Lord, I love your com-mands.

Lord, I love your com-mands. Lord, I love your com-mands.

929 Seventeenth Sunday in Ordinary Time B, Ps. 145

The hand of the Lord feeds us; he an-swers all our

To repeat *To verses* *Last time*

needs, he an-swers all our needs. The needs. needs.

930 Seventeenth Sunday in Ordinary Time C, Ps. 138

Lord, on the day I called for help,

1. 2.

you an - swered me.

Eighteenth Sunday in Ordinary Time A *See no. 929* 931

Eighteenth Sunday in Ordinary Time B, Ps. 78 932

RJS

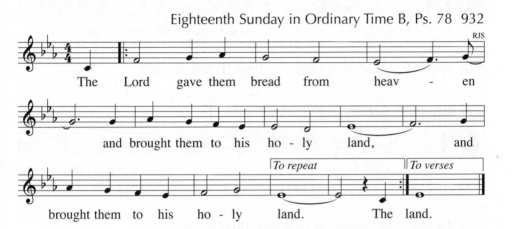

The Lord gave them bread from heav - en

and brought them to his ho - ly land, and

To repeat   *To verses*

brought them to his ho - ly land. The land.

Eighteenth Sunday in Ordinary Time C *See no. 822* 933

Nineteenth Sunday in Ordinary Time A *See no. 795* 934

Nineteenth Sunday in Ordinary Time B, Ps. 34 935

MG

Taste and see the good - ness of the Lord.

Nineteenth Sunday in Ordinary Time C, Ps. 33 936

LR

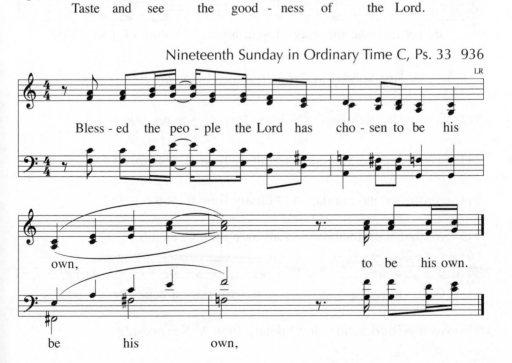

Bless - ed the peo - ple the Lord has cho - sen to be his

own,   to be his own.

be his own,

937 Twentieth Sunday in Ordinary Time A, Ps. 67

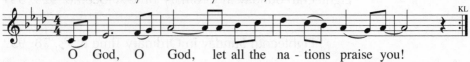

O God, O God, let all the na-tions praise you!

938 Twentieth Sunday in Ordinary Time B *See no. 827*

939 Twentieth Sunday in Ordinary Time C, Ps. 40

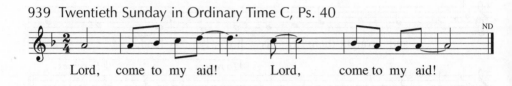

Lord, come to my aid! Lord, come to my aid!

940 Twenty-First Sunday in Ordinary Time A, Ps. 138

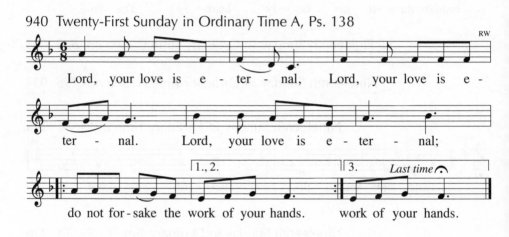

Lord, your love is e - ter - nal, Lord, your love is e -

ter - nal. Lord, your love is e - ter - nal;

┌ 1., 2.   ┌ 3.   *Last time* ⌢

do not for-sake the work of your hands.   work of your hands.

941 Twenty-First Sunday in Ordinary Time B *See no. 827*

942 Twenty-First Sunday in Ordinary Time C *See no. 906*

943 Twenty-Second Sunday in Ordinary Time A *See no. 915*

944 Twenty-Second Sunday in Ordinary Time B *See no. 927*

945 Twenty-Second Sunday in Ordinary Time C, Ps. 68

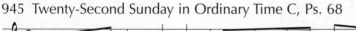

God, in your good-ness, you have made a home for the poor.

946 Twenty-Third Sunday in Ordinary Time A *See no. 822*

Twenty-Third Sunday in Ordinary Time B, Ps. 146 947

KL

Praise the Lord, praise the Lord, praise the Lord, praise the Lord, praise the Lord, my soul!

Twenty-Third Sunday in Ordinary Time C, Ps. 90 948

NP

In ev-'ry age, O Lord, you have been our ref-uge.

You have been our ref-uge in ev-'ry age, O Lord.

Twenty-Fourth Sunday in Ordinary Time A, Ps. 103 949

MRH

The Lord is kind and mer-ci-ful, slow to

To verses │ Final ending

an - ger, and rich in com-pas - sion.

Twenty-Fourth Sunday in Ordinary Time B See no. 820 950

Twenty-Fourth Sunday in Ordinary Time C, Ps. 51 951

RW

1.

I will rise and go to my fa - ther, go to my fa - ther;

2.

I will rise. go to my fa - ther; I will rise.

952 Twenty-Fifth Sunday in Ordinary Time A, Ps. 145

ND

The Lord is near to all who call on him. The

Lord is near to all who call on him.

953 Twenty-Fifth Sunday in Ordinary Time B, Ps. 54

ND

The Lord up-holds my life.

954 Twenty-Fifth Sunday in Ordinary Time C, Ps. 113

RW

Praise the Lord, praise the Lord who lifts up the poor. poor.

955 Twenty-Sixth Sunday in Ordinary Time A, Ps. 25

RT

Re - mem - ber your mer - cies, O Lord.

Re - mem - ber your mer-cies, O Lord.

956 Twenty-Sixth Sunday in Ordinary Time B, Ps. 19

WCP

The pre - cepts of the Lord give joy to the heart;

1. give joy to the heart; give joy to the heart. The

2. give joy to the heart.

957 Twenty-Sixth Sunday in Ordinary Time C *See no. 947*

Twenty-Seventh Sunday in Ordinary Time A, Ps. 80 958

The vine-yard of the Lord is the house of Is - ra - el.

Twenty-Seventh Sunday in Ordinary Time B, Ps. 128 959

May the Lord bless us, may the Lord bless us and pro -

tect us all the days of our lives.

Twenty-Seventh Sunday in Ordinary Time C *See no. 822* 960

Twenty-Eighth Sunday in Ordinary Time A, Ps. 23 961

Oh, I shall live in the house of the

Lord all the days of my life.

Twenty-Eighth Sunday in Ordinary Time B, Ps. 90 962

Fill us with your love, O Lord, and we will sing for joy!

Fill us with your love, O Lord and we will sing for joy!

Twenty-Eighth Sunday in Ordinary Time C *See no. 866* 963

964 Twenty-Ninth Sunday in Ordinary Time A, Ps. 96

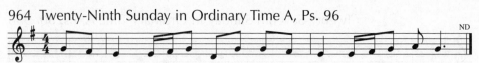

ND

Give the Lord glo-ry and hon-or. Give the Lord glo-ry and hon-or.

965 Twenty-Ninth Sunday in Ordinary Time B *See no. 819*

966 Twenty-Ninth Sunday in Ordinary Time C, Ps. 121

LR

Our help is from the Lord,

who made heav-en, heav - en and earth.

967 Thirtieth Sunday in Ordinary Time A, Ps. 18

WCP

I love you, Lord. I love you, Lord.

I love you, Lord, my strength.

968 Thirtieth Sunday in Ordinary Time B *See no. 796*

969 Thirtieth Sunday in Ordinary Time C, Ps. 34

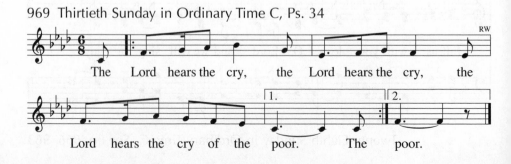

RW

The Lord hears the cry, the Lord hears the cry, the

1.　　　　　　2.

Lord hears the cry of the poor. The poor.

Thirty-First Sunday in Ordinary Time A, Ps. 131 970

In you, O Lord, I have found my peace.

Thirty-First Sunday in Ordinary Time B, Ps. 18 971

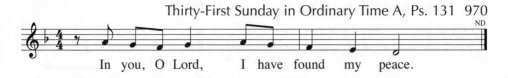

I love you, Lord, my strength. I strength.

Thirty-First Sunday in Ordinary Time C *See no. 864* 972

Thirty-Second Sunday in Ordinary Time A *See no. 915* 973

Thirty-Second Sunday in Ordinary Time B *See no. 947* 974

Thirty-Second Sunday in Ordinary Time C, Ps. 17 975

Lord, when your glo-ry ap - pears, my joy, my joy will be

full, my joy, my joy will be full. joy will be full.

Thirty-Third Sunday in Ordinary Time A, Ps. 128 976

Bless-ed are those who fear the Lord. fear the Lord.

Thirty-Third Sunday in Ordinary Time B *See no. 840* 977

978 Thirty-Third Sunday in Ordinary Time C, Ps. 98

The Lord comes to rule the earth with jus- tice.
The Lord comes to rule
Rule the earth. The Lord comes to
rule the earth with jus - tice.

979 Our Lord Jesus Christ, King of the Universe A *See no. 825*

980 Our Lord Jesus Christ, King of the Universe B, Ps. 93

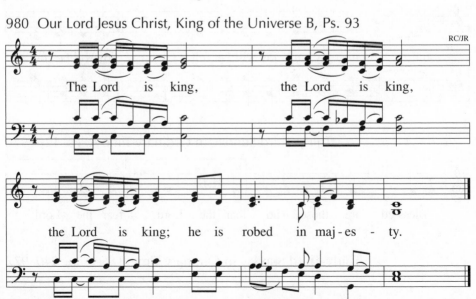

The Lord is king, the Lord is king,
the Lord is king; he is robed in maj-es - ty.

Our Lord Jesus Christ, King of the Universe C *See no. 791* 981

February 2: Presentation of the Lord / Blessing of Candles and Procession 982

Antiphon

Be - hold, our Lord will come with pow'r, to en - light - en the eyes of his ser - vants, al - le - lu - ia.

Verses

1. Your	word	is a lamp for		my	feet,
		I have sworn an oath and af -		firmed	it,
2. I	am	deeply afflicted,		O	LORD;
		Accept, LORD, my freely offered		hom -	age,
3. Your	de -	crees are my heritage for -		ev -	er,
		I incline my heart to carry out your		stat -	utes

D.C.

and a	light	for	my		path.
to obey	your	just	judg -		ments.	R̶.
by your	word,	give	me		life.
and	teach	me	your	de -	crees.	R̶.
the	joy	of	my		heart.
for -	ev -	er,	to	the	end.	R̶.

Text: Psalm 119:105–108, 111–112, *The Revised Grail Psalms,* © 2010, Conception Abbey and The Grail, admin. by GIA Publications, Inc.;
antiphon, ICEL, © 2010
Music: Chant Mode VIII; acc. by Richard Proulx, © 1985, GIA Publications, Inc.; antiphon, ICEL, © 2010

When the candles have been blessed, the priest sings:

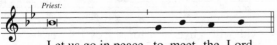

Let us go in peace to meet the Lord.

Or:

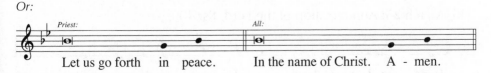

Let us go forth in peace. In the name of Christ. A - men.

983 *During the procession, the following may be sung:*

Antiphon

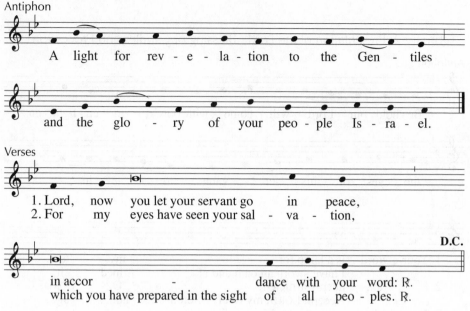

A light for rev - e - la - tion to the Gen - tiles

and the glo - ry of your peo - ple Is - ra - el.

Verses

1. Lord, now you let your servant go in peace,
2. For my eyes have seen your sal - va - tion,

D.C.

in accor - dance with your word: ℞.
which you have prepared in the sight of all peo - ples. ℞.

Text: Luke 2:29–32, trans. ICEL, © 2010
Music: Chant Mode VIII; acc. by Richard Proulx, © 1985, GIA Publications, Inc.; antiphon, ICEL, © 2010

984 February 2: Presentation of the Lord, Ps. 24

WCP

Who is this king, king of glo-ry? It is the Lord, it is the Lord!

Who is this king, king of glo-ry? It is the Lord!

985 March 19: Joseph, Husband of Mary, Ps. 89

ND

The son of Da - vid will live for ev - er.

986 March 25: Annunciation of the Lord, Ps. 40

ND

Here am I, O Lord; I come to do your will.

June 24: Nativity of St. John the Baptist—Vigil Mass, Ps. 71 987

ND

Since my moth-er's womb, you have been my strength.

June 24: Nativity of St. John the Baptist—Mass During the Day, Ps. 139 988

WCP

I praise you, O Lord. I praise you, O Lord,

for I am won - der - f'lly made.

June 29: Sts. Peter & Paul, Apostles—Vigil Mass, Ps.19 989

LR

Their mes-sage goes out through all the earth; goes

out through all the earth.

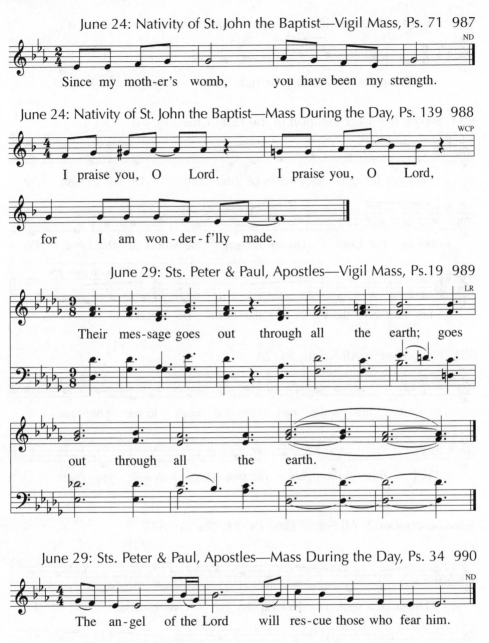

June 29: Sts. Peter & Paul, Apostles—Mass During the Day, Ps. 34 990

ND

The an - gel of the Lord will res-cue those who fear him.

August 6: Transfiguration of the Lord *See no. 871* 991

August 15: Assumption of Mary—Vigil Mass, Ps. 132 992

ND

Lord, go up to the place of your rest, you and the ark of your ho-li-ness.

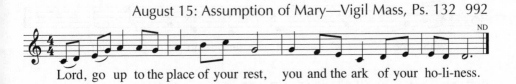

993 August 15: Assumption of Mary—Mass During the Day, Ps. 45

The queen stands at your right hand, ar-rayed in gold.

994 September 14: Exaltation of the Holy Cross, Ps. 78

Do not for-get the works of the Lord. Do not for-get the

works of the Lord. Do not for-get the works of the Lord. Do

1., 2.　3.　Last time

not for-get the works of the Lord. Do works of the Lord.

995 November 1: All Saints, Ps. 24

Lord, this is the peo - ple that longs to see your face.

Lord, this is the peo - ple that longs to see your face.

996 November 2: All Souls' Day, Ps. 23 *See no. 825*

Or:

Though I walk in the val - ley of dark - ness, I

fear no e - vil, for you, for you are

with me, I fear no e - vil.

997 November 2: All Souls' Day, Ps. 25 *See no. 793*

Or:

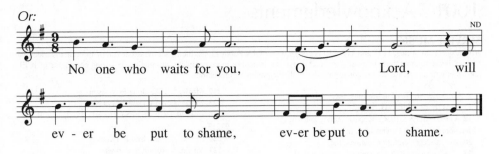

No one who waits for you, O Lord, will ev-er be put to shame, ev-er be put to shame.

November 2: All Souls' Day, Ps. 27 *See nos. 821* 998

Or:

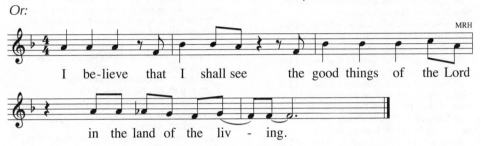

I be-lieve that I shall see the good things of the Lord in the land of the liv - ing.

November 9: Dedication of the Lateran Basilica, Ps. 46 999

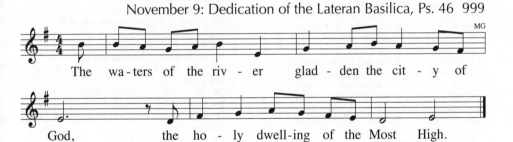

The wa-ters of the riv - er glad - den the cit - y of God, the ho - ly dwell-ing of the Most High.

December 8: Immaculate Conception, Ps. 98 1000

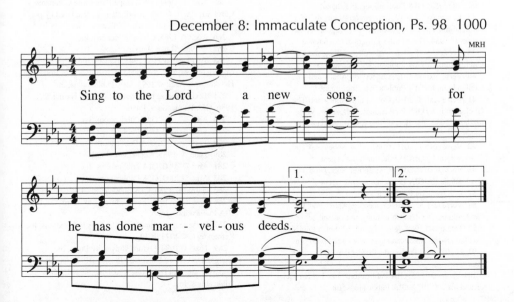

Sing to the Lord a new song, for he has done mar - vel - ous deeds.

1001 Acknowledgments

Acknowledgments/*continued*

461 Arr.: © 2008, Iona Community, GIA Publications, Inc., agent

462 © 1997, 2003, GIA Publications, Inc.

463 © 1979, Les Presses de Taizé, GIA Publications, Inc., agent.

466 © 2012, GIA Publications, Inc.

467 © 1982, Bob Jay Music Co.

468 © 2002, World Library Publications, Franklin Park, IL wlpmusic.com 800-566-6150 All rights reserved. Used by permission.

469 Text and Tune: © 2003, Mr. Que Publishing (BMI). Arr. © 2012, GIA Publications, Inc.

470 Tune: © 1987, Timothy Gibson

471 Arr.: © 2012, GIA Publications, Inc.

472 © 2002, Integrity's Praise! Music and Pace's Vision Music, admin. at EMICMGPublishing.com. All Rights Reserved. Used by Permission.

474 © 1998, Leon Roberts. Published by OCP Publications, 5536 NE Hassalo, Portland, OR 97213. All rights reserved. Used with permission.

476 © 1971, Bud John Songs (ASCAP), admin. at EMICMGPublishing.com. All Rights Reserved. Used by Permission.

477 © 1940, Singspiration Music (ASCAP). A div. of Brentwood-Benson Music Publishing, Inc., admin. by Music Services. All Rights Reserved. Used by Permission.

478 Arr.: © 2000, GIA Publications, Inc.

479 Text and tune: © 1970, New Song Music. Arr.: © 2000, GIA Publications, Inc.

482 © 1996, GBGMusik

483 © 1948 (renewed), Martin and Morris Studio, Inc. All Rights Administered by Unichappell Music, Inc. This arr. © 2011, Martin and Morris Studio, Inc. All Rights Reserved. Used by Permission of Alfred Publishing Co., Inc.

484 © 1984, Bernadette B. Salley. Administered by GIA Publications, Inc.

485 Text and tune: © Rev. Earl Pleasant Publishing, Arr.: © 2000, GIA Publications, Inc.

486 Text: © 1939, 1966, E. C. Schirmer Music Co., Boston Massachusetts. Harm.: © The Royal School of Church Music, 19 The Close, Salisbury SP1 2EB, UK. www.rscm.com

487 Text: English adapt., © 2000, GIA Publications, Inc. Tune: © 1990, Christ Church Gospel Band. Arr.: © 1990, Iona Community, GIA Publications, Inc., agent

489 Arr.: © 2000, GIA Publications, Inc.

490 © Legré Publishing Co. (BMI)

492 © 1923, renewed 1951, Hope Publishing Co., Carol Stream, IL 60188. All rights reserved. Used by permission.

493 Text: © 1968, John T. Benson Publishing Co. (ASCAP). A div. of Brentwood-Benson Music Publishing, Inc., admin. by Music Services. All Rights Reserved. Used by Permission.

495 Arr.: © 2000, GIA Publications, Inc.

496 Arr.: © 2000, GIA Publications, Inc.

497 © 1975, Word Music, Inc. (ASCAP), 65 Music Square West, Nashville, TN 37203, admin. by Warner/Chappell

498 Arr.: © 2000, GIA Publications, Inc.

499 © 1973, 2000, Davike Music Co./Fricon Music Co.

500 Harm.: © 1975, GIA Publications, Inc.

502 Arr.: © 2000, GIA Publications, Inc.

504 © 1993, Malaco Music, Inc. International Copyright Secured. All Rights Reserved. Reprinted by permission of Hal Leonard Corporation.

505 © 1982, Bud John Songs (ASCAP), admin. at EMICMGPublishing.com. All Rights Reserved. Used by Permission.

506 Arr.: © 2012, GIA Publications, Inc.

507 Arr.: © 2000, GIA Publications, Inc.

508 © Rev. Maceo Woods. Administered by GIA Publications, Inc.

509 Text and tune: © 1993, Jessy Dixon Music Company, administered by Larry Spier Music LLC, New York, NY. All rights reserved including right of performance. International copyright secured. Arr.: © 2000, GIA Publications, Inc.

510 Arr.: © 2000, GIA Publications, Inc.

512 © 2001, GIA Publications, Inc.

519 © 1994, Betty Gadling. Administered by GIA Publications, Inc.

521 © 1989, Chenaniah Publications, Inc.

522 Arr.: © 2000, GIA Publications, Inc.

523 © 1982, Full Armor Music and Whole Armor Music. Admin. by the Kruger Organization, Inc. International Copyright Secured. All rights reserved. Used by Permission.

524 Arr.: © 2000, GIA Publications, Inc.

526 Harm.: © 1981, GIA Publications, Inc.

527 © 1991, Glenn Burleigh (Burleigh Inspirations Music)

528 Arr.: © 2000, GIA Publications, Inc.

531 Arr.: © 2000, GIA Publications, Inc.

532 © 1953, 1981, Clara Ward. Assigned to Gertrude Music (SESAC). This is a new arrangement.

533 © 1982, Les Presses de Taizé, GIA Publications, Inc., agent

534 Text adapt. and arr. © 1978, Mar-Vel

535 Arr.: © 2000, GIA Publications, Inc.

536 Text and tune: © 1978, Bridgeport Music, Inc. (BMI). Arr.: © 2000, GIA Publications, Inc.

537 Harm.: © Estate of Wendell Whalum

538 © 1953 (renewed), Doris M. Akers. All Rights Administered by Chappell & Co., Inc. This arr. © 2011, Doris M. Akers. All Rights Reserved. Used by Permission of Alfred Publishing Co., Inc.

540 © 1987, 1988, 1991, GIA Publications, Inc.

541 © 1980, 2012, Savgos Music, Inc. and Grundy Boys Music. International Copyright Secured. All Rights Reserved. Reprinted by permission of Hal Leonard Corporation.

542 Text: © Lutheran World Federation. Tune: © Peace of Music Publishing AB, All Rights Administered by Walton Music Corporation. International Copyright Secured. All Rights Reserved.

543 Text tr.: © 1990, Iona Community, GIA Publications, Inc., agent

544 Text: © 1997, GIA Publications, Inc.

546 Text and tune: © 1940 (renewed), Warner-Tamerlane Publishing Corp. This arr. © 2011, Warner-Tamerlane Publishing Corp. All Rights Reserved. Used by Permission of Alfred Publishing Co., Inc.

547 © StepKey Music

548 © 1965, renewed 1993, Manna Music, Inc./ASCAP (admin. by ClearBox Rights). All Rights Reserved. Used by Permission.

549 © 1944 (renewed), Martin and Morris. All Rights Administered by Unichappell Music, Inc. This arr. © 2011, Martin and Morris. All Rights Reserved. Used by Permission of Alfred Publishing Co., Inc.

Acknowledgments/*continued*

Acknowledgments/*continued*

746 Text: © 1982, The Jubilate Group. Administered by Hope Publishing Company, Carol Stream, IL 60188. All rights reserved. Used by permission. Acc.: © 1999, GIA Publications, Inc.

747 Text adapt.: © 2009, GIA Publications, Inc. Arr.: © 2000, 2009, GIA Publications, Inc.

748 © Century Oak Publishing Group/Richwood Music (BMI), admin. by Conexion Media Group, Inc.

749 Text and Tune: © 1985, 1987, Amity Music Co. Arr.: © 2012, GIA Publications, Inc.

750 ©1983, GIA Publications, Inc.

751 © 1986, GIA Publications, Inc.

753 © 1984, Les Presses de Taizé, GIA Publications, Inc., agent

754 Text: © 1971, rev. 1995, Hope Publishing Co., Carol Stream, IL 60188. All rights reserved. Used by permission. Harm.: © 1938 (Renewed) The H. W. Gray Company. All Rights Controlled and Administered by Belwin-Mills Publishing Corp., a Division of Alfred Music Publishing. All Rights Reserved. Used by Permission of Alfred Publishing Co., Inc.

755 © 1966, 1970, 1986, 1993, GIA Publications, Inc.

757 © 1977, Archdiocese of Philadelphia. Published by International Liturgy Publications, PO Box 50476, Nashville, TN 37205. www.ILPmusic.org

758 © 1975, Hope Publishing Company, Carol Stream, IL 60188. All rights reserved. Used by permission.

759 Vss. 1–3, 5–9 tr.: © 2011; Harm.: © 1986, GIA Publications, Inc.

762 © 1998, Antilles Episcopal Conference

763 © 1995, 1997, GIA Publications, Inc.

764 © 1988, Bob Hurd and Pia Moriarty. Published by OCP. 5536 NE Hassalo, Portland, OR 97213. All rights reserved. Used with permission.

765 Verse Text: © 1969, James Quinn, SJ, Selah Publishing Co., Inc., North American agent. www.selahpub.com. Refrain Text, and Tune: © 1989, GIA Publications, Inc.

766 Harm. © 1979, George E. Mims

770 Harm.: © 1992, Carl Haywood

771 Text: © 1980, ICEL

772 Tune: © 2012, GIA Publications, Inc.

773 Text and tune: © S. Boddie. Arr.: © 2000, GIA Publications, Inc.

774 Arr.: © 2012, GIA Publications, Inc.

775 © 1994, 1997, GIA Publications, Inc.

776 Text: © 1997, GIA Publications, Inc.

777 © 1994, Malaco Music, Inc. International Copyright Secured. All Rights Reserved. Reprinted by permission of Hal Leonard Corporation.

779 © 1963, Hanna Street Music. All rights controlled by Gaither Copyright Management. Used by permission.

780 © 1938 (renewed), arr. © 1994, Warner-Tamerlane Publishing Corp. All Rights Reserved. Used by Permission of Alfred Publishing Co., Inc.

781 Arr.: © 2000, GIA Publications, Inc.

786 Text: © 1983, 2003, GIA Publications, Inc. Arr.: © 2000, GIA Publications, Inc.

790 © 1998, Antilles Episcopal Conference

791 Music: © 1981, 1997, GIA Publications, Inc.

792 Music: © 1996, 2012, Leon C. Roberts. Published by OCP. 5536 NE Hassalo, Portland, OR 97213. All rights reserved. Used with permission.

793 Music: © 1997, 2012, GIA Publications, Inc.

794 Music: © 2001, Light the Fire! Music

795 Music: © 1987, GIA Publications, Inc.

796 Music: © 2007, GIA Publications, Inc.

797 Music: © 2012, GIA Publications, Inc.

798 Music: © 2012, GIA Publications, Inc.

799 Music: © 2012, GIA Publications, Inc.

800 Music: © 1996, GIA Publications, Inc.

801 Music: © 2012, GIA Publications, Inc.

804 Music: © 2007, GIA Publications, Inc.

805 Music: © 2007, GIA Publications, Inc.

806 Music: © 1987, GIA Publications, Inc.

809 Music: © 1963, The Grail, GIA Publications, Inc., agent

809 Music: © 2012, GIA Publications, Inc.

809 Music: © 2012, GIA Publications, Inc.

810 Music: © 2012, GIA Publications, Inc.

811 Music: © 1987, GIA Publications, Inc.

812 Music: © 2005, 2012, World Library Publications, Franklin Park, IL wlpmusic.com 800-566-6150 All rights reserved. Used by permission.

813 Music: © 2012, GIA Publications, Inc.

814 Music: © 2012, GIA Publications, Inc.

815 Music: © 2012, GIA Publications, Inc.

817 Music: © 2012, GIA Publications, Inc.

818 Music: © 1980, GIA Publications, Inc.

819 Music: © 1993, GIA Publications, Inc.

820 Music: © 2012, GIA Publications, Inc.

821 Music: © 1983, GIA Publications, Inc.

822 Music: © 2008, World Library Publications, Franklin Park, IL wlpmusic.com 800-566-6150 All rights reserved. Used by permission.

823 Music: © 2012, GIA Publications, Inc.

824 Music: © 2012, GIA Publications, Inc.

825 Music: © 1987, GIA Publications, Inc.

826 Music: © 2012, GIA Publications, Inc.

827 Music: © 1983, GIA Publications, Inc.

828 Music: © 1987, GIA Publications, Inc.

829 Music: © 2012, GIA Publications, Inc.

831 Text and music: © 2010, ICEL. Acc.: © 1985, 2011, GIA Publications, Inc.

833 Music: © 1987, GIA Publications, Inc.

834 Music: © 2012, GIA Publications, Inc.

835 Text tr.: © 1969, James Quinn, SJ. Selah Publishing Co., Inc., North American agent. www.selahpub.com. Acc.: © 1964, GIA Publications, Inc.

836 Music: © 2012, GIA Publications, Inc.

839A Music: © 1987, GIA Publications, Inc.

839B Music: © 2012, GIA Publications, Inc.

840 Music: © 2012, GIA Publications, Inc.

841 Music: © 2012, GIA Publications, Inc.

842 Music: © 2012, GIA Publications, Inc.

845 Music: © 2012, GIA Publications, Inc.

848 Music: © 1981, GIA Publications, Inc.

849 © 2010, ICEL

850 Text and music: © 2010, ICEL. Acc.: © 2011, GIA Publications, Inc.

853 Music: © 1997, GIA Publications, Inc.

854 Text tr.: © 1983, Peter J. Scagnelli. Acc.: © 1975, GIA Publications, Inc.

855 Music: © 2012, GIA Publications, Inc.

856 Music: © 1998, GIA Publications, Inc.

857 Music: © 2007, World Library Publications, Franklin Park, IL wlpmusic.com 800-566-6150 All rights reserved. Used by permission.

858 Music: © 2012, GIA Publications, Inc.

859 Music: © 2012, GIA Publications, Inc.

860 Music: © 2012, GIA Publications, Inc.

861 Music: © 2003, GIA Publications, Inc.

863 Music: © 2012, GIA Publications, Inc.

864 Music: © 2012, GIA Publications, Inc.

865 Music: © 2012, GIA Publications, Inc.

866 Music: © 1994, 1998, GIA Publications, Inc.

867 Music: © 2009, World Library Publications, Franklin Park, IL wlpmusic.com 800-566-6150 All rights reserved. Used by permission.

868 Music: © 1987, GIA Publications, Inc.

869 Music: © 2012, GIA Publications, Inc.

870 Music: © 2012, GIA Publications, Inc.

871 Music: © 2012, GIA Publications, Inc.

874 Text: ©1983, Peter J. Scagnelli. Acc.: © Interkerkelijke Stichting voor het Kerklied

875 Music: © 2012, GIA Publications, Inc.

876 Music: © 2012, GIA Publications, Inc.

877 Music: © 2012, GIA Publications, Inc.

878 Music: © 2012, GIA Publications, Inc.

879 Music: © 2012, GIA Publications, Inc.

880 Music: © 2012, GIA Publications, Inc.

881 Music: © 2012, GIA Publications, Inc.

884 Music: © 1994, 1998, GIA Publications, Inc.

885 Music: © 2012, GIA Publications, Inc.

886 Music: © 1987, GIA Publications, Inc.

887 Music: © 2012, GIA Publications, Inc.

888 Music: © 2012, GIA Publications, Inc.

889 Music: © 2012, GIA Publications, Inc.

890 Music: © 1993, 2012, GIA Publications, Inc.

891 Music: © 2012, GIA Publications, Inc.

892 Music: © 1975, GIA Publications, Inc.

893 Music: © 2012, GIA Publications, Inc.

894 Music: © 2012, GIA Publications, Inc.

895 Music: © 2012, GIA Publications, Inc.

896 Music: © 1993, 2012, GIA Publications, Inc.

897 Music: © 2012, GIA Publications, Inc.

899 Music: © 2012, GIA Publications, Inc.

901 Music: © 1975, GIA Publications, Inc.

903 Music: © 2012, GIA Publications, Inc.

904 Music: © 2012, GIA Publications, Inc.

905 Music: © 2012, GIA Publications, Inc.

906 Music: © 2012, GIA Publications, Inc.

907 Music: © 2012, GIA Publications, Inc.

911 Music: © 2012, GIA Publications, Inc.

912 Music: © 2012, GIA Publications, Inc.

913 Music: © 2012, GIA Publications, Inc.

914 Music: © 1993, 2012, GIA Publications, Inc.

915 Music: © 2005, 2012, World Library Publications, Franklin Park, IL wlpmusic.com 800-566-6150 All rights reserved. Used by permission.

920 Music: © 2012, GIA Publications, Inc.

922 Music: © 2007, World Library Publications, Franklin Park, IL wlpmusic.com 800-566-6150 All rights reserved. Used by permission.

924 Music: © 2012, GIA Publications, Inc.

925 Music: © 2012, GIA Publications, Inc.

927 Music: © 2012, GIA Publications, Inc.

928 Music: © 2012, GIA Publications, Inc.

929 Music: © 1993, 2012, GIA Publications, Inc.

930 Music: © 2012, GIA Publications, Inc.

932 Music: © 1993, GIA Publications, Inc.

935 Music: © 1994, 1998, GIA Publications, Inc.

936 Music: © 2012, GIA Publications, Inc.

937 Music: © 2012, GIA Publications, Inc.

939 Music: © 2012, GIA Publications, Inc.

940 Music: © 2012, GIA Publications, Inc.

945 Music: © 2012, GIA Publications, Inc.

947 Music: © 2012, GIA Publications, Inc.

948 Music: © 2012, GIA Publications, Inc.

949 Music: © 2012, GIA Publications, Inc.

951 Music: © 2012, GIA Publications, Inc.

952 Music: © 2012, GIA Publications, Inc.

953 Music: © 2012, GIA Publications, Inc.

954 Music: © 2012, GIA Publications, Inc.

955 Music: © 2012, GIA Publications, Inc.

956 Music: © 2012, GIA Publications, Inc.

958 Music: © 2012, GIA Publications, Inc.

959 Music: © 2012, GIA Publications, Inc.

961 Music: © 2012, GIA Publications, Inc.

962 Music: © 2001, 2012, GIA Publications, Inc.

964 Music: © 2012, GIA Publications, Inc.

966 Music: © 2012, GIA Publications, Inc.

967 Music: © 2012, GIA Publications, Inc.

969 Music: © 2012, GIA Publications, Inc.

970 Music: © 2012, GIA Publications, Inc.

971 Music: © 2012, GIA Publications, Inc.

975 Music: © 1993, GIA Publications, Inc.

976 Music: © 2012, GIA Publications, Inc.

978 Music: © 2005, 2012, World Library Publications, Franklin Park, IL wlpmusic.com 800-566-6150 All rights reserved. Used by permission.

980 Music: © 2005, World Library Publications, Franklin Park, IL wlpmusic.com 800-566-6150 All rights reserved. Used by permission.

982 Antiphon text and music: © 2010, ICEL. Antiphon acc.: © 2011, GIA Publications, Inc. Verse text: © 2010, Conception Abbey and The Grail, admin. by GIA Publications, Inc., agent. Verse acc.: © 1985, GIA Publications, Inc.

983 Text and antiphon music: © 2010, ICEL. Antiphon acc.: © 2011, GIA Publications, Inc. Acc.: © 1985, GIA Publications, Inc.

984 Music: © 2012, GIA Publications, Inc.

985 Music: © 2012, GIA Publications, Inc.

986 Music: © 2012, GIA Publications, Inc.

987 Music: © 2012, GIA Publications, Inc.

988 Music: © 2012, GIA Publications, Inc.

989 Music: © 2012, GIA Publications, Inc.

990 Music: © 2012, GIA Publications, Inc.

992 Music: © 2012, GIA Publications, Inc.

993 Music: © 2012, GIA Publications, Inc.

994 Music: © 2012, GIA Publications, Inc.

995 Music: © 2012, GIA Publications, Inc.

996 Music: © 2012, GIA Publications, Inc.

997 Music: © 2012, GIA Publications, Inc.

998 Music: © 2012, GIA Publications, Inc.

999 Music: © 1994, 1998, GIA Publications, Inc.

1000 Music: © 2012, GIA Publications, Inc.

Scripture Passages Related to Hymns/*continued*

Scripture Passages Related to Hymns/*continued*

150:2   Praise Him! Praise Him! 441
150:3-4   Praise to the Lord 466
150:6   How Excellent Is Thy Name 462

PROVERBS
3:5—4:18   Leaning on the Everlasting Arms 592
8:22   O Come, O Come, Emmanuel 231
16:20   Trust and Obey 565
18:24   Jesus Is All the World to Me 370

SONG OF SONGS
2:4   God Be with You till We Meet Again 545

SIRACH (ECCLESIASTICUS)
50:22   Now Thank We All Our God 488

WISDOM
18:14-15   Creator of the Stars of Night 239

ISAIAH
2:2-3   Holy, Holy, Holy! Lord God Almighty! 335
2:4   O God of Every Nation 663
6:2-3   All Hail the Power of Jesus' Name! 342
6:2-3   All Hail the Power of Jesus' Name! 343
6:2-3   Holy God, We Praise Thy Name 465
6:2-3   Holy, Holy, Holy! Lord God Almighty! 335
6:8   Here Am I 636
6:8   Here I Am, Lord 643
7:14   Emmanuel, Emmanuel 234
7:14   O Come, O Come, Emmanuel 231
7:14   The King of Glory 341
9:1-3   Goodness Is Stronger than Evil 313
9:2   Brightest and Best 272
9:5   Hark! The Herald Angels Sing 247
9:5   His Name Is Wonderful 372
9:5   Jesus, the Light of the World 274
9:5   Wonderful Counselor 256
9:5-7   O God of Every Nation 663
11:1   All Hail the Power of Jesus' Name! 342
11:1   All Hail the Power of Jesus' Name! 343
11:1   Lo, How a Rose E'er Blooming 263
11:1   O Come, O Come, Emmanuel 231
22:22   O Come, O Come, Emmanuel 231
25:6-9   Come to the Feast 684
34:4   It Is Well with My Soul 569
35:1   Lo, How a Rose E'er Blooming 263
35:4   Be Strong! 573
35:6   O for a Thousand Tongues to Sing 438
35:10   We're Marching to Zion 706
40:3-4   Prepare Ye the Way of the Lord! 235
40:3-4   Prepare Ye the Way of the Lord 237
40:3-5   On Jordan's Bank 240
40:9   Behold Your God 280
40:9   Prepare Ye the Way of the Lord 237
40:10   How Firm a Foundation 555
40:11   Praise Him! Praise Him! 441
40:25-26   God of Our Fathers 787
41:13   Precious Lord, Take My Hand 780
43:1   Hush, Hush, Somebody's Callin' My Name 624
43:1-2   Precious Lord, Take My Hand 780
43:1-2   The Solid Rock 561
43:1-7   Eternal Father, Strong to Save 539
43:2-3   Be Not Afraid 583
43:19   I Will Do a New Thing 535
49:    In Christ There Is No East or West 664
49:7   Great Is Thy Faithfulness 492
49:13-16   Wash, O God, Our Sons and Daughters 737

49:15   We Gather Together 669
51:11   We're Marching to Zion 706
52:7   Come, O Long-Expected Jesus 238
52:7   O Holy Night! 255
53:4   Praise Him! Praise Him! 441
53:4   What a Friend We Have in Jesus 361
54:7   Come, Ye Disconsolate 590
55:8-9   O Dawn of All Creation 338
55:8-9   We'll Understand It Better By and By 574
57:19   Nearer, My God, to Thee 784
61:1   Hold Us in Your Mercy: Penitential Litany 291
61:1-2   Come, O Long-Expected Jesus 238
61:1-2   O for a Thousand Tongues to Sing 438
62:3   All Hail the Power of Jesus' Name! 342
62:3   All Hail the Power of Jesus' Name! 343
63:3   Mine Eyes Have Seen the Glory 694
66:1   Mine Eyes Have Seen the Glory 694
66:10-11   Wash, O God, Our Sons and Daughters 737

JEREMIAH
8:22   There Is a Balm in Gilead 502
29:11   Great Is Thy Faithfulness 492
37:17   Is There a Word from the Lord? 422

LAMENTATIONS
3:22-23   Great Is Thy Faithfulness 492
3:23   Jesus in the Morning 391

EZEKIEL
11:19   Here I Am, Lord 643
21:14-15   Mine Eyes Have Seen the Glory 694
36:27   Spirit of God, Descend upon My Heart 323
43:5   The Glory of the Lord 607

DANIEL
6:1—7:28   The Glory of These Forty Days 284
7:9   Come Now, Almighty King 334
7:13-14   O Christ, What Can It Mean for Us 348
7:22   Come Now, Almighty King 334
12:3   We Gather in Memory 686

HOSEA
6:3   Mine Eyes Have Seen the Glory 694

JOEL
2:12-18   Remember You Are Dust 287

JONAH
1:    You Better Run 721
1:15-16   The Storm Is Passing Over 595

MICAH
5:2   O Little Town of Bethlehem 250
7:18   Love Divine, All Loves Excelling 494

HABAKKUK
2:20   The Lord Is in His Holy Temple 672

HAGGAI
2:7   Angels, from the Realms of Glory 264
2:7   Come, O Long-Expected Jesus 238
2:7   O Come, O Come, Emmanuel 231

Scripture Passages Related to Hymns/*continued*

1003   Liturgical Index

Liturgical Index/*continued*

Liturgical Index/*continued*

Topical Index/*continued*

517 Sweet Hour of Prayer
327 Sweet, Sweet Spirit
704 Swing Low, Sweet Chariot
375 Take the Name of Jesus with You
596 The Angels Keep A-Watchin'
383 The Blood Will Never Lose Its Power
591 The Joy of the Lord
341 The King of Glory
601 The King of Love My Shepherd Is
572 The Lord Is My Light
561 The Solid Rock
595 The Storm Is Passing Over
705 The Sweet By and By
502 There Is a Balm in Gilead
511 There's a Wideness in God's Mercy
637 This Little Light of Mine
584 Through It All
565 Trust and Obey
532 Until I Found the Lord
652 We Shall Overcome
361 What a Friend We Have in Jesus
500 What Wondrous Love Is This
687 When Morning Gilds the Sky
770 Yield Not to Temptation

COMMISSIONING
646 Go Make of All Disciples
321 Go to the World!
322 Go Ye Therefore
643 Here I Am, Lord
553 I Say "Yes," Lord / Digo "Sí," Señor
627 Lord, When You Came / Pescador de Hombres
645 Lord, Whose Love in Humble Service
619 Take, O Take Me As I Am
622 The Summons

COMMITMENT
628 A Follower of Christ
552 A Living Faith
707 Ain't-a That Good News!
431 Blessed Assurance, Jesus Is Mine!
385 Certainly, Lord!
747 Certainly, Lord! (RENEWAL OF BAPTISMAL PROMISES)
744 Changed Mah Name
743 Come to Jesus
433 Come, Thou Fount of Every Blessing
623 Completely Yes
629 Done Made My Vow to the Lord
336 Father, I Adore You
625 Give Me a Clean Heart
350 Give Me Jesus
646 Go Make of All Disciples
392 God Is
513 Have Thine Own Way, Lord!
785 He Understands; He'll Say, "Well Done"
636 Here Am I
643 Here I Am, Lord
640 I Am on the Battlefield for My Lord

525 I Am Thine
613 I Have Decided to Follow Jesus
553 I Say "Yes," Lord / Digo "Sí," Señor
639 I Shall Not Be Moved
616 I Surrender All
766 I Will Arise
576 I Will Trust in the Lord
620 I'll Be Somewhere Listening for My Name
386 I've Been 'Buked
626 I've Decided to Make Jesus My Choice
660 Is Your All on the Altar
671 Jesu Tawa Pano / Jesus, We Are Here
370 Jesus Is All the World to Me
773 Just Let Him In
515 Keep Me Every Day
662 Let There Be Peace on Earth
645 Lord, Whose Love in Humble Service
2 Morning Hymn
514 My Faith Looks Up to Thee
527 Order My Steps
503 Rock of Ages
523 Sanctuary
289 Stations of the Cross
701 Steal Away to Jesus
619 Take, O Take Me As I Am
622 The Summons
638 Thuma Mina / Send Me, Jesus
518 Thy Way, O Lord
647 Till I Die, Till I Die
565 Trust and Obey
642 We Must Work
361 What a Friend We Have in Jesus
659 What Shall I Render
621 Where He Leads Me
631 You Walk along Our Shoreline

COMMUNION
See Liturgical Index: Eucharist

COMMUNION OF SAINTS
552 A Living Faith
343 All Hail the Power of Jesus' Name! (CORONATION)
342 All Hail the Power of Jesus' Name! (DIADEM)
752 Alleluia! Sing to Jesus
728 For All the Saints
480 For the Beauty of the Earth
346 He Is King of Kings
335 Holy, Holy, Holy! Lord God Almighty!
555 How Firm a Foundation
762 Let Us Enter into Covenant
849 Litany of the Saints
756 Lord, Who at Your First Eucharist
716 Shall We Gather at the River
544 Sing Praise to God for Friends
317 Sing with All the Saints in Glory
606 The Church's One Foundation
393 'Tis the Ol' Ship of Zion
722 Transform Us
686 We Gather in Memory
719 We Shall Rise Again
574 We'll Understand It Better By and By

697 Where Shall I Be?
730 Ye Watchers and Ye Holy Ones

COMMUNITY
683 All Are Welcome
473 Bless the Lord
605 Blest Be the Tie That Binds
679 Enter into Jerusalem
677 Gather, Christians
676 Gather Us In
754 I Come with Joy
668 I Need You to Survive
294 Jesu, Jesu, Fill Us with Your Love
760 One Bread, One Body
608 Somebody Prayed for Me
610 To Be the Body
686 We Gather in Memory
604 We Will Walk with God / Sizohamba
295 Where True Love and Charity Are Found / Ubi Cáritas

COMPASSION
676 Gather Us In
645 Lord, Whose Love in Humble Service
494 Love Divine, All Loves Excelling
45 Luke 1:68–79 / Now Bless the God of Israel
46 Now Let Your Servant Go in Peace
771 Our Father, We Have Wandered
764 Pan de Vida
682 Risen Lord, We Gather Round You
301 Were You There

COMPLACENCY
690 God of Day and God of Darkness
774 Sinner, Please Don't Let This Harvest Pass
612 The Church of Christ Cannot Be Bound

CONFESSION *See Repentance*

CONFIDENCE *See Trust*

CONVERSION
495 Amazing Grace!
505 Can't Nobody Do Me Like Jesus
385 Certainly, Lord!
747 Certainly, Lord! (RENEWAL OF BAPTISMAL PROMISES)
744 Changed Mah Name
389 Glory, Glory, Hallelujah! (Williams)
404 Glory, Glory, Hallelujah! (Bradley)
402 Great Change Since I've Been Born
329 Holy Spirit, Flow through Me
240 On Jordan's Bank
527 Order My Steps
771 Our Father, We Have Wandered
366 Precious Jesus
283 Somebody's Knockin'
403 Something on the Inside

Topical Index/*continued*

Topical Index/*continued*

Topical Index/*continued*

Topical Index/*continued*

Topical Index/*continued*

LOVE FOR GOD

623 Completely Yes
336 Father, I Adore You
408 God Is a Good God
557 His Eye Is on the Sparrow
675 I Just Came to Praise the Lord
588 I Love the Lord, He Heard My
    Cry
437 I Love You, Lord
661 I've Got Peace Like a River
391 Jesus in the Morning
436 Praise Him, All Ye Little
    Children
464 Praise, My Soul, the King of
    Heaven
403 Something on the Inside
323 Spirit of God, Descend upon
    My Heart

LOVE FOR JESUS CHRIST

431 Blessed Assurance, Jesus Is
    Mine!
296 Calvary
505 Can't Nobody Do Me Like
    Jesus
618 Close to Thee
350 Give Me Jesus
557 His Eye Is on the Sparrow
372 His Name Is Wonderful
640 I Am on the Battlefield for My
    Lord
525 I Am Thine
459 I Love You, Lord, Today
367 I Really Love the Lord!
616 I Surrender All
483 I Thank You, Jesus
420 I Want to Walk as a Child of the
    Light
740 I've Just Come from the
    Fountain
425 In the Garden
368 Is There Anybody Here Who
    Loves My Jesus?
671 Jesu Tawa Pano / Jesus, We Are
    Here
447 Jesus
370 Jesus Is All the World to Me
357 Jesus Is Real to Me
491 Jesus Loves Me
599 Jesus, You Brought Me All the
    Way
783 Just a Closer Walk with Thee
559 Just a Little Talk with Jesus
369 Lamb of God
592 Leaning on the Everlasting
    Arms
363 More Love to Thee
514 My Faith Looks Up to Thee
364 My Jesus, I Love Thee
351 No, Not One!
371 Now Behold the Lamb
353 O Holy Savior!
365 O How I Love Jesus
297 O Sacred Head, Sore Wounded
366 Precious Jesus
736 Take Me to the Water
647 Till I Die, Till I Die
617 We Are Climbing Jacob's
    Ladder
725 When I Survey the Wondrous
    Cross

LOVE FOR OTHERS

683 All Are Welcome
605 Blest Be the Tie That Binds
385 Certainly, Lord!
648 Go in Peace, Go in Love
546 God Be with You
313 Goodness Is Stronger than Evil
254 He Came Down
658 He Had a Dream
636 Here Am I
643 Here I Am, Lord
754 I Come with Joy
358 I Know Jesus
668 I Need You to Survive
553 I Say "Yes," Lord / Digo "Sí,"
    Señor
576 I Will Trust in the Lord
644 I'm Available to You
661 I've Got Peace Like a River
395 If You Live Right
294 Jesu, Jesu, Fill Us with Your
    Love
435 Joyful, Joyful, We Adore You
758 Let Us Talents and Tongues
    Employ
387 Lord, I Want to Be a Christian
627 Lord, When You Came /
    Pescador de Hombres
756 Lord, Who at Your First
    Eucharist
551 Old Time Religion
609 Renew Thy Church, Her
    Ministries Restore
682 Risen Lord, We Gather Round
    You
608 Somebody Prayed for Me
612 The Church of Christ Cannot Be
    Bound
589 The Gift of Love
745 There Is One Lord
511 There's a Wideness in God's
    Mercy
524 This Day
547 Till We Gather Again
295 Where True Love and Charity
    Are Found / Ubi Cáritas
757 You Satisfy the Hungry Heart
631 You Walk along Our Shoreline

LOVE OF GOD FOR US

683 All Are Welcome
316 At the Lamb's High Feast We
    Sing
332 Come Down, O Love Divine
688 Day Is Done
480 For the Beauty of the Earth
499 God Has Smiled on Me
787 God of Our Fathers
313 Goodness Is Stronger than Evil
492 Great Is Thy Faithfulness
635 He Has Done Great Things for
    Me
354 He's So Real
643 Here I Am, Lord
339 Hidden Here before Me / Adóro
    Te Devóte
291 Hold Us in Your Mercy:
    Penitential Litany
555 How Firm a Foundation
405 How Great Thou Art
525 I Am Thine
754 I Come with Joy
598 I Heard the Voice of Jesus Say

588 I Love the Lord, He Heard My
    Cry
501 I Love to Tell the Story
558 I Must Tell Jesus
759 I Receive the Living God
384 I've Got the Joy, Joy, Joy
660 Is Your All on the Altar
294 Jesu, Jesu, Fill Us with Your
    Love
491 Jesus Loves Me
667 Jesus Loves the Little Children
435 Joyful, Joyful, We Adore You
559 Just a Little Talk with Jesus
369 Lamb of God
614 Lead Me to Calvary
762 Let Us Enter into Covenant
401 Lord, Keep Me Day by Day
756 Lord, Who at Your First
    Eucharist
494 Love Divine, All Loves
    Excelling
 45 Luke 1:68–79 / Now Bless the
    God of Israel
611 Make of Our Life a House of
    Praise
579 My Heavenly Father Watches
    over Me
476 My Tribute
371 Now Behold the Lamb
 46 Now Let Your Servant Go in
    Peace
488 Now Thank We All Our God
348 O Christ, What Can It Mean for
    Us
338 O Dawn of All Creation
438 O for a Thousand Tongues to
    Sing
497 O How He Loves You and Me
365 O How I Love Jesus
299 O Sacred Head, Surrounded
302 Only Love
771 Our Father, We Have Wandered
764 Pan de Vida
448 Praise God from Whom All
    Blessings Flow
436 Praise Him, All Ye Little
    Children
441 Praise Him! Praise Him!
464 Praise, My Soul, the King of
    Heaven
466 Praise to the Lord
439 Praise to the Lord, the Almighty
444 Revive Us Again
769 Softly and Tenderly Jesus Is
    Calling
562 Standing on the Promises
327 Sweet, Sweet Spirit
750 Taste and See
596 The Angels Keep A-Watchin'
601 The King of Love My Shepherd
    Is
397 The Master's Love
622 The Summons
511 There's a Wideness in God's
    Mercy
524 This Day
547 Till We Gather Again
610 To Be the Body
442 To God Be the Glory
565 Trust and Obey
500 What Wondrous Love Is This
725 When I Survey the Wondrous
    Cross

Topical Index/*continued*

Topical Index/*continued*

Topical Index/*continued*

Topical Index/*continued*

662 Let There Be Peace on Earth
649 Lift Every Voice and Sing
627 Lord, When You Came /
    Pescador de Hombres
645 Lord, Whose Love in Humble
    Service
689 Mary's Canticle
694 Mine Eyes Have Seen the Glory
265 Star-Child
612 The Church of Christ Cannot Be
    Bound
622 The Summons
745 There Is One Lord
652 We Shall Overcome

SONG

407 All Creatures of Our God and
    King
343 All Hail the Power of Jesus'
    Name! (CORONATION)
342 All Hail the Power of Jesus'
    Name! (DIADEM)
674 All People That on Earth Do
    Dwell
752 Alleluia! Sing to Jesus
316 At the Lamb's High Feast We
    Sing
414 Be Still, God Will Fight Your
    Battles
275 Behold the Star!
431 Blessed Assurance, Jesus Is
    Mine!
314 Christ Has Arisen, Alleluia /
    Mfurahini, Haleluya
433 Come, Thou Fount of Every
    Blessing
478 Count Your Blessings
344 Crown Him with Many Crowns
679 Enter into Jerusalem
728 For All the Saints
677 Gather, Christians
650 Go Down, Moses
724 Hail, Holy Queen Enthroned
    Above
452 Halleluja! Pelo Tsa Rona /
    Halleluya! We Sing Your
    Praises
636 Here Am I
465 Holy God, We Praise Thy Name
335 Holy, Holy, Holy! Lord God
    Almighty!
501 I Love to Tell the Story
471 I Will Sing Hallelujah
717 I'll Be Singing Up There
248 It Came upon the Midnight
    Clear
315 Jesus Christ Is Risen Today
345 Jesus Shall Reign
435 Joyful, Joyful, We Adore You
475 Let All the People Praise Thee
486 Let All Things Now Living
649 Lift Every Voice and Sing
251 Messiah Now Has Come
364 My Jesus, I Love Thee
784 Nearer, My God, to Thee
438 O for a Thousand Tongues to
    Sing
312 O Sons and Daughters
412 Over My Head
448 Praise God from Whom All
    Blessings Flow
441 Praise Him! Praise Him!
439 Praise to the Lord, the Almighty

716 Shall We Gather at the River
317 Sing with All the Saints in
    Glory
419 Siyahamba / We Are Marching
562 Standing on the Promises
705 The Sweet By and By
686 We Gather in Memory
500 What Wondrous Love Is This
460 When in Our Music God Is
    Glorified
687 When Morning Gilds the Sky
730 Ye Watchers and Ye Holy Ones

SORROW *See Grief*

SPIRITUALS

707 Ain't-a That Good News!
275 Behold the Star!
296 Calvary
385 Certainly, Lord!
747 Certainly, Lord! (RENEWAL
    OF BAPTISMAL
    PROMISES)
744 Changed Mah Name
506 Come Out the Wilderness
702 Deep River
629 Done Made My Vow to the
    Lord
522 Every Time I Feel the Spirit
710 Fix Me, Jesus
654 Free at Last
350 Give Me Jesus
389 Glory, Glory, Hallelujah!
306 Go and Tell Mary and Martha
650 Go Down, Moses
253 Go Tell It on the Mountain
718 Good News!
537 Guide My Feet
307 He Arose
346 He Is King of Kings
411 He's Got the Whole World in
    His Hand
624 Hush, Hush, Somebody's
    Callin' My Name
781 I Know the Lord Has Laid His
    Hands on Me
639 I Shall Not Be Moved
712 I Wanna Be Ready
388 I Want Jesus to Walk with Me
576 I Will Trust in the Lord
717 I'll Be Singing Up There
386 I've Been 'Buked
740 I've Just Come from the
    Fountain
695 In That Great Gittin' Up
    Mornin'
396 It's Alright
387 Lord, I Want to Be a Christian
693 My Lord, What a Morning
651 Oh, Freedom
714 Plenty Good Room
293 Ride On, Jesus, Ride
692 Ride On, King Jesus
258 Rise Up, Shepherd, and Follow
597 Shine on Me
774 Sinner, Please Don't Let This
    Harvest Pass
283 Somebody's Knockin'
516 Standin' in the Need of Prayer
701 Steal Away to Jesus
704 Swing Low, Sweet Chariot
736 Take Me to the Water
489 Thank You, Lord

502 There Is a Balm in Gilead
393 'Tis the Ol' Ship of Zion
738 Wade in the Water
399 Walk Together, Children
617 We Are Climbing Jacob's
    Ladder
655 We've Come a Long Way, Lord
301 Were You There
729 When the Saints Go Marching
    In
256 Wonderful Counselor

STEWARDSHIP

481 Come, You Thankful People,
    Come
644 I'm Available to You
660 Is Your All on the Altar
565 Trust and Obey
659 What Shall I Render

STRENGTH

577 All My Help Comes from the
    Lord
573 Be Strong!
688 Day Is Done
728 For All the Saints
499 God Has Smiled on Me
392 God Is
313 Goodness Is Stronger than Evil
492 Great Is Thy Faithfulness
557 His Eye Is on the Sparrow
566 Hold Back the Night
555 How Firm a Foundation
582 I Can Do All Things through
    Christ
515 Keep Me Every Day
538 Lead Me, Guide Me
401 Lord, Keep Me Day by Day
285 Lord, Who throughout These
    Forty Days
514 My Faith Looks Up to Thee
383 The Blood Will Never Lose Its
    Power
284 The Glory of These Forty Days
591 The Joy of the Lord
572 The Lord Is My Light
637 This Little Light of Mine
457 Total Praise

STRUGGLE

556 A Mighty Fortress Is Our God
788 America the Beautiful
776 Cast Down, O God, the Idols
311 Christ the Lord Is Risen Today
490 Every Day Is a Day of
    Thanksgiving
728 For All the Saints
350 Give Me Jesus
555 How Firm a Foundation
786 I Call You to My Father's
    House
388 I Want Jesus to Walk with Me
498 I'm So Glad
396 It's Alright
290 Jesus, Tempted in the Desert
599 Jesus, You Brought Me All the
    Way
559 Just a Little Talk with Jesus
632 Just As I Am
656 Keep the Dream Alive
593 Leave It There
649 Lift Every Voice and Sing
579 My Heavenly Father Watches
    over Me

Topical Index/*continued*

415 My Help Cometh from the Lord
245 Night of Silence
560 O God, Our Help in Ages Past
533 O Lord, Hear My Prayer
510 Oh, What He's Done for Me
585 On Eagle's Wings
713 On Jordan's Stormy Banks
412 Over My Head
570 People Need the Lord
446 Praise Him!
575 Savior, Lead Me Lest I Stray
703 Soon-a Will Be Done
782 Stand by Me
562 Standing on the Promises
701 Steal Away to Jesus
517 Sweet Hour of Prayer
704 Swing Low, Sweet Chariot
750 Taste and See
572 The Lord Is My Light
561 The Solid Rock
502 There Is a Balm in Gilead
745 There Is One Lord
580 There's a Bright Side Somewhere
584 Through It All
457 Total Praise
565 Trust and Obey
669 We Gather Together
652 We Shall Overcome
574 We'll Understand It Better By and By
655 We've Come a Long Way, Lord
548 We've Come This Far by Faith
549 Yes, God Is Real

TRUST IN JESUS CHRIST
583 Be Not Afraid
431 Blessed Assurance, Jesus Is Mine!
681 Christ Is Our Peace
506 Come Out the Wilderness
753 Eat This Bread
630 Follow Jesus
350 Give Me Jesus
404 Glory, Glory, Hallelujah!
507 He's Done So Much for Me
360 He's Sweet, I Know
557 His Eye Is on the Sparrow
555 How Firm a Foundation
582 I Can Do All Things through Christ
598 I Heard the Voice of Jesus Say
558 I Must Tell Jesus
520 I Need Thee Every Hour
616 I Surrender All
388 I Want Jesus to Walk with Me
569 It Is Well with My Soul
396 It's Alright
370 Jesus Is All the World to Me
300 Jesus, Keep Me near the Cross
491 Jesus Loves Me
97 Jesus, Remember Me
559 Just a Little Talk with Jesus
773 Just Let Him In
538 Lead Me, Guide Me
592 Leaning on the Everlasting Arms
633 Lift Him Up
299 O Sacred Head, Surrounded
362 One Day
767 Pass Me Not, O Gentle Savior
378 Praise the Name of Jesus
780 Precious Lord, Take My Hand

575 Savior, Lead Me Lest I Stray
597 Shine on Me
283 Somebody's Knockin'
562 Standing on the Promises
701 Steal Away to Jesus
601 The King of Love My Shepherd Is
561 The Solid Rock
584 Through It All
719 We Shall Rise Again
550 We Walk by Faith
361 What a Friend We Have in Jesus
715 When We All Get to Heaven

TRUTH
339 Hidden Here before Me / Adóro Te Devóte
694 Mine Eyes Have Seen the Glory
359 You, Lord, Are Both Lamb and Shepherd

UNDERSTANDING
384 I've God the Joy, Joy, Joy
663 O God of Every Nation
574 We'll Understand It Better By and By

UNITY
683 All Are Welcome
605 Blest Be the Tie That Binds
681 Christ Is Our Peace
279 Epiphany Carol
658 He Had a Dream
754 I Come with Joy
668 I Need You to Survive
664 In Christ There Is No East or West
667 Jesus Loves the Little Children
656 Keep the Dream Alive
756 Lord, Who at Your First Eucharist
611 Make of Our Life a House of Praise
337 O God, Almighty Father
760 One Bread, One Body
764 Pan de Vida
682 Risen Lord, We Gather Round You
606 The Church's One Foundation
421 The Word
745 There Is One Lord
406 This Is My Father's World
610 To Be the Body
666 Unity (Psalm 133:1)
665 We Are One
652 We Shall Overcome
295 Where True Love and Charity Are Found / Ubi Cáritas
757 You Satisfy the Hungry Heart
631 You Walk along Our Shoreline
761 Your Sacrifice

UNIVERSE
480 For the Beauty of the Earth
465 Holy God, We Praise Thy Name
405 How Great Thou Art

VICTORY OVER SIN AND DEATH
556 A Mighty Fortress Is Our God
20 Abide with Me
316 At the Lamb's High Feast We Sing

303 Because He Lives
314 Christ Has Arisen, Alleluia / Mfurahini, Haleluya
311 Christ the Lord Is Risen Today
344 Crown Him with Many Crowns
416 For God So Loved the World
545 God Be with You till We Meet Again
578 God Never Fails
313 Goodness Is Stronger than Evil
307 He Arose
635 He Has Done Great Things for Me
507 He's Done So Much for Me
640 I Am on the Battlefield for My Lord
558 I Must Tell Jesus
367 I Really Love the Lord!
639 I Shall Not Be Moved
376 In the Name of Jesus
315 Jesus Christ Is Risen Today
355 Jesus Is a Rock in a Weary Land
357 Jesus Is Real to Me
726 Lift High the Cross
438 O for a Thousand Tongues to Sing
441 Praise Him! Praise Him!
349 Rejoice, the Lord Is King!
281 Satan, We're Gonna Tear Your Kingdom Down
317 Sing with All the Saints in Glory
562 Standing on the Promises
308 The Strife Is O'er
777 Victory Is Mine
652 We Shall Overcome
319 We Walk His Way / Ewe, Thina
634 What a Mighty God We Serve
715 When We All Get to Heaven
770 Yield Not to Temptation

VOCATION
646 Go Make of All Disciples
644 I'm Available to You
619 Take, O Take Me As I Am
642 We Must Work

WATER
746 Baptized in Water
684 Come to the Feast
598 I Heard the Voice of Jesus Say
736 Take Me to the Water
738 Wade in the Water
737 Wash, O God, Our Sons and Daughters

WAY, TRUTH, AND LIFE
51 Go Now in Peace
759 I Receive the Living God
700 Jesus Christ Is the Way
765 Take and Eat

WELCOME
683 All Are Welcome
685 As We Gather at Your Table
786 I Call You to My Father's House
96 In Paradísum / May Choirs of Angels
611 Make of Our Life a House of Praise
682 Risen Lord, We Gather Round You

Topical Index/*continued*

612 The Church of Christ Cannot Be
     Bound
603 The Reign of God

WISDOM
413 Awesome God
475 Let All the People Praise Thee
338 O Dawn of All Creation
737 Wash, O God, Our Sons and
     Daughters

WITNESS
552 A Living Faith
685 As We Gather at Your Table
414 Be Still, God Will Fight Your
     Battles
431 Blessed Assurance, Jesus Is
     Mine!
306 Go and Tell Mary and Martha
646 Go Make of All Disciples
321 Go to the World!
452 Halleluya! Pelo Tsa Rona /
     Halleluya! We Sing Your
     Praises
635 He Has Done Great Things for
     Me
785 He Understands; He'll Say,
     "Well Done"
507 He's Done So Much for Me
354 He's So Real
360 He's Sweet, I Know
636 Here Am I
329 Holy Spirit, Flow through Me
509 I Am Redeemed
501 I Love to Tell the Story
644 I'm Available to You
368 Is There Anybody Here Who
     Loves My Jesus?
700 Jesus Christ Is the Way
758 Let Us Talents and Tongues
     Employ
633 Lift Him Up
398 Lord, Be Glorified
438 O for a Thousand Tongues to
     Sing
609 Renew Thy Church, Her
     Ministries Restore
523 Sanctuary
544 Sing Praise to God for Friends
427 Something Within
524 This Day
638 Thuma Mina / Send Me, Jesus
610 To Be the Body
722 Transform Us
686 We Gather in Memory
642 We Must Work
739 We Offer Christ
460 When in Our Music God Is
     Glorified

WORD OF GOD
556 A Mighty Fortress Is Our God
495 Amazing Grace!
685 As We Gather at Your Table
334 Come Now, Almighty King
539 Eternal Father, Strong to Save
423 From the Dawning of Creation
321 Go to the World!
787 God of Our Fathers
542 Hamba Nathi / Come, Walk
     with Us
759 I Receive the Living God
553 I Say "Yes," Lord / Digo "Sí,"
     Señor
422 Is There a Word from the Lord?
660 Is Your All on the Altar
290 Jesus, Tempted in the Desert
 45 Luke 1:68–79 / Now Bless the
     God of Israel
611 Make of Our Life a House of
     Praise
 46 Now Let Your Servant Go in
     Peace
663 O God of Every Nation
527 Order My Steps
609 Renew Thy Church, Her
     Ministries Restore
562 Standing on the Promises
765 Take and Eat
397 The Master's Love
421 The Word
584 Through It All
518 Thy Way, O Lord
565 Trust and Obey
548 We've Come This Far by Faith
359 You, Lord, Are Both Lamb and
     Shepherd

WORK *See Daily Life and Work*

WORLD
344 Crown Him with Many Crowns
480 For the Beauty of the Earth
411 He's Got the Whole World in
     His Hand
664 In Christ There Is No East or
     West
662 Let There Be Peace on Earth
347 To Jesus Christ, Our Sovereign
     King

WORSHIP AND ADORATION
343 All Hail the Power of Jesus'
     Name! (CORONATION)
342 All Hail the Power of Jesus'
     Name! (DIADEM)
413 Awesome God
275 Behold the Star!

451 Bless the Lord
519 Bless This House
470 Blessing and Honor and Glory
     and Power
272 Brightest and Best
282 Down at the Cross
336 Father, I Adore You
443 Hallelujah, Amen!
304 He Is Lord
467 He's Worthy
339 Hidden Here before Me / Adóro
     Te Devóte
454 High Praise
372 His Name Is Wonderful
465 Holy God, We Praise Thy Name
335 Holy, Holy, Holy! Lord God
     Almighty!
469 Holy Is the Lord
462 How Excellent Is Thy Name
525 I Am Thine
437 I Love You, Lord
479 I Will Bless Thee, O Lord
458 I Will Call upon the Lord
576 I Will Trust in the Lord
472 I Worship Thee
456 In the Beauty of Holiness
447 Jesus
345 Jesus Shall Reign
274 Jesus, the Light of the World
251 Messiah Now Has Come
364 My Jesus, I Love Thee
476 My Tribute
430 O Come, Let Us Adore Him
255 O Holy Night!
297 O Sacred Head, Sore Wounded
424 Oh, the Glory of Your Presence
377 Perfect Praise
446 Praise Him!
439 Praise to the Lord, the Almighty
455 Praise You
464 Praise, My Soul, the King of
     Heaven
366 Precious Jesus
609 Renew Thy Church, Her
     Ministries Restore
692 Ride On, King Jesus
672 The Lord Is in His Holy Temple
397 The Master's Love
347 To Jesus Christ, Our Sovereign
     King
737 Wash, O God, Our Sons and
     Daughters
670 We Have Come into This House
273 We Three Kings of Orient Are
340 We Will Glorify
673 We've Come to Worship You
634 What a Mighty God We Serve
434 Worship Him
     See also Praise

Index of Composers, Authors and Sources/*continued*

Index of Composers, Authors and Sources/*continued*

Index of Composers, Authors and Sources/*continued*

7 8 7 7 WITH REFRAIN
WHAT A MORNING   693

7 8 7 8 77
GROSSER GOTT   465

7 8 8 8 WITH REFRAIN
WADE IN THE WATER   738

7 9 7 8
I'VE BEEN 'BUKED   386

8 3 8 3 77 8 3
STAND BY ME   782

8 4 8 4 777 4 5
SALVE REGINA COELITUM   724

8 4 8 4 888 4
AR HYD Y NOS   688

8 4 8 4 WITH REFRAIN
JUDGMENT DAY   697

8 6 6 6 WITH REFRAIN
SMILED ON ME   499

8 6 8 3 6 8 3
I WANT TO BE A CHRISTIAN   387

8 6 8 66 6 8 6
CLEANSING FOUNTAIN   381

8 6 8 6 7 6 8 6
ST. LOUIS   250

8 6 8 6 8 6
CORONATION   343

8 6 8 6 88 8 3
ALL THE WORLD   370

86 10 7 WITH REFRAIN
THE BLOOD   383

8 7
THUMA MINA   638

8 7 77 11
CHILDREN   667

8 7 8 7 8 7 7
DIVINUM MYSTERIUM   266

8 7 8 7 66 66 7
EIN' FESTE BURG   556

8 7 8 7 77
IRBY   270

8 7 8 9 WITH REFRAIN
HE TOUCHED ME   779

88 44 6 WITH REFRAIN
KINGS OF ORIENT   273

88 7
STABAT MATER   286

888 6
HOLY SAVIOR   353

888 6 WITH REFRAIN
SOON-A WILL BE DONE   703

88 88 88
MELITA   539

88 8 9
WALK WITH ME   388

888 9 WITH REFRAIN
NORRIS   621

888 9 66 9 76 9
SOMEWHERE LISTENING   620

888 10
GUIDE MY FEET   537

88 9 11
HE'S SWEET   360

88 10 7
WHEN THE SAINTS   729

8 9 8 12 WITH REFRAIN
GOD IS REAL   549

8 9 10 7 WITH REFRAIN
GARDEN   425

8 10 8 10 WITH REFRAIN
BE READY   712

9 4 9 4 WITH REFRAIN
I'LL FLY AWAY   709

9 6 8 6 8 7 10 WITH REFRAIN
TWO OAKS   683

9 7 9 6
WE WILL GLORIFY   340

9 8 8 9 WITH REFRAIN
GOD BE WITH YOU   545

98 98 WITH REFRAIN
FEEL THE SPIRIT   522

9 8 9 12 WITH REFRAIN
RESURRECTION (Gaither)   303

9 9 9 3
HEALING   505

99 9 7 WITH AMEN
COME HERE JESUS   534

999 7 WITH REFRAIN
GLORY TO HIS NAME   282

9 10 9 9 WITH REFRAIN
ASSURANCE   431

10 5 10 5 16 10 5
GOOD NEWS   707

Metrical Index/*continued*

1008 Index of Service Music

1009 Psalm Refrains Set to Music

A light for revelation to the Gentiles and the glory of your people Israel. 983

A light will shine on us this day: the Lord is born for us. The Lord is born for us. 805

All the ends of the earth have seen the saving power of God. 806

Alleluia. 848

Be merciful, O Lord, for we have sinned. 815

Be with me, Lord, when I am in trouble, be with me, Lord, I pray. 35 818

Behold, our Lord will come with power, to enlighten the eyes of his servants, alleluia. 982

Blessed are they who dwell in your house, O Lord. 32 809

Blessed are they who follow the law, follow the law of the Lord! 895

Blessed are they who hope in the Lord, who hope in the Lord. 897

Blessed are those who fear the Lord. 976

Blessed be the Lord, blessed be the Lord, for he has come to his people and set them free. 5

Blessed the people the Lord has chosen to be his own, to be his own. 876 936

Blessed the poor in spirit; the kingdom of heaven is theirs. 889

Create in me a clean heart, O God. Create in me a clean heart. 30 829

Cry out with joy and gladness: cry out, for among you is the great and Holy One, cry out, the great and Holy One of Israel. 799

Day and night, day and night I cry to you, my God. 34

Do not forget the works of the Lord. Do not forget the works of the Lord. Do not forget the works of the Lord. Do not forget the works of the Lord. 994

Do not hide your face from me; in you I put my trust. 42

Father, into your hands I commend my spirit. 836

Fill us with your love, O Lord, and we will sing for joy! Fill us with your love, O Lord, and we will sing for joy! 962

For ever I will sing the goodness of the Lord, the goodness of the Lord. 801

Give thanks to the Lord for he is good, his love is everlasting. 855

Give thanks to the Lord, give thanks to the Lord, his love is everlasting. 914

Give the Lord glory and honor. Give the Lord glory and honor. 964

Glory and praise for evermore. Glory and praise for evermore. Glory and praise, glory and praise, glory and praise for evermore. 875

Go out to all the world and tell the Good News. Go out to all the world and tell the Good News. 906

God, in your goodness, you have made a home for the poor. 945

God mounts his throne to shouts of joy: a blare of trumpets for the Lord. 868

Good ground, the seed that falls on good ground will yield a fruitful harvest. 922

Have mercy, Lord. Have mercy, Lord. Have mercy, Lord, and hear my prayer. 25

He who does justice will live in the presence of the Lord. 927

Here am I, Lord; here am I, Lord; I come to do your will. 884

Here am I, Lord; I come to do your will. 986

I believe that I shall see the good things of the Lord in the land of the living. 998

I believe that I shall see, I believe that I shall see the good things of the Lord in the land of the living. 869

I love you, Lord, my strength. 971

I love you, Lord. I love you, Lord. I love you, Lord, my strength. 967

I praise you, O Lord. I praise you, O Lord, for I am wonderfully made. 988

I turn to you, Lord, in time of trouble, and you fill me with the joy of salvation. 896

I will praise you, Lord, for you have rescued me. 842

I will praise you, Lord, in the assembly of your people, in the assembly of your people. 863

I will praise you, Lord. I will praise you, Lord. I will praise you, Lord, for you have rescued me. 858

I will praise your name for ever, my king and my God. 43 864

I will rise and go to my father, go to my father; I will rise. 951

I will sing, I will sing of your salvation. 891

I will take the cup of salvation, and call upon the name of the Lord. 879

I will walk before the Lord in the land of the living. 820

If today you hear his voice, harden not your hearts, harden not your hearts. 36 890

If today you hear his voice, harden not your hearts. 822

In every age, O Lord, you have been our refuge. You have been our refuge in every age, O Lord. 948

In the morning I will sing, sing glad songs of praise to you; I will sing glad songs of praise to you. 3

In the sight of the angels, I will sing your praises, sing your praises, Lord. 894

In the silent hours of night, in the silent hours of night, bless the Lord, bless the Lord. 41

In you, my God, my body will rest, my body will rest in hope. 27

In you, O Lord, I have found my peace. 970

Justice shall flourish in his time, and fullness of peace for ever. Justice shall flourish, shall flourish in his time. 794

Let all the earth, let all the earth, let all the earth cry out to God with joy. 31 865

Let my tongue be silenced, if I ever forget you! 826

Let the Lord enter, let the Lord enter, let the Lord enter; he is king of glory. 800

Let us go rejoicing to the house of the Lord, to the house of the Lord. 791

Let us sing to the Lord; he has covered himself in glory. 841

Like a deer that longs for running streams, my soul longs for you. My soul longs for you, my God, my soul longs for you. 845

Lord, be my rock of safety. 904

Lord, come to my aid! Lord, come to my aid! 939

Lord, every nation on earth will adore you, every nation on earth will adore you. 811

Lord, forgive the wrong I have done. Please, Lord, forive the wrong I have done. 912

Lord, go up to the place of your rest, you and the ark of your holiness. 992

Lord God, be my refuge and strength, be my refuge and strength. 29

Lord, heal my soul, for I have sinned against you. 899

Lord, I love your commands. Lord, I love your commands. Lord, I love your commands. Lord, I love your commands. 928

Lord, in your great love, answer me, answer me. 913

Lord, it is good to give thanks to you, it is good to give thanks to you. 911

Lord, it is good, good, good to give thanks, thanks, thanks, to give thanks to you. 903

Lord, let your face shine on us, let your face shine on us. 857

Lord, let your mercy be on us, as we place our trust in you. 819

Lord, Lord, come and save us. 797

Lord, make us turn to you; let us see your face and we shall be saved. 792

Lord, on the day I called for help, you answered me. 930

Lord, send out your Spirit. Lord, send out your Spirit. Lord, send out your Spirit, and renew the face of the earth. 839A

Lord, this is the people that longs to see your face. Lord, this is the people that longs to see your face. 995

Lord, when your glory appears, my joy, my joy will be full, my joy, my joy will be full. 975

Lord, you are good and forgiving, good and forgiving. 33

Lord, you are good and forgiving, you are good and forgiving. 925

Lord, you have the words of everlasting life, of everlasting life, of everlasting life. 28 823

Lord, you will show us the path of life. 856

Lord, your love is eternal, Lord, your love is eternal, Lord, your love is eternal; do not forsake the work of your hands. 940

May God bless us in his mercy. Bless us in his mercy. 810

May the Lord bless us, may the Lord bless us and protect us all the days of our lives. 959

My God, my God, why have you abandoned me? 833

My prayer shall rise like incense, my hands like an evening oblation. 12

My soul is thirsting for you, O Lord, thirsting for you, my God. 915

My soul rejoices in my God. My soul rejoices in my God. 798

Night holds no terrors for me sleeping under God's wings. 35

No one who waits for you, O Lord, will ever be put to shame, ever be put to shame. 997

O bless the Lord, bless the Lord, my soul. 814

O blessed are those who fear the Lord and walk in his ways. 807

O God, let all the nations, let all the nations praise you! 867

O God, O God, let all the nations praise you! 937

O Lord, let us see your kindness. O Lord, let us see your truth. O Lord, let us see your kindness, and grant us your salvation. 795

O Lord, our God, how wonderful your name, how wonderful your name in all the earth! 26 877

Oh, I shall live in the house of the Lord all the days of my life. 961

Our blessing-cup is a communion with the Blood of Christ. 834

Our eyes are fixed on the Lord; our eyes are fixed on the Lord; our eyes are fixed on the Lord, pleading for, pleading for his mercy. 920

Our help is from the Lord, who made heaven, heaven and earth. 39 966

Out of the depths I cry to you, O Lord. 40

Praise the Lord, Jerusalem. Praise the Lord, Jerusalem. 878

Praise the Lord, praise the Lord, who heals the brokenhearted. 893

Praise the Lord, praise the Lord who lifts up the poor. 954

Praise the Lord, praise the Lord, praise the Lord, praise the Lord, praise the Lord, my soul! 947

Proclaim his marvelous deeds to the nations. 885

Protect us, Lord, as we stay awake; watch over us as we sleep, that awake we may keep watch with Christ, and, asleep, rest in his peace. 23

Remember your mercies, O Lord. Remember your mercies, O Lord. 955

Rest in God alone, rest in God alone, my soul, my soul. 901

Since my mother's womb, you have been my strength. 987

Sing to the Lord a new song, for he has done marvelous deeds. 37 1000

Sing with joy to God! Sing with joy to God! Sing with joy to God, to God our help! 905

Taste and see the goodness of the Lord. 935

Taste and see, taste and see the goodness of the Lord. 827

Teach me your ways, O Lord. 887

The Almighty has done great things for me, and holy is his name, and holy is his Name. 14

Psalm Refrains Set to Music/*continued*

The angel of the Lord will rescue those who fear him. 990

The earth is full of the goodness of the Lord. 839B

The hand of the Lord feeds us; he answers all our needs, he answers all our needs. 929

The just man is a light in darkness to the upright. 892

The Lord comes to rule the earth with justice. The Lord comes to rule the earth with justice. 978

The Lord gave them bread from heaven and brought them to his holy land, and brought them to his holy land. 932

The Lord has done great things for us; we are filled with joy. 796

The Lord has revealed to the nations his saving power, his saving power. 866

The Lord has set his throne in heaven. 870

The Lord hears the cry, the Lord hears the cry, the Lord hears the cry of the poor. 969

The Lord is kind and merciful, slow to anger, and rich in compassion. 949

The Lord is kind, the Lord is kind and merciful. 824

The Lord is king, the Lord is king, the Lord is king; he is robed in majesty. 980

The Lord is king, the Most High over all the earth. 871

The Lord is my light and my salvation, of whom should I be afraid, of whom should I be afraid? 821

The Lord is my light and my salvation. 54 886

The Lord is my shepherd; there is nothing I shall want. 825 859

The Lord is near to all who call on him. The Lord is near to all who call on him. 952

The Lord remembers his covenant for ever. 808

The Lord upholds my life. 953

The Lord will bless his people, the Lord will bless his people, the Lord will bless his people, bless them with peace. 812

The Lord's kindness is everlasting, everlasting to those who fear him. The Lord's kindness is everlasting to those who fear him. 881

The precepts of the Lord give joy to the heart; give joy to the heart; give joy to the heart. 956

The queen stands at your right hand, arrayed in gold. 993

The son of David will live for ever. 985

The stone rejected by the builders has become the cornerstone. 860

The vineyard of the Lord is the house of Israel. 958

The waters of the river gladden the city of God, the holy dwelling of the Most High. 999

Their message goes out through all the earth; goes out through all the earth. 989

This is the day the Lord has made; let us rejoice and be glad in it! This is the day the Lord has made; let us be glad, be glad, be glad, be glad and rejoice in it! 853

Though I walk in the valley of darkness, I fear no evil, for you, for you are with me, I fear no evil. 996

To the upright I will show the saving power of God. 907

To you, O Lord, I lift my soul. To you, O Lord, I lift my soul. 793

Today is born our Savior, Christ the Lord. 804

Turn to the Lord in your need, and you will live. 924

We are his people, the sheep of his flock, we are his people, the sheep of his flock, we are his people, the sheep of his flock, where he leads us we will surely go. 38 861

Who is this king, king of glory? It is the Lord, it is the Lord! Who is this king, king of glory? It is the Lord! 984

With the Lord there is mercy and fullness of redemption. 40 828

You are a priest for ever, in the line of Melchizedek. 880

You are my inheritance, inheritance, inheritance. You are my inheritance, O Lord. 840

You will draw water joyfully from the springs of salvation. 813

Your ways, O Lord, are love and truth to those who keep your covenant. 817

Your words, O Lord, are Spirit and life. 888

Index of First Lines and Common Titles/*continued*

Index of First Lines and Common Titles/*continued*

Index of First Lines and Common Titles/*continued*

Index of First Lines and Common Titles/*continued*

Index of First Lines and Common Titles/*continued*

Index of First Lines and Common Titles/*continued*

Index of First Lines and Common Titles/*continued*